MISSION TO AMERICA

Sportsman's Hall, built in 1790 by Father Theodore Brouwers, served as the first pastoral residence and chapel of the parish that became Saint Vincent.

JEROME OETGEN

MISSION TO AMERICA

A History of Saint Vincent Archabbey,
The First Benedictine Monastery
in the United States

The Catholic University of America Press
Washington, D.C.

The paper used in this publication meets the minimum requirements of American National Standards for Information Science-Permanence of Paper for Printed Library materials, ANSI Z39.48-1984.

∞

LIBRARY OF CONGRESS CATALOGING-IN-PUBLICATION DATA

Oetgen, Jerome, 1946–

Mission to America : a history of Saint Vincent Archabbey, the first Benedictine monastery in the United States / by Jerome Oetgen.

p. cm.

Includes bibliographical references and index.

1. Saint Vincent Archabbey (Latrobe, Pa.)—History. 2. Latrobe (Pa..)—Church history. I. Title.

BX2525.S28047 2000

271′.1074881—dc21

99-34694

ISBN 0-8132-0957-9 (alk. paper)

CONTENTS

PREFACE

Benedictines have traditionally had a passion for history, particularly their own. They have chronicled it, meditated on it, studied it formally and informally, and passed it down with loving care from one generation to the next in both written and oral form. The rich historical sources preserved in European monastic archives, as well as the work of monastic historians from the medieval chroniclers through Jean Mabillon in the seventeenth century to Jean Leclercq and David Knowles in the twentieth, bear witness to that long-nurtured passion and provide students of church history with an astonishingly thorough historical record of the Benedictine Order.

One reason that this record has survived virtually intact is that from the time of St. Benedict to the present, Benedictine men and women have been unfailingly conscious of their participation in a forward-moving tide of human history that has been given meaning, direction, and purpose by the birth, death, and resurrection of Christ; and since at least the time of the Venerable Bede, Benedictines have faithfully remembered and recorded the important monastic events in that tide, always focusing on the Providence that directs human affairs and always delighting in telling stories of those moments when God has dramatically and unexpectedly revealed Himself to them and to their communities. With the single exception of the study of sacred scripture, no other intellectual pursuit has engaged Benedictines quite so fully as has the preservation and study of monastic history.

American Benedictines have not been remiss in following in the footsteps of their ancestors. From the beginning, they have been mindful of their heritage, preserving important documents and letters in their archives, recording their stories in manuscripts, chronicles, and histories, and analyzing in scholarly studies the ideas and events that shaped them and their monastic communities. Since 1873, when Oswald Moosmüller published *St. Vincenz in Pennsylvanien* to commemorate the twenty-fifth anniversary of the first Benedictine abbey in the United States, more than 250 books and articles have appeared that examine the history of the Benedictines in North America. While not all these works have been distinguished by scholarly rigor and precision, they all reflect the deep interest American Benedictines have consistently had in their monastic heritage. Moreover, some of these works are indeed distinguished by their scholarship, notably the carefully researched studies of such Benedictine historians as Regina Baska, Colman Barry, Peter Beckman, Grace McDonald, Edward Malone, Joel Rippinger, Paschal Baumstein, Ephrem Hollermann, and Judith Sutera, to name just a few of those who have made substantial contributions not only to American Benedictine, but also to American Catholic history.

The present study was written to commemorate the 150th anniversary of the founding of Saint Vincent Archabbey, Latrobe, Pennsylvania. Perhaps more importantly, however, it was written to fill a significant gap in American Benedictine studies. The histories of most of the older Benedictine houses of men and women in the United States—including those of many of the communities that had their origins in Saint Vincent—have already been published. But the story of the foundation and development of the first Benedictine monastery in the United States has not been adequately told since Moosmüller's 1873 work. Subsequent brief histories in English by Vincent Huber (1892), Louis Haas (1905), and Gerard Bridge (1922) drew mainly on Moosmüller.

To remedy this deficiency, the Benedictine community of Saint Vincent commissioned the present study, which covers the period from the founding of the Sportsman's Hall parish in 1790 to the election of Rembert Weakland as seventh archabbot of Saint Vincent Archabbey in 1963. The two chapters covering the Benedictine arrival in the United States (1846) to the death of Boniface Wimmer (1887) make extensive use of materials developed more fully and with a slightly different focus in my biography of Wimmer, *An American Abbot,* published by the Catholic University of America Press in 1997.

In preparing this history of Saint Vincent, I have depended upon American and European archival sources as well as the various published works (including those of Moosmüller, Huber, Haas, and Bridge) listed in the notes and bibliography. My purpose has been to provide a detailed history of Saint Vincent and its apostolates within the context of both monastic history and the history of the American Catholic Church.

My debt to a succession of archivists at Saint Vincent and other American Benedictine monasteries is incalculable. Their diligent service over the past 150 years in collecting, cataloguing, and maintaining all the important sources of American Benedictine history has made the preparation of this history of Saint Vincent a lesser task than it otherwise might have been. I am especially indebted to Father Omer Kline and the late Brother Philip Hurley, Saint Vincent's archivist and assistant archivist, for their enormous assistance and cheerful good will in taking time off from busy schedules to search for and locate crucial documents which had been logically filed many years ago and which I, illogically and unsuccessfully, had tried to find in all the wrong places. To attempt to name all those who have assisted and encouraged me in this work would be futile and, besides, would run the risk of serious omission. Nonetheless, I want to express my deep thanks to Father Vincent Tegeder, archivist of St. John's Abbey, Collegeville, Minnesota, and Father Paschal Baumstein, archivist of Belmont Abbey, Belmont, North Carolina, who were especially helpful.

Father Omer Kline, Archbishop Rembert Weakland, Archabbot Egbert Donovan, Archabbot Paul Maher, Father Demetrius Dumm, Father Terrence Kardong, Father Joel Rippinger, Father Paschal Baumstein, and Father Joseph Chinnici carefully read the manuscript and offered many pertinent and helpful suggestions for improvements, which in most cases I have followed. Any errors, inconsistencies, misstatements, and infelicities that remain, of course, are entirely my own. Archabbot Douglas Nowicki provided me unparalleled support and encouragement throughout the project, and the entire community of Saint Vincent offered me hospitality, friendship, and a quiet and prayerful ambience in which to carry out my research. To all of them I am deeply grateful and express my sincerest thanks.

Finally, I want to acknowledge the great debt I owe to the spirit and wisdom of St. Benedict and the Benedictine Order, which have guided me in this work and throughout my life. With Bede, the proto-Benedictine historian, "I earnestly ask all who may hear or read this history to ask God's mercy on my many failings and beg that they may grant me the favor of frequent mention in their devout prayers."

Jerome Oetgen
MADRID

ABBREVIATIONS

AACC	Archives of the American Cassinese Congregation
AAB	Archives of the Archdiocese of Baltimore
ABelA	Archives of Belmont Abbey
ACPF	Archives of the Congregation for the Propagation of the Faith
ACSA	Archives of the Collegio di Sant' Anselmo
ADL	Archives of the Diocese of Linz
AND	Archives of the Diocese of Newark
ADP	Archives of the Diocese of Pittsburgh
AHCA	Archives of Holy Cross Abbey
ALMV	Archives of the Ludwig Missionsverein
AMA	Archives of Metten Abbey
ASA	Archives of Scheyern Abbey
ASBA	Archives of St. Benedict's Abbey
ASJA	Archives of St. John's Abbey
ASPA	Archives of the Abbey of St. Paul's Outside the Walls
ASVA	Archives of Saint Vincent Archabbey
RAB	Royal Archives of Bavaria

MISSION TO AMERICA

ONE

A PARISH ON THE FRONTIER (1789–1846)

SAINT VINCENT ARCHABBEY, Seminary, and College were founded in 1846 by Boniface Wimmer, a Benedictine priest from the Bavarian abbey of Metten who came to America with the intention of establishing the Order of St. Benedict in the New World, educating the sons of German immigrants, and training a native clergy for the German-speaking people of the United States. Settling in Westmoreland County, Pennsylvania, on the site of a parish founded in 1790 for German, Irish, and English Catholics, Wimmer created at Saint Vincent the first Benedictine monastery in North America as well as the first Catholic educational institution in the United States specifically devoted to the education of German-speaking priests for the American missions.

An integral part of Wimmer's plan was to transplant the Benedictine Order from Europe to the New World. The Benedictines had already experienced a long and notable history in Europe when Wimmer introduced them to America. They had founded centers of spirituality, learning, and culture throughout the Old World; and these centers, for nearly thirteen centuries, had made unparalleled contributions not just to the dissemination but, at times, to the very survival of Western civilization. During the early Middle Ages Benedictine communities, and the schools attached to them, had kept the light of Christian faith and classical learning alive as barbarian tribes descended upon Europe, destroying the fabric of the old Roman civilization. And in the nineteenth century, when Europe was once again devastated by invasion, war, economic uncertainty, and spiritual decline, a Benedictine revival in Germany, France, and Italy confronted a rampant secularism and reasserted those Christian values that for centuries had formed the spiritual and intellectual foundation of Western culture.

From the beginning education had played an important role in Benedictine tradition. Schools were an essential part of the monasteries from the earliest times, and there had developed in them a heritage of humane and liberal learning centered on such Benedictine values as stability, community, hospitality, and moderation. "We intend to establish a school for the Lord's service," St. Benedict wrote in his sixth-century monastic rule. "In drawing up its regulations, we hope to set down nothing harsh, nothing burdensome."[1]

Wimmer's aim was to imitate the models of his Benedictine predecessors and establish strong, stable communities of monks who would devote their lives to the service of God, the pursuit of learning, the preaching of the Gospel, and the education of youth. He believed that America was fertile soil for the planting of this ancient tradition and that the tradition itself would contribute a new and vital spiritual energy to the young nation. He wrote, "I am determined to have our monasteries not only schools of religion and of the sciences, but also nurseries of the fine arts in order to develop a better taste for these things and to keep from our people the American mercenary spirit which thinks of nothing but how to make a living, because necessity demands it and example encourages it."[2]

With the aid of several American churchmen, as well as friends and benefactors in Europe (including King Ludwig I of Bavaria, Cardinal Karl von Reisach of the Roman Curia, and Archbishop Gregory Scherr of Munich), Wimmer established at Saint Vincent the community he had envisioned. Then, for the remaining forty years of his life he worked tirelessly to strengthen the monastery and school in Pennsylvania and to establish others throughout the United States. From Saint Vincent he founded Benedictine communities and schools in Minnesota, Kansas, New Jersey, North Carolina, Illinois, Alabama, Georgia, and elsewhere. In 1855 Pope Pius IX elevated Saint Vincent to the rank of abbey and named Wimmer its first abbot. Wimmer thus became the first Benedictine abbot in North America, and by 1887, when he died, he was recognized throughout the American

Church as an outstanding missionary, ecclesiastical leader, builder, and educator—a worthy successor of St. Boniface, his patron and the Benedictine who had introduced Christianity to Germany.

Wimmer brought the Benedictines to a region of the United States that just fifty years before had been part of the American frontier. It was a territory that had been contested first by French and English armies, then by land-hungry Pennsylvania and Virginia farmers, and finally by Indian hunters and American settlers who skirmished in obscure battles of the American Revolution, which for the settlers were part of an epic struggle for independence and for the Native Americans a final desperate effort to preserve the land between the ridges of the Allegheny Mountains and the forks of the Ohio as hunting grounds for themselves and their posterity. In the end, the settlers defeated the hunters and drove them westward, and to the land came new pioneers from the East, farmers and traders, good people and rogues, men and women seeking new opportunities for themselves and their families in the rich soil of western Pennsylvania. Among the newcomers were Irish and German immigrants who established the first Catholic parish in western Pennsylvania, and it was this parish that would come to be called Saint Vincent.

THE HUNTING GROUND

The earliest inhabitants of the land that became Saint Vincent were Native Americans. Evidence of their presence can be found in artifacts recovered from the fields around the monastery and college and on the banks of Twelve Mile Run and Fourteen Mile Run, tributaries of the Loyalhanna Creek that flow through the monastery lands across an ancient forest trail twelve and fourteen miles west of the old Indian village of Loyalhanna, today known as Ligonier. Among the artifacts found in the area are stone tools, projectile points, and pottery shards, and they indicate that the land was used as hunting grounds by parties of Native Americans who camped and foraged here for hundreds of years before the arrival of the Europeans.

The first hunters were Algonquin-speaking peoples who entered and settled in the forests of the Ohio Valley about A.D. 1000. Those who settled and hunted in the region that is now southwestern Pennsylvania developed a distinct forest culture known to archaeologists as the Monongahela Woodlands Complex. They established villages on bottom land near major streams, on saddles between hills, and on hilltops often at a considerable distance from water sources. The Monongahela people subsisted on fishing, the hunting of deer and small game, the gathering of edible plants, and the cultivation of corn, beans, and squash. Several of their villages located in present-day Allegheny, Fayette, Washington, Somerset, and Westmoreland counties have been excavated and studied.[3]

During the Beaver Wars at the end of the seventeenth century these sedentary people were driven from the region by other tribes that included the Iroquois, the Susquehannock, and the Shawnee. For a time southwestern Pennsylvania was depopulated and came to serve as hunting lands for indigenous groups dwelling to the north, east, and south. Historians conjecture that diseases contracted from white traders brought epidemics that played a part in the depopulation of the region. In the 1740s southwestern Pennsylvania was repopulated once again with groups of Shawnee and Delaware from the east and Wyandot from the northwest. When the English moved into the area two decades later, they identified the peoples with whom they came into conflict as Shawnees, Delawares, Miamis, Mingoes, Muncies, and Cornplanters.[4]

At the time of the French and Indian War both France and the colony of Virginia claimed the land that is now southwestern Pennsylvania. In 1754 Governor Robert Dinwiddie of Virginia sent Major George Washington with a force of 150 Virginia militia on an ill-fated expedition to drive the French from Fort Duquesne on the forks of the Ohio. The French defeated Washington at the Battle of Fort Necessity in present-day Fayette County, and the Virginians withdrew. The following year General Edward Braddock marched into the region with an army of twenty-five hundred British regulars and militia from Virginia and Pennsylvania. The English army followed a line of march that took them through present-day Westmoreland County about twenty miles from the future site of Saint Vincent. Again the French and their Indian allies defeated the invaders in a battle that resulted in more than half the English and colonial forces being killed or wounded. Braddock himself was killed, and his army retreated south in panic. Braddock's disastrous defeat took place on the Monongahela River eleven miles from Fort Duquesne in what is now Allegheny County, and marked the nadir of English power on the western frontier. Three years later, in September 1758, the military and political order was reversed when the British launched a third offensive against the French. Six thousand men, including British, Maryland, Virginia, and Pennsylvania regiments, assembled in Raystown (now Bedford), Pennsylvania, and marched west under the command of General John Forbes. Establishing a base camp at Fort Ligonier, site of the Indian village of Loyalhanna, they blazed a path twelve feet wide through the thick forest to Fort Duquesne (modern Pittsburgh). The

French retreated, and the Ohio Valley fell into British hands. Forbes Road, the military path built by the English and colonial troops, ran adjacent to the site that later became Saint Vincent and opened the region to settlement by English-speaking pioneers.[5]

The pioneers came from Virginia, Maryland, and eastern Pennsylvania, and settled on land whose title was in dispute. Indian tribes continued to regard the region between the mountains and the Ohio River as their proper hunting grounds and raided the English farms and settlements despite the presence of colonial troops at Fort Ligonier and Fort Pitt. The colony of Virginia still claimed much of the region, as did the Proprietors of Pennsylvania, who discouraged all settlements in the disputed territory until the boundary between Virginia and Pennsylvania was defined. Nonetheless the English settlement continued under military permits that encouraged the cultivation of lands near the English forts to provide food for the garrisons at Ligonier and Fort Pitt. Unauthorized settlements also increased as land-hungry farmers from the east moved westward along the Braddock and Forbes Roads and squatted in the valleys and along the rivers and streams of southwestern Pennsylvania on lands to which they hoped eventually to gain title.[6]

The Treaty of Paris (1763) ended the French and Indian War, but the French surrender of their lands in the Ohio Valley as stipulated by the treaty caused an intensification of the conflict between the English settlers and the Native Americans for control of the region. The uprising of 1763 known as Pontiac's War threatened English settlements as far east as the Susquehanna River. British forts north of Pittsburgh fell to indigenous war bands. Settlers were attacked and massacred. Fort Pitt and Fort Ligonier were in imminent danger of capture. In July 1763 Colonel Henry Bouquet led a force of five hundred British regulars to the relief of Fort Pitt, which was under siege. He reached Fort Ligonier on August 2, and after allowing his troops two days' rest, he set out along the Forbes Road toward the English stronghold on the forks of the Ohio. Bouquet's force camped the first night on ground west of Chestnut Ridge, about two miles south of the future site of Saint Vincent, and on August 5 they continued their march fifteen miles northwest toward a place called Bushy Run, midway between Fort Ligonier and Fort Pitt. A mile from Bushy Run the four regiments were attacked by a superior force of warriors from the Six Nations under the Seneca chief Guyasuta. The battle lasted twenty-four hours and ended only when a desperate Bouquet feigned retreat, then turned on the attackers, caught them in a withering cross fire, and drove them from the field.

Bouquet's victory at the Battle of Bushy Run brought the relief of Fort Pitt, led to the eventual defeat of Pontiac and his allies, and ultimately assured that the region of southwestern Pennsylvania would be settled by English-speaking rather than French-speaking peoples.[7]

In November 1768 representatives of the Proprietors of Pennsylvania signed the Treaty of Fort Stanwix with the Native American leaders whose people claimed the Ohio Valley. In this treaty the Indians sold their lands south of the Ohio River and east of the Allegheny River to the Province of Pennsylvania for about ten thousand dollars in provisions and an unlimited supply of rum. In April 1769 the province opened a land office for the sale of warrants for lands in the Stanwix Purchase, and thus a mechanism for gaining legal title to property in southwestern Pennsylvania was established. A land rush followed that during the next twenty-five years brought more than 60,000 settlers to the region.[8]

The vast majority of pioneers who came to southwestern Pennsylvania after 1769 were Scotch-Irish Presbyterians, who cut the trees, cleared the land, and established modest family farms in the dense forest. They brought with them strong Calvinist principles of hard work, independence, and righteousness; they fought savagely against the Native Americans who continued to raid their settlements, and when it came, they embraced the revolutionary fight for liberty with a courage and perseverance that inspired their fellow revolutionaries on the Atlantic Coast.

In 1773 the Proprietors of Pennsylvania established Westmoreland County to include the whole region west of the Allegheny ridges. Virginia also claimed much of this land, and a key purpose for establishing the new county was to create a civil administration under Pennsylvania jurisdiction for the region. The Virginia militia had occupied Fort Pitt, and the southern colony claimed all lands west of the Monongahela River. The Pennsylvanians established the Westmoreland county seat at Hannastown on the Forbes Road, a little less than halfway between Fort Ligonier and Fort Pitt, and sent protests about the Virginian "invasion" to the governor of Pennsylvania in Philadelphia.

But the presence of the Virginians was not the greatest concern of the Westmoreland County settlers. Conflict with the native peoples continued to be the gravest threat to their safety and survival. Because of the depredation wrought by the continuing raids of Indian war parties, the white farmers began to build small forts and blockhouses throughout the county. These included a number of fortified houses along the Forbes Road between Fort Ligonier and Hannastown, places such as Fort Wallace, Fort

Barr, Shield's Fort, Fort Walthour, Fort Allen, and Fort Shippen which served as refuges for farmers and their families during the decade between 1774 and 1784 when native incursions were at their height. The last of these strongholds, Fort Shippen, was built in 1774 by Colonel John Proctor, sheriff of Westmoreland County, at his property near the Forbes Road on Fourteen Mile Run, only a mile from the site that eventually became Saint Vincent.[9]

In the American Revolution the frontier communities of Westmoreland County not only provided their full quota of troops for the Continental Army in the East but also defended the settlers with varying degrees of success against British-supplied Indian war parties who raided them with increasing frequency beginning in 1774. In May 1775 a convention of Westmoreland citizens assembled at Hannastown and adopted the Hannastown Resolves which called for armed opposition "should troops be sent from Great Britain to enforce the late arbitrary acts of its Parliament." In order to put teeth into the resolution, the Hannastown delegates organized a battalion of volunteers under the command of Colonel John Proctor. Westmoreland County volunteers served with Washington's army throughout the Revolution, while others remained behind to defend the county against Indian raids. Dozens of such raids took place during the Revolution, most of them involving small bands of Tory and Native American marauders. The American response was to send several expeditions against the Indian villages in the Allegheny Valley. The severest blow inflicted by the British and their Indian allies against Westmoreland County occurred in July 1782 when sixty Canadian rangers and one hundred Seneca attacked Hannastown and burned it to the ground.[10]

With the end of the Revolution, Indian raids in the county diminished and finally ended, and the region was opened to settlement once again. New pioneers came across the eastern mountains and settled on the rich farmlands of the Loyalhanna Valley between Ligonier and Hannastown. Most of these new settlers were Irish and German immigrants who established themselves either in and around the new county seat of Greensburg or on lands at a greater distance from the old Forbes Road than the farms of the earliest settlers. Some of the new arrivals were Catholics. The stretch of land along the Forbes Road between Ligonier and Hannastown was the most desirable in the area because the road gave access to markets in both the East and West. The plantations established along the road were generally three-hundred-acre plots sufficient to sustain a family and produce enough surplus to be sold at market for the family's cash income. Postrevolutionary records show that among those holding tracts along the Forbes Road on either side of the Chestnut Ridge were Hugh White, John Pollock, James Gurdie, Arthur O'Hara, Mary Rowan, William Lochry, William Grier, John Proctor, James Hunter, and Joseph Hunter.[11] Some of those on the list—William Lochry, John Proctor, and James Hunter for example—were long-time residents of Westmoreland County and veterans of the American Revolution. Others were newcomers. Exactly how long Joseph Hunter had lived in the county is not known. What is clear, however, is that in 1790 he received from James Hunter, possibly his father, a tract of a little more than three hundred acres on the Forbes Road where it intersects with Twelve Mile Run and that because of its popularity with hunters the tract was known locally as Sportsman's Hall.

SPORTSMAN'S HALL

As a result of the liberal Quaker policy of religious toleration, Pennsylvania could claim during the colonial period the second largest concentration of Catholic settlers in British North America after Maryland. The earliest Catholic immigrants to the colony were Irish servants accompanying the English and Welsh Quakers who founded Philadelphia in 1682, and evidence suggests that the first public Masses were celebrated, in violation of English penal laws, as early as 1707 in Philadelphia. In the 1730s Father Joseph Greaton, a Jesuit missionary, was openly celebrating Mass in the City of Brotherly Love for a small, predominately Irish congregation, and by mid-century a significant number of German Catholics, taking advantage of the Pennsylvania authorities' nonenforcement of British colonial anti-Catholic legislation, had settled in the colony as well. A census taken in 1756 reveals that Pennsylvania's Catholic population had grown to almost fourteen hundred adults. About four hundred of these lived in Philadelphia, but the rest, primarily farmers driven by war from the Rhineland and Palatinate regions of Germany, had established themselves in the rich farmlands of the Susquehanna, Schuylkill, and Lehigh River valleys. Mixing with English-speaking Catholics from Maryland, German Catholic farmers in the rural districts of eastern Pennsylvania formed worshiping congregations served by German-speaking Jesuits in Conewago, Lancaster, and Goshenhoppen during the 1740s. By 1784, when Rome named John Carroll superior (with the title of prefect apostolic) of the Catholic missions in the United States, the number of Catholics in Pennsylvania had risen to seven thousand, and six years later the state's estimated Catholic population was ten thousand. Most of them were Germans.[12]

Before the Revolution, the number of Catholics in the western regions of the colony of Pennsylvania was insignificant. From the evidence of prerevolutionary civil documents and postrevolutionary parish lists, however, it is possible to identify some Catholics who settled in Westmoreland County prior to 1776. In several petitions sent to Governor John Penn seeking military protection from the incursions of the Indians and redress of certain injuries suffered from the land claims of settlers from Virginia, we find the names of Catholics who would later play a role in establishing the first Catholic worshiping congregation in Westmoreland County. One such petition, sent in 1774 from Fort Shippen, the home of Colonel John Proctor on Fourteen Mile Run, was signed by Patrick Archibold; another, sent from Fort Allen in Hempfield Township, was signed by Richard Archibold, and a third, sent from Hannastown, the county seat, contained the names of William Freeman and Patrick Culgan. The Archibold, Freeman, and Culgan families were among the earliest Catholic settlers of Westmoreland County.[13]

After the Revolution several Catholic families from eastern Pennsylvania journeyed along the Forbes Road to Westmoreland County and settled in the vicinity of Greensburg. They came from the settlement of Goshenhoppen near Perkiomen Creek in Berks County, forty-five miles northwest of Philadelphia, a region settled by German Catholic and Mennonite farmers in the 1730s. In 1741 Father Theodore Schneider, S.J., arrived in Berks County to organize the Catholic community, and two years later the Catholic settlers, with the help of their Mennonite neighbors, built St. Paul's Chapel at Goshenhoppen, which Schneider used as a base for his missionary activities in Berks, Lehigh, and Bucks counties. By 1757 the number of Catholics in and around Goshenhoppen had risen to 228, and Schneider attended 364 more at his other regular mission stations in the farming region north of Philadelphia.[14] The first group of Catholics from Goshenhoppen arrived in Westmoreland County in 1787 and included, from the Austrian province of Tyrol, the three Ruffner brothers, Simon, Christian, and George, and their wives and children. The following year more Catholic families from Goshenhoppen came west and settled eight miles east of Greensburg in Unity Township, not far from Sportsman's Hall. This second group included Henry Kuhn, the brother of Christian Ruffner's wife Ottilia.

On March 13, 1789, six Catholic laymen—John Probst, John Young, Patrick Archibold, Simon Ruffner, Christian Ruffner, and George Ruffner—purchased a plot of ground near Greensburg to build a Catholic church and lay out a Catholic cemetery. The seller was Philip Freeman, one of the prerevolutionary Catholic settlers in Westmoreland County, and the price was the nominal sum of five shillings. In 1789 the small Catholic community began to construct a log church on the property. The heads of the families who joined together to build the church were, in addition to those mentioned above, Henry Kuhn, John Topper, Patrick Griffin, and Philip Hartmann. Because of developments that led to the building of another church near the farm of Henry Kuhn in Unity Township, construction of the Greensburg church was never completed. An attempt to finish the church in 1800 also failed, although Bishop John Carroll mentioned it in 1799 as a place where religious services were sometimes conducted.[15] After that the trustees of the congregation, who retained title to the plot of ground, sold the unfinished building to a local builder who dismantled and removed it. In 1847, a year after they came to Westmoreland County, the Benedictines built Most Holy Sacrament Church on the site of the unfinished log chapel.[16]

The German Catholics who settled in Westmoreland County hoped to obtain the services of a resident pastor, and even before leaving Goshenhoppen in 1787 they had solicited help from Catholic priests in Philadelphia, Goshenhoppen, and Conewago. According to some historians, Father Peter Helbron, a German Capuchin, visited the Westmoreland Catholics as early as 1787, and then again in 1789, to administer the sacraments. Helbron had been their priest in Goshenhoppen and undertook these pastoral visits in fulfillment of a promise he had made before they migrated beyond the Alleghenies that he would not neglect them once they moved west. As will be seen, Helbron became pastor in Westmoreland County in 1799, and his permanent establishment at Sportsman's Hall would be followed by a further migration of Catholic families from Goshenhoppen to Westmoreland County.[17] Tradition also records that in March 1789 Father John Baptist Cause, O.F.M., of Conewago made a brief pastoral call on Greensburg and during his stay celebrated Mass in the house of John Probst, ten miles west of the county seat near the site of modern-day Harrison City. Some have called this the first Mass celebrated for the German settlers from the East, but that presumes that Helbron did not visit earlier. Cause remained in western Pennsylvania only a few days before returning to Conewago, but it may have been at his suggestion, and in the hope of obtaining a permanent pastor, that the small community purchased the land for a church and cemetery at Greensburg, a transaction that occurred in the same month as his purported visit.

The third priest to visit the Westmoreland Catholics was Father Theodore Brouwers, O.F.M., who arrived in Greensburg in mid-November 1789, eight months after the departure of Father Cause. Brouwers came not as a temporary missionary but as permanent pastor of the new congregation, sent by the newly designated bishop of Baltimore, John Carroll. To prepare for his residency Father Brouwers had purchased, before his arrival, a farm of 162 acres (with 43 perches for road allowance) called O'Neill's Victory. The farm lay on the Loyalhanna Creek in Derry Township, about nine miles northeast of Greensburg and eight miles north of the Forbes Road. Brouwers bought it in August 1789 for £106 17s. from Arthur and Mary O'Neill of Chester County, Pennsylvania.[18]

Brouwers was a fifty-one-year-old native of Rotterdam who had entered the Franciscan Order at Louvain in 1757. After his ordination in 1762 he taught theology and philosophy at the seminary of Venlo in the province of Limburg, Holland. In 1770 his superiors sent him to the Franciscan monastery in Brussels to teach sacred scripture to young students of the order. Six years later, in July 1776, the Holy See transferred the missions of Curaçao in the West Indies from the Belgian Dominicans to the Belgian Franciscans, and Father Peter Schmising, Franciscan provincial in the Netherlands, called for volunteers for this new mission field. Theodore Brouwers was one of the volunteers, and Schmising appointed him superior of the missionary band that left for the Netherlands Antilles, off the coast of Venezuela, in September 1776. The voyage from Amsterdam to Willemstad, capital of Curaçao, lasted two months. Shortly after he arrived, the Holy See appointed Brouwers prefect apostolic of the Dutch West Indies (the same title that John Carroll held in the United States before being named bishop of Baltimore), and for eleven years he served the people of the islands. He left Curaçao, probably because of ill health, sometime after April 1787, when his name is last recorded in the baptismal record of the Willemstad mission. He next appears in January 1789 in Philadelphia, where his name is recorded on the subscription list for a book entitled *The Unerring Authority of the Church.* In Philadelphia Brouwers first assisted Father John Baptist (Charles) Helbron, O.F.M. Cap., brother of Father Peter Helbron, at the newly established German parish of Holy Trinity and then went to the German congregation in Conewago where he worked for several months under Father James Pellentz, pastor of Sacred Heart Church. In November 1789 John Carroll appointed him pastor of the Catholic congregation in southwestern Pennsylvania.

Brouwers spent the winter of 1789–90 as a guest in the home of Christian and Ottilia Ruffner, whose farm lay five miles northeast of Greensburg, near the ruins of Hannastown and not far from the present-day town of Crabtree. During the winter he celebrated Mass in the Ruffners' farmhouse and visited his parishioners to administer the sacraments and organize the congregation. When spring came he went to O'Neill's Victory with the intention of selecting a site to build a house for himself and a chapel for the congregation, but learning that the land was not as fertile as he had been led to believe and that its location, removed from the main body of the Catholic community and eight miles distant from the Forbes Road, was inconvenient for his flock, he reconsidered his original plan. Advised by Christian Ruffner and Ruffner's brother-in-law, Henry Kuhn, Brouwers decided that he needed more fertile land and a centrally located site more accessible to the main road of the region for the first parish church in Westmoreland County, and it happened that just at that time Sportsman's Hall, the 313-acre farm of Joseph Hunter on the north side of the Forbes Road at Fourteen Mile Run, was advertised for sale. Kuhn, whose own farm was nearby, urged Brouwers to seize the opportunity and buy the land. Brouwers agreed, and on April 16, 1790, he received from Joseph Hunter the deed for the Sportsman's Hall tract, which contained 313 acres with 8 perches for road allowance, in exchange for "Four Hundred and Seventy-Five Pounds Specie Good and Lawful money of Pennsylvania." This tract had previously been part of the estate of James Hunter, probably Joseph Hunter's father. James Hunter had purchased it in 1768 from John Fraser, who received it under military permit in 1766 from the commander of Fort Pitt.[19]

When Theodore Brouwers bought the Sportsman's Hall tract, it consisted chiefly of forested land. About a hundred acres were cleared ground, sixty of which were under cultivation while the other forty awaited the plough. A small building existed on the property, but it was hardly more than a hut and certainly not suitable for divine services. With help from his parishioners Father Brouwers began constructing a log house seventeen feet square and one and a half stories high to serve as both pastoral residence and chapel. When the structure was completed, Brouwers moved in and hired Christian and Maria Andrews to tend the farm at a salary of £26 a year. He continued, however, to say Sunday Mass at the home of Christian and Ottilia Ruffner, about five miles northwest of Sportsman's Hall, where the Catholics of the area were accustomed to assemble for worship.

Brouwers' health deteriorated in the months that followed his move to Sportsman's Hall, and one Sunday in June 1790, while celebrating Mass, he collapsed at the altar. He sent to Greensburg for a lawyer to help him write his will, and William Maghee, county registrar, came to assist him. Over the next several weeks Father Brouwers recovered sufficiently to return to his ministry, but recognizing that his end was near, he wrote Jesuit Father James Pellentz, pastor of Sacred Heart Church in Conewago, asking for a priest to take over the pastoral care of the Westmoreland congregation and to be on hand when the moment came for him to be given the last rites of the Church. The priest whom Pellentz sent from Conewago was John Baptist Cause, who had visited Westmoreland County in March 1789 and who now returned to Sportsman's Hall in the early autumn of 1790 with the ostensible purpose of assisting Father Brouwers.

While the vast majority of Catholic clergy who served the faithful in the United States during the late eighteenth and early nineteenth centuries were men of integrity and often even of heroic sanctity, the early history of the Church in the United States also records stories of self-serving clerics who left Europe under clouds of scandal and ecclesiastical censure, seeking refuge in America where they hoped to be free to pursue their own ends untroubled by religious superiors and ecclesiastical authority. Throughout his episcopacy Bishop John Carroll was troubled by such vagabond European priests, whom he referred to in exasperation as a "medley of clerical characters." Regrettably, Father John Baptist Cause was one of these.

A German Recollect friar, whose name in religion was Fidentianus (or Fidelis), Cause had abandoned his monastery in Germany sometime before 1784 and gone to Philadelphia where Father Ferdinand Farmer, pastor of St. Mary's Church, took pity on the fugitive and helped him obtain pardon from his superiors in Germany. John Carroll, newly appointed superior of the missions in the United States, conditionally accepted him as a member of the American clergy, gave him faculties, and appointed him to serve the German congregation in Lancaster, Pennsylvania.[20] But Cause soon manifested signs of the instability and lack of discipline that led to his excommunication seven years later. Abandoning his post at Lancaster, he returned to Philadelphia and from there went to Boston. He spent the next two years wandering the Northeast and seeking his fortune wherever opportunity led him. From Boston he moved to Quebec, then to Halifax, Nova Scotia, and finally back to Philadelphia in 1787. Carroll, hard-pressed for German-speaking priests to minister to the Catholics of eastern Pennsylvania, agreed to accept Cause on trial once again and reassigned him to Lancaster where he worked quietly in the parish for a while and served as a founding trustee of Franklin College (later Franklin and Marshall). In 1789 he returned to Philadelphia, but the following year he pulled up stakes again and went to the German Catholic colony of Conewago to work under Father James Pellentz. It was soon after Cause's arrival in Conewago that the call came from Theodore Brouwers for a priest to assist with the pastoral care of the congregation at Sportsman's Hall, and Father Pellentz made the unfortunate decision to send the wayward Franciscan to Westmoreland County.[21]

When Cause arrived in western Pennsylvania, he found Father Brouwers on the verge of death. Rather than attend to the spiritual needs of the dying priest and the welfare of the flock he had come to serve, however, he immediately turned his attention to mundane matters and asked to see a copy of Brouwers' will. Upon reading it he expressed his displeasure over the disposition of the pastor's personal effects and demanded that certain alterations be made. Specifically, he pressed Brouwers to bequeath his property to the priests of Conewago, of whom he himself was one. Clearly he intended to take possession of all Brouwers' property upon the older priest's death, but even though Cause refused to administer the last sacraments to him until he altered his will, Brouwers resisted. When Brouwers, desperate for the sacraments, at last indicated his willingness to make concessions, Cause summoned William Maghee, the county registrar, from Greensburg to help draw up the new will. Maghee transcribed several wills dictated by Father Brouwers but none of them satisfied Cause. At last Maghee, seeing that Father Brouwers was near death, protested against his being forced to make any further concessions.

Thus five days before his death Father Brouwers signed the final version of his will in the presence of Maghee, Cause, and Christian Andrews, the hired hand who tended the farm at Sportsman's Hall. He left fifty dollars to his "beloved Sister" Gertrude Brouwers; his farm animals and farm utensils to Christian Andrews as payment for the services he had rendered; his books, clothing, furniture, and personal effects to Father James Pellentz in trust "for the use of the Poor Roman Catholic Priest, that does or shall live at the Chappel, on Connewagga"; and all his land, both at Sportsman's Hall and O'Neill's Victory, with their appurtenances, "to a Roman Catholic Priest that shall succeed me in this said place, to be Entaild to him and to his Successors in trust and so left by him who shall succeed me to his successors and so in trust and for the use herein mentioned in succession for ever." Finally he enjoined his successors to offer four Masses a year in perpetuity for the repose of his soul.[22]

Theodore Brouwers died on October 29, 1790, at the age of fifty-two, and in accord with his wishes the congregation buried him in the cemetery at Sportsman's Hall. Father John Baptist Cause officiated, and a local stonemason, Peter Cole, constructed a small stone wall around the grave for which he was paid one dollar by Christian Ruffner and Henry Kuhn, the executors of the will.

After his death a number of pious legends grew up around Father Brouwers. He was venerated by his parishioners as a holy man who selflessly devoted his life to the priestly vocation to which he had been called as a youth, and to the Catholic congregation of Westmoreland County, which he had served for only a year before he died. It was said that during his yearlong ministry at Sportsman's Hall he had frequently expressed the hope of creating there a Catholic community at least as strong and devout as the one at Conewago, and that he had also planned to begin a school on his property for young men who aspired to the priesthood. One historian even records an oral tradition that Father Brouwers often said he hoped Sportsman's Hall would become "a nursery for many priests."[23] Those who passed on the legend of Brouwers' aspirations for a seminary at Sportsman's Hall had the advantage of hindsight, of course, but it is not beyond reasonable speculation that the former professor of theology and holy scripture in the Franciscan seminaries of Holland and Belgium did indeed hope one day to create a school on his property in western Pennsylvania where priests could be trained for the American missions. Whatever his intentions, Brouwers did not live to open a school at Sportsman's Hall, although he did, by an unusual clause in the will John Baptist Cause forced him to sign, make it possible for such a school eventually to take root there. Much scandal and trouble would intervene, however, before that hidden purpose would be revealed.

A MEDLEY OF CLERICAL CHARACTERS

The most important item in Father Brouwers' will was the clause in which he bequeathed to his successors as pastors of Sportsman's Hall the 475 acres of land he had bought from Arthur O'Neill and Joseph Hunter. As the reputed new pastor of the Westmoreland congregation, John Baptist Cause, immediately after the Dutch Franciscan's death, claimed rights to the property. He took possession of both the estate and Brouwers' personal effects and sent to Conewago for a four-horse team and wagon to haul away the movables. Cause remained at Sportsman's Hall only until the wagon came from the East. Then he loaded up the books, clothing, and furniture and made preparations to abandon his religious obligations (though not his property claims) at Sportsman's Hall. He told the parishioners that he was obliged to go to Philadelphia on business but that he would return in the spring. Father Brouwers, who had been a frugal man throughout his life, had left on deposit in a Philadelphia bank the considerable sum of $1,146. Because he was not authorized to receive the money, Cause asked the executors, Christian Ruffner and Henry Kuhn, to grant him power of attorney to do so, and he offered when he traveled to Philadelphia to withdraw the funds and bring the cash back to them, thus saving them the trouble, expense, and inconvenience of so tedious a journey.

Ruffner and Kuhn, who had not interfered when Cause took possession of the house nor when he removed the personal property of Father Brouwers, now became suspicious. They hesitated to grant him power of attorney, but he appealed to their loyalty to the Church, saying that good Catholics did not mistrust the word of a priest and that if they showed such lack of confidence in him, he could not possibly continue as their pastor. His argument had the desired effect, and in November 1790 Cause departed Westmoreland County with a wagonload of Father Brouwers' possessions and written authorization from Ruffner and Kuhn to withdraw Brouwers' money from the bank.

The suspicions of Ruffner and Kuhn proved in the end to be well grounded. When he arrived in Philadelphia, Cause withdrew the money from the bank, but instead of returning to Westmoreland County, he went on a spending spree. He bought a traveling circus or minstrel show called "Jerusalem" and toured the countryside where he gave performances and "abandoned himself to every vice." Learning of the scandal caused by Cause's behavior, Father James Pellentz, vicar general for Germans in the Diocese of Baltimore and pastor of Conewago, sent a messenger to Sportsman's Hall to inform the executors of Cause's actions. He advised them to have Cause arrested or to empower him as vicar general to act for them. Ruffner and Kuhn sent Pellentz power of attorney, and Pellentz brought charges against Cause for misusing the property and money of Father Brouwers. Cause was arrested and jailed in York, Pennsylvania, and the court summoned Ruffner and Kuhn to York to testify against him. Cause found bail and gave bond of £361. In order to avoid a prison sentence, he also signed documents formally relinquishing all claims to Brouwers' property in Westmoreland County.[24]

In February 1792 Bishop John Carroll excommunicated Cause, accusing him of immorality and of attempting to set up a schismatic church in Baltimore "with a few of the worst of his countrymen." Carroll wrote Cardinal

Leonardo Antonelli, prefect of the Roman Congregation for the Propagation of the Faith, that Cause had

> spread the report that as he was a religious he did not need episcopal authorization to act as a pastor of souls. By letter he dared to make this statement to me. He was active in calumniating me and others whom he disliked. Eventually, on the advice of the priests at hand, I resorted to the extreme measure of excommunication; but this did not deter him, nor did it induce his followers to absent themselves from his meetings. They seemed to think that by coming to America, besides attaining civil liberty, they could now, with impunity, oppose the pastors of souls.[25]

In May 1793 Cause wrote Bishop Carroll expressing repentance for what he had done and seeking reconciliation with the Church. The bishop wrote at once expressing his willingness to remove "the censures under which you now are, as soon as you give satisfactory proofs of the sincerity of your repentance, & readiness to repair public scandals,"[26] but no further correspondence in the Carroll papers indicates whether Cause followed through with his intention to repent and reconcile with the Church. After June 1793 his name disappears from the records. By then, however, another scandal was brewing in Westmoreland County which would bring the fledgling Sportsman's Hall congregation into disrepute and cause turmoil and conflicts, both internal and public, lasting until the end of the century. Again, the troubles began with the arrival of a self-serving, unscrupulous priest.

In July 1789 Father Francis Rogatus Fromm, a German Franciscan friar who had been ordained in 1773 for the Archdiocese of Mainz, arrived in Baltimore with commendatory letters from the vicar general of the archbishop of Mainz and Cardinal Leonardo Antonelli of the Sacred Congregation for Propaganda Fide to the superior of the American missions, Father John Carroll. While events later proved that Fromm had obtained these letters under false pretenses, Carroll accepted them at face value and conditionally received Fromm into the mission, assigning him to the German congregation of Conewago under the authority of Father James Pellentz.[27] In Conewago Fromm made the acquaintance of fellow Franciscan Father Theodore Brouwers shortly before Brouwers' departure for Westmoreland County, and also met Father John Baptist Cause, who at the time was serving the German congregation in Lancaster. When the peripatetic Cause went to Philadelphia late in 1789, Pellentz appointed Fromm to Lancaster, where he remained until March 1791.

Fromm's tenure as pastor of St. Mary's Church, Lancaster, was not a happy one. The parishioners complained to Carroll, who had been consecrated bishop of Baltimore in August 1790, that he was unable to preach, hear confessions, or teach their children in English; that he failed to celebrate daily Mass; that he rejected the traditional devotional texts that nourished their spiritual lives; that he planned to introduce a new catechism whose orthodoxy they suspected; and that he was "harsh and morose" in his dealings with them, an aspect of his character especially evident in his heavyhanded public treatment of a widow of the parish. The congregation asked the bishop to send them another pastor, and Carroll wrote Fromm informing him that he intended to do so.

> As you have not as yet been admitted officially to the American clergy, but only allowed to engage in certain ministerial works until some decision could be arrived at concerning your position, I have finally come to the conclusion that it would be better for you to return to a monastery in Germany. Whether it is from some weakness of your character or because of the prejudices of others it seems that your labors will bear no fruit for the spreading of the faith here.[28]

By now the parish at Sportsman's Hall was without a priest. Father Brouwers had died in October, and Father Cause had abandoned the congregation and gone east in November. About the time Fromm received Carroll's letter recommending that he return to Germany, he learned either from Cause himself or perhaps from the priests at Conewago of the unusual bequest in Father Brouwers' will. On March 3 he wrote the bishop, defending his actions and claiming that he had been slandered by the parishioners in Lancaster. He asked Carroll to appoint another pastor for these headstrong people and said that he intended to go west to work among the Catholics of Westmoreland County.

On April 5 Carroll wrote him a conciliatory letter, admitting the possibility that reports about his behavior in Lancaster had been inaccurate and offering to allow him to continue as pastor there "if you can maintain the station . . . in peace and with benefit to religion." He said, however, that he could not consider appointing him to Westmoreland County until he had additional information about the needs of the congregation there.[29] Shortly after receiving this letter, Fromm defiantly set out for western Pennsylvania with the intention of assuming charge of the Sportsman's Hall parish and laying claim, in accordance with the will, to the 475 acres of land that Brouwers had bequeathed to his successor. He arrived at Sportsman's Hall on May 2, 1791, and announced to the congregation that he was their new pastor.

It is clear that in the beginning at least the Westmoreland parishioners were delighted that Fromm had come and that they again, after a six-month hiatus, had a resident pastor. Fromm took up residence in the log house that Brouwers had built and from Sportsman's Hall began his ministry among the Catholics of the neighborhood. To secure his position, he persuaded the congregation to draw up and sign a document acknowledging him as their "Catholic priest and pastor for the time of his Life and Lawfully elected Sucsesor in the name of the r[ev]. theo[dore Brouwers], who has by his Last will and testament Constituded his Sosesor[s] in his estate [as] heirs and trustees of his place called Sportsman hall. [sic]"[30] It is noteworthy that Fromm did not claim to have been appointed by Bishop John Carroll but to have been "Sent as Catholicion missionaries by the rite re[v]. arch bishop of ments [i.e. Mainz] according [to] the witness of his authentick Letter." The lay trustees at Sportsman's Hall, unversed in ecclesiastical law, did not realize that the archbishop of Mainz had no authority to assign a pastor to them and were understandably impressed by the document Fromm showed them, purportedly signed by the vicar general of the German archbishop. Their own ecclesiastical superior, John Carroll, was to their way of thinking merely a bishop, and living in Baltimore as he did, he was for all practical purposes almost as distant from them as was the much more impressively titled archbishop of Mainz. Over the next several years Carroll fought an uphill battle to convince the Westmoreland Catholics that only he, as bishop of Baltimore, had jurisdiction to appoint pastors in the United States. Throughout the subsequent controversy Fromm continued to claim rights in western Pennsylvania based upon credentials he claimed from the archbishop of Mainz. It is ironic that in the end the "authentick Letter" Fromm presented to the congregation at Sportsman's Hall proved to be a forgery.[31]

In July Fromm went to Philadelphia to collect furniture and other materials for his new home at Sportsman's Hall, and from there he wrote Bishop Carroll that he had taken charge of the Westmoreland congregation and, with the acquiescence of its leaders, had assumed ownership of the Brouwers estate. In the meantime the bishop had received reports from Greensburg that Fromm was moving dangerously close to schism by encouraging the congregation to declare its independence from the authority of the bishop of Baltimore. Carroll answered Fromm's letter several weeks later with a harsh denunciation of the German priest's presumption and a stern warning against further attempts to alienate the Westmoreland Catholics from the bishop.

> [Y]ou left Lancaster and went to Greensburg without consulting me, or even mentioning your plans to me. I state the facts as I heard them; whether they are true or not, you know well enough. First: that you desire to alienate the parishioners, and

especially the German parishioners, from me, their Bishop, by suggesting that I am not solicitous of them, and do not care for them: Second: that you ostentatiously presumed to insinuate that I enjoyed no right to the distribution of goods, which Rev. Mr. Browers, of pious memory, applied to sacred uses. Actually, I never interfered in that business, except inasmuch as a Bishop should, by reminding Mr. Cause of his duty: Thirdly: you declared that you could exercise and that you intended to exercise the sacred ministry wherever you wished and without my consent. Before another parish will be assigned you, I await a reply to these charges, one without evasions, and also an explicit acknowledgment of my ordinary jurisdiction, extending throughout all the provinces of the United States. This I do because a story was designedly circulated by Mr. Cause, perhaps by others also, and spread by Germans, to the effect that I am in no way their Bishop. Your letter seems to imply that you took fifty books from the effects of Rev. Mr. Browers. By what right you did so, I do not know. However, that affair must not be transacted with me, but with the Executors of his will, upon whom falls the obligation of accounting for everything to Rev. Mr. Pellentz. What you add about the scandal arising from the civil action against Rev. Mr. Cause, is, it seems, indirectly aimed at me, although I had no part in it, I gave no advice, and knew nothing of the affair. But now, since action has been resorted to, I both approve it and judge it necessary. If any scandal results, let it recoil on him who made it necessary. Would that nothing more serious and more unbecoming happens.[32]

When he received this letter, Fromm realized that Carroll had no intention of confirming his pastorship in Westmoreland County and that probably the bishop planned to send another priest to take charge of Sportsman's Hall. In defiance of the bishop he wrote Christian Ruffner and Henry Kuhn instructing them not to allow "any priest, whom P. Pellentz may send, to take possession of Father Brouwers' house, otherwise we may lose everything," and began making plans for his immediate return to the western parish. Fromm arranged to ship his personal effects from Lancaster to Greensburg, and he met with Father Cause in York to settle the debts Cause had left unpaid when he abandoned the parish. He reported to the executors of Father Brouwers' estate that Cause continued to refuse to surrender Brouwers' personal property—his books, clothing, furniture, and other movables—to Father Pellentz "because the will says 'for the use of the poor roman Catholic Priest of the Chappel at Conewagge' and there is no other 'poor roman Catholic Priest' there [except Cause] since all the rest belong to the very rich community of the ex-Jesuits, who own over 10,000 acres of land in America and consequently are not to be counted among the 'poor roman Catholic Priests.'"[33]

Fromm returned to Sportsman's Hall in September and for almost two years functioned as pseudo-pastor, apparently to the general satisfaction of the people. Despite the efforts of James Pellentz of Conewago, vicar general of the diocese, and of emissaries such as Father Michael Levadoux, S.S., whom the bishop sent to remonstrate with him, Fromm refused to acknowledge Carroll's jurisdiction and effectively led the congregation into schism. He publicly maligned both Pellentz and Carroll and told the people that they owed allegiance not to the bishop of Baltimore but to himself personally as representative of the archbishop of Mainz. Gradually he compounded his offenses by sliding from schism into heresy. Carroll wrote that Fromm "panegyrized Luther. He preached against the Holy Sacrifice of the Mass although he was ready to celebrate it any number of times just to retain possession of the manor. He harangued against devotion to the Blessed Virgin, and against clerical celibacy. Finally, again and again he sought to marry."[34] His patience tried to the limit, the bishop finally issued a formal revocation of Fromm's priestly faculties and ordered him once again to surrender charge of the parish at Sportsman's Hall. On May 13, 1793, Bishop Carroll wrote the intransigent priest: "In order to curb such intolerable excesses as far as possible, to protect from further danger the sheep entrusted to my care, and to forestall all evasions, by this letter, I revoke whatsoever faculties I ever gave you for discharging any sacred ministry. And all faculties revoked at my orders by one of my Vicars General are hereby again revoked. Insofar as needed I declare them to be null and void."[35]

As he pondered ways to resolve the impasse that had developed in Westmoreland County, John Carroll received an inquiry from England that for a while he thought would lead to a practical and advantageous solution to the problem of what to do with the Brouwers estate once Fromm was ejected from it. The inquiry came from Father Michael Pembridge, an English Benedictine who was seeking a refuge for monks of the English Congregation expelled from France in the wake of the French Revolution. Pembridge wrote Carroll to explore the possibility of establishing an English Benedictine foundation for this purpose in the United States, and Carroll replied that he would welcome a colony of up to a dozen monks, "including, at least, four good laborious lay Brothers." He offered Sportsman's Hall "in the neighborhood of the town, called Pittsburg, in Pennsylvania" as the "properest place for a settlement and a school." And in case the English monks feared the dangers of settling in what was then the American West, the bishop wrote that "this situation is far remote from, & as secure as London, from the Indians, and there is a continual communication and regular posts from that settlement to Balt[imor]e, Phila[delphia], and all the trading towns on the Atlantic." In the end the English Benedictines chose not to found a monastery in the Diocese of Baltimore, and more than fifty years would pass before monks from Bavaria would finally settle at Sportsman's Hall and introduce Benedictine life to North America. It is noteworthy, however, that as early as 1794 John Carroll had identified the Brouwers estate as the "properest place" for a Benedictine community in the United States.[36]

Meanwhile, as Carroll corresponded with the English Benedictines, the parishioners at Sportsman's Hall had begun to grow uneasy about their anomalous status with respect to the bishop of Baltimore, and to question Father Fromm's claims of having proper authority to assume pastoral rights over the Westmoreland congregation. A majority of them insisted that he reconcile with Bishop Carroll, submit to his jurisdiction, and obtain credentials from him to serve as pastor of Sportsman's Hall. They presented an ultimatum that unless within one year he became reconciled with Carroll and received his approval to continue as their pastor, he must step down from his position and relinquish all claims to the property he held under the Brouwers will.

Fromm reluctantly signed an agreement with the lay leaders of the congregation acceding to these demands, but when he received another letter from the bishop rejecting his argument that Brouwers' will gave him the right to assume title to the Sportsman's Hall property and censuring him for his continued insubordination, Fromm realized that because of his agreement with the congregation he was likely to lose the property before the year was out.[37] He therefore conspired to seize the document he had signed, and when he had it in his possession, he ripped off his signature and declared to the startled people, "I am not your priest and you are not my congregation!" His plan now was to claim title to Sportsman's Hall by virtue of his fulfilling the will's stipulation that Brouwers' successor offer four Masses a year for the repose of his soul. The majority in the congregation rejected this interpretation, and when they received a letter from Bishop Carroll confirming that Fromm had "never been commissioned to exercise pastoral functions amongst you" and that the bishop had suspended him from celebrating Mass, they instituted civil proceedings against him in the Westmoreland County Court of Common Pleas with the intention of ejecting him from the property.[38]

In his letter to the Sportsman's Hall Catholics, Bishop Carroll instructed them not to assist at any Masses offered by Fromm but "to sanctify the Sundays and feasts by private religious exercises at y[ou]r homes, till it shall please heaven to grant you a pastor, for which blessing I will labour immediately." The pastor that Carroll found for them was Father Lawrence Sylvester Phelan (sometimes written Whelan), an Irish Capuchin who arrived in Westmoreland County in September 1795. Because Fromm continued to hold Sportsman's Hall, Father Phelan took up residence in the home of Simon Ruffner and began to minister to the Catholics of the county. He reported to Carroll that the people were very poor and that the imbroglio caused by Fromm's contumacy had divided them. Most of the Irish families had left the settlement, and the Germans who remained were split into two groups, those who supported Fromm and those who opposed him. Conditions had deteriorated to such an extent that some of the parishioners seemed ready to resort to violence. One night an unknown assailant shot a musket through Fromm's bedroom window in an obvious attempt to drive him away from Sportsman's Hall. In the wake of the attack Fromm brought suit against Phelan and several members of the congregation and then drew up his last will and testament.[39]

As the conflict escalated between Fromm and the congregation, as well as within the congregation itself, some of the cooler heads among the parishioners came together and attempted to reach a compromise. Even Fromm's supporters, among whom was Henry Kuhn, realized by now that no good could come from the continued standoff. They therefore agreed that Fromm should submit to the authority of Bishop Carroll and seek to be lawfully instated as pastor at Sportsman's Hall. Accordingly, in January 1796 three lay leaders of the parish—Henry Kuhn, Christian Ruffner, and Simon McBonsol—together with Fromm himself, drafted a letter to Carroll stating that because of "the high opinion all entertain of your Moderation, Prudence and Christian Virtue" they would abide by his decision either to permit Fromm to remain as pastor of Sportsman's Hall or "to be settled elsewhere."[40]

Bishop Carroll continued to insist, however, that Fromm leave Sportsman's Hall, though he indicated his willingness to "bury in oblivion" Fromm's offenses and find another place for him "provided that you satisfy me in certain essential points, which must be the grounds of my confidence." One of the essential points was that Fromm relinquish all claim to Father Brouwers' property.[41] Under these conditions Fromm refused to leave Sportsman's Hall, and both he and the parishioners resigned themselves to fighting the matter out in the courts. Frustrated with his inability to resolve the conflict and considering himself unable to minister to the parish effectively as long as Fromm remained, Father Lawrence Phelan left Westmoreland County in the middle of 1796. Carroll sent Father Patrick

Lonergan, O.S.F., to replace him, but Lonergan, too, found conditions impossible for the normal fulfillment of his pastoral duties. Divisiveness within the congregation continued to drive many families away, and shortly after his arrival, Lonergan gave up in exasperation and led a group of Sportsman's Hall families westward, first to Washington County and then to Greene County where they attempted unsuccessfully to establish Catholic colonies.[42]

The suit to eject Fromm from Sportsman's Hall came before Judge Alexander Addison, president of the Court of Common Pleas for the Fifth Circuit of Pennsylvania, at Greensburg in the December term, 1798. Representing the executors of the Brouwers will (collectively the plaintiff) was a Catholic lawyer from Maryland, Dominic Young, brother-in-law of Dominican Father Edward D. Fenwick, later bishop of Cincinnati. Representing Fromm (the defendant) was Hugh Brackenridge, a prominent Pennsylvania lawyer and a Protestant. Bishop Carroll provided information to the plaintiff's counsel outlining the history of Fromm's scandalous behavior and his subsequent suspension, explaining the nature of episcopal jurisdiction according to canon law, and detailing evidence to prove that the letter, allegedly from the archbishop of Mainz, which Fromm had used to claim authority to function as a priest in western Pennsylvania, was in fact a forgery.[43]

After the case had been presented and the charges read, Brackenridge offered a series of arguments to prove that Fromm, and not the executors of Father Brouwers' will or the bishop of Baltimore, was legal owner of the Sportsman's Hall and O'Neill's Victory tracts. He argued that the executors had no authority over the property because the will did not give them any; that the bishop of Baltimore had no claim to the property under law; that Carroll's suspension of Fromm was invalid because it had not been preceded by three warnings as required by canon law; that even if the suspension were judged valid, Fromm remained a priest and could administer the sacraments "though under a mortal sin" because "the laying on of hands Gives the holy Spirit which Cannot be Taken away"; and that as a priest with the power to administer the sacraments, Fromm, in accordance with the stipulations of the will, had the right to assume ownership of the Brouwers estate because "this Estate was Vacant and Acquirable by the first Occupant, qualified for performing the condition" of saying the foundation Masses for the repose of Brouwers' soul and because "Occupancy is a Title known to the law, the taking possession of things Belonging to no Body, [and] this Estate was of that Description."

In his response Dominic Young argued that since Pennsylvania and U.S. law protected the rights of all religions, the Sportsman's Hall case had to be decided in light of the laws of the Roman Catholic Church; that under the laws of the Church a priest could function as a pastor only with the consent of the local bishop, and that Fromm did not have that consent; that it was "Too Absurd to be Supposed" that merely by celebrating the foundation Masses called for in the will Fromm was fulfilling the intention of Brouwers, who had given the estate "to Enable a poor Catholick Congregation to support a priest Regularly Admitted to Administer Instruction and the sacraments to a flock which he loved"; that because he did not have the consent of the bishop of Baltimore, Fromm was not "regularly inducted" to perform this function and therefore did not meet the conditions of the will; that the executors of the will had the right and obligation to see that Brouwers' intentions were fulfilled; and that the executors therefore had the right to eject Fromm from the estate because the bishop of Baltimore had not authorized him to function as a pastor of souls.

Calling it a case that had been "argued with ingenuity" and regretting that "people will apply to ignorant men to Write wills and other papers affecting property," presiding judge Alexander Addison sided with the executors of Brouwers' will and instructed the jury to find for the plaintiff. In a judgment that set a precedent in American jurisprudence for recognition of the rights of Roman Catholic bishops to have sole authority over the spiritual and temporal affairs of the churches in their dioceses, Judge Addison said:

> [T]he bishop of Baltimore has, and before, and at the Time of Fromm's taking possession of this Estate, had the sole Episcopal authority over the Catholick Church of [the] United States[.] Every Catholick Congregation within the United States is subject to his inspection, and without Authority from him, no Catholick priest can Exercise any pastoral Functions over any Congregation within the United States[;] without his appointment or permission to Exercise Pastoral Functions over this Congregation, no priest Can be Entitled, under the will of Brower's to Claim the Enjoyment of this Estate. Fromm has no such appointment or permission and is, therefore, incompetent to discharge the duties or Enjoy the benefits which are the Objects of the will of Browers.[44]

The jury's verdict was for the plaintiff, and Fromm was ordered to surrender Sportsman's Hall to Brouwers' executors. Refusing to accept the Circuit Court's judgment, Fromm appealed to the Superior Court in Philadelphia, and in the spring of 1799, leaving his agent John Topper at Sportsman's Hall to protect his interests, he traveled east to pursue his case. In Philadelphia Fromm met Father Peter Helbron who urged him unsuccessfully to accept the original verdict and become reconciled with Bishop Carroll. He pressed forward with his appeal, but before the Superior Court could consider it, Fromm succumbed to the yellow fever epidemic then raging in Philadelphia and died sometime in the summer of 1799.

ORDER OUT OF CHAOS

Fromm's death marked the end of a decade of turmoil in the Westmoreland Catholic congregation. In the fall of 1799 Bishop Carroll appointed Father Peter Helbron as the new pastor of the parish, and in November Helbron arrived at Sportsman's Hall. His coming signaled the beginning of a sixteen-year period of peace and order after the chaos wrought by Cause and Fromm. Helbron was a Capuchin friar whom a contemporary characterized as "an estimable priest, a courteous whole-souled gentleman, cheerful, affable, kind to all, excellent company, and most thorough and exact in his spiritual duties with a soldier-like discipline and careful regard to details."[45]

Peter Helbron had come to the United States in 1787 with his brother and fellow Capuchin, Father John Baptist (Charles) Helbron, in response to calls for German priests to serve the growing numbers of German-speaking Catholics in the American Church. Peter Helbron's first assignment in America was at Goshenhoppen, Pennsylvania. In 1791 Bishop John Carroll appointed him pastor of Holy Trinity Parish, Philadelphia, to replace his brother. In 1796 the trustees of Holy Trinity forced him out of the pastorate by electing Father John Nepomucene Goetz in his place, and when Bishop Carroll refused to recognize their action, the trustees rejected the jurisdiction of the bishop and the parish entered into a schism that lasted until 1802. Helbron left Holy Trinity and took up residence at St. Joseph Parish, Philadelphia. Three years later, in October 1799, Carroll named him pastor in Westmoreland County.

Helbron's tenure at Sportsman's Hall opened a new era for the Catholics of the region. For the first time since the death of Theodore Brouwers, regular and peaceful relations among parishioners, pastor, and bishop became possible. After obtaining a court order to eject Fromm's agent, John Topper, from the property, Helbron took possession of Sportsman's Hall and set up residence in the small log house built a decade earlier by Brouwers. Because of losses caused by the scandals resulting from the actions of Cause and Fromm, the Westmoreland parish numbered fewer than fifty families when Helbron took charge of it.

The physical conditions he encountered at Sportsman's Hall upon his arrival were appalling. It was a "wrecked place in the wilderness" with a skeleton of a house for a dwelling and a dark, stuffy room for the celebration of Mass. "The house of Mr. Brouwers is very bad," he wrote, "because the rain comes through it. I wish I could take the 1,600 dollars of Mr. Brouwers from the bank which brought the unhappy Cause from Jerusalem, (and with which the unhappy Cause bought the show Jerusalem). I could build a fine church and house."[46] He counted only seventy-four Easter communicants in 1801, but by Easter 1809 the number of communicants in the parish had almost tripled.[47]

Peter Helbron devoted the next sixteen years of his life to serving the Catholics of western Pennsylvania, attending the spiritual needs of the people at Sportsman's Hall, and providing the leadership and pastoral care that transformed the poor congregation into a unified and flourishing community of faith. His selfless and painstaking labors reversed a decade of decline and healed the damage and divisiveness brought on by the scandalous conduct of his predecessor. Benedictine Father Gerard Bridge, an early historian of the Benedictine community at Saint Vincent, said of him:

> The arduous labors which he underwent in the missions of western Pennsylvania; his journeys across trackless forests without even the semblance of modern facilities of traveling; his constant struggle against the inroads of a disease which he evidently knew must terminate fatally; the restrictions imposed upon him by his unfamiliarity with the language of some of the parishioners; the readiness with which he was willing to spend and be spent for Christ: all these mark [Helbron] a man of God, a worthy associate of the early pioneers of this country, and an admirable example of patience and endurance so strikingly manifest in the great servants of God.[48]

In the year following Helbron's arrival at Sportsman's Hall the congregation constructed a new house, twenty-six by twenty-eight feet, for their pastor, and shortly afterward they built an extension to it which served as a temporary chapel. Henry Kuhn and George Ruffner did the carpentry work. In January 1801 Helbron wrote a friend in the East: "My little chapel which I built here is completed. I blessed it in the name of Jesus, and entitled it the chapel of the Holy Cross. I intend next spring to repair the other at Greensburg."[49] To accommodate the growing number of parishioners at Sportsman's Hall, the congregation constructed in 1810 a log church, forty by twenty-six feet. The heads of seventy-three families contributed a total of $206.50 towards the building expenses, and Henry Kuhn, the ever-active parish lay leader, traveled across the mountains to Carlisle to purchase the nails needed for construction.[50]

Helbron was the first pastor at Sportsman's Hall to keep a parish register of baptisms, marriages, burials, and Easter communions. Analysis of the data he recorded between 1800 and 1815, as well as of the names contained on the 1810 list of contributors to the building fund, indicates that 56 percent of the congregation's families were German, 37 percent Irish, and 7 percent English. The English and some of the Irish parishioners came from the old Catholic settlements of western Maryland, where many of the family names recorded at Sportsman's Hall are found a generation earlier (e.g., Noel/Noll, Wade, Topper, Burgoon, and Maguire). Names from the Goshenhoppen colony dominate among the German families recorded at Sportsman's Hall during Helbron's pastorate (e.g., Kuhn/Coon, Ruffner/Roofner, Heinrich/Henry, Aren/Aaron, Bruck/Bridge, Reinzel/Reintzel, and Flower). The immigration pattern for German Catholics settling in the neighborhood of Sportsman's Hall, therefore, appears to have included intermediate settlement in the German Catholic colonies of eastern Pennsylvania, especially in the Goshenhoppen area. Only a few families came to Westmoreland County from Conewago. The majority of Irish parishioners apparently immigrated directly from the old country. Before settling in Westmoreland County some Irish and German colonists stopped first in Cambria County where their names are recorded in the parish registers kept at Loretto by Father Demetrius Gallitzin, the famous Russian prince and Catholic missionary who came to be known as the "Apostle of the Alleghenies." These colonists included the Cantwells, Diamonds, Rheys, Trucks, and Riffles. Some intermarriage between the Catholic families of Loretto and Westmoreland County occurred. William Weakland of Loretto, for example, went to Sportsman's Hall to marry Mary Barbara Ruffner in 1804.[51]

A steady increase in the number of Easter communions between 1800 and 1810 points to Father Helbron's success in stemming and then reversing the defections by emigration and abandonment of the faith which occurred during Fromm's pseudo-pastorate. Many new families joined the parish after 1799, perhaps as many as eighty of them attracted to Westmoreland from Berks County by the presence of Father Helbron, who had been their curate in Goshenhoppen from 1787 to 1791. Helbron's parish register records an impressive number of baptisms during the decade and a half that he served as pastor of Sportsman's Hall. No fewer than 815 infants were baptized during this period, and nineteen adult baptisms were recorded as well. Adult converts included Lutherans, Methodists, Quakers, Calvinists, and those of "no religion," most of whom seem to have entered the Church when they married Catholic spouses. During the same period the register records forty-seven marriages and nine burials, the majority of which were of children under the age of twelve. The extremely high ratio of infant baptisms to adult deaths between 1799 and 1815 reveals that Helbron's was a vibrant, young, and growing Catholic congregation. The fact that the average number of Easter communions remained fairly constant, at about 150 per year, for the same period seems to indicate that Westmoreland County was often a temporary home for families who later continued their journey westward.[52]

From his base at Sportsman's Hall, Helbron assumed the pastoral care of Catholic settlers throughout western Pennsylvania. His missionary journeys took him south to Greene County on the Pennsylvania-Virginia border, and possibly as far north as Lake Erie. He visited the Irish colony of Donegal at Sugar Creek in present-day Armstrong County, and the Catholic settlements at Slippery Rock in Butler County and Brownsville on the Monongahela River in Fayette County. He often traveled as far as 160 miles from Sportsman's Hall to bring the sacraments to the scattered Catholics of the region. He celebrated Mass for the small Catholic community of Pittsburgh where in 1806 Colonel James O'Hara gave him a plot of land at Liberty and Washington Streets for St. Patrick's, the first Catholic church in the city.[53]

It was during Helbron's tenure that the Diocese of Baltimore was divided and the Diocese of Philadelphia, which included the parish of Sportsman's Hall, was created. In 1808 Father Michael Egan, O.F.M., was named the first bishop of Philadelphia, and in August 1811 he visited Sportsman's Hall for the first and only time to meet the congregation and administer the sacrament of confirmation. When Egan died in 1814, John Carroll, now archbishop of Baltimore, named Father Louis de Barth administrator of the Philadelphia diocese, a post he held until 1820 when Father Henry Conwell was named second bishop of Philadelphia. The Sportsman's Hall parish functioned under the jurisdiction of the bishop of Philadelphia from 1808 until 1843, when Rome divided the Diocese of Philadelphia and created that of Pittsburgh.

Helbron received no salary from the Westmoreland congregation for his labors. He neither asked for nor expected remuneration, since Theodore Brouwers' will provided income from the land at Sportsman's Hall and O'Neill's Victory for support of the resident pastor. Helbron, however, was not a careful steward of the property, and during his pastorate the estate fell into disrepair and debt. He kept too much livestock on the farm and did not sell the crops when prices were favorable. He also failed to pay punctually the farmer he had hired to manage the land. As a consequence the farmer neglected his duties, and the congregation's lay leaders grew apprehensive about the temporal affairs of the parish. Helbron, however, was a conscientious—indeed indefatigable—spiritual leader and pastor who earned the deep respect and love of the people. In 1815 ill health compelled him to travel east for an operation to remove a tumor from his neck. The parishioners collected money for his journey and treatment, but the surgery, performed by a doctor in Philadelphia, was unsuccessful. On his return journey to Sportsman's Hall, he stopped in Carlisle, Pennsylvania, at the home of a Catholic couple, Thomas and Mary Hagan. Nursed for several weeks by Mary Hagan, he finally succumbed to the illness which had plagued him for five years, and died on April 24, 1816. He was buried in the cemetery of St. Patrick's Church, Carlisle.

IRISH PASTORS AND LAY TRUSTEES

After the death of Father Helbron, the people of Sportsman's Hall had no resident pastor for almost two years. Father William Francis Xavier O'Brien of St. Patrick's Church, Pittsburgh, visited the congregation every three or four months, and other priests—including Demetrius Gallitzin of Loretto and James Pellentz of Conewago—occasionally came to administer the sacraments. Two of the parish's lay leaders, Simon Ruffner and John Rogers, assumed charge of the congregation's temporal affairs, and in May of 1816 they took up a collection to defray the costs of building an altar in the church Helbron had constructed in 1810. The collection yielded $310, contributed by sixty-two heads of parish households. The list of contributors included the names of many new Irish members of the congregation, most of whom had recently come to the region to help build the turnpikes being constructed in western Pennsylvania at the time.[54]

In the fall of 1817 Father Louis de Barth, administrator of the Diocese of Philadelphia, appointed Father Charles B. Maguire, O.S.F., as the third resident pastor of Sportsman's Hall. Maguire was a forty-nine-year-old native of County Tyrone, Ireland, who had experienced an eventful life before coming to the United States. He had studied for the priesthood at Louvain and after ordination had worked in parts of Holland and Germany. When Napoleon's armies invaded Holland, Maguire and other clergymen who opposed the French invaders were proscribed and arrested. Maguire was sentenced to death, but as he was being taken to the guillotine, a cooper who knew him managed to free him and he escaped. The heroic cooper was not so fortunate. He was seized by the infuriated mob and beaten to death. From Holland Maguire went to Rome where he taught theology at the college of St. Isidore for six years. In 1815 he was back in Belgium, working in Brussels where he ministered to sick and wounded soldiers after the Battle of Waterloo. In 1817 he immigrated to the United States, arriving in Philadelphia where he offered himself to Father de Barth as a missionary in good standing with his European superiors. As a linguist fluent in both German and English he was an ideal candidate for missionary work in the Diocese of Philadelphia, encompassing as it did the whole state of Pennsylvania with its German Catholic congregations and thousands of German immigrants.

Father Maguire arrived at Sportsman's Hall on November 27, 1817, and took up his duties at once. He found the farm neglected and the barn in need of repairs, so he appealed to the congregation for funds to build a new barn and put the land into profitable production once again. Maguire hired his brother to manage the farm and his sister-in-law to keep house for him, and he leased the best part of the farm to David Mulholland for a term of seven years. An unexpected drop in farm prices in 1819 led to a financial crisis throughout Pennsylvania, and at Sportsman's Hall Maguire found himself unable to repay the loans he had contracted in 1818 in order to build the barn and restock the farm with cattle.

In the spring of 1820, when Father William F. X. O'Brien resigned as pastor of St. Patrick's Church, Pittsburgh, Maguire left Westmoreland County and assumed charge of the Pittsburgh parish. He had given the parishioners at Sportsman's Hall assurances that he would remain their resident pastor permanently, and they regarded his move to Pittsburgh as a betrayal. Even though he continued to visit them occasionally to administer the sacraments, he had left the farm with a debt of almost $250 and once again without a resident priest. The lay leaders of the congregation were angry and decided to seek control of the property so that they could manage it without the interference of transient pastors. To this end they petitioned the state legislature to vest the property in a board of trustees, and despite a counterpetition from Father Maguire, the legislature approved a bill on March 7, 1821, placing the tracts of land mentioned in Brouwers' will in the hands of five "Trustees of the Roman Catholick Church in Westmoreland County, and their successors, who shall be Duly and Regularly appointed, according to the rules of the said Congregation, in trust for the uses mentioned and Declared in the last will and testament of the said Reverend Theodore Browers."[55] The first trustees were Dennis O'Connor, Edward Shivlin, Frederich Kintz, Conrad Henry, and Henry Kuhn.

Much has been written about the trustee system in the American Catholic Church during the eighteenth and nineteenth centuries. Earlier historians tended to emphasize the negative aspects of the system: the propensity of lay trustees to usurp authority canonically reserved for bishops and pastors, disagreements between laity and clergy over distribution of temporal goods, lay demands for the right to choose clergy to serve them, and administrative and doctrinal disputes which in several notable cases led to interdict or schism. More recently historians of the American Church have examined the system with greater sympathy for the point of view of the lay leaders who promoted it and have formulated more balanced assessments of this uniquely American institution within the universal Church. Patrick Carey, for example, sees the trustee system as part of a widespread attempt in the Catholic community of the United States "to adapt the European Catholic Church to American culture by identifying that Church with American republicanism,"[56] and Jay Dolan has pointed out that the system's emergence in almost every major city and parish in the United States provides evidence of a movement toward democratization of ecclesiastical life that signaled a new understanding of the Church.[57] As one of the trustees of the Catholic congregation in Charleston, South Carolina, observed, American Catholics wanted to "rear a National American Church, with liberties consonant to the spirit of Government, under which they live; yet, in due obedience in essentials to the Pontifical Hierarchy, and which will add a new and dignified column to the Vatican."[58]

Abuses did arise, and strong disagreements between lay trustees and clerical church leaders led to conflicts and schisms in Philadelphia, Baltimore, New York, Boston, Charleston, and Norfolk, Virginia. Nonetheless, the American vision of a "democratized" national Church independent of foreign temporal jurisdiction and endorsing pluralism and toleration of all religions—a vision of which the trustee system was an important manifestation—was shared even by such luminaries in the American hierarchy as Bishop John England of Charleston and (at least initially) Archbishop John Carroll of Baltimore.[59]

What the lay leaders at Sportsman's Hall sought in gaining legal control of the property left by Theodore Brouwers was to protect the parish's patrimony against the mismanagement of unwise clerical stewards and to ensure its proper use for the purposes and ends intended by their first pastor. In their petition to the Pennsylvania legislature, they had asserted that Brouwers' trust had "not been faithfully Executed but abused," and by establishing the trustee system at Sportsman's Hall, they sought to remedy that abuse.

Conflict between the lay trustees' interpretation of the rights and responsibilities they held with respect to the temporalities of the parish and the clergy's understanding of their jurisdiction in both spiritual and temporal affairs arose soon after the arrival of the next resident pastor in Westmoreland County. Father Terrence McGirr came to Sportsman's Hall at the beginning of Lent 1821, appointed by Bishop Henry Conwell of Philadelphia. Like his predecessor, McGirr was a native of County Tyrone, Ireland. Born in 1782, he had studied for the priesthood at St. Patrick's College, Maynooth, and there had received a doctor of divinity degree. He was ordained in 1806 and sometime after 1810 immigrated to the Diocese of Philadelphia where he served various congregations before his appointment to Sportsman's Hall.

Father Vincent Huber, another early historian of Saint Vincent, described McGirr as a "singular character" who was "good at heart, faithful to his duties, ready for every hardship, humble, obliging and kind to the poor; but his outer deportment was not in keeping with the dignity of his priestly character. In conversation he was rough, uncivil, unreserved, harsh, and often extremely overbearing and imperious."[60] It was this "overbearing and imperious" manner that brought McGirr into conflict with the trustees. When he arrived at Sportsman's Hall, McGirr discovered that Father Maguire's brother still occupied the parish house, so he took up residence for several months in Youngstown, a village two miles distant from the church. When Maguire left the property in 1822, Father McGirr hired his own brother, Bernard McGirr, as tenant farmer, and himself moved into the parish house. He took these actions without consulting the trustees, whom he generally ignored, and the trustees began to resent what they regarded as his arrogant indifference to their prerogatives.

Other members of the congregation also found McGirr's behavior antagonistic and abrasive. On Sundays he preached sermons that revealed an irritable and resentful temper, and he scheduled Masses at early, inconvenient hours without consulting the parishioners. Soon they were complaining to the bishop in Philadelphia. In 1823 the trustees petitioned Bishop Conwell to remove Father McGirr from Sportsman's Hall and send them another priest. Conwell did not reply to their request, and relations between the pastor and the people worsened. When McGirr attempted to usurp control of the board of trustees, the trustees met and passed several resolutions designed to prevent him from doing so. They prohibited, for example, "the clergyman or present incumbant [*sic*], for the time being, to superintend at any Election for Trustees, and that in case of such illegal interference the old Trustees shall continue to act for the ensuing year." They also passed a resolution that "no Relatives of the present Clergyman by marriage or otherwise or of any other person or persons living on the plantations belonging to the said Congregation, shall be considered Eligable [*sic*] to serve or to be Elected a Trustee for the said Congregation."[61]

When McGirr attempted to lease the land at O'Neill's Victory to a tenant farmer, the trustees rejected his decision and leased it instead to parishioner George Aaron. McGirr tried to have Aaron ejected, but courts in both Greensburg and Philadelphia upheld the authority of the trustees to oversee and determine use of the property. The trustees then appointed one of their number as treasurer with the power to receive the entire income of the two tracts of land. McGirr railed against these encroachments upon what he regarded as his property and jurisdictional rights, but to no avail.

Despite conflicts with the trustees and parishioners at Sportsman's Hall, Father McGirr continued to minister to their spiritual needs. He seems to have had some success in winning the respect and even affection of the poorer Irish members of his flock, and in 1822 he built a small log chapel for them about six miles north of Sportsman's Hall, near the village of New Derry where many of the Irish turnpike workers had settled. He dedicated the chapel to Our Lady of Mount Carmel. He also carried the sacraments to Irish Catholics in Armstrong and Butler counties.

In 1828 the trustees made another attempt to have McGirr removed as pastor. In the absence of Bishop Conwell, who had gone to Rome for extended consultations, they sent a petition, signed by a majority of the parishioners and including the signature of Father Charles Maguire, to Father William Matthews, vicar general and administrator of the Diocese of Philadelphia. In it they accused McGirr of scandalous behavior that involved a supposed relationship with a woman of the parish and demanded that he be replaced. Before Father Matthews could respond, Father Demetrius Gallitzin of Loretto rushed to McGirr's defense. Pledging "with the help of Divine Providence" to "exert all lawful means in my power to render abortive and harmless to Mr. McGirr the machinations of the impious Catholics of Westmoreland district," Gallitzin wrote both Matthews and Maguire to deny the accusations of those he called "the Westmoreland rebels." "More than thirty-three years spent on the mission," he said, "have taught me that Catholics will go to any length when animated by a spirit of hatred against their pastors."[62]

When Father Matthews responded, appointing Father Maguire to investigate the case against Father McGirr and instructing McGirr to abide by the judgment of Maguire, Gallitzin again wrote Matthews objecting to the appointment of a judge who had been one of McGirr's accusers. This effectively delayed the investigation, and the case dragged on without resolution for two more years. Conflict and animosity continued to mark the relationship between pastor and people at Sportsman's Hall, with Father Gallitzin supporting the pastor and Father Maguire the people. In October 1829 the trustees appointed Henry Kuhn and Edward Shivlin as their representatives and authorized them "to demand from Rev. Terance McGill [*sic*] all the personal property he has received from the Catholick Congregation." Eleven months later they appointed parishioners Denis Connor and John Rhey to comprise "a committee to apply to the Rt. Rev. Francis P. Kenrick, Bishop of Arath, and Coadjutor of Philadelphia, on his arrival in this Neighborhood for to use every honorable means, in Removing Our present Clergyman the Rev. Mr. McGirr and supply our Congregation in Westmoreland County with another Clergyman in his place."[63]

Kenrick, who had been named coadjutor bishop of Philadelphia in February, came to Westmoreland County in October 1830 to conduct a visitation of the congregation and administer the sacrament of confirmation. After hearing out the petition of the trustees' ad hoc committee and listening to the further complaints of other members of the congregation, he met with Father McGirr and urged him to resign the pastorate. "There has been much trouble between the Rev. Terence McGirr and the faithful under his charge," Bishop Kenrick wrote in his journal, "so that he can no longer exercise the pastoral office among them without evident peril to souls. I counseled him, therefore, to resign the charge within one month from the nineteenth day of October; otherwise I would be forced to remove him."[64]

McGirr resigned shortly after the bishop's departure and went to Loretto to stay with his friend Demetrius Gallitzin. He spent the last twenty-one years of his life in Cambria County, occasionally serving the congregations at St. Patrick's, Cameron's Bottom; and St. Joseph's, Hart's Sleeping Place. But his experience at Sportsman's Hall had broken him, and he never again held a parish from the bishop. He died on August 11, 1851, and was buried in Ebensburg.

A PLACE CALLED SAINT VINCENT

Bishop Kenrick wasted little time in appointing a new pastor to Sportsman's Hall. In November 1830 he offered the position to recently ordained Father James Ambrose Stillinger of Maryland. Stillinger was a native of Baltimore and descendant of German and French immigrants, and his command of German ideally suited him for the pastoral care of the ethnically mixed Catholic congregation of Westmoreland County. Born in 1801, he studied at Mount St. Mary's College and Seminary in Emmitsburg, Maryland, and was ordained to the priesthood by Baltimore Archbishop James Whitfield on February 28, 1830. Immediately after ordination Stillinger returned to western Maryland where he served Catholic congregations at Libertytown and in the Catoctin Mountains for the nine months before his assignment to Sportsman's Hall.

Because Stillinger was a priest of the Archdiocese of Baltimore, Bishop Kenrick had to obtain permission from Archbishop Whitfield for his incardination into the Diocese of Philadelphia, but while Whitfield agreed to the transfer, other Baltimore priests objected. When Father John B. Purcell, president of Mount St. Mary's College and later bishop of Cincinnati, protested the withdrawal of Stillinger from western Maryland, Bishop Kenrick wrote him that he was "forced to take him from you." He went on to say that

> [t]he congregation of Westmoreland seems absolutely to require him, whose piety, and knowledge of the German tongue render him peculiarly adapted to fill the vacancy which has occurred. Had you witnessed the tears of the good people, you would scarcely hesitate to give them this good Pastor, who may console them for years of spiritual desolation. I, who am charged with their salvation, could not but feel the most anxious solicitude to give them one whom I deem the most proper to heal their wounds. Do not, I pray you, put an obstacle in the way of so much good. If you have claims, are you not rewarded for your sacrifice by the consideration that you have formed a worthy priest, whose prayers will draw down benedictions on his benefactors?[65]

Stillinger assumed his duties at Sportsman's Hall on the first Sunday of Advent, November 25, 1830. Because the trustees had leased the house on the property to the farmer hired to manage the land, he decided to take up residence in the village of Blairsville, fifteen miles away, where Bishop Kenrick had also assigned him as pastor of the recently organized parish of Ss. Simon and Jude. An even more compelling reason for Stillinger's decision to settle in Blairsville, however, was the continued insistence by the trustees at Sportsman's Hall that they alone possessed the legal right to administer the Brouwers estate. By now the American hierarchy had determined to suppress the trustee system because of the abuses that had arisen from it, and Stillinger recognized that if he resided on the property at Sportsman's Hall, he would be tacitly acknowledging the rights the trustees claimed. He avoided confrontation, however, and using his considerable diplomatic and pastoral skills worked slowly but steadily to bring the trustees around to his, and the hierarchy's, point of view. The measure of his success is the warmth with which the congregation received him and the cordial relations which he established from the beginning with the trustees. Unlike his predecessor, Father McGirr, he earned the respect and love of the people, and consequently, when Bishop Kenrick paid his second pastoral visit to the Catholics of Westmoreland County, the trustees at Sportsman's Hall were ready to reconsider their position.

Kenrick came to Sportsman's Hall in August 1831 to administer the sacrament of confirmation and to discuss with the congregation their legal claims to the administration of the two church farms. He told them that as he had acceded to their wishes by providing them with an excellent pastor, he now wanted them to respect the pastor's rights and leave the property entirely under Stillinger's management. In a document he drew up before leaving them, he summarized his arguments for transferring the administration back to the pastor and urged them to comply with his wishes. The property, he said

> was originally purchased, not by the Congregation with their money, but with the money of the Revd. Mr. Brouwers, who bequeathed it to the Catholic Pastor for support. The Will of the dying Man should be sacredly guarded. In extraordinary circumstances the Legislature created a corporate Body to protect the Pastor's rights, by preserving the Farm from devastation during the Vacancy of the Pastorship; but these circumstances being changed, it does not appear Just or conscientious to use a Charter obtained in that emergency, particularly as its use would defeat the disposition of the Will. The dying Man meant to leave his successors in the Pastorship an honorable and independent Maintenance, subject to no control. The Congregation has therefore no right to interfere, under any pretext, since the property is not theirs. As several Congregations are now destitute of a Pastor who, if sent to them, would be left free of all Lay interference, the bishop cannot consent to oblige the Rev. Mr. Stillinger to remain in the Sportsman's Hall Congregation should the Management of his property be denied him. Rev. Mr. Stillinger will consent to suffer the present Occupants to remain during the Term for which they rent the Farms, provided the Trustees forthwith cease from all interference, and leave him to manage his affairs by himself or by such persons as he may appoint. August 24, 1831.[66]

Despite the reasonableness and civility with which the dialogue between bishop and people was conducted, the trustees did not immediately acquiesce to Kenrick's request. For their part, the bishop and Father Stillinger decided not to press the issue. Recognizing the sensitive nature of the question and not wishing to offend the democratic sensibilities of the congregation, they now stood back from the debate and waited patiently while the people discussed the matter among themselves. It took the parishioners nine months to resolve their misgivings and reach a decision. In the end, however, they decided to accede to the bishop's request. The trustees called a parochial meeting for May 28, 1832, at which sixty-six members of the parish agreed by unanimous vote "that there should be no more elections for the future for trustees—but that all should be done by the appointment of the Bishop and the Pastor." The resolution was signed by four of the five trustees—Jacob Kuhn, George Miller, Conrad Henry, and John Rogers—as well as by the sixty-six parishioners who voted in favor of it. The minority who did not agree—including presumably the fifth trustee, Henry Kuhn—absented themselves from the meeting. As soon as the resolution passed, Stillinger appointed Jacob Kuhn, Conrad Henry, and John Rodgers as trustees for the following year.[67] A new petition sent by the parish to the state assembly in 1832 resulted in legislation reversing the 1821 law that had vested the trustees with legal title to the Brouwers estate.

Stillinger's success in resolving the prickly issue of trustee rights at Sportsman's Hall clearly illustrates the extraordinary pastoral skill, leadership, and sensitivity that marked his priestly ministry. For the next fourteen years he faithfully served the parish at Sportsman's Hall, and even after he left that congregation to devote his full attention to the Catholics of Blairsville, the people of Sportsman's Hall continued to honor him as their good friend and spiritual father.

In July 1833 Stillinger received permission from Bishop Kenrick to move forward with his plans to construct a new church and parochial residence at Sportsman's Hall. "As to the erection of a new church at Sportsman's Hall," the bishop wrote, "you have my free permission to undertake it, as I rely on your judgment as to its practicability. The docility of these good people . . . deserves to be rewarded by exertions on our part to console them and give them all the benefits of Religion."[68]

The congregation met on July 24, and 103 heads of households pledged a total of $4,162 for the church. Stillinger himself pledged $500, the largest amount of anyone. The leading contributors among the lay people were Dr. Patrick McGirr, Henry Kuhn Sr., Frederick Kintz, Conrad Henry, John Henry, Martin Miller, and Jacob Kuhn, who represented some of the oldest families in the parish. Ninety-nine of the 103 contributors pledged between five and sixty dollars, and of the thirteen who contributed a hundred dollars or more, nine were Germans, three Irish, and one English. Based on the distribution of family donations, it is clear that the wealthiest families in the congregation were the Germans. The overwhelming majority of Irish contributed ten dollars or less, though the largest single benefactor after the pastor was Dr. Patrick McGirr who contributed $300. The list of contributors reveals that the ethnic composition of the Sportsman's Hall parish had shifted since the pastorate of Peter Helbron. Now 40 percent of the families were German while the proportion of Irish families, many of whom had only recently come to the region in order to build the turnpikes, had increased to 53 percent. The proportion of families with English surnames remained constant at 7 percent.[69]

Stillinger contracted with the Pittsburgh firm of Anthony Kerrins and Jonathan Wilson, Master Builders, to construct a "gothic style brick church" fifty feet by eighty-five feet and a brick residence forty feet square. The total cost of materials and construction was almost ten thousand dollars. The congregation assumed a six-thousand-dollar debt to complete the buildings, but because he was dissatisfied with the faulty construction of the church's foundation, Stillinger withheld fourteen hundred dollars from the builders for damages. They sued him and the congregation to recover the money, and the suit was not resolved until 1843 when a jury in Greensburg found in favor of Stillinger and the parish.

Construction of both church and residence was completed in the summer of 1835, and in July Bishop Kenrick came to Sportsman's Hall to dedicate the new church, which he described in his journal as "spacious and beautiful (*ampla et pulchra*)." Father Stillinger celebrated the dedication Mass and the bishop preached. Four other priests of the Diocese of Philadelphia participated in the ceremony: Fathers Patrick Rafferty, Francis Maurice Masquelet, Hugh Mohan, and Peter Henry Lemke. As was his custom, Kenrick named the church after the saint on whose feast day its dedication occurred. July 19 was the feast of Saint Vincent de Paul, and so the parish at Sportsman's Hall, once known as Holy Cross, was henceforth called Saint Vincent. That afternoon the congregation assembled again for the celebration of pontifical Vespers, and at this solemn service Father Peter Henry Lemke, an assistant to Father Demetrius Gallitzin in Loretto who would later be instrumental in bringing the Bavarian Benedictines to western Pennsylvania, preached the sermon in German. The following day Bishop Kenrick confirmed fifty-five persons in the newly dedicated church and noted in his diary that nearly one hundred parishioners received Holy Communion. "God grant," he wrote, "that the consolation which I experienced here by reason of the piety of the priest in charge and the good will of the people under his care may long endure."[70]

With the church and residence completed, Stillinger moved from Blairsville to Sportsman's Hall where he remained for the next nine years.

He established an elementary day school for the children at Saint Vincent and attended other Catholic congregations in Westmoreland, Indiana, and Fayette counties.[71] In 1837 when the American bishops recommended the creation of a diocese in western Pennsylvania, Bishop Kenrick submitted Stillinger's name to Rome as one of three candidates to be considered for bishop of the new diocese. In July of the following year Kenrick paid his third pastoral visit to Sportsman's Hall and confirmed an unspecified number of communicants. He noted in his journal that the parish now had 150 families and that the previous year Father Stillinger had baptized thirty-five infants, performed seven marriages, and buried five parishioners. On a subsequent visit in 1839 Kenrick confirmed ninety-four people and in an 1842 visit, ninety-five.[72]

A COLLEGE AND SEMINARY AT SPORTSMAN'S HALL

In 1843 Rome created the Diocese of Pittsburgh from the western counties of Pennsylvania and named Michael O'Connor, Kenrick's vicar general in western Pennsylvania, as first bishop. Born in Cobh, Ireland, in 1810, O'Connor had received his primary education in Ireland before going to the Urban College of the Propaganda Fide in Rome for his secondary and theological studies. In June 1833 he was ordained to the priesthood by Archbishop Gaetano Patrizi and two months later received his doctorate in sacred theology. After ordination O'Connor served as professor of sacred scripture and vice rector of the Irish College in Rome until recalled to Ireland by his bishop in 1835. For the next three years he worked as curate and chaplain in the Diocese of Cloyne and Ross, and in 1838 he immigrated to America where Bishop Kenrick named him president of St. Charles Seminary, Philadelphia. In 1841 Kenrick assigned him as pastor of St. Paul's Church, Pittsburgh, and two years later O'Connor was named first bishop of Pittsburgh.[73]

Stillinger remained at Saint Vincent for a year after the establishment of the new diocese, but in 1844 he moved back to Ss. Simon and Jude Church in Blairsville. To replace him at Sportsman's Hall, O'Connor named Father Michael Gallagher, who had been a missionary priest in western Pennsylvania since his ordination in 1837. Born in Drommore, Ireland, in 1806, Gallagher had immigrated to the United States when he was fifteen years old and studied for the priesthood at the diocesan seminary in Philadelphia. After ordination he had worked in Washington, Greene, Fayette, and Somerset counties before being assigned to Sportsman's Hall.

In notes he made in the diocesan registry shortly after his elevation to the episcopate, O'Connor indicated that the Catholics of Westmoreland County now numbered one thousand souls. Three churches served this population: Saint Vincent near Youngstown, Ss. Simon and Jude in Blairsville, and Mount Carmel Chapel near New Derry. In 1845 two priests—Michael Gallagher at Saint Vincent and James Stillinger at Ss. Simon and Jude—attended the needs of these Catholics as well as those of the small congregation in Indiana, Pennsylvania.[74]

As early as 1831 Father James Stillinger had suggested Sportsman's Hall as an ideal place for a college and seminary to train priests for the missions. He wrote Father Simon Gabriel Bruté, S.S., of Mount St. Mary's College, Emmitsburg, of the idea, and Bruté responded that "as for that good idea of a little college and seminary at Sportsman's Hall . . . you do well to submit it to your bishop."[75] Stillinger's efforts to resolve the question of trustee governance at Sportsman's Hall prevented him from pursuing the matter, but eleven years later, shortly after a visit to Westmoreland County, Bishop Kenrick noted in his diary that the plan to use the Sportsman's Hall property and buildings for a college and seminary was acceptable to Father Stillinger and Father O'Connor, the vicar general.[76]

Upon becoming Pittsburgh's first bishop, Michael O'Connor counted it a high priority to establish a seminary in the new diocese, and because of Saint Vincent's extensive property and salubrious location, his thoughts turned to the parish as the ideal site for such a school. He approached Father John Timon, C.M., superior of the Vincentian Fathers in the United States and later first bishop of Buffalo, about the possibility of staffing a seminary at the rural parish, but Timon responded that he had no available professors to assign to the diocese. Despite this reversal, O'Connor continued to regard Saint Vincent as a prime location for a school, and in September 1844 he wrote his brother, Father James O'Connor, that "we are about to start a college also at Youngstown. After tomorrow I am to be there and I think I will then make arrangements for a beginning be it ever so small. It will be as a kind of preparatory seminary also."[77]

As the months passed, the project for creating a college and minor seminary at Saint Vincent moved forward. Father Gallagher proposed that a community of brothers be established on the property to work the land and thus support not only themselves but the students in the projected school. Bishop O'Connor believed the proposal had merit and instructed Gallagher to proceed with implementing it. O'Connor also came to an agreement with Bishop John B. Purcell of Cincinnati to establish the seminary at Saint Vincent as a joint venture, and Purcell sent Cincinnati priest

Father Joseph O'Mealy to Westmoreland County to help organize the school. Meanwhile Father Gallagher gathered at Saint Vincent a group of six young Germans and Irishmen who had aspirations for the religious life and with them attempted to establish the diocesan brotherhood he envisioned. The community did not prosper, however, and the six novices soon left. At the same time Bishop O'Connor failed in his efforts to raise sufficient funds to open a seminary, and O'Mealy left Sportsman's Hall after only a year when it became clear that the Pittsburgh-Cincinnati seminary project would not bear fruit.[78] At the end of 1845 O'Connor temporarily suspended plans for a college and seminary at Saint Vincent and invited a community of Sisters of Mercy to the property.

The Sisters of Mercy had come to the Diocese of Pittsburgh from Ireland in 1843, and under the leadership of Mother Mary Frances Warde, R.S.M., had settled in the episcopal city where they gave religious instructions to children and adults at St. Paul's Cathedral. In 1844 Henry Mathias Kuhn, son of the Henry Kuhn who had played such a prominent role in the early history of the parish, donated to the diocese 108 acres of prime land adjacent to the Forbes Road and half an hour's ride from the Sportsman's Hall tract for a Catholic female academy. In return for this donation Kuhn asked that twelve Masses a year be offered for his intentions and that the diocese care for himself and his unwell adopted daughter until their deaths.[79] Bishop O'Connor accepted the terms and turned the property over to the Sisters of Mercy who agreed to establish a boarding school on it. In the summer of 1845, as construction of the convent and school on the Kuhn estate progressed, seven sisters moved from Pittsburgh to Saint Vincent, where they began teaching classes for about ten girls at "Mount St. Vincent Academy" while awaiting completion of the building on their own land a mile and a half away.[80]

Despite the failure of his first attempt to establish a seminary at Saint Vincent, Bishop O'Connor remained optimistic about the possibility of creating such an institution on the land at Sportsman's Hall. Meanwhile in 1845 he authorized Father Peter Henry Lemke, who at the time was serving the congregation at Hart's Sleeping Place in Cambria County, to travel to Germany to recruit missionary priests for German-speaking Catholics of the Diocese of Pittsburgh, and it was Lemke's journey that initiated the events that brought the bishop's hopes for a seminary at Saint Vincent to fruition.

Peter Henry Lemke was one of the more colorful figures in the history of the Catholic Church in western Pennsylvania. Born in 1796 at Rhena, in the state of Mecklenburg-Schwerin, he had served in the Prussian army before entering the Lutheran seminary at Rostock to pursue theological studies. Ordained a Lutheran minister in 1819, he served briefly in parishes in Mecklenburg before becoming disenchanted with the rationalist-influenced Lutheran theology of his day. In 1823 he abandoned the ministry and traveled to Catholic Bavaria where he continued his studies of theology under the ultramontanist bishop of Regensburg, Johann Michael Sailer. Sailer, who would later become a key figure in the restoration of Benedictine monasticism in Bavaria, received Lemke into the Catholic Church on April 21, 1824, and two years later, at the age of thirty, Lemke was ordained a priest. For the next ten years he served in various pastoral positions in Bavaria. During this period he witnessed the restoration of the Benedictine monastery of Metten (1830), and for a time even considered becoming a monk there. The *Wanderlust* that led him in his long lifetime to visit and live in many parts of Germany and America now took control of his destiny, however, and rather than enter the monastery he decided to become a missionary. He sought incardination into the Diocese of Philadelphia, and in 1834 he traveled to America where Bishop Kenrick accepted him as a priest of the diocese and assigned him as assistant pastor of Holy Trinity Parish in the City of Brotherly Love. Within a few months a confrontation between the sometimes irascible and always opinionated Lemke and the lay trustees of Holy Trinity led to his departure from Philadelphia. He next set out on a two-month missionary journey to the German Catholics of western Pennsylvania. He visited Pittsburgh, Blairsville, and Sportsman's Hall, and in December 1834 Bishop Kenrick assigned him as assistant to Father Demetrius Gallitzin, pastor in Loretto, Pennsylvania, in the Allegheny Mountains. Lemke faithfully served the Catholics of the region for the next six years, and when Gallitzin died in 1840, he assumed charge of the missions of Cambria County. From his base at St. Joseph's Church, Hart's Sleeping Place, he undertook the pastoral care of the Catholics in Centre and Clearfield counties as well. In 1840 he purchased land near St. Joseph's and began planning the establishment of a Catholic settlement there which eventually would become the community of Carrolltown, Pennsylvania.[81]

At the end of 1844 he announced he was ready for an extended vacation, and when early in 1845 Bishop O'Connor gave him permission to take a leave of absence, stipulating that he combine rest with an effort to recruit priests for the Diocese of Pittsburgh, he set out for his homeland. An underlying motive for the trip seems also to have been the raising of funds and recruitment of immigrants for his projected community at Carrolltown, a project in which he had already invested most of his capital. Lemke's return after a ten-year absence to the scenes of his earliest work as a Catholic priest had enormous repercussions for the Church in western Pennsylvania in general and for the parish of Saint Vincent in particular.

In Munich Lemke paid a call at the Benedictine Priory of St. Boniface, and there he met Father Boniface Wimmer, a teacher of Latin and Greek in the Ludwigs-Gymnasium, a prestigious secondary school in the Bavarian capital which had been established and endowed by King Ludwig I of Bavaria five years earlier. Lemke's encounter with Wimmer in May 1845 was a transitional moment in the lives of both men. Ever since his conversion to Catholicism the restless priest had held the Benedictines and their monastic heritage of work and prayer in the highest esteem, and during the years he had served as a missionary in western Pennsylvania he had sometimes wondered why the newly restored Benedictine communities in Bavaria had not sent missionaries to the United States. For his part, Wimmer had, during the course of the previous three years, focused his attention on the American missions and at the time of his meeting with Lemke was seeking permission from his superiors to go to America to establish a monastery and school to train priests for the German-speaking Catholics of the United States. It is a happy accident of history that both men recorded their impressions of that first meeting.

Lemke, who would later become a monk at Saint Vincent, wrote:

> One day I dined with the Benedictine Fathers who were members of the abbey of Metten and had charge of a Latin School. They were very inquisitive about America, and I told them among other matters that I was authorized by the bishop of Pittsburgh to engage German priests and that I would be pleased to become their leader. They only smiled at such an idea, because in those days the good people of Bavaria bothered themselves no more about America than about the moon. After dinner, Father Boniface Wimmer, one of the professors, took me aside and told me that for a long time he had felt inclined to come to America as a missionary. "It is easy," I said, "for a religious to get a dispensation for such work. I know several priests of different orders, even a Benedictine from St. Peter's, Salzburg. How would it be if you were to go with associates having the authorization to found a Benedictine monastery? I have plenty of land and several congregations about me and could easily settle you there. Besides, you may find a candidate in me, for I was present with Bishop Sailer sixteen years ago when Metten was reopened and intended to become one of the first candidates of this venerable house. You may read in the *Katholik* of Mainz, published in 1835, a long letter in which I said, 'Why don't the Benedictines come to America?' This would be the very land for them, if they would commence in the same way as their predecessors did more than a thousand years ago in the impenetrable forests of Germany."[82]

Wimmer himself wrote his abbot, Gregory Scherr of Metten:

> A few weeks ago the missionary Peter Lemke, a good friend of our deceased Father Placidus and of the present prince-bishop of Diepenbrock, arrived here and visited us. He came to Europe to obtain priests and funds, but he was not very successful. He is stationed in the state of Pennsylvania, in the mountains between the Allegheny and Susquehanna Rivers, the only priest in a district of 90 German square miles with 6,000 Catholics. He has charge of six churches. Although he is still very robust, his strength is inadequate for all this work. Your Lordship can easily imagine that his descriptions revived all my sympathies for America after they had subsided somewhat of late. When my confreres introduced me to him as a friend of the missions, we soon became acquainted, and I needed little persuasion to follow him. He regretted very much that our order is not yet represented in America and believes that it would be the one most suited for American ways if we again take up the same work as did our forefathers centuries ago.

Lemke offered Wimmer a farm he owned near St. Joseph Church, Hart's Sleeping Place, in Cambria County, sixty miles from Saint Vincent, as the site for a Benedictine monastery and school, and Wimmer, even without seeing the place, wrote enthusiastically to his abbot that the location was ideal for his purposes. The land, he said, consisted of a parish with 150 families, a farm of four hundred acres, a residence, and a church. Lemke was creating the German Catholic community of Carrolltown near the farm, and this settlement, Wimmer said, would become the nucleus from which young boys with vocations to the priesthood could be recruited for the proposed Benedictine seminary. At St. Joseph the Benedictines could begin to educate "an American clergy" for German immigrants "and the whole Church would profit thereby." The monks, of course, would "be obliged to work again with the hoe and the plow" to support their monastery and school, but "Father Lemke would at once transfer these four hundred acres to us, one hundred of which are already under cultivation. He says everything can be raised there in abundance, even without fertilizing the soil. The air is healthful and the climate similar to Italy."[83]

Thus, as a result of a fortuitous meeting between Peter Lemke and Boniface Wimmer, the scene was set for the establishment of a Benedictine monastery and school in western Pennsylvania. The plan, of course, consisted at this stage of only the barest outline and was subject to much modification. But still it held promise of accomplishing all the immediate goals of Lemke, Wimmer, and Bishop O'Connor himself. For Lemke it meant an institution that would attract Catholic settlers to his proposed community at Carrolltown; for Wimmer it allowed for the transfer of the Benedictine Order to the United States and the creation of a foundation he had dreamed of making for three years; and for O'Connor, though he had not yet been consulted, it provided a means of achieving his twin goals of establishing a seminary and obtaining German-speaking priests for his diocese. From Lemke's and Wimmer's perspective the plan was an excellent one. Bishop O'Connor too, when he learned of it, would think it an idea worthy of consideration. But before the bishop gave his approval, he would recommend a slight modification, and this modification would not only bring about a change in the location of the proposed foundation from St. Joseph in Cambria County to Saint Vincent, but also result in a conflict between Lemke and Wimmer that would take years to resolve. In the meantime, however, Lemke reported the happy results of his meeting to Bishop O'Connor, and Wimmer, the visionary, set about the difficult task of convincing his superiors in Bavaria and Rome to approve his project for establishing a Benedictine monastery and school in Pennsylvania.

TWO

THE *PROJEKTENMACHER* OF METTEN (1846–1855)

BY THE END of the eighteenth century Benedictine monasticism in virtually every part of Europe had fallen on hard times. The ancient charism of following the Gospel and the Rule of St. Benedict through work and prayer had lost much of its appeal to Europeans influenced by rationalism, and many of the monasteries of Europe were in need of spiritual and disciplinary reform. Added to this was a strong antimonastic bias among social and political leaders of the day. They regarded monasteries as moribund holdovers from an earlier, less enlightened age, centers of lassitude and superstition harboring unproductive men and women who made little contribution to social progress and holding a monopoly on large tracts of land and property that inhibited the economic development of the continent.

As a consequence of political events following the Napoleonic conquests of the late eighteenth century, as well as of the anticlerical prejudices of many European intellectuals and leaders of the day, Benedictine monasteries in large sectors of Europe were closed, their properties confiscated, and the monks and nuns forced to seek their livelihood outside the cloister. The monastic suppression in Bavaria occurred in 1803. In that year a decree of the Diet of Regensburg ordered that "all goods and properties of institutions, abbeys, and monasteries . . . [be] placed at the free and complete disposition of the respective princes of these territories, to be used to meet the expenses of divine services, education, and other purposes of the common good, as well as to ease their own financial burdens."[1] With this decree the eleven-century-old Benedictine tradition in Bavaria appeared to have definitively come to an end. The buildings, land, and moveable property of the abbeys, priories, and convents were taken over by the government and distributed among secular institutions and minions of the state whose own wealth and property had been lost in the Napoleonic wars.[2]

The anticlerical government of King Maximilian I Joseph had overseen the secularization of Bavarian religious institutions and the suppression of the Bavarian monasteries, but with the king's death in 1825 and the coronation of his thirty-nine-year-old son Ludwig, the stage was set for the Catholic Revival of the 1820s and 1830s. After reestablishing diplomatic relations with the Vatican, King Ludwig, with the help of Bishop Johann Michael Sailer of Regensburg and Prime Minister Karl von Abel, set about rebuilding the religious institutions that had suffered so much during his father's reign. He summoned Catholic scholars from all over Europe to the newly constituted Ludwig Maximilian University in Munich; invited the Franciscan, Redemptorist, Jesuit and other orders to reestablish communities in Bavaria; created the Ludwig Missionsverein to support the work of Catholic missionaries in the Near East, Asia, and North America, and began the gradual process of restoring the Benedictine Order in the kingdom.[3]

The first monastery to be restored was the Abbey of St. Michael at Metten in the Diocese of Regensburg, a community that traced its origins to a foundation by Charlemagne in the eighth century. In 1827 the king issued a decree reversing the suppression of 1803 and calling on the bishop of Regensburg to summon the displaced monks back to the cloister. By then, however, only six Bavarian Benedictine monks were still alive. Four of these chose to remain in retirement as secular priests, but two, Fathers Roman Raith and Ildephonse Nebauer, agreed to return, and on June 3, 1830, Raith and Nebauer officially reintroduced Benedictine monastic life to Bavaria in a ceremony at the monastery of Metten attended by Bishop Johann Michael Sailer and Johann Mulzer, president of Lower Bavaria. Metten thus became the first of the Benedictine monasteries restored by King Ludwig I. Others soon followed at Augsburg, Scheyern, Munich, Eichstätt, and Weltenburg.[4]

Full restoration of monastic life at Metten, however, required more than the presence of two aged monks, so Bishop Sailer invited volunteers from the secular clergy to enter the community as novices. Five priests of the Regensburg diocese accepted the invitation, and in December 1832 they were invested at Metten with the Benedictine habit. The first novices to enter the community after the restoration were Gregory Leonard Scherr, Rupert Anthony Leiss, Francis Xavier Wolfgang Sulzbeck, Pius Joseph Bacherl, and Boniface Sebastian Wimmer. Both Gregory Scherr and Rupert Leiss would later make important contributions to the growth and development of Benedictine monastic life in North America, and Boniface Wimmer would become the founder of the monastery and school at Saint Vincent.

WIMMER'S VISION

Born on January 14, 1809, of humble parents (his father was a tavern-keeper) in the small farming village of Thalmassing, Bavaria, Wimmer studied philosophy and theology first under Sailer at the diocesan seminary in Regensburg and then at the newly restored Ludwig Maximilian University in Munich where his professors included some of the leading Catholic intellectuals of Europe. Among them were Friedrich Wilhelm Schelling, who taught him philosophy; Francis Xavier Baader, his professor of dogmatic theology; Joseph Allioli, the famous translator and his professor of sacred scripture; Joseph von Görres, the renowned historian, and Johann Ignaz Döllinger, a young priest who taught Wimmer church history and canon law and who would later achieve fame as the chief European opponent of papal infallibility. Wimmer's three years at the university imbued him with a lifelong love of history and sacred scripture.

He was ordained to the priesthood for the Diocese of Regensburg in 1831, and his first assignment was to the community of diocesan priests who served the Marian shrine at Altötting. For over a year he attended the spiritual needs of the thousands of pilgrims who annually visited the medieval apparition site and also assisted at nearby parishes. Wimmer's experience living in the community of secular priests at Altötting, as well as his earlier experience of the common life at the Gregorium, a residence college for theology students in Munich, formed a lasting impression on him of the value of religious community life. As a student of Johann Ignaz Döllinger he had also come to understand and appreciate the Bavarian Benedictine tradition and heritage. So when word spread through the Diocese of Regensburg that the newly restored Benedictine Priory of Metten was seeking priest candidates to enter the monastery, he began to consider the monastic vocation.[5]

Wimmer sought the advice of his confessor and superior at Altötting and by May 1832 had decided to become a Benedictine. "In the monastery under your supervision and in union with virtuous and well-educated men," he wrote Prior Ildephonse Nebauer of Metten, "I could work out my own salvation as well as that of others."[6] In December he was received into the novitiate with the four other Regensburg priests, and a year later, on December 29, 1833, he pronounced solemn vows of stability, conversion of morals, and obedience. He was twenty-five years old.

During his sixteen years as a monk of Metten before emmigrating to the United States, Wimmer actively participated in King Ludwig I's monastic restoration and educational reform programs. Immediately after his solemn vows, he was assigned as assistant pastor to the parish in Edenstätten which was served by monks of the Metten community. He worked in Edenstätten for twenty-two months and was then assigned to the second Benedictine monastery revived by the king, St. Stephen's Abbey, Augsburg, to assist in the establishment of a Benedictine college there. Wimmer spent the 1835–1836 academic year teaching at the college in Augsburg. In September 1836 he returned to Metten where he took up parochial duties once again. By now, under the leadership of Rupert Leiss who had replaced Ildephonse Nebauer as prior, the Metten monks had committed themselves to two principal apostolates, parish work and the operation of a gymnasium (Latin secondary school) for boys. During this period Wimmer gained valuable experience not only as a Benedictine pastor of souls but also as a monk involved in the planning and direction of a monastic school. It was experience that would deepen in the years ahead and that he would put to practical use when he established the monastery and school at Saint Vincent.

In 1838 King Ludwig reopened the monastery of Scheyern and called upon Metten to provide the initial group of monks to introduce monastic life once again to the priory. Rupert Leiss was named prior of Scheyern and the Metten monks chose Gregory Scherr to replace him as their superior. In the summer of 1839 Scherr appointed Wimmer procurator (business manager) at Scheyern, a post he held for one year. Again the experience was formative. As procurator Wimmer was responsible for the financial well-being of the community and, under Prior Rupert, directed its daily administrative operations. He proved himself a careful steward and learned important lessons about the economics of monastic life that would later serve him in America.

The Benedictine restoration in Bavaria had now reached full momentum, and Wimmer found himself deeply involved in every phase of the movement. Having participated in the restoration of the first three foundations—Metten, Augsburg, and Scheyern—he became a key figure in the establishment of the fourth. In 1840, shortly after the Priory of Metten had been elevated to the rank of abbey and Gregory Scherr elected abbot, King Ludwig opened a Latin school (the Ludwigs-Gymnasium) in Munich and called upon Abbot Gregory to send monks to the capital city to staff it. Scherr assigned Wimmer and eight other Metten monks to Munich where they founded the Priory of St. Boniface and took up posts as professors in the Latin school. Wimmer taught Latin and Greek and served as prefect at the Hollandeum, a residence for boarding students of the Ludwigs-Gymnasium.

In Munich Wimmer contributed to the monastic revival both by his active participation in the Benedictine educational apostolate and by his efforts to ensure greater autonomy for the order and to expand its presence in Bavaria. Already he had led a successful movement to secure for Metten its independence which had been threatened by the government's attempt to place all the Benedictine monasteries under the jurisdiction of the abbot of St. Stephen's, Augsburg. He had also been successful in leading the fight to secure for the Metten monks the right to elect their own superior at a time when the government, backed by leading Bavarian bishops, wanted to make the position appointive. With these successes behind him Wimmer now began to develop a plan for the revival of a fifth Benedictine house in Bavaria. He obtained financial support from several lay benefactors for the restoration of the monastery of Mallersdorf, twenty miles south of Regensburg, and urged the establishment of a secondary school at Mallersdorf where young men could begin preparation for the Benedictine priesthood. In 1841 he presented his proposal to King Ludwig I, but Abbot Gregory Scherr, observing that Metten lacked sufficient resources to undertake such a project, refused to support it. As a consequence the king rejected the proposal, and Wimmer found himself the butt of criticism among his own confreres at Metten who mockingly branded him the community's *Projektenmacher,* their impractical planmaker.[7] Wimmer was profoundly disappointed by his failure to restore Mallersdorf and equally frustrated by his brother monks' failure to share his vision for the development of the Benedictine Order in Bavaria. Disillusioned, he now turned his attention to another project that would eventually take him away from his Bavarian homeland and lead to the establishment of the Benedictine monastery and school at Saint Vincent.

While German immigration to America had been significant since colonial times, the 1830s witnessed dramatic new developments in this historic movement of peoples. The decade began with a modest annual migration of about ten thousand Germans to the New World, but within twenty years the flow increased to more than one hundred thousand people per year. Many of these immigrants were Catholics who found in the United States a land brimming with economic opportunity but lacking in the spiritual and cultural institutions that had sustained them in their homeland. Their calls for assistance had resulted in the establishment of the Austrian Leopoldinen Stiftung in 1829 and the Bavarian Ludwig Missionsverein in 1838, mission societies whose purpose was to aid German Catholics in the United States with money and German-speaking priests. By 1840, however, complaints had begun to filter back across the ocean that the intentions of the mission societies were being thwarted by the Irish bishops of America who were using the funds they received from Germany and Austria to support non-German institutions and parishes.[8]

The publication in Philadelphia of an anonymous pamphlet entitled *Die katholisch-irisch- bischöfliche Administration im Nordamerika (The Irish Catholic Episcopal Administration in North America)* fueled the controversy. This pamphlet, which criticized the American hierarchy for ignoring the spiritual plight of German Catholics in America, was widely circulated in Austria and Bavaria, and together with other reports from German Catholic communities in the United States caused the directors of the Leopoldinen Stiftung to undertake an investigation. In 1842 they sent Canon Josef Salzbacher from Vienna to examine conditions among German-speaking Catholics in North America and to report on the manner in which the American bishops were using the resources of the mission societies. In 1845 Salzbacher published his findings in a pamphlet entitled *Meine Reise nach Nord-Amerika im Jahre 1842 (My Journey to North America in the Year 1842).* While exonerating the Irish American bishops of misappropriation of German mission funds, Salzbacher confirmed that many German-American Catholics were being lost to the faith because of the lack of German-speaking priests to minister to them, and he called for the establishment of a mission seminary in either the United States or Europe to train priests for the German missions of America.[9]

Boniface Wimmer arrived in Munich and assumed his duties at the Ludwigs-Gymnasium at the precise moment when the debate over how best to address the needs of the German Catholic immigrants in America was beginning to unfold. He followed the debate in the German Catholic press and in the many discussions taking place among the clergy of the

Bavarian capital, and in 1842, when his Mallersdorf project failed, he determined to volunteer for the American missions. He sought permission from Abbot Gregory Scherr to become a missionary, but citing the needs of Metten for priests and professors to carry on the parochial and educational work of the community, Scherr refused to release him.

Wimmer's initial thought was to go to America as a solitary missionary and offer his services to one of the American bishops, and while he viewed Scherr's refusal as a setback, he did not abandon his plan. He wrote the abbot that he could "not discard the thought that everyone who feels drawn toward the vocation has the obligation of dedicating himself to a missionary life. I very sincerely believe that priests belonging to religious orders are bound to carry out such designs more strictly than the secular clergy, and it is a disgrace if we shirk that duty." Wimmer went back to his teaching at the Ludwigs-Gymnasium, but his desire to become a missionary in America did not abate, and a year later, after his plans had further matured, he returned to the theme with renewed enthusiasm. By now his idea had developed into something larger than the original one of going to the United States as a single missionary. He now urged that Metten establish a "mission house" in Munich to train young men to become missionaries. The students would reside at the mission house under the supervision of Benedictine priests and pursue their education at the Ludwigs-Gymnasium and the University of Munich. Many of them, he suggested, would become Benedictines and these, once they reached America, would form the nucleus of a new branch of the Order in the New World. "They . . . could be transferred to the other side of the ocean to establish firm centers for Catholic life and Benedictine monasticism," he wrote. He pointed out that this was the way Europe had been evangelized during the Middle Ages, and he bluntly charged that the Benedictine Order in Bavaria was abdicating an important responsibility if it failed to heed the call of the missions. "The harvest is ready," he said, "but there are no laborers. Let us not become isolated or transfer this work to others. We belong to the whole world. The heretics are spreading to all parts of the earth, and we are keeping warm behind the stove."[10]

But once again Abbot Gregory Scherr refused to support his irrepressible Projektenmacher's proposal. Frustrated but undaunted, Wimmer continued to prepare for the day when his superiors would release him. Soon his plan evolved into its third and final stage. Now he proposed not to become a solitary missionary in the United States, nor to train students in Munich for the missions, but rather to go to America with a band of volunteers and establish there a monastery and school where missionaries to German-speaking immigrants could be trained. To that end he gathered around him a group of priests, students, and manual laborers who, fired with his enthusiasm, had expressed the desire to accompany him to the United States. It was about this time that Father Peter Henry Lemke arrived in Munich looking for priests to serve the German-speaking Catholics of the Diocese of Pittsburgh. Wimmer's meeting with Lemke at St. Boniface Priory, Munich, in May 1845 proved to be a crucial moment in the evolution of Wimmer's plan. Not only did Lemke come armed with authorization from Bishop Michael O'Connor of Pittsburgh to recruit priests for the German Catholics of the diocese, but he was prepared to offer Wimmer four hundred acres of land in Cambria County, Pennsylvania, to establish a monastery. Lemke encouraged Wimmer to attempt once again to obtain the permission of his abbot. He urged him as well to seek the approval of Rome for embarking on the American missions and establishing the first Benedictine monastery in the United States. Within days of their first meeting Lemke accompanied Father Boniface to the offices of the papal nuncio to the kingdom of Bavaria, Archbishop Carlo Morichini. Wimmer outlined his proposal to Morichini, and the nuncio promised to forward it to the Holy See. When Lemke departed Munich, Wimmer sat down and wrote Abbot Gregory Scherr of his meetings with Lemke and Morichini, asking once more to be permitted to go to the American missions.[11]

The relationship between Wimmer and Scherr during this period was strained. It is clear that the abbot was reluctant to lose one of his most trusted and energetic monks. He doubted, moreover, the feasibility of the plan to establish a Benedictine community in the United States. Wimmer's persistence in the face of Scherr's continued refusal annoyed the abbot, who admonished Father Boniface to put aside his thoughts of America and focus his energies on his work as a teacher and prefect in Munich. Wimmer, however, was not to be dissuaded. He continued to promote his project among leading Bavarian churchmen, including Archbishop Karl von Reisach of Munich, president of the Ludwig Missionsverein, and Father Joseph Ferdinand Müller, a director of the Missionsverein and chaplain to the court of King Ludwig I. Through Müller Wimmer obtained an audience with the king and laid out his proposal. The monarch showed great interest and indicated his willingness to provide financial support when and if Father Boniface received permission from his abbot and from Rome to undertake the mission. Encouraged by the reception his idea had received from the king and the archbishop of Munich, Wimmer proceeded with preparations for his journey to America.[12]

He was in the midst of these preparations when he received news from Rome that the permission he hoped for had been denied. Cardinal Giacomo Filippe Fransoni, prefect of the Sacred Congregation for the Propagation of the Faith, wrote Archbishop Morichini that

taking into account the work of restoration in which [Father Boniface Wimmer] is currently engaged and the good which this religious is accomplishing in his labors, and considering the qualities he has demonstrated in his labors and towards his superiors, as well as the evil effects that might result from his departure for the missions and the fact that there is not such an urgent need as to warrant depriving the understaffed Abbey of Metten of a person of his abilities, it does not seem to me opportune to send this religious to the infidels.[13]

Wimmer sent Fransoni's letter to Abbot Gregory with the wry comment that "the nuncio [Morichini] is urged to advise me for the future to fulfill my duties in my present vocation, which is of great importance since I can serve the Church equally well and can obtain a greater reward from God. That means, in other words, 'Mount your horse and stick to your job.'" Doubtless Scherr thought (and hoped) that Rome's refusal would mean the end of the Projektenmacher's pipe dream. But Wimmer was not so easily diverted from his purpose. Observing that the reasons for Rome's refusal were "not sufficient" and that the motives of the Propaganda Fide were "incorrect," he said he intended to appeal the decision. He hinted that he suspected Abbot Gregory of giving "inaccurate reports" about him to Rome that resulted in Cardinal Fransoni's decision and promised to visit Metten before the end of summer vacation to discuss the matter with the abbot.[14]

In the months that followed, Wimmer inundated Abbot Gregory with letters explaining his project and pleading for permission to go to America. "For three consecutive years I have been put off from one year to the next," he wrote. "It is just as if I were a child with some caprice that would easily pass away if one just stalled a bit." He argued that the Benedictine Order had an historical imperative to take up the mission cross and that he himself felt called by God to do so. "My poor and forlorn fellow countrymen stand before me and call for help," he said. "I desire to go—as firmly as can be desired—with several others or alone, whichever is possible and more convenient. I will not rest until I have succeeded." As for the abbot's objection that he was needed at Metten, Wimmer wrote:

I have paid my debt to Metten as well as I could. In my thirteen years as a monk I have been kept at home for only two. Thus by letting me help out all over—in

Augsburg, Scheyern, and Munich—Metten has already clearly indicated that as much as my weak strength permits, I am to labor more for the good of the whole order than for Metten itself. I am willing to do it; surely you would not want to hold me back."[15]

Meanwhile, he once again petitioned Rome through the papal nuncio and continued to discuss his ideas with Archbishop von Reisach, Father Müller, and the other directors of the Ludwig Missionsverein. He sought the advice of Father Frederick von Held, C.Ss.R., provincial of the Redemptorists' Belgian province, to which the Redemptorist missions in the United States were subject, and he recruited candidates for the priesthood and lay brotherhood to accompany him to America. Then in November 1845 he published an anonymous article in the *Augsburger Postzeitung* laying out for public scrutiny his proposal to establish a Benedictine monastery in the United States and to evangelize German immigrants there. Wimmer's article was a blueprint for the ambitious project to which he devoted the next forty-two years of his life.

Acknowledging the achievements of both the secular clergy and religious orders such as the Jesuits and Redemptorists in the American missions, Wimmer argued that a lasting solution to the problem of providing spiritual and educational assistance for German Catholic immigrants could be achieved only by establishing stable, self-supporting religious communities in the United States that could minister to the spiritual needs of the people, establish educational institutions for the poor, and train a native, German-speaking clergy to carry on missionary work among Germans throughout America. The Jesuits, who operated excellent colleges, were not suited for such an undertaking, he said, because their educational work focused on the well-to-do upon whom they depended for their economic support. The Redemptorists, who did admirable parochial work in American cities, were not prepared to operate schools and seminaries because their statutes required them to devote themselves exclusively to missionary labors. On the other hand, the Benedictine Order, he said, was by its nature and tradition ideally qualified to provide a permanent answer to the question of how to address the spiritual and educational needs of German Catholics in America.

Wimmer pointed out that Benedictines had successfully addressed those same needs during the Middle Ages by sending missionaries and establishing monastic communities and schools in England, Germany, the Scandinavian countries, Hungary, and Poland. Bavaria itself had been evangelized in the eighth century by Benedictine missionaries working out of the more than forty monasteries they established there. He observed that "conditions in America today are like those of Europe a thousand years ago, when the Benedictine Order attained its fullest development and effectiveness by its wonderful adaptability and stability." With this historical precedent in mind, then, he called for the establishment in rural America of a Benedictine monastery with "three priests and ten to fifteen brothers skilled in the most necessary trades." Sustaining itself by working the land, this community would first undertake missionary labors among local German Catholics and then gradually expand its evangelization efforts to more distant regions. The monks would soon open a Latin school, and because the monastery would be self-sustaining, the school could educate the "poorer classes of boys who could pay little or nothing." Wimmer envisioned that some of these boys, influenced by their Benedictine teachers, would discover they had vocations to the priesthood (either as diocesan or Benedictine priests) and could be trained in a seminary operated by the monks. These new priests (a "native clergy") would then become missionaries among the German-speaking populace. Eventually the monastery, which would certainly attract new members from among the immigrants, would plant its roots so deeply in American soil that it could establish monasteries and seminaries in other parts of the United States. Thus would the spiritual needs of German immigrants in America be satisfied, and at the same time the Benedictine Order would establish itself in the New World.[16]

Wimmer's anonymous article attracted the attention of King Ludwig I who asked to meet its author. Again Father Joseph Ferdinand Müller arranged a royal audience for Wimmer, and during this meeting the king promised to provide financial assistance for a Benedictine foundation in the United States. With support from the king, the archbishop of Munich, the Ludwig Missionsverein, and the papal nuncio, and with a letter of invitation from Bishop O'Connor of Pittsburgh in hand, Wimmer once more turned to Abbot Gregory for permission to become a missionary, and this time, as if to unburden himself of a heavy cross, Scherr relented. He said that he could go to America and gave Wimmer an *exeat* that stated: "With this document I freely dismiss Boniface Wimmer, a professed monk of this house in good standing, to this end: that he may labor in the American missions for the honor of God and the salvation of souls and that with legitimate authority he may establish one or more monasteries of the Order of St. Benedict. Nor do I intend to revoke this permission except for grave cause or unless the project fails."[17]

A month later Wimmer received authorization from the Sacred Congregation for the Propagation of the Faith to undertake the mission to the United States. By now he had collected a band of perhaps thirty-five men who wanted to help establish a Benedictine monastery in North America. The band included several priests (including two or three Benedictine confreres and at least two diocesan priests), six students, and about twenty-five candidates for the lay brotherhood who had expressed interest in accompanying him.[18] As the time drew closer for the departure, however, some of them began to have second thoughts. The six students, who had volunteered for the mission with the intention of becoming Benedictine priests in America, wrote Father Boniface asking to be allowed to complete their studies in Bavaria before joining him later in America. He replied in a lengthy letter that he could not agree to their request. If they made their novitiate in a Bavarian monastery, he said, they would "soon become accustomed to many things that you will not find in America." This would lead to disappointment and discouragement when they later joined him. For that reason he insisted that they decide before the journey began whether they truly had a vocation to the missionary life. "I am willing to take you along because I am confident that you will gladly share my joys and sorrows in the service of God and of our neighbor. If you join me, you must be animated by the same confidence in me. If you cannot have this confidence in my integrity, my honesty, my zeal, my experience and my determination, do not go with me. . . . I do not know the future. I only show you the cross."[19]

In the end, two of the six students decided not to go to America with Wimmer. None of the priests who had originally expressed interest accompanied him, and about half the brother candidates also dropped out. Thus when Wimmer and his group of Benedictine postulants finally set out for America, they numbered four priesthood students, fourteen candidates for the lay brotherhood, and one priest—Wimmer himself. They came from five southern Bavarian dioceses: Munich, Regensburg, Augsburg, Eichstätt, and Passau. The four students, all of whom became priests at Saint Vincent and persevered in their Benedictine vocation until their deaths, were Benedict Lawrence Haindl (1815–87), Placidus John Döttl (1818–52), Charles Martin Geyerstanger (1820–81), and Celestine Charles Englbrecht (1824–1904). The brother candidates, all of whom entered the novitiate at Saint Vincent, were Conrad Joseph Reinbolt (1818–96), a dairyman; Felix Michael Hochstätter (1817–65), a farmer; Joseph Sailer (1820–91), a weaver; Michael Böhm (1822–62), a weaver; Stephen James Weber (1817–70), a mason; Bernard Joseph Eggerdinger (1819–67), a mason; James Reitmayer

(1812–87), a carpenter; Andrew Binder (1812–91), a leather worker; Englebert Nusser (1814–80), a blacksmith; Placidus James Wittmann (1814–67), a locksmith; Francis Pfaller (1820–53), a baker; Peter Seemüller (1816–96), a miller; George Wimmer (b. 1824), nephew of Father Boniface and a farmer; and Leonard Hiller (b. 1818), also a farmer. Of the fourteen lay brothers all but Peter Seemüller, George Wimmer, and Leonard Hiller remained Benedictines the rest of their lives.[20]

FOUNDATION IN PENNSYLVANIA

In the early morning hours of July 25, 1846, Wimmer and his eighteen companions gathered at St. Michael's Church, Munich, to attend Mass offered by Archbishop von Reisach. After bidding farewell to friends and family, they boarded a train for the first leg of their journey, which took them through Augsburg, Ulm, and Stuttgart to Mainz. From Mainz they traveled by boat down the Rhine to Rotterdam where on August 10 they embarked on a sailing ship, the S.S. *Iowa,* for the United States. After a relatively quiet sea voyage of thirty-seven days, they landed on September 15 in New York, where Wimmer immediately sought out three German priests to whom he had been given letters of reference: Monsignor John Stephan Raffeiner, vicar general for Germans in the Diocese of New York and pastor of St. Nicholas Parish in Williamsburg (Brooklyn); Father Gabriel Rumpler, C.Ss.R., pastor of Holy Redeemer Parish on Third Street; and Father Nicholas Balleis, O.S.B., an Austrian Benedictine from St. Peter's Abbey, Salzburg, who had been serving as a missionary among Germans in America for ten years and who was now pastor of St. Mary's Parish, Newark, New Jersey. Wimmer explained the reason for his coming to America to each of these priests and they all had the same advice. He should dismiss the brother candidates, they said, find places for the students in an American seminary, and himself apply for incardination in one of the American dioceses. They all regarded his plan to establish a monastery and school in the rural districts of western Pennsylvania as pure folly and doomed to failure.[21]

Almost as disappointing as the German priests' reaction to his plans was Father Peter Henry Lemke's failure to meet the Benedictine group in New York as he had promised. After three days Lemke had still not arrived, so Wimmer and his men gathered their baggage from the customs house and prepared to travel to Cambria County, Pennsylvania, without a guide. On September 19 they went to Grand Central Station to purchase their tickets, and there they encountered Lemke. "I hurried to New York," he later wrote, "and behold my Benedictines had arrived. Benedictines did I say? There were nineteen persons whom I met: four students of theology and fourteen others who had agreed to enter as lay brothers. These were tailors, shoemakers, blacksmiths, hostlers, and brewers, as Father Wimmer could gather in Munich. I must confess, I felt sadly disappointed and doubted that anything could be achieved with such help. But I had given my word to settle them, and took the whole company with their abundant luggage four hundred miles to Carrolltown.[22]

Lemke's reaction upon encountering the missionaries was almost as negative as that of the German priests in New York. He had been given to believe that Wimmer was bringing a company of experienced priests and brothers to establish the first Benedictine foundation in the United States, but of the eighteen candidates only one (Geyerstanger) had ever been inside a Benedictine monastery. The others were novices in the fullest sense of the word. Wimmer's boldness in implementing his project was nowhere better illustrated than in the fact that he intended to begin Benedictine life in the United States with inexperienced neophytes. He would mold the community from raw clay, though his plan to do so was regarded by more experienced churchmen and missionaries as evidence not so much of his boldness as his recklessness.

The journey to Cambria County took them first to Philadelphia, where they changed trains, and then to Harrisburg. In Harrisburg they left the train and continued the journey by canal boat to Hollidaysburg in Blair County, Pennsylvania, where two of the company, Conrad Reinbolt and Felix Hochstätter, were left behind because they had contracted typhoid fever. At Hollidaysburg the canal boat was lifted up the Allegheny Mountains by inclined plane on the famous Portage Road, an engineering marvel that deeply impressed the Bavarian travelers. At the summit of the Alleghenies they left the Portage Road and traveled twenty miles on foot, their baggage following by wagon, to Lemke's holdings at St. Joseph in northern Cambria County. They arrived on September 30, 1846, two months after they had set out from Munich.[23]

Father Demetrius Gallitzin (1770–1840), the Russian prince who had converted to Catholicism, become a priest, and then served the Catholics of Cambria County for more than forty years, had founded St. Joseph Church in 1830 on the site of a small settlement called Hart's Sleeping Place. Father Peter Henry Lemke had taken charge of the church in 1837 and later bought four hundred acres of land nearby where he planned to establish the farming community of Carrolltown. When the Benedictine missionaries arrived at St. Joseph in 1846, however, the village of Carrolltown had still not taken shape. In Munich Lemke had offered to sell the four hundred acres to the Benedictines at a favorable price and to turn over the pastorate of St. Joseph Church to Wimmer, but when they had an opportunity to survey the land that Lemke offered, Wimmer and his men were disappointed. Little of the land was under cultivation, and the fields that had been cleared were full of stones and studded with tree stumps. The roads leading in and out of the valley were rough, stony, and hilly, and on the property itself there were only a poorly constructed farmhouse and a barn, both three miles from the church. The single advantage of the place, from Wimmer's point of view, was that the region was settled by more than three hundred German Catholics, the people whom the Benedictines had come to serve.[24]

Soon after the Benedictine mission arrived, Bishop Michael O'Connor wrote Wimmer welcoming him to the diocese and inviting him to join him in Pittsburgh for the dedication of St. Philomena German Church. Wimmer accepted the invitation and traveled to Pittsburgh where he met the bishop on October 4. When he explained to O'Connor his disappointment with the land Lemke had offered him in Cambria County, the bishop told him that there was another property in the diocese ideally suited for a Benedictine settlement: a parish with a large church, several sturdy buildings, and two fertile and prospering farms where he had long hoped to establish a seminary. O'Connor offered to show Wimmer the place and Wimmer agreed. The next day they went to Saint Vincent where the bishop introduced Father Boniface to the pastor of the parish, Father Michael Gallagher, and some of the leading parishioners. O'Connor offered to turn Saint Vincent over to the Benedictines so that they could establish a monastery and seminary there, and Father Gallagher said that he would be pleased to surrender the pastorship to Father Boniface and even join the monastery as a novice.

Wimmer was delighted by the bishop's offer and eager to accept it. But he had signed a preliminary contract with Lemke for the property in Cambria County and had already made a down payment of four hundred dollars. He was not sure that he could cancel the arrangement and get a refund of his money. He told the bishop that he would consult with his companions at St. Joseph and together they would decide what to do. When he returned to Cambria County, Father Boniface called a meeting of the missionary band. He explained the situation and the bishop's offer. He told them that Saint Vincent was in an "uncommonly beautiful and fertile region" and that the land was much more arable than the acreage at St. Joseph. Brother Stephen Weber, acting as spokesman for the group, urged that because of the more suitable farmland in Westmoreland County the community establish itself there. The others echoed his opinion, complaining that the stumps and stones in the fields at St. Joseph hampered their efforts to plant the winter wheat crop. The community was of one mind. They should leave Cambria County and move to Saint Vincent.[25]

Meanwhile, the parishioners at Saint Vincent held a meeting in the parish church and drafted a letter of invitation to Wimmer. Observing that the Benedictines would never find a better place in Pennsylvania to establish a monastery and school, they urged him to come to Saint Vincent. They promised, moreover, to give him every possible assistance in settling permanently there and pledged that the trustees would never interfere with his rights as pastor under Theodore Brouwers' will.[26]

On October 15 Wimmer ordered his men to collect their baggage and prepare to move to Saint Vincent. He left open the possibility that he would purchase some of the Carrolltown property at a later date, but he rebuffed the efforts of Lemke and the St. Joseph parishioners to have the Benedictines remain in Cambria County. When he attempted to get Lemke to refund the down payment of four hundred dollars, Lemke refused, saying that he had already spent the money. This left Wimmer in a difficult financial position because he had already spent most of the funds he had brought from Bavaria and badly needed cash. Thus began the uneasy and often conflictive relationship between Wimmer and Lemke which continued even after Lemke became a Benedictine at Saint Vincent.[27]

On October 16 Wimmer and most of his companions set out on foot from St. Joseph for Westmoreland County. Stopping in Blairsville, where they stayed overnight with Father James Ambrose Stillinger at Ss. Simon and Jude Church, they arrived at Saint Vincent on October 18. The remainder of the community, accompanying the sick brothers, left St. Joseph a day later and arrived on October 19. Because the German parishioners in Cambria County refused to help with the move, Wimmer had to hire several Irishmen to haul the baggage to Saint Vincent.[28]

On October 24, 1846, Wimmer invested the four students and twelve of the lay brothers with the Benedictine habit in the church at Saint Vincent. Because there were only six habits available for all the novices, as one was invested he would retire to the sacristy, change back into secular dress, and return the habit to the sanctuary for use in the investiture of another novice. The two sick brothers, Conrad Reinbolt and Felix Hochstätter, were invested as novices sometime later, and on the feast of the Immaculate Conception (December 8) Father Michael Gallagher also joined the community and entered the novitiate.

When the Benedictines settled at Saint Vincent in 1846 the parish was fifty-six years old. Its two farms—one of 313 acres surrounding the parish church and the other of 162 acres at O'Neill's Victory, seven miles away—were those that Father Theodore Brouwers had left in trust to his successors in perpetuity, and by naming Wimmer pastor, Bishop O'Connor in effect granted the land to the Benedictines at no cost to them. Since the bishop retained the right to appoint a new pastor whenever he wished, however, Father Boniface did not feel secure in his title to the land. Nonetheless, O'Connor's promise to "regulate the matter in such a way that the superior of the Benedictine monastery to be established here will always be pastor and have full and complete rights to this property" mollified him, at least for the moment.[29] He and his confreres therefore settled into the regular observance of monastic life at Saint Vincent on October 24, 1846, happy to have found what Wimmer called "one of the most beautiful and salubrious spots in America for a Benedictine monastery."[30]

As their first winter in America approached, the community made their home in the two-story schoolhouse built by Father Gallagher two years earlier. To accommodate the needs of so many new people on the property, the brothers set about constructing an outdoor kitchen and latrine. The schoolhouse, located about 150 feet southwest of Saint Vincent Church (built by Father James Ambrose Stillinger in 1835), had originally been intended for the minor seminary Bishop O'Connor and Father Gallagher unsuccessfully attempted to establish at Saint Vincent in 1845. As for the other buildings on the property and their inhabitants, the seven Sisters of Mercy, with eighteen female students, continued to reside in the parochial residence, which had been constructed at the same time as the church and which was located fifty paces east of it, and the tenant farmer, John Schowalter, lived with his family in Sportsman's Hall, sixty paces south of the church. Sportsman's Hall, the oldest building on the land, had been constructed by Father Theodore Brouwers in 1790 to serve as a priest's residence and church. Now used as a farmhouse, it formed part of a complex that included several "miserable" farm buildings. Except for Sportsman's Hall and the farm buildings, which were made of hewn logs, all the other structures on the property were of brick. Surrounding the church and the other buildings were wheat fields and grazing meadows, and beyond these lay an oak forest. A pump inside the schoolhouse and a spring next to

Sportsman's Hall provided water.[31] The Benedictines lived in the two-story schoolhouse until John Schowalter sold the fall harvest and left Saint Vincent. After this some of the lay brothers moved into the log structure, thus easing congestion in the schoolhouse. In May 1847, when the Sisters of Mercy moved with their students to the newly constructed convent of St. Xavier a mile and a half away, Wimmer, Gallagher, and the four clerical novices occupied the parochial residence.

The daily schedule of the monks during their first year in America was similar to that of the Abbey of Metten. Closely following the horarium prescribed by the Rule of St. Benedict, it evenly divided the day into periods of prayer, work, and spiritual reading. The monks rose at 3:45 a.m. and went to the parish church for prayer. At 4:00 a.m. Wimmer, Gallagher, and the clerical students recited the hours of Matins and Lauds (in Latin) in the choir loft while the lay brothers recited the first five decades of the Rosary (in German) in the sanctuary. At 5:00 a.m. all observed an hour of meditation before the Blessed Sacrament, and at 6:00 a.m. they attended conventual Mass, after which the lay brothers, before going to work, took a light breakfast, while the clerical monks recited the hour of Prime and listened to readings from the Benedictine Martyrology and a chapter from the Rule of St. Benedict. (Wimmer and the clerical students did not break their fast until 11:00 a.m.) At 7:00 a.m. the students went to class and the lay brothers to their assigned jobs. At 9:00 a.m. the clerical monks interrupted their studies to recite the hours of Terce, Sext, and None. Then at 10:45 a.m. everyone gathered in the church for adoration of the Blessed Sacrament and particular examination of conscience. The community ate "dinner" at 11:00 a.m., followed by recreation for the clerics and instruction in the religious life for the brothers. At 1:00 p.m. the clerical students returned to class and the brothers to their work. At 3:00 p.m. Wimmer, Gallagher, and the students gathered in the church to recite Vespers, after which classes continued for another hour and a half, and at 5:00 p.m. the entire community gathered in the church for spiritual reading and an explanation of the Rule of St. Benedict. At 6:00 p.m. they had supper, followed by recreation and housework until 7:30 p.m., when the brothers recited the final five decades of the Rosary and the clerical monks prayed Compline. Night prayers and a general examination of conscience concluded the day. Everyone retired at 9:00 p.m.[32] This was the basic schedule the monks at Saint Vincent followed for more than a century.

Wimmer's original plan was to have the entire community—clerical monks and lay brothers alike—recite the Divine Office together, but because few of the lay brothers had more than an elementary education, he decided early on to allow them to pray the Rosary in German while the clerical monks (priests and students preparing for the priesthood) chanted and sang the full round of the Benedictine Office in Latin.

The institution of the lay brotherhood traced its origins to the Cistercian monastic reform of the late eleventh century. The early Cistercian monasteries had accepted men in their communities who took vows, wore the habit, and followed the monastic rule, but who were not bound to the daily recitation of the Divine Office. Rather, these lay brothers worked the fields, tended the flocks, and devoted themselves to the humbler tasks necessary for the economic well-being of the monastery, leaving the rest of the community (the ordained choir monks) free to celebrate the liturgy in the manner prescribed by St. Benedict.[33]

From his readings of monastic history Wimmer knew that the medieval Cistercian communities had prospered to a great extent on account of the lay brotherhood, and he drew on that knowledge when formulating his plan to establish the Benedictine Order in the United States. His introduction of the lay brotherhood in America was innovative insofar as he recreated an historic monastic phenomenon at Saint Vincent for which there was no precedent in the restored Bavarian monasteries. (Metten had only three lay brothers at the time, and the economic success of the community in no way depended on them.) What this meant, of course, was that from the earliest days there existed a division at Saint Vincent between the clerical choir monks and the lay brothers, a division founded upon each group's distinct responsibilities and functions within the community. At times this division resulted in problems and conflicts, but as in the medieval Cistercian communities, it was clearly a key element in the spiritual and economic success of the monastery in Pennsylvania. The lay brotherhood continued at Saint Vincent and in the monasteries founded from it for nearly one hundred and twenty years. It was not until 1966, when English became the language of the Divine Office at Saint Vincent, that the division ended and the clerical monks and lay brothers came together in the choir to form a single praying community.

EARLY DAYS AT SAINT VINCENT MONASTERY

Historians of the American Church have often asserted that the establishment of the first Benedictine monastery in the United States was the result of Boniface Wimmer's boldness and persistence in pursuing a goal that many in Bavaria and America thought quixotic and unattainable. While this assertion is essentially true, it is equally certain that Wimmer could not have achieved his goal without the assistance of generous benefactors on both sides of the Atlantic. Wimmer and his eighteen companions were able to undertake the mission to America only because of substantial financial support from the Abbey of Metten, the Ludwig Missionsverein, Bishop Gregory Ziegler of Linz, Austria, and countless anonymous contributors throughout Bavaria. The community of Metten provided the first Benedictine mission in America with money and supplies valued at nearly five hundred Bavarian florins. The Ludwig Missionsverein gave a nonreimbursable grant of six thousand florins. Bishop Ziegler, a former Benedictine abbot, contributed about six hundred florins for travel expenses, and Wimmer raised another three hundred florins from clerical and lay friends in Munich. In addition, some of the lay brother candidates contributed personal funds to the enterprise amounting to about six hundred florins. Later both King Ludwig I of Bavaria and Archduke Maximilian of Austria made substantial monetary contributions to the Pennsylvania foundation, but in the final analysis the establishment of the first Benedictine monastery in the United States was done on a shoestring. Wimmer wrote that he doubted "such an institution has ever been established for six or eight thousand florins, as seems will be the case here."[34] A recent historian has estimated that a Bavarian florin, worth about half a U.S. dollar in the 1840s, would be equivalent to twenty U.S. dollars in the 1990s, and if this estimation is accurate, it means that the Benedictines founded the monastery and school at Saint Vincent with the equivalent of $120,000 to $160,000 in modern (1997) American currency.[35]

In America Bishop Michael O'Connor's grant of the land and buildings at Saint Vincent was valued at twenty-five thousand dollars. Though the Benedictines' title to the property would not be secure for several years, O'Connor's unexpected donation was crucial and assured the ultimate success of the foundation. Moreover, the parishioners at Saint Vincent assumed the debts of the parish, amounting to about thirty-five hundred dollars, including five hundred dollars that Father Michael Gallagher had contracted in the course of constructing the schoolhouse and extending the parochial residence.[36]

Nonetheless, the community's financial plight during its first years at Saint Vincent bordered on the desperate. Wimmer spent most of the money he had received in Bavaria on expenses related to the journey. He lost another $400 when Father Peter Henry Lemke refused to return the down payment for the failed settlement in Cambria County. As a consequence, the community depended during the first several years not only upon contributions from Europe, but also upon the pew rent from the parish of Saint Vincent (about $700 a year), the income from the two farms ($120 a year), and credit given by local Protestant merchants. "We are poor in general and in particular," Wimmer wrote to his Bavarian friends.[37]

Money continued to flow in regularly from Bavaria but at a much slower rate than Wimmer had hoped for. Bishop Ziegler contributed an additional eighteen hundred florins in the fall of 1847, and the Ludwig Missionsverein made regular annual contributions of approximately six thousand florins in the years that followed. But it was not until the beginning of 1851 that the monastery was on a sound financial footing. In January of that year King Ludwig I provided an endowment of ten thousand florins (about $200,000 in modern U.S. currency) which resolved most of the critical economic problems the Benedictines at Saint Vincent still faced.[38]

The parish farms' fall harvest (wheat, oats, and corn) had been almost completely gathered when the Benedictines arrived. Wimmer purchased the harvested grain from tenant farmer John Schowalter, and the lay brothers (with periodic help from the clerical novices and Wimmer himself) set about planting the winter wheat crop. The monks found the land fertile and much more tillable than Lemke's farm in Cambria County. Using credit and what little money remained of the funds he had brought from Bavaria, Wimmer purchased four horses, five cows, six pigs and twenty-eight piglets. He regretted that he did not have enough money to buy sheep. He also bought plows, wagons, leather harnesses for the horses, and furnishings for the blacksmith shop (an anvil, bellows, iron). The total cost for all this was about six hundred dollars. When spring came, the brothers returned to the fields and planted wheat, oats, and corn. From the parish farms Wimmer expected the monks to raise six to seven hundred bushels of wheat, five hundred bushels of oats, and nine hundred to a thousand bushels of corn. He estimated that this would sustain a community of 30 to 40 monks and students, but already in the spring of 1847 he was projecting that he would eventually have to support a community of 140 priests, brothers, and students, for which he would need to acquire more land. If this projection seemed overly optimistic, he reminded his Bavarian friends "that God can raise children of Abraham from stones."[39]

He complained that local millers expected one-third of the grain brought to their mills for grinding as payment, and he told the directors of the Ludwig Missionsverein that he would have to build a gristmill at Saint

Vincent as soon as possible to avoid this additional expense. He also planned to build a sawmill, which would significantly reduce the cost of lumber when time came to erect new buildings, and to buy poultry, sheep (to "furnish most of [our] clothing"), and additional cattle and horses. His goal was to make the monastery completely self-sufficient. "That I brought *so many* brothers along," he wrote, "is rather a profit than a loss. I only wish that I had twenty more with me. The number I have is *not enough*. . . . If I wanted to have a Benedictine monastery, I could not have done it in any other way. Had I set out alone with only two or three men, the undertaking [would have failed]." In the meantime, however, he still needed financial support from Bavaria.

As for the food that sustained the monks during the early days, meat (served three times a week) and bread were staples, supplemented by potatoes and pumpkins. Wimmer said that water was the only drink. "We have neither beer nor wine nor apple cider, etc., which is to be found in every American home. Our dishes, made of flour, contain no eggs (which now are very expensive)." Only Father Gallagher used butter because "he is accustomed to having it and cannot all at once do without it."[40] To increase both the variety and quantity of food and drink available to the community, the monks planted a vegetable garden, laid out a fruit orchard, began a dairy, established a poultry farm, and acquired a brewery within five years of their settlement at Saint Vincent.

A proto-seminary began operating at Saint Vincent immediately after the Benedictine settlement with Wimmer and Gallagher as instructors and the four Benedictine clerics and a subdeacon from the Diocese of Pittsburgh as students. All the Benedictine clerics arrived at Saint Vincent with Bavarian classical educations. Benedict Haindl (age thirty-one) had completed his studies at the Old Gymnasium in Munich; Placidus Döttl (age twenty-three) had been educated at the Latin school in Burghausen, Bavaria, and the New Gymnasium in Munich, and Celestine Englbrecht (age twenty-two) at the New Gymnasium in Munich. Each of these needed the full three-year course in theology before being ordained. Only Charles Geyerstanger (age twenty-six), who had completed classical and philosophical studies in Salzburg, Austria, was close to ordination, having finished two years of theology at the University of Munich before joining the Benedictine mission to the United States. The diocesan subdeacon, whose name has not been recorded, had also completed nearly all his pre-ordination theological studies.[41]

During the first year (1846–1847), Wimmer taught the students logic, homiletics, monastic spirituality, and chant, and Father Gallagher taught them theology. Because he did not know German, Gallagher gave classes to the Benedictine clerics in Latin while the subdeacon from Pittsburgh taught them English. Later, after Gallagher left the community and reinforcements arrived from Bavaria, Father Peter Lechner of Scheyern and Father Thaddeus Brunner of Metten took charge of instructing the seminarians in theology. Toward the end of 1846 Wimmer announced in several German-American Catholic newspapers that the Benedictines would begin accepting boys for secondary instruction that would lead eventually to the study of theology. By Easter 1847, however, only two such boys had come to Saint Vincent, though Wimmer reported that "many" had applied for admission the following year. The Redemptorists in Pittsburgh had promised to send him students if he could accept most of them gratis, and he estimated that he could eventually accommodate as many as fifty of these nonpaying students provided he could acquire more land and offset costs by receiving paying students as well.[42] A key Benedictine goal continued to be to serve the educational needs of the poor.

Wimmer wrote Archbishop von Reisach that "monastic life was my first aim," and his establishment of the Metten horarium at Saint Vincent was only the first step in the spiritual development of the community. During the first year in Pennsylvania Father Boniface gave daily lessons in monastic spirituality to the novices (both the clerics and lay brothers). His method, he said, was to "explain the Holy Rule to them and say what they have to do." He found in all the novices "a joyful compliance, which has not slackened for a moment, to lead a life pleasing to God according to the trusty Rule of St. Benedict. I cannot thank God enough that, driven by His Holy Spirit, such a considerable number of staunch people have gathered around me. If all are not equally industrious and thoroughly permeated by their vocation, most are, and these have such a salutary effect through word and example on the others, who are not so advanced in the spiritual life, that they gladly follow."[43]

After four months of monastic life at Saint Vincent, Wimmer reported that the three traditional religious vows were being faithfully observed by the monks. Poverty was perhaps the easiest to follow since the condition of the community was such that temptations to break this vow did not exist. He said that chastity was not endangered ("except in our own hearts") and that he frequently encouraged his confreres "to rely on Him who was born of the Immaculate Virgin and who keeps His own pure." Obedience was also "practiced faithfully." Thus, with regard to observance of the vows,

Wimmer had no complaints about the brethren, whose conduct, he said, was "praiseworthy." As for other aspects of traditional monastic discipline, the monks observed the Great Silence from Compline until Prime, though because they lived so close together they could not observe absolute silence during the day. On the other hand, "jesting and personal conversation are allowed only during recreation." All in all, Wimmer was very pleased with the manner in which Benedictine observance had taken root in Pennsylvania. "I doubt," he wrote, "if a monastery exists anywhere (except perhaps for the Trappists) in which monks live more faithfully the Rule of St. Benedict than here."[44]

PASTORAL WORK

The Benedictines began their pastoral work among German immigrants and their children immediately upon their arrival at Saint Vincent. At first only Wimmer—the sole priest in the mission—attended to the spiritual needs of the people. In March 1847, however, Bishop O'Connor ordained Charles Geyerstanger (the first Benedictine monk to be raised to the priesthood in the United States), and after that there were always at least two German-speaking priests attending to the needs of the German Catholics in Westmoreland County.

At the end of October 1846 Wimmer took over the duties of pastor at Saint Vincent from Father Michael Gallagher. As Wimmer's assistant, Gallagher assumed responsibilities for the English-speaking members of the congregation. Judging from the names of the fifty-eight heads of households who signed the letter inviting the Benedictines to Saint Vincent on October 10, 1846,[45] about two-thirds of the parish families were of German heritage, and the remaining third of Irish and English extraction. This corresponds with what Wimmer himself wrote to Bavaria shortly after settling at Saint Vincent. The congregation, he said, was predominantly German, though there were eighteen or twenty Irish families.[46] If these figures are accurate, they indicate that the number of families in the parish had declined since Bishop Kenrick's episcopal visitations of the late 1830s, but it is more likely that Wimmer was counting only those parishioners in the immediate vicinity of Saint Vincent who regularly attended services there. It is probable that many Irish families in the parish attended Mass at Mount Carmel Chapel in New Derry, six miles north of Saint Vincent. This chapel had been founded for Irish turnpike workers in 1822 by Father Terrence McGirr and continued to be served from Saint Vincent by Father Michael Gallagher.

Out of a total population of forty-two thousand in Westmoreland County, Wimmer (drawing on figures provided by Bishop O'Connor) estimated that there were perhaps two thousand Catholics, about half of whom were Germans. The parishes of Saint Vincent and Ss. Simon and Jude in Blairsville nominally served these Catholics, but in fact most of these people did not have the regular services of a priest. Wimmer reported that he had encountered many Germans who were formerly Catholics but who had fallen away from the Church because of the lack of German-speaking priests to minister to them. He also reported that there were large numbers of German Protestants in the region, some of whom had invited him to preach to them. One thing that all German families had in common, Wimmer said, was that they were losing touch with their cultural and linguistic heritage.

It has developed in the course of time that most of the German children hardly understand German any more, and after not many more years only the newly immigrated families (about twelve to fifteen from the Würzburg and Baden areas) have retained their mother tongue for a while. I can at any rate say that I preside over a German, if not purely German congregation. And besides the German Catholics, a lot, indeed a far greater number of German Protestants live here, of whom many attend my talks, so in its origin and direction my mission is German and extremely important for the Germans, and it will contribute essentially toward keeping the Germans German.

Wimmer emphasized his work among the Germans because that was the purpose for which he had come and for which the directors of the Ludwig Missionsverein and other benefactors had given money to the American mission. Nonetheless, he discovered early in his pastoral experience in Pennsylvania that if he hoped to succeed he could not limit himself to serving German Catholics alone. He would also have to serve the Irish because there were few purely German Catholic settlements in America.

Usually Germans and Irish, or anglicized Germans, live mixed with one another, and usually the Germans are in the minority. Even in St. Joseph where I originally wanted to go, and where in fact I went for a while, there is no purely German Catholic population. It is very mixed. . . . I bring this up only because, as I gather from a letter from Bavaria, the notion reigns there now and then that I let myself be misled by the Irish and to some extent have betrayed the Germans.[47]

Wimmer moved quickly to respond to the criticism from Bavaria, explaining in numerous letters home that conditions in America did not permit him to neglect Irish Catholics for the sake of Germans. He emphasized again and again that while he would give preference to Germans, he and his monks were prepared to serve both nationalities. This meant that he would even accept Irish boys for the school, as Bishop O'Connor expected. There was a logic to this that even the directors of the Ludwig Missionsverein could understand. The Benedictines would teach their Irish students German at the same time they taught their German students English. Thus they would educate bilingual priests who could serve both German and Irish Catholics. Meanwhile, Wimmer and his confreres turned to their own study of English with a renewed sense of purpose.

From Saint Vincent Wimmer, and later Geyerstanger, sought out German Catholics throughout Westmoreland County, very soon expanding their activities to Indiana County in the north where Wimmer estimated sixteen thousand people lived, most of them Germans. In 1847 he organized Catholic congregations and built churches in Greensburg, Saltsburg, and Indiana. He and Geyerstanger also visited and brought the sacraments to Catholics in Mt. Pleasant, Bobtown, Adamsburg, Possolstown, Kittanning, and Ligonier (where the Benedictines built a church in 1854). During this early period (1846–1848), the Benedictine field of missionary activity extended forty miles east and west of Saint Vincent and ninety miles north and south. Wimmer said that he had the Catholics in nineteen small towns in his care.[48] Typical of the requests for pastoral care that came to Saint Vincent at the time was a letter Wimmer received from Karl Schell of Kittanning, Pennsylvania: "With these lines I pray you, shepherd of my soul, to look up a sheep who has gone astray. I and my small family could not attend mass for a year, and now, as God has blessed us with a child, we ask you to come and baptize it, and give us a chance to receive the sacraments. We live two miles from Kittanning. When you come, only ask for the German tinner. Everybody knows me."[49]

From time to time on special occasions the Benedictines joined together with lay people to celebrate the liturgy in mission churches served from Saint Vincent. For instance, after completing construction of Blessed Sacrament Church in Greensburg (accomplished with financial help from both Irish Catholics and German Protestants), they assisted Bishop O'Connor at the dedication on the second Sunday of Advent 1847. The *Pittsburgh Catholic* reported that the church was completely filled for the ceremony and that many people had to stand outside. Wimmer celebrated the Mass, Bishop O'Connor preached, and the Benedictine community sang the liturgy. "There is yet no organ in the church," said the reporter from Pittsburgh, "but the rich, deep tones of eight or nine German voices, combined in admirable harmony, more than supplied this want."[50]

Wimmer made his mission rounds in a biweekly circuit that brought him to the towns of Saltsburg and Indiana, for example, twice a month for Mass. He often stayed in the homes of parishioners and on those occasions he functioned not only as priest but "also as schoolmaster and catechist." He gave religious instruction to adults and children, celebrated Mass, and then moved on to the next station. His schedule was grueling. "For several weeks I was at home only two days back to back," he wrote in June 1848. "Otherwise, I am seldom at home. A bad chair is now and then my bed, on which I sleep sitting up. Sun and moon are my road guides in the beautiful oak forests. My shield is my Jesus, whom I always have near me, as well as most of the time everything needed for the offering of the Holy Sacrifice of the Mass. Thus my horse is a wandering chapel."[51]

During his first two years in America Wimmer's solitary journeys on horseback through the Pennsylvania forest, along difficult roads in winter and summer, bore abundant fruit. He instructed the ignorant in the truths of the Catholic faith. He baptized nominal Catholics—children, adolescents, and adults—who had never seen a priest. He brought God's forgiveness to penitents who had not been shriven for half a century. He reconciled people to the Church who had not belonged to it for years. He celebrated Mass for hundreds who had last received the Eucharist before they had come to America or who had never received it at all. And he gave last rites in the hour of death to men and women who had never expected to end their lives with the comfort of the sacraments. "The more I get to know especially the more remote parishioners," he wrote, "the more wretchedness I find."[52] But he relieved the burdens and eased the pain of those to whom he ministered. These were the people the Bavarian monks had come to America to serve, and the work Wimmer and his confreres did among them during those first impoverished years at Saint Vincent was not just a fulfillment of the Projektenmacher's impractical hopes and aspirations but a paradigm for the labors the Benedictines would undertake in America over the next 150 years.

CONFLICT WITH THE BISHOP

Diocesan and Benedictine goals coalesced in remarkable fashion at Saint Vincent in 1846. Wimmer's objectives were virtually the same as those of Bishop O'Connor: to minister to the spiritual needs of German-speaking Catholics and to establish a seminary to educate American-born priests. O'Connor had authorized Father Peter Henry Lemke to recruit German-speaking priests in Bavaria in 1845 to accomplish the first objective, and he had attempted to establish a diocesan seminary at Saint Vincent in 1844 to accomplish the second. When the Benedictines arrived in the Diocese of Pittsburgh in 1846, therefore, they must have seemed the answer to the bishop's prayers. Their plan was to do precisely what O'Connor had hoped to achieve since becoming bishop of Pittsburgh. For that reason O'Connor turned the valuable parish of Saint Vincent over to them and promised to arrange things in such a manner that the parish lands would become Benedictine property in perpetuity.

The bishop believed that such generosity merited an appropriate response, and six months after they settled at Saint Vincent, he wrote Wimmer informing him of how the Benedictines could repay the debt. He had already spoken to Father Boniface of his intention to send boys to Saint Vincent from Pittsburgh to be educated for the priesthood. Now, in April 1847, he wrote that he wanted to send seven of these boys as soon as the Sisters of Mercy and their students left Saint Vincent. Since the sisters were scheduled to move to St. Xavier in May, he expected the Benedictines to begin preparing for the arrival of the Pittsburgh students at once. "I will consider it a great favor if you would be able to take them without too much trouble," he said. "If you wish (and most probably this will be necessary now), I can send an English[-speaking] priest along who will give them instructions."[53]

Wimmer's response was immediate and negative. He was not prepared to receive the bishop's students so soon. He and Father Gallagher had enough on their hands attending to the needs of the parishioners, visiting Catholics in distant towns and villages, and preparing the Benedictine clerics and the bishop's subdeacon for ordination. Moreover O'Connor's plan to send seven English-speaking diocesan students, along with a diocesan priest to have charge of them, meant that the school at Saint Vincent would be in jeopardy of becoming predominantly Irish and diocesan rather than German and Benedictine.

From the beginning Wimmer's plan was to establish a Latin secondary school at Saint Vincent modeled on the Bavarian gymnasium. He expected to attract to this school the children of German immigrants who would first receive a classical Bavarian education and then enter the major seminary he planned to establish at Saint Vincent. But in the spring of 1847 he had neither the professors nor the financial resources to open a German school at Saint Vincent, much less an English one for the bishop's students. He and the Benedictine clerics still lacked proficiency in English, and he feared that by accepting the Pittsburgh students and an Irish diocesan priest to take charge of them, he would irrevocably surrender control of the educational institution he hoped eventually to create. He was therefore adamant in his refusal to accept the bishop's students.[54]

O'Connor responded in a conciliatory manner. He proposed that he and Wimmer draw up a written contract to avoid future miscommunication. He said that his understanding of the oral agreement he and Father Boniface had come to in October 1846 was that he would turn Saint Vincent over to the Benedictines on three conditions. First, he expected that Wimmer and his priests would take pastoral charge of the parishioners at Saint Vincent and do missionary work in Westmoreland County. If the German Benedictines could not adequately minister to the English-speaking Catholics in their charge, the bishop reserved the right to assign Irish or American priests to Saint Vincent whom the monks would be obliged to support. Second, he expected that the monks would provide pastoral services for the Sisters of Mercy at St. Xavier Convent, celebrate daily Mass for them, and act as their confessors. Finally, he expected that the Benedictines would open a minor seminary as soon as possible and accept diocesan candidates for the priesthood at reduced rates, receiving them gratis once the monastery had achieved a stable financial footing.[55]

Much of this was news to Wimmer. Perhaps the problem lay in the fact that neither he nor the bishop spoke the other's native language. They conducted their discussions in Latin, a tongue in which both were fluent, but they came from different European cultures, and their cultural differences easily led to misinterpretations of what the other was saying. This was not a problem unique to Boniface Wimmer and Michael O'Connor. Throughout the nineteenth century cultural differences and misunderstanding plagued an American Church in which Irish and German interests were often sharply divided.[56] Wimmer was surprised that the bishop was making so many demands on the Benedictines at a time when the monastic community clearly did not have enough ordained monks to meet the challenge. In May 1847 the monastery at Saint Vincent had only Charles Geyerstanger, Michael Gallagher, and Wimmer himself to manage its extensive pastoral and educational commitments. These three priests were responsible for administering the parish of Saint Vincent, preparing three Benedictine clerics for ordination, and covering about thirty-six hundred square miles of mission territory, including Catholic congregations in Greensburg, Saltsburg, Indiana, Ligonier and almost twenty other Pennsylvania towns and villages. Father Gallagher, moreover, had already expressed his intention of leaving Saint Vincent to join the Irish Augustinians in Philadelphia, and promised reinforcements from Benedictine communities in Bavaria had not yet arrived.

Thus Wimmer felt he had no choice but to refuse most of the bishop's conditions. His understanding of their verbal agreement, he said, was that in exchange for the land at Saint Vincent the Benedictines would care for the parish at Saint Vincent and the German population of Westmoreland County. They would also celebrate Mass and hear confessions for the Sisters of Mercy on Sundays and holy days. Beyond that, however, they would expect stipends for any services they performed for the sisters and would accept responsibility for mission work outside of Westmoreland County only when the bishop requested them to care for specified congregations and agreed to recompense them for the extra work. Finally, he said, they would not be bound to receive the bishop's English-speaking students except on a case-by-case basis and then only if the bishop were willing to pay the customary fees.[57]

O'Connor responded that he hoped Wimmer would not be distressed "if within certain limits I am expecting the diocese to derive the first fruits of your labors." He continued to insist upon the conditions he understood to have been agreed upon beforehand and implied that he would not give the Benedictines permanent rights to the land unless they met his requirements.[58] Wimmer refused. He knew that by accepting the bishop's conditions, he would jeopardize the monastery's independence. He also understood that unless the bishop gave the Benedictines indisputable title to the land, future bishops (or O'Connor himself) could grant the pastorship of Saint Vincent to another priest, resulting in the Benedictines' loss of the property that Theodore Brouwers had willed to the pastor of the parish. Unless they were secure in their property rights, the Benedictines could not hope to found a permanent monastery at Saint Vincent. Wimmer therefore began to look for another place to settle the community. He informed the bishop that the monks would leave Saint Vincent, and he began exploring possible alternative sites for a monastery. He had received invitations from Bishop John Martin Henni of Milwaukee to settle in Wisconsin, from Father Nicholas Balleis, O.S.B., to settle in New Jersey, and from the land company that in 1845 had established the German colony in St. Marys, Pennsylvania, to settle in St. Marys. He considered all these place, concluding that St. Marys was the least desirable since it was in Bishop O'Connor's diocese. "I am torn between Newark and Wisconsin, to which the *German* Bishop Henni has earnestly invited me three times. I thought of St. Teresa and intend to have nothing further to do with this Irish scoundrel. In reality this changes nothing except the place. We are best under Germans, and never again will I have anything to do with acting as a pastor for the Irish."[59]

When he learned that Wimmer was planning to leave the diocese, Bishop O'Connor reconsidered his position. In November 1847 he offered to accept the Benedictines on their own terms and agreed to withdraw the conditions he had placed on granting them the land at Saint Vincent in perpetuity.[60] A month later he issued a decree giving Wimmer and his successors as the superior of the Benedictine monastery of Saint Vincent "the right to the two estates which the Reverend Theodore Brauer [*sic*] granted in his will to the pastor of the church of Saint Vincent."[61] By this document the Benedictines were assured permanent ownership of the property, and thus the settlement of the Benedictine Order in Westmoreland County was ratified and confirmed. Wimmer later wrote that his disagreement with the bishop was unavoidable. "I could understand the mind of the bishop," he said. "In spite of the testimonials from the abbot of Metten and the bishops of Munich and Regensburg, I was still a stranger to him. He granted me the two properties by appointing me pastor, but in case of my death he could have given them to another priest, and in such a case the brothers would have had to leave the place. He could even remove me at his pleasure from the parish. All this caused me great anxiety."[62]

In the fall of 1848 the Benedictines accepted several of the bishop's students at reduced rates, and tensions between Wimmer and O'Connor eased. Meanwhile Wimmer was taking action in a matter that would lead to a second conflict with the bishop. In June 1848 he petitioned the Holy See through the offices of John Martin Henni, bishop of Milwaukee and the only German in the American hierarchy, to have the monastery at Saint Vincent raised to the rank of canonical priory, declared independent of the Abbey of Metten, and made exempt from the jurisdiction of the bishop of Pittsburgh in its internal administrative and spiritual affairs. In Europe, Benedictine monasteries were traditionally independent and exempt from episcopal control, and Wimmer saw his petition as part of the standard procedure for founding a Benedictine monastery. In America, however, there existed no exempt monasteries, and neither O'Connor nor the other American bishops were eager to see them established, since to a certain extent exemption limited a bishop's power to manage and direct church affairs in his diocese.

Wimmer's decision to petition for exempt canonical rank without first seeking O'Connor's approval, as well as his rather maladroit attempt to sidestep the bishop of Pittsburgh by submitting his request to Rome through the bishop of Milwaukee, further alienated O'Connor. Then in 1849 Wimmer made another decision which, though it seemed eminently reasonable to him and his German friends, the Irish bishop regarded as imprudent and injudicious. The decision was to take over the operation of a brewery.

Since the Middle Ages German monasteries had operated breweries not only to generate income but also to supply monastery tables with beer. As a good German, Wimmer saw no difficulty with Benedictines being involved in the beer trade. Michael O'Connor, on the other hand, had become a leader of the temperance movement in the American Church and saw Benedictine operation of a brewery as inconsistent with diocesan policy and gravely scandalous to the faithful.

The brewery was in Indiana, Pennsylvania, where the monks from Saint Vincent served a small community of German Catholics. It had been bought by a nephew of Wimmer's who had borrowed the money from his uncle. When the nephew failed in the business, Wimmer took it over, hired a brewer, and leased the tavern attached to the brewery to a previous owner. When Bishop O'Connor learned of the monks' involvement in the beer trade, he ordered them to sell the brewery and tavern at once. Wimmer refused, claiming rights that every Benedictine monastery in Bavaria possessed. O'Connor reminded him that Saint Vincent was not in Bavaria but in the United States, where conditions and rules were different.[63] When Wimmer continued to resist, the bishop responded by refusing to execute the decree that had recently arrived from Rome establishing Saint Vincent as a canonical priory.

With matters at an impasse Wimmer decided to travel to Europe to organize support for his monastery. He had three goals in mind: (1) to secure canonical rank for the monastery at Saint Vincent, (2) to gain exemption from the jurisdiction of the bishop, and (3) to obtain confirmation of the monastery's right to operate a brewery. In Munich Wimmer received the powerful support of Archbishop Karl von Reisach and the Ludwig Missionsverein and learned that King Ludwig I was ready to speak with Vatican officials on his behalf as well. Rather than go to Rome, Father Boniface remained in Bavaria working with von Reisach and Father Joseph Ferdinand Müller, treasurer of the Ludwig Missionsverein, on the strategy his friends in Rome would use to promote his cause. King Ludwig, who at this time gave the substantial grant of ten thousand florins to the monastery in Pennsylvania, instructed Bavarian diplomats in Rome to speak to Vatican officials on the American Benedictines' behalf, and Wimmer himself carried on a campaign by letter to convince the Sacred Congregation for the Propagation of the Faith to grant all the petitions he had submitted.[64]

Bishop O'Connor, on the other hand, was not without his Roman friends. He wrote priests at the Irish College in Rome and asked their support in presenting his case to the Propaganda, explaining that Wimmer had "set me at defiance" by continuing to operate the brewery. Bishop John Hughes of New York happened to be visiting the Vatican at the time, and when officials of the Propaganda asked his opinion, Hughes came out with a spirited defense of the bishop of Pittsburgh.[65]

It took Vatican officials more than a year to resolve the case. Their resolution was a classic compromise that gave a little and kept a little from each party in the dispute. For the Benedictines, the cardinals granted canonical status to the monastery as well as the right to brew beer "provided every disorder is avoided." For the bishop, they declared that the monastery would be nonexempt and that the monks would not be permitted to sell beer by the glass. In other words, a brewery to provide beer for the monastery table was allowed, and the monks could even distribute it "by the barrel" (wholesale) to meet costs, but they were prohibited from engaging in the retail trade. The tavern would have to go.[66] In the end—in order to placate the bishop and also because the operation was losing money—Wimmer sold the brewery and turned the tavern into a residence for the monks assigned to Indiana County. But the Benedictines did not entirely abandon their hopes for a brewery. In 1860, after Bishop O'Connor had resigned the See of Pittsburgh and entered a Jesuit novitiate, they dusted off the Roman decree of 1852 and built a brewery at Saint Vincent that provided beer for the monastery table for the next sixty years.

REINFORCEMENTS FROM BAVARIA

In August 1847, less than a year after the first Benedictine mission settled in the United States, Father Peter Lechner, prior of the Abbey of Scheyern, and seventeen candidates for the lay brotherhood arrived at Saint Vincent, sent by Abbot Rupert Leiss to assist Wimmer and his confreres in their efforts to establish a permanent center of Benedictine monastic observance in the United States. The coming of the Scheyern contingent marked a decisive turning point in the history of Saint Vincent. Not only did the arrival of so many men double the number of monks in the community and bring encouragement and hope to the pioneers who had endured their first impoverished year in America, but it also signaled the beginning of the long hoped-for support from the Bavarian Benedictine abbeys.

Until then many in the Bavarian communities had stood back waiting to see the outcome of the Projektenmacher's latest idea. Now that it seemed as if the Benedictine mission to America would succeed, others came forward to join. The volunteers included not only Peter Lechner and the seventeen brother candidates from Scheyern, but also Father Thaddeus Brunner and the cleric Adalbert Pums from Metten and Father Andrew Zugtriegel from Augsburg.[67] The new lay brothers joined the original band to work the farms and perform the other manual labor necessary for the community's economic sustainability, and the new priests divided their time between instructing the students and ministering to the faithful. Wimmer assigned Lechner, Brunner, and Pums to teach the seminarians and preparatory students who had begun to enroll at Saint Vincent, while he, Zugtriegel, and Geyerstanger undertook the pastoral care of Catholics in Westmoreland and Indiana counties. On April 20, 1849 Bishop O'Connor ordained Benedict Haindl, Placidus Döttl, and Celestine Englbrecht to the priesthood. Thus two and a half years after the settlement at Saint Vincent, there were eight Benedictine priests from Bavaria laboring in the missions of western Pennsylvania.

Wimmer named Lechner prior and novice master at Saint Vincent and gave him responsibility for training the Benedictine and diocesan students in the seminary. To Brunner he assigned the task of organizing the gymnasium (or Latin school), which eventually became Saint Vincent College. Both Lechner and Brunner were experienced educators. The former had for many years overseen the theological program for Benedictine clerics at Scheyern, and the latter had taught in the gymnasium at Metten. Their scholarly interests were broad and their educational standards high. In many ways they were precisely the right people to be in charge of establishing the schools at Saint Vincent. On the other hand, they lacked a fundamental awareness of and appreciation for the need to adjust European ideals to American realities. Their insistence upon applying Bavarian standards and practices in the seminary and gymnasium at Saint Vincent led to serious disagreements between them and Boniface Wimmer.

The first clash came when Lechner challenged Wimmer on his decision to assign physical work to the seminarians during a portion of each day. Lechner said the students could not possibly keep up with the course of studies he had designed for them if they were required to devote time to working in the fields. Wimmer replied that manual labor was an important element in monastic formation, from which the novices and clerics would derive spiritual benefits, and that everyone needed to work in the fields if the community were to become economically self-sustaining. Lechner gave in to these arguments but continued to complain that the young monks' spiritual and intellectual development suffered adversely from Wimmer's pragmatic approach to their formation.[68]

A second disagreement over how the educational programs at Saint Vincent should develop arose when Brunner complained about the standards of admission for students in the gymnasium. The academic level of the young boys who came to Saint Vincent in the late 1840s and early 1850s was, he said, abysmally low. These boys arrived illprepared for secondary studies, sometimes hardly able to read and write, and Brunner identified the source of the problem as Wimmer's insistence on recruiting students from rural communities of poor German immigrants. Brunner suggested that academic standards (not to mention the community's economic security) would increase dramatically if the monks recruited English-speaking boys from well-to-do families in the cities. Wimmer responded forcefully that "this would stamp me as a traitor to my cause. I did not come to America to make money, and not for the rich English students, but to educate my poor countrymen. I would rather suffer want and continue to work under these poor conditions than serve the world, have a better income, and live comfortably."[69]

The sharpest criticism of Wimmer's administration, however, did not have to do with academic matters but rather with the quality of religious observance in the monastery. Lechner, Brunner, and Zugtriegel were of one mind that monastic standards at Saint Vincent were distressingly low. They complained that the novices did not have the opportunity to develop sufficiently their spiritual lives before being assigned to the missions, that the monks lacked time for spiritual reading, that monastic silence was not strictly enforced, that there was no proper monastic enclosure, and that Saint Vincent was "a farm and no monastery" where the superior had "entirely given himself over to business affairs, acquiring more land, more cows, and more sheep."[70]

Wimmer was thrown on the defensive and wrote Abbot Rupert Leiss of Scheyern that he was seriously "worried about the difference of opinions with regard to our daily routine. Some consider it too strict, others too lax. Among the latter is Father Peter who told me that he has complained to you about the manual labor of the students and the monastic enclosure."[71] Still, Wimmer insisted that his pragmatic approach to monastic observance—focusing on the essential elements and introducing traditional but nonessential customs and practices only gradually—was the surest way of establishing a lasting Benedictine presence in America. Fathers Peter, Thaddeus, and Andrew came from the restored Bavarian abbeys which had had the advantage of two decades of development and experience preparing the younger monks in the observance of the customs and practices of traditional Benedictine life. Such observance would eventually become the rule rather than the exception in America too, but in the meantime one had to plow the fields and plant the crops. "I cannot do many things as they should be done," Wimmer said. "Even now Father Peter is bothering me about the enclosure, but it is not *possible* to have one. After I have worked one more year I can comply. I cannot introduce *total* silence in the daytime at work—we would have to become Trappists."[72]

Following a strict, "Trappist" observance, however, was an ideal that continued to inspire Lechner, Brunner, and Zugtriegel. At first they asked Wimmer for permission to found their own community with a number of like-minded clerics who had come to Saint Vincent to enter the novitiate. When Wimmer refused, claiming that dividing the community so soon after the roots had been planted would mean that neither Saint Vincent nor the new community would survive. Lechner then began privately to advise some of the clerics and novices, who under his influence had expressed dissatisfaction with the level of monastic observance at Saint Vincent, to join the Trappist monastery at Gethsemani, Kentucky. In the summer of 1849 Zugtriegel, along with six clerics and brothers, including the monastery musicians, Leonard and Wendelin Mayer, did precisely that. Soon afterwards Lechner himself said that he wanted to leave the community, and Wimmer, exasperated by the "good-natured, sanguine fanaticism" of the would-be reformers, gave him his *exeat.* He wrote Lechner's abbot, Rupert Leiss: "The consciousness of being surrounded by false confreres, the everlasting opposition, the endless series of impractical proposals, the perpetual complaining when I cannot conjure up everything—this is difficult. But I am unremitting, always well, and delight in the Lord, for it is also a comfort to suffer, especially when it comes not from wickedness but from well meaning but misdirected zeal."[73]

Little more than a year later the monks who had gone to Gethsemani returned. They had found life in the French Trappist monastery too exacting for Germans who knew no French and who had even to go to confession through an interpreter. Wimmer received the humbled monks like the father of so many prodigal sons and wrote: "My Trappists have come back, also the musicians, and the loss of several hundred florins, which I suffered on account of them, is compensated by the radical cure of Trappist fever which resulted."[74]

Lechner, Brunner, and Zugtriegel, however, did not come back. They all decided to return to Bavaria to pursue their visions of the monastic life, so different from Wimmer's. Peter Lechner went back to Scheyern where he spent the remainder of his life in prayer and study, publishing numerous spiritual and theological works. His three-volume commentary on sacred scripture was published by the Archabbey Press at Saint Vincent in 1881. Thaddeus Brunner returned to Metten and eventually became conventual prior of St. Denis Priory at Schäftlarn, near Munich. Andrew Zugtriegel left the Benedictines and became a Trappist, ending his days as abbot of the Cistercian Abbey of Oehlenberg in Alsace.

Despite the dissension they caused in the fledgling community, these three "reformers" nonetheless made important contributions to Saint Vincent in the short time they were in America. Not only did Lechner and Brunner help shape the seminary and gymnasium along lines that both schools followed for the next half-century, but all three raised issues related to monastic observance that continued to inform the consciousness and to shape the debate at Saint Vincent long after they had gone. After 1850 Wimmer accepted no more professed monks from Bavarian abbeys into the community. He decided that he would have to build the Benedictine Order in the United States with "raw recruits" whose monastic formation would take place entirely in America and in accord with his own vision of the Benedictine ideal. Still, the tension between the contemplative ideal of prayer and scholarship represented by Lechner, Brunner, and Zugtriegel and the active ideal of missionary work, teaching, and pastoral care represented by Wimmer continued to act as a creative force within the monastery of Saint Vincent, helping to define the community's character for the next century and a half. Neither pole of the Christian monastic dynamic—action and contemplation, work and prayer—ever gained complete ascendancy at Saint Vincent, and throughout the history of the community neither was completely overshadowed by the other. Both remained vital forces in the monastic life of the American Benedictines, just as they had always been in monasteries that followed the Rule of St. Benedict.

THE COLLEGE AND SEMINARY, 1846–1855

Meanwhile, even as conflict marked the early stages of monastic life at Saint Vincent, academic life developed steadily and impressively during the first decade of the Benedictine presence in Pennsylvania. Saint Vincent College was one of forty-two Catholic colleges founded in the United States between 1786 and 1850 and one of ten of the early Catholic colleges that survived into the late twentieth century. Like many of the other surviving institutions, Saint Vincent was established in conjunction with a seminary, and at the beginning its chief purpose was to prepare young men for later theological study and eventual ordination to the priesthood. Like the others, its early curriculum was principally that of a secondary school, with elementary classes provided for very young pupils. It developed more advanced courses only gradually and over a fairly long period of time. Unlike the other early American Catholic colleges, however, Saint Vincent was founded as a school for German Catholic students, and even though it began to accept non-German English-speaking students early in its history, German language and culture continued to dominate throughout its formative period.[75]

The Benedictines in Pennsylvania modeled their school on the Bavarian gymnasium (or Latin school), a nine-year institution of elementary and secondary learning designed to prepare students for German universities. The curriculum in the Bavarian gymnasium was based upon the study of the classics, with required courses in Latin, Greek, German, mathematics, history, geography, the natural sciences, and religious instruction. Students entered the gymnasium as young as ten years of age, completing their work at about age eighteen. They then entered a university (or theological seminary) where the course of studies normally lasted three years.[76]

This system was modified by the Bavarian Benedictines in Pennsylvania in response to the resources available to them and to the needs of the students who enrolled. In the early years the college lacked experienced professors in some of the disciplines taught in Bavarian gymnasiums. Latin, Greek, German, and religion constituted the main courses, but instruction in mathematics was sporadic at the beginning and in the natural sciences instruction was not provided at all during the first decade. The early students were taught principally by Benedictine clerics (theology students) who themselves were only recently graduated from Bavarian gymnasiums. Most of the students who came to Saint Vincent before 1855 were the children of German immigrants and ranged in age from ten to fifteen years old. These students were already well on their way to becoming fully bilingual, and English instruction was therefore a basic need. In the beginning none of the German-speaking monks had sufficient proficiency to teach English, so they called on a few Irish priesthood candidates in the seminary to instruct the younger students in the college.[77]

At least one and possibly two boys came to Saint Vincent during the first academic year (1846–47) for secondary-level instruction in the "college" (gymnasium). Nothing is known of these students except that they were German and that one of them was recommended by the Redemptorist priests in Pittsburgh.[78] Though these boys received instruction at Saint Vincent, there was nothing even faintly resembling a full-fledged secondary school during the first year. The students received individualized instruction according to their need. In the fall of 1847 eight students arrived to pursue secondary studies,[79] and during the second academic year (1847–48) the seeds of the six-year college program that eventually developed at Saint Vincent were planted. By the third academic year (1848–49) there were twelve students enrolled in the college: five from Westmoreland County, one from Pittsburgh, two from Philadelphia, three from St. Marys, and one from Butler, Pennsylvania.[80]

Wimmer himself had charge of the education of the college students during the first few years. He was assisted by the Benedictine seminarians (clerics) who did most of the teaching. The method and content of instruction were doubtless governed as much by the previous academic preparation of the students as by the educational backgrounds and capabilities of the young monks assigned to teach them. Then in 1849 Father Thaddeus Brunner, an experienced educator from Metten, took charge of the college. While he disagreed with Wimmer on the details of monastic observance and on the necessity of making Saint Vincent a school primarily for poor Germans, Brunner was a competent administrator who laid a strong foundation for the fully functioning Latin school that eventually developed.

During the fourth academic year (1849–50) thirteen young boys who did not plan to enter the priesthood arrived at Saint Vincent from the German colony of St. Marys, Pennsylvania, to begin their secondary education. Added to the seven priesthood students, this influx brought the total enrollment of the college to twenty. Like the priesthood candidates, the "commercial" students followed the classical curriculum of Latin, Greek, German, English, history, and Christian doctrine. Only later was a special "commercial" course offered to them. Music and art were very important elements in the curriculum from the earliest years. Beginning in 1849 Father Luke Wimmer (the superior's nephew) taught art appreciation and drawing to the students, and Fathers Leonard and Wendelin Mayer, music.

Wimmer expressed his views about the education the Benedictines intended to give all the students at the college when he wrote the Ludwig Missionsverein: "My heart is in this work, and I will spare no expense to teach the students first what is necessary, then what is useful, and finally what is beautiful so long as it contributes to their refinement."[81] By 1852, there were sixty students in the college, a little more than half of whom intended to become priests. Describing the college to the archbishop of Munich in 1852, Wimmer wrote:

> In our minor seminary the instructions in Latin are the same as in Germany, but English is the main branch for the Germans and German the most important for English-speaking boys. Some of these beginners who already show signs of a beard are declining *mensa, mensae* or are conjugating *amo, amas*. Greek is taken less thoroughly. The students are graded in different branches according to their progress but receive instructions in common in penmanship, drawing, and music. One priest is director of the school, and he has two clerics as prefects: one for the ecclesiastical, the other for the commercial students. They rise at 4:30 and retire at 8:30. They take care of their own apartment and in this way we follow the motto: help yourself.
>
> Their meals are the same as ours. This arrangement causes difficulties because our diet differs from theirs at home. At times they show this disposition openly. On abstinence days they hate the "Bavarian dumplings," which they call "metaphysics." Our terms are sixty dollars for board and tuition and five dollars for laundry. Generally, however, they pay less and several orphans are kept entirely free.[82]

The arrival of the "commercial" students in 1849 is sometimes taken to mark the beginning of Saint Vincent College. The evidence is clear, however, that academic instruction began on the secondary level at Saint Vincent at least as early as 1847, when eight boys arrived at the monastery, and Wimmer's letters indicate that some sort of preparatory instruction may have been taking place as early as 1846. The date of the establishment of the seminary, on the other hand, has never been questioned. Formal theological instruction began in October 1846, as soon as the Benedictines founded their monastery.

As in Bavaria, the seminary the Benedictines established at Saint Vincent provided a three-year course of study in philosophy and theology. The first year was devoted to philosophy, the second and third years to theology. For admission to the seminary a student was expected to have completed the equivalent of a classical education in a Bavarian gymnasium. The first students in the seminary were the four Benedictine postulants who accompanied Wimmer to America in 1846 and a diocesan subdeacon sent by Bishop O'Connor. They ranged in age from twenty-two to thirty-one. Wimmer and Father Michael Gallagher instructed them in theology during the first academic year (1846–47), but in the second year (1847–48), after Father Gallagher's departure from the community, Father Peter Lechner, assisted by Fathers Thaddeus Brunner and Adalbert Pums, took charge of the seminarians' education. By then three more postulants who had finished their classical studies in Bavarian gymnasiums had arrived to join the monastery and begin their studies for the priesthood. In the fall of 1848 seven additional Benedictine candidates came to Saint Vincent from Bavaria and began their philosophical studies under Lechner. Thus by the third academic year (1848–49) there were thirteen young Benedictines studying philosophy and theology at Saint Vincent Seminary.[83]

The fourth academic year (1849–50) opened with the addition of seven seminarians from the dioceses of Pittsburgh, Milwaukee, Baltimore, Philadelphia, and New York. Together with the Benedictine clerics, this increased enrollment in the seminary to about twenty. Except for two Irish theological students from Pittsburgh and an Irish-born Franciscan brother who awaited dispensation from Rome to become a Benedictine, the seminarians were all first- or second-generation Germans. By the end of 1850 eight Benedictine clerics had been ordained to the priesthood, and by the end of 1855 twenty Benedictine and twelve diocesan seminarians had been ordained.[84]

The ninth academic year (1854–55) is the first for which seminary and college records are fairly complete, and they reveal remarkable progress in the schools at Saint Vincent. By then the Benedictine educational program was divided into four academic departments. The first two departments (theology and philosophy) constituted the major seminary, the second two (classical and elementary) constituted the college. The seminary had an enrollment of twenty-eight students (twenty-one theologians and seven philosophers) and a faculty of three professors, one of whom was himself a seminarian who had come to Saint Vincent after completing his philosophical studies in Bavaria. The rector of the seminary was Father Demetrius di Marogna, a Bavarian nobleman and secular priest who had come to Saint Vincent in 1852 and entered the Benedictine Order at the age of forty-nine.

The college had an enrollment of eighty-eight students, fifty-four of whom were in the classical department and thirty-four in the elementary department. Its director was Father Ulric Spöttl, a twenty-three-year-old Benedictine who had recently been ordained after completing his studies in the seminary. The classical department (modeled on the Bavarian gymnasium) was divided into six classes taught by a faculty of nine Benedictine priests and clerics. The curriculum included Christian doctrine, Latin, Greek, German, English, French, history, geography, mathematics, music, and drawing. The youngest students were eleven to twelve years old, the oldest eighteen to nineteen years old. The elementary department (or "English School") was divided into three classes taught by four Benedictine clerics. Elementary students, who ranged in age from seven to eleven years old, followed a course of study that included catechism (in English and German), reading, spelling, and writing (in English and German), arithmetic, history, geography, English grammar, music, and drawing.

Of the 113 students in the seminary and college in 1855, 75 percent were of German and 25 percent of Irish heritage. On the other hand, 70 percent of the students were American-born while the remainder were European-born. Naturally, the vast majority of the European-born came from the various kingdoms and principalities of Germany—Bavaria, Württemberg, Baden, Prussia, and Lorraine. But there were also three students from Ireland and one from Switzerland. While the majority of American-born students came from Pennsylvania (Pittsburgh, Philadelphia and the three "Benedictine" counties of Westmoreland, Cambria, and Elk), a significant number came from centers of German immigrant settlement in other parts of the United States (New York, Baltimore, Milwaukee, St. Louis, and rural communities in Ohio, Indiana, Illinois, Michigan, and Wisconsin).[85]

EARLY STUDENTS

The college and seminary quickly set about achieving Wimmer's goals of educating the children of German immigrants, preparing German-speaking priests for the American missions, and firmly establishing the Benedictine Order in the United States. A look at some of the students who studied at Saint Vincent in the 1840s and 1850s, together with brief outlines of their subsequent careers, illustrates the success the Benedictine educational efforts at Saint Vincent had from the very beginning. Sketchy enrollment records in the early years necessarily limit an examination of student population to boys and young men who went on to become Benedictine priests and for whom biographical files are therefore available in the monastery archives. It must be remembered, however, that many of the students during this period never intended to enter the Benedictine Order but instead became diocesan priests or pursued careers in business, law, and medicine after leaving Saint Vincent. Unfortunately information about these latter two groups during the decade 1846–55 is severely limited.

Among the first students to come to Saint Vincent from the German colony of St. Marys, Pennsylvania, were the brothers Peter and John Pilz, who arrived at the monastery in the summer of 1848 when Peter was twelve and John thirteen years old. Born in Möggenford, Bavaria, they immigrated to America with their parents and settled in St. Marys during the mid-1840s. They entered the college when Father Thaddeus Brunner was director and were among the poor immigrant boys with deficient academic preparation whom Brunner believed prevented the school from achieving high academic standards. When they became Benedictine novices in 1853 (at the ages of eighteen and nineteen), Peter received the religious name Placidus and John became Gerard. They pronounced temporary vows a year later and began their studies of philosophy and theology in the seminary. During their last two years of study they both served as prefects and teachers in Saint Vincent College.

Father Placidus Peter Pilz subsequently served as a pastor in Butler, Pennsylvania, spent a short while with the Benedictine mission in Kansas, and was pastor in Greensburg, Pennsylvania, before joining the Benedictine mission to North Carolina. He served as director of the school and prior of Maryhelp Priory in North Carolina, and in 1889 went to the Benedictine missions in Colorado. In 1892 he became prior of the monastery at St. Marys, Pennsylvania, and in 1896 was named prior at Saint Vincent by Archabbot Leander Schnerr. He retired from administrative work in 1902 and became chaplain for the Benedictine Sisters in Allegheny, Pennsylvania. He died in 1911 at the age of seventy-six.

After ordination Father Gerard John Pilz served as assistant pastor in the Benedictine parishes of Covington, Kentucky, Erie, Pennsylvania, and Allegheny, Pennsylvania. Later Wimmer sent him to the Royal Academy in Munich to study art, and upon his return he taught at Saint Vincent College. In 1882 he became prior of St. Mary's Priory in Newark, New Jersey, and in 1885 was transferred to St. Joseph's Priory in Chicago, Illinois. He founded the Benedictine mission in Florida that eventually became St. Leo's Abbey, and when the Florida mission became part of Maryhelp Abbey (1888), Father Gerard transferred his vows to the North Carolina monastery where he died in 1891.[86]

Another boy who arrived at Saint Vincent College when Father Thaddeus Brunner was director was eleven-year-old Herman Krug. Born in Hünfeld, Hesse, he immigrated to Baltimore with his parents and entered the lower grades at Saint Vincent in 1849. He was invested with the Benedictine habit in 1851, when he was thirteen years old, and became a novice in 1856, taking the name Boniface in religion. After completing his classical, philosophical, and theological studies in the college and seminary, Boniface Krug was ordained to the priesthood in 1861 and Wimmer immediately named him director of Saint Vincent College. In 1862, when several Benedictines at Saint Vincent were drafted into the Union Army, Wimmer sent a few of them, including Krug, to Canada to avoid military service. Krug taught for a while at Assumption College in Sandwich, Ontario, at the time one of Saint Vincent's educational apostolates. Unable to return to the United States because of his draft evasion, Krug went to Italy where he transferred his vows to the Archabbey of Montecassino, the proto-Benedictine monastery founded by St. Benedict himself. He was named prior of Montecassino in 1874, elected abbot of the monastery of Cesena in 1888, and became archabbot of Montecassino in 1897. He returned to Saint Vincent for a visit in 1908 and died at Montecassino in 1909.[87]

In 1850, at the age of fourteen, Otto Schnerr came to Saint Vincent from Baltimore to study for the priesthood. His family had emigrated from Gommersdorf, Baden, where Otto had been born in 1836. In 1856 he became a Benedictine novice, taking the name Leander. Completing his classical and theological studies in the college and seminary, he was ordained in 1859. With the exception of a brief period in the 1860s at Assumption College in Canada, Father Leander Schnerr spent the next thirty-three years of his priestly life in Saint Vincent's parish apostolates. He worked as a curate at Benedictine parishes in Newark, New Jersey, and Covington, Kentucky, and in 1868 Wimmer named him prior at St. Joseph's Priory, Chicago. Six years later he was transferred to St. Mary's Priory, Erie, Pennsylvania, where he was again made prior, and then in 1877 he went as prior to St. Mary's Priory, Allegheny, Pennsylvania There he remained until 1892 when, at the age of fifty-six, he was elected third archabbot of Saint Vincent. He died in 1920.

Another Bavarian-born immigrant who came to America as a boy and entered the college in the 1850s was Charles Hipelius who began his studies at Saint Vincent in 1851 when he was fifteen years old. Hipelius entered the novitiate in 1854, taking the religious name Edward, studied theology in the seminary, was ordained in 1858, and assumed duties as professor and prefect in the college. A brilliant student, Father Edward Hipelius was the first Saint Vincent monk to go to Europe for advanced studies. In 1861 Wimmer sent him to England to study sacred scripture with the English Benedictines, and the following year he went to Rome for courses in canon law at the Sapienza University. Hipelius returned to Pennsylvania after the Civil War and became one of the most valued members of the monastic community. He taught sacred scripture and canon law in the seminary, served as secretary of the monastic chapter, and became a key advisor to Boniface Wimmer in matters relating to both the monastic and the educational affairs of the community. Because he believed that monastic life at Saint Vincent did not compare favorably with the observance of the new abbeys in Europe (especially that of Beuron) he had a falling out with Wimmer, who transferred him to St. Marys, Pennsylvania. Frustrated by his failure to interest the Saint Vincent community in a reform of monastic observance based upon Beuronese practices, he left the community in 1879 to care for his young brothers and sisters after the death of their parents. He was incardinated into the Diocese of Albany and worked as a diocesan priest until his death in 1900.

Matthew Hintenach, the fourteen-year-old son of German immigrants from Schollbrunn, Baden, came to Saint Vincent College from Baltimore in 1852. He entered the novitiate in 1857, at the age of nineteen, and took the religious name Athanasius. Three years later he was ordained to the priesthood. Father Athanasius Hintenach served as curate in several of Saint Vincent's Pennsylvania parishes before becoming pastor of Most Holy Sacrament Church, Greensburg, Pennsylvania, in 1880. In 1883 Wimmer sent him to establish the Benedictine mission in Alabama that eventually became St. Bernard Abbey. He returned to Saint Vincent in 1885 and held various offices in the monastery, including that of master of novices, assistant procurator, and subprior. After his retirement he became chaplain for the Benedictine sisters in Ludlow, Kentucky, and died at Saint Vincent in 1923 when he was eighty-five years old.

An immigrant from Huefingen, Baden, Charles Müller was eleven years old when he began his studies at Saint Vincent College in 1853. He entered the novitiate at the age of seventeen and took the name Adalbert in religion. Another brilliant student, he completed his classical and theological studies at Saint Vincent with highest honors and was ordained in 1865. Wimmer sent Father Adalbert Müller to Rome for graduate studies, and he received his doctorate in philosophy from the Sapienza University in 1870. From 1871 to 1880 he was professor of philosophy and theology at Saint Vincent Seminary. In 1880 Wimmer sent him back to Rome as superior of St. Elizabeth's House of Studies, the residence for American Benedictine students in the Eternal City. Three years later Müller returned to the United States and taught theology at St. Benedict's College, Atchison, Kansas, until 1887. In 1888 he was summoned to Rome by the Holy See to become professor of theology at the International Benedictine College, Sant' Anselmo. Shortly afterwards he was named prior of Sant' Anselmo, a position he held until his death at Rome in 1906.[88]

Another young immigrant from Baden who came to Saint Vincent in 1854 was Tobias Hintenach, brother of Matthew. Born in Schollbrunn, Baden, and brought by his parents to Baltimore at a young age, Tobias was only ten years old when he entered Saint Vincent College. He became a novice with the religious name Andrew at the age of sixteen, and after completing his classical, philosophical, and theological studies at Saint Vincent was ordained in 1867. Over the next two decades Father Andrew Hintenach served as a professor of classics in the college and as master of novices, subprior, and prior of the abbey. In 1886 he was appointed superior of Saint Vincent's Alabama missions, and little more than a year later, upon the death of Wimmer, he was elected second archabbot of Saint Vincent after his classmate Innocent Wolf had refused to accept the election. Himself reluctant from the beginning to accept the responsibilities of the abbacy, Hintenach resigned the position in 1892 and served afterwards as chaplain to several communities of nuns in Colorado and Pennsylvania. He returned to Saint Vincent in 1921 and died six years later at the age of eighty-three.[89]

William Wolf, a native of Schmidheim, Rheno-Prussia, came to Saint Vincent as an eleven-year-old student in 1854. Taking the religious name Innocent, he entered the novitiate with Andrew Hintenach in 1860 and was ordained in 1866. He went to Rome with Adalbert Müller to study theology, and when he returned to America in 1870, he taught moral theology, sacred scripture, and liturgy in Saint Vincent Seminary. He became prior at Saint Vincent in 1874 and was elected first abbot of St. Benedict's Abbey, Atchison, Kansas, in 1877. In 1888 he won election as second archabbot of Saint Vincent but opted to remain abbot of the Kansas monastery. Innocent Wolf continued as abbot of St. Benedict's Abbey for the remainder of his life, concurrently serving as president of the American Cassinese Congregation from 1896 to 1902. He died in 1922 when he was seventy-nine years old.[90]

Scores of pre-adolescent and adolescent sons of German immigrants came to Saint Vincent in the mid-1850s to study for the priesthood, and expanding enrollment in the college confirmed Boniface Wimmer's conviction that America needed a college for German Catholic youth. Many of these boys became Benedictines, some of them rising to prominent positions in the Order. But immigrant youngsters between the ages of ten and fifteen were not the only pool Saint Vincent drew on for its monastic recruits during this period. Older candidates, who had already finished their secondary education and who sometimes had university educations as well, came to America directly from Germany with the intention of becoming Benedictines at Saint Vincent. Many of them played important roles in the early development of the college and seminary, as well as in the development of the Benedictine missions in the United States.

Caspar Christoph, a native of Regensburg, Bavaria, where he had completed his classical education in the Regensburg gymnasium, came to Saint Vincent in 1851, when he was twenty years old, and applied for admission to the novitiate, taking the name Aegidius (Giles) in religion. He spent two years in the college as professor of Latin and prefect, and entered the seminary in 1853 for the three-year course in philosophy and theology. Ordained in 1856, Father Aegidius Christoph became one of Wimmer's most trusted subordinates. He served as prior in the monasteries of Carrolltown, Atchison, Chicago, and Covington, and from 1869 to 1871, when Wimmer was in Rome attending the Vatican Council, he directed affairs at Saint Vincent as prior. His last assignment was in Covington, Kentucky, and when he died in 1887 at the age of fifty-seven, the people asked that he be buried in the church near the confessional where he had consoled so many souls. When St. Joseph Church, Covington, was razed in 1971, his remains were disinterred and reburied in the abbey cemetery at Saint Vincent.

Like Christoph, Michael Bliemel was a Bavarian student from Regensburg. He had completed his classical education in the gymnasium at Metten and in 1850 decided to join the Benedictines in the United States. Arriving at Saint Vincent at the age of nineteen, he was admitted to the novitiate in June 1851 with the name Emmeran. In 1852 he entered Saint Vincent Seminary, where he completed the required philosophy courses and began his studies of theology, and in 1856 he was ordained to the priesthood. Father Emmeran Bliemel was a talented mathematician, and during his years of theological study, he taught mathematics in Saint Vincent College. After ordination he worked in the Benedictine parishes of Johnstown, St. Marys, and Butler, Pennsylvania. Then in 1860, when Bishop James Whalen, O.P., of Nashville asked the Benedictines to work among German Catholics in his diocese, Wimmer sent Bliemel to Tennessee where he became pastor of the small German parish of the Assumption in Nashville. The Civil War broke out a year later, and in 1863, when many of his parishioners had entered the Confederate Army, Bliemel sought and received permission to join them as their chaplain. He served with the 10th Tennessee Regiment during the Tennessee Campaign, and in August 1864, during the Battle of Atlanta, he was killed when a shell struck his head as he administered last rites to a dying soldier. He was thirty-three years old when he died. In 1889 Bliemel's friend and classmate, Father Otto Kopf, who arrived with him at Saint Vincent in 1851, found his grave on the old battlefield and brought his body to Tuscumbia for reburial in the cemetery of Tuscumbia's Benedictine parish.[91]

Augustine Francis Wirth was another Metten student who joined the Benedictine mission in the United States. Born in 1828 in Lohr, Bavaria, he spent part of a year in the novitiate at Metten before coming to Saint Vincent in 1851 at the age of twenty-three. He completed his theological studies in the seminary, during which he also taught Latin in the college, and was ordained in 1852. After ordination Father Augustine Wirth continued to teach in the college for several years and then was appointed pastor at Blessed Sacrament Church, Greensburg. In 1857 Wimmer tapped him to lead the Benedictine mission to Kansas. He was prior at St. Benedict Priory, Kansas, from 1857 to 1868, when he went to Minnesota to work in the Benedictine missions there. In 1874 he returned to Saint Vincent where he was reassigned as pastor in his old parish at Greensburg. In the 1880s he transferred his vows to St. Mary's Abbey, Newark, and worked in the New Jersey abbey's parish apostolates until his death in 1901. During his lifetime Wirth published several volumes of sermons which made his name prominent among the American Catholic clergy.[92]

Another seminarian at Saint Vincent in the 1850s was William Moosmüller, a young man who would become one of the most talented and active Benedictine missionaries in the United States. Moosmüller was born in Aidling, Bavaria, in 1832 and completed his gymnasium studies at Metten. He came to Saint Vincent with Augustine Wirth in 1851, entered the novitiate in 1854 with the religious name Oswald, and was ordained in 1856. He taught Latin and history at Saint Vincent College in the 1850s. During his long and fruitful monastic career Father Oswald Moosmüller worked as a missionary in Kentucky, Brazil, Kansas, Georgia, and Alabama. He served as superior of Saint Vincent's daughterhouses in Sandwich, Ontario; Atchison, Kansas; and Savannah, Georgia; and in St. Elizabeth's House of Studies in Rome. He was a noted historian who published several books on the European discoveries of America, the history of Saint Vincent, and the life of Boniface Wimmer. In 1885 he was elected first abbot of Maryhelp Abbey, North Carolina, but declined the honor. He returned to Saint Vincent from the South in the 1890s and became prior at the abbey. In 1892 he established New Cluny Priory in Wetaug, Illinois, where he spent the remainder of his life in prayer and study. He died in 1901.[93]

Ulric Spöttl came to Saint Vincent from Bavaria in 1851, when he was twenty-one years old. He had studied at the Latin school of St. Stephen's Abbey, Augsburg, graduated from the Wilhelm-Gymnasium in Munich, and had begun his course of philosophy at the University of Munich when he decided to become a missionary in America. Retaining his baptismal name (Ulric) in religion, he entered the novitiate, completed his theological studies at Saint Vincent Seminary, and was ordained to the priesthood in 1854. Wimmer immediately named Father Ulric Spöttl director of Saint Vincent College, a post he held for only four years, resigning in 1858 because of poor health. A biographer noted that Father Ulric "loved to teach and among other changes during his directorship he introduced weekly conferences of the professors to build up a more efficient educational staff." Spöttl's early death from tuberculosis in 1859 cut short a promising career at Saint Vincent College.[94]

John Heimler was born in Bavaria in 1832. He had been a brilliant student at the gymnasium at Regensburg as well as at the University of Würzburg, but was denied admission to the priesthood because of a congenital deformity of his right hand. In 1854, at the age of twenty-one, he came to Saint Vincent and entered the novitiate, taking the name Alphonse. Wimmer arranged for surgery on the hand to make it possible for him to celebrate Mass, and obtained permission from Rome to ordain him. Father Alphonse Heimler became the first monk at Saint Vincent to receive a postgraduate academic degree when he was awarded a master of arts in physics and astronomy from Georgetown College in 1860. In 1862 Wimmer appointed him president of Saint Vincent College, and under his leadership the college received a state charter to grant degrees in 1870. Heimler was president of the college for ten years and then went to New Jersey to teach in the Benedictine college at Newark. In 1890 he returned to Pennsylvania and served as a pastor in Cambria County until his death in 1909.[95]

Many other young men came to Saint Vincent in the 1850s, entered the monastery, studied in the seminary, and left their marks on Benedictine communities in Pennsylvania and throughout the United States. Alto Sebastian Hörmann (1829–67), a student at Metten, came to Saint Vincent at the age of twenty-three, entered the monastery, finished his theological studies in Saint Vincent Seminary, and after ordination volunteered for the Benedictine mission to Texas. He published several novels in German and died at Saint Vincent in 1867 of tuberculosis contracted in Texas. Louis Michael Fink (1834–1904) came to Saint Vincent from Bavaria in 1852, completed his theological studies in the seminary, and was ordained in 1857. He taught at Saint Vincent College and St. Benedict's College, Newark, before serving in the Benedictine missions in Kentucky, Illinois, and Kansas. In 1871 he was named coadjutor bishop of the Kansas Vicariate—the first American Benedictine to be raised to the episcopate—and in

1874 became bishop of Leavenworth. Francis Thomas Cannon (1811–86), a native of Ireland, was a Franciscan brother in Loretto, Pennsylvania, when he applied for admission to the monastery at Saint Vincent. Wimmer obtained permission from Rome for him to become a Benedictine, and he entered the novitiate in 1852. After studies in the seminary and ordination in 1858, he was sent as a missionary to Nebraska. In the 1860s he served on the faculty at Saint Vincent College, teaching mathematics and bookkeeping. He left the monastery in 1874 and went to Ireland where he died in 1886. Another religious who transferred to the Benedictines at Saint Vincent in the 1850s was Peter George Baunach (1815–68), a Redemptorist priest who came to Saint Vincent in 1854. Baunach served as novice master and prior in Pennsylvania and volunteered for the Texas missions in 1859. He died of tuberculosis contracted in Texas in 1868.[96]

These and all the other students who came to the college and seminary in the 1840s and 1850s received an education modeled on that of contemporary Bavarian schools and modified according to the needs of the monastic community at Saint Vincent. In the beginning and for long afterwards, the principal needs were to prepare young boys to enter the Benedictine Order and to train priests for the American missions. Wimmer and his monks considered Christian doctrine, languages (Latin, German, English), rhetoric, music, art, and history as essential for the proper preparation of the younger students who felt called to the monastic vocation, and they therefore concentrated their resources on developing these subjects in the college. For the seminarians, the concentration was on philosophy (especially logic, metaphysics, and ethics), dogmatic and moral theology, sacred scripture, homiletics, church history, and liturgy. During the first decade of the Benedictine presence at Saint Vincent the breadth and depth of the academic programs were limited by the lack of an adequately trained and sufficiently large faculty. Much of the instruction, both in the college and seminary, was given by younger monks who themselves had only recently completed the courses they were now teaching. Still, as they worked to develop the academic quality of the schools and build an adequate corps of professors, Wimmer and his monks succeeded in preparing a generation of missionaries for the American Church. The rapid expansion of the Benedictine mission in Pennsylvania provides clear evidence of their success.

PRIORIES IN PENNSYLVANIA

Wimmer's master plan was first to found a monastery and a school in the United States where Benedictine missionaries could be trained, and then, when the roots of the initial foundation had taken hold, to send those missionaries out to establish new foundations in other parts of the country. Two years after the settlement at Saint Vincent, he initiated the second phase of his plan.

In October 1848 Bishop Michael O'Connor added Cambria County to the missionary territory for which the Benedictines were responsible. Wimmer immediately reopened negotiations with Father Peter Henry Lemke to purchase property near Carrolltown, sixty miles east of Saint Vincent, where the Benedictines had originally intended to settle. Lemke sold him 300 acres of land, and in November Father Peter Lechner and several lay brothers went to St. Joseph's Church, Hart's Sleeping Place, to establish Saint Vincent's first dependent priory. In the summer of 1849 Wimmer recalled Lechner to Saint Vincent and appointed Father Benedict Haindl prior at St. Joseph. Six months later Father Celestine Englbrecht replaced Haindl, and Wimmer assigned several more brothers to Cambria County. Shortly after taking over the Cambria County mission, the Benedictines began constructing a church in the village of Carrolltown to replace St. Joseph as the center of Catholic worship in the area, and in December 1850 they dedicated their new church to St. Benedict. From then on St. Benedict Priory, Carrolltown, became the center of Benedictine missionary activity among Catholics of northern Cambria and southern Clearfield counties. Wimmer's plans to build a college in Carrolltown never materialized, but by 1852 the monks from Saint Vincent had a fully functioning dependent priory in Cambria County, with four priests and seven brothers in residence. By 1855 they had acquired eight hundred additional acres in and around Carrolltown and had constructed a monastery to accommodate a dozen monks. Ten brothers worked the farm and three priests provided pastoral care for the mixed Irish and German congregation in Carrolltown itself as well as for German Catholics in Loretto, Summit, and Summerhill in Cambria County and for others in southern Clearfield County.[97]

In December 1849 monks from Saint Vincent founded a second dependent priory in Elk County, Pennsylvania, at St. Marys. The colony of St. Marys, 120 miles north of Saint Vincent, had been established in 1843 by German Catholic settlers escaping anti-Catholic bias on the East Coast. Redemptorist priests attended the spiritual needs of the colony during the early years, but in 1849 the Redemptorists withdrew and Bishop O'Connor asked the Benedictines to take charge. Wimmer transferred Father Benedict Haindl from Carrolltown to St. Marys and assigned Father Andrew Zugtriegel from Saint Vincent to join him. The initial Benedictine foundation in St. Marys failed when fire destroyed the church and school and badly damaged the monastery. Haindl and Zugtriegel returned to Saint Vincent in the summer of 1850, but little more than a year later Wimmer sent Haindl back to St. Marys, accompanied by Father Charles Geyerstanger and four lay brothers. The Benedictines purchased eight hundred acres of land and established St. Mary's Priory from which they would minister to the people of Elk County for the next century and a half, down to the present time.

By 1855 there were three priests and eleven lay brothers assigned to St. Marys. The brothers worked the farm and operated a sawmill and gristmill while the priests attended the spiritual needs of four hundred German Catholic families in St. Marys as well as Irish and German Catholics in nearby Kersey, Williamsville, Warren, and Brookville. The Benedictines of St. Mary's Priory also had charge of the spiritual welfare of a community of Bavarian Benedictine nuns from St. Walburga Priory, Eichstätt, whom Wimmer had invited to open an elementary school at St. Marys in 1852.[98]

Benedictines from Saint Vincent began missionary work in Indiana County, Pennsylvania, in 1847, and in 1852, after ending their brewery operations in the town of Indiana, established St. Bernard Priory there. They purchased a three-hundred-acre farm outside of the town and transformed the renovated tavern into a monastery. By 1855 there were five lay brothers from Saint Vincent working the farm as well as one priest, Father Valentine Felder, ministering to the Catholics of Indiana County. As at Carrolltown and St. Marys, the priory at Indiana, located sixty miles north of Saint Vincent, became the hub of Benedictine missionary activity in the region, but the monks' work in Indiana ended shortly after the Civil War when the parish of St. Bernard and its missions were turned over to the bishop of Pittsburgh.[99]

A fourth priory was established from Saint Vincent at Butler, Pennsylvania, where two priests, Fathers Utho Huber and Charles Geyerstanger, and two lay brothers took up residence in 1854. Priests from this priory (St. Peter's) attended Catholics in Butler, Great Western, and parts of Armstrong County for more than a decade, but in the 1860s the monks turned the parish and missions over to the diocese and returned to Saint Vincent.[100]

In addition, between 1848 and 1852 priests from Saint Vincent attended the spiritual needs of the Irish workers constructing the Central (later the Pennsylvania) Railroad between Harrisburg and Pittsburgh, and in 1852, when the rail line was completed and regular passenger traffic began, they quickly made use of the new service to extend their pastoral work among

Catholics all along the line as far as Altoona. In 1852 the first regular religious services were held for Germans at St. Joseph's Church in Johnstown by Father Ildephonse Böld.[101]

Thus, within a decade of their settlement in the United States, the Bavarian Benedictines had established monastic communities at five locations in western Pennsylvania. Priests from these communities carried on missionary work among both English- and German-speaking Catholics in Westmoreland, Cambria, Elk, Indiana, Butler, Clearfield, and Armstrong counties and attended dozens of parishes and mission stations on a regular basis. They even served a small French- speaking congregation in Frenchville, Pennsylvania, where Father Joseph Billon, a secular priest from France who became a Benedictine at Saint Vincent in 1853, was pastor. In 1854 the Saint Vincent community was incorporated under the laws of Pennsylvania as "The Benedictine Society in Westmoreland County" and thus received the right to transact business and purchase property in the name of the corporate entity. Until then the land and property purchased by the monks had to be registered in the names of individual members of the community. The Act of Incorporation, signed by Governor William Bigler on April 19, 1854, stated that the "essential objects of said corporation shall be the relief and support of sick, destitute and dependent persons, the maintenance of orphans, the care and education of youth, and the establishment of churches and conducting of services therein."[102]

By 1855, then, Wimmer's vision of a Benedictine presence in America was well on its way to being fulfilled, and the time had now arrived for Rome to consider confirming the work by raising the monastery of Saint Vincent to abbatial rank.

AN EXEMPT ABBEY

The process of establishing Benedictine monasteries during the nineteenth century normally consisted of three stages. The first involved sending a small group of monks from an independent community (usually an abbey) to settle in a new location where they would institute public celebration of the Divine Office and undertake some appropriate work (often education) which would provide sufficient income to make the community viable. Invariably it was also during this stage that the new monastery acquired the land and property necessary for its economic security and independence.

When the community had achieved a measure of administrative and financial stability, had proven itself capable of faithfully observing the monastic rule, had secured a stable source of future vocations, and no longer depended upon its community of origin (motherhouse) for monks or money, then it petitioned Rome for recognition as a canonical priory. Once the Holy See granted canonical status, the new community effectively became independent in its spiritual, administrative, and financial affairs from the community of origin. Each monk transferred his vow of stability from the motherhouse to the recently independent monastery, although they normally maintained close fraternal bonds with the community of origin and continued a mutual exchange of ideas on matters related to the observance of the monastic rule.[103]

The third stage in the process involved the independent priory's elevation to the rank of an exempt abbey, a step that occurred only after another period of trial when the quality of monastic observance and the economic viability of the community were again tested. This step also required the approbation and action of the Holy See. The elevation to abbatial rank signified that the monastery was independent not only of its community of origin but, with respect to the management of its internal spiritual, administrative, and financial affairs, independent of the local bishop as well. Exempt abbeys were the only ecclesiastical institutions within a diocese that did not fall under the direct control of the diocesan bishop, and European bishops traditionally attempted to limit the number of them within their jurisdictions. By the middle of the nineteenth century exemption had still not taken root in America, and American bishops were reluctant to see a precedent established.

The 1846 settlement of Wimmer and his companions in Westmoreland County marked the achievement of the first stage in the establishment of a Benedictine monastery in the United States. For the first five and a half years, Saint Vincent was dependent on Metten and under the authority of Gregory Scherr, Metten's abbot. When the Holy See declared it a canonical priory in 1852, Wimmer transferred his vow of stability from Metten to Saint Vincent and received the vows of the clerics and brothers who had joined him in America but who, until the American monastery became independent, could not (according to canon law) make a vowed commitment of lifelong stability to the community.

As soon as Saint Vincent achieved canonical independence, Wimmer immediately began preparing the groundwork for the community's elevation to the rank of abbey. In November 1853 he submitted his petition to the Sacred Congregation for the Propagation of the Faith, and wrote Archbishop Carlo Morichini, former papal nuncio in Munich and now an offi-

Boniface Wimmer, O.S.B. (1809–87), who in 1846 founded the Benedictine monastery of Saint Vincent. He became the monastery's first abbot in 1855 and archabbot in 1883.

cial in the Vatican, asking for his support. In December he met with Archbishop Gaetano Bedini, papal nuncio to Brazil and special envoy from the Holy See to the bishops of the United States, and sought his support as well. In the petition to Rome Wimmer asked (1) that Saint Vincent be made an abbey, (2) that the abbey be exempt from the jurisdiction of the local bishop, (3) that the priests of the abbey have the right to elect their abbot, and (4) that the abbot's tenure be for life.[104]

Wimmer's efforts to gain exempt abbatial status for Saint Vincent met with opposition from Bishop Michael O'Connor of Pittsburgh. O'Connor believed that raising Saint Vincent to the dignity of an abbey so soon after its establishment as a canonical priory was premature and inopportune, and he explained to the Holy See that in his view the priests of Saint Vincent, though very generous in attending to the needs of the Catholics of the diocese, were young, inexperienced, and limited in their education and training. Moreover, he said that Wimmer, because of his imprudence in the matter of the brewery and his spirit of independence from episcopal authority, was not suited to become an abbot.[105]

O'Connor's opposition brought the process of securing abbatial status for Saint Vincent to a halt. The Holy See would not rule in favor of the Benedictine petition without the approbation of the local ordinary; and so, convinced that he could not accomplish anything from a distance, Wimmer decided in December 1854 to travel to Rome to fight for his cause in the place where the future of his monastery would be decided. He arrived in Munich in February 1855 and devoted a month to marshaling support from his Bavarian friends. He then traveled over the Alps to the Eternal City, arriving on the Wednesday of Holy Week, April 4, 1855. He spent the next five months arguing his case before officials of the Sacred Congregation of the Propagation of the Faith, trying to convince the cardinals that Saint Vincent should be made an exempt abbey. With the help of Bavarian prelates in Rome he even obtained a private audience with Pope Pius IX, who pointed out to him that whatever the final decision, Saint Vincent could not expect to be allowed to operate a tavern.[106] The fact that the beer controversy continued to cloud the issue of Saint Vincent's status surprised Wimmer, who believed the matter had been laid to rest in 1852 with the community's elevation to the rank of a canonical priory.

Bishop O'Connor had made it clear that he was not opposed in principle to the elevation of Saint Vincent to abbey rank. He simply thought the time was not right. He also made it clear that if and when the abbey were established, it should not be exempt, its abbot should be appointed for a limited period, and Wimmer should not be considered for the position. In addition, the bishop reopened the matter of the seminary and said that before he would acquiesce to any change in the status of the monastery, the Benedictines would have to agree to accept into their schools "a fair number of diocesan students (one-half or one-third as the Holy See may deem proper) gratis or at a very low rate for board and tuition." He insisted, moreover, that these students should be selected and approved by the bishop and not by the Benedictines.[107]

Again the bishop had raised an issue Wimmer had thought resolved in 1852 when the Holy See made Saint Vincent a canonical priory. The monks in Pennsylvania were already accepting the bishop's students, but to open half or even a third of the college to nonpaying or partially paying students would spell financial disaster for the monastery. Wimmer therefore informed the cardinals that he would not agree to Bishop O'Connor's conditions.

Wimmer's refusal to compromise on this and other issues early in the negotiations caused some officials in the Propaganda Fide to look upon him and his case with disfavor. They regarded his resistance as intransigence, downright German stubbornness. "Prince Hohenlohe believes that I will not be made abbot," Wimmer wrote King Ludwig I, "because Monsignor Barnabo told him that I write too harshly and need to be mortified. It is true. I speak plainly even in Latin. But if I must defend right against wrong, I have a still franker language."[108]

By this time Wimmer had won the support of a very able advocate, the Benedictine abbot Angelo Pescetelli, procurator of the Italian Cassinese Congregation. The prefect of the Propaganda Fide had appointed Pescetelli promoter of the American Benedictine case, and the Italian abbot proved himself an adroit and effective diplomat in countering the objections of Bishop O'Connor. Pescetelli reminded the cardinals that the Bavarian Benedictines had been sent to America by the Ludwig Missionsverein to work among Germans and that the Holy See itself had blessed the mission in 1846. "This contract should be kept," he wrote. Abbot Pescetelli argued for raising Saint Vincent to an exempt abbey with the right to elect its own abbot, pointing out that this was the custom in Europe and that no innovations should be made to it in America.[109]

As the weeks passed Wimmer began to realize that O'Connor's concerns focused on two main issues: exemption and the right of his students to attend the seminary free of charge. In consultation with Pescetelli, Wimmer determined that exemption for the abbey was not a matter on which he could afford to surrender. "Ecclesiastical history shows very well," he said, "that monasteries have sought exemption for this reason: that bishops with their sometimes troublesome requests and recommendations exhausted those who were not able to resist or did not dare to do so. [Bishop O'Connor] does not love the religious if he cannot use them as he chooses. . . . He has no principles of justice and order as his guidelines, except that of utility." With respect to the seminary, however, he now felt there was room for compromise, particularly if it meant that Bishop O'Connor would give in on the fundamental question of an exempt abbey. At the suggestion of one of the cardinals of the Propaganda Fide he agreed to grant two of the bishop's students free room, board, and tuition each year, and wrote Prior Demetrius di Marogna at Saint Vincent: "It is certain that we must rather give up material advantages than sacrifice a principle. Thus it will be better to burden ourselves with the education of a few boys than put the school under the supervision of the bishop."[110]

Meanwhile Saint Vincent's cause was receiving valuable new support from prominent ecclesiastical and lay leaders in both Italy and Bavaria. Along with Abbot Angelo Pescetelli, several Italian abbots came to Wimmer's defense, as did Archbishop Karl von Reisach of Munich, Bavarian Ambassador Ferdinand von Verger, and King Ludwig I, who returned to his Roman residence in April 1855 and brought his considerable influence to bear on behalf of the American Benedictines. In addition, Wimmer wrote that Saint Vincent could count on "a good many powerful patrons among the cardinals of the Propaganda."[111]

The Saint Vincent case was presented to the cardinals of the Propaganda Fide in June, and a month later they issued a decree, formally promulgated in an apostolic brief dated August 24, 1855, in which the Benedictines in Pennsylvania were granted virtually everything they had asked for. Saint Vincent was raised to the rank of an abbey; the abbey was made exempt; the priests of the abbey were given the right to elect their abbot; and the abbot was to hold a lifetime tenure. In addition the cardinals imposed upon the new abbey a special obligation to maintain a seminary to which diocesan seminarians would be admitted "provided that they meet the expenses of their education," and in a concession to Michael O'Connor, they granted the local diocesan bishop the right "to watch over the education and morals" of his seminarians. Finally, the decree established an American Benedictine congregation to which Saint Vincent and all future independent monasteries founded from it would belong. The new congregation was to follow the statutes of the Bavarian Congregation and to be affiliated with the Italian Cassinese Congregation. (It later came to be called the American Cassinese Congregation.)[112] Three weeks after publication of the apostolic brief of August 24, 1855, the Propaganda Fide issued a second decree announcing that Pope Pius IX had named Wimmer abbot of Saint Vincent "in consideration of [his] eminent services . . . in behalf of the monastery." Wimmer was appointed for a three-year term, after which the priests of Saint Vincent would exercise their right to elect an abbot "according to the regular method."[113]

The decisions of the Propaganda Fide represented a clear victory for the Benedictines in their controversy with Bishop O'Connor. Not only was the community elevated to abbatial rank and given the right (after three years) to elect its abbot, but it was also removed from the jurisdiction of the bishop and made exempt. The seminary was to remain a monastic school under

Benedictine jurisdiction, and any students the bishop sent would have to pay full costs. Wimmer agreed informally to accept two of the bishop's students gratis each year, but by insisting upon the Benedictines' rights to control all aspects of the school's operations, he protected its financial interests and assured its independence of action.

In the aftermath of the controversy Bishop O'Connor wrote Abbot Boniface congratulating him on his promotion to abbot and saying that, with respect to "the seminary matter," he regretted that "unfounded" apprehensions had led to conflict between them. "Notwithstanding the light in which I am represented," he continued, "you may rest assured that I feel the most lively interest and entertain the brightest hopes of the success of your community. Though I may sometimes differ in opinion as to the propriety of some measures, I think I may say with sincerity that it will always afford me pleasure to contribute everything in my power that will increase its prosperity and usefulness."[114]

The elevation of Saint Vincent to the rank of abbey marked one of the most important milestones in the history of the community. Not only did it represent the Roman Catholic Church's formal recognition of the impressive achievement of the Bavarian Benedictine mission in the United States, but it also signaled a fundamental change in the identity of that mission. No longer was Saint Vincent simply a German monastery in America. It had now become an American institution whose roots, though Bavarian in origin, were deeply planted in American soil. The creation of the abbey confirmed and fulfilled the early vision of the *Projektenmacher* of Metten. That the fulfillment of his vision had been achieved so quickly—only ten years had elapsed since Wimmer had outlined his project in the *Augsburger Postzeitung*—was a cause for astonishment and admiration in both Europe and the United States. Now, at the end of 1855, the American Benedictines were poised for new challenges, new missions. This was no time for the monks in Pennsylvania to rest on their laurels. America was expanding westward, and the Benedictines of Saint Vincent prepared to follow the immigrants.

THREE

MONKS, MISSIONARIES, AND TEACHERS (1856–1887)

PRIOR DEMETRIUS DI MAROGNA had charge of the monastery, schools, and missions at Saint Vincent during the year that Boniface Wimmer was in Munich and Rome attempting to secure abbatial status for the Pennsylvania community. The scion of a noble Italian family that had immigrated to Bavaria in the early nineteenth century, Carlo di Marogna was ordained for the Diocese of Augsburg in 1826 and spent the first two decades of his priestly life serving parishes in Bavaria. Then in 1847 he immigrated to the United States and spent four years working as a missionary among German Catholics in Illinois. In 1852, when he was forty-nine years old, he came to Saint Vincent and entered the novitiate. To symbolize his commitment to the missionary life, he took the name Demetrius in religion after Father Demetrius Gallitzin who had worked so long among the Catholics of Cambria County. A year later di Marogna pronounced solemn vows, and Wimmer, delighted to have among his monks an experienced priest solidly educated in the Bavarian tradition, soon appointed him prior of the monastery and rector of the seminary. Di Marogna was the man Bishop O'Connor had hoped would become abbot of Saint Vincent instead of Boniface Wimmer. When Pope Pius IX intervened and named Wimmer abbot for a three-year term, di Marogna continued as prior and rector until Wimmer assigned him to lead the Benedictine mission to Minnesota in 1856.[1]

Di Marogna was a judicious superior who, despite difficult circumstances, governed the community well during Wimmer's absence in Rome. Though only recently professed as a monk, he guided the monastic observance, oversaw the operations of the seminary and college, and directed the monks' pastoral and missionary work in western Pennsylvania. The monastery he temporarily governed consisted of 19 priests, 110 brothers, and almost 60 clerics and novices. The priests, based at Saint Vincent and its dependencies in Carrolltown, St. Marys, Indiana, and Butler, carried on missionary work throughout western Pennsylvania and taught in the college and seminary at the motherhouse. The brothers did the manual labor that sustained the community, and the clerics and novices prepared themselves through prayer and study for the monastic life and the priesthood.[2]

Dissension erupted in the monastery, however, during di Marogna's tenure, when some of the monks objected to the prior's manner of administering the temporal affairs of the community. In Wimmer's absence he had ordered the construction of a new building, which many regarded as unnecessary and poorly built, and after the fall crop failed, he had borrowed three thousand dollars to buy food, fuel, and clothing to sustain the monks and students through the coming winter. None of di Marogna's administrative decisions was unwarranted or beyond the scope of his authority, but they occurred at a time when the United States was entering a period of economic depression, and many of the younger priests feared that by burdening the community with more debt, di Marogna was jeopardizing its future financial security. There was also the matter of his being a recent arrival. Despite the fact that he was twenty years older than most of the priests at Saint Vincent, they regarded the prior as a newcomer, junior to them in profession, a man less knowledgeable and experienced in the monastic life than they. Because of this, a number of them were not reluctant to express their resentment at having to follow his orders.

Wimmer returned to Saint Vincent in December 1855 and found the community in turmoil. He wrote Abbot Gregory Scherr that under di Marogna's leadership "more than one thing went wrong." He immediately set about the task of putting the community's financial affairs in order and of soothing the ruffled feathers of both the prior and the young priests who had opposed him. Di Marogna himself was grateful for the reprieve and eagerly surrendered the reins of government to the abbot. Wimmer was not censorious. He took note of the dissension in the house and concluded that "in the long run everyone followed the dictate of his conscience as well as he could, and this naturally made me very happy." Considering everything, the abbot expressed his relief "that all had a good ending. I know too well that no one, not even the most capable, could handle such a complicated business in so short a time."[3]

The Christmas of Wimmer's return was a very special one at Saint Vincent. Despite the disagreements that had occurred during the previous year, the monastic community joyfully celebrated both the Nativity of Christ and the birth of the abbey with liturgies, concerts, and banquets attended by lay and clerical friends. On Christmas Eve the monks and students prepared a solemn liturgical ceremony highlighted by the chant of the monastic choir and the music of the college orchestra. The ceremony culminated with Wimmer's celebration of his first solemn Pontifical Mass. That day a violent snowstorm swept over the countryside, and everyone worried that the ceremony would be marred by sparse attendance. But at midnight, when the abbot and the monastic community entered the church to begin the liturgy, they found the pews and aisles crowded with people. Emotions ran high as Abbot Boniface intoned the *Gloria* and the orchestra and choir followed with the strains of Haydn. The Mass was a memorable occasion for the Benedictines, students, and parishioners of Saint Vincent and was spoken of for many years afterwards.[4]

MISSIONS WEST

On January 11, 1856, the priests of the new abbey gathered at Saint Vincent for the first general chapter of the American Cassinese Congregation. After only a decade the Benedictine mission in the United States had grown and prospered in ways that few had anticipated, and the monks were now eager to consolidate their gains and spread out beyond the limits of their original settlements. The two principal items on the general chapter's agenda, therefore, were to organize their communities into a congregation and to plan for the expansion of their missionary activity outside of Pennsylvania.

Rome had established the American Cassinese Congregation at Wimmer's request to ensure that Benedictine missionary work in the United States would be coordinated among the independent American monasteries. At the time, however, there was only one independent American Benedictine monastery: Saint Vincent. The fact that the priories in Carrolltown, St. Marys, Indiana, and Butler continued to be dependent on the motherhouse created an anomaly. According to both Church law and Benedictine tradition a congregation supposed the existence of three independent monasteries which, joined together in a loose confederation, provided mutual support and encouragement in the common task of working, praying, and following a monastic regimen according to an agreed-upon interpretation of the Rule of St. Benedict.

The American Cassinese Congregation was created with the expectation that independent priories would soon develop from the dependencies that had already sprung from Saint Vincent. The communities in Carrolltown and St. Marys seemed especially ripe for independence, so at the congregation's first general chapter the capitulars (all the ordained monks of the abbey) discussed not only the implementation of the statutes of the old Bavarian Congregation in the abbey and priories but also the steps necessary to secure independent status for the monasteries in Carrolltown and St. Marys.[5]

The second principal agenda item at the general chapter of 1856 was planning for the Order's expansion beyond the borders of Pennsylvania. During the previous decade a number of American bishops had sent inquiries to Saint Vincent about the possibility of establishing Benedictine monasteries, parishes, and schools in their dioceses. Because of a lack of personnel, Wimmer had been forced to decline most of these invitations, though in the early 1850s he was able to send priests temporarily to the dioceses of Philadelphia and New York at the request of Bishops John Neumann and John Hughes. In January 1856 the monks of Saint Vincent had six new offers from American bishops to found monasteries and schools. These offers came from Archbishop John B. Purcell of Cincinnati, Archbishop Peter Kenrick of St. Louis, Bishop Mathias Loras of Dubuque, Bishop Frederic Baraga of Northern Michigan, Bishop John Martin Henni of Milwaukee, and Bishop Joseph Cretin of St. Paul in the Minnesota Territory.

The Saint Vincent priests concluded that they were capable of responding favorably to only one of these requests. The question was, which would it be? Father Bruno Riess, one of the pioneer Benedictines in Minnesota, later explained how the choice was made.

It happened in January 1856 that six American bishops sent petitions to the late Abbot Wimmer for the introduction of the Benedictine Order and erection of monasteries in their dioceses. The movement caused some perplexity. Widely divergent opinions and proposals were brought to the front in a chapter in which these applications were considered—one favored acceptance of this, another of that post. The Abbot listened, no conclusions were reached. Finally he arose and said: "We will commit the whole affair to the hands of God—may He decide where we should make the beginning. I shall," he said, "write each of the bishops and tell him of our needs, i.e., the conditions upon which we will be able to correspond with his request. All of these letters I will mail at the same time and the first bishop who will reply satisfactorily shall have our priests." And behold, the voice of God came from the West, from St. Paul, the most distant point which the mails only reached via Dubuque and thence per stage; from St. Paul came the first unconditional call for Benedictine monks.[6]

There was clear agreement that the first foundation outside Pennsylvania would be in the West, where immigrants from Europe were daily settling and where the future of America lay. There was also agreement on the conditions the chapter would impose before sending monks to a new diocese. In order to avoid a repetition of the problems they had experienced with Bishop O'Connor, Wimmer and his monks expected first of all to have complete and unencumbered title to the land they settled on. Their second condition was that the new foundation be subject in all internal and monastic matters to the jurisdiction of the abbot of Saint Vincent and not the host bishop. Finally, the Saint Vincent chapter wanted assurances from the local bishop that he would not prevent the new foundation from developing into an exempt abbey like the motherhouse in Pennsylvania.

The first bishop to respond positively to all of these conditions was Joseph Cretin of Minnesota, who urgently invited the Benedictines of Saint Vincent to establish a monastic colony in his diocese and work among the thousands of recent German immigrants in central Minnesota. Perhaps with the exception of Northern Michigan, Minnesota—with its harsh winters, primitive conditions, and remoteness—was the most difficult and challenging of all the places the Benedictines could have accepted. Still, the abbot and monks of Saint Vincent eagerly embraced the challenge, and Prior Demetrius di Marogna volunteered to lead the missionaries westward.

The mission group, consisting of one priest, two clerics, and two lay brothers, departed Saint Vincent for Minnesota on April 5, 1856. They traveled via Pittsburgh to St. Louis where Archbishop Peter Kenrick attempted unsuccessfully to have them abandon their Minnesota plans and remain in his diocese. From St. Louis they traveled up the Mississippi by riverboat and arrived in St. Paul on May 2. The journey from St. Louis to St. Paul was not uneventful. Near Davenport, Iowa, the boilers of the riverboat immediately behind them overheated and exploded, and hundreds of passengers were killed. News came to Pennsylvania that the Benedictine missionaries had also been killed, and funeral services were held for them in the abbey church. Only weeks later did the monks at Saint Vincent learn that their five confreres had safely reached their destination.[7]

In addition to di Marogna, the group consisted of the clerics Bruno Riess and Cornelius Wittmann, both of whom had come to Saint Vincent from Bavaria in 1852 and only recently had completed their theological studies in the seminary, and lay brothers Benno Muckenthaler and Patrick Greil. Muckenthaler, a forty-one-year-old native of Bavaria, had been a monk at Saint Vincent since 1851. He was a carpenter and his latest job at the motherhouse was that of chief cabinetmaker. Greil was a thirty-three-year-old Bavarian who had been a cook at Saint Vincent since 1852.[8]

Bishop Cretin welcomed the monks warmly and gave them lodging in the episcopal residence. On May 17 he ordained Riess and Wittmann to the priesthood, and two days later the five Benedictines set out on an eighty-mile trek to St. Cloud, near the confluence of the Mississippi and Sauk rivers. There, on the banks of the Mississippi below St. Cloud, they established a monastery on 320 acres of land donated by the brothers Louis and Wilhelm Rothkopp, two elderly German Catholics who asked in return only that they be allowed to reside with the Benedictines until their deaths.[9]

Brothers Benno and Patrick set about refurbishing the Rothkopps' two primitive log cabins which would serve as monastery and chapel, while Fathers Demetrius, Bruno, and Cornelius attended the spiritual needs of Catholic settlers in a twenty-four-hundred-square-mile region. The Benedictines had charge of German congregations in St. Cloud, St. Augusta, Sauk Rapids, St. Joseph, St. James Prairie, and Richmond, Minnesota, attending these missions from the priory in St. Cloud. The first year in Minnesota was one of dire poverty. The Benedictines from Pennsylvania survived on a spare diet of bread, potatoes, coffee, and a few strips of bacon that were available from time to time. In addition to the manual work required to establish and sustain the monastery and missionary labors among the Catholics of central Minnesota, the monks strove from the very beginning to maintain the monastic horarium they had followed at Saint Vincent. The priests chanted the Divine Office, and the brothers recited the Rosary three times a day. When Boniface Wimmer visited Minnesota for the first time in the fall of 1856, he arrived at the priory at five o'clock in the morning and found the monks reciting the Divine Office. Father Bruno

Riess reported that the abbot "was greatly pleased and edified at the disposition and religious zeal which prevailed. He did not interrupt our prayers, but patiently waited behind the curtain-door of our chapel, until we had finished our Office, and the two Brothers had recited the Rosary in the kitchen."[10]

Wimmer brought with him six monks from Saint Vincent that autumn to reinforce the small band of missionaries who had originally settled in St. Cloud. From then on, despite hardships and contretemps, the community grew and developed into a major center of monastic life and missionary, liturgical, and educational activity in the Midwest. In 1858 it became an independent priory and in 1866, an abbey. The monks in Minnesota established a college and seminary, and a 140 years after its founding, the institution (as St. John's Abbey and University) continues to flourish as a vital hub of Benedictine and Catholic life in the American Church.

A year after the first missionaries from Saint Vincent set out for Minnesota, two other monks departed Pennsylvania for Kansas. The origins of the Kansas foundation, however, predated the official mission from Saint Vincent. The beginnings of St. Benedict's Abbey, Atchison, the third independent monastery in the American Cassinese Congregation, were the result of an unauthorized initiative by the free-spirited priest who had invited Wimmer to Pennsylvania, Peter Henry Lemke.

When he finally sold his land in Cambria County to Wimmer in 1848, Lemke had left Carrolltown and sought incardination in the Diocese of Philadelphia, whose bishop, Francis Patrick Kenrick, assigned him to the German parish of St. Peter's in Reading, Pennsylvania. Lemke settled into his parochial duties and pursued the literary work he had always aspired to. While at Reading he completed a German translation of Father Demetrius Gallitzin's pamphlet, *A Defense of Catholic Principles,* and began research for a life of Gallitzin that he eventually published in 1861.[11] He remained in Reading for a year, but his volatile temper and authoritarian manner alienated his parishioners, and at the end of 1849 he returned to Carrolltown. In 1852 Wimmer received him into the Benedictine community and assigned him to St. Benedict Priory, Carrolltown, under Father Ildephonse Böld, the twenty-nine-year-old prior. As a Benedictine the fifty-four-year-old Lemke fared no better controlling his curmudgeonly temperament than he had as a secular priest, and he soon came into conflict with the young monks with whom he lived. In October 1855, while Wimmer was still in Europe, Lemke abandoned Carrolltown once again and went to Pittsburgh where he intended to secure passage to Kentucky in order to enter the Trappist monastery at Gethsemani. In Pittsburgh Lemke met a Trappist who described the regimen the monks in Kentucky followed. The description convinced him that he was not called to a Cistercian vocation after all, and he decided to abandon his aspirations to become a Trappist and instead to accompany a group of German families on their way to Kansas. He offered to be these immigrants' spiritual guide and promised to establish a Benedictine monastery in the place where they finally settled.[12]

When Wimmer returned to Saint Vincent in December 1855 and learned of Lemke's unauthorized departure, he ordered the fiercely independent priest back to the abbey. But the abbot had mixed feelings about his order. Lemke had proven to be a divisive presence in the priory at Carrolltown, and Wimmer doubted that he could ever adjust to communal monastic life. "I hope he will obey," he wrote. "In a way, though, I would rather not see him come, unless it be dangerous for his eternal salvation if he fails to comply."[13] As it happened, Lemke did not obey. Instead he settled down among the immigrants he had accompanied from Pittsburgh and wrote Wimmer asking for three lay brothers to assist him in establishing a monastery. The abbot did not send the brothers, but he did give permission for Lemke to remain among the German settlers at Doniphan, Kansas, on the Missouri River. It was this mission that became the seed of Saint Vincent's second foundation in the West.[14]

Lemke set about purchasing land and planning for a permanent monastery at Doniphan. He spoke with Bishop John Baptist Miége, S.J., vicar apostolic of Kansas, and urged him to invite Wimmer to send more monks. This Miége did in the summer of 1856, and the abbot put the matter before the capitulars at Saint Vincent. The abbey chapter voted to accept the bishop's invitation, and in April 1857 Wimmer sent Father Augustine Wirth and Brother Casimir Seitz to Kansas. In addition to the usual conditions he placed on foundations in new dioceses, the abbot insisted that Bishop Miége not require the Saint Vincent monks to live with Lemke. The bishop agreed and provided the Benedictines with property in Doniphan from which they could carry out their mission to the German settlers. Prohibited from taking up residence with Wirth and Seitz, Lemke, complaining that he had been discarded "like a pair of worn-out wooden shoes," went to Bendena, Kansas where he remained until the following November.[15]

The two monks Wimmer sent to the Kansas vicariate were typical of the young Bavarians who had come to Saint Vincent in the 1850s. Both had received their secondary education in Bavarian gymnasiums and had completed their theological studies at Saint Vincent Seminary. The twenty-nine-year-old Wirth had come to Saint Vincent in 1851, been ordained in 1852, and served as professor in Saint Vincent College and pastor of Blessed Sacrament Church, Greensburg, Pennsylvania, before being assigned to lead the Kansas mission. Seitz, age twenty-eight, joined the monastery of Saint Vincent in 1854 and pronounced solemn vows in 1856. Two and a half weeks after his arrival in Kansas, Bishop Miége ordained him to the priesthood.[16]

In Doniphan Wirth and Seitz led a quasi-monastic life marked by missionary labors among German settlers on farms and in the river towns along the Missouri. Their pastoral care embraced the region along the river from Atchison north to Omaha, Nebraska. Like their confreres in Minnesota, the Kansas monks experienced great poverty during the early days in Doniphan. They lived in a shanty without floors, windowpanes, or stove, and subsisted on a diet of potatoes, cabbage, cornmeal, bread, and eggs, with occasional quantities of fresh meat, smoked ham, and bacon. They were also burdened with the debts that Lemke had contracted and were able to satisfy the creditors only with the help of local Catholics. Seitz wrote: "The creditors were satisfied, and the constables kept off our necks. The windows were fitted with glass, the church received a floor, bedsteads and a table arrived from St. Joseph, the sacks we had brought along were filled with prairie grass and shavings. With six bricks we built a fireplace for cooking, and I declared myself ready to function as cook. We considered ourselves gentlemen, praised God's providence for His children, gave a toast to monastic poverty, and hoped for better times."[17]

The foundation in Kansas developed slowly and fitfully over the next decade. Saint Vincent sent additional monks and provided financial assistance, but the Kansas community continued to suffer from poverty, indebtedness, and a paucity of vocations throughout its early history. Still, it struggled valiantly to overcome these difficulties and was grateful for the support it received, both in personnel and money, from the motherhouse in Pennsylvania. In 1858 it became an independent priory, and a year later the community transferred to Atchison, ten miles south of Doniphan, where the monks opened a college. The Kansas monastery's relationship with the abbey in Pennsylvania remained extremely close during its first twenty years. During this period its novices and clerics were educated at the motherhouse; many monks from Saint Vincent went to Atchison to provide temporary assistance in the missions and the college, and in 1876, when St. Benedict's Priory was raised to the rank of abbey, Prior Innocent Wolf of Saint Vincent was elected the community's first abbot.

Saint Vincent's third priory in the West did not fare so well. In the summer of 1859 the abbey chapter voted to accept the invitation of Bishop John Mary Odin, C.M., of Galveston to establish a monastery in Texas. Bishop Odin offered the Benedictines the buildings and land of the Franciscan mission of San José, five miles south of San Antonio on the San Antonio River. San José was one of a group of missions, including the famous Alamo, seven miles to the north, founded by the Franciscans in the eighteenth century to care for the Indians of Texas. By the mid-nineteenth century the region had been thickly settled by German immigrants, and it was to serve these immigrants that the Benedictines went to the Lone Star State.[18]

Three priests and two lay brothers volunteered for the mission, and on July 1, 1859, set out from Saint Vincent. They traveled by rail to Cairo, Illinois, where they boarded a riverboat for the trip down the Mississippi to the Gulf of Mexico. The leader of the group was Father Alto Hörmann, a thirty-year-old Bavarian who had completed his theological studies at Saint Vincent Seminary and was ordained in 1855. With Hörmann were forty-four-year-old Father Peter Baunach, a former Redemptorist who had joined the monastery in Pennsylvania in 1856 and pronounced his solemn vows a year later, and Father Aemilian Wendel, a recently ordained priest from Bavaria who had entered the monastery at Saint Vincent in 1854. The lay brothers were Michael Böhm, a thirty-seven-year-old cook who had come to America with Wimmer in 1846, and Norbert Rossberger, age fifty-one, who had joined the Pennsylvania community in 1852 and had served as the monastery baker.

Bishop Odin met the missionaries in New Orleans and took them by steamer to Galveston. By the end of July they had settled into the mission at San José and began refurbishing the buildings. In October 1859 King Ludwig I sent a donation of three thousand florins to the Texas community, and Wimmer wrote enthusiastically that "conditions in Texas are so favorable that we can hope for success. The bishop transferred San José to us. It consists of a magnificent church and a large monastery which are in the midst of 720 acres of fertile land."[19]

The monks from Saint Vincent found an abundant field of labor in the region surrounding the monastery. They provided pastoral care for German congregations in San Antonio, Castroville, Neubraunfels, Fredericksburg, and D'Hanis, and struggled to make the 720-acre farm productive. More monks came from Saint Vincent in 1860, including several brothers and three priests: Fathers Amandus Kramer, Theodore von Gründer, and Gallus Erhardt. In 1862 the general chapter of the American Cassinese Congregation voted to petition Rome for the independence of San José Priory, but by now the community in Texas was encountering severe and debilitating problems.

The first of these was the difficulty of establishing a regular monastic observance at the priory. Even with six priests (two of whom, Theodore von Gründer and Gallus Erhardt, later abandoned the monastic life) the community found that its extensive and exhausting pastoral commitments made it all but impossible to maintain the daily round of prayer and devotions essential for Benedictine communal life. The outbreak of the Civil War also adversely affected the community's ability to remain financially solvent. Communications with Saint Vincent were broken, and much needed money and personnel from the motherhouse were cut off. In addition, the local populace became suspicious of the monks, so recently arrived from Pennsylvania, and questioned their loyalty to the Confederate cause. Finally, the most significant problem the community faced was illness. Many of the monks in Texas contracted tuberculosis. Both Brothers Michael Böhm and Norbert Rossberger died of the disease while still at San José, and though Fathers Alto Hörmann and Peter Baunach returned to Saint Vincent in the 1860s, they also succumbed to the illness contracted in Texas.

As a result of these insurmountable difficulties, the Saint Vincent chapter withdrew its recommendation for the priory's independence and in 1867, after a lengthy debate, voted to return San José, its properties and missions to the bishop of Galveston. The failure of the Benedictine mission to Texas, which consumed eight years, four lives, and incalculable resources, provides dramatic and sobering testimony to the challenges facing the Benedictine missionaries from Saint Vincent who went west in the 1850s. The story of San José also serves to bring into sharp focus the extraordinary achievements of the Saint Vincent monks who managed to create monasteries, missions, and schools in Minnesota and Kansas that continue to flourish 140 years later.

OTHER FOUNDATIONS FROM SAINT VINCENT

During the 1850s and 1860s monks from Saint Vincent established a dozen additional foundations that extended the work of the Pennsylvania community into six new American states and Canada. Although only one of these foundations eventually gained independence and became an abbey, the others played important roles in advancing the pastoral and educational apostolates of the American Benedictines.

Benedictines from Saint Vincent had worked in New Jersey, off and on, since 1849 when Wimmer sent Father Placidus Döttl to Newark to assist Father Nicholas Balleis, the Austrian Benedictine who had greeted the Bavarian Benedictine mission when it arrived in New York in 1846 and who was founding pastor of St. Mary's Church, Newark. Döttl remained only seven months as assistant to Balleis before being recalled to Pennsylvania to become prior at Saint Vincent. In 1852 Father Charles Geyerstanger went from Pennsylvania to New Jersey to assist Balleis and remained until 1854.

As early as 1847 Father Nicholas Balleis had offered to turn the parish in Newark over to the Benedictines of Saint Vincent, but in its first years the Pennsylvania community had neither the manpower nor the financial resources necessary to administer a large parish so far from home. Then in 1854, after an anti-Catholic riot nearly destroyed St. Mary's Church, Balleis grew despondent and announced his intention of leaving the city. Bishop James Roosevelt Bayley of the newly established Diocese of Newark turned to the Benedictines at Saint Vincent once again and invited them to take over the parish. Wimmer and his monks were still hesitant to accept the offer. Father Boniface told the bishop that the principal reason for this reluctance was the monks' conviction that the best places for them to establish foundations were in rural districts where they could lead a monastic life of work and prayer undisturbed by the multiple distractions of cities. "In the country, far from the noise of cities, we lead a happy life," he said. The Benedictines believed that all they had accomplished in the farm country of Pennsylvania "would be impossible in a city to be done; the country, the soil, the industry of the lay brothers, the zeal and frugality of the young priests, and above all the blessing of Almighty God never separated from religious poverty is doing it. Will you blame me then, if in sight of such facts, I am not desirous of a congregation in a city?"[20]

Bishop Bayley accepted the Benedictines' decision and turned the parish over to the Redemptorists. In 1857, however, when the Redemptorists were forced suddenly to leave, Wimmer agreed to come to the bishop's aid and sent three monks to Newark. The leader of the Benedictine mission to New Jersey was Father Valentine Felder, a twenty-seven-year-old Bavarian who had come to Saint Vincent in 1851, completed his theological studies in Saint Vincent Seminary, and been ordained in 1854. Felder had served for three years in the Pennsylvania missions before being appointed to Newark. Accompanying him were Eberhard Gahr, a twenty-three-year-old cleric who had just finished his studies at Saint Vincent, and Brother Luke Zeume who was to serve as cook for the small community.

The Benedictines arrived on April 17, 1857, and a month later Bishop Bayley ordained Gahr to the priesthood. On May 19 Father Valentine wrote the abbot that all was going well. The Benedictines were attending the spiritual needs of the six thousand German Catholics of the city. They had purchased three houses adjacent to the parish property and were making one of them ready for a group of Benedictine sisters from St. Marys, Pennsylvania, who were expected soon to open an elementary school in the parish.[21] Less than two weeks later tragedy struck.

On May 28, while in New York City to arrange construction of a new parish church, Father Valentine Felder was run down in the street by a trolleycar and killed. The death of the young priest sent shock waves back to Saint Vincent. Wimmer wrote Bishop Bayley that "struck with astonishment as I was at the sad and sudden news, I did not know what to do at first." He decided against going to Newark and opted instead to go to St. Marys, Pennsylvania, where he dispatched the prior of St. Mary's Priory, Father Rupert Seidenbusch, to New Jersey.[22]

Seidenbusch, a twenty-seven-year-old native of Munich, had entered the monastery at Saint Vincent in 1851 and been ordained in 1853. He had served in St. Marys since ordination and was appointed prior there in 1856. Wimmer called him "superior in ability and intelligence" and had come to depend on Seidenbusch as a troubleshooter, assigning him the task of settling controversies that had developed between the monks and the Benedictine nuns in St. Marys. Seidenbusch, who eventually became first abbot of the Minnesota foundation, remained in Newark for six years and during that time oversaw the development of monastic life in the priory and parochial work in the parish. In 1868, under Prior Roman Hell (1825–73), St. Mary's Priory, Newark, opened St. Benedict's College, and in 1884 the priory became independent from Saint Vincent and was elevated to the rank of abbey.[23]

Another priory established by Saint Vincent in 1857 was at Bellefonte, Pennsylvania, in the Diocese of Philadelphia. At the invitation of Bishop John Nepomucene Neumann, C.Ss.R., Wimmer assigned Fathers Odilo Vandergrün and Louis Fink, both recently ordained graduates of Saint Vincent Seminary, to attend the spiritual needs of German immigrants in Bellefonte and the surrounding towns of Snow Shoe, McVeytown, Lewiston, and Sinnemahoning. Two brothers accompanied the priests to St. John's Church, Bellefonte, and together they established a priory which Wimmer hoped would develop into an independent community. The priory did not prosper, however, and after the Civil War the monks returned the parish to the bishop and came back to Saint Vincent.[24]

A far more successful priory was founded in Covington, Kentucky, in 1858. At the invitation of Bishop George A. Carrell, S.J., of Covington, the Saint Vincent chapter accepted charge of the German congregation of St. Joseph's in the see city, and Wimmer sent Fathers Roman Hell and Oswald Moosmüller to establish a priory there. A year later he assigned two more priests (Alphonse Heimler and Aemilian Wendel), a cleric (Lambert Kettner), and three brothers to Kentucky. The Benedictines built a church and opened a short-lived Latin school for boys at St. Joseph's Priory. They also invited a community of Benedictine nuns from Erie, Pennsylvania, to establish a priory in Covington and open a school for girls.[25] The monks of St. Joseph's provided the pastoral care for several hundred German families in Covington as well as for four rural Catholic congregations outside the city. Once a month Father Oswald Moosmüller journeyed 150 miles to the Virginia border to care for one hundred English-speaking Catholic families he had discovered on his missionary rounds. Wimmer wrote that these families "did not know that there were so many of them and [they] had to be gradually organized into smaller congregations."[26] The priory in Covington survived into the twentieth century and was eventually downgraded to the rank of parish. It never developed into the independent abbey that Boniface Wimmer and the Saint Vincent chapter had hoped for, but it served the Catholics of Covington for more than a century before the monks were finally recalled to the motherhouse.[27]

Other pre–Civil War foundations from Saint Vincent included St. Joseph Parish, Johnstown, Pennsylvania (1852); St. Philomena Parish, Omaha, Nebraska (1858); St. Mary's Priory, Erie, Pennsylvania (1859); Assumption Parish, Nashville, Tennessee (1860); St. Mary's Priory, Richmond, Virginia (1860); and St. Joseph Priory, Chicago, Illinois (1860). During the Civil War missionary activity by the monks in Pennsylvania necessarily came to a standstill. Nonetheless, as the conflict raged the chapter in Pennsylvania authorized the establishment of two new parishes in New Jersey—St. Henry's in Elizabeth City (1863), founded by the irrepressible missionary, Father Peter Henry Lemke, and St. Benedict in Newark (1864), founded from St. Mary's Priory—and accepted an invitation to staff Assumption College in Sandwich, Ontario (1862).

The decision to go to Canada was spurred by the outbreak of the Civil War and the threat of military conscription that hung over many of the monks at Saint Vincent. Draft notices began to arrive at Saint Vincent toward the beginning of 1862, and about that time Abbot Boniface received a request from Bishop Pierre Adolphe Pinsonnault of London, Ontario, that the Benedictines of Saint Vincent take over operation of Assumption College in Sandwich. The people of the Canadian diocese were largely French and Irish, with few if any German Catholics, and under normal circumstances Wimmer would have declined the offer. He sensed, however, Saint Vincent's need for a refuge outside of the United States in the event that political and economic chaos erupted during the Civil War. He also wanted a place to send the young priests and clerics most threatened by military conscription. The Saint Vincent chapter therefore accepted Bishop Pinsonnault's offer, and in the summer of 1862 about eight monks (priests, clerics, and lay brothers), under the leadership of Father Oswald Moosmüller, went to Canada to take over administration of the college with its enrollment of forty-five students.[28] Among the clerics sent to Ontario to avoid conscription were Leander Schnerr, who would become third archabbot of Saint Vincent, and Boniface Krug, who later went to Italy, entered the monastery of Montecassino, and became archabbot there in 1897. The Saint Vincent monks remained at Assumption College until the end of the Civil War, when they returned the school and property in Ontario to the bishop and moved back to Saint Vincent.

By 1866 Saint Vincent monks were working in seven American states: Pennsylvania, Minnesota, Kansas, New Jersey, Kentucky, Virginia, and Illinois. (The missions in Tennessee, Nebraska, and Ontario had been withdrawn.) Wimmer's vision of planting Benedictine communities throughout America was well on its way to being fulfilled.

SAINT VINCENT AND THE CIVIL WAR

The effects of the Civil War on the monastery and college were immediate and grave. Economic conditions at the abbey, and indeed in all the American Benedictine monasteries, grew precarious, and communications among Benedictine missionaries throughout the United States became increasingly difficult. Two months before the conflict began, Wimmer wrote Abbot Angelo Pescetelli that Saint Vincent's missions in the South were almost entirely cut off from the motherhouse. "Our fathers in Texas, Nashville, Richmond, and Covington, and most probably in Kansas," he said, "have been separated from us so completely that we cannot communicate with them by letter."[29] Then, when the war finally did break out, missionary activity ground to a halt.

After 1862 no communication at all was possible with the monks in Texas. Brother Michael Böhm died in San José in December 1862, but the war was nearly over before word of his death reached Saint Vincent. Eventually communication with the Kentucky priory was restored, and contact between the monks in Pennsylvania and those in Kansas was never effectively broken. In Richmond, however, Father Leonard Mayer was completely isolated from Saint Vincent until the city fell to Union forces in the spring of 1865.

In January 1861, when communication with the South was still possible, the Saint Vincent chapter answered a call for assistance from Bishop James Whelan, O.P., by sending Father Emmeran Bliemel from the priory in Covington to the Diocese of Nashville. Father Emmeran, who for a while had been professor of mathematics at Saint Vincent College, took up residence at the German parish of the Assumption in Nashville, but soon after his arrival most of his male parishioners were drafted into the Confederate army. Bliemel asked Bishop Whalen's permission to follow them. Two years passed before he could get the bishop to agree, but in October 1863 he enlisted in the 10th Tennessee Regiment and went to Georgia where he joined the soldiers from his parish. Less than a year later, during the Battle of Atlanta, he was killed while administering the Church's last rites to wounded soldiers near Jonesboro, Georgia. He is remembered as the only chaplain of either army to be killed during the war.[30]

Besides the burdens it placed on the monks and missions in the South, the war caused considerable hardship at Saint Vincent itself. In the 1862–63 academic year, 20 of the 142 students in the college came from Southern states and were unable to return to their homes when the fighting began. Wimmer wrote Archbishop Scherr of Munich in 1863 that these students "already owe us six thousand dollars for board and tuition, and most probably we will never receive payment." The abbot's patience and charity were tried, moreover, when the Southern students seemed bent on aggravating trouble with their Yankee classmates. On one occasion the patriotic fervor of the "Rebels" caused serious difficulties with local farmers. According to an account written forty years after the event, several of the southern boys prevailed upon a local seamstress to make a Confederate battle flag for them. In the dark of night they unfurled the banner atop one of the high buildings at Saint Vincent, and at dawn it waved bravely over the abbey and college. When neighboring farmers, taking their produce to market in Latrobe, saw the Rebel flag, they angrily marched up to Saint Vincent and demanded an explanation. The abbot had not been aware that the flag was flying over his preserve. When it was brought to his attention, he summoned the Southern students and directed them to furl their colors. They did, and a peace of sorts came to the Yankee campus once again.[31]

But more serious problems faced Wimmer and the American Benedictines in 1862 on account of the war. The Union's Conscription Act was passed that year, and as a result several of the monks at Saint Vincent were drafted. Wimmer sent some of these priests and brothers to Assumption College in Canada to escape military service, and in November 1862, with the help of Archbishop Francis Patrick Kenrick of Baltimore, he successfully petitioned the War Department in Washington to exempt from military service several of the monks who had been drafted.[32] But early in 1863 Congress passed a new, more stringent draft law, and more Benedictines were called up for military duty. In February 1863 Brother Bonaventure Gaul was drafted and assigned to the 61st Pennsylvania Regiment. A month later Brother Ulric Barth followed him. In all six priests and eight brothers were drafted: in addition to Bonaventure and Ulric, they included Brothers Ildephonse Hoffmann, George Held, Leo Christ, and Gallus Maier from Saint Vincent; Father Valentine Lobmayer from St. Joseph's Parish, Johnstown, Pennsylvania; Fathers Bernard Manser, Casimir Seitz, and Erhard Vanino from St. Mary's Parish, Erie; Father Benno Hegele from Newark Priory; and Father Isidor Walter and Brothers Martin Beck and Philip Bernard from St. Benedict's Priory, Carrolltown. Two priests and two brothers were released when the monastery paid the three-hundred-dollar exemption fee for each, and four others were declared unfit to bear arms by army doctors. But five brothers—Ildephonse, George, Leo, Ulric, and Bonaventure—served in the army until the war ended: and Gallus Maier was wounded at Antietam and after a brief hospitalization returned to Saint Vincent in 1863.

In June 1863 Wimmer wrote President Lincoln asking that his monks be released from military service on account of their total unsuitability as warriors. He argued that "at no time among civilized nations ever a law existed by which clergymen or monks had been obliged to go to war" and that Christian monks could not "go to war unless we act in a grievous manner against our conscience."[33] Lincoln endorsed the letter and forwarded it to the War Department where Secretary of War Edwin Stanton issued an order transferring the drafted monks to the Hospital Corps. They were released from the onus of bearing arms, but for two years they served the wounded on the battlefield amid the horrors of war.

Some of the war correspondence of the brothers has survived and interesting anecdotes of their military service abound. Thus Brother Bonaventure wrote from Virginia during the final campaign of the war, "We dug trenches so close to the rebels that we could talk to them." Brother Leo Christ was severely wounded in the leg during the Petersburg Campaign of

1865 and suffered from the wound until his death in 1883. Brother Bonaventure was with Grant's army during the last days of the war, and three days after Lee's surrender he wrote his confrere, Brother Ildephonse Hoffmann, describing the surrender at Appomattox.

> On Palm Sunday, at 5 p.m., General Lee handed over his sword, and just as we were attacking again, his troops surrendered to the Sixth Corps. It was a glorious moment to witness, to hear the shouting and to listen to the Hurrahs. To me it was worth a thousand dollars. Then all the divisions of the Sixth Corps celebrated the event. Finally ration wagons were sent to save the troops that had surrendered. This assistance was very necessary. At that time we were only a short distance from the rebels. . . . I hope the war will be over soon. Thanks to God a thousand times. These hardships will not easily be forgotten.

The Benedictines were discharged from the army during the summer of 1865. Brother Gallus Maier, who after being wounded had returned to Saint Vincent in 1863, later decided to leave the Order, but the others remained. Brother Bonaventure Gaul earned a reputation in subsequent years as infirmarian of the college. Well trained in military hospitals during the war, he brought from the army a recipe for liniment that was popularly called "wizard oil" at the school and that helped heal a host of student sports injuries. Brothers Ulric, Leo, George, and Ildephonse all remained at Saint Vincent until their deaths, quietly and unobtrusively fulfilling the duties they had been called from to go to war.[34]

Four weeks after the Confederate surrender at Appomattox the effects of the war were brought home even more dramatically to Saint Vincent when the funeral train carrying the body of Abraham Lincoln passed through the monastery lands along the main line of the Pennsylvania Railroad less than a mile from the abbey and college. Monks and students lined the tracks to pay their final respects to the man who had saved the Union.

THE GHOST STORY

As the Civil War raged, threatening to tear the nation asunder, another kind of conflict developed at Saint Vincent which proved far more threatening to the peace and unity of the abbey. The episode known as "the ghost story" involved deception, disobedience, and sexual misconduct and nearly fragmented the American Cassinese Congregation. There followed seven years of divisiveness and deep distrust within the Saint Vincent community before the problems caused by the alleged apparitions could be resolved.

The event that triggered the long, unhappy story, however, was first viewed as God's blessing on the community: a vision from beyond the grave designed to inspire greater religious devotion among the monks of Saint Vincent. In September 1859 Paul George Keck, a twenty-three-year-old novice from Rheno-Prussia who before entering the novitiate at Saint Vincent had studied acting in Europe, claimed to have been visited by a ghost while recovering from an illness in the monastery infirmary. The ghost, he said, was that of "a Benedictine monk in choir garb with his head covered by a cowl and holding a cross in his right hand." The spirit told Keck that he had come from Purgatory to ask that prayers and Masses be said for the repose of his soul. Keck informed the novice master, Father Wendelin Mayer, who at once gave the news to Wimmer and the subprior, Father Othmar Wirtz.[35]

It appears that Mayer and Wirtz almost at once accepted the story as true. Wimmer at first was skeptical, but after interviewing the novice, he wrote to Abbot Angelo Pescetelli in Rome that he could "hardly doubt the phenomenon." Keck was told to communicate with the ghost, which continued to appear regularly to the former actor and revealed that "of the five priests who had already died at the abbey, no one was yet in Heaven, but suffering in Purgatory." By February newspapers in Pittsburgh had begun to publish reports of the alleged visions, and Wimmer felt obliged to set the record straight and correct certain misinformation contained in the press articles. He sent a letter to the *Pittsburgh Dispatch,* the *Pittsburgh Catholic,* and the *Wahrheitsfreund* of Cincinnati in which he asserted the truth of the apparitions but denied that the ghost had claimed, as reported by the *Pittsburgh Dispatch,* that in the whole history of Christianity only two Catholic priests had ever found their way to heaven.[36]

Despite the fact that many inside and outside the community maintained a healthy skepticism about the alleged apparitions, the phenomenon continued to grow, bringing with it a kind of religious hysteria at Saint Vincent. Claiming to have received further revelations, Keck informed the community that it was the divine will that a stricter monastic regimen be observed in the monastery. He directed that certain pious practices be adopted by all the monks, that each, for example, attach a Rosary to his belt and follow the Cistercian custom of affixing "Maria" to his name in religion. Perhaps the fame of the apparitions in Lourdes two years earlier had inspired Keck to concoct his own revelations, and it is likely that the perennial agitation on the part of some of the monks at Saint Vincent, among whom were both the novice master and subprior, for a more contemplative, devotional life in the monastery had suggested the proposed reforms. In any event, Keck's visions became the center of an intense controversy not only at Saint Vincent but in the priories of Minnesota and Kansas as well.

Led by Fathers Wendelin Mayer and Othmar Wirtz, a strong party of reformers gathered around the young novice. They all adopted the name "Maria" and called for a more contemplative and ascetic form of monastic life at Saint Vincent. Division within the community was immediate. Those who believed in the supernatural origins of the visions aligned themselves with Mayer and Wirtz and demanded a thorough reformation of the monastic regimen. The skeptics opposed any efforts at reform. The controversy split the community into two strong camps whose acrimonious debates built in a crescendo of angry exchanges and hard feelings until they reached a head at a chapter in August 1860. At that chapter more than half the community voted to reject Keck's petition to make religious vows, and this vote resulted in his expulsion from the community. It is a measure of the divisions the ghost story caused in the congregation that immediately after being dismissed from Saint Vincent, Keck was accepted into the community in Minnesota.[37]

Within nine months of his dismissal the climate at Saint Vincent changed, and the chapter voted to receive Keck back into the novitiate. Wimmer wrote that "at first the members of the house opposed [Keck]. But gradually the majority became his friends and supporters."[38] At the abbey once again, the seer began to have more visions, and before long a form of hysteria swept through the monastery. Two more monks claimed to be visited by spirits and to have received the gift of prophecy. These "prophets" informed Wimmer and the community that hardship and misfortune would be their future lot if they did not follow the directives of Keck who, they claimed, was relaying authentic messages of the divine will delivered to him by an angel in the form of "a beautiful young boy." In November 1861 Keck said that Martin Luther had appeared to him and revealed that he was not in hell but in purgatory, a revelation that was greeted by the staunchly Catholic Bavarians of Saint Vincent with considerable consternation. Other apparitions claimed by Keck revealed that unless an immediate reform took place in the Pennsylvania monastery the entire community would be drafted into the army, a revelation that gained much credibility when the draft notices began to arrive soon afterwards.

In April 1862 Keck pronounced simple triennial vows and entered the seminary. By now he had surrounded himself with a number of clerics and priests who regarded him as an authentic interpreter of God's will. Wimmer himself was not unimpressed with the young cleric's behavior and the effect his revelations had on the community. With regard to the visions and revelations Wimmer wrote, "I doubted many very strongly, but I considered several as authentic since many prophecies were fulfilled exactly, and several real miracles have been worked. For example, a noticeable cure, the conversion of a calloused sinner on his deathbed, etc."

The case reached "sensational heights" and almost all the monks in the house were divided for or against the seer. To the abbot, those monks who were Keck's friends seemed more zealous for the monastic life than ever before. They followed the Rule more carefully and became model religious. Those who opposed the seer, on the other hand, were "the more lax ones," the shirkers who often missed Morning Office and tended not to be scrupulous observers of the Rule. Wimmer himself felt that Keck's influence had a positive effect on his own spiritual life. "It was impossible for a long time for me to decide what I should think of the matter," the abbot wrote, "particularly since I myself could give evidence that I became more zealous in good deeds through it, as was also certain to a greater or lesser degree with all his friends."[39]

But in the end Keck's carefully woven deception began to unravel. The young cleric informed Wimmer that his heavenly visitors had instructed him to seek immediate ordination. Wimmer responded that heavenly visitors or not, Keck would have to complete his theological studies before being ordained. Then for the first time since the affair began Keck turned on the abbot. He accused Wimmer of playing into the Devil's hands by refusing to allow him to be ordained, and he was able to convince many of his supporters that this was the case. With two of these supporters he set out for Pittsburgh to seek ordination from Bishop Michael Domenec. When Domenec refused, Keck went to Erie to attempt to convince Bishop Josue Mary Young to ordain him.

Though denied ordination by Bishop Young, Keck was received warmly by the Benedictines of St. Mary's Priory, Erie. His confreres in Erie stood in awe of the visionary from the motherhouse, and one evening several of them took him to the home of a parishioner so that the people of the parish could meet him. The monks and laypeople talked and drank and sang well into the night in what Wimmer described as a secular environment totally inappropriate for a monk. Returning to the priory with one of the priests, whom Keck later claimed to be intoxicated, the visionary attempted to seduce the man. The priest angrily rejected the cleric's homosexual advances and denounced him before the community. Keck defended himself vehemently. He insisted that he had done nothing wrong, arguing that he had taken off the priest's clothes because the priest, in a drunken state, was unable to do so himself. He claimed further that he had merely given the priest the kiss of peace, a custom which Keck had encouraged many of his followers to practice as part of the spiritual renewal taking place in the monastic community under the influence of the visionary's alleged revelations. Keck said, moreover, that it had been the priest and not himself who had attempted the seduction.[40]

Upon hearing the news, Wimmer rushed back to the abbey from Sandwich, Ontario, where he had been on visitation at Assumption College. Understandably he was horrified by the turn of events. He summoned the monks who had attended the party in Erie and questioned them thoroughly. He took testimony from the priest who accused Keck and interrogated the visionary himself. He met with both the supporters and opponents of Keck at Saint Vincent and carefully examined the devotional practices that had developed in the community under the visionary's influence. The evidence he accumulated pointed to the appalling conclusion that the spiritual reformation in the monastery concealed a homosexual subculture whose leading proponent was Keck himself.

Wimmer was aghast at what he had discovered. In a report to the Sacred Congregation for the Propaganda Fide, he said that Brother Paul "was accustomed to embrace his friends most tenderly and to kiss them by putting his tongue in their mouths, as scarcely any chaste friends would do and which . . . I consider gravely impure. His manner of comportment manifested a certainly womanly tenderness and effeminacy, even when he sang, for which he was looked upon askance by many laymen and clerics."[41] As a result of his investigations, the abbot expelled Keck from the monastery and attempted to end the influence the young cleric's friends continued to exercise over religious observance at Saint Vincent. Many of those friends were indignant at the expulsion and loudly complained about Wimmer's dismissing them from positions of authority in the monastery. Novice master Wendelin Mayer abandoned the abbey and went to Minnesota, where Keck had gone to seek assistance from his friends among the Benedictine community in St. Cloud.[42]

In Minnesota Father Othmar Wirtz (now prior in St. Cloud) gave refuge to Keck and Mayer and attempted to have the cleric ordained. With the help of Prior Louis Fink in Chicago (who, like Wirtz and Mayer, believed that Keck had been maligned and unjustly treated by Wimmer) Father Othmar petitioned Bishops Thomas Grace of St. Paul and James Duggan of Chicago for Keck's ordination, but as the bishops of Pittsburgh and

Erie had done earlier, Grace and Duggan refused. Thwarted in the West as he had been at Saint Vincent, but continuing to receive the support of important members of the American Benedictine community who still believed in the authenticity of his visions, Keck now boldly decided to bring his case before the Holy See. In March 1863 he left Minnesota for Rome to defend himself.[43]

Abbot Angelo Pescetelli again assumed the role of advocate for the American Benedictines and defended Wimmer before the cardinals of the Propaganda Fide against the attacks now leveled at him by Keck, Wirtz, and Mayer. These attacks focused on the manner in which the abbot oversaw the observance of the monastic Rule at Saint Vincent. The "reformers" complained that because of the abbot's inattention to the details of religious life it was impossible for the monks "to pray the Divine Office together. . . . [E]ven other holy exercises are often neglected, and the holy discipline has disappeared and has made room for secular customs. Frequently young monks have to rely upon themselves and live without supervision or example, or help and counsel, and often the greatest temptations and scandals occur."[44] They also asserted that the charges brought against Keck were the result of opposition to the young visionary's efforts to reform a corrupt monastery.

Saint Vincent's dirty laundry was being aired in the capital of Christendom, and for a while Wimmer feared not only that his days as a religious superior would be over, but also that his hopes for creating a strong Benedictine presence in the American Church were about to be crushed. Abbot Angelo Pescetelli, however, once again proved himself an adroit advocate and good friend of the American Benedictines. He defended Wimmer's decisions regarding Keck and the "reformers," and he thwarted an attempt by Father Othmar Wirtz to obtain abbatial rank for the priory in Minnesota with Wirtz named as abbot. The reformers at Saint Vincent and St. Cloud had pinned their hopes on establishing a reform abbey in Minnesota under the direction of the leading proponents of the movement inspired by Keck's visions. When that effort failed, their movement began to disintegrate.

In June 1864 Keck, who by now had abandoned his aspirations for the priesthood and had enlisted in the Papal Zouaves, was summoned before the Holy Office of the Inquisition to answer questions about his alleged visions. Wimmer himself was summoned to Rome at the end of 1864 to present his side of the ghost story and all that emanated from it. Because of the Civil War he was not able to travel until February 1865, but in April, after first visiting Bavaria, he arrived in the Eternal City. He had many matters to discuss with Vatican officials, but the most pressing was the matter of Paul Keck and those who continued to support him. The case dragged on for months, but at last in September 1865 the cardinals of the Holy Office handed down their decision. They declared "that the visions and revelations of George Keck deserve no credence. On the contrary, they contain grave errors, and the two monks who are their principal supporters must be placed under surveillance."[45] On October 11, 1865, the decree was formally promulgated, and six days later Abbot Boniface wrote Prior Othmar Wirtz in St. Cloud informing him of the decision of the Holy Office and relieving him of his duties as superior in Minnesota. Following instructions of the Holy See, Wimmer also directed that all capitulars of the American Cassinese Congregation sign a document renouncing support for Paul George Keck and declaring their submission to the decision of the Holy Office.[46]

Father Othmar informed Wimmer that he would abide by the Roman decision and wrote Father Wendelin Mayer in December that he wished to comply entirely with the repudiation of Keck. His hopes of founding a "reformed" monastery finally dashed, he submitted in every way to his superiors. From St. Cloud Father Othmar went to St. Paul, Minnesota, where he worked as assistant to Father Clement Staub in Assumption Parish until his death in 1874.[47] Father Wendelin Mayer continued for a while to oppose the decision of the Inquisition. His faculties were suspended, and he was severely censured by the cardinals. Finally, convinced of his error, he requested absolution from the Congregation De Penitentiaria in May 1866. After formally declaring his submission to the Roman decree concerning Paul Keck's visions and apologizing to Abbot Boniface for the calumnies he had spoken against him and the scandals he had brought to Saint Vincent, Mayer was absolved of all censures by the Roman Congregation.[48] He returned to the United States in September, and for the next fifteen years he worked quietly in parishes in Pennsylvania and New Jersey until his death in 1881. Of Paul Keck, the actor and arch-imposter who for nearly seven years had occasioned unparalleled furor and contentiousness in the Benedictine communities of the American Cassinese Congregation, no more was ever heard.

AN ERA OF TROUBLES

The decade between 1856 and 1866 was a stressful and difficult one for the monks of Saint Vincent. Not only were their resources and energies tried to the limit by the extensive missionary activities they undertook, but the grave internal problems resulting from the masterful hoax of Paul Keck created tensions and divisiveness within the American Benedictine family that threatened to destroy the young community. Saint Vincent confronted several other crises during the decade as well, and the characterization of this period by Benedictine historian Felix Fellner as an "era of troubles" is both accurate and understated. At no other time in the history of Saint Vincent did the monastic community face such severe challenges to its well-being and survival, and that it overcame them all, damaged but intact, is a tribute to both the leadership of Boniface Wimmer and the single-minded dedication of the majority of the monks to the Benedictine monastic, pastoral, and educational mission in the United States.

The episode that came to be known as the "insurrection of the brothers" had its roots in Wimmer's plan to introduce a large number of lay brothers at Saint Vincent. By 1856 there were 110 of these lay brothers in a community that totaled 188 monks. Wimmer's original plan was to integrate the brothers, clerical students, and priests into a single community in which they would all possess the same privileges, share the responsibilities of instructing the German students, and participate jointly in the communal prayer life, specifically in the recitation of the Divine Office. This plan emerged not from contemporary practice in Bavarian monasteries but from exigencies in America and from Wimmer's own innovative thinking based on his reading and knowledge of the institution of the lay brotherhood in medieval Cistercian communities. Anticipating criticism of such integration, Wimmer wrote the Ludwig Missionsverein that the brothers would contribute not only to the material good of the monastery but also, by their simple piety, to its spiritual development as well.[49]

Not long after the monks' arrival in America, however, it became apparent that the plan was not practicable. It soon became apparent that a distinction between the lay and clerical members of the monastery, based upon social class, education, and function in the community, was unavoidable. The young clerical candidates who arrived at Saint Vincent to study for the priesthood generally came from families who belonged to the small landowning and mercantile classes of the Bavarian bourgeoisie, families who could usually provide secondary and sometimes even university education for their sons. Those, on the other hand, who came as candidates for the nonclerical brotherhood were skilled and unskilled laborers, generally from the poorer classes, who normally had only an elementary education. The differences between the two groups, as well as the economic and educational needs of the community itself, led to an inevitable division of labor and status at Saint Vincent and in the priories founded from it.

The clerical members of the community devoted their energies before ordination to study, and then afterwards to teaching, sacramental ministry, and the organization and administration of Catholic congregations, first in Pennsylvania and later in Minnesota, Kansas, New Jersey, Kentucky, and Texas. Upon the nonclerical members, or lay brothers, devolved the responsibility of filling the great demand for manual laborers necessary for building the monasteries, farming the lands, and feeding and clothing the American Benedictine communities. Thus while the priests taught and catechized, the brothers worked in the fields, kitchens, and craft shops.

By 1860 the social structure that divided clerical and lay members of the monastic community was firmly institutionalized, and this caused dissatisfaction among many of the lay brothers at Saint Vincent. True, since the elevation of the monastery to the rank of canonical priory in 1852, the lay brothers, like the clerical monks, had been permitted to pronounce solemn rather than the less binding simple vows. But now the brothers, the majority in the community, were no longer permitted to participate in the deliberations and decisions of the monastic chapter, a right reserved in canon law to ordained monks. Some of them began to feel that in democratic America they were being treated like second-class citizens in their own community.

In April 1861, Brother Joseph Sailer, one of the pioneers of 1846, addressed a lengthy letter of complaint to Pope Pius IX in which he alleged that the brothers at Saint Vincent were being treated unfairly and even taken advantage of by the abbot and the other clerical monks. Sailer said that when they were leaving Europe in 1846 Wimmer had promised that in America there would be no distinction made between the brothers and the priests, that all would enjoy the same rights and privileges. Sailer said, for example, that Wimmer had promised the brothers separate cells such as the priests would have and that they would be given the right to vote as full-fledged members of the monastic chapter. According to Sailer, none of these promises was kept. He complained that the brothers were looked down upon by the priests and clerics, who did not consider them part of the community; that they could be dismissed by Wimmer at the abbot's whim, solemn vows notwithstanding; that they were forced to work so hard "that no slave in America is treated with greater severity"; and that several brothers had been dismissed for no reason. "A thousand times" they had been promised the statutes that would instruct them in their rights and privileges, Brother Joseph said, but they had never received them, and it was a hard thing "to have spent one's youth and lost one's health in working hard, and then to be sent away or to be treated in such a manner as to be obliged to go away and close one's life in a poorhouse, in a country where one cannot even speak the language." Finally Brother Joseph protested that though great demands were made of the brothers, who were bound by the "gravest obligations," no corresponding rights and privileges were granted them.[50]

The matter was referred to the Sacred Congregation for the Propagation of the Faith, which directed Bishop Michael Domenec of Pittsburgh and Bishop Josue Mary Young of Erie to conduct an investigation. In September Bishop Domenec, accompanied by his German-speaking secretary, Father John Stibiel, visited the monastery and interviewed the brothers and priests. He reported to the Holy See that while some of the promises made to the brothers could not be kept, the abbot had followed canon law in all matters relating to nonclerical members of the community and had treated the lay brothers justly and equitably.[51] Bishop Young visited the priory in St. Marys, Pennsylvania, where he carried on his own investigation and reported to Rome that he had heard "no whisper of complaint" from the brothers. He noted that he would "be more ready to accuse [the abbot] of excess of indulgence towards the fractious and erring, than being severe with any one."[52] In October the chapter at Saint Vincent, composed of priests and clerics in major orders, met to debate the matter and after discussing the charges of Brother Joseph determined that there was no substance to them. They drafted a letter to Rome indicating the results of their deliberations and exonerating the abbot of any fault.[53] Finally, Wimmer himself wrote Cardinal Alessandro Barnabo, prefect of the Propaganda Fide, denying the allegations and calling the accusation that he had borne himself arbitrarily against the lay brothers "a pure lie."[54]

In the end the Holy See concluded that Brother Joseph's complaints had no substance and absolved Wimmer and the clerical monks of any wrongdoing. Tensions subsided at the abbey, and everyone returned to his respective labors. After 1861, however, the lay brothers at Saint Vincent and the other monasteries of the American Cassinese Congregation were not permitted to take solemn vows (which implied full membership in the monastic community and the right to participate in the deliberations of the monastic chapter), and for the next century they lived and worked at Saint Vincent bound by simple vows and forming what many regarded as a separate, subordinate community within the monastery.[55]

A second crisis that the monks of Saint Vincent confronted during the era of troubles was their failure to elect a permanent abbot despite three attempts to do so. This failure left the community insecure in its leadership, and to some extent reflected fundamental internal divisions which were not satisfactorily resolved until 1866.

Although the Propaganda Fide had ruled in 1855 that the abbot of Saint Vincent should be elected for life by the monastery chapter, Pope Pius IX had overridden the decision and appointed Boniface Wimmer abbot for a three-year term after which an election was to take place "according to the regular method." Wimmer's term expired in September 1858, and in anticipation of the election he wrote the Propaganda Fide in April requesting guidance on electoral procedures. By August Rome had still not responded to Wimmer's questions, but in order to ensure that monks from distant priories could participate, he sent out announcements of the election and summoned all the capitulars to the motherhouse. Thirty-nine priests responded to the summons; four others appointed proxies. When the chapter met on September 10, Wimmer informed the monks that the Propaganda Fide had not formally authorized the election nor provided answers to the procedural questions submitted in April, but the capitulars unanimously voted to proceed, presuming that the papal decree of September 1855, which directed that after a term of three years an election take place "according to the regular method," was authorization enough. Thus the election took place, with the result that on the first ballot Wimmer was chosen permanent abbot of Saint Vincent by a vote of thirty-nine to three. (One proxy vote was disqualified after being accidentally opened before balloting began.)[56]

The outcome was a decisive victory for Abbot Boniface who had feared that many of his monks had grown tired of his rule. Indeed, some of the younger priests had begun to question his leadership. They feared that by sending so many monks to distant missions, he was jeopardizing the security and future of the motherhouse in Pennsylvania. Nonetheless, when the matter came to a vote, virtually everyone agreed that Wimmer was the most qualified person to lead the community. It came as a profound shock, then, when the cardinal prefect of the Propaganda Fide communicated in December that the Holy See had voided the election. The Roman cardinals chided the chapter for proceeding without answers to the procedural questions submitted the previous April. They ruled that Wimmer had not been legally elected abbot of Saint Vincent for life and appointed him for another three-year term.[57] The Roman decision was discouraging for the community and humiliating for the abbot, but with no alternative available to them, the Pennsylvania monks acquiesced and, turning their attention to the missions, followed the advice of Abbot Angelo Pescetelli, who wrote: "You must, like a sturdy oak, spread your roots deeper and deeper, extending your branches farther and farther."[58]

Three years later the Holy See advised the Saint Vincent chapter that because of the unsettled political situation in the United States, which would make it difficult for all the priests in the far-flung missions to assemble at the motherhouse, the monks should postpone the election one more year. Meanwhile, Wimmer would remain abbot "at the pleasure of the Holy See."[59] For the second time the community's hopes of electing a permanent abbot were frustrated.

In September 1862 the capitulars again gathered at the motherhouse to hold an election. By now, however, the Keck controversy was in full flower, and many of the monks were of the opinion that Wimmer was not sufficiently enthusiastic about the reforms Keck and his adherents called for. With the help of Father Augustine Wirth, prior in Kansas, and Father Edward Hipelius, a Saint Vincent monk studying in Rome, some of the younger priests mounted a full-blown effort to deprive him of the abbacy. The election protocol approved by Rome assigned the responsibility of electing an abbot to clerical monks in solemn vows. Before the election could begin, however, Wirth produced a document, obtained by Hipelius in Rome, indicating that a recent decision by the Holy See in the case of abbatial elections in certain European monasteries gave electoral rights not only to clerical monks in solemn vows but to monks in simple vows as well. Wirth and his supporters demanded that the lay brothers also be allowed to vote. Since the lay brothers were the majority in the community, the Wirth faction knew that a block vote by them would carry the election, and they planned to convince the brothers to support the candidacy of either Father Alphonse Heimler or Wirth himself.[60]

The maneuver brought the proceedings to a halt. The capitulars who supported Wimmer were reluctant to continue with the election because they feared whatever decision they made—to include or not to include the lay brothers—would result in Rome's overturning for the second time their election of an abbot. They were concerned that if they did not permit the lay brothers to vote, they might be acting contrary to the wishes of the Holy See as expressed in the document produced by Hipelius and Wirth. On the other hand, they realized that if they did permit them to vote, it was likely that the lay brothers, aligned with the more fanatical members of the Keck faction and recently frustrated in their own efforts to obtain a more substantial voice in community decisions, would choose either

Heimler or Wirth, both of whom many priests in the community regarded as undesirable candidates. Heimler was a contentious, uncompromising individual who had alienated potential allies because of his transparent ambition, and Wirth was a secret alcoholic. Both seemed ready to promise the lay brothers greater involvement in community affairs in return for their support. The capitulars voted, therefore, to postpone the election yet again until they received guidance from Rome as to the right of simply professed monks to participate.

For the third time in five years the community had been thwarted in its attempt to elect a permanent abbot, but this time the reason for the impasse had rather to do with quarrels and divisions within the monastery than with procedural errors or Vatican directives.

A third controversy during this period of turmoil had to do with the Benedictine nuns who had come to America in 1852. While the conflict between Abbot Boniface and the nuns had no direct impact on the missionary and educational work of the monks at Saint Vincent, it was a matter serious enough to raise questions in Bavaria and Rome about Wimmer's judgment and leadership of the Benedictine mission and consequently added to the burdens of both abbot and community during the era of troubles. Because a number of historians have sufficiently detailed the story in recent years, no more than a summary treatment is necessary here.[61]

The first group of Benedictine women arrived at Saint Vincent from the Bavarian Priory of St. Walburga, Eichstätt, in July 1852. The Eichstätt community had been invited by Wimmer to participate in the Benedictine missionary efforts in America, and this first contingent of five Benedictine sisters regarded themselves (and were regarded by Wimmer) as partners with the monks in the work of educating German Catholic immigrants in the United States. Wimmer arranged for the five sisters to settle in St. Marys, Pennsylvania, where they established a monastery and opened a school.

Wimmer's plan was for the community in St. Marys eventually to attain independence from its motherhouse at Eichstätt and to develop along lines similar to those of the communities of monks. He even envisioned that the nuns' community in America would become exempt from episcopal control, a status that no European monastery of Benedictine women had enjoyed since the Middle Ages. Wimmer recognized, however, that America was *terra nova,* where even a conservative Bavarian Catholic like himself was not always bound to follow European precedents and traditions when pragmatic considerations suggested the need for innovation. Thus Wimmer assumed that exemption was possible for the Benedictine women in the United States, just as it had proven to be for the monks. His goal was to establish independent, exempt communities of Benedictine nuns who, like the communities of men, would follow the statutes of the Bavarian Benedictine Congregation, embrace missionary work and education as their principal apostolic activities, and be united with the communities of men within a single congregational structure under the authority of the abbot president of the American Cassinese Congregation.

Unfortunately for Wimmer, some of the nuns he had invited to the United States did not share this vision. Chief among those who disagreed was Mother Benedicta Riepp, superior in St. Marys. Riepp believed that the Benedictine communities of women should be exempt in their internal administrative and spiritual affairs not just from episcopal control but also (and especially) from control by Benedictine men, including the president of the American Cassinese Congregation. She sought greater autonomy for the nuns and came into conflict with Wimmer over whether the abbot of Saint Vincent had ultimate jurisdiction over the Benedictine sisters in the United States.

In the summer of 1857 Mother Benedicta left Pennsylvania and returned to Bavaria to seek support in her effort to clarify the limits of Wimmer's authority. With the assistance of Bishop George von Öttl of Eichstätt and Archbishop Karl August von Reisach, formerly archbishop of Munich and now a member of the Roman curia, she presented her case to the Holy See. In April 1858 Wimmer heard of Riepp's complaints against him from Cardinal Alessandro Barnabo, prefect of the Sacred Congregation for the Propagation of the Faith, and responded with a series of petitions to the Propaganda Fide. First, he asked that the convents in St. Marys, Erie, and Newark be recognized as independent priories and incorporated into the American Cassinese Congregation under the jurisdiction of the congregation's president.[62] Second, he urged that the sisters be permitted to make solemn vows without being obliged to adhere to the customary monastic enclosure. Third, he requested that they be allowed to teach in public and private schools; and finally, he proposed that on account of their teaching burdens, they be permitted to substitute the Little Office of the Blessed Virgin for the Benedictine Office in their community prayer.[63] His petition to Rome was part of his overall strategy to establish a unified Benedictine response to the exigencies of the American missions and, at the same time, to create for the nuns an institutional structure that would assure them independence from episcopal control and organize them in a manner consistent with Benedictine tradition and conducive to their work and monastic observance in the United States.

It took Rome more than a year to review the case, but finally, in December 1859, the Holy See handed down a decision. The decree reached America several weeks later, and from it Abbot Boniface learned that all of his most important petitions had been denied. Jurisdiction over the Benedictine nuns in America would henceforth rest not with the president of the American Cassinese Congregation but rather with the bishops of the three dioceses in which the sisters had settled. In addition, the sisters would no longer be bound to solemn but now only to simple vows. The decision settled the problem of *clausura* and the obligation to recite the Divine Office because as simply professed religious they were not bound to either.[64]

The Roman decision was a grave disappointment for Wimmer, not so much because he had been denied jurisdiction over the nuns but because he recognized that by refusing the Benedictine women in America the right to profess solemn vows and by placing them under the authority of the bishops, Rome had put them in the same category as contemporary diocesan sisterhoods and compromised their uniquely Benedictine identity.

Nonetheless, despite Wimmer's failure to incorporate the monasteries of Benedictine women into the American Cassinese Congregation, the monks of Saint Vincent continued to work closely with the sisters in the American missions. Indeed, the nuns' foundations closely tracked those of the monks, and by the end of the nineteenth century Benedictine women had established flourishing communities in most of the places where the monks had established priories. These included St. Marys (1852), Erie (1856), St. Cloud (1857), Newark (1857), Covington (1859), Chicago (1861), Atchison (1863), Richmond (1868), and Carrolltown (1870).

TWENTY-FIVE YEARS IN AMERICA

Virtually all the serious problems confronting the Saint Vincent community during the era of troubles were resolved by the middle of 1866, but the resolutions had not come without pain and great effort on the part of the monks and their energetic abbot. Wimmer had spent nineteen months in Munich and Rome attempting to "clean up a mess of ten years."[65] The result was a series of Roman decisions in 1865 and 1866 that addressed all the issues which had perplexed the Benedictines in Pennsylvania during the previous decade: resolution of the controversy over Paul Keck and his purported visions, the decree concerning the status of the lay brothers, and in 1866 confirmation of the earlier decision concerning the status of Benedictine nuns in the United States. As for the often postponed question of a permanent abbot, Propaganda officials decided against ordering another election and instead recommended to Pope Pius IX that in view of Wimmer's having "contributed to the faith in a wonderful way," the pope name him abbot of Saint Vincent for life. This the Holy Father did on July 27, 1866. Finally, to confirm and show its approval for the work of the American Benedictines during the previous twenty years, the Holy See raised the priory in Minnesota to the rank of an abbey.[66]

Thus when Wimmer returned to Saint Vincent at the end of September 1866, he brought the good news to the community that the troubles of a decade were behind them. The monks and students greeted him with joy. The students gathered logs from the surrounding woods and built huge bonfires all around the campus. The brothers placed candles in the windows of the monastery and college. When the midnight train arrived at the station in Latrobe, a delegation of priests met the abbot and escorted him in a triumphal procession back to Saint Vincent. As the abbot's carriage, surrounded by black-clad horsemen, climbed the hill to the abbey, the bonfires and candles were lit and the student band trumpeted a welcome. At the monastery gate Prior Rupert Seidenbusch greeted the abbot with a short speech, and the monks and students cheered his return. It was a dramatic and moving moment, but Wimmer was exhausted and after a few brief words of thanks, he urged everyone to go to bed. The next day he celebrated a pontifical High Mass for the community and later was guest of honor at a reception and dinner the monks prepared for him.[67]

The months that followed were busy ones at Saint Vincent. Not only was there work to be done consolidating and extending the missionary activities of the community, but also renewed attention had to be given to the schools and their academic programs. In November twelve Saint Vincent monks transferred their vows to the new abbey in Minnesota, and a month later they elected Father Rupert Seidenbusch, prior at Saint Vincent, as the second abbot in the American Cassinese Congregation.[68]

One of the most pressing needs in the schools was the development of an adequate faculty. In October Fathers Oswald Moosmüller, Adalbert Müller, Innocent Wolf, and Hilary Pfrängle departed for Rome to establish an American Benedictine house of studies in the Eternal City. Wimmer wrote that the priests were going to spend "three or perhaps four years in Rome, in order to qualify themselves as professors for our College," and he hoped to send others soon.[69] The Saint Vincent monks founded St. Elizabeth's House of Studies and pursued courses in philosophy and theology at the Sapienza University under the Dominicans. In addition, Moosmüller, the leader of the group, undertook historical studies in the Vatican Archives; Müller, a talented linguist, studied oriental languages; and Wolf studied mathematics and physics. In 1869 two more clerics from Saint Vincent—James Zilliox and Xavier Baltes—arrived at St. Elizabeth's to study philosophy and theology.

As the twenty-fifth anniversary of the founding of Saint Vincent monastery approached, the monks could look with pride at their accomplishments over the previous quarter-century. Wimmer wrote that upon the arrival of the monks in Pennsylvania,

> future prospects were naturally quite gloomy. I do not know whether, apart from me, even one of them had the firm expectation that we would bring a monastery into being. Despite many difficulties and dangers from within and without, however, the work we began went forward, flourished, and became consolidated once it obtained papal authorization. [Since then] it has spread mightily into eleven dioceses and eight states! Is it not wonderful how here also God is glorified by bringing into being a great work with insignificant means? I say a *great* work because if calamitous events don't disturb us, without any doubt our Order will spread all over America and through the care of souls and the teaching and training of priests will exercise a great influence on the population.[70]

It was for the care of souls and the teaching and training of priests, of course, that the Benedictines had come to America, and as the Order spread to distant states and territories, Benedictine parishes and schools multiplied proportionately. By 1871 there were two abbeys and one independent priory in the United States, and the American Benedictines were operating nineteen parishes and serving nearly thirty other congregations with nonresident pastors. Benedictine sisters taught in elementary schools at most of the parishes in Pennsylvania, Minnesota, Kansas, New Jersey, Kentucky, and Illinois, and the monks administered and taught in six secondary schools ("colleges") that they had established in Pennsylvania, Minnesota, Kansas, New Jersey, Kentucky, and Virginia. The total enrollment in the colleges was more than five hundred students, three hundred of whom were candidates for the Benedictine Order. In addition, major seminaries at the abbeys of Saint Vincent and St. Louis on the Lake (later called St. John's) prepared nearly sixty young men from a dozen American dioceses for the priesthood.[71]

At Saint Vincent itself there were fifty-nine priests, twenty-one clerics, ninety-eight lay brothers, and ten novices. The ecclesiastical seminary had twenty-one Benedictine clerics and fifteen diocesan seminarians studying for the priesthood. The college boasted 250 students, and priests from the abbey ministered to Catholics in six dioceses.

In the Diocese of Pittsburgh, priests from Saint Vincent were engaged in the pastoral care of ten thousand Catholics in Westmoreland, Indiana, Armstrong, Butler, and Allegheny counties. From the parish church at

Saint Vincent they held regular services at St. Xavier's Convent, St. Boniface Chapel on Chestnut Ridge, Holy Trinity Church in Ligonier, St. Matthew's Church in Saltsburg, Immaculate Conception Church in New Germany, Assumption Church in Penn, and the small Catholic chapel in Irwin. From time to time they assisted at other places, including Pittsburgh itself.

At St. Benedict's Priory in Carrolltown four priests and seven brothers served a large parish of two thousand souls, and Benedictine sisters taught one hundred pupils in the parish school. Priests from Carrolltown held regular services at St. Joseph's Mission at Hart's Sleeping Place, St. Lawrence Church in St. Lawrence (Glen Connell), St. Boniface Church in St. Boniface, and St. Nicholas Church in Nicktown.

Other Benedictine parishes with resident pastors in the Pittsburgh Diocese included St. Mary's Priory, Allegheny City, where four priests had charge of a large parish and several chaplaincies, Blessed Sacrament Church in Greensburg, St. Peter's Church in Butler, St. Bernard's Church in Indiana, St. Joseph's Church in Johnstown, and St. Mary's Church in Cambria City. In the parochial schools attached to the Benedictine parishes in the Diocese of Pittsburgh there were fourteen hundred pupils.

In the Diocese of Erie, Saint Vincent monks staffed priories in St. Marys and the episcopal city. At the priory in St. Marys five priests and eleven brothers worked in a parish of four thousand souls and served a thousand more Catholics at nine mission stations in three counties. The Benedictine sisters taught 140 pupils in the parish school of St. Marys. St. Mary's Priory, Erie, had three priests who served a twenty-four-hundred-member congregation and a parish school with 500 pupils directed by the Benedictine sisters. One priest from the Erie priory also served as pastor of St. John's Church in the see city.

In the Diocese of Newark five priests and two brothers were stationed at St. Mary's Priory in Newark and administered a parish with thirty-seven hundred souls and a high school with 50 students. Monks from St. Mary's Priory also staffed St. Benedict's Church in Newark, St. Walburga's Church in Elizabeth City, and St. Mary's Church in Stony Hill. The Benedictine sisters in New Jersey taught eight hundred pupils in the two parishes at Newark and in St. Walburga's Parish, Elizabeth City.

In the Diocese of Covington, four priests were assigned to St. Joseph's Priory in the see city. They conducted services for a congregation of over two thousand members in Covington and attended six other parishes, with a total of twenty-two hundred parishioners, in five Kentucky counties. The

Benedictine nuns in Covington taught seven hundred children in four of the Kentucky parishes served by the Benedictine priests.

In the Diocese of Richmond, two priests were stationed at St. Mary's Church, Richmond. They had charge of eleven hundred German Catholics in the city, conducted a high school of 50 students, and operated a parish school with 160 pupils taught by the Benedictine sisters. They also served a mission in Louisa County, Virginia.

In the Diocese of Chicago five priests were stationed at St. Joseph's Church, Chicago, and had the pastoral care of more than five thousand souls and eight mission stations in four Illinois counties. Five hundred pupils, taught by a community of Benedictine nuns, attended St. Joseph Parochial School. The Benedictine church and school in Chicago had been destroyed by the great fire of 1871, but at the time of Saint Vincent's silver jubilee Prior Leander Schnerr, a future archabbot of Saint Vincent, was busily organizing the congregation's efforts to raise money for reconstruction.[72]

By 1871, principally under the direction of the community's two architects, Brothers Stephen Weber and Ewald Horn, a quadrangle of buildings at Saint Vincent had been constructed on the north side of the abbey church. Lower down the hill on which stood the church, monastery, and college were the barn, stables, brewery, gristmill, sawmill, printery, and workshops of the brothers. Each of these buildings, except the church, Sportsman's Hall, and the original parish house which the monks found when they arrived at Saint Vincent, had been constructed by the lay brothers, who had charge of every aspect of construction from the cutting of timber and the making of bricks to the placement of crosses on the turrets. Saint Vincent was a busy and vibrant center of work and prayer in 1871, and the monks had a great deal to celebrate on the twenty-fifth anniversary of their coming to America.

The jubilee celebration took place on October 24, and present for the festivities were Bishop Michael Domenec of Pittsburgh and two neighboring pastors, Fathers James Ambrose Stillinger of Blairsville and Jerome Kearney of Latrobe. That morning Abbot Boniface celebrated a solemn pontifical Mass, and three of the four clerical students who, twenty-five years before, had been invested as novices at the same altar, assisted in the sanctuary. Father Benedict Haindl, claustral prior in Minnesota, served the abbot as archpriest; Father Celestine Englbrecht, conventual prior of St. Mary's Priory, Allegheny City, was master of ceremonies, and Father Charles Geyerstanger served as chaplain to Abbot Rupert Seidenbusch who had come from Minnesota for the celebration. The pioneer brothers Andrew Binder, Jacob Raitmayer, Engelbert Nusser, and Conrad Reinbolt assisted in the sanctuary.

Bishop Michael Domenec delivered the anniversary sermon and praised the Benedictines for their contributions to the Diocese of Pittsburgh and the American Church. He said that "the great success of the sons of St. Benedict is my success. The honor given them is my honor. Saint Vincent is already called the 'Montecassino of America'! May it become a similar light in the New World as the home of St. Benedict was in the Old World!"[73]

The mass was followed by a banquet in the monastery refectory attended by lay as well as clerical guests. A reporter from the *Pittsburgh Catholic,* a student at the college in the 1850s, was present and wrote that

> even in the years 1853–1856, when your correspondent had the honor—then thought a misfortune—of being one of St. Vincent's boys, such a change [as has come about at St. Vincent] was considered impossible. In those days of "Charley-come-back" and what we expected to be soup, the monks fared still worse. I don't think that Father Superior, now abbot, would have considered it a misfortune to the house if all the boys would have run away. The trials of the infant colony were terrific and required more than human courage and perseverance to overcome them. But by the blessing of God he has overcome them, and now finds himself at the head of a flourishing Order of zealous, hardworking men, and of a College holding a foremost rank among such institutions in the United States.[74]

To memorialize the occasion, the jubilee committee initiated plans for the construction of a bell tower in the monastery quadrangle, and Father Oswald Moosmüller was commissioned to write a history of the American Benedictines.[75] The fire in Chicago, however, which had destroyed St. Joseph's Priory and Church, cast a pall over the festivities, and Abbot Boniface wrote that he had decided to permit only a "family feast" on account of it. He had ignored the promptings of the community and invited only a few special friends. Soon after the celebration ended, he left for Chicago to see what could be salvaged there. The work the Benedictines had set out to do was still not completed, and there was really little time for the "frivolous" merrymaking that some of their well-wishers would foist upon them.[76]

COLLEGE AND SEMINARY

By 1871 Saint Vincent College had developed into a healthy and thriving institution that prepared young men not only for the priesthood but also

Bell tower at Saint Vincent, built in 1871 to commemorate the twenty-fifth anniversary of the arrival of the Benedictines in the United States. For many years a landmark at Saint Vincent, it was destroyed by fire in 1963.

for advanced studies in medicine and law. Another important goal of the college was to provide practical training for students interested in pursuing careers in business. On April 18, 1870, the school received its charter, granted by an act of the Pennsylvania legislature and signed into law by Governor John W. Geary. This charter established "a college for the education of youth in the various branches of science, literature, and the arts by the name and style of St. Vincent college in the State of Pennsylvania" and authorized that "the president and professors for the time being of the said college shall have power to grant and confer such degrees in the arts and sciences to such students of the college and others when by their proficiency in learning, professional eminence or other meritorious distinction they shall be entitled thereto as they may see proper or as are granted in other colleges or universities in the United States, and to grant to graduates or persons on whom such degrees may be conferred diplomas or certificates as is usual in colleges and universities."[77]

The charter of 1870, drafted by several Catholic legislators who had befriended the Benedictines, was a remarkable document which, in effect, gave unlimited power to Saint Vincent to bestow any academic degrees that other colleges and universities in the nation granted. The college used this power with restraint, though it did award several master's and doctor's degrees in the course of the next fifty years. The usual degree, however, was the bachelor of arts, the first of which were granted to Maximilian Betzel of Staten Island, New York, and Michael Bergrath of Westphalia, Michigan, in 1871. Also at the 1871 commencement William A. Sweeney of Wilbur, New York, received the first "master of accounts" degree granted by the college. According to the college catalogue, the bachelor of arts degree was conferred upon students who succcessfully passed examinations "in all the languages and sciences taught in the classical course." Those who graduated with a bachelor of arts could "obtain the degree of Master of Arts by devoting two years to a learned profession, or to literary or scientific studies."

There were now four clearly defined programs of study offered by the college. In the first of these, the ecclesiastical course, eight Benedictine clerics and eleven diocesan seminarians were enrolled in 1871. The diocesan students came from Pittsburgh, Erie, Philadelphia, New York, Milwaukee, and Toledo. A student normally began the ecclesiastical course at age nineteen or twenty, although older men were sometimes accepted if recommended by a bishop or accepted by the monastic chapter. The ecclesiastical course offered a three-year program of theology to young men who had completed their "classical" studies either at Saint Vincent or in some other

Scholastics at Saint Vincent, 1869. The bearded priest in the left foreground is Father Ignatius Trueg, O.S.B. (1827–1910), director of the Scholasticate.

Catholic institution. Benedictine students were required to undergo a year's novitiate before beginning the course. The curriculum consisted of classes in moral theology, dogmatic theology, sacred scripture, biblical languages, liturgy, and ecclesiastical history. Students who were native English speakers were expected to learn German, and native German speakers, English. All had to know Latin and German thoroughly, for theology classes were taught in those languages. In the 1860s and 1870s there was still no formal administrative division between the college and seminary, though the ecclesiastical course was clearly a separate program for advanced students. It would later be detached from the college and become Saint Vincent Seminary. But even in the 1870s the ecclesiastical course was normally referred to as "the seminary."

The second program of study was the "classical course" or Latin school. The classical course consisted of a six-year program of study encompassing the traditional liberal arts disciplines taught in Bavarian gymnasiums. The principal disciplines were classical and modern languages (Latin, Greek, English, and German), history, mathematics, science, music, and religion. The fifth year of the classical course was devoted to rhetoric and the sixth to philosophy. Optional courses in French, Italian, Spanish, music, drawing, and painting were available. Students in the classical course ranged in age from thirteen to twenty. Most were candidates for the priesthood, though some planned after graduation to enter universities and professional schools in order to study medicine and law. Those among the classical students who desired to enter the Benedictine Order lived, worked, recreated, and prayed together in the "scholasticate," but their program of studies was the same as that of the other classical students.

The commercial course was the third division at Saint Vincent College in the 1870s. It provided a three-year course of study for students who desired practical preparation for careers in business, but there was also a strong liberal arts component in the curriculum. Boys in the commercial course were of the same age as those in the classical course and often attended the same classes. They studied modern languages (English, German, and French), mathematics, history, bookkeeping, penmanship, geography, natural philosophy, chemistry, and religion. In 1871 there were 116 students enrolled in the classical course and 69 in the commercial course.

A fourth educational program operated by the monks in Pennsylvania (and part of the "college") was the elementary course. The Benedictines had established this school shortly after their arrival at Saint Vincent in order to afford children from poor families in the neighborhood, "especially those of German descent, an excellent opportunity of acquiring a thorough knowledge of elementary principles of the English and German languages." Its curriculum embraced the study of reading, spelling, writing, religion, penmanship, arithmetic, and geography. In 1871 there were twenty-three pupils (called "minims") between the ages of ten and thirteen enrolled in this course.[78]

The Saint Vincent faculty and administration in the 1870–1871 academic year numbered twenty-two professors of whom all but one was a monk. Lay professor Joseph Maurice Schwab, a Bavarian-born instructor of music, was the exception.[79] The faculty included young monks who would later become leaders at Saint Vincent and in some of the independent abbeys founded from it. Among them were Innocent Wolf (first abbot of St. Benedict's Abbey, Atchison, Kansas), Andrew Hintenach (second archabbot of Saint Vincent), Hilary Pfrängle (second abbot of St. Mary's Abbey, Newark, New Jersey), Leo Haid (first abbot of Maryhelp Abbey and bishop of North Carolina), Benedict Menges (first abbot of St. Bernard's Abbey, Alabama), Rhabanus Gutman (leader of the Benedictine mission to Colorado that became Holy Cross Abbey), and Wenceslaus Kocarnik (leader of the mission to the Czech Catholics in Nebraska that was later transferred to Illinois where it became St. Procopius Abbey). The president of the college in 1871 was Father Alphonse Heimler, a brilliant but tempestuous man who had received his degree in philosophy from the University of Munich before coming to Saint Vincent in 1854. Heimler was renowned for the breadth, if not the depth, of his learning. He was an accomplished Latinist who, as president, insisted that the students in the ecclesiastical and classical courses be proficient in reading, writing, and speaking Latin.

In 1859 Wimmer had sent Heimler to study physics and astronomy at Georgetown College where he earned a master's degree in 1860. He was the first Benedictine to obtain a graduate degree from an American university. Upon his return to Saint Vincent Heimler expected to be named president of the college, but when Wimmer failed to appoint him to the post immediately, he allied himself with those in the congregation who opposed the abbot and for a while promoted himself as Wimmer's successor. In 1862 he joined the successful effort by Father Augustine Wirth and some of the younger monks to thwart Wimmer's election as lifetime abbot of Saint Vincent. It is a measure of the abbot's tolerance and patience with the talented young monks who often challenged his leadership that shortly afterwards Heimler was appointed to the position he longed for, a position he held for the next ten years.[80]

Other Benedictine professors at Saint Vincent in the late 1860s and early 1870s included Father Edward Hipelius, the first Saint Vincent monk to be sent for advanced studies to Europe, where he took courses in hermeneutics (sacred scripture) in England and received his doctorate in canon law from the Sapienza in Rome, and Father Ulric Spöttl, who had studied philosophy and theology at the universities of Munich and Würzburg before entering the novitiate at Saint Vincent. Besides Heimler, Hipelius, and Spöttl, the monks teaching at Saint Vincent in 1871 had all received their postsecondary educations in the ecclesiastical course of the college in Pennsylvania. In many cases professors in the college were clerics working as part-time instructors in the classical and commercial courses while they completed their theological studies in the ecclesiastical course. Wimmer complained that the Benedictine professors during this period were on the whole academically undistinguished. He recognized the monks' need for more thorough intellectual training and for that reason established St. Elizabeth's House of Studies in Rome where Fathers Oswald Moosmüller, Adalbert Müller, Innocent Wolf, and Hilary Pfrängle lived and studied from 1866 to 1870. Other Saint Vincent monks who received European educations during the 1860s and 1870s included Cyril Elder and William Walter, who studied theology and history at the University of Munich; Xavier

Baltes and James Zilliox, who studied theology and sacred scripture first with the Dominicans at Rome and then with the Jesuits at Innsbruck; and Gerard Pilz, Bonaventure Ostendarp, and Cosmas Wolf (a lay brother), who studied art at the Royal Bavarian Academy in Munich.[81]

The academic year at Saint Vincent began during the first week of September and finished at the end of June. It consisted of two sessions of five months each, at the conclusion of which an examination of all the classes was made and reports sent home to the parents of the students "to inform them of the conduct, health, and improvement of their sons or wards." When a student presented himself for admission, which could be granted at any time during the year, he was examined and placed in a class "for which his previous attainments may have fitted him." Those coming to the college from other institutions were required to produce satisfactory recommendations from the faculties of those institutions.[82]

Students in the college were recruited primarily from those dioceses in which the Benedictines had parishes. The administration placed special emphasis on providing the means for poor boys to study for the priesthood at Saint Vincent. "It used to be said that American boys had no inclination for the priesthood," Wimmer wrote.

> But this is not true. The sons of wealthy parents, of course, seldom dedicate themselves to the religious life, but this is general. The poor, however, especially in large cities do so if they can find the opportunity. [The poor] frequently find it difficult to achieve independent positions in the populated areas. It is easier for them in the country districts. Thus we recruit mostly from our city parishes, where we select the best and most talented boys from the school for ourselves. All the orders do the same, as do the bishops. . . . We have more candidates for our Order than for the secular clergy. This scarcely needs justification. But in the end the proportion adjusts itself, for some of our scholastics leave before entering the novitiate or making profession and become secular priests. It is not uncommon for them to make profession but leave the Order before solemn profession or give such indications of a lack of a religious vocation that we do not admit them to solemn vows but turn them over to the secular clergy. In this way we have sent very many secular priests to the bishops.[83]

Two such candidates for the Benedictine Order who left the scholasticate in the 1860s and entered the secular priesthood were John A. Watterson of Blairsville, Pennsylvania, and Joseph A. Rademacher of Westphalia, Michigan. In 1880 Watterson was named bishop of Columbus, Ohio, and in 1883 Rademacher became bishop of Nashville, Tennessee, and ten years later assumed leadership of the Diocese of Fort Wayne, Indiana.[84]

The annual registration fee at Saint Vincent was $5, and tuition (which included "board, bedding, washing and mending of linen") was $180 per year. Students who took chemistry and "natural philosophy" (general science) were charged an additional $10 a term, as were those who opted to take courses in drawing and painting. The cost of instruction in music, French, Italian, and Spanish was set by the individual professors of these courses. There was also a graduation fee of $5. Many of the students were too poor to pay all the costs of their education, but if they showed signs of a vocation to the priesthood, they were charged lower fees or even educated gratis.

STUDENT LIFE

College regulations stipulated that all students, whether Catholic or Protestant, attend morning Mass and daily religious devotions ("for the sake of order and uniformity"). The use of tobacco was not allowed, but this particular regulation seems to have been honored in the breach rather than strictly observed since student memoirs of the period mention frequent escapes to the "Cherry Path" on the edge of the campus for conversation, walks, and smokes. Students were strictly forbidden from going "out of bounds," i.e., off campus, except in groups organized by senior prefects and authorized by the president. They were also prohibited from having money in their possession, though moderate amounts of pocketmoney sent by parents were distributed by the college treasurer "as prudence may suggest or occasion require." Letters, papers, and books sent and received by the students were subject to inspection "by the President or his substitute."

Extracurricular activities were limited during the first quarter-century of the college's existence to a few popular pastimes. Student organizations included the Saint Vincent's Debating Society, founded in 1861 "to afford the students of Rhetoric and Belles-Lettres practical exercises in elocution and dialectics"; the Students' Library Association, whose purpose was "to encourage good reading, and to procure the most interesting and useful works of modern writers"; the Senior Dramatic Association, which performed two or three dramas a year but whose rehearsals were "held during recreation hours only"; the Sodality of the Most Blessed Sacrament, which endeavored "to foster and promote tender devotion to Jesus in the Holy Sacrament of the Altar, by daily visits and semi-monthly Communions"; and the Students' Altar Society of St. Joseph, whose special aim was "to inspire its members with filial love for the holy Catholic Church and its ministers, and to assist in adorning and beautifying the Altar in the Students' chapel."

Students diverted themselves with organized hikes through the countryside (including fall and spring treks to the monastery property on Chestnut Ridge, ten miles away, for overnight campouts), occasional trips to Latrobe, swimming and ice skating on the Loyalhanna Creek, and sports activities which were highlighted by baseball in the spring.

Baseball was introduced at Saint Vincent shortly after the Civil War and became wildly popular. Organized and managed by Benedictine clerics like Leo Haid and James Zilliox, college teams played endless rounds of intramural games and challenged local teams from Latrobe, Youngstown, and Greensburg. The college club was named Excelsior and the scholastics' team, Eureka. These were the days when "the game was for runs and not [a] pitchers' battle," and scores were usually in the double digits. On May 6, 1868, for example, the Excelsiors defeated the Mutuals of Greensburg by a score of fifty-two to thirty-nine.[85]

Despite the college's relative isolation in the rural farmlands of Westmoreland County, students at Saint Vincent in the fourth quarter of the nineteenth century found themselves in the midst of a rich cultural ambience that the monks had devoted considerable effort and expense to bring from Bavaria to western Pennsylvania. Art, music, drama, and literature all played important roles in student life. Boniface Wimmer himself set the tone for this development in 1852 when he wrote the Ludwig Missionsverein that "a monastic school that does not strive to advance art as much as studies and religious instruction will be deficient in its work."[86] From the beginning the academic program at Saint Vincent accentuated the artistic and cultural heritage of Catholic Bavaria, especially in the fields of painting and music.

With the assistance of Father Joseph Ferdinand Müller, treasurer of the Ludwig Missionsverein, the monastery and college received hundreds of works of art between 1847 and 1851 from benefactors in Bavaria. The majority of these came from the collection of Father Pius Reiser, a diocesan priest of the Munich cathedral chapter who had been a seminary classmate of Boniface Wimmer's in Regensburg, but others came from the royal collection of King Ludwig I. Because of these and other donations from Europe, the school's art department was especially well equipped. The first instructor of painting and drawing at Saint Vincent was Father Luke Wimmer, the founder's nephew, who studied art in Munich before coming to America and entering the monastery at Saint Vincent in 1847. Later, Fathers Gerard Pilz (1834–1891) and Bonaventure Ostendarp (1856–1912) went to Italy and Bavaria to study art and returned to teach in the college. The French-born

Father John Sommer (1815–86) taught drawing and painting to Saint Vincent students for nearly a quarter-century.[87]

The study of literature was also stressed, and students were urged to read deeply if not widely. The focus was on Latin and German classics, with few books of English literature and no modern fiction reading encouraged. Creating a library at Saint Vincent was one of the first concerns of the early monks. The nucleus of the library was formed by the textbooks and reference books Wimmer and his companions brought with them in 1846. In 1851 the college and monastery received a shipment of six large crates of books donated by Father Heinrich Brestlmayer, pastor in Ried, Austria. Father Joseph Müller was also instrumental in obtaining books for the Saint Vincent library from the Bavarian National Library, and donations were made by many others, including King Ludwig I and Bishop Gregory Ziegler of Linz, Austria. In 1851 Wimmer wrote Archbishop von Reisach of Munich that because of the generosity of Bavarian patrons, the library in Pennsylvania contained the works of "almost all the Latin and Greek authors of prominence." The theology, philosophy, and history sections were especially well supplied and contained books of "both old and new authors and books essential for the study of Scripture."[88] In addition, the library owned a collection of incunabula donated by King Ludwig and other wealthy contributors in Bavaria. Visitors to Saint Vincent often took note of the book collection the monks had gathered. The Austrian priest Joseph Salzman, who founded the Salesian seminary in Milwaukee, spent several days at the monastery in 1850, and afterwards wrote that the library was "well-stocked and considering that the books were acquired by donations, they represent a good selection, particularly in history and patrology."[89] By 1860 the library contained over twelve thousand volumes, and it continued to grow during the nineteenth century through donations and purchases.[90]

Musical activity was another important source of cultural diversion and entertainment for the students. Under the direction of Joseph Maurice Schwab, the college's Munich-born *Kappelmeister* who lived and worked at Saint Vincent from 1851 until his death in 1875, a student orchestra, choir, and brass band were formed and gave regular concerts throughout the year. The musical level of the college and monastery during the 1860s and 1870s was remarkably high, and performances included works by Joseph and Michael Haydn, Handel, Mozart, Weber, Cherubini, Beethoven, Rossini, and Strauss. Jesuit Father Hugh Erly, a student at the college in the 1850s, asserted that the choir and orchestra at Saint Vincent were the first in the United States to perform Mozart's Twelfth Mass and Requiem.[91] Monks and students joined together to form ensembles that presented string quartets, overtures, piano chamber music, flute concertos, violin concertos, marches, and waltzes. Dozens of motets and Masses by German composers were sung in the abbey church on Sundays and holy days, and comic opera was also performed during the academic year.

Over twenty-five hundred separate pieces of music, in printed and handwritten scores, survive in the college music department, testifying to the importance and richness of the musical tradition at Saint Vincent during the nineteenth century. Some of them, like the eighteen pieces by German composer Joseph Matthias Kracher (1752–1830) and several works of Michael Haydn, are unique to the Saint Vincent collection. In describing the musical activity at Saint Vincent during the nineteenth century, musicologist Fred J. Moleck observed that the college choir's

> repertoire of Haydn and Mozart Masses and nineteenth-century motets and Masses presents [it] as an organization that might have equalled any European cathedral choir. An impressive factor that surrounds the choir and orchestra is the setting in which they performed. Uprooted from their Bavarian household, the St. Vincent monks promulgated a section of nineteenth-century culture in an American setting removed from metropolitan centers. These men performed music that won acclaim only from a passing visitor or an interested priest. They performed their Masses and motets within the spirit of the monastic life and a monastic school. As monks of the Order of St. Benedict, their interest in music flowed from their duties to the office and choir; music was a means of enhancing the liturgical functions of the church and of supplying more solemnity to the feast by providing fitting concerts later in the day.[92]

The June commencement exercises (called "exhibitions") became popular occasions for students to display their musical and dramatic talents. Special trains were chartered to bring music and theatre lovers from Pittsburgh to Saint Vincent where they were treated to day-long entertainments. The Saint Vincent barn was transformed into an auditorium and stage, and student performers presented such plays as Cardinal Wiseman's *The Hidden Gem* and the two-act German operetta *Das Steckenpferd* by Georg Willenborg to appreciative audiences. In an age when oratorical skills were highly valued, the musical and dramatic performances were interspersed with formal student orations, debates, and dialogues in English, German, and Latin. Among the topics offered were "The Advantages of Education," "The Germans in America," "The Pedants: A Dialogue," "Die Standeswahl: A German Dialogue," "Eine gute Erziehung ist besser als Reichthum," "Deutsche Literatur," "De Metaphysicis quibus corporum existentia explicatur," and "Strophilium ad Georgium Washington."[93]

An interesting account of student life at Saint Vincent during this period survives in the "fugitive recollections" of Henry Ganss, who attended the college from 1868 to 1878. Ganss became a priest in the Diocese of Harrisburg and gained a modest reputation as a Reformation scholar and a composer of sacred music. In his memoirs, written about 1909 in the florid style of the period, he said that in the 1870s Saint Vincent was an unprepossessing place whose buildings

> were few in number; space being a constant and crying demand. Architecturally they could lay claim to no beauty, not even symmetry. Simple to the point of ugliness in architectural character; meagre to the point of hardship in academic comforts; primitive to the point of destitution in class room equipment; medieval from the standpoint of hygienics,—they were all the same filled by such an enthusiastic, ambitious, hardworking body of intelligent students,—encouraged by such a devoted, zealous, helpful, competent body of professors, that I frequently since strengthened the unsettled conviction in my mind, that the years from 1868 to 1873, were years of such a striving of intellectual activity, mutually fostered by the energetic and purposeful body of professors and students, as to eclipse all the subsequent years I spent there.

Ganss, who entered the classical course at age thirteen and completed the ecclesiastical course nine years later, described in ironic detail many of the "characters" who made up the college community of his day. Pride of place was enjoyed by Father Alphonse Heimler, president of the college until 1872. According to Ganss, "no man could be more suave and gracious in manner, more urbane and presentable in company, more deeply concerned about the physical comforts and mental helps of his students" than Father Alphonse. But Heimler's personality was marred by a deep flaw, namely "his own misanthropic, drastic temperament, no doubt ascribable to pathological conditions." Ganss observed that if the easily angered president had been able to "divest himself of his irascibility, which was chronic," and add "temperamental poise to his otherwise splendidly-rounded character," he would have been an ideal educator. Alas, that was not the case. Everyone at Saint Vincent, at one time or other, experienced the heat of his anger. "Even the saintly Father Abbot, in my hearing, pleading for a poor fellow who smuggled contraband drinkables into the college, received such a harsh and defiant excoriation, that I could hardly trust my ears."[94] And yet during Heimler's decade-long tenure as president, the college developed into a creditable academic institution and obtained its state charter to grant degrees.

The lay brothers, in their own humble and kindly way, exercised a moderating influence on the atmosphere of rigid discipline demanded by Father

Alphonse. For twenty years Brothers Gothard Nadermann and Frank Stelzle were the cooks at Saint Vincent, honored and loved by the students. Their kitchen was a place of escape for homesick and unhappy boys who needed a refuge from the disciplinary excesses of prefects and faculty. Brothers Gothard and Frank would lend a sympathetic ear to their problems while plying them with off-hour portions of soup and slices of the delicious Saint Vincent bread. Brother Stephen Weber, one of the pioneers of 1846, had charge of the beer cellar and performed the same acts of kindness and charity as the cooks. Understandably, Brother Stephen's domain was "a favorite haunt of the students," but Ganss noted "in spite of a pretty liberal consumption of beer by the students . . . drunkenness only effected an entrance into the college precincts and grounds through smuggled goods." Brother Bonaventure Gaul's "studio, cobbler shop, and emergency hospital" was also a place where students could go. Ganss wrote that "the good brother was real clever at woodcarving, and himself surveyed his artistic creations with unfeigned admiration; he repaired shoes at fabulously cheap prices and long credit; his hospital experience during the Civil War made him quite adept in setting broken bones and reducing slight fractures" which usually occurred in the winter on the frozen surface of the Loyalhanna Creek and in the spring on the baseball field.

Another honored "character" at the college during Ganss's time was Professor Joseph Maurice Schwab. Singularly unattractive in his personal appearance—with "a face florid to the point of inflammation; a drooping gray mustache; a nose almost bulbous; his walk, in spite of his inseparable cane, shambling; his defective eyes screened by glasses of heavy lenses; partially paralyzed, which not only impaired his left side but also caused involuntary salivation; his knowledge of English most elementary"—Schwab, "the most capable musician the institution ever had," was universally loved among the students. When Ganss arrived at Saint Vincent in 1868, Professor Schwab recognized his musical talents and gave him special instruction that emphasized fundamental technique and artistic discipline. Ganss's first lesson was brief but memorable. "The short-sighted old man surveyed me critically from head to foot, made a few inquiries about my previous studies, examined my hands with some care, laconically stated that nature had adapted me for a *Klavierspieler oder Taschendieb* (pianist or pickpocket) . . . and asked me to sit down at the rubber covered square piano and play—a scale." The boy was eager to demonstrate his dexterity by playing several difficult pieces he had brought from home, but Schwab insisted on the scale and "dutifully pinioned me down to scales, and nothing but scales—

for three years." Thus Professor Schwab made him return to the basics. "My status as a prodigy was fixed."

Ganss remembered with fondness the wonderfully rich musical environment at Saint Vincent during the 1870s. An especially memorable part of that environment was the string quartet formed by four Benedictine faculty members: Nepomucene Jaeger, Raymond Daniel, Cornelius Eckl, and John Sommer. All of them were excellent musicians, but Ganss reserved his highest praise for Father John Sommer—"John the Superb, man of culture and refinement, true priest and real gentleman, born artist and exemplary monk . . . *Nihil tetigit quod non ornavit"* (everything he touched turned to beauty). "Many a time I crept into the deep doorway leading to the kitchen opposite the Band Room, and feasted my ears on the strains that were then as ravishing as any performance of the Joachim or Kneissel Quartet was in after life. It may sound strange, even incredible, but I venture to state that today, after the lapse of forty-one years, I can give the notation of some of the themes I heard at those rehearsals!"

Students in Ganss's day came principally from Pennsylvania, but the states of New York, New Jersey, and Ohio also provided many. Among those Ganss remembered were Max Betzel from New York City, who had "an overweening fondness for the German classical drama"; Al Bachman from Buffalo, New York, who was a "bright student but irrepressible practical joker"; Francis X. Reuss from Columbia, Pennsylvania, "a splendid singer, promoter of theatricals, and the subject of many an exciting college escapade," who went on to become a professor of music and biographer of Abbot James Zilliox, first abbot of St. Marys Abbey, Newark; John Ulrich from Brooklyn, New York, "one of Brother Stephen's most frequent visitors," who "wound up . . . becoming a discalced Capuchin"; Henry Hesse from Brooklyn, "of quick mind and temper, who lapsed into a medical career"; Barney McNeirney from Easton, Pennsylvania, whose "jaunty walk, geometrically parted hair, Lord Dundreary whiskers . . . were the admiration of the rustic female world"; Hoppy O'Brien from Ashland, Pennsylvania, "whose attempts at singing were usually as commendable as the results were disastrous"; Joe Bruns from Westphalia, Missouri, "lean, lank, cadaverous, the 'Knight of the Sorrowful Figure'"; Lawrence Flick from Carrolltown, Pennsylvania, who became a nationally renowned medical doctor and devoted the rest of his life to helping those afflicted with tuberculosis; and Joe Hanselman from Brooklyn, NewYork, whose "decadence grew apace with years until he became a Jesuit, nor did it stop there until he became Provincial of the New York–Baltimore Province." Of these and other

Saint Vincent College "minims" in 1883. Minims were boys between the ages of ten and thirteen preparing to enter the college's secondary school. The priests, from left to right, are Leonard Walter, O.S.B. (1857–1936), professor of Latin; Mark Kirchner, O.S.B. (1856–93), chief disciplinarian and professor of mathematics; Hilary Pfrängle, O.S.B. (1843–1909), president of the college and later abbot of St. Mary's Abbey, Newark, New Jersey; Leo Haid, O.S.B. (1849–1924), college chaplain and later abbot of Belmont Abbey, North Carolina; and William Hein, O.S.B. (1867–1918), prefect of the minim department.

Saint Vincent students of the 1860s and 1870s, Ganss says: "On the whole a jollier, better natured, or more studious body of men could not be thrown together, and in spite of occasional friskiness, deviltry, and student pranks, usually at the expense of the Director, real hard work was done and a high mark of scholarship attained."

The "golden years" Ganss wrote of were marked by significant changes at the college. Father Alphonse Heimler resigned as president in 1872, and Father Hilary Pfrängle, who had earned his doctorate at the Sapienza in Rome, replaced him. At this time the title of president was assumed by Abbot Boniface Wimmer, and Pfrängle was named "director." But for all practical purposes the day-to-day administration of the college was in the hands of the director, while Wimmer and his abbatial successors retained general control over academic and financial policy in their position as president.

Pfrängle was the first American-born monk to lead the college, and he assumed the directorship at a time when a growing number of other American-born Benedictines were becoming influential members of the faculty. This changing of the guard from Bavarian to American leadership had important ramifications for the students. Ganss referred to the Bavarians as "severe taskmasters" whose approach to discipline was characterized by "wrath and punishment" and had a good deal of "military precision" about it. While the Bavarians "ruled by fear and respect," the Americans under Pfrängle ruled "by reverence and affection." The new regime understood "the spirit and foibles of the American boy. On the whole the prefects were exemplary men, distinguished alike for their sense of duty and obligation of piety" and their ability to handle "the skittish Yankee." Father Hilary (born in Butler, Pennsylvania) "could be approached without your heart sticking in your throat." Father Leo Haid (born in Westmoreland County, Pennsylvania) "had nothing of leonine ferocity about him." Father Dominic Block (a native of East Orange, New Jersey) was "from the first . . . one of the boys." And Father Lawrence Haas (who grew up in Erie, Pennsylvania) was "a man of much personal charm, deep piety and deserved popularity." To be sure, German language and German culture continued to exercise strong influence in the monastery and school at Saint Vincent, but by the mid-1870s the English language and American culture were beginning to shape the changes that would mark the future of the abbey and college.

MISSIONS SOUTH

Despite extensive pre–Civil War activities, the Saint Vincent community did not undertake major missionary work again until more than a decade after the conflict ended. In the interim it was necessary to consolidate the work they had begun earlier as well as to recover from the effects of the nation's postwar economic slump. When missionary activities did get underway again, however, it was with the same energy that had marked the first period. Now, though, instead of west, the Pennsylvania monks turned south, to the devastated states of the old Confederacy.

Monks from Saint Vincent had been working in the South since 1858 when they had accepted Bishop George A. Carrell's invitation to take charge of the German parish in Covington, Kentucky. In 1859 the chapter had sent missionaries to San José in Texas; in 1860 Father Leonard Mayer was assigned to Richmond, and in 1861 Father Emmeran Bliemel went to Nashville. In each of these cases the parishes the Saint Vincent Benedictines accepted consisted of German-speaking congregations. But now they began to consider requests to establish missions among exclusively English-speaking Catholic congregations in the South, including missions to the freed black slaves. The new phase of expansion would take the Pennsylvania monks to North Carolina, Alabama, Georgia, and Florida.

In August 1875 Wimmer received a request from Bishop James Gibbons, bishop of Richmond and vicar apostolic of North Carolina, for monks to work in the western part of the North Carolina vicariate. An estate of five hundred acres in Gaston County near Charlotte had recently been donated to Bishop Gibbons by Father Jeremiah J. O'Connell, a priest who had worked in the Carolina and Georgia missions for thirty years. Gibbons wrote that he had immediately thought of turning to the Benedictines of Saint Vincent, "whose brethren, I trust, are destined to cultivate souls and land in North Carolina, as they had done in Europe" during the Middle Ages. The bishop said that since the land was well situated on the Richmond and Atlanta Railroad, it would be an ideal spot to establish a college. He reminded the abbot that no Catholic school of this kind existed between Washington and Mobile "except in Georgia." The property in North Carolina that Gibbons offered the Benedictines was valued at more than ten thousand dollars, and the only condition Father O'Connell had placed on the gift was that he be allowed to occupy a room on the premises during his lifetime, "which in the order of nature is not destined to be long, as he is old and feeble." Gibbons said that there were scarcely any Catholics in the immediate vicinity of the property, and that the mission would provide a great opportunity for the sons of St. Benedict to do serious proselytizing in a heavily Protestant region. "May God inspire you to accept this offer."[95]

There was considerable opposition among the capitulars to accepting Gibbons' offer. For one thing, the financial condition of the abbey was still tenuous. The national economic decline following the Civil War continued to have adverse repercussions at the monastery and school in Pennsylvania, and many capitulars believed that it was not judicious to commit resources to the missions until the financial situation at the motherhouse improved. For another thing, many noted, as Bishop Gibbons himself admitted, that there were scarcely any Catholics in the region which was being offered them. And what was probably worse for the Saint Vincent monks, there were no Germans either, Catholic or otherwise. When the chapter met to consider the matter, therefore, it was obvious that a growing consensus was developing to reject Gibbons' offer. Abbot Boniface, however, made it clear that he was in favor of accepting the mission in North Carolina. The place was poverty-stricken, Protestant, and "godless," and had as yet not recovered from the ravages of a catastrophic civil war. But the bleaker the prospects the more eagerly Wimmer seemed to want to take them on. This was not the sort of challenge he had turned away from in the past, and the opportunity to create an oasis of monastic and academic life out of the Protestant and primitive land of western North Carolina stirred his spirit. Monks of old had turned deserts into fertile fields, swamps into rich pastures, wasteland into flourishing agricultural centers. Wimmer saw no reason why his men could not also turn North Carolina into something worthwhile. Such rhetoric had its effect on the monks. After a lengthy discussion, the formerly reluctant capitulars "unanimously" advised Wimmer to accept Bishop Gibbons' offer, and the following day Wimmer wrote Father Benno Hegele, prior in Richmond, instructing him to inform Gibbons of the chapter's decision.[96]

The abbot detached Father Herman Wolfe, O.S.B., a sixty-year-old native of Holstein and a convert from Lutheranism, from Richmond, where he had been serving as assistant to Father Benno, and assigned him to lead the mission to North Carolina.[97] Wolfe, who had served as a doctor in the Confederate army, was an excellent choice as first Benedictine superior in North Carolina. His service to the South during the war would offset whatever objections Protestant North Carolinians might raise to a Catholic presence in their state. With characteristic humility Wolfe wrote that "had I been at Saint Vincent I would have voted in favor of accepting the place but certainly would not have chosen the man who is to go there to start it." He said that "at first I hoped that the bishop would raise objections on account of my age, but this wish came to naught. The community must assist me with its prayers."[98]

Father Herman visited the North Carolina property in February and wrote that he hoped to open a school there in the very near future.[99] After much planning and preparation, Wolfe finally settled on the O'Connell estate in April 1876. Wimmer visited North Carolina in May, and when he returned to Saint Vincent, he sent Brothers Bartholomew Freundl, Ulric Barth, Placidus Draude, and Philip Cassidy to assist in establishing a monastery. In July Father Herman wrote that "we are all well. The first work which I did on the place was to fit up a room in the house for a chapel. I blessed it, and from the first morning holy Mass was offered every day. May God assist us that this Sacrifice will never be interrupted here."

Bishop Gibbons had entrusted the Benedictines with the care of souls in the western North Carolina counties of Gaston and Mecklenburg, and Father Herman spent the early weeks of his assignment traveling about and visiting the scattered Catholics. He wrote that "the people are very earnest about their religion, and I have good hopes of being able to take care of them in spiritual matters. I intend to visit them once a month, going about by railroad. This means that I must start on Sunday mornings at 4:30 and come back at 10:30 in the evening." The monks were making plans to erect a building that would serve as a school, and the superior reported that nine students were expected for the first school year. "So far we have three resident students; two from Richmond who are scholastics and pay fifty dollars and another from the neighborhood who pays a hundred and fifty dollars." There were also six day students, and Wolfe said he was "expecting help from Saint Vincent, a priest or at least a cleric."[100]

Wolfe had named the monastery Mariastein, Mary's stone, on account of a large circular stone he found on the property. An oral tradition held that the stone served at one time as a sacrificial altar for Indians in the region and more recently as a block upon which black slaves were sold.[101] Father Joseph Keller soon came from Saint Vincent to assist Father Herman, and together with Father O'Connell, who became an oblate in the community, the two priests and the several brothers busily set about laying the groundwork for the monastery and school that eventually would become Belmont Abbey. Brother Philip Cassidy, a former Irish School Brother who was sent to teach at the new foundation, wrote that "the plantation is well-timbered with oak and pine; the ground is level and seems easy to cultivate. The place in general looks well, and I think it is healthy as the country is a rolling land. . . . It seems primitive enough but it has signs of improvement."[102]

Meanwhile the establishment of a second new southern mission was underway. About the same time that Bishop Gibbons offered the Benedictines the property in Gaston County, North Carolina, several requests for priests had come to Saint Vincent from German settlers in Tennessee and northern Alabama, and in August 1875 Abbot Boniface dutifully presented a proposal to the monastic chapter to send monks into Tennessee. The large German congregation at Lawrenceville in the Diocese of Nashville had been unable to find a priest to attend to its spiritual needs, and with the encouragement of Bishop Patrick A. Feehan of Nashville they had turned to Saint Vincent. Although Wimmer favored establishing a mission in rural Tennessee, at the time internal opposition to his missionary activity had reached one of its frequent high water marks at Saint Vincent. In addition to being concerned about the abbey's financial problems, the capitulars thought it wiser to conserve manpower at the motherhouse than to spread thin the monastic ranks by sending more missionaries into the field. The major concern of most of the monks at Saint Vincent was for the development of the college and the seminary. They feared that by opening more new missions, no matter how beneficial to the Church, they would drain talented teachers and essential resources from the schools at Saint Vincent. Their fears were not unwarranted. From the beginning of his work in America Wimmer had shown an inclination to send his best men to distant missions where for all practical purposes they were lost to the faculties of the college and seminary in Pennsylvania. The schools invariably suffered when missions were accepted, and when the monastic chapter met on August 30, 1875, to discuss the Tennessee proposal, they decisively voted it down.[103]

Six months later, however, the mood of the chapter had changed. In March, after agreeing to accept the property in North Carolina, the monks received a request from Bishop John Quinlan of Mobile to establish a Benedictine mission among a German colony that had been founded in northern Alabama in conjunction with the one in Lawrenceville, Tennessee. This second colony, near Huntsville, was called St. Florian. Bishop Quinlan offered to give the community at Saint Vincent "charge of Cullman Station, where there are one hundred families, of St. Florian, with its thirty families, and all the property under my control. I will also give you charge of Huntsville." The bishop said that in Huntsville a church had already been constructed for which nineteen thousand dollars had been expended. The debt the Benedictines would have to assume amounted to little more than three thousand dollars. When the abbot brought this proposal before the chapter, he pointed out the advantages of accepting a mission where much of the groundwork—such as the building of a church and the gathering of a worshiping congregation—had already been laid. A lengthy debate ensued in which some objected to the commitment of financial and human resources the mission would entail, while others pointed out the advantages Alabama, with its German congregations and completed church, had over the mission in North Carolina. Wimmer urged the monks to accept the mission, and in an about-face that frequently characterized the decisions of the chapter, the community, with only two dissenting votes, agreed to send a band of monks to Alabama.[104]

The abbot assigned Father Gabriel Guerster from the priory in St. Marys, Pennsylvania, as well as Brothers Majolus Mathey and Thaddeus Weber from Saint Vincent, to St. Florian, and in April 1876 he accompanied the three monks to Alabama where, in addition to the land given him by the bishop, he purchased one thousand acres for thirty-five hundred dollars. He spent two weeks in Alabama, meeting the bishop, familiarizing himself with the mission, and introducing himself and his monks to the people. Soon the Benedictine mission in Alabama expanded to include fifty-six hundred square miles of territory. In addition to the German settlement of St. Florian, the monks cared for Catholic congregations in Tuscumbia, Huntsville, Florence, Decatur, and Cullman Station and served the spiritual needs of hundreds of immigrant Czechs, Slovaks, and Italians digging canals along the Tennessee River. Forced by ill health to relinquish his post, Father Gabriel Guerster returned to Pennsylvania in 1877 and was replaced as superior of the Alabama missions by thirty-seven-year-old Father Benedict Menges, a native of Bavaria who had served in the Benedictine priories of Chicago and Pittsburgh. Fourteen years later Menges would be elected first abbot of St. Bernard Abbey. Other priests from Saint Vincent who served in the Alabama missions in the years before the establishment of the abbey included Athanasius Hintenach, Emmeran Singer, Joseph Keller, Oswald Moosmüller, and Andrew Hintenach.[105] Many years elapsed before monastic life could formally be instituted in Alabama. The monks from Pennsylvania were few in number and spread out over a wide mission field, which precluded their coming together to pray the Divine Office and celebrate other communal devotions. From the beginning, however, their intention was to establish a functioning Benedictine monastery and college in northern Alabama, and though a decade and a half would elapse before they could accomplish their goal, the work that they did between 1876 and 1890 laid a strong foundation for St. Bernard Abbey and College.

By 1877 Saint Vincent had men working in four southern states—Kentucky, Virginia, North Carolina, and Alabama—and when Bishop William Gross, C.Ss.R., of Savannah requested priests from Pennsylvania to take over a small monastery in Georgia, Wimmer agreed to provide them. In 1874 Gross had invited monks from the French province of the Benedictine Subiaco Congregation of the Primitive Observance to establish a community in Savannah and care for the emancipated black population. Two French monks arrived in the spring of 1874, and settling on the Isle of Hope, some nine miles east of Savannah, they built a monastery and opened a novitiate. Two years later yellow fever struck the community and carried off the superior, Father Gabriel Bergier, as well as several novices and candidates. The remaining monks withdrew from Savannah and went to Oklahoma where they formed part of the nucleus that eventually became Sacred Heart Abbey.[106] Bishop Gross then turned to Abbot Boniface for help in restoring the monastery on the Isle of Hope, and in February 1877, after the Saint Vincent chapter voted to accept the mission, the abbot sent Fathers Oswald Moosmüller from Kansas and Maurice Kaeder from Saint Vincent to Savannah.[107]

Moosmüller and Kaeder arrived in Georgia in March, and immediately took possession of the small monastery on the Isle of Hope. Three black brothers, the only remaining members of the original community, joined the two priests in their efforts to reestablish monastic life in the Georgia mission, and Prior Oswald wrote that plans were underway to establish a school for Negro boys near Savannah. Because the monastery on the Isle of Hope was still infected with yellow fever, Moosmüller said that he was investigating the possibility of purchasing land on nearby Skidaway Island where he had found a more suitable place for a monastery and school. In the meantime he reported that Bishop Gross and the people of Savannah had warmly received the Benedictines from Pennsylvania and that prospects for the community in Georgia were bright. The monks obtained a state charter for their monastery under the title "The Benedictine Order in Georgia." They claimed capital of ten thousand dollars invested in real estate on Skidaway Island, property the bishop had given them "for the education of youth, especially of the Colored Race."[108] As Moosmüller began construction of a monastery and manual labor school for blacks on Skidaway Island, Kaeder set out on a missionary journey through central Georgia to bring the sacraments to Catholics scattered along the railroad that extended three hundred miles from the coast to the interior of the state.[109]

In September Moosmüller opened a school for black students at the Isle of Hope, and eight months later the Benedictines moved to their newly constructed monastery and school on Skidaway Island across the Skidaway River. Twelve boys entered the school, and four additional monks arrived from St. Vincent, including Brother Philip Cassidy and Brother Rhabanus Cononge, a black monk from New Orleans who had recently entered the monastery at Saint Vincent, to assist in the teaching of the students and in the agricultural work of the seven-hundred-acre farm Bishop Gross had given to the Benedictines. Moosmüller's plan was to establish an agricultural school for the black population of coastal Georgia, but when he discovered that many of the families he hoped to serve preferred that their sons have the opportunity for professional studies, he modified the plan and created a school "designed to benefit two classes of students: . . . those who wish to get a business education qualifying them for such positions" and those "whose circumstances or wishes incline them to seek a more limited and practical course of instruction in farming as a profession." Moosmüller intended that the institution would "elevate the vocation of farmer, and give him a scientific as well as a practical instruction for his pursuits." The school would do this by putting the student "in possession of knowledge of the most improved methods of cultivation which are now used." The Benedictines' purpose in establishing the school was "to counteract the increasing tendency against manual labor, especially vindicating its dignity by showing that it is compatible with intellectual culture and social refinement."[110]

In order to develop further opportunities for the conversion of the five hundred African Americans living on Skidaway Island, Moosmüller arranged for the appointment of the young black cleric, Siricius Palmer, as schoolmaster in the public school on the island. He wrote that "if Siricius is a good teacher, he has the chance to convert these children and with them the whole population of the island to the Catholic Faith."[111] At the same time the Benedictines began working among the black population of Savannah. In 1879 Father Oswald moved from Skidaway to Savannah where he established a parish (Sacred Heart) for African Americans. Father Melchior Reichert, a twenty-seven-year-old native of Bavaria, who had recently been a professor at Saint Vincent College, replaced Moosmüller as superior of the monastery and school on Skidaway Island.[112] Other priests from Saint Vincent who served in Georgia during the 1870s and 1880s included Daniel Hefti, Joseph Keller, Alexius Grass, Cyprian Creagh, and George Lester. Hefti was killed on Skidaway, the victim of a gun accident. In 1884, when the Benedictine community in North Carolina was raised to the rank of an abbey, the monastery and school on Skidaway became a dependency of the new abbey. In the 1890s the school was closed and the monks moved to Savannah where in 1902 they established Sacred Heart Priory and Benedictine College.[113]

The fourth southern mission founded from Saint Vincent after the Civil War was in Florida. In May 1886 the monastic chapter voted to accept the offer of Bishop John Moore of St. Augustine to take charge of a large German colony in Hernando County. Father Gerard Pilz had gone to Florida the previous month to examine the proposed mission field and wrote that it was "most beautiful in every respect. San Antonio is a splendid district for people to settle in and to make a good living."[114] When the chapter agreed to accept the colony of San Antonio, Florida, Wimmer assigned Father Cyprian Creagh from Georgia and Brother Francis de Sales Zwiesler from Saint Vincent to assist Pilz in establishing a parish and a college (high school) in Hernando County. Later Father Constantine Leber came from Saint Vincent. The Benedictines had charge of Catholic congregations in Hernando, Pasco, and Citrus counties, including the towns of San Antonio, Brookville, St. Thomas, and Topkinsville. In 1888 the Florida missions were transferred from Saint Vincent's jurisdiction to that of Maryhelp Abbey in North Carolina. The community in Florida became an independent priory in 1894 and St. Leo's Abbey in 1902.[115]

MONASTIC OBSERVANCE

Not all the monks at Saint Vincent were happy with the renewal of missionary activities in the 1870s. A fundamental problem the community faced was how to maintain a spiritually sound monastic observance while at the same time serving the pastoral needs of the American Church. As early as 1847 reformers led by Father Peter Lechner of Scheyern had questioned the appropriateness of extensive missionary work for the Benedictines in America and had urged the adoption of a more contemplative, scholarly, liturgically oriented life at Saint Vincent. In the years that followed, reformers periodically called for a stricter monastic regimen—as in 1862 when the adherents of Paul George Keck, led by Prior Othmar Wirtz and novice master Wendelin Mayer, initiated a movement to reform the American Cassinese Congregation.[116] These reform-minded monks regarded missionary labor as at best a temporary necessity caused by conditions in the American Church, and at worst a debilitating distraction from what they believed to be the authentic Benedictine life of prayer, study, and liturgical praise carried on within the confines of the monastery.

There existed within the abbey strong disagreement over how best to strike a balance between the active life of the missions and the contemplative life of the cloister. Life in the monastery continued to center on the daily celebration of the Holy Eucharist and the communal chanting of the Divine Office, which had continued uninterrupted at Saint Vincent since October 24, 1846; and prayer, scriptural study, *lectio divina,* private devotions, and manual labor continued to be essential elements in the spiritual life of the community. Still, the progress the Benedictines had made in the missions during their first quarter-century in America had not been achieved without a degree of compromise with respect to monastic observance. Monks in the missions often found it impossible to follow the daily round of community prayer, meditation, and spiritual reading called for by the Rule of St. Benedict, and even at Saint Vincent some of the priests excused themselves from attending Divine Office and other community functions with the claim that their work in the college or in the parishes prevented them from observing the finer points of the monastic regimen. By the late 1870s some of the monks had begun to complain that Saint Vincent was becoming more a factory for missionaries than a place where they could quietly pursue their monastic vocation.

The first signs of this new reform impulse occurred in 1878 when Father Ignatius Trueg, director of music at the abbey, attempted to introduce Gregorian chant at Saint Vincent. Gregorian chant, the ancient plainsong of the Church, had been revived by the French Benedictines of the Abbey of Solesmes in the 1830s, and by the 1870s had become central to the liturgical observance of Benedictine monasteries in Europe that derived from Solesmes and the German Abbey of Beuron (restored in 1863). This newly recovered form of music both characterized and symbolized the contemplative orientation of the Benedictine revival in France and Germany during the second half of the nineteenth century, and Trueg's effort to introduce it at Saint Vincent represented more than just a change in liturgical taste and practice. It also implied an attempt to refocus the life of the monks in Pennsylvania from the active work of external apostolates to the contemplative tradition of study, meditation, and prayer.

Trueg and his supporters hoped to reform monastic observance among the American Benedictines, and Wimmer, always disposed to listen to new ideas that might contribute to the spiritual and monastic development of the community, agreed to allow the introduction of Beuronese methods of celebrating the liturgy. Opposition from other members of the community, however, quickly developed. Many of the older monks at the abbey were entirely satisfied with the traditional Bavarian music and liturgical practices they had known since entering the monastery, and they succeeded in frustrating Trueg's reform efforts. Deeply disappointed by his failure, Trueg petitioned the Holy See to have his vows transferred to the Beuronese congregation, and soon afterwards left Saint Vincent.[117]

Despite the departure of Father Ignatius, the reform movement gained momentum. In June 1879, just before the annual monastic retreat, Wimmer uncovered what he described as a plot by two of his most trusted monks who had encouraged a group of young clerics to seek a more contemplative life in stricter monastic communities. He wrote Abbot Innocent Wolf in Kansas that "a number of clerics were ready to leave the monastery on account of the low state of religious discipline and go to the Trappists or Beuron. And now it develops that the prior and master of novices are part of the plan, the latter also ready to go along with them. I found this out through the Abbot of Gethsemani."[118]

The agents of the "plot" were Prior Andrew Hintenach, who had given his blessing to the clerics' plans, and Father James Zilliox, the thirty-year-old novice master whose spiritual instruction had inspired them. Wimmer moved quickly to thwart what he regarded as "treachery to me and to the monastery of Saint Vincent under the pretext of piety and zeal." He censured the prior, forbade the clerics to leave the monastery, and dismissed Zilliox as novice master. But what Wimmer regarded as injudicious zeal and misguided piety, the reformers considered essential for authentic observance of the Benedictine Rule.

James Zilliox, the American-born leader of the reformers and one of the most respected of the young members of the American Benedictine community, had studied theology in Rome, Austria, and Germany from 1869 to 1875, and had become enamored of the contemplative monasticism he had observed in the Beuronese houses of Europe. He was distressed by what he believed to be the lax monastic observance at Saint Vincent and continued to call for change. Zilliox's reputation among his confreres, and even with his abbot, remained high despite the imbroglio caused by his promoting the clerics' departure. The regard in which he was held is nowhere better illustrated than by the fact that little more than a year and a half after dismissing him as novice master, Wimmer appointed him prior of the monastery.

As prior Zilliox continued to be troubled by the apparent lack of religious commitment on the part of the majority of the monks at Saint Vincent, and he grew frustrated by the abbot's failure to discipline those who refused to measure up to the high standards of monastic observance set by the reformers. Unable to convince the abbot to institute the changes he believed essential, Zilliox conspired to bring the state of spiritual affairs at Saint Vincent to the attention of the Holy See. In August 1881 he joined with Father Maurice Kaeder—a monk whom many in the community regarded as both insincere and manipulative and one who was sometimes cited as among the greatest offenders against monastic discipline—in composing a letter of protest to the pope.[119]

Several months later Wimmer received a startling communiqué from Cardinal Giovanni Simeoni, prefect of the Sacred Congregation for the Propagation of the Faith, informing him that the Propaganda Fide had received a document from two monks of Saint Vincent that raised serious questions about monastic observance in the abbey and even the moral behavior of the members of the community. "It is reported that your monks do not observe any law of enclosure, that they go out and wander here and there, that they talk and feast with women outside the cloister, that sometimes they go to the city to visit the theater, that they receive women within the enclosure as well as in the dormitories of the abbey. And so it happens that monks are considered most scandalous, ensnared in shameful habits, pursuing earthly, not heavenly things."[120]

The letter struck Wimmer like a lightning bolt. The seventy-three-year-old abbot reeled back from the blow in shock and dismay, and wrote Abbot Innocent Wolf of Kansas: "Father Maurice and Father Prior have brought accusations against me at the Vatican to the pope. They have made charges for a hearing. The affair will probably end with my resignation. They are hounding me to death. Of course I will give account of my actions. But it will be a sorry story for Saint Vincent and for the entire congregation on account of the way in which we have been portrayed."[121]

Others came to the defense of Wimmer and the community. Abbot Innocent, who had served as prior at Saint Vincent before his election as abbot of St. Benedict's, expressed his outrage at what Zilliox and Kaeder had written, and Abbot Alexius Edelbrock of St. John's Abbey wrote that "certainly Father James Zilliox as well as Father Maurice Kaeder will be considered very scandalous because of their lie against their monastery and their abbot, burdened with years and merits as he is."[122] The bishop of Pittsburgh also came to the defense of Saint Vincent. Fortuitously, when the letter of protest arrived in Rome, Bishop John Tuigg had been at the Holy See on his *ad limina* visit consulting with officials of the Propaganda Fide. Cardinal Simeoni questioned him about the accusations against Wimmer and the abbey, and he responded by denouncing the charges of Kaeder and Zilliox as vicious lies and by giving a glowing report on conditions at Saint Vincent and on the probity and judiciousness of Wimmer as abbot. In a spirited defense of Abbot Boniface, Tuigg wrote:

> Alone he planted and watered in the United States the Benedictine tree, which now has spread over the whole land. He created St. Vincent Abbey out of nothing. He can be judged by the fruits, and these fruits show a most kind-hearted man of unbounded charity, indefatigable in work, eminent in learning and prudence, wise in temporal as well as in spiritual matters. As I know him well, I cannot be convinced that he should have done or omitted anything through his fault and that he will do or omit anything from which Religion or his subjects should suffer harm. I visit the abbey several times a year for ordinations or other purposes, and I must confess that I never saw anything which would be considered a grave violation of the Rule of religious perfection. On the contrary I was always highly edified by the monastic silence which the monks observe.[123]

In addition to this unexpected support from the bishop of Pittsburgh, Wimmer was gratified to discover that he commanded greater respect and support among the monks of Saint Vincent than he had at first realized. Most of the monks did not like Father Maurice at all, and though they generally respected Father James, they nevertheless repudiated the prior's action and rallied around the abbot. Father Leo Haid, rector of the major seminary at Saint Vincent, expressed the sentiments of many of his fellow monks when he wrote:

> Our discipline is not only very lax, but in a word we have no monastic discipline. We go to theaters, loaf around the country *ad libitum,* eat and drink whatever and whenever we please, take women into our cells, etc. Hang it! The recital alone is enough to make St. Hermenegild lose his patience. . . . We are not all saints, but after all we try to be Benedictines. I have been here for nearly twenty-one years and only once did I see a woman in the monastery—accidentally having lost her way. And good Father Charley of happy memory nearly threw the poor thing down the stairs.

Father Leo said that only malice "and a good dose of crankiness" could have caused Kaeder to pen such accusations. He was sorry that Abbot Boniface's "declining years should be embittered by such ingratitude. He need not fear. His fathers love him and will gladly defend him against every attack. Had he given us our way, we would have smoked the coon out and given him a chance to face all his slandered brethren in the Chapter."[124]

So with strong support from the Saint Vincent chapter, the abbots of the American Cassinese Congregation, and the bishop of Pittsburgh, Wimmer prepared to answer the charges. "The coarsest allegations," he wrote, "were characteristically presented by Father Maurice" who had apparently been motivated by resentment over missionary assignments (such as the one to Georgia) that he did not think worthy of his talent. The abbot forgave both men, however, though he reluctantly admitted that he would have to remove Father James from the office of prior. With less reluctance he dismissed Father Maurice from the seminary faculty and transferred him to a parish in Illinois. In the meantime, after he had "cooled off," he drafted a reply to Rome. "I did not make any recriminations but reported that choir is being faithfully attended—even by Father Maurice."[125]

The Holy See exonerated Abbot Boniface of any wrongdoing and took no steps to institute a canonical inquiry into monastic discipline at Saint Vincent. Clearly the assertion of Zilliox and Kaeder that religious observance at the abbey was at an intolerably low level was a gross exaggeration, but their protest to Rome had a sobering effect on the monks, and everyone's consciousness was raised with regard to the potential problems that

The seven abbots who attended the Third Plenary Council of Baltimore, 1884. From left to right: Fintan Mundwiler of St. Meinrad's Abbey, Indiana; Boniface Wimmer of Saint Vincent; Rupert Seidenbusch, first abbot of St. John's Abbey, Minnesota, and at this time bishop of Northern Minnesota; Benedict Berger of the Trappist Abbey of Gethsemani, Kentucky; Alexius Edelbrock, second abbot of St. John's, Minnesota; Innocent Wolf of St. Benedict's Abbey, Kansas; and Frowin Conrad of Conception Abbey, Missouri.

the community's continued commitment to extensive missionary activity could pose both for morale and monastic observance. To be sure, missionary work did not end, nor even appreciably decline, during the next decade. Increasingly, however, responsible members of the Saint Vincent chapter questioned the wisdom of focusing the community's energies and resources on external apostolates, and urged that more attention should be given to strengthening the religious observance and spiritual life of the abbey. It would not be until after Wimmer's death that the reformers gained the upper hand and began the process that would result in Saint Vincent's reassessment of its broad commitment to the missions. By then, of course, conditions in the American Church had also changed and the need for monastic missionaries was diminishing.

DEATH OF THE *PROJEKTENMACHER*

In the meantime there was still much work to be done. In December 1884 the Holy See raised Saint Vincent's dependent priories in New Jersey and North Carolina to abbatial rank, and two months later the Saint Vincent capitulars elected Father James Zilliox as abbot of St. Mary's Abbey, Newark, and Father Oswald Moosmüller as abbot of Maryhelp Abbey, North Carolina. Moosmüller declined the honor, choosing to remain a monk of Saint Vincent, and in a second election, conducted by ten monks who had volunteered to transfer their vows to the North Carolina abbey, Father Leo Haid, rector of the seminary at Saint Vincent, was elected abbot of Maryhelp. The election of the abbots of New Jersey and North Carolina marked a new phase in the history of the Benedictine Order in the United States. Haid, a native of Westmoreland County, Pennsylvania, and Zilliox, a native of Newark, were American-born, and their election signified that a new, native-born generation was taking over leadership of the Benedictine Order in the United States.

New patterns of immigration were opening other missionary fields to the Benedictines of Saint Vincent as well. By the mid 1870s large numbers of Catholic immigrants from central Europe were settling in the American Midwest, and in response to calls for missionaries to the Czech settlers in Nebraska, the Saint Vincent chapter accepted charge of St. Wenceslaus Parish, Omaha, in the summer of 1877. Father Wenceslaus Kocarnik, a monk of Saint Vincent, served the Czech Catholics of Omaha for nearly eight years before turning the parish over to a secular priest. In January 1885 the Saint Vincent chapter accepted an invitation from Archbishop Patrick A. Feehan and assumed charge of the large Czech parish of St. Procopius in Chicago. Wimmer sent Kocarnik, along with Nepomucene Jaeger and Sigismund Singer, two other Czech priests at Saint Vincent, to take over operations at St. Procopius. The plan was to establish a Czech Benedictine monastery in Chicago that would serve central European Catholic immigrants just as Saint Vincent had been created forty years before to serve German immigrants. In November 1885 Jaeger wrote that "every month we have one hundred baptisms, a dozen marriages, and twenty-five funerals. The school has nine hundred and thirty children in ten classes." Father Wenceslaus had traveled to Prague for the purpose of raising money for the future abbey and had returned with twenty-five hundred dollars and promises of equal contributions the following year. Although Kocarnik found no young men willing to come to America to join the Benedictines, Jaeger felt confident that numerous Czech candidates for the Order could be found among the people of Chicago.[126] In the months that followed the monks in Chicago made good progress. They purchased more property and opened St. Procopius College in the fall of 1886. A year later, upon the petition of the Saint Vincent chapter, Rome elevated St. Procopius to the rank of independent canonical priory, and in 1894 the community was made an abbey. It was the sixth monastery founded from Saint Vincent to achieve abbatial status.[127]

Another missionary undertaking accepted by the Saint Vincent chapter in the 1880s was in Colorado. In September 1886 Bishop Joseph P. Machebeuf, vicar apostolic of Colorado and Utah, visited Saint Vincent and asked for priests to work in his vicariate. In December Father Rhabanus Gutmann, pastor of the Saint Vincent Parish, and Father Eusebius Geiger, socius of novices at the abbey, went to Colorado to assume charge of the missions in and around Breckenridge which Bishop Machebeuf had offered the Benedictines. The Saint Vincent monks arrived in Denver on December 17, 1886. As Father Rhabanus later wrote, they "found the bishop at home and were cordially received, but says the bishop you must leave this evening for Breckenridge at 8 o'cl. So we did and arrived at Breckenridge at 4 a.m., pitch dark, station closed, zero and below, 4 feet of snow, & no path to be seen. We will freeze to death I said to P. Eusebius, but behold at once we saw a light. The bishop had informed Mr. McNamara to meet us at the station, came a little late yet in time."[128]

In Breckenridge the monks took up their duties, which included serving the Catholic missions in eight nearby small towns. On December 18 Father Rhabanus wrote that he did "not know whether we are going to freeze this winter or not." The following month he wrote that "as far as our parish is concerned, which embraces two counties, we do not think that we shall suffer any great want. The people are willing and very generous, also devoted to the priest."[129] Both Gutmann and Geiger suffered debilitating illnesses during their early months in Colorado, and for a while Geiger had to be hospitalized in the Union Pacific Railroad hospital in Denver. Nevertheless, they continued their work among the Catholics of Breckenridge and its vicinity and explored the possibilities for a more permanent Benedictine settlement in Colorado. The seeds they planted in 1887 eventually took root and grew, becoming the origins of Holy Cross Abbey, the tenth independent abbey founded from Saint Vincent.

The 1880s also witnessed a renewed effort on the part of the Saint Vincent chapter to establish a house of studies in Rome. In October 1880, after a hiatus of ten years, the chapter reestablished St. Elizabeth's House of Studies which had been closed after the French invasion of 1870. The American Benedictines were able to secure a new lease on the property, and Abbot Boniface immediately assigned Father Adalbert Müller as rector and sent four students from Saint Vincent to Italy: Vincent Huber, Philip Kretz, Clement Stratman, and Robert Monroe. Upon their arrival in Rome these students took up residence at St. Elizabeth's and began courses of study in philosophy and theology under the Jesuits of the German College.[130] A year later they were joined by two more Saint Vincent clerics, Hugo Paff and John Kops. The new venture at St. Elizabeth's lasted only three years. The property was condemned by the Rome City Council to make room for a road, and in August 1883, after failing in their attempt to rent another facility, the Saint Vincent monks returned home. Three of them had received their doctorates in philosophy, however, and two others their licentiates in theology.[131]

Though two attempts to establish an American Benedictine house of studies in Rome ended in failure, Saint Vincent's efforts, in part at least, helped motivate Vatican officials to reconstitute the Benedictine Collegio di Sant' Anselmo in February 1887. Sant' Anselmo was originally established in the eighteenth century as a Benedictine house of studies by Pope Innocent XI, but had been suppressed during the Napoleonic upheavals. Wimmer had proposed its reestablishment during a meeting of Benedictine abbots at Montecassino in the spring of 1880, and in October 1886 the Italian Cassinese abbots, meeting at the Abbey of Melk, Austria, passed a resolution urging Pope Leo XIII to restore the old college as an international house of studies for the Benedictine Order.[132] The monks of Saint Vincent strongly supported the Italian plan, and when the college opened in September 1887, two of them, Fathers Adalbert Müller and Robert Monroe, were appointed to the faculty. In addition, three Saint Vincent clerics went to study theology in the first class organized at Sant' Anselmo after the restoration: Candidus Eichenlaub, Raphael Wieland, and Lawrence Haas. During the next year the Saint Vincent chapter donated more than eight thousand dollars to the international Benedictine college.

During the summer of 1887 Bishop Peter Schumacher of Portoviejo, Ecuador, came to Saint Vincent seeking Benedictines to establish a colony in his diocese; but even though several priests expressed interest in volunteering for the mission, there was general agreement among the capitulars that the community was overcommitted and could not immediately send monks to South America. Wimmer himself was inclined to assist Bishop

Schumacher, but he was an old man now and his thoughts were turning more and more to his approaching death. He regretted that he had to turn down the offer to establish a foundation in South America, but he wrote his nephew, Father Luke Wimmer, that perhaps his successor would be in a better position to help those whom he himself could not.[133] In the meantime, he arranged for several Benedictine nuns from the convent in Elizabeth, New Jersey, to go to Ecuador to assist Bishop Schumacher.[134]

Wimmer died four months later, on December 8, 1887. Forty-one years had elapsed since his arrival in the United States, and in that time the monastery of Saint Vincent had grown under his leadership from a small community of four students and fourteen candidates for the lay brotherhood to a large and thriving abbey with two hundred monks. Enrollment in Saint Vincent College had reached 296 students, and there were forty-five seminarians studying theology in the major seminary. In addition, Saint Vincent monks staffed ten dependent priories and served the Catholics of more than forty parishes in the states of Pennsylvania, Maryland, Kentucky, Georgia, Alabama, Illinois, and Colorado. Four independent abbeys, with their own schools, dependent priories, and parishes, had been founded from Saint Vincent and now flourished in Minnesota, Kansas, New Jersey, and North Carolina. In 1887 *Sadlier's Catholic Directory* said of the abbey in Pennsylvania: "Nothing in the growth of the Church in this country exceeds the wonderful development of this community." But Wimmer's success could not be counted simply in numbers and statistics. Rather, it was the lives he had touched and the hearts he had changed by remaining faithful to the vision he had received in Munich more than forty years before that revealed the fullest measure of the man. Thousands of people throughout the United States had grown in the Catholic faith under the guidance of his monks; thousands of students had been educated in Benedictine schools; and more than four hundred secular priests educated by the monks of Saint Vincent now served in parishes throughout the nation. Father Adalbert Müller, a Saint Vincent monk teaching in Rome, summarized the feelings of many when he wrote:

> From my eleventh year he lodged and fed and clothed and educated me. Whatever I know and whatever I am able to do, I owe next to God to our deceased Abbot. May God forgive me all the sorrows and heartaches which I caused dear Abbot Wimmer, and may He reward him for all the kindness he showed me and my confreres. Archabbot Boniface worked most zealously for the glory of God and for what he believed to be the true interest of our order. His zeal and his childlike confidence in God enabled him to do great things.[135]

FOUR

CONSOLIDATION AND RENEWAL (1888–1892)

THE DEATH OF BONIFACE WIMMER marked the end of an era at Saint Vincent. For four decades he had guided the community through its extended formative phase, overseeing the development of Benedictine observance in Pennsylvania, building a college and seminary that by 1887 had earned an honored place in the educational life of the American Church, training hundreds of priests for American dioceses, and sending missionaries throughout the United States to create new centers of monasticism, education, and pastoral care. No aspect of the prayer and work of the community lacked the imprint of his powerful and visionary personality, and now that he was gone the monks of Saint Vincent felt apprehensive.

In the face of increasingly complex challenges, Wimmer had managed to hold the major factions and diverse commitments of the community together by his determination, singlemindedness, and sheer force of will. Now the monks wondered who would lead them in the next phase of their development as religious, educators, and missionaries. The crucial question they confronted was who among them possessed the strength, character, and vision to reconcile their differences and bring unity and coherence to their common life of work and prayer?

The conflict within the community between those who shared Wimmer's commitment to apostolic work and the expansion of the Benedictine Order in America and those who desired a more contemplative, prayer-centered life of silence and withdrawal from the world within the confines of the monastery had intensified in the final years of the old archabbot's life; and when the time came to choose a new abbot, the priests of the abbey were in disagreement over which of the various candidates was best suited for the job. Those who wanted to maintain the active missionary monasticism promoted by Wimmer divided their support among three candidates: Michael Hofmayer, prior at Saint Vincent; Hilary Pfrängle, who had recently succeeded James Zilliox as abbot of St. Mary's Abbey, Newark; and Innocent Wolf, abbot of St. Benedict's Abbey, Kansas. Those who sought a stricter monastic regimen and gradual withdrawal from the missions supported Fathers Placidus Pilz and Andrew Hintenach, both priests of Saint Vincent.

Two months elapsed between the death of Wimmer and the day the monks of Saint Vincent gathered to choose his successor. The election took place on February 8, 1888. That morning the community celebrated a solemn High Mass of the Holy Spirit in the abbey church, and after breakfast Abbot Alexius Edelbrock of St. John's Abbey, president of the American Cassinese Congregation, led the electors into the monastery choir chapel to begin the balloting.[1] One hundred priests of the abbey were eligible to vote. The statutes of the congregation stipulated that they could choose any priest in the congregation who was at least thirty years old, and that a simple majority of votes would decide the outcome. Seventy-one of the electors were present; twenty-nine others had appointed proxies. After the election of tellers and a final prayer of intercession to the Holy Spirit for guidance, the voting began. On the first ballot Innocent Wolf received twenty-four votes, followed by Hilary Pfrängle with fourteen, Placidus Pilz with thirteen, Andrew Hintenach with twelve, and Michael Hofmayer with ten. The remaining twenty-seven votes were spread out among nine other priests. The inconclusive results confirmed what all the monks suspected: the community lacked a clear consensus as to what direction Saint Vincent should take in the post-Wimmer era. None of the leading candidates had gained even a quarter of the votes, and the fact that the two highest vote-getters—Wolf and Pfrängle—were not even monks of Saint Vincent indicated that many of the capitulars believed that differences within the community could be reconciled only by bringing in a relative outsider to lead them.

The second ballot was equally inconclusive. This time Wolf received thirty-one votes, Pilz nineteen, Pfrängle seventeen, and Hintenach fifteen, while Prior Michael Hofmayer dropped to two votes and withdrew from consideration. After the second turn neither the faction supporting the status quo (represented by those who cast a total of forty-nine votes for Wolf, Pfrängle, and Hofmayer) nor the one seeking to change the direction of monastic life at Saint Vincent (represented by the thirty-four monks who cast their votes for Pilz and Hintenach) had managed to garner a majority.

The third ballot, however, decided the issue. Pilz and Hintenach maintained their strong showing with a combined total of thirty-five votes, but Wolf not only gained the support of those who had earlier voted for Hofmayer but also won eleven votes from Pfrängle's supporters, as well as an additional twelve votes from those who had previously cast ballots for other candidates. The result was a majority of fifty-six votes out of a total of one hundred. Prior Michael Hofmayer immediately telephoned the Western Union office in Latrobe and dictated a message to be telegraphed to Abbot Innocent in Kansas: "You have been elected abbot. Please accept."[2]

The news reached Wolf at St. Benedict's Abbey shortly after lunch. Later he recorded his reaction in his diary:

> I went at once to my room and wrote back an answer: "Give thanks to chapter for confidence, but cannot accept." After I had written this, the thought came that this perhaps was a sign of God's will, and then I got very nervous, so that at that moment I could not have written a word. After a short prayer I rang for my confessor, confessed and then I was quiet again, and telephoned my answer to the Western Union.
>
> Thereupon I went to the chapter room where all were anxiously waiting for news. I let them guess, and then told them that I had been elected. There was a pause of silence which I broke by saying: But I have answered already that I will not accept. Then there was an outburst of clapping and cheering. Afterwards I heard that there was much anxiety about my action, as there was also in St. Vincent's.[3]

The forty-five-year-old Wolf, who had been among the first monks of Saint Vincent to be educated in Rome, had entered Saint Vincent College in 1854 at the age of eleven and been ordained in 1866. He had taught moral theology, scripture, and liturgy in Saint Vincent Seminary for six years, and served as prior of Saint Vincent for two, before being elected first abbot of St. Benedict's Abbey, Kansas, in 1877. Although ten years had elapsed since he had been a member of the Saint Vincent community, he was well known to and highly respected by the monks, and his election as second abbot had been the fulfillment of Wimmer's own hopes. It was generally known that Wimmer had expected his successor to be either Wolf or Hilary Pfrängle, both of whom supported the old archabbot's monastic policies. Wolf's refusal to accept the office, therefore, was both a shock and a profound disappointment to the capitulars.

The telegram announcing Abbot Innocent's decision reached Saint Vincent on the afternoon of February 8, and that evening, after Vespers and supper, the monks assembled in the choir chapel once again to vote for an abbot. In a surprising turn of events, most of those who had voted for Wolf on the final ballot of the first election now swung their support not to Pfrängle, who until just a year before had been rector of Saint Vincent Seminary, but to Andrew Hintenach, a key leader among the reformers. On the first ballot of the second election Hintenach received fifty-three votes, Placidus Pilz twenty-one, and Abbot Hilary Pfrängle a mere six. A sudden and unexpected wind had seemed to stir among the capitulars, and the result was that the reformers had scored an unforeseen victory. Even those who had earlier supported Innocent Wolf were delighted. Hintenach, however, was distressed. The official election results reveal that he "accepted very reluctantly," and oral tradition relates that he responded to the outcome with tearful pleading that he be allowed, like Wolf, to refuse. But his confreres would not hear of a second failed election, and so with a heavy heart Andrew Hintenach submitted to the will of the community and became the second abbot of Saint Vincent.

Hintenach, elected when he was forty-four years old, had come to Saint Vincent College at the age of ten. Ordained in 1867, he had at various times served as professor of Latin and theology in the college and novice master, subprior, and prior in the monastery. He was one of the few members of the community who had lived virtually his entire monastic life at Saint Vincent. In June 1887 Wimmer had appointed him superior of the Alabama missions, his first and only assignment away from the abbey. He had served in Alabama only eight months when he was elected abbot.[4] Immediately after the election Hintenach withdrew into seclusion and went to St. Marys, Pennsylvania, for an extended retreat. In the opening days of April, when word arrived from Rome that the Sacred Congregation for the Propagation of the Faith had confirmed his election, he returned to Saint Vincent and entered upon his new office. "May God in His merciful kindness," he wrote, "give me the necessary prudence and firmness to discharge the duties imposed upon me."[5]

SPIRITUAL RENEWAL

After attending the episcopal ordination in Baltimore of Abbot Leo Haid, whom Rome had recently named vicar apostolic of North Carolina, Hintenach was blessed as abbot at Saint Vincent on July 5, 1888. Several weeks later he learned that the Holy See had granted him the honorific title of archabbot. Wimmer himself had been named archabbot in 1883, and after 1892, when Rome raised Saint Vincent to the rank of archabbey in recognition of its status as the first Benedictine abbey in the United States, all the abbots elected by the community held the title by virtue of their office. But Hintenach, like Wimmer, was named archabbot by special indult of the Holy See.

Archabbot Andrew began at once to institute a program of monastic reform and spiritual renewal both at Saint Vincent and in its dependent houses. To assist him in his efforts, he summoned Father Oswald Moosmüller back to the abbey from the southern missions and appointed him prior. Despite his long experience as a missionary (or perhaps because of it), Moosmüller was one of the most ardent and articulate critics of Wimmer's policy of committing the community's men and resources to extensive external apostolates. Like Hintenach and the other reformers, he advocated retrenchment in the missions and greater emphasis on developing monastic observance at the abbey. Archabbot Andrew now turned to him for support in the effort to reorient the community and renew its spiritual life.

Hintenach's program of spiritual renewal had three principal goals: (1) to reawaken the spirit of prayer and religious devotion at the abbey and inspire the monks to greater faithfulness in attendance at Divine Office; (2) to form small independent monasteries from as many of the dependent missions as possible in order to make it easier for the monks to lead a monastic life of work and prayer in unified, focused communities while avoiding the risk of distraction and fragmentation on account of a wide range of apostolic activities; and (3) to ensure that Saint Vincent monks working in parishes had, to the extent possible, an opportunity to lead a Benedictine life of communal prayer and monastic observance.

At the time of Hintenach's election two-thirds of the priests of Saint Vincent were serving in priories, parishes, or small mission stations away from the abbey. The spiritual life of these priests was a key concern for Archabbot Andrew, and a month after he assumed office, he sent a circular letter to all members of the chapter announcing his plan to revitalize monastic discipline in the parishes. "Whether living in the Monastery or in the Parish," he wrote,

> as Religious we are obliged to observe our Holy Rule. Since practical seculars always gain by living up to the proverb: "Keep thy shop and thy shop will keep thee"—we must apply the same adage for ourselves in regard to the Holy Rule. However, for various reasons it is obvious that in a parish the regulations and divisions of time for the Divine Office, for Meditation, Spiritual Reading, and Examination of Conscience, the observance of the Nocturnal Silence cannot be observed in the same manner as it is done in the Abbey; nevertheless it is necessary to have certain regulations for the same adapted to the circumstances of the place.

Noting that "the chief duty of the Abbot is to watch over the discipline" of the community, Hintenach directed that all the monks serving as pastors in the missions submit a statement on how monastic life was being observed in their parishes. He asked for detailed descriptions of the order and manner in which the Divine Office and traditional spiritual exercises were being followed; he inquired into whether any abuses existed "touching the vows of Obedience, Chastity, and Poverty," and he invited suggestions on "any point in which you think there may be room for improvement, or whatever you may consider advisable for the future."[6]

The priests in the far-flung parishes dutifully submitted their reports. The response of Father Severin Laufenberg, a Saint Vincent monk serving as pastor of St. Mary's Parish in Anna, Illinois, was typical. Father Severin reported that he and his assistant, Father Engelbert Leist, rose at 5:00 a.m. in the summer and 5:30 a.m. in the winter; prayed Prime, Terce, Sext, and None at 6:30 a.m.; celebrated Mass at 7:30 a.m.; had breakfast at 8:30 a.m., followed by "reading the news, the studying & reading spiritual books" until the noon meal. During the meal they had ten minutes of "table reading" from the New Testament, and afterwards they visited the Blessed Sacrament for meditation and prayer. The two priests prayed Vespers and Compline at 2:00 p.m. and spent the afternoon "either in sick calls or walks for recreation or reading according as circumstances may direct." They ate their evening meal at 6:00 p.m., during which there was ten minutes of reading from the Old Testament, and then at 7:30 p.m. they prayed "anticipated" Matins and Lauds, after which they retired for the night.[7]

Despite the evidence of good discipline and high standards of Benedictine observance in the missions that the responses to Archabbot Andrew's circular provided, the reformers at Saint Vincent were not satisfied that parish life was compatible with a Benedictine vocation. Prior Oswald Moosmüller wrote that "the great majority of us are living like secular

Andrew Hintenach, O.S.B. (1844–1927), second archabbot of Saint Vincent, resigned in 1892 after serving only four years.

priests, scattered over the country from 1,000 to 2,000 miles and even farther apart." The result of so many priests being assigned to the care of souls outside Saint Vincent was that many of them "don't care about the monastery any more," regarding it as "good enough for a training school and perhaps as a refuge for disabled men," but not as the praying community that sustained their spiritual lives and to which they had pronounced solemn vows of stability, obedience, and conversion of life.[8]

Moosmüller was deeply distressed by what he regarded as the lack of monastic fervor not only among the parish priests but also among many of the monks living at the abbey. "St. Vincent's is too large," he wrote to his friend Adalbert Müller, the Saint Vincent priest who had become prior of Sant' Anselmo in Rome. And "neither too large convents nor too small ones can keep up discipline." Moosmüller believed that in order "to keep discipline and control . . . instead of *one* monastery we should have *three.*" Moosmüller also thought that the monks at Saint Vincent neglected their vow of poverty. As evidence of this neglect he pointed to the fact that "[t]here may be priests in this house who smoke Cigars in one day, worth as much as one of our Priests stationed out alone can afford to pay for his dinner."[9]

The purported lack of religious zeal at the abbey also concerned the archabbot. Hintenach regularly admonished the monks at chapters and other community gatherings that they should be more diligent in attending choir, particularly in the early morning; that priests should be conscientious in the celebration of daily Mass; that clerics should not fail to attend conventual Mass; and that all should strictly observe the prohibition against leaving the monastery without the explicit permission of the prior. When his words of admonition seemed to fall on deaf ears, the archabbot suspended the monks' afternoon *haustus* (an hour of community recreation during which beer was served) and threatened further sanctions.[10]

Despite the allegations of a minority that monastic observance did not meet even minimum standards, an objective assessment of conditions at Saint Vincent during the years of Hintenach's abbacy suggests that the abuses cited by the reformers consisted of only minor infractions against the monastic rule by monks overburdened with the community's educational and pastoral commitments. Indeed, after the regular visitation of 1890 Abbots Leo Haid of North Carolina and Innocent Wolf of Kansas noted a "marked improvement in the discipline of the abbey since the last visitation."[11] Still, tension continued to exist between the reformers and the majority of the monks who saw little need for altering the customs and practices they had always followed. The result was an impasse. Archabbot Andrew, supported by a handful of idealists, persisted in his efforts to promote internal reform, while the main body of monks, the pragmatists, resisted any effort to change the outward-looking missionary character that had always marked the community. When asked by the reformers why they refused to consider change and continued to persist in the old ways, the pragmatists responded with unassailable German logic, "Es war immer so" ("Because we always did it this way").

Among the reformers, Prior Oswald Moosmüller became particularly discouraged. He saw few prospects for creating at Saint Vincent the environment of contemplation and monastic peace the reformers envisioned as the Benedictine ideal. His alternative to attempting to change prevailing attitudes at the abbey was to leave Saint Vincent altogether and establish in another place the kind of community he desired. "I came to a conclusion which I dare not express to anyone," he wrote his friend Adalbert Müller. "When I see a chance open again, I will go to the poorest place, provided it shall be organized as an independent Priory, and I will publish again a monthly magazine like the *Geschichtsfreund,* that would build up and support a Monastery and train young Scholastics and Clerics to literary work."[12]

A PRIORY IN ECUADOR

Others at Saint Vincent had earlier come to the conclusion that the only way to lead the kind of monastic life they felt called to live was to establish an independent house in a remote place. The opportunity offered itself even before Wimmer's death, when Bishop Peter Schumacher of Portoviejo, Ecuador, visited the abbey and asked for priests to assist with the care of souls in his distant diocese. Wimmer had wanted to help, but his own illness and the community's other commitments at the time prevented him from sending monks to South America in 1887. After the election of Archabbot Andrew, a group of Saint Vincent monks expressed their desire to undertake the mission. Their intention, however, was not to found another dependency of Saint Vincent but rather to make a clean break with the abbey and establish at once an independent monastery where they could follow the Benedictine Rule according to their own monastic ideals.

In fact, it was only under this condition that Archabbot Andrew and the council of seniors would agree to authorize the mission. The reformers were determined to limit long-term commitments by Saint Vincent to new and distant missions, the burden of which they believed not only jeopardized the development of monastic renewal at the abbey but drained its financial and human resources. Hintenach and the council of seniors would thus support new foundations only if they had the prospect of quickly becoming independent. When three priests—Augustine Schneider, Clement Stratman, and Conrad Ebert—and the cleric Macarius Schmitt expressed their desire to found a monastery in Ecuador, Archabbot Andrew attempted to ensure the rapid independence of the new community by asking the monks to sign a document renouncing their affiliation with Saint Vincent. Interestingly, they agreed.[13]

Schneider, leader of the group, was a forty-year-old native of Rheno-

Bavaria, who had entered Saint Vincent in 1868 and been ordained in 1873. He had served as professor of Hebrew and liturgy in the seminary, as well as director of clerics and prefect of the seminary. His only missionary work had involved a short assignment to Benedictine parishes in southern Illinois. Born in Pittsburgh, Stratman was twenty-nine when he joined the Ecuador mission. He had completed his theological studies at the Collegio di Sant' Anselmo in Rome in 1883 and been ordained to the priesthood in 1884. During the next four years he taught philosophy at Saint Vincent Seminary. The twenty-eight-year-old Ebert was a native of New York City who had come to Saint Vincent at the age of thirteen, entered the novitiate in 1877, and been ordained in 1884 after serving a year as a professor at Maryhelp Priory in North Carolina. The Bavarian-born Schmitt had come to Saint Vincent as a seminarian in 1882 at the age of twenty, entered the novitiate in 1884, and had made solemn vows a year before volunteering for the Ecuador mission. All four were among the idealists who sought a more focused monastic life in a small community.

The monks set off for South America in the summer of 1888 accompanied by George Schabacker, Mathias Schieber, and William Lange, three scholastics from Saint Vincent College who had applied to become novices in the new monastery. Bishop Schumacher arranged for the band from Pennsylvania to settle in the town of Bahía de Caraquez on Ecuador's Pacific coast, where they established their residence in a dilapidated wooden building and took charge of a commercial college of thirty-three students. The bishop also assigned them the pastoral care of Catholics in three parishes in the provinces of Manabí and Esmeraldas, and in November ordained Macarius Schmitt to the priesthood.

In October 1888 Father Augustine, with support from Bishop Schumacher in Ecuador and Abbot Bernard Smith, procurator general for the American Benedictines in Rome, submitted a petition to the Holy See asking Pope Leo XIII to elevate Holy Spirit Monastery in Bahía to the rank of independent canonical priory with the right to open a novitiate and receive novices.[14] Rome acted quickly on the petition, and in December 1888 the Sacred Congregation of Bishops and Religious issued a decree establishing the canonical monastery and granting it all the rights and privileges of an independent Benedictine community.[15] Father Augustine Schneider was elected prior, and the three scholastics—joined now by a fourth, Michael Henry Kruse, who in 1886 had been refused admittance to the novitiate at Saint Vincent because of ill health—were invested as novices.

The community operated the commercial college in Bahía and had the care of souls in an extensive missionary field in parts of two Ecuadorian provinces. Father Augustine reported to Abbot Bernard Smith: "We have here a territory for our holy Order larger than any kingdom." Traveling along the coast in boats and over muddy roads on horses that sometimes sank into mud up to their bellies, the priests brought the sacraments to Catholics in the coastal region of Ecuador who had not received them in years. Schneider wrote of the many hardships they encountered and noted: "Such is our life, yet we are happy to see people frequent holy Mass, as they never or seldom for sixteen years had a chance to hear Mass or receive the holy sacraments."[16] To Archabbot Andrew he wrote: "You don't know how poor we are, yet I must confess, that I would not like to trade with you—we live happily and peacefully."[17]

But the happy and peaceful life that Schneider described was not to continue. Not long after the news arrived of the monastery's elevation to canonical rank, Father Conrad Ebert returned to the United States because of ill health and went to St. Benedict's Abbey, Kansas. Soon two of the novices also left. Then, shortly after the departure of Father Conrad, Fathers Augustine and Clement had an argument over the way Schneider was managing the temporal affairs of the priory. The disagreement resulted in Stratman's going to work as a missionary among the Indians and blacks of Esmeraldas, and Schneider was left in Bahía with two novices and the recently ordained Macarius Schmitt. Continuing their work in the commercial college and the coastal missions, the small community struggled to survive, but a final, devastating blow struck in April 1889 when Father Augustine Schneider suffered a heart attack and died. Father Clement returned from Esmeraldas to assist Father Macarius in Bahía, but by now it was clear that Holy Spirit Priory's days were numbered. Schmitt and Stratman asked the Saint Vincent chapter to send money and reinforcements, but at the end of May the chapter decided by a vote of thirteen to twelve not to provide "help and assistance to the monastery and college in Bahia, Ecuador." In July 1889 Archabbot Andrew, declaring that the document they had earlier signed renouncing their affiliation with Saint Vincent was invalid, summoned the two priests back to Saint Vincent.[18]

Father Clement Stratman remained another year in Ecuador working among the Indians and blacks of Esmeraldas before returning to Pennsylvania. Father Macarius Schmitt went back to Saint Vincent in the fall of 1889 but later decided to transfer his vows to the Benedictine monastery of São Bento in São Paulo, Brazil. The two remaining novices left the monastery and returned to the United States. One of them, Michael Henry Kruse, became a priest in the Diocese of Newark and for six years served as curate and pastor in several New Jersey parishes. In 1897 he returned to Latin America and, like Macarius Schmitt, became a Benedictine at São Bento in São Paulo, where he was later elected abbot. Kruse became a noted Benedictine missionary in Latin America during the early twentieth century, and he always credited Boniface Wimmer, whom he had known as a student at Saint Vincent, for the inspiration that led him to work in the missions.[19]

MISSION TO NATIVE AMERICANS

Even as the monks of Saint Vincent debated among themselves the question of limiting their commitment to external apostolates and withdrawing from the community's far-flung missions and parishes, pleas for assistance continued to pour in from bishops and priests throughout the United States, but in most cases Archabbot Andrew did not even present the requests to the chapter for consideration. The consensus at Saint Vincent was that the community's missionary era had ended and that the moment had arrived for consolidation and even retrenchment. In 1889 Saint Vincent turned over its missions in Florida to Maryhelp Abbey, and later that year Archabbot Andrew recalled the Saint Vincent priests who were still serving in Kansas. When Archbishop Michael A. Corrigan of New York offered an attractive mission in the Bahamas to the community, the chapter politely refused.[20]

Some requests were more difficult to turn down. In the fall of 1888 Katharine Drexel, a Philadelphia heiress who devoted her life and fortune to supporting Catholic missionary and educational work among Indians and blacks, approached the Benedictines of Saint Vincent and asked them to staff the Indian School of St. Joseph's in Rensselaer, Indiana. Drexel, who would later found the Sisters of the Blessed Sacrament as a missionary society to labor among Native Americans and African Americans, had already provided considerable assistance to Martin Marty, the Benedictine bishop of the Dakota Territory, in developing Catholic missions among Native Americans of the northern plains, and in the early twentieth century she would support the efforts of St. John's Abbey, Minnesota, and Belmont Abbey, North Carolina, in their missions to Indians and blacks.[21]

The prospect of contributing to Catholic missionary efforts among the Indians of the United States appealed to the monks of Saint Vincent, some of whom envisioned establishing a small monastery in the West whose work would be to educate and evangelize Native Americans and to prepare missionaries to labor among them. When the question came before the chapter, therefore, the capitulars voted by a margin of twenty-two to two to accept the offer in Indiana.[22] Two months later the Saint Vincent monks learned to their disappointment that Bishop Joseph Dwenger of Fort Wayne had decided to offer the school to another religious order. In January 1889 Katharine Drexel wrote Archabbot Andrew expressing regret that the bishop had not given St. Joseph's to the Benedictines and suggesting that Saint Vincent consider instead a mission to the Navajo Indians of New Mexico. "Will you, Rt. Rev. Father, think of these seventeen thousand eight hundred & thirty eight souls when you are before the same Infant Jesus whom the Three Kings found with Mary his Mother?"[23]

Hintenach consulted with the council of seniors and wrote Drexel that he "hesitated very much to say 'No' with regard to undertaking a Mission among the . . . Navajoes." He asked for detailed information about the projected mission and learned that Father Joseph A. Stephan of the Bureau of Catholic Indian Missions wanted the Benedictines to send two priests and two or three lay brothers to open an industrial and agricultural school for Navajo boys in New Mexico. Stephan said that while he hoped the Benedictines would take over the Navajo missions, there were other Indian missions in the Southwest that were also in need of schools, and he suggested that the Saint Vincent chapter consider them as well.[24]

In April 1889 the chapter agreed by an almost unanimous vote to accept one of the Indian missions in the Southwest, and Archabbot Andrew set out with Abbot Innocent Wolf of St. Benedict's on a six-week journey to investigate the best locations for the community's new work. Hintenach and Wolf visited New Mexico, Arizona, and California, and when they returned, the chapters in Kansas and Pennsylvania each decided to assume responsibility for one of the missions that had been offered the Benedictines. St. Benedict's Abbey would take charge of St. Catherine's Indian School in Santa Fe, New Mexico; and Saint Vincent, of St. Boniface Indian School in Banning, California. Both institutions would be built with funds provided by Katharine Drexel and operated with financial support from the Bureau of Catholic Indian Missions.[25] Hintenach wrote Bishop Francis Mora of Monterey–Los Angeles explaining that "the uniform practice of Benedictines has been to establish themselves permanently in one place which then becomes a centre as it were from which operations are conducted in a certain locality or territory." While the beginnings at Banning would be modest, the Saint Vincent chapter hoped eventually to found a monastery in southern California and open a college and seminary that would serve the needs not only of Indians but of whites as well. They also hoped to be "employed in the *Cura Animarum* [care of souls]" in the bishop's diocese, "not only among the Indians but also among the whites, in order that the field of their usefulness and labors may not be too restricted."[26]

In June 1889 Father Bernardine Dolweck and Brother Fridolin Rosenfelder set out from Saint Vincent for southern California, arriving in Banning at the end of the month. In August Father Dominic Block joined them. Dolweck, a sixty-one-year-old native of Alsace-Lorraine, had been ordained in 1853 and served in the missions most of his monastic life. Archabbot Andrew appointed him superior in California. Rosenfelder, a sixty-year-old native of Baden had become a lay brother at Saint Vincent in 1864 and worked on the farms of both the abbey in Pennsylvania and the missions in Georgia and North Carolina before taking charge of agricultural activities in California. Block, age forty, a native of East Orange, New Jersey, had served as a professor and administrator in Saint Vincent College since his ordination in 1874, and in 1887 had succeeded Hilary Pfrängle as director of the college. He went to California to oversee the founding and development of the Indian School in Banning.

The Pennsylvania monks immediately encountered difficulties. Shortly after arriving in Banning, Father Bernardine contracted pneumonia and was hospitalized in Los Angeles. Father Dominic made contact with the Indians the Benedictines had come to serve but discovered that they spoke no English, only Spanish and their native language. In addition, the house the monks expected to live in was not completed at the time of their arrival so they had to stay at a hotel in Banning for several months, an expense they had not anticipated. The result was that by October their money had run out, and expected support from the Bureau of Catholic Missions had not come. In frustration Father Dominic wrote, "I have already had enough of sand and sunshine to do me for the balance of my natural life."[27]

Still the Saint Vincent monks held out hopes of establishing a monastery and opening a school for Native Americans in the lovely valley between the foothills of the Grayback and the San Jacinto mountains. The location was about a mile north of the desert community of Banning and included a ranch of about one hundred acres with a fruit orchard, a vineyard, and an apiary that produced about ten tons of honey a year. Father Dominic and Brother Fridolin moved out to the ranch in September and occupied the eight-room house that had recently been completed for them. They made arrangements for the construction of a school building and began agricultural operations on the ranch. Block wrote Archabbot Andrew:

"I have attentively studied the economy of running this ranch, & my conclusion is that it can be made to pay us well if we run it with our own men."[28]

Hintenach was unable to send more brothers to assist with the manual labor, and Father Dominic was forced to hire local workers at rates the monks could hardly afford. Father Bernardine recovered from his illness and in mid-October rejoined Father Dominic and Brother Fridolin in Banning. The two priests carried on limited missionary work among the Indians of nearby villages. But as the new year approached the financial condition of the Banning mission grew bleaker. Father Dominic wrote: "We have now several months ahead of us during which we have not a cent of income and as our purse is more than empty, where is the means of our subsistence to come from?" He noted that if assistance did not come soon, the three monks would "have to pack our gripsacks & seek shelter under our father's roof."[29]

The Bureau of Catholic Missions had failed to provide the promised funds to keep the mission in Banning solvent. In January Father Joseph Stephan wrote Archabbot Andrew that a new anti-Catholic administration in the federal Bureau of Indian Affairs had contrived to cut off funds for Catholic schools in the Indian missions. The Bureau of Catholic Indian Missions depended on federal money to support the mission schools, and with no prospect of receiving that money, Father Stephan was unable to provide the necessary assistance to the Benedictines in California.[30]

The news from Washington decided the issue. The Saint Vincent chapter determined that without federal support it would be unable to subsidize the mission school in Banning. In March Hintenach recalled the monks from California and the community's missionary work among Native Americans ended. But the mission in Banning did not close. The Bureau of Catholic Missions took charge and sent Father Florian Hahn to continue the work of the Benedictines. Hahn enlisted the aid of the Sisters of St. Joseph of Carondolet, and when federal money became available again he opened the school the Benedictines had constructed before their departure. He directed St. Boniface Indian School for the next twenty-five years.[31]

ST. BEDE'S COLLEGE

A more successful foundation had its origin in the plan of the Saint Vincent priests at St. Joseph's Priory in Chicago to gain independence from the motherhouse. St. Joseph's, founded in 1859, had become one of the most prosperous and successful of Saint Vincent's dependent priories, and by the late 1880s many of the capitulars regarded it as ripe for independence. In 1889 the monks in Chicago—Fathers Celestine Englbrecht, Utto Huber, Casimir Elsesser, and Boniface Wirtner—sent a joint letter to the chapter at Saint Vincent urging the establishment of a Benedictine college near Chicago.[32] Their idea was to use the resources of St. Joseph's Priory to create a small, independent monastery in rural Illinois. The principal apostolates of the new foundation would be parish work and education, but before the monastery could become independent, a college would have to be established that would provide sufficient income for the new monastery.

Bishop John Lancaster Spalding of Peoria supported the idea and offered to assist Saint Vincent in acquiring suitable land in central Illinois for the college. The chapter agreed to the proposal of their Chicago confreres, but not before an extended debate and what some believed to be unseemly manipulation by supporters of the project. Oswald Moosmüller reported to Adalbert Müller that the maneuvering was "to be compared to acts of politicians in the legislature."

> [First] a grant of $30,000 for the building was voted on; afterwards when $70,000 were asked, it fell through, & then in another Chapter at night the same day, after a few more members to attend the Chapter had been hunted up—it was set up again for reconsideration but fell through again. In the meantime agitation was practiced for 5 or 6 weeks; promoters of the plan went around from member to member and collected subscriptions of their names for their vote, & when the required number was secured, another Chapter was held, the number of votes was already known before balloting & it passed.[33]

The difficulty in getting the votes to approve funding for the new foundation reflected the fact that many in the chapter opposed new foundations on principle, fearing that they would drain critical resources and manpower from the abbey and would make it difficult for the community in Pennsylvania to meet commitments to its various apostolates, including the college and seminary. Others saw the creation of small, autonomous monasteries as a means of ensuring the survival of authentic Benedictine observance in America. These monks had all but given up on reforming Saint Vincent according to their own vision of the monastic ideal. They sought now to establish independent communities elsewhere in which they could live the life they desired.

After the chapter had finally authorized funds for the new college, Archabbot Andrew, with Bishop Spalding's assistance, purchased a farm of 203 acres on the Illinois River near Peru, Illinois. The land included the farm of the famous American statesman and orator Daniel Webster, whose house still stood on the property. The Chicago architectural firm of Bauer and Hill was contracted to design the building, and in the summer of 1889 Hintenach sent Father Casimir Elsesser and Brother Wolfgang Traxler to central Illinois to supervise construction.[34]

The five-story brick and stone structure, with space for 150 students, was completed in less than two years. The new college was called St. Bede's in honor of the eighth-century English Benedictine scholar and saint who had spent his entire life devoted to prayer, work, and study within the confines of his monastery at Jarrow. The building was dedicated by Bishop Spalding on October 12, 1891. Hintenach appointed Father Albert Robrecht, a forty-year-old professor of Latin at Saint Vincent College, as rector, and assigned Fathers Alexius Grass, John Müller, Eusebius Geiger, Alcuin Maucher, James Canavin, and Winfrid Kollmansperger to the faculty. The college opened its doors on September 1, 1891, with forty-five boarders and twenty-three day students. The curriculum at St. Bede's was modeled on that of Saint Vincent College and offered two courses of study, a classical course of six years and a commercial course of two years. There was also a preparatory department that offered instruction to boys "not yet sufficiently advanced in the elementary branches to enter either the Classical or Commercial course."[35]

St. Bede's College was slow in developing, and the plan to establish an independent monastery connected with it was delayed. But unlike Saint Vincent's foundations in Ecuador and California, St. Bede's endured and thrived and became the nucleus of an independent abbey established two decades later.[36]

AN ABBEY IN ALABAMA

By 1890 many of the capitulars at Saint Vincent had reached the conclusion that the only way to institute a coherent and well-regulated monastic life for the abbey was to establish from the larger entity several independent houses in which small groups of monks could live a disciplined religious life, united in prayer and a common labor under the rule of an abbot or conventual prior. By now most of them agreed that Saint Vincent was too large, that it was undesirable to have two-thirds of the priests living away from their monastic home, and that one man as archabbot could not possibly oversee the temporal and spiritual welfare of a community of two hundred monks, many of whom were scattered around the country at great distances from the motherhouse. The solution that many had come to support was not to found new communities but to raise existing priories and missions to independent status. "By this plan," Oswald Moosmüller wrote, "the whole character of our system & the spirit of our members would soon be improved."[37] The principal candidates for independence were the priories in Carrolltown, Pennsylvania, St. Marys, Pennsylvania, and Covington, Kentucky, and the missions in Colorado and Alabama.

In May 1890 Hintenach sent a letter to the priests of the abbey outlining the difficulties distant missions posed for the spiritual development of the individual monks and for the satisfactory administration of the abbey's temporal affairs. "The character of a Benedictine life presupposes a family life," he wrote.

> [T]he members of a Benedictine Monastery should enjoy the privilege; yes, have the right to live together in a Community—to enjoy mutual intercourse and such benefits as are to be found only when Brethren live together in fraternal charity.
>
> The whole number of professed Priests, belonging to St. Vincent, is fully one hundred; but of this number, scarcely one-third is in the Abbey itself; whilst the other two-thirds are living outside, a greater or smaller distance from the Monastery.
>
> This condition of things brings with it many inconveniences of a truly serious nature. Thus it happens, that our Fathers, being so far and widely scattered, become more and more estranged to each other for want of an opportunity to meet occasionally at the annual Retreat or at Chapter-meetings. Matters of the greatest importance are decided by a comparatively small minority, as under *our present circumstances,* it is altogether impracticable to assemble all, or even the greater portion of the Fathers, especially from the far South or the distant West.
>
> I need not dwell upon the many spiritual disadvantages to which our Fathers are subjected by the fact, that in many respects, because they are laboring singly in their Missions, which are distant from the common centre, their mode of life resembles that of the secular clergy with all its dangers but without its privileges and conveniences, which, as Religious, they dare not enjoy.

The time had come, Archabbot Andrew said, to consolidate the distant missions and erect independent monasteries. Saint Vincent's parishes in both Alabama and Colorado possessed sufficient lands and revenues "to enable a small band of Monks, animated by the spirit of the Holy Rule and filled with zeal for the honor of God and His Church, not only to subsist, but to make steady and substantial progress." He asked for volunteers from among the priests to establish two new monasteries.[38]

Saint Vincent monks had been serving in the Alabama missions since 1876. In 1890 six priests and three brothers from the abbey were living in five parishes (located in Cullman, Tuscumbia, St. Florian, Huntsville, and Decatur) and visiting scattered Catholic congregations in eight northern Alabama counties. The work was arduous but rewarding since it provided the missionaries with an opportunity to serve the spiritual needs of hundreds of the faithful who otherwise would have had no access to the sacraments. The chapter at Saint Vincent, the monks in Alabama, and Bishop Jeremiah O'Sullivan of Mobile all agreed that an independent monastery in northern Alabama could serve as a vital center for educational and missionary work that would benefit both the Church and the Benedictine Order.[39]

In July 1890 Hintenach petitioned Rome to establish an abbey in the Diocese of Mobile whose members would have the right to choose an abbot and receive novices, and in May 1891 the Holy See granted the petition.[40] It was the fifth abbey founded from Saint Vincent. Upon creation of the new monastery, twelve monks of Saint Vincent transferred their vow of stability to Alabama: Father Benedict Menges (prior in Carrolltown, Pennsylvania), Father Dennis Stolz (pastor in Decatur, Alabama), Father Severin Laufenberg (pastor in St. Florian, Alabama), Father Urban Tracy (pastor in Cullman, Alabama), Father Fridolin Meyer (assistant pastor in Cullman, Alabama), Fraters Theodosius Osterrieder and Bernard Menges (clerics in the theological course at Saint Vincent Seminary), and Brothers Roman Veitl, Emilian Kopps, Rhabanus Cononge, and Placid Schiesser.[41]

On September 29, 1891, the community gathered at Sacred Heart Church, Cullman, Alabama, and with Bishop Leo Haid of North Carolina presiding, the priests of the new abbey elected Father Benedict Menges as their abbot. A native of Obermohr, Bavaria, the fifty-one-year-old Menges had gone to Saint Vincent as a theological student in 1865. As a cleric he had taught Latin and served as a prefect in Saint Vincent College, and after ordination in 1872 he had worked first in the Benedictine missions in Illinois and then in Alabama. From 1888 to 1891 he was prior of St. Benedict's Priory, Carrolltown.

The Alabama monks decided to call their new abbey St. Bernard's in honor of the twelfth-century Cistercian abbot and doctor of the Church, St. Bernard of Clairvaux. For the first year the abbey was located in the spacious rectory of Sacred Heart Church in Cullman, but the monks began at once to build a monastery and college about two miles outside of Cullman on land earlier purchased by Father Gamelbert Brunner. The buildings were completed in the summer of 1892 and dedicated on September 15 by Bishop O'Sullivan of Mobile and Bishop Joseph Rademacher of Nashville, an alumnus of Saint Vincent College. About forty students entered St. Bernard's College in the fall of 1892.[42]

The establishment of St. Bernard's Abbey and College in Alabama proved to be much less complicated than the attempt to erect an independent monastery in Colorado. Monks from Saint Vincent had first gone to the western state in 1886, and by 1890 they had established parishes in three western Colorado counties, including Sacred Heart Church in Boulder. The Saint Vincent chapter's hope of creating an abbey in Colorado met resistance from Bishop Nicholas Chrysostom Matz of Denver, who wrote that the Benedictines were "as yet in no condition to stand on [their] own independent basis" in the diocese. He asked Archabbot Andrew "to allow the little child of St. Benedict in the far west a few more years to grow stronger."[43] Without support from Matz, there was little prospect for a successful petition to Rome, and the chapter decided to postpone plans to establish an independent monastery in Colorado. In the meantime, however, the Saint Vincent monks agreed to accept the bishop's offer of a German parish in the town of Pueblo, which became the nucleus of an independent priory established three decades later.[44]

THE PARISH APOSTOLATE

St. Mary's Church in Pueblo, Colorado, was one of four new parishes accepted by the monastic chapter during Hintenach's abbacy, and the monks assumed charge of it only after returning the missions in Breckenridge and Fairplay to the diocese. Between 1888 and 1892 the Saint Vincent chapter also authorized the establishment of Sacred Heart Parish in Jeannette, Pennsylvania (1889); St. Bernard Parish in Hastings, Pennsylvania (1890); and St. Cecilia Parish in Whitney, Pennsylvania (1891). Sacred Heart and St. Cecilia's were served by priests based at the abbey and St. Bernard's by priests from St. Benedict's Priory, Carrolltown.

Despite efforts by the reformers to limit the number of parishes under the care of the abbey, parochial work continued to be a principal apostolate for Saint Vincent during the Hintenach years. The monks recognized their obligation to serve the pastoral needs of the Church and continued to respond to those needs as they had always done. By 1892 priests from the abbey had charge of the pastoral care of thirty-six thousand Catholics in forty-six parishes in Pennsylvania, Kentucky, Illinois, Colorado, and Maryland. Attached to these parishes were parochial schools enrolling more than six thousand pupils who were taught, for the most part, by Benedictine sisters. Eight of the larger parishes (St. Benedict's in Carrolltown, Pennsylvania; St. Mary's in St. Marys, Pennsylvania; St. Joseph's in Johnstown, Pennsylvania; St. Mary's in Erie, Pennsylvania; St. Mary's in Allegheny City, Pennsylvania; St. Joseph's in Covington, Kentucky; St. Joseph's in Chicago, Illinois; and Sacred Heart in Boulder City, Colorado) were designated as priories and had up to six priests and brothers assigned to them. Others had one or two priests in residence or were served by priests from one of the priories.[45]

An important aspect of these parishes was their distinctive Benedictine character. Far from being isolated congregations, they formed part of a greater Benedictine family and shared in the spiritual life of the abbey in Pennsylvania. In 1890 Archabbot Andrew sought and received from Rome authorization to establish in the United States a confraternity of St. Benedict to which many of the parishioners eventually belonged.[46] This confraternity offered laymen and laywomen the opportunity to become oblates of St. Benedict and participate in a Benedictine spirituality which gave deeper meaning to their lives. In the 1890s the monks also established a Confraternity of the Holy Ghost at Saint Vincent which spread to the parishes and spiritually united them with one another as well as with the abbey itself.[47] The Benedictine character of the parishes was strengthened and enhanced, moreover, by the fact that virtually all of the American-born men who came to Saint Vincent as candidates for the priesthood and lay brotherhood during the nineteenth and early twentieth centuries came from parishes under the care of Saint Vincent priests.

The close bond that existed between the abbey and the parishes is illustrated by Saint Vincent's response to the destruction of St. Joseph's Priory in Johnstown during the great flood of 1889. The St. Joseph's parish school was swept away in the flood waters, the church was badly damaged, and 110 parishioners lost their lives. The day after the disaster, Archabbot Andrew dispatched five brothers and a workman from Saint Vincent to assist Prior Corbinian Gastbiehl and the parishioners in recovery efforts. The monastic chapter provided money to assist parishioners as well as to restore the parish church, which after preliminary repairs was temporarily turned over to the Flood Commission for use as a relief center. A year later, when the church had been restored, Hintenach went to Johnstown to celebrate a pontifical Requiem Mass for the flood victims, who included the families of several Saint Vincent students.[48]

The oldest parish served by priests from the abbey was that of Saint Vincent itself. In 1892 it was still a relatively small congregation, consisting of only 520 parishioners. Because its members were scattered over the rural farmlands that surrounded the town of Latrobe, making it difficult for their children to attend school at a central location, the parish sponsored five one-room schools strategically located in the countryside surrounding the abbey. These schools enrolled 160 pupils who were taught by lay teachers from the parish.[49]

The church at Saint Vincent, built in 1835, served the lay congregation as well as the monastic community, and by 1890 it was clearly inadequate to meet the needs of both. On April 16, 1890, at the centennial celebration of the founding of the Sportsman's Hall Parish by Father Theodore Brouwers, Archabbot Andrew called a meeting of the congregation at which he announced plans for construction of a new church. He asked the parishioners for their support, and the parishioners, as one historian of Saint Vincent noted, "[a]ll entered heartily into the project and promised to aid cheerfully towards its accomplishment."[50]

Plans for a new abbey church had been on the drawing board for twenty years, but resources for the work had not been available as long as Saint Vincent was committing its major energies to the establishment of missions and parishes throughout the United States. Now that the policy had changed to one of consolidation and even retrenchment in the missions, the chapter at Saint Vincent decided that it was time to build a suitable church for public worship and celebration of the monastic liturgy. Contracts were drawn up with the local construction companies of Brown Brothers and John Kirchner to quarry stone at Donohoe Station and the nearby Kuhn farm; the Marble-Hill Quarry Company of Pittsburgh was contracted to face the foundation stone; and Mr. Sebastian Wimmer, nephew of the late archabbot and a civil engineer, was selected to lay out the ground and superintend construction of the foundation. Men from the parish volunteered to haul stone to the building site, and the Saint Vincent brickyard began to produce twelve thousand bricks a day. By the beginning of winter there were one million bricks on hand.[51]

The site chosen for construction was the east side of the monastery quadrangle. Ground breaking ceremonies took place on December 21, 1891, and about 140 children of the parish took part in the gala event. After a solemn High Mass in the old church, the children assembled at the porter's gate and then "fell into file, the boys going two by two, followed by the girls in the same order." At a signal from Father Edward Andelfinger, pastor of the parish, they set to work digging the ground where the church was to rise.

> For fully an hour the little ones worked as though for life. Earth and stones and fragments of dirt flew through the air as missiles in a sweeping storm. Fathers laughed and shouted their little ones on to greater activity. Mothers holding infants in their arms placed small piece of ground in their tiny hands and made them deposit it in the standing carts. . . . After several carts had been filled and carried away, Father Edward thanked the children for their earnest labor, urged them to be ever faithful and zealous in this truly great work of God and then dismissed them to return to their homes and cherish the memory of the day.[52]

Many of the parish children who participated in the ground breaking bore the names of the earliest Catholic families in the region, such as the Bridges, Henrys, Kintzes, Kuhns, Kellys, Millers, Noels, and Staders, many of whom had welcomed the Benedictines to Saint Vincent in 1846 and some of whom had been among Theodore Brouwers's first parishioners in 1790. That children from these and other parish families played so prominent a role in the ground breaking ceremony held a significance beyond the event itself, for it linked the parish community's present with its past as well as its future. These children would see the abbey church rise above the farmlands of western Pennsylvania to become a center of community life and worship for themselves, their children, and their children's children. Moreover, their participation reflected the close relationship between the people and the monastic community, a relationship that continued to endure through the century that followed.

Monks and parishioners expected the new abbey church to be completed by 1896, the fiftieth anniversary of the Benedictines' arrival at Saint Vincent. But a national economic depression, resulting in a long period of financial uncertainty for the abbey and the parish, delayed construction, and the church was not finished until 1905, fourteen years after the work began.

DEVELOPMENTS IN THE COLLEGE AND SEMINARY

Educational advances in the college and seminary during the years of Hintenach's abbacy were modest. With one significant exception, the curriculum established in the 1860s remained basically unchanged through the 1890s. The traditional division into the theological, classical, commercial, and elementary departments was maintained, with the principal resources and largest number of faculty being devoted to the theological and classical departments. Now, however, a two-year philosophy program was added to the classical curriculum, expanding the course of studies in that department from six to eight years, while both philosophical and theological instruction became increasingly dominated by the influence of Thomistic scholasticism.[53]

The two-year elementary school, whose purpose was "to prepare boys for one of the higher courses in the College," continued to attract an average of two dozen students a year, most of them from western Pennsylvania but some from as far away as Bavaria. The three-year course in the commercial department annually enrolled about eighty students whose studies led to careers in business and trade. Students who successfully completed the commercial course and passed a series of examinations received a master of accounts degree, the most frequently conferred degree at the college in the 1890s.

The bachelor of arts degree was awarded relatively infrequently during the final decade of the nineteenth century. Theoretically every student who completed the eight years of classical studies (including the two final years of philosophy) was eligible, but in fact the B.A. was conferred only upon those who sat a rather rigorous examination "in all the languages and sciences taught in the classical course." Between 1887 and 1900 the college granted only twenty-four bachelor of arts degrees, compared with ninety-seven masters of accounts degrees during the same period. This was despite the fact that there was always a larger enrollment in the classical course than in the commercial course. Students who earned a B.A. and then "devot[ed] two years to a learned profession, or to literary or scientific studies" could earn a master of arts degree. The college awarded ten of these between 1887 and 1900.

The classical course, now divided into a Latin curriculum of six years and a philosophy curriculum of two years, began in the 1890s to take on the character of a combined secondary and collegiate program. The first two years of the Latin curriculum were designated "preparatory," the second four "collegiate." As its name implied, the Latin curriculum emphasized classical language studies, as well as English, German, history, geography, math, and religious instruction. It also included science courses in botany, chemistry, natural history (biology and geology), and natural philosophy (physics). The average enrollment in the classical course during this period was 155 students, of whom an average of thirty-five priesthood students followed the advanced philosophy curriculum.

Students who had completed the six years of the Latin curriculum and who intended to become priests entered the philosophy program. At the Third Council of Baltimore (1884) the bishops of the United States had set down standard requirements for American seminaries. These requirements firmly fixed the organization, discipline, and studies of minor and major seminaries, stipulating a two-year program in philosophy followed by a three-year program in theology.[54] Both the philosophy and the theology curricula at Saint Vincent in the 1890s conformed to the new standards.

Courses in the philosophy curriculum included the history of philosophy, ethics, logic, ontology, cosmology, natural theology, introduction to sacred scripture, and Hebrew. Philosophy students also undertook advanced studies in Latin and Greek and attended classes in mathematics, physics, and chemistry. Following the guidelines established by the Council of Baltimore, and in conformity with the instruction of Pope Leo XIII in the encyclical *Aeterni Patris* (1879), the philosophical and theological programs at Saint Vincent became increasingly centered on the thought of St. Thomas Aquinas. In order to prepare faculty to teach courses in scholastic philosophy and theology the Saint Vincent chapter continued the practice of sending Benedictine clerics and priests to Rome to study at the international college of Sant' Anselmo. Among those who went to the Eternal City in the final decade of the nineteenth century were Lawrence Haas, Raphael Wieland, Candidus Eichenlaub, Leopold Probst, Ambrose Kohlbeck, Ernest Gensheimer, and Virgil Niesslein.

Priesthood students who completed the classical course continued on to theological studies in the Saint Vincent major seminary. As yet there was no absolute administrative division between the college and the seminary. During the 1890s enrollment in the three-year theology course averaged forty seminarians, about a fourth of whom were Benedictine clerics and the rest diocesan seminarians. The diocesan students came principally from the Pennsylvania dioceses of Pittsburgh, Erie, Harrisburg, Scranton, and later Altoona, but there were also major seminarians from the dioceses of Covington, Columbus, Cleveland, Brooklyn, Buffalo, Trenton, La Crosse, Green Bay, Marquette, Galveston, Sioux Falls, and Helena, and the archdioceses of Chicago and New York.

Following the decrees of the Third Council of Baltimore, the theology curriculum included courses in dogmatic theology, moral theology, sacramentology, church history, liturgy, sacred eloquence, and Gregorian chant. (The study of scripture was completed in the two years of the philosophy program.) The principal texts were Schouppe's *Theologia Dogmatica* and *Res Sacramentaria,* Sabetti's *Theologia Moralis,* Brueck's *Historia Ecclesiastica,* Drecker's *Eloquentia Sacra,* the *Rituale Romanum,* the *Brevarium Romanum* and *Brevarium Monasticum,* and Wapelhorst's *Liturgia Sacra.* The prominence of Thomistic theology is evidenced by the fact that by 1891 there were eighteen copies of the *Summa Theologica* in the seminary library.[55] To ensure that they would first be able to study the most important primary and secondary theological sources in the original languages and afterwards serve the needs of German-speaking Catholics in American dioceses, the seminarians were required to be proficient in both Latin and German.[56]

The 1890s were a period of controversy and intellectual ferment in the American Catholic Church. Major disagreements arose between progressives who advocated exploring legitimate ways of adapting the ancient

Catholic Church to contemporary American life and values, and European-bound traditionalists who considered American culture as fundamentally secular and Protestant and who regarded any attempt to reach a compromise with that culture as a betrayal of traditional Catholic teaching tantamount to heresy. For the first time in its hundred-year history the American hierarchy did not speak with one voice. Liberal bishops such as James Gibbons of Baltimore, John Ireland of St. Paul, and John Lancaster Spalding of Peoria held a deep-rooted conviction that there was a fundamental harmony between American democratic ways and Catholicism. They supported the "Americanization" of the millions of European Catholic immigrants who had come to the United States during the nineteenth century, and they advocated the Church's acceptance of public education for Catholic children as a means of achieving assimilation. Conservative bishops such as Michael Corrigan of New York, Bernard McQuaid of Rochester, and the German bishops of the American Midwest viewed American culture and values as basically incompatible with Catholicism, and they opposed any attempt at assimilation. The conservatives strongly supported parochial schools and the right of Catholic immigrants from Europe to preserve their languages and religious traditions within their own ethnic communities as a means of keeping the faith that they had inherited from their ancestors.[57]

Monks and seminarians at Saint Vincent closely followed the issues dividing the American Church in the 1890s. The seminary subscribed to all of the journals in which the controversies were played out publicly: *The Catholic World, The American Ecclesiastical Review, The American Catholic Quarterly Review,* and *The Century.* An examination of contemporary volumes of these journals in the Saint Vincent Library indicates that they were heavily used and carefully read.[58] The almost constitutional conservatism of the American Benedictines left little doubt as to where the sympathies of the vast majority of monks and seminarians at Saint Vincent lay. The monastic community strongly supported the position of Archbishop Corrigan and the German bishops of the Midwest, and the conservative bishops demonstrated their appreciation of this support by frequently sending their priesthood candidates to Saint Vincent for theological studies.

The conservative effort to preserve ethnic identity, language, and values among the immigrants was also strongly supported by the Saint Vincent community. Despite the fact that the majority of the monks were now American-born, the German heritage of the monastery and school was everywhere in evidence in the 1890s. The German language predominated in the monastery; English-speaking seminarians were required to learn German and English-speaking college students were encouraged to do so as well; German-language books and periodicals filled the library shelves and reading rooms; public events were usually marked by at least one address in German; and priests from the abbey continued to serve parishes that were predominately German. While the American Benedictines on the whole remained aloof from the bitter debates between liberal and conservative Catholic leaders of the period, Archabbot Andrew attended the second annual *Katholikentag* of German-American Catholics in Cincinnati in 1888, a meeting organized by the German-American Priests' Society to oppose the "Americanization" program of the liberals and "to promote loyalty to the Holy See, the parochial school system, and the preservation of German language and culture among German-American Catholics."[59]

Turnover in the academic leadership of Saint Vincent College occurred with an unusual frequency in the 1890s, reflecting not only the difficulties of developing and maintaining an academically sound program in the college and seminary but also the increased pressures upon the Benedictine community to provide talented administrators for the missions, parishes, and schools distant from Saint Vincent. Between 1888 and 1900 no less than eight priests served as directors of the college. Father Dominic Block, director from 1887 to 1889, was sent to California on the ill-fated mission to open an Indian school in Banning. He returned to the abbey in 1890 only to die a year later, at the age of forty-two, from tetanus. Block's successor, Father Louis Haas, held the directorship for only one year (1889–90) before becoming prior at St. Joseph's Priory, Covington. Haas was succeeded by Father Mellitus Tritz, a forty-three-year-old professor of Latin who died of pneumonia within a year of his appointment (1890–91). The next director, twenty-nine-year-old Father Martin Singer, served a one-year term (1891–92) before going to Manchester, New Hampshire, to assist the Benedictines of Newark establish Saint Anselm College in that city. The five-year tenure of Singer's successor, Father Vincent Huber, was longer than that of any other director of the 1890s. He successfully led the college from 1892 to 1897, when he left to assume the directorship of St. Bede's College, Peru, Illinois. Thirteen years later he was elected abbot of St. Bede's when that community was elevated to the rank of abbey. Huber was followed as director of Saint Vincent College by Father Raphael Wieland, a professor of sacramentology in the seminary who had recently returned from theological studies at Sant' Anselmo in Rome. Wieland was director for two years (1897–99) before being appointed prior of St. Joseph's Priory, Covington,

Kentucky. In 1899 Father Germain Ball, a thirty-nine-year-old mathematics professor from Johnstown, Pennsylvania, assumed the directorship, which he held until 1905. His six-year tenure was the longest since the time of Father Alphonse Heimler who had piloted the college for a decade in the 1860s and 1870s.

The faculty of the college and seminary during the final decade of the century was composed entirely of Benedictine priests and clerics, for the increase in monastic vocations during the 1880s and 1890s had eliminated the necessity of employing lay professors. The faculty averaged thirty members throughout this period, and there was frequent turnover as clerics were ordained and assigned to parishes, and priests were recalled from the parishes to serve as professors in the college. The academic backgrounds and teaching talents of many of the monks, moreover, assured the institution of a distinguished and dedicated professorate that provided Saint Vincent students of the day with a quality, if somewhat insular, education. Among the faculty during this period was Father Oswald Moosmüller, professor of history, who had studied in both Bavaria and Rome and whose historical researches in American and European archives had resulted in the publication of works on the history of the Benedictines in the United States as well as on the pre-Columban European explorations of America.[60] Father Maurice Kaeder, a noted public lecturer in both English and German and author of *Lectiones in Jure Canonico,* was professor of moral theology, canon law, and homiletics. Teaching rather than research and publication, however, occupied most of the energies of faculty members at Saint Vincent in the 1890s. Professors held in especially high regard by the students included Father Mark Kirchner (physics, astronomy, and mathematics), Father Julian Kilger (who had taught philosophy at Montecassino), Father Raymond Daniel (music), Father Gallus Hoch (sacred scripture), Father Jerome Schmitt (Latin), Father Daniel Kaib (bookkeeping), and Father Baldwin Ambros (pastoral theology and liturgy).

Students in the college during this period came principally from Pennsylvania, but the states of Connecticut, Indiana, Kentucky, New Jersey, New York, Maryland, Ohio, and West Virginia were amply represented as well. In addition, each year a handful of students came from Europe, especially from Bavaria, Austria, Prussia, Württemberg, and the German-speaking parts of Bohemia. In the 1890s the four divisions of the college had an average annual enrollment of 300 students, which represented a 10 percent decline from the average enrollment of 330 students in the 1870s, and an even greater decline from the average of 350 students enrolled in the 1880s.

One reason for the decline was a shortage of housing in the college and monastery, both of which, though separated into different quarters, shared the same facilities. Between 1886, when the south wing of the main quadrangle was completed, and 1907, when Alfred Hall was built, no new dormitory space became available at Saint Vincent, and during Hintenach's abbacy not only did monastic vocations increase but a significant number of priests in the parishes and missions were brought back to live at the abbey. Thus, the need for room to house the influx of monks limited the amount of space available to house students, and fewer students may have been accepted. An even greater reason for the decline in student enrollment, however, was the economic depression that struck the nation in the mid-1890s. Fewer families had the resources now to pay the three-hundred-dollar annual charge for tuition, board, and fees, and as a result, by 1898 enrollment had declined to a twenty-five-year low of 268 students.[61]

Student life changed little at Saint Vincent between the Civil War and the last decade of the century. Students still lived a strictly regulated, quasi-monastic life consisting of classroom lessons, study hall, community meals (with table reading), common recreation, and regular religious devotions. Like their Catholic classmates, non-Catholic students were required to attend daily Mass and other prayer services, but they were exempt from religious instruction classes.

Sports continued to be an important part of student life. Regular field days were held in the fall and spring at which seminarians, college students, and elementary school pupils competed with others in their own age groups. Events on field days consisted principally of races. One such competition held in the spring of 1892 involved the hundred-yard dash, a sack race, a three-legged race, a wheelbarrow race, a hop-step-jump competition, a tug-of-war, and a "peanut scramble."[62] Baseball, football, handball, and tennis were also popular, and some of the most intense competition on the playing fields was between the college students who were preparing to enter the Benedictine Order (the scholastics) and their classmates who were preparing themselves for other vocations (the "collegiates"). Other student activities during the 1890s included day trips to Saint Vincent's property on Chestnut Ridge, nine miles from the college; organized hikes through the countryside around the college; excursions to Idlewild Park near Ligonier; and trips to nearby Loyalhanna Creek for ice-skating in winter and swimming in summer. One evening in June 1891 a swimming party in the Loyalhanna ended in tragedy when senior student Charles F. Ayers of Elizabeth, New Jersey, drowned.[63]

Student societies during the 1890s included the Sodality of the Blessed Sacrament, the Students' Altar Society of St. Joseph, the League of the Sacred Heart, the St. Boniface Literary Society, the St. Vincent Debating Society, the Senior Dramatic Society, the St. Vincent College Choir, the St. Benedict Orchestra, and the St. Vincent Military Band. In 1885 the St. Thomas Literary and Dialectic Society had been formed in the seminary. Its purpose was "to develop and perfect the intellectual and oratorical powers of its members by debates, sermons and lectures" and to inculcate in its members greater knowledge of the intellectual heritage of St. Thomas Aquinas. Each year on March 7 its members celebrated the feast of the Angelic Doctor with formal lectures on the life and work of their patron. An account of the celebration in 1891 reported that

> [i]n Latin, English, and German did the members of the Society expatiate upon the virtues and general sanctity of the most saintly among the Learned; in various languages did some of our honorary members depict the studiousness, the untiring diligence, the depth and breadth of intellectual grasp, the analytic and synthetic powers, the force, clearness, and simplicity of diction of the most learned among the Saints. The addresses were not mere eulogies or panegyrics; they were instructive and animating, and we flatter ourselves that not a small part of the enthusiasm for St. Thomas, his works and doctrines, which now abounds at St. Vincent's, was called forth by the eloquence, which fired the souls of the speakers and audiences at the annual recurrence of the feast of St. Thomas.[64]

In 1891 the society made a lasting contribution to Saint Vincent by founding the *St. Vincent's Journal,* a monthly publication containing news about faculty, students, and alumni; editorials on contemporary national, international, and religious issues; and essays and articles on various topics. The first volume contained articles on the poetry of Tennyson, the life of Thomas More, the contribution of St. Benedict to Western civilization, the religion of Shakespeare, the history of St. Vincent, and Pope Leo XIII's condemnation of the African slave trade. The *Journal,* which later came under the editorial administration of college students, continued its uninterrupted publication until 1956 when it was replaced by the *St. Vincent Review.*

JUBILEE AND RESIGNATION

In April 1892 Archabbot Andrew marked the twenty-fifth anniversary of his ordination. In the months leading up to the anniversary a committee of priests at the abbey worked quietly to organize a celebration to honor a superior whom the members of the Saint Vincent community had come to genuinely love. The planned celebration was to be a simple "family feast" in deference to the archabbot's "well known modesty." Noting that "any public manifestation of honor or attention [was] naturally painful" to him, the organizers hoped to arrange an unpretentious commemoration that would demonstrate the monks' affection for their spiritual father without causing him to feel ill at ease. They planned to invite a few special guests and keep the festivities low-key, but as it turned out the jubilee evolved into a much more elaborate affair than originally conceived and the effort to conceal the plans from the archabbot failed when one of the invited guests sent him a letter expressing regret at not being able to attend.

On the day preceding the anniversary many of the Saint Vincent priests serving in the parishes arrived at the abbey to take part in the celebration. They were joined by Abbot Innocent Wolf of Kansas, Abbot Bernard Locnikar of Minnesota, Abbot Benedict Menges of Alabama, Abbot Fintan Mundwiler of St. Meinrad's Abbey in Indiana, and Bishop Richard Phelan of Pittsburgh. After vespers the Saint Vincent orchestra serenaded Archabbot Andrew who was then invited to the chapter room where the monks had prepared a festive reception in his honor. Gifts and messages of congratulations had poured in from friends and confreres in the United States and Europe, and a special greeting and apostolic blessing had come from Pope Leo XIII. The telegrams and letters were read and the gifts presented. Father Celestine Englbrecht, prior of St. Joseph's Priory in Chicago and one of the students who had come to Saint Vincent with Boniface Wimmer in 1846, acted as spokesman for the community. He congratulated the archabbot upon the occasion of his silver jubilee and thanked him for his fatherly care of the monks over the previous four years. Hintenach responded graciously but with evident distress. The *St. Vincent's Journal* reported that he "said that he himself owed a great deal of gratitude to St. Vincent's, which had always treated him like a mother except on one occasion when it played him a trick from the effects of which he still suffers from being deprived of the peace and quiet, which he had enjoyed as a private religious."

The following morning the guests, who now included alumni and friends of Saint Vincent and members of the Hintenach family, gathered in the abbey church for a solemn pontifical High Mass at which Abbot Benedict Menges preached the sermon. After Mass, the monks sang the *Te Deum* "with a volume of voice that betokened the feelings of gratitude to God, which filled every heart." In the afternoon almost two hundred guests gathered in the monastery refectory to attend a banquet in the jubilarian's honor at which toasts were offered by Bishop Phelan, the abbots, and several priests. When the meal was over everyone went to the front of the monastery quadrangle where the first stone of the new abbey church was laid. Clergy and laity "took an active part with trowel and hammer" and prayers were said for the Church, for Saint Vincent, and for Archabbot Andrew that God would "grant him a long and useful life in our midst as the head of this institution."[65]

The elaborate celebration, organized with the best of intentions and designed to express the community's reverence and love for the archabbot, proved to be a difficult and embarrassing moment for him. As everyone recognized, his naturally retiring disposition and introverted personality made any public display of honor or deference disquieting, but on this occasion the demonstrations of affection and esteem and the warm wishes of the community for his long and fruitful reign as archabbot were particularly painful, for hidden in his heart was a secret that Hintenach had shared with no one at the abbey. Three months before, he had submitted to Rome his resignation as archabbot of Saint Vincent.

Andrew Hintenach had never wanted to be archabbot. Except for eighteen months when he was superior of the Alabama mission, he had lived his whole life in the shadow of the monastery, quietly, faithfully following the monastic rule of prayer, work, and study. He wanted nothing more than to be able to continue to lead that simple, unassuming life. He had greeted the surprise of his election with anxiety and tears and had begged his confreres to let that particular cup pass from his lips. But in the spirit of monastic humility and obedience, he had finally accepted the responsibilities imposed upon him by his brothers.

Less than two years after his election, however, he had secretly written to the Holy See asking to be relieved of office. The reasons he gave revealed his own personal sense of inadequacy in dealing with the spiritual and temporal problems confronting the community as well as his frustration at being unable to reform monastic life at Saint Vincent according to his own spiritual and monastic ideals. Specifically Hintenach said that the reasons for his desire to step down were: (1) the intrinsic difficulties of governing a religious community, (2) the even greater difficulty of governing a large religious community whose members lived in various places distant from the monastery, and (3) the fact that he himself lacked the necessary qualities and character to govern the community properly. Hintenach said that these were the same reasons he had given his confreres when he tried to refuse the election in February 1888 and that he had finally agreed to become abbot only "aegro animo" ("with a sick heart"). After almost two years of serving the community as superior, he feared that if he continued in the abbacy, the monastery would suffer both spiritual and temporal harm (*"concludit se damnum sive spirituale sive temporale Monasterii timere"*).[66]

Cardinal Joannes Simeoni, prefect of the Sacred Congregation for the Propagation of the Faith, informed both Abbot Leo Haid, president of the American Cassinese Congregation, and Abbot Bernard Smith, procurator general for the American Benedictines in Rome, of Archabbot Andrew's request and asked for their advice. Both Haid and Smith said at once that they opposed the resignation. Haid wrote that the reasons Hintenach offered for wanting to resign were inadequate.

> I know that he accepted the dignity with a sick heart, but the reasons for his accepting are still in force. The difficulties of governing the monastery will remain for his successor. Archabbot Andrew is a pious, prudent, truly religious, and humble man. His fear of failure has no foundation. In the visitation held at his monastery in September 1890 I found monastic discipline to be excellent. . . . I know the monks all have a sincere love for the archabbot and hold him in the highest esteem.[67]

Haid told Abbot Smith that he believed Hintenach's "diffidence and a desire to be somewhat more retired" were the real reasons for his petition to Rome, but it was clear that "[n]o successor could escape the difficulties inseparable from the government of a large community with extensive temporal interests to be attended to. . . . I don't see that any better one can be found—and there are many chances to get those less fit to rule. At all events his resignation should not be accepted now—in 8 or 10 years things may change so as to relieve him."[68]

And so, to Archabbot Andrew's great distress, the Holy See refused to relieve him of the burdens of office. He accepted the decision with equanimity and never said a word to anyone at Saint Vincent, but he continued to pray for a remedy. A year passed and his sickness of heart persisted. The stress of responsibility weighed heavily on his spirit and he longed for release. His growing depression and withdrawal into himself were regarded by the monks as signs of his holiness and the deepening of his search for God. His self-effacement and increased periods of silence were interpreted as evidence of his devotion to the contemplative monastic ideal, and his dark night of the soul only served to endear him more to his spiritual sons.

Hintenach worked diligently in the year after his petition had been rejected to create for the monks of Saint Vincent an environment of prayer and work in which they could find the peace and order embodied in the Benedictine Rule. He sought to limit their isolation in distant parishes and to form model communities where they could grow in wisdom and grace.

In January of 1892 he received the happy news that the election of Abbot Benedict Menges in Alabama had been confirmed by the Holy See, thus ratifying his efforts to establish another center of Benedictine observance in America where priests and brothers could both serve the Church and develop their interior lives. He wrote, "May it please God to bless our enterprises, for they are undertaken to promote His honor and glory."[69]

But as one twentieth-century commentator on his life observed, Archabbot Andrew was a man who knew his limits.[70] To him it seemed as if he had failed, and he was now convinced more than ever that he was not the superior to do for the monastery of Saint Vincent what had to be done. Moved by an authentic Christian humility and recognizing his limits, he once again sought to free himself from the burdens and responsibilities of the abbacy. In January 1892 he wrote Abbot Bernard Smith asking for his help. "You are aware that a little over a year ago I petitioned the Propaganda for the permission to resign and retire from the office and position I held since April 1888," he said.

> In this petition were embodied the different reasons which urged me on to take such a step. In order to avoid as much as possible all unnecessary delay I sent the petition direct to Propaganda, believing that thereby it would escape the attentions of those who I thought might out of misplaced charity and friendship for me in some way or other interfere with said petition and perhaps prevent its being granted. However I have since found out that my plan had failed and that my anxiety to keep the matter secret was not a success. Notwithstanding that my first attempt proved a failure, yet I feel myself urged on in my own mind and heart *to try again*, and may it please God with better success. Would you kindly take my part in this matter and to the best of your ability defend my cause! I have hardly anything more to add to my former petition. The reasons given *then* I also urge now with still greater emphasis. I cannot believe that a change of Superior here would embarrass our Community. On the contrary it will rather be a benefit, and the future will show such to be the case.[71]

Hintenach pleaded with Abbot Leo Haid to support the new petition, and this time Haid agreed. "Tho' I am very sorry that he insists in resigning," the bishop of North Carolina wrote, "and tho' I still consider his reasons insufficient, yet I feel that he is suffering agonies, and out of charity—I withdraw all objections."[72]

Haid had already sent his endorsement to Rome when Archabbot Andrew learned of preparations for the jubilee celebration in his honor. Embarrassed at the possibility that he would have to announce his resignation shortly after the monks had publicly honored him for his twenty-five years of devoted service as a priest, he asked Abbot Leo to postpone the endorsement of his resignation until a later time. Haid immediately wrote Abbot

Bernard Smith asking him to ignore his letter sent ten days before. He said he had recently learned that Archabbot Andrew "has reconsidered the matter, and I now hope he will not resign."[73] But Smith had already forwarded the resignation and endorsement to the Propaganda Fide, and deliberations had begun that would lead, four weeks later, to the Holy See's officially accepting Hintenach's resignation and calling for the election of a new archabbot of Saint Vincent.

The Sacred Congregation for the Propagation of the Faith issued a decree on May 25, 1892, relieving Hintenach of the abbatial office and instructing the Saint Vincent capitulars to elect a new superior.[74] The decree was sent to Bishop Leo Haid, who met with Archabbot Andrew in Baltimore on June 12 and informed him of the decision. On the same day Haid sent a letter to Father Vincent Huber, prior at the abbey, informing him of the Roman decree and instructing him to keep the matter secret until Archabbot Andrew had an opportunity to return to Saint Vincent and tell the community the news himself. "I am very sorry this is done," Haid wrote; "yet, in all things, God has His ends, and let us hope that the present cloud will give way to light in the near future."[75]

Archabbot Andrew returned to the abbey on June 13 and the following day composed a letter to the monks of Saint Vincent telling them that he was no longer their abbot. Rome, he said, had "granted my earnest desire to be relieved of my present position as Superior of St. Vincent Abbey. Of this fact you are herewith officially notified. On this occasion I most heartily express to you my gratitude for the kind feelings shown towards me during my term of office; and I also beg your indulgence for any shortcomings on my part in the exercise of my duties during the same. May God's blessing rest upon dear St. Vincent's Abbey." He signed the letter, "Your sincere Confrere, Andrew Hintenach, O.S.B."[76]

Father Louis Haas reported that the news struck the community "like a thunderbolt from a clear sky."[77] Another contemporary reporter observed that "to say that the community was surprised would be a mild form of expressing the agitation that prevailed."[78] Many of the monks were incensed with Abbot Leo Haid for the part he had played in the archabbot's resignation. In a passionate outburst marked by shock and pain and outrage, the normally tranquil prior of Saint Vincent, Father Vincent Huber, wrote the abbot of North Carolina:

> What have you done!!! You have shaken the very foundations of this great Abbey by depriving us of our superior by your execrable officiousness. You have deprived us of a superior whose only fault is his humility. He is the most worthy of all our Benedictine prelates, and there is not a superior in this great land who was and is

more loved and respected by his subjects than he. But humility caused him to hand in his resignation and Rome placed and (as the result showed) misplaced a matter of such momentous importance in your hands by stating that the resignation would not be accepted if not endorsed by the Praeses. That disposed of the first attempt at resignation. The good Archabbot then had recourse to you; at first you refused to endorse, but later on you lost all backbone and made St. Vincent's an orphanage. . . . The air is full of execrations against you and in my opinion you deserve them all.[79]

Father Edward Andelfinger, pastor of Saint Vincent Parish, wrote Abbot Leo in a similar vein:

[T]he entire community at St. Vincent's is in the state of frenzied agitation over the resignation of our Father Abbot, and to a man it is incensed against you for the part you have taken in effecting the present unhappy condition of our monastery, leaving upon it an everlasting stigma of dishonor, infamy and disgrace; blighting and blasting the fondest hopes of the cradle of your own greatness. . . . No matter what may have been the motive, a personal consideration of the Archabbot, you should have some respect for the community. You have injured us greatly. The only thing left is to right the wrong and restore to us our first and last and only choice, Abbot Andrew. As a Bishop/Abbot and priest, I beg pardon for my boldness. But never will you receive forgiveness from St. Vincent's.[80]

On June 16 the Saint Vincent chapter met and elected Father Vincent Huber and Father Athanasius Hintenach (brother of Archabbot Andrew) as vicar of the chapter and temporal administrator of the abbey respectively until a new archabbot could be elected. The chapter then took up the question of what the community should do in face of the crisis confronting it. An overwhelming majority of the priests at the abbey urged that the chapter send a petition to Rome asking the Holy See to withdraw its acceptance of Archabbot Andrew's resignation. Others were in favor of proceeding with the election of a new archabbot.[81]

Because the matter was so important, the chapter decided to poll the priests in the parishes before determining which option to choose. On June 18, therefore, Huber sent a circular letter to all the priests of the community, both at the abbey and in the parishes, asking them to vote on whether to petition Rome to withdraw its acceptance or to proceed with the immediate election of Hintenach's successor.[82] A week later Huber announced the results of the poll. An absolute majority of the capitulars voted in favor of the immediate election of Hintenach's successor.[83]

Two elements seem to have converged to bring about this decision. First, some of the monks at the abbey who originally supported petitioning Rome for a reversal of the decree apparently learned that Archabbot Andrew wanted them to cease all efforts to reinstate him. These monks, who had always supported Hintenach and the reforms he had attempted to introduce, now accepted his resignation as a fait accompli and reluctantly agreed to the election of a new leader. On the other hand, Hintenach had never enjoyed strong support among the priests serving in parishes. Many of them had regarded his monastic reform program at the abbey as a reflection of a lack of understanding and appreciation for the value of the work they did. The vote of the parish fathers, the critical element in the chapter's final decision not to attempt to reverse the Roman decree, was overwhelmingly in favor of proceeding with the election of a new leader. They had never been satisfied with the direction Saint Vincent had taken since Archabbot Andrew had assumed the abbacy, and they now saw an opportunity to change things by electing one of their own.

In the end the monks put the shock of the archabbot's resignation behind them and began to plan for the future. The election was scheduled for July 15, and Father Vincent Huber wrote Abbot Leo Haid inviting him to preside. Haid had feared that the animosity some of the monks felt toward him would make him unwelcome at Saint Vincent, but Huber, apologizing for his earlier harsh words, assured him that he was expected to come and would be welcome. "I hope that all will pass off quietly," he wrote. "By all means come yourself to preside at the election; your very presence will explain many things and will assist in restoring good and friendly [feelings]. I feel that I owe you an apology for the tone of my first letter and I hereby sincerely tender you my apology. The letter was written under the excitement of the deep feelings that raged in my heart."[84]

Meanwhile Archabbot Andrew had left Saint Vincent and gone to the Monte Cassino Priory in Covington, Kentucky. He wanted to spend time in silence and prayer in the small, isolated community, and was happy to escape the maelstrom into which the abbey had descended since the announcement of his resignation. He maintained a studied silence in the weeks that followed, communicating with no one at the abbey. He did, however, break his silence on one occasion in order to write to his old friend, Father Adalbert Müller, prior of Sant' Anselmo in Rome. His letter to Müller is the only surviving document in his hand that reveals his feelings about his decision and his state of mind immediately following his resignation. "The reason I write you now," he said,

> is not to inform you of the great change that has taken place at St. Vincent (of which you had notice ere this) but to express to you as an old friend the satisfaction I feel that such a heavy responsibility—to be Superior of St. Vincent—is taken

from me. May it fall upon the shoulders of one better qualified to bear it. Of course, at first it caused great surprise, and to some extent dissatisfaction, which, however, will pass off in a short time.

The manner in which Rome granted me my freedom seems somewhat strange—still, since it has granted what I so earnestly longed for, I can have no reason for complaint. I am keeping myself here for some time till the election of [the] new abbot has taken place. I have not yet made any definite plans for the future and hence cannot say what I shall do. Please make a memento for me. Your Confrere, Andrew, O.S.B."[85]

Andrew Hintenach's brief reign as archabbot of Saint Vincent was a time when the community attempted to redefine its purpose and character. During those four years the monks made a concentrated and in many ways successful effort to renew their commitment to the Benedictine ideal of prayer and work. But the hopes of those who desired to limit the abbey's active involvement in external apostolates and to focus the community's resources and energies entirely upon perfecting monastic life in the cloister never achieved fulfillment. Some, like Oswald Moosmüller, left Saint Vincent to discover or create their own ideal communities elsewhere. But most remained, convinced that the monastery to which they had pronounced their vows of stability was the place where God intended them to live out their lives and monastic vocations.

Saint Vincent would continue to be home for both idealists and pragmatists, and the differing views of individuals and groups within the community would continue to act as leaven in the loaf. Despite the tensions and occasional discord of the Hintenach era, the community did not fragment. The monks in fact learned that argument need not lead to divisiveness and that honest disagreement might even prove a creative force, so long as together, like brothers, they continued to strive for unity and renewal of their common life of prayer and work.

FIVE

ENTERING THE NEW CENTURY (1892–1918)

The election of Andrew Hintenach's successor took place on July 15, 1892. Ninety-one priests of the abbey, many of whom had come from Saint Vincent's far-flung missions and parishes, were present, and nine others had appointed proxies. Bishop Leo Haid of North Carolina, abbot of Maryhelp Abbey and president of the American Cassinese Congregation, arrived at the abbey a few days before the event to oversee the proceedings, and at nine o'clock in the morning, after a solemn High Mass of the Holy Spirit, the doors of the church were locked and the voting began. On the first ballot no one received a majority of fifty-one votes, but Father Leander Schnerr, with forty-six votes, was the clear favorite. The only other strong candidates were Prior Vincent Huber, with twenty-five votes, and Father Casimir Elsesser, with eleven votes. On the second ballot Schnerr was elected with sixty-three votes, and the *St. Vincent Journal* reported that "it was . . . with relief and satisfaction and demonstrative applause that [the electors] heard him announce, with agitated voice, his readiness to accept the burden which they had placed upon him." Haid formally declared Schnerr third abbot of Saint Vincent, pending confirmation by the Holy See, and the monks immediately intoned the *Te Deum*. Then the church doors "were thrown open, and the bells of the monastery, large and small, proclaimed *urbi et orbi—et ruri* [to the city and the world—and to the countryside], that we were no longer orphans, that we had an Abbot."[1]

Fifty-five-year-old Leander Schnerr, like Andrew Hintenach, was a native of the Grand Duchy of Baden whose family had immigrated from Germany to Baltimore in the 1840s. He had come to Saint Vincent in 1850 as a boy of fourteen, entered the novitiate in 1853, and after completing his studies in the college and seminary had been ordained to the priesthood in 1859. Except for a brief period in the 1860s when he served on the faculty of Assumption College in Sandwich, Ontario, he had spent his entire priestly life before becoming abbot laboring in the parish apostolate as curate and pastor of Saint Vincent's parishes in Newark, Covington, Chicago, and Erie. Since 1877 he had been prior of St. Mary's Priory, Allegheny, Pennsylvania.[2]

During his tenure as prior in Allegheny, Schnerr had demonstrated noteworthy administrative skills. He had canceled the parish debt of eighty-three thousand dollars, refurbished the parish church, founded a school for boys, built a beautiful new priory adjoining St. Mary's church, bought and blessed a new cemetery in which he erected a sexton's residence, and established the parish of St. Boniface in Pittsburgh to accommodate the overflow of Catholics from St. Mary's. A prototypical "parish father" among the Saint Vincent monks, he was precisely the kind of leader the other parish fathers longed for, an active and competent administrator, affable, practical, and outgoing, who enjoyed dealing with the nuts and bolts of managing a large and vibrant enterprise. He was, moreover, in full accord with those who regarded parochial work as entirely consistent with a Benedictine vocation. As Saint Vincent historian Father Louis Haas noted: "The executive ability displayed in the administration of parish affairs, temporal as well as spiritual, coupled with his engaging qualities of heart and mind, made him the choice of his brethren to rule the community, and augured well for the future of St. Vincent's."[3]

A month after the election the papers of confirmation arrived from Rome. The Roman confirmation included a decree raising the monastery to the rank of archabbey and making every future abbot of Saint Vincent ipso facto an archabbot. On the feast of St. Placidus, October 5, 1892, Bishop Richard Phelan of Pittsburgh came to Saint Vincent for the formal blessing of the new archabbot. Three hundred of Schnerr's former parish-

The monastic chapter of Saint Vincent on July 15, 1892, after the election of Leander Schnerr as third archabbot. Leo Haid, abbot president of the American Cassinese Congregation, who oversaw the election, is in the center (front row). Archabbot Leander is on his left, and Father Vincent Huber, prior of the archabbey, on Haid's right.

ioners traveled by train from Pittsburgh to join three hundred Benedictines, other clergy, and friends and family of Archabbot Leander for the three hour and fifteen minute ceremony in the crowded abbey church. Later that day, after a banquet attended by four hundred guests, Bishop Phelan laid the cornerstone of the new abbey church, the construction of which had begun ten months earlier.[4]

Saint Vincent Archabbey in 1892 was the largest Benedictine monastery in America and one of the largest in the world. It was home for 231 monks, of whom 106 were priests, 14 clerics, 11 clerical novices, and 102 lay brothers. In addition to the parish, college, and seminary at the archabbey itself, the community served forty-six parishes and missions in eight American dioceses (in Pennsylvania, Kentucky, Maryland, Illinois, and Colorado) and operated St. Bede's College in Peru, Illinois. During the abbacy of Andrew Hintenach many of the parish priests had been brought back to the abbey, and the acceptance of new parishes and missions had been severely curtailed. Nevertheless, when Leander Schnerr assumed the leadership of Saint Vincent, fifty-five priests were still directly involved in the parish apostolate and almost half the community (priests and brothers) lived outside the motherhouse.[5] Under Archabbot Leander the community's commitment to parish work would expand, and an even greater proportion of the ordained monks would find themselves spending most of their monastic lives away from the archabbey.

NEW CLUNY PRIORY

A small minority of the priests continued to regard this situation of the expansion of the parish apostolate as intolerable, and some of them left the community on account of it. In 1891, even before the resignation of Archabbot Andrew, Father Oswald Moosmüller sought permission to establish an independent priory on property owned by Saint Vincent in Wetaug, Illinois, and there he founded the monastery of New Cluny hoping to create the kind of contemplative life focused on prayer, work, and study that he believed represented the true heritage of the Benedictine Rule. Saint Vincent Fathers Bruno Riess, Macarius Schmitt, Eberhard Gahr, and Engelbert Leist, Brother Alphonse Thumel, and four scholastics—Rudolph Ruprecht, Erhard Wiesneth, John Heinzelmeier, and Robert Reitmeier—joined Moosmüller at New Cluny and inaugurated monastic observance in rural Illinois. The community was welcomed by Bishop John Janssen of the Diocese of Belleville, and in August 1892 the Holy See formally recognized it as a canonical priory with the right to receive novices.[6]

Moosmüller quickly set about creating at the new priory a simple monastic regimen modeled on the observance of Beuron. He established the statutes of the medieval Benedictine abbey of Cluny as the basis for his new foundation and closely followed his old plan of making historical research and literary activity the chief work of the monks. His aim was to translate the *Acta Sanctorum* of the Bollandists into German, adapting its style to the general reader, and to that end he began publishing in 1892 *Die Legende,* a monthly journal devoted to translating the Latin lives of the saints. The journal continued publication for six years.[7]

In addition to literary work, the monks of New Cluny devoted themselves to labor on the farm attached to the priory and to parish work in the village of Wetaug. Moosmüller made it clear, however, that his conception of the monastic life did not include the possibility of commitment to work in distant missions and parishes. "There is a view to be corrected," he wrote,

> that it is necessary for the vocation of a priest, be he a secular or a regular, to labor in a parish or in the care of souls. It has indeed been customary at all times for the religious to look after the needs of the souls of Catholics living in the immediate vicinity of the cloister. But this custom does not warrant the conclusion that these religious therefore regard the care of souls as their vocation. No religious order—neither the Benedictines, nor the Franciscans, nor the Jesuits, Redemptorists or others—was founded for the purpose of parish administration. They may indeed engage therein by way of exception, but if they make this their principal object, they are failing in the fulfillment of their vocation.[8]

Monastic life at New Cluny embodied the ideals and practices that the reformers had wanted to institute at Saint Vincent, but the mere size of the motherhouse and its diverse commitments to educational and parochial apostolates had rendered their reform efforts there futile. In a spirit of resignation and regret, Moosmüller wrote Bishop Leo Haid that "[i]t is most probable that this poor place will attract no one from St. Vincent, and therefore the community is to be raised by a novitiate. If novices for this place are to be trained at St. Vincent, then their vocation will be put upon a severe trial when they come here, not only on account of the great contrast of the buildings, comforts, diet, beer, etc., but also in the climate, between St. Vincent and this place, so that it is to be feared that they would become discontent and would not like to stay here."[9]

New Cluny Priory continued in existence for a decade, attracting a few priests and brothers from Saint Vincent and other monasteries of the American Cassinese Congregation, as well as the occasional novice. But the monastic ideal espoused by Moosmüller and other "reformers" among the Saint Vincent monks never really took root, and in the end Moosmüller's experimental community failed. After his death in 1901 the monks of New Cluny elected first Father Maurus Hartmann and then Father Leo Eichenlaub as their prior. Both were monks of Saint Vincent and both declined their election. This forced Abbot Innocent Wolf, now president of the American Cassinese Congregation, to petition Rome to appoint a prior at New Cluny, and Father Alfred Mayer of St. John's Abbey was recommended. Mayer accepted charge of the small community of eleven members, but after a year he became convinced that it had no future.

The monks considered transferring their monastery to New York, California, or Colorado, but in the end they decided to move north, to Saskatchewan, Canada, where the Canadian Pacific Railroad had recently opened up the Canadian prairies to settlement by European immigrants. Among the immigrants in western Canada were many German Catholics, and in 1903 the monks of New Cluny went there to serve them. Thus the monastery founded as an alternative to Saint Vincent and the other active missionary communities of the American Cassinese Congregation itself undertook a mission to German Catholics in Saskatchewan. In 1911 it was raised to the rank of abbey under the patronage of St. Peter, the ninth abbey founded from Saint Vincent.[10]

Like Moosmüller and his companions at New Cluny, several other monks left Saint Vincent in the 1890s to pursue their vocations in other communities or to join the secular clergy. Most of the Saint Vincent monks, however, had come to recognize that a commitment to apostolic work both in parishes and schools was an authentic manifestation of Benedictine tradition, and as a result, the debate between the idealists and the pragmatists waned. By the turn of the century the community in Pennsylvania was as outward-looking as it had been during the great missionary era of Boniface Wimmer.

SAINT VINCENT IN THE 1890S

The first years of Archabbot Leander's abbacy were a period of financial crisis and economic depression in the United States. The panic began in February 1893 when the Reading Railroad went bankrupt, and by the end of the year five hundred banks and sixteen thousand businesses had been financially ruined. In the months that followed, the country settled into a deep depression from which it did not fully recover until the beginning of the twentieth century.[11]

The effects of the depression at Saint Vincent were serious but did not cause grave hardship since the community was still basically self-sufficient, was not in debt, and had few investments in the financial institutions that failed. The wealth of the archabbey was in the lands and buildings it owned, both at Saint Vincent and its dependencies, as well as in the annual income from the schools and parishes. That income decreased, of course, as the depression deepened, and a 20 percent drop in enrollment in the college and seminary during the second half of the decade was cause for concern. Construction of the abbey church slowed and even ceased for long periods of time, and other building projects were delayed or indefinitely postponed. Still, despite the hard times, life at Saint Vincent continued at a regular and uninterrupted pace. The farm continued to produce the food necessary to sustain monks and students; the coal mines of the abbey (which had been worked by the lay brothers since the 1850s) continued to provide fuel to heat the buildings in winter; and if material prosperity noticeably declined, difficult conditions gave the monks more reason to extol the virtues of monastic poverty and offered them an excellent opportunity to stress to their students the vanity of worldly comforts.

Schnerr took seriously his role as leader of an outward-looking community that had an important role to play in the Benedictine Order and the American Church. His first few years as archabbot found him frequently on the road representing Saint Vincent at national and international meetings. Even before his blessing he attended the sixth annual *Katholikentag*, the convention of German-American Catholics, held in Newark in September 1892. There he met Archbishop Michael A. Corrigan of New York, Bishop Winand N. Wigger of Newark, and other conservative leaders of the American Church, and by his presence demonstrated Saint Vincent's support for the principles they championed.[12]

In April 1893 Schnerr departed the archabbey for Rome where he attended the first international congress of Benedictine abbots at the Collegio di Sant' Anselmo. In Rome he consulted with Vatican officials and fellow Benedictine abbots from around the world, participated in the laying of the cornerstone for the new church at Sant' Anselmo, attended an audience with Pope Leo XIII, and took part in the deliberations that led to the creation of the post of abbot primate of the Benedictine Order. While in Europe Schnerr also took advantage of opportunities to visit the Benedictine monasteries of Downside and Erdington in England; Maredsous in Belgium; Munich, Metten, Scheyern, Eichstätt, Augsburg, Maria Laach, and Salzburg in Germany and Austria; Einsiedeln in Switzerland; and Montecassino and other abbeys in Italy.[13]

He returned to Saint Vincent in July 1893, attended the annual retreat at the archabbey, and then traveled to Chicago for the triennial general chapter of the American Cassinese Congregation. The general chapter took place August 23–25, and in the course of it the abbots and delegates promulgated new statutes for the congregation. Since 1855 monasteries of the American Cassinese Congregation had followed the statutes of the Bavarian Congregation, but conditions in late nineteenth-century America were different from those of Bavaria in the seventeenth century, when the older statutes had been written, and monks in American Cassinese houses had been demanding for more than a decade a modern constitution more consonant with the needs and conditions of the American houses.[14] Some of the leaders of the congregation complained that the new statutes diminished the power of abbots,[15] but Schnerr and the monks of Saint Vincent were pleased with the practical and more democratic character of the new rules governing the monasteries. Archabbot Leander also took advantage of his stay in Chicago to visit the World's Fair, where Saint Vincent College was featured in the Catholic Educational Exhibit.[16]

Schnerr spent much of 1894 and 1895 visiting the priories, parishes, and missions of Saint Vincent. In October 1895 he attended the Eucharistic Congress in Washington, D.C., and in 1896 he returned to Washington to participate in a ceremony at which the apostolic delegate to the United States, Archbishop Francesco Satolli, received the red biretta of a cardinal. The constant travel and activity proved detrimental to Schnerr's health, and he suffered from a recurrence of malaria which he had picked up in Rome in 1893 and which subjected him to frequent chills and fevers.[17] Still, he maintained a heavy schedule of travel and continued to represent the archabbey at meetings and conferences around the country. It became more and more evident that in Leander Schnerr the monks of Saint Vincent had a peripatetic abbot in the mold of Boniface Wimmer.

During his frequent journeys, Schnerr depended upon Prior Joseph Keller and members of the council of seniors to maintain discipline and attend to the day-to-day operations of the monastery, but when he was at home, he himself managed the community's temporal and spiritual affairs. The perennial problem of maintaining high standards of monastic discipline both at the motherhouse and in the dependent houses occupied his attention much of the time. He insisted upon a careful observance of the monastic rule in the abbey, and like Andrew Hintenach also required monks in the priories and parishes to observe a strict monastic regimen.

In October 1895 and again in May 1897 he issued directives to the priests serving in "the smaller houses of our monastery, that is in priories, colleges, and in every house where three or more monks live," to follow the same schedule as the monks at the archabbey and to divide their time equally between "prayer, studies, and pastoral duties," because "otiositas inimica est animae" ("idleness is the enemy of the soul").[18] Priests were required to say daily Mass at hours designated by the local superior; meals were to be taken in common and accompanied by table reading from the sacred scriptures, the Holy Rule, and other religious books; the monks were to avoid "chorearum theatrorumque aditus" ("going to dances and theaters"); laypeople were prohibited from entering the houses where the monks lived "except for reasons of duty or charity"; and all recreation was to be taken in common.[19] That the archabbot felt obliged to issue such directives regularly suggests that the rules were not always strictly observed by priests in the parishes.

Nonetheless, both the monastery and the parishes continued to maintain high standards of discipline and monastic observance. Despite restrictions such as those against monks leaving the monastery to go to theaters or students leaving the campus without specific permission, life at Saint Vincent in the 1890s was characterized more by regularity and a spirit of celebration than by prohibitions. The visit in 1894 of Archbishop Francesco Satolli, the apostolic delegate to the United States, was an occasion of immense joy for the entire community and an opportunity for monks and students to honor the pope's representative in America, to demonstrate their loyalty to the Holy See, and at the same time to celebrate their own identity and self-understanding as a dynamic and unified Benedictine community. Archbishop Satolli spent two days at Saint Vincent, and his presence gave palpable expression to the Holy See's approval of the work the Benedictines had been doing in America for the last forty-eight years. The delegate was warmly received by the priests, brothers, and students who had prepared for his arrival by decorating the campus with hundreds of papal and American flags. He was welcomed by church bells and "a hearty and prolonged cheer from 300 throats." At the gates of the monastery Father Raphael Wieland greeted him with a speech in Latin, to which the visitor replied in the same language, "paying a glowing tribute to Archabbot Wimmer, of happy memory, express[ing] the hope that the Benedictine colony erected by him in America might become for the church in the United States what the early Benedictines had been to the Old World." Archbishop Satolli participated in the monastic liturgy during the two days he was at the archabbey, celebrated pontifical High Mass, attended a banquet held in his honor, and was entertained by the monastery orchestra and the student dramatic society. Before departing he even sat through a few innings of a student baseball game, which he witnessed "with evident pleasure."[20]

Throughout the 1890s liturgical festivals and community celebrations marked the course of each year, from the opening of school in September to commencement exercises in June. Ecclesiastical feasts and national holidays were celebrated with Masses, processions, dramatic performances, games, and festive meals attended by monks, students, alumni, and friends

Leander Schnerr, O.S.B. (1836–1920), third archabbot of Saint Vincent, led the community from 1892 to 1920.

of Saint Vincent. The beginning of the academic year was highlighted by a student retreat followed by a community picnic. Thanksgiving was celebrated by a Mass of thanksgiving and the traditional turkey dinner. The Christmas season found students away from the school, and on the day itself most of the priests were away from the archabbey helping out in parishes throughout western Pennsylvania. But the Christmas midnight Mass, celebrated by the archabbot and sung by the monastery choir, drew hundreds of lay folk from Latrobe and the surrounding countryside. Other important feast days at which special liturgical and community observances were held included St. Benedict's Day, the feast of St. Thomas Aquinas, and the feast of St. Leander (in honor of the archabbot). Holy Week was a solemn period of prayer and liturgical functions, and students normally remained at the college and seminary to attend them, leaving the campus for Easter vacation only on Holy Saturday. Spring was welcomed with picnics at Idlewild Park, field days, baseball games, and liturgies in honor of the Blessed Virgin, and summer was introduced by a celebration of the feast of Corpus Christi when monks, students, laypeople, and visiting clergy accompanied the Blessed Sacrament in procession through the fields and grounds of the archabbey, stopping at stations along the way for Benediction. The school year culminated in June with commencement exercises that included the granting of degrees and diplomas, the awarding of academic prizes, concerts by the community's orchestra and glee club, and dramatic presentations by student drama groups.

Indeed, dramatics were part of virtually every important feast and holiday in the course of the year. Since the days of Boniface Wimmer theater performances had been a favorite pastime of Saint Vincent students, and by the 1890s hardly a month passed without a play being performed by one or the other group of college or seminary students. Tastes ran to operettas and melodramas. Some of the works produced during the period included *Major André* by the literary abbot of Belmont, Leo Haid; the German comic opera *Jägerlatein* by August Bolz; the German melodrama *Gott schützt das Recht* by Stanley Weyman; *Hermigild,* or *The Two Crowns* by Rev. J. Oechtering; William O'Brien's *English Rule and Irish Rebels;* Richard Brinsley Sheridan's historical play *Pizarro;* and Shakespeare's *Julius Caesar* and *Macbeth.* Every performance was enhanced by the music of the student-faculty orchestra. A feature of dramatic performances at Saint Vincent throughout much of this period and well into the twentieth century was that, in accordance with college regulations, female characters were never depicted on stage. Thus classical works were altered so that only male characters appeared. In the production of *Macbeth* presented by the St. Thomas Literary and Dialectic Society in 1897, for example, the witches were men and a new character, Menteith, was added to the cast. Described as "brother to Macbeth and keeper of Macbeth Castle," Menteith took the lines Shakespeare had written for Lady Macbeth.[21]

One of the most memorable celebrations at Saint Vincent during the 1890s took place in 1896 to mark the fiftieth anniversary of the arrival of

Boniface Wimmer and his companions in America. The monks had hoped that the new abbey church would be completed for the jubilee, but because of the depression, construction had been delayed and the celebration was kept small. The American Cassinese superiors—Peter Engel of St. John's, Innocent Wolf of St. Benedict's, Hilary Pfrängle of St. Mary's, Leo Haid of Belmont, Benedict Menges of St. Bernard's, Nepomucene Jaeger of St. Procopius, and Charles Mohr of St. Leo's in Florida—joined the Saint Vincent monks for the festivities, which took place August 17–19 in conjunction with the general chapter of the congregation. The celebration included liturgies, concerts, lectures, and a pontifical Requiem Mass for the deceased members of the Order. The guest of honor was Father Celestine Englbrecht, the sole surviving member of the pioneer Benedictine band in America, who had recently retired to the archabbey from his post as prior of St. Joseph's Priory, Chicago. The seventy-two-year-old Englbrecht was still in excellent health, and the *St. Vincent Journal* noted that "[h]is head is white with the snows of age, his years have exceeded the scriptural three score and ten, but his heart is as light, his spirit as blithe, his disposition as lovable as it was fifty years ago, when as a young man he crossed the Atlantic." Two years later the monks gathered once again, this time to celebrate the golden jubilee of Englbrecht's religious profession. At the banquet following the jubilee Mass, Father Celestine told amusing stories about the early days at Saint Vincent. One day soon after their arrival in America, he said, the pioneer monks were served corn bread. "It had a rich yellow color and the young greenhorn thought that eggs must be very plentiful; but when he tasted it, he concluded that matters must be pretty bad when they were compelled to eat sawdust. Many a time afterwards he was glad to have it."[22]

Founded in 1885, the Saint Vincent Alumni Association held annual meetings in Pittsburgh during the 1890s. Father J. F. Regis Canevin, chancellor and later bishop of the Diocese of Pittsburgh, was an early president who believed that organizations such as the college's alumni association could "be made to play an important part in maintaining the control of religion over the public actions of men and in shaping the destiny of people."[23] It was a lofty vision but one in full accord with the goal of the college and seminary to educate priests to serve the Church and Catholic laymen to bear witness to the Faith as they assumed their roles within American society. By now hundreds of former Saint Vincent students were living and working in various parts of the country. Many of them were priests, and some of these had gained high rank in the American Church.

Saint Vincent lay brothers at the fiftieth anniversary celebration of the establishment of the Benedictine Order in the United States, 1896.

Others were laymen whose success in their respective professions sometimes brought them to regional and even national attention. Virtually all of them regarded their education at Saint Vincent as crucial to the success they had achieved, and they proudly looked upon themselves as "Saint Vincent men."

Alumni of the college and seminary who had or would become bishops in the American Church during the nineteenth and early twentieth century were Rupert Seidenbusch of Northern Minnesota, Louis Fink of Leavenworth, Leo Haid of North Carolina, Joseph Rademacher of Fort Wayne, John Watterson of Columbus, Joseph Cotter of Winona, James Trobec of St. Cloud, James A. McFaul of Trenton, Joseph Schrembs of Cleveland, J. F. Regis Canevin and Hugh Boyle of Pittsburgh, and George Mundelein of

Chicago (who was later raised to the dignity of cardinal). Other notable priests who had studied at Saint Vincent included James F. Mooney, vicar general of the Archdiocese of New York; nationally renowned composer Henry G. Ganss; Michael A. O'Byrne, rector of the Cathedral of St. John the Baptist in Savannah, Georgia; Andrew A. Lambing, author and historian of the Church in western Pennsylvania; and Boniface Krug, archabbot of Montecassino.

One graduate of Saint Vincent Seminary who achieved distinction in a way that saddened his former professors was Joseph Hodur (1866–1953). Born in Poland in 1866, Hodur studied theology in his native land before coming to the United States as a priesthood candidate for the Diocese of Scranton in 1892. He completed his studies at Saint Vincent, and in August 1893 was ordained to the priesthood by Bishop William O'Hara. In 1897, when members of Scranton's Polish community established an unauthorized parish and invited Hodur to serve as their pastor, the young priest defied his bishop and accepted the invitation. In September 1898 he was formally excommunicated, whereupon he founded the schismatic Polish National Catholic Church. He was elected bishop of the breakaway church in 1904 and served in that position until his death in 1953.[24]

Lay alumni who maintained close contact with and brought honor to their alma mater included Francis X. Reuss of Philadelphia, a noted professor of music and American church historian; Dr. Isidore P. Strittmatter of Philadelphia, a prominent internist; Dr. Lawrence Flick, whose research into the causes of tuberculosis led to effective treatment and an eventual cure of the dread disease; Dr. Sebastian Wimmer of New York, grandnephew of Saint Vincent's founder and author of several medical texts that became standard in the United States; W. L. Maginnis, chief justice of the Wyoming Supreme Court; Villers S. Brandt, U.S. Justice Department official in the Philippine Islands; James C. McNally, a U.S. diplomat who served in Colombia, China, Belgium, Germany, and Switzerland; Robert Joseph Kennedy, who held the chair of American Jurisprudence at the Catholic University of America; and Aloysius Frauenheim, president of the Pittsburgh Brewing Company. The educational programs at Saint Vincent had begun to focus more and more on the formation of young men for the secular professions and on the education of a lay Catholic leadership. In the 1890s many students of the college went on to become doctors, lawyers, and businessmen.

As the Benedictines increasingly came to recognize their responsibility to educate a truly Catholic and truly American laity, the mission of the college began to be articulated in new ways. In 1892 Father Francis P. McNichol of Pittsburgh, an alumnus of the college, addressed the faculty, students, and alumni on the topic "The Apostolate of the Educated Catholic Layman." His lecture reflected the college's broadened understanding of its mission in American society. "Too long have educated Catholic laymen remained unreminded of the duties and obligations of their position in life," McNichol said. "Too long have they deemed that the accumulation of wealth, the acquiring of social and political position, and the enjoyment of the world was to be the sole object of their creation." He urged the students and alumni to place high value on their Catholic faith and commit themselves to creating stable Christian families, opposing divorce laws, and practicing justice and charity not only in the family but within the workplace as well.

> Whilst dwelling on the family, it is well to remember that justice and charity should be extended to employees who were honored in other days as members of the family. If that Christian spirit could only reenter into modern business relations, how readily the questions of employer and employee, of capital and labor, could be solved.
>
> Moreover, the educated Catholic layman should set the example of, not Spartan, but of Christian simplicity in the family. . . . Passing from the duties of the educated layman to the family, we come to his obligations to the States, as an educated citizen, voter, and perhaps office-holder. It is a well-known principle that to whom God has given education and position, of him a stricter accounting will be required than from the less favored.
>
> But, gentlemen, even as Catholic American citizens you have nothing to be ashamed of. The Catholic religion is inseparably connected with this fair land. Discovered by a Catholic, the first religious ceremony upon its soil was the Holy Sacrifice of the Mass. The black robe of the priest was honored among the untutored savage long before the Pilgrims had landed on Plymouth Rock or the Cavaliers had entered the James River. . . . Therefore, gentlemen, you have no reason to blush at the name of Catholic. But your religion may have cause to blush for you. You have a duty to do. . . . Beware of the traps and snares, the secret organizations with benevolent features, the surrounding infidelity and disrepect for all authority.

Father McNichol concluded by urging his listeners to help the poor and assist the pastor in his labors.[25]

Despite the continued influence of its Bavarian heritage, Saint Vincent in the 1890s was becoming increasingly Americanized. To be sure, the culture of the monastery, where the German language and German traditions still prevailed, remained predominately German. More than three-quarters of the monks were German-born, while most of the rest were second-generation German-Americans. On the other hand, all but a few of the students in the seminary and college were American-born, and of these more than a third were of non-German, principally Irish, heritage. The presence of so many American-born students necessarily changed the complexion of the once thoroughly Bavarian institution, contributing substantially to the process by which in the twentieth century it would become fully assimilated into the mainstream of American life.

Signs of change were everywhere, and perhaps the clearest of them was the active interest taken by students during the late 1890s in the nation's political life. The presidential election of 1896, which pitted Republican William McKinley against Democrat William Jennings Bryan, caused a major stir at Saint Vincent. The *St. Vincent Journal* reported that 80 percent of the students, like the vast majority of their Catholic countrymen, were enthusiastic supporters of the Democrat Bryan, and they expressed their support vociferously. On the eve of the election more than a hundred of them marched through the streets of nearby Youngstown "to the music of tin horns and the classical strains of *Marching through Georgia"* to rally the citizenry to Bryan's cause, and even though their candidate lost the election, the students were proud of their patriotic demonstration, which had been "a creditable outburst of enthusiasm on the part of American students" and evidence, the *Journal* said, that the anti-Catholic American Protective Association was wrong when it accused American Catholics of being unpatriotic.[26]

The outbreak of the Spanish-American War unleashed another spurt of patriotic fervor at Saint Vincent. Initially the mood at the college was cautious. After the sinking of the battleship *Maine* on February 15, 1898, the *St. Vincent Journal* editorialized that everyone's hope was that "this deplorable incident will not lead to war. It cannot unless the hystero-epilepsy of the belligerent tooters, who cannot speak of Spain without gnashing their teeth, has more influence with the government than we would fain hope. So far the balance of opinion and of probability and of reason and of common sense is for the theory of internal accident." But when Congress declared war on April 25, 1898, the *Journal* reported that there was "a surplus of bottled up enthusiasm in the hearts of the students that had waited patiently for a fitting occasion of egress." In the wake of President McKinley's call for 150,000 volunteers to join the fight against Spain, the college administration organized a patriotic demonstration. On June 16 Father Raphael Wieland, director of the college, declared a free day and that afternoon the students marched in a body around the campus "with martial tread and colors flying." Then, after some "patriotic airs" by the college's brass band, they raised Old Glory to the top of the new water tower. Father Edward Andelfinger delivered a patriotic address while "a miniature cannon kept booming away, zealously trying to make up in noise what it lacked in size and beauty." After more patriotic music from the band the students dispersed, now "more loyal and patriotic . . . as a result of the day's exercises."[27]

Saint Vincent students had little opportunity to enlist in the armed forces after the school year ended, for the war was over by the middle of August. But a number of alumni who were members of the Pennsylvania National Guard went on active duty and participated in military action in the Philippines. Among them were Greensburg residents Lawrence Kienzle and Benedict Wirtner, brother of Fathers Boniface and Anthony Wirtner of Saint Vincent.[28] Patriotism at the college was not so extreme, however, as to prevent criticism of the way military commanders treated inhabitants of the conquered Spanish colonies, and a fact that caused unease among students and monks at Saint Vincent, as it did among American Catholics generally, was that the war was conspicuously a conflict between a Protestant nation and a Catholic one.

There is little doubt that underlying the patriotic and humanitarian idealism that led the United States to declare war on Spain and seek independence for Cuba was a substratum of anti-Catholicism that still festered in American society. Spain was preeminently Catholic, while as an heir of the English Reformation America had inherited Anglo-Saxon religious and cultural prejudices against it that went back three hundred years. In addition, in the 1890s anti-Catholic prejudice, championed by such ostensibly respectable organizations as the American Protective Association, had once again raised its ugly head in American society. It was a short leap from this native American anti-Catholicism to a "politically correct" contempt for Spain, Spanish culture, and Spanish religion.

While American Catholics were quick to support the political rationale for a declaration of war with Spain, they remained vigilant against making the war an excuse for their non-Catholic countrymen to give vent to nativist animosity toward Catholicism. Students and faculty at Saint Vincent shared this vigilance. Thus when an American naval officer was quoted as saying that the U.S. Navy would make Spanish "the prevailing language of Hell," the *St. Vincent Journal* pointed out that when the admiral, as was to be hoped, eventually reached Heaven, he would surely "hear more Spanish than if he landed in the tropics of the hereafter." The *Journal* also editorialized that though there was no question that Spain had grossly misgoverned

Cuba "politically and ecclesiastically" and therefore deserved to lose it, nonetheless "our philanthropic crusaders against 'Spanish cruelty' would be as indifferent to its existence under England in Cuba as they are to its existence under England in India and elsewhere." Reported insults by American military officers against priests, nuns, and the Catholic religion in Cuba, Puerto Rico, and the Philippines, moreover, were roundly condemned in the pages of the *Journal* during the war and for several years afterwards.[29]

BEER CONTROVERSY

Among the traditions that the monks had brought with them from Bavaria and that continued into the 1890s was beer brewing. The conflict between Boniface Wimmer and Bishop Michael O'Connor over the issue had been settled by the Holy See in 1855, and since 1860 the monastery in Pennsylvania, like many Benedictine houses in Germany, had operated a brewery. In the beginning beer was produced at Saint Vincent only for the community's own consumption, but Rome's 1855 decree had allowed for wholesale distribution, and in time the monks began to sell barrels of "St. Vincent's Beer" to saloons in Pittsburgh and other parts of western Pennsylvania. The practice raised no objections for several decades, but in the 1880s temperance advocates in both the Protestant and Catholic communities began to criticize the monks for engaging in the beer trade. At the Third Plenary Council of Baltimore (1884), Bishop John J. Keane of Richmond, with the support of Archbishop John Ireland of St. Paul and other progressive members of the American hierarchy, attempted to ban beer brewing in American Benedictine monasteries, but after a spirited debate in which the practice was defended by Benedictine Bishop Rupert Seidenbusch of Northern Minnesota, the move was defeated.[30]

Still, the brewery at Saint Vincent was a burr under the saddle of many members of the American Catholic clergy who were devoting much of their pastoral efforts to promoting temperance among hard-drinking Catholic immigrants. These pastoral efforts were by no means limited to the Irish-American clergy. Two of the harshest critics of Saint Vincent's beer-brewing tradition were German-American priests who helped bring the issue to national attention. In 1895 Father Ferdinand Kittel, pastor of St. Michael's Parish, Loretto, Pennsylvania, wrote Archabbot Leander calling on the Benedictines to withdraw from the beer trade: "No complaint is made of the brewery itself, or of your making and using beer; that is your own affair with which we have no right to meddle. But the fact of your *sell-*

ing it, and of its being advertised in secular papers as 'on tap' in various saloons, is regretted by the clergy of the diocese without exception, for it brings odium on the Church and shame on our people."[31]

Schnerr responded by pointing out that when Saint Vincent was elevated to the rank of abbey the Holy See had granted the monks permission to brew and sell beer wholesale and that American Benedictines therefore had the right to continue the practice. But the response did not satisfy Kittel, who fulfilled his threat of sending a protest, signed by twenty Pennsylvania priests, to the apostolic delegate in Washington, Archbishop Francesco Satolli. Satolli reacted diplomatically, acknowledging the right of the Saint Vincent monks to brew and sell beer but asking them to refrain from large-scale production and sales in light of the "evil of intemperance" and of the current crusade in the United States to combat it.[32]

The controversy died down for a while, but then flared up anew when another German-American priest, Father George Zurcher of Buffalo, N.Y., published a pamphlet entitled *Monks and Their Decline.* In this intemperate philippic Zurcher excoriated American Benedictines in general and the monks of Saint Vincent Archabbey in particular for their continued refusal to conform to the ideals of the Catholic temperance movement. "The monk priests are largely to blame," he wrote, "that the temperance laws [*sic*] of the Catholic Church in America are not observed in so many sections of the country." He sarcastically interpreted O.S.B. (Order of St. Benedict) as the "Order of Sacred Brewers" and petulantly contrasted the German monks of Saint Vincent with upstanding examples of temperance advocacy among other priests in the American Church.[33]

Zurcher's pamphlet introduced the controversy to a wider audience and brought unwanted national attention to the brewery at Saint Vincent. In April 1898 a Catholic editor in Philadelphia, Martin I. J. Griffin, sent a letter to the *New York Voice* drawing the newspaper's notice to beer brewing at the archabbey. "I can only openly protest against a clerical scandal in my native state," he wrote. "I know it will be effective some time in closing up the rumshop of the Holy Brewers at Beatty [i.e., Saint Vincent]. We Catholics are so overawed about our clergy that I wish the New York *Voice* would expose this Holy Brewery as it has the Protestant colleges."[34]

The newspaper, an independent, secular journal, took up the challenge and sent a reporter to Pennsylvania. On April 21, 1898, it published a sensationalized exposé, datelined Latrobe, which began:

> A mile and a half to the west of this place is the famous St. Vincent's Arch-Abbey, College, Monastery, Theological Seminary, Cathedral [*sic*], Grist-Mill, and Brew-

ery, an unholy combination that has scandalized the Catholic Church for upward of half a century. Three hundred and ten students are here, 50 of whom are students of theology preparing for the priesthood, more than 30 professors nearly all of whom are doctors of divinity, and 75 monks, including an extensive collection of abbots, friars [*sic*], priors, chaplains, and priests. Everything is the property of the abbey: 600 acres of land drained by the Loyalhanna creek, with mills, stables, brickyard, and the famous brewery. The brewery is owned by the monks, the beer is made by the monks, it is sold by the monks, and much of it is drank [*sic*] by the monks of holy St. Vincent. If you want to make arrangements to have your boy educated for the priesthood, you address a letter to "The Reverend Director." If you wish a carload of beer, you write the same official. The yearly output of priests and beer is extensive. More than 500 American Catholic priests have been trained here for their work. The annual crop of beer is not so large. Until recently, the output has been upward of 3,000 barrels per year. Since the work of building the new $250,000 cathedral [*sic*] was begun some years ago, this has been increast [*sic*] so as to provide beer for the big church pow-wows which are held for the benefit of the construction fund.[35]

The article was a prime example of the sensational "yellow journalism" of the day. It combined fact with inaccuracies and self-righteous posturing, and included anecdotes and quotes presented in a way that made the monks look like fools and hypocrites. It was a humiliating experience for the entire community to be portrayed in such a light, but rather than respond publicly to the article and thus fuel the controversy, the monks decided to remain silent. The only allusion to the newspaper attack in the *St. Vincent Journal* was a good-humored remark in an announcement about an end-of-year picnic held by the college drama society. "We wish to state for the benefit of the *New York Voice* reporter," the announcement said, "that lemonade was the strongest beverage on the bill of fare."[36]

Public criticism of beer brewing at the archabbey caused chagrin among the monks but did not bring the practice to an end. The tradition was too deeply ingrained, and the attacks were regarded simply as new examples of the anti-Catholicism of American Protestants on the one hand and of the anti-German sentiments of Irish-American Catholics on the other. Beer production at Saint Vincent never reached the proportions reported by the *New York Voice.* In the 1890s the brewery produced about one thousand barrels annually and paid about two thousand dollars a year in federal taxes. Operations continued until 1919 when ratification of the Eighteenth Amendment to the U.S. Constitution sealed the fate of beer brewing at Saint Vincent. For the next seven years the small brick brewery, which had caused so much controversy, was used as a storehouse for the farm, and in January 1926 it was destroyed by fire.

ETHNIC DIVERSITY

In the first decade of the twentieth century the ethnic composition of the student body in the seminary and college at Saint Vincent changed dramatically. Through most of the 1890s two out of three students were of German heritage, but by 1910 the proportion of German to non-German names on the college roster had reversed. Now nearly two-thirds of the students were the sons of non-German immigrants. The vast majority of these were second-and even third-generation Irish-Americans, but other nationalities—Polish, Slovak, Czech, Hungarian, Lithuanian, Italian, and Cuban —were also strongly represented.[37] The change reflected the new immigration patterns affecting the American Church as thousands of new Catholics from the countries of eastern Europe and Italy arrived on the shores of the United States between 1890 and 1910. In the case of the Slovaks alone, one historian estimated that more than 450 students of Slovak origin studied at Saint Vincent College and Seminary between 1902 and 1936.[38]

The dominant group at the college during this period was the Irish. As early as 1896 Irish students had come to exercise such an influence on life in the college that the school colors were changed from the traditional Bavarian blue and white to green and gold. A student journalist noted that the reason for this change was that "*gold* is a recognized emblem of victory, and *green*—well, it goes without saying that green is a beautiful color, and at present very *bon ton,* quite the thing, you know." The two colors, the commentator said, were a combination "Irishmen [could] . . . wear proudly and by their conduct make them the mark of scholarly gentlemen and the honored emblem of their *Alma Mater.*"[39] By 1905 the Irish presence in the college was so prominent that the college journal jokingly suggested that it might publish a Gaelic edition.[40]

But other nationalities vied with the Irish for recognition in the melting pot that Saint Vincent was becoming. Some referred humorously to the seminary as a "tower of Babel" because of all the languages spoken there, and the *St. Vincent Journal* said: "Would that the tower of Babel were never put in course of erection: since it has caused our Seminarians to waste so much energy in overcoming direful consequences. Imagine 'a sprig of the Emerald Isle' racking his brain in his eagerness to master the tongue of the Teuton; the offspring of sunny Italy and downtrodden Poland slowly cutting their way through the meshes of English grammar, and you have a picture of every-day life amongst us."[41] In 1902 Slovak was added to German as a language taught in the seminary to better prepare priesthood students for their pastoral work after ordination, and in 1908 the seminary's St. Thomas Literary and Homiletic Society organized a Slovak-language division.

The new immigrants made their presence felt at Saint Vincent in other ways as they moved into the region around the monastery. By the turn of the century coal mining had become the principal industry of Pennsylvania, and many Polish, Lithuanian, Hungarian, and Slovak laborers had settled with their families in the western part of the state to work the coal mines. Most of the coal miners were Catholic, and the bishops of Pennsylvania were hard-pressed to provide priests for the coal mining communities. The dioceses of Pittsburgh and Altoona were particularly short of resources, both material and human, to attend the pastoral needs of the new immigrants, and the bishops of these dioceses called upon the monks of Saint Vincent to assist in the work. Archabbot Leander wrote to Bishop Leo Haid of North Carolina that "the foreigners in the surrounding country—Bohemians, Poles, Slovaks, Krainers, Magyars, Lithuanians & Italians—give us a great deal of trouble. They are uneducated people especially in religion and fall an easy prey to the Socialists. We have not a sufficient number of priests for them. Our young clerics must learn these languages, but it will be some time before they can be ordained & be of any service to these people."[42]

Archabbot Leander's lifelong commitment to the parish apostolate now had the firm support of the monastic chapter, and Saint Vincent's response to the bishops' calls for assistance in the pastoral care of the western Pennsylvania coal miners and their families was rapid and enthusiastic. During Schnerr's abbacy the community established parishes for the eastern European immigrants in the western Pennsylvania towns of Vandergrift (St. Gertrude and Holy Trinity), Patton (St. George), Forbes Road (St. Mary), Bovard (St. Bede), New Alexandria (St. James), Marguerite (St. Benedict), Trauger (Forty Martyrs), Greensburg (St. Bruno), and Slickville (St. Sylvester). In addition, they founded the Italian parish of the Ascension in Jeannette. Other parishes established or taken over by Saint Vincent during Schnerr's abbacy included St. Benedict, Baltimore, Maryland; St. Paul, Chicago, Illinois; and Sacred Heart, St. Marys, Pennsylvania.

Concurrently with the commitment to the pastoral care of Slovak, Polish, Lithuanian, and Hungarian coal miners in western Pennsylvania, Saint Vincent was also experiencing significant change in the ethnic composition of its monastic population. In the twenty years between 1892 and 1912 two significant shifts in that population occurred. First, the proportion of American-born monks had increased to 53 percent of the total (in 1892 it

Saint Vincent in 1897.

had been 31 percent). Second, the proportion of monks of German extraction had fallen from 87 to 80 percent. Now other ethnic groups had begun to be represented at the archabbey, admittedly in small numbers but still in a way that reflected American Catholic immigration patterns in the last decade of the nineteenth and first decade of the twentieth century. In addition to Czechs, who had been represented at Saint Vincent as early as 1880, now Slovaks, Poles, Hungarians, and Italians were joining the monastery and proceeding to solemn vows and ordination. Irish representation also increased slightly. The list of monks published in 1913 indicates that of 140 priests and clerics at Saint Vincent at that time, 8 were Czech, 7 Irish, 6 Slovak, 2 Polish, and 1 Italian.[43]

As a result of the missionary efforts of Saint Vincent monks among African Americans in the South after the Civil War, a few black candidates for the monastic life joined the monastery in Pennsylvania. Those who did included Brother Rhabanus Cononge, who entered the novitiate in 1878 and served in Saint Vincent's missions in Georgia and Alabama before joining Father Oswald Moosmüller's community of New Cluny; Brother Siricius Palmer, a cleric who served in Georgia; Brother Albert Mason, who spent five years as a lay brother at Saint Vincent before leaving the monastery and assuming a role as lay leader among black American Catholics; and Brother Innocent Carter, a former slave on the Eastern Shore of Maryland who entered the monastery in 1877 and served as cook for the Saint Vincent community until his death in 1912.[44]

Despite the increase in non-German monks at Saint Vincent, the archabbey remained an overwhelmingly German-American institution. The German language continued to be the first language of the cloister, as reflected by the fact that German continued to be used for table-reading and for conversation at recreation. Before World War I, novices who entered the community from other language groups had to learn German in order to communicate with the older members of the community; in the seminary diocesan seminarians were taught German, which vied with Latin and increasingly English in the theology classes; and though the predominate language of the college classroom was English, the students came into daily contact with German and still produced German plays on a regular basis.

A COLLEGE IN COLORADO

Although Archabbot Andrew Hintenach's efforts in 1890 to organize the Benedictine missions in Colorado into an independent abbey had proved unsuccessful, the Saint Vincent chapter hoped for better results in the future and to that end continued accepting missions in Colorado and planning for the creation of a Benedictine college there. By the middle of 1895 there were six Benedictine priests from Pennsylvania serving in the Colorado missions. Three attended the Benedictine parish in Boulder, thirty miles northwest of Denver; two attended the parish in Pueblo, a hundred miles south of Denver; and one, retired Archabbot Andrew, served as chaplain for the Benedictine sisters at St. Scholastica Academy in Canon City, forty miles west of Pueblo. Father Placidus Pilz, former prior at Saint Vincent, was superior of the Colorado missions. In 1895 Saint Vincent also assumed responsibility for the pastoral care of Catholics in the coal-mining towns of Canon City, Rockvale, Florence, Williamsburg, and neighboring areas. Czech, Slovak, and Polish immigrants had settled in the region to work the coal mines, and Saint Vincent priests fluent in their languages, such as Fathers Cyril Rettger and Benno Staudigl, were now assigned to Colorado.

However, negotiations with Bishop Nicholas Chrysostom Matz of Denver for the establishment of a college and an independent monastery in the western diocese dragged on. The bishop explained to Archabbot Leander that while he himself had no objection to the ounding of a canonical priory in his diocese, the Jesuits, who had been engaged in educational work in Colorado for some time, were opposed to the establishment of a Benedictine college because such a competing institution would adversely affect their own educational efforts in the diocese. In view of the Jesuit objections, Bishop Matz proposed that the Benedictines postpone opening their own school for five years. Schnerr responded that "it is not our intention to cause you any inconvenience, nor do we intend to commence with the college at once. But if you wish us to take charge of Canon City and its missions . . . we should also have permission to establish a monastery and college . . . as we have at St. Vincent's, St. John's, and the other Abbeys."[45]

Archabbot Leander was clearly reflecting the mind of the Saint Vincent chapter when he insisted upon the establishment of both a college and monastery in Colorado. The chapter recognized that American Benedictine communities had flourished only in those places where the monks had also been able to establish colleges for the education of young men. The abbeys in Pennsylvania, Minnesota, Kansas, New Jersey, and North Carolina depended upon their colleges for financial support as well as for vocations to the monastic life. In those places where monasteries were established without colleges—for example, in San José, Texas; Creston, Iowa; and Wetaug, Illinois—the communities had foundered and died. The Saint Vincent chapter, therefore, had no desire to commit its resources to the creation of an independent monastery in Colorado without the bishop's assurance that they would also be permitted to open a college.

After prolonged discussions, however, the chapter finally acquiesced to the bishop's request for a delay. In July 1895 Archabbot Leander sent a petition to the Vatican requesting (1) that the missions in Canon City and surrounding mining towns be transferred to the Benedictines of Saint Vincent *in perpetuum;* (2) that because of the great distance of the Colorado missions from Saint Vincent, an independent priory be immediately established in Canon City or its environs with the right to open a novitiate and elect a canonical prior; and (3) that the Holy See grant "apostolic approbation" for a college and seminary to be established by the new monastery sometime after 1898.[46]

Rome's initial response was disappointing. In November 1895 the Sacred Congregation for the Propagation of the Faith issued a decree confirming the transfer of the missions in Canon City and its vicinity to the Benedictines, but it did not agree to the establishment of a monastery or college because of opposition from the Jesuits and the lack of clear support from the diocesan clergy.[47] Having obtained renewed confirmation of support from Bishop Matz, and with assistance from Abbot Primate Hildebrand de Hemptinne, Archabbot Leander again wrote to Rome, pressing for the creation of an independent priory in Colorado, and this time permission was granted.[48] The opposition of the Jesuits and Bishop Matz's own lukewarm support, however, discouraged most of the priests and clerics at Saint Vincent from applying to join the new monastery. Archabbot Leander wrote Bishop Leo Haid that only two priests of the abbey had indicated a desire to transfer their vows of stability to the proposed independent community. The reason for this lack of enthusiasm, Schnerr surmised, was the monks' concern about ecclesiastical conditions in the Diocese of Denver.

> The fathers out there as far as I know are altogether displeased with the bishop and his way of acting. One of the fathers writes to me, the Jesuits for some time suspected that the Benedictines wished to establish themselves in Colorado and perhaps would commence a college. Their Superior P. Mara asked the Bishop about it, and his Lordship answered, that the Benedictines had only permission to establish a monastery in Canon City and educate their own men. Considering affairs in the Diocese of Denver I cannot feel contented. The Bishop and the greater part of the clergy as also a great portion of the laity are at variance with each other. . . . The priests agitating against the Bishop and hostile to him, would also be hostile to us, and the Jesuits would look upon the establishment of another college with great dissatisfaction, especially since the Bishop asserted that we have no such permission.[49]

Under these circumstances the chapter decided to delay not only the opening of a college but the establishment of an independent monastery as well. At the end of 1897 Archabbot Leander assigned Father Meinrad Jeggle as superior of the mission in Colorado. Jeggle was a sixty-three-year-old Bavarian who had entered the monastery at Saint Vincent in 1856 at the age of nineteen. Ordained in 1861, he had served in Saint Vincent's parishes in Chicago and Baltimore before being named prior of St. Mary's Priory, Allegheny, Pennsylvania, the post he held immediately before his assignment to Colorado. Father Meinrad arrived in Pueblo on December 19, 1897, and was met with a "grand reception" at Saint Mary's Church, Pueblo, by the priests of the Colorado mission. These included Fathers Chrysostom Lochschmidt, Gregory Zeilnhofer, Henry Hohman, Cyril Rettger, Edmund Butz, Benno Staudigl, Modestus Wirtner, and Archabbot Andrew Hintenach—all monks of Saint Vincent.

The accession of Jeggle seems to mark the first serious efforts of the monks to initiate communal monastic life in Colorado. Until then they had worked singly or in small groups in various parts of the diocese without enjoying the opportunity to live in community and pray the divine office in common. Their pastoral responsibilities still precluded full-scale monastic observance in Colorado at that time, but under Jeggle they were able to come together on special occasions for common religious devotions. Thus in April 1898 four of them, including Father Meinrad, "assembled at Pueblo for the Solemn Office of Holy Week," and in August all but Father Modestus Wirtner were able to come together at Pueblo for a community retreat given by Prior Joseph Sittenauer of Saint Benedict's Abbey, Kansas.[50]

In November 1898 a local chapter of the Benedictines in Colorado was held at Saint Mary's Church, Pueblo. At this meeting the monks considered the question of whether they should establish an independent priory in Colorado and, if so, where it should be located. Their answer to the second question was much more easily arrived at than to the first. Everyone agreed that the future monastery should be established in the vicinity of Canon City, an ideal location, the healthy climate and lovely scenery of which appealed to all who visited it. With regard to the question of whether to establish a monastery at all, however, the Colorado monks were less sanguine. "Nothing [can be done] by the Colorado Fathers with their present resources," they concluded. "If the Archabbey of Saint Vincent's would like to make a start—no less than fifty thousand ($50,000) would be required according to the judgment of all the Fathers." Because of the depression of the 1890s, the community in Pennsylvania was hardly in a position to put such resources into Colorado, and once again the project to establish an independent priory and college there was postponed. A sense of resignation, if not resentment towards the motherhouse, descended upon the monks in Colorado. When Archabbot Leander visited them in 1901, their anonymous chronicler noted: "His Lordship did not seem very favorably impressed with our slow progress in acquiring property for the 'new monastery and college.' He also did not favor the idea of a high school in Pueblo, as proposed to Fr. Gregory by Bishop Matz; nor did he like the locations around Canon City shown him by Archabbot Andrew and Fr. Gregory. The trouble seems to be either his Lordship's unwillingness or the lack of means to help Colorado materially."[51]

It was not until 1903 that the project finally got off the ground. In February of that year, after Bishop Matz had offered the Catholic congregation in East Pueblo to the care of the Benedictines and recommended the location as an ideal site for a monastery and college, the Saint Vincent chapter voted an initial sum of three thousand dollars for construction of a twenty-five-thousand-dollar college and monastery in East Pueblo. In May the chapter voted a loan of eight thousand dollars to the new foundation to complete the building.[52]

St. Leander's College opened in October 1903 with five monks from Saint Vincent on the faculty and with twenty-five day students enrolled. A former director of Saint Vincent College, Father Vincent Huber, was named director of St. Leander's, and Fathers Gregory Zeilnhofer, Hilary Kaib, Agatho Strittmatter, and James Spalding were assigned to assist him. Archabbot Leander sent Brother Matthias Peter to serve as the community's cook, and a year later appointed Father Alexius Grass to replace Huber as director.[53] The college in Pueblo soon came to be known simply as Benedictine College, and the monks both in Pennsylvania and Colorado had high hopes for its future. In 1907 Father Alexius wrote Archabbot Leander that despite consistently low enrollment and chronic economic problems, he was hopeful for the school's ultimate success.

> Looking over the whole situation, I for my part, am not in the least dismayed. I feel that our condition financially is good, and that the future of the Benedictine family is bright. Aside from the clamor of the papers and the boosting of various associations, there is real material progress in the State, and the number of inhabitants is continually and effectively on the increase. To me the future looks rosy. I am somewhat of an optimist, but withal unbiased; and given a few more years the college will come up to reasonable expectations.[54]

Saint Vincent continued to pour men and resources into the college in Pueblo and the Colorado missions generally, and by 1908 there were eighteen priests, one deacon, and two lay brothers from Pennsylvania at the school in Pueblo and the parishes in Canon City and Boulder.[55] To the dismay of Archabbot Leander, however, prospects for the establishment of an independent monastery in Colorado were as dismal as ever. With the monks living in three locations at great distances from one another and devoting themselves to a variety of pastoral and educational work, there was little cohesiveness in the mission and little opportunity for a unifying community spirit to develop. The Colorado monks themselves, moreover, showed little inclination to alter their status as capitulars of Saint Vincent on temporary assignment in the West. Archabbot Leander was shocked when none of them responded to a circular letter sent to all the priests and clerics of Saint Vincent inviting volunteers to transfer their vows of stability to a proposed independent abbey in Colorado. "To the best of my knowledge," he wrote Prior Hilary Kaib in Pueblo,

> all of them are glad to be out there; why should they not feel disposed to align themselves with the movement towards monastic establishment in Colorado so that this matter could finally come to a decision? It strikes me that the fathers do not want to have an abbot or an abbey so that they could be more independent because everyone feels that a superior who is in a subordinate position does not have the same power of enforcement that is held by one who is in complete control. Such a state of mind of course should not be admissible, but it is so just the same, especially where the superior who is in complete authority exercises his subjects far removed from them as is the case of Colorado.[56]

Prior Hilary disagreed with the archabbot's assessment and responded with an explanation of his own. The monks in Colorado were reluctant to affiliate themselves with a new independent abbey in the West, he said, not because they preferred to be distant from their monastic superior but because they did not want to be in Colorado at all. They all longed to go back to Saint Vincent. "We did not ask to be sent to Colorado," he wrote. Moreover, after seven years of existence, with only twelve students enrolled,

> the College [in Pueblo] seems less assured than ever. Yes, dear Father Abbot, if you only knew how depressing and discouraging it is to work in the class-room year after year with a ridiculously small number of boys of all ages and attainments and to feel that your work and sacrifices [are] wasted, humanly speaking, then you would understand that there were times when in the past it took all the strength of my vows and all the efforts of my will strengthened by the supernatural considerations to keep me here at all. . . . I will do all I can for Colorado and the College in the future as in the past, if your desire is that I stay here longer. But I am not ready now to detach myself from St. Vincent and join a new monastery where I feel I could

neither find peace and contentment by any evident service to God and man or further the interests of my salvation.[57]

Confirmation of Father Hilary's observation that none of the monks from Saint Vincent really wanted to be in Colorado is to be found in the frequent turnover in personnel in the Colorado missions. Priests assigned there usually stayed for only a few years before returning to Pennsylvania, as others took their places. Even the prior begged to be relieved so that he could return to the archabbey. It seemed that the only monks who appreciated the opportunity of being in Colorado were those suffering from asthma, tuberculosis, chronic bronchitis, and other respiratory diseases. For them the pure mountain air and healthy climate were ideal for treatment of their illnesses, but because of their physical weakness, they were usually unable to perform all the work required of those assigned to teaching or pastoral duties and were often more a burden on the mission than a help. Moreover, when they recovered, they too were eager to return to Pennsylvania.

Meanwhile, the college struggled to survive. In September 1914 Father Walter Stehle replaced Father Hilary Kaib as prior and director. Stehle was a thirty-seven-year-old native of the German Duchy of Württemberg who had served for eight years as director of Saint Vincent College. That Archabbot Leander chose to assign him to Colorado illustrates the importance Schnerr and the Saint Vincent chapter placed in the work of establishing a strong Benedictine community and college there, for Father Walter was one of the most talented and respected leaders in the Pennsylvania community.

When Stehle arrived in Pueblo he discovered that conditions were every bit as dismal at the college as reports had indicated. After eleven years of existence, Father Walter said, the college had "no standing and no reputation for anything definite. To do anything we must begin to work hard and to overcome prejudices against the place." The principal "prejudice" against Benedictine College seems to have been its lack of academic credibility among Catholics of the state. Families who could afford to send their sons to a private Catholic secondary school preferred the Jesuit college in Denver. The Benedictines' college in Pueblo had a commercial course and an elementary school but lacked a classical curriculum altogether. Stehle reported that the three-story building with fourth-floor dormers that the monks had built in 1903 was inadequate since it did not accommodate boarding students. Moreover, "the number and quality of Catholics in this city does not, at present, justify the hope that we shall be able to get day-students enough to make the place self-supporting." The monks in Colorado were demoralized and held out little hope for the success of the school, but Father Walter urged them to persevere, telling them "that it is not a question of success for us, but of obedience and that it is our business to make every reasonable effort and to show our good will and to leave the success of the whole thing to God who always blesses obedience in some way."[58]

To build a reputation for the school and attract students, Stehle spent the summer of 1915 on a "preaching (advertising) crusade" in the area. He also published a pamphlet on Catholic education that he hoped would bring students to the school. "We have to overcome the prejudice," he wrote to Archabbot Leander, "and convince the people that we are ready and able to keep our promises and to do more for their sons in an educational way than any other educational agency . . . can do."[59]

The Saint Vincent chapter, meanwhile, was beginning to have second thoughts about its commitment to operating a college in Colorado. In the spring of 1916 Archabbot Leander informed Stehle that if he were unable to resolve the problems and make the college self-supporting within two years, the chapter would vote to close it. Stehle replied that he would do whatever Schnerr and the community in Pennsylvania wished, noting that "the circumstances are disheartening to the Fathers [in Colorado], but not to me." In January of 1918 he happily reported that the college was free from debt for the first time in fifteen years.[60] The overall debt burdening the Benedictines in the Colorado missions, however, continued to be high, and that, together with the threat to the school's enrollment resulting from the new military conscription law and the unlikely prospects for improving the academic standing of the college without draining Saint Vincent of more professors, led to the chapter's decision on March 19, 1918, by a vote of twenty-six to two, to give up the Benedictine College of Pueblo.[61]

The college closed its doors at the end of May 1918, and Archabbot Leander recalled the professors to Saint Vincent, leaving a contingent of about twelve priests and brothers to continue the parochial and missionary work that monks from Pennsylvania had been doing in Colorado for over thirty years. In July 1922 the Holy See established the independent priory of Saint Leander in Pueblo, and nine priests and one deacon transferred their vows of stability to the newly independent monastery. Father Cyprian Bradley, a professor at Saint Vincent College and prefect in the seminary who had previously served on the faculty of the Benedictine College in Pueblo, was elected first conventual prior.[62] In 1923 the monastery was transferred to Canon City, and its name was changed to Holy Cross Priory.

Two years later it was elevated to the rank of abbey, and Bradley, a native of Port Vue, Pennsylvania, who had come to Saint Vincent in 1898 as a fourteen-year-old scholastic, was elected its first abbot. Holy Cross in Colorado was the tenth abbey to be established from Saint Vincent.

AN ABBEY IN ILLINOIS

Meanwhile Saint Vincent had continued to staff St. Bede's College in Peru, Illinois. St. Bede's had been established by the Pennsylvania Benedictines in 1891 and during its early years had struggled with the twin problems of low enrollment and financial insecurity. In 1897 Archabbot Leander sent Father Vincent Huber, the forty-two-year-old director of Saint Vincent College, to assume the duties of both director of the college and prior of the monastery at St. Bede's. Huber, a native of Carrolltown, Pennsylvania, who had come to Saint Vincent as a boy, entered the monastery in 1874, and been ordained in 1880, had received his theological training in Rome and served as professor of dogmatic theology, seminary prefect, and prior of the archabbey before being named director of Saint Vincent College in 1892. He had held this latter position for five years before his assignment to Illinois.

Shortly after his arrival in Peru, Father Vincent wrote Archabbot Leander that "the prospects are good for the future of St. Bede's and I sincerely hope it will be able to repay at least a little to St. Vincent's before many years shall have passed." The beginning of Huber's tenure witnessed an economic recovery that followed the great national depression of the 1890s, and under his leadership the college's enrollment grew dramatically. After only a year Father Vincent reported that there were seventy-eight boarders and eleven day students at St. Bede's, and he asked Schnerr to send more professors from Saint Vincent.[63] By the end of 1898 student enrollment had passed the one hundred mark, and eight years later it had nearly doubled to two hundred.[64]

The success of the college encouraged the chapter at Saint Vincent, and many of the monks in Pennsylvania volunteered to serve on the faculty. By 1905 both the Benedictine community and the student body at St. Bede's had grown to such an extent that the administration found it necessary to expand the original building. The Saint Vincent chapter voted thirty thousand dollars for the expansion, and the Chicago architectural firm of Bauer and Hill was contracted to do the work. In the spring of 1906 a new wing with three floors and a sixteen-foot basement was completed, doubling the amount of space available for the college and priory. By now there were almost 150 students enrolled and fifteen Saint Vincent priests on the faculty, and thus the success of the college seemed assured.[65]

In February 1906, amid great optimism both in Pennsylvania and Illinois for the future of St. Bede's, the tragic death of Father Gilbert Simon, a twenty-seven-year-old professor of Latin and Greek who had been ordained at Saint Vincent two years before, along with that of three students, cast a pall over the community. The deaths resulted from a skating accident. When a group of students fell through the ice of the Illinois River, Father Gilbert had rushed to their assistance and managed to save seven of them before succumbing to the cold and sinking beneath the water. In its eulogy, the *St. Vincent Journal* noted that Father Gilbert was "endowed with exceptional talent, with a fine, frank, genial disposition, radiating irresistible cheerfulness, with a splendid physique, which served him so nobly in his last moments." His life, the *Journal* said, "glowed rich with promise, never, alas, to be fulfilled. But his death has hallowed his life; his name will be indissolubly linked with his last grand action; in one short, heroic moment he has grown beyond the fruition of many years."[66]

Despite the gloom that descended on students and faculty because of the accident, optimism in the college and monastery recovered and life continued to move forward at an ever-increasing tempo. In addition to operating the college, which was the principal apostolate of the monastic community, the Benedictines in Peru, like their brethren in Pennsylvania, were also involved in parochial work. They had charge of St. Joseph's Parish in Peru as well as St. Benedict Parish in Ladd (with its missions in the neighboring mining towns of Cherry and Seatonville) and St. Francis German Parish in Ottawa.[67] Unlike Saint Vincent, however, St. Bede's did not develop extensive commitments to parish work; rather, the monks focused their energies on developing the college and building monastic life at the priory.

In August 1908 the sixteenth general chapter of the American Cassinese Congregation was held at St. Bede's, and one of the issues discussed by the abbots and delegates was the advisability of elevating the priory to the rank of independent abbey.[68] The proposal met with the general approval of the abbots and delegates and the enthusiastic support of the monks in Peru. A year passed as preparations were made for the creation of a new independent abbey in Illinois. Bishop Edmund Dunne of Peoria, who had succeeded John Lancaster Spalding in 1908, gave his approval, and on August 17, 1909, the Saint Vincent chapter voted almost unanimously to petition the Holy See for St. Bede's elevation to abbatial rank. The chapter also voted to relieve the community in Illinois of the obligation to repay the money loaned to it over the years by Saint Vincent and to cede to it all the Benedictine parishes and missions in the Diocese of Peoria.[69]

In January 1910 the Holy See granted Archabbot Leander faculties to erect St. Bede's into an exempt abbey. Granting such faculties to the archabbot of Saint Vincent was an entirely new procedure. Until now independent abbeys in the United States had been created by direct papal action. The new procedure indicated recognition by the Vatican that the monastery of Saint Vincent had come of age and was prepared to share with the Holy See responsibilities for the status of the monasteries founded from it.[70] Thirteen Saint Vincent priests volunteered to transfer their vows to St. Bede's, and later they were joined by three clerics and two lay brothers from Saint Vincent.

Archabbot Leander called for the election of an abbot and set March 29, 1910, as the date for elevating the priory to the rank of abbey. On that day Abbot Peter Engel of St. John's, president of the American Cassinese Congregation, arrived in Peru and read the decree whereby the priory became an exempt abbey. The following day, after an early morning solemn High Mass in honor of the Holy Spirit, twelve of the thirteen capitulars of the new abbey gathered in the monastery chapter room to elect an abbot. On the first ballot Father Vincent Huber of Saint Vincent was chosen unanimously and Abbot Peter cabled him with the news. Huber, who had served as prior and director of the college at St. Bede's between 1897 and 1908, was teaching dogmatic theology in Saint Vincent Seminary at the time of his election. The Holy See confirmed the election a month later, and on June 29, 1910, he was blessed as the first abbot of St. Bede's Abbey, a position he held for the next thirty-one years.[71]

THE NEW ARCHABBEY CHURCH

Even as the energies and resources of the archabbey were contributing to the development of monastic foundations in Colorado and Illinois, other energies and resources were being devoted during the opening years of the twentieth century to monastic and academic initiatives at Saint Vincent itself. Among the most ambitious of these was construction of the archabbey church, a work begun in 1891 that twelve years later was still in progress. The *St. Vincent Journal* noted in 1903 that there seemed no end to the construction effort. The work was slow, the structure itself Massive and expensive. "The rule," said the *Journal* was "pay as you go, and go as you pay. . . . there are no magical developments from the operation of such safe economic principles."[72] The economic depression of the 1890s had delayed progress, but by the first years of the new century conditions had improved and the building was dramatically taking shape amid the farmlands of central Westmoreland County.

The Romanesque church, built of red brick and locally quarried stone, had been designed by William Schickel of New York, and construction was under the supervision of Brother Wolfgang Traxler of Saint Vincent. Bricks for the edifice were fabricated at the Saint Vincent brickyard, and lay brothers from the archabbey and volunteers from the parish contributed to the work, though most of the skilled and manual labor was done by hired workmen. By the spring of 1904 much of the work had been completed, and the monastic chapter set August 24, 1905, as the date for the church's solemn consecration, a date which marked the fiftieth anniversary of Saint Vincent's elevation to the rank of abbey.

When guests and dignitaries arrived at the archabbey for the ceremony, they found an imposing structure that had been fourteen years in the making. The church was 230 feet long from the entrance on the east to the apse on the west. The nave and aisles of the cruciform church, as well as the choir and its aisles, were 75 feet wide, while the transepts (or arms of the cross) measured 122 feet in length. The height of the nave and choir ceiling was 62 feet and that of the transepts, 68 feet. Two rear towers rose to a height of 150 feet, and two towers in the front of the church had reached 120 feet. The original plan was to bring these main towers to a height of 250 feet. The supporting wall beneath them was clearly sufficient to hold the projected weight, but the work on the front towers was never completed because of the lack of funds.

Inside the church red granite columns from Aberdeen, Scotland, supported the clerestory and galleries. The main altar was located at the intersection of the nave and transepts. Before it were pews accommodating six hundred people and behind it choir stalls for the monks of the archabbey. Eight other altars graced the church: two were located in the extreme ends of the transepts and six in the sanctuary behind the choir stalls. The white marble altars were made in Carrara, Italy; the inlaid work was fashioned from yellow Sienna marble, the panels of purple Pavonazzo marble. The side and transept altars were dedicated to St. Benedict, St. Scholastica, St. Vincent de Paul, St. John the Baptist, the Guardian Angels, St. Joseph, the Blessed Virgin, and the Sacred Heart. The pews and choir stalls, like the pulpit and confessionals, were crafted by master carpenters among the lay brothers of Saint Vincent largely from oak trees harvested on nearby Chestnut Ridge.

The twenty-seven stained-glass windows were made in Munich by the Stoltzenberg Company; the twenty-two windows of the clerestory and the rose windows were filled with glass made in the United States. The windows in the nave presented various scenes from the life of Christ—the Nativity, the Epiphany, the Child Jesus Teaching in the Temple, the Holy Family, the Baptism of Christ, the Transfiguration, Christ Blessing the Children, the Resurrection, the Ascension, and the Descent of the Holy Spirit. Windows in the transepts depicted the Sacred Heart, the Good Shepherd, the Prodigal Son, the Pharisee and the Publican, the Good Samaritan, St. John the Baptist, St. Martin of Tours, and St. Boniface. In the sanctuary the windows showed the Guardian Angels, the Meeting of St. Benedict and St. Scholastica, the Death of St. Benedict, St. Vincent de Paul, and in the apse, the founders of five monastic orders: St. Benedict, St. Romuald, St. Bernard of Clairvaux, St. Dominic, and St. Francis of Assisi.

Frescoes decorating the ceiling of the church were the work of Pittsburgh artist Joseph Reiter. Above the main altar were paintings of the four Evangelists and above the choir stalls the nine Choirs of Angels and the four great Doctors of the Church: St. Augustine, St. Ambrose, St. Jerome, and St. Gregory the Great. The stone carvings were done by Polish artist Ladislaus Vitalis, who chiseled the capitals throughout the church and the group above the main entrance which depicted Christ giving the keys to St. Peter in the presence of the other Apostles. The Stations of the Cross were half reliefs in ivory-tinted stone crafted by the Bavarian Art Company.[73]

An important feature of the church was the double organ designed by the internationally renowned English organ builder Robert Hope-Jones and constructed by the Austin Organ Company of Hartford, Connecticut. The organ consisted of fifty-two stops powered by two rotary blowers driven by electric motors of ten and three horsepower. The main organ of thirty-eight stops was in the gallery above the entrance to the church and the smaller organ of fourteen stops in the sanctuary. Two four-manual consoles, one placed in the sanctuary, the other in the east gallery, were connected electrically so that they could be played together or separately from either position.[74]

The organ was inaugurated on the day preceding the church's consecration by Professor Caspar P. Koch, organist at Carnegie Hall, Pittsburgh, who presented a festive concert that included Bach's Toccata and Fugue in D Minor, Böllman's *Gothic Suite, In Paradisum* and *Fiat Lux* by Dubois, the Largo from Handel's *Xerxes,* and Rossini's *William Tell* Overture. At the same concert the Saint Vincent Parish choir sang the *Domine Deus* by

Stehle and the monastery's *Männerchor* (male voice choir) performed the *Jesu Dulcis* by Zeller and Kösporer's *Ave Maria.*

Hundreds of guests came to Saint Vincent for the consecration of the church on August 24, 1905. Bishop J. F. Regis Canevin of Pittsburgh, an alumnus of the college and seminary, was the principal celebrant, assisted by dozens of abbots and bishops, including Archbishop Diomede Falconio, apostolic delegate to the United States. The ceremony began at 7:00 a.m. on August 24 with a procession around the new church during which Bishop Canevin blessed the foundation, walls, and doors and the monastic *schola* (small choir) chanted the prayers "using the pure and time-honored melodies of Solesmes." At 8:30 a.m. the relics were brought into the church in a solemn procession, and Bishop Canevin and eight other bishops consecrated the nine altars. Taking part in the consecration of the altars were Archbishop Sebastian G. Messmer of Milwaukee; Archbishop Francesco A. Symon of the Vatican nunciature in Washington; Bishop Henry Richter of Grand Rapids, Michigan; Bishop Camillus P. Maes of Covington, Kentucky; Bishop Leo Haid, O.S.B., of the vicariate of North Carolina; and three other Pennsylvania bishops: Eugene A. Garvey of Altoona, John W. Shanahan of Harrisburg, and John E. Fitzmaurice of Erie.

Following the consecration of the altars, Archbishop Falconio celebrated a solemn pontifical High Mass during which Bishop James A. McFaul of Trenton, New Jersey, preached the sermon. The church was packed with more than eight hundred people, including ten abbots and three hundred priests, most of whom were alumni of Saint Vincent. After the Mass, guests were invited to a special banquet, hosted by the Benedictine community, at which Archbishop Falconio, Bishop Canevin, and Bishop Haid gave speeches. That evening Archabbot Leander was principal celebrant at a solemn pontifical Vespers in the new church. Schnerr, who had been bedridden for several months with a lung ailment, had recovered his health sufficiently to preside over the long and tiring liturgy, and the *St. Vincent Journal* reflected the views of the entire community when it noted that the archabbot's participation was itself a cause for celebration, "for to his labor and zeal and energy is largely due the successful completion of the magnificent structure."[75]

The consecration of the church was also marked by the publication of two historical works by monks of the archabbey. Father Felix Fellner's German work *Die St. Vincenz Gemeinde und Erzabtei* was one of this noted Benedictine scholar's earliest studies of Saint Vincent and American Benedictine history, and Father Louis Haas's *St. Vincent's: Souvenir of the Conse-*

cration of the New Abbey Church was a brief but important history of Saint Vincent that has the distinction of being the first such work written in English.[76]

In all, the completion and consecration of the archabbey church marked a significant milestone in the history of the Benedictine community. With a monastic population of nearly 230 monks, Saint Vincent was now the largest Benedictine monastery in the world. Its priests taught six hundred students in the seminary and college at Saint Vincent as well as at the colleges in Illinois and Colorado, and served forty-one thousand Catholics in forty-two parishes in Pennsylvania, Maryland, Kentucky, Colorado, and Illinois. The new archabbey church was a symbol of both the stability and vitality of the Saint Vincent Benedictines.

DEVELOPMENTS AT SAINT VINCENT COLLEGE

Under Archabbot Leander Schnerr Saint Vincent College entered the twentieth century fully prepared to meet the challenges confronting it as it underwent the changes that would turn it into a modern undergraduate institution. By 1905 there was clear differentiation among the seminary, or ecclesiastical course, which offered a four-year program of theological studies; the undergraduate college, which offered a four-year classical course to students who had completed their secondary education; and the four-year secondary school, which was divided into classical and commercial tracks. Altogether there were 430 students in these three academic programs, the highest enrollment yet in the schools of Saint Vincent and one that remained steady over the next decade.

The undergraduate college itself was divided into two residence halls: the college proper, and the scholasticate. The scholasticate was a six-year program in which candidates for the Benedictine Order completed four years of secondary education and two years of undergraduate work before entering the novitiate. The college catalog for 1904–5 explained: "the Scholasticate—which, studies excepted, is altogether distinct and separate from the College—forms the preparatory Seminary for such as feel themselves called to become members of the Benedictine Order; hence, only those are received who intend to become Benedictines. The discipline is calculated to impress on the minds of the aspirants a due sense of the requirements of monastic life."[77]

But even for those students not planning to become Benedictines, the regimen at Saint Vincent in the beginning of the twentieth century was decidedly monastic, as their weekday schedule attests. The students rose at

5:00 a.m. and attended Mass at 6:00 a.m. The rest of their day was as follows:

6:30 a.m.	Breakfast, followed by recreation
7:10 a.m.	Study hall
8:00 a.m.	Classes
11:30 a.m.	Lunch, followed by prayer and recreation
1:45 p.m.	Classes
5:30 p.m.	Supper, followed by recreation
7:00 p.m.	Study hall
8:30 p.m.	Night prayers and bed

The students' spiritual development was a primary goal of the faculty and administration of the college, and the daily round of prayers and religious devotions within the ambience of the Benedictine liturgy was an essential part of the educational program. Moreover, the monks held firm to the belief that "boys have not the sense and not the will of men. Their sense and their will must be developed and made strong and fit to cope with the manifold temptations and occasions for wrong-doing in our modern civilization. A place away from city life and town pleasures and temptations is, therefore, good for the education of the average boy and the only means of saving some boys from physical and moral ruin."[78]

The college catalog made it quite clear that the students were at Saint Vincent to develop not merely their intellectual skills but their spiritual life and moral character as well:

> In the moulding of a staunch, fearless, upright character, good traits must be encouraged and developed, vicious habits must be checked and eliminated, natural inclinations must be carefully directed or corrected. To the attainment of these ends it is very important that the relations existing between the students and the Faculty of the College be not mistaken or misunderstood. Superiors and Professors mingle with the students not in the role of detectives and severe taskmasters, but rather in the capacity of true friends and wise moderators, whose only ambition is to secure the temporal and eternal welfare of their subjects and pupils.
>
> The discipline at St. Vincent is strict, but not severe. It is enforced more by moral suasion than by forceful measures. No well disposed student, who realizes why he is at College, will find great difficulty in observing the . . . Rules of Conduct.[79]

Student life in the early 1900s, however, was not all rules of conduct and monastic regimen. The faculty was determined to educate the whole person, which required careful attention to the students' physical well-being and social adjustment. During this period baseball, football, basketball, gymnastics, hockey, tennis, and bowling were popular intramural activities, and every student participated in at least one team sport. Indeed, physical exercise, team sports, and communal recreational activities were at the heart of the educational program. The college catalog offered this attractive description of extracurricular activities at the school:

If there is anything that lends enchantment to a student's life and tends to lighten the burden and relieve the monotony of daily study, it is an inviting campus where he may find relaxation in healthful games and pastime-pleasures, and to add to his moral and mental culture that physical development which will render him hale of body and rugged of constitution. The College play-grounds are admirably adapted to the attainment of these objects. They are so fashioned by nature and art as to render them a place of welcome to all students, howsoever varied their dispositions and inclinations may be. The grounds comprise twenty-five acres, seven of which are a grove of primeval oaks, in the centre of which is a generous spring of purest water which has stood the test of ages. Circling paths wind beneath the shady trees. Five hand-ball courts are pleasantly located in the grove and afford many an hour of mirthful and invigorating exercise.

Five base-ball diamonds grace the campus and offer ample opportunities to the lovers of the great national sport, whilst games of a less violent nature have their allotted places. A large ice-pond and the Loyal Hannah close by are resorts of pleasure to the lovers of skating.

In wet weather and during the dreary months of winter, the students spend most of their recreation time in the Gymnasium. Thus every possible advantage to build up and develop a strong and healthy constitution, which contributes so much to the happiness of man and to his utility in society, is offered to the student during his sojourn at the College.[80]

One of the features of the college that attracted many to it was its lovely rural setting. College recruiters regularly highlighted this feature in advertising the college to the public. The description of the campus in the catalog portrayed a tranquil and idyllic place, far from the madding crowd and secluded from the purportedly unhealthful influences of city life and industrial America.

The landscape surrounding St. Vincent is indeed beautiful. The most fertile valleys of Pennsylvania, the thickly wooded Chestnut Ridge stretching along the eastern horizon, undulating fields with primeval forests serving as a background—these are some of the charms of nature by which the student of St. Vincent is environed and inspired. The hand of man has not dared to destroy the natural beauties of our immediate vicinity. We are encompassed by coal-mines and coke-works, by steel-mills and glass factories, but they are several miles away and do not mar the enchanting scenery which nature has thrown around our College home. On the contrary, ingenuity and assiduous labor have helped to make this an ideal garden of beauty. Spacious lawns, beds of flowers, blooming shrubbery, vines, and ferns, and hundreds of ornamental bushes and shapely shade-trees have added to the charms

Saint Vincent College baseball team, 1902. Bat boys: Kenna Jennings and William Coyne. Seated: Victor Dzmura, Father Mark Kistner, O.S.B., Edward Abbaticchio, Thomas Wilson, Alphonse Bour, Joseph Gallick (later Father Cuthbert, O.S.B.). Standing: Victor Follen, Harry Treschler, John Coyne, William Hogan, John Barrett (later Father Regis, O.S.B.), Charles Peterman, Martin O'Hara, Aloysius O'Reilly, Otto Weaver.

which the Creator has showered with a lavish hand over the knoll that bears St. Vincent.[81]

Situated as they were in western Pennsylvania, where the coal and steel industries had destroyed thousands of square miles of forest and polluted the air and water, the faculty and students of Saint Vincent were particularly aware of their responsibility to preserve the environment for future generations. In January of 1905, when President Roosevelt called for a commission to study ways of protecting the forests of North America from destruction by commercial interests, the *St. Vincent Journal* applauded the initiative and called readers' attention to conditions in their own backyard. "Take our own local forests," the editorialist wrote. "The trees are mercilessly slaughtered, and no care taken of the young saplings." Also, "the mines in our immediate neighborhood consume an immense number of pit posts yearly." The writer called for environmental conservation and protection by the government, and remarked that "if our country could boast of a few more men like Mr. Roosevelt, who not only looks after the present welfare of his country but also deems it the duty of every true and loyal citizen to look out for posterity, the American family and the American forest would follow the scriptural injunction, and increase wonderfully in numbers."[82]

In the years leading up to the First World War, significant academic developments occurred in the college. These developments were part of a nationwide effort by Catholic colleges to bring some coherence and uniformity to their academic curricula. In April 1899 representatives from Catholic institutions of higher education throughout the country met in Chicago to discuss such issues as curriculum development, academic standards, and higher education administration. Monsignor Thomas J. Conaty of the Catholic University of America, Washington, D.C., chaired the meeting, which was a response to modern developments in American higher education generally. The key question confronting the delegates was how Catholic colleges and universities should change to meet the growing needs of their students and to compete with secular institutions of higher learning.

Father Vincent Huber, former director of Saint Vincent College and now director of St. Bede's College, Peru, Illinois, was Saint Vincent's representative at the meeting, and when he returned to St. Bede's he wrote Archabbot Leander recommending that Benedictine college administators hold their own meeting to consider establishing uniform curricula, entrance requirements, and standards for conferring degrees at Benedictine institutions in the United States. Schnerr consulted with other abbots of the American Cassinese Congregation, who all agreed that such a meeting was necessary.[83]

As a result of Huber's initiative, representatives of eight American Benedictine colleges—Saint Vincent, St. John's in Minnesota, St. Benedict's in Kansas, Maryhelp College in North Carolina, St. Benedict's in New Jersey, St. Bernard's in Alabama, St. Bede's in Illinois, and St. Anselm's in New Hampshire—met at St. John's Abbey in August 1899 and then again at Saint Vincent in July 1900 to "devise plans of uniformity as to courses, methods, text-books, etc." in the Benedictine colleges of the United

States.[84] A significant result of these meetings was a consensus that the classical (liberal arts) course would continue to be the core component of academic programs in American Benedictine colleges, despite the growing enthusiasm of students for the commercial course. The Benedictine administrators also fixed the cycle for the commercial course at four years of secondary-school work and the classical course at eight years: four of "academic" high-school work and four of liberal arts studies at the "undergraduate" level.[85] The meetings at St. John's and Saint Vincent led to the establishment in 1919 of the National Benedictine Educational Association, whose member institutions included colleges and seminaries in both the American Cassinese and the Swiss-American Congregations and whose purpose was "to increase excellence in American Catholic education in general and American Benedictine education in particular."[86]

An important consequence of the meetings of Benedictine educators at the turn of the century was a new awareness at Saint Vincent of the need to improve the curriculum and raise academic standards to levels commensurate with those of other colleges in the United States. It was generally recognized that one of the significant weaknesses of American Benedictine colleges was the lack of adequate programs in science, an area in which other American colleges and universities excelled. The administration at Saint Vincent focused with some success on improving scientific study at the college during the period before the First World War. Old courses in chemistry and physics were revised and new ones introduced in biology, physiology, zoology, botany, and astronomy. Talented young Benedictines like Fathers Mark Kistner and Fabian Heid were trained in science and became members of the faculty.

In January of 1912 the archabbey's council of seniors voted to permit young priests and clerics "who show special talents in certain branches" to be sent to secular universities for advanced studies.[87] Until then, monks from Saint Vincent had gone only to Catholic universities in the United States and Europe. It was in the secular universities of the United States, however, that the programs were offered that would prepare members of the faculty to develop the scientific curriculum of the college. The archabbot was reluctant to send the young priests and clerics into what he considered the lion's den, but, like the council of seniors, he recognized that the college would have to have an adequately trained faculty if it were to compete with other institutions of higher learning in the country. He therefore reluctantly agreed to the council's recommendation, with the stipulation that the young monks would go only to universities near Benedictine parishes and that they would live in the parishes during their studies rather than on campus.

Among the first clerics to go out under this new initiative were Alcuin Tasch and Florian Bergmann, who spent summers studying biology, chemistry, and physics at Johns Hopkins University while living at Fourteen Holy Martyrs Parish in Baltimore.[88] As in the past, other young monks from Saint Vincent continued to be sent to study in Europe, including Ignatius Groll, who studied liturgical music at Beuron, and Francis Mersinger and Lambert Daller, who studied theology at Sant' Anselmo in Rome.

In 1915 a significant change took place in the curriculum of Saint Vincent College when a scientific course was added to the classical and commercial courses. The scientific course was a four-year program intended to permit a student to "prepare himself for admission to the technical schools and premedical courses of the schools of medicine." In addition to Latin, English, history, modern languages, and religious instruction, students in the scientific course received a firm grounding in mathematics and the sciences. At the same time as the introduction of the scientific course, the college also introduced a modern language requirement in the classical and commercial courses and offered four languages from which students could choose: German, Italian, French, and Slovak.[89]

Despite changes in the curriculum designed to modernize the academic program at Saint Vincent, student life during the early years of the twentieth century altered little from the pace set in the days of Boniface Wimmer. Social life still centered on the campus, and the old traditions of plays, concerts, debates, and sports were maintained. Religious, literary, and musical societies such as the League of the Sacred Heart, the Debating Society, and various liturgical, classical, and popular music groups continued to occupy the students' time and interest. Formal debates held on campus centered on such propositions as: "that the government ought to construct an extensive system of irrigation works," "that country life is preferable to city life," "that life imprisonment with work should be substituted for punishment by death for crime," and "that immigration to the United States should be further restricted by law"—all of which, except the last, were won by teams defending the affirmative position.

For theater enthusiasts, melodramas and operettas—with titles like *The Blind Prince, Old Glory,* and *The Triumph of Justice*—were still the preferred fare, and field trips to Chestnut Ridge and the Kuhn's Farm in the fall and to Idlewild Park in the spring continued to be regular events. A popular gathering place on campus for students during this period was the "sweets shop" called "The Shack," where since the 1890s students had been able to purchase toiletries, candy, and tobacco. Father Agatho Strittmatter ran the Shack during the early years of the century, and when he was assigned to the missions in Colorado, he was replaced as manager by senior students, including one named Nagidac who inspired the following doggerel:

> Our friend Nagidac now tends to the Shack
> And kindly dispenses the wool and soft soap.
> Important as Mars, he hands out cigars,
> Forgetting the matches and "dope."
> He puts down five slabs, then the quarter he grabs;
> Such manners! A saint t'would provoke.
> We tell him he's tight, he then laughs outright:
> "I'd rather be tight than be broke."[90]

"Dope" in this innocent age, of course, meant not illicit drugs but "gossip."

In 1911, Father Thomas H. Bryson, an alumnus of the college, published a novel entitled *The Juniors of St. Bede's,* which was based on Bryson's experiences as a student at Saint Vincent. A brief review of the novel in the *St. Vincent Journal* observed that the author had "presented a very interesting story of college boys [describing] their hardships and their troubles, their fun and escapades," and that the story was told "in a very interesting manner and keeps the attention of the reader throughout."[91]

The Saint Vincent Alumni Association, originally founded in 1885, was revived in 1905 at the time of the consecration of the new archabbey church, and Father William Kelty of Crafton, Pennsylvania, was elected president. The following year Father Hugh Boyle, a Pittsburgh priest who would later succeed Regis Canevin as bishop of Pittsburgh, was elected the association's president, and in the years that followed such distinguished alumni as Pittsburgh businessman Edward Diebold, Elk County attorney James A. Gleason, Philadelphia physician Lawrence F. Flick, and Pittsburgh priest David Hegarty held the position. For the first time the alumni association, under the direction of its indefatigable secretary, Benedictine Father Gerard Bridge of Saint Vincent, took on the task of raising funds for the college and established two Alumni Association Scholarships for needy students. Members of the association who made significant donations or established individual scholarships during this period included Father James Hickey, rector of St. Thomas Church, Braddock, Pennsylvania; Francis Rocks of Connellsville, Pennsylvania; Dr. Isidore P. Strittmatter of Philadelphia; and several anonymous donors.

SAINT VINCENT SEMINARY

The principal reason that Boniface Wimmer had come to the United States in 1846, of course, was to establish a seminary where young men could be prepared for the priesthood. From the beginning, the Benedictines of Saint Vincent had regarded the seminary as their most important apostolic work, and by the turn of the century it had become one of the oldest and most respected institutions of its kind in the United States. Though Wimmer's original intention was to educate German youth for holy orders, seminarians from other Catholic ethnic groups—first the Irish, then Czechs, Poles, Slovaks, Hungarians, Lithuanians, and Italians—soon contributed to the mix and quickly became part of the melting pot of this truly American seminary.[92]

Since 1846 hundreds of Pittsburgh priests had received their theological training there. Seminarians came from dozens of other American dioceses as well, and by the turn of the century few dioceses in the United States—from Savannah to Boston and from New York to San Francisco—did not have at least one parish priest on their rolls who had been educated at Saint Vincent. In addition, the vast majority of Benedictine priests in the American Cassinese Congregation had also been educated there.

Between 1846 and 1912, according to one study done by the seminary, nearly 1,200 American priests pursued all or part of their philosophical and theological studies at Saint Vincent. More than two-thirds of these alumni were non-Benedictine (mostly diocesan) priests, and of these more than 500 were still active in the ministry in 1912. Of the 330 Benedictine priests who had been educated at Saint Vincent between 1846 and 1912, more than 200 were still alive at the time of the study. In addition, eleven American bishops had received part or all of their priestly training in the seminary at Saint Vincent. Among those still active in 1912 were Regis Canevin of Pittsburgh, Joseph B. Cotter of Winona (Minnesota), James A. McFaul of Trenton, James Trobec of St. Cloud, Joseph Schrembs of Toledo, and George Mundelein of Brooklyn, who in 1915 would become Archbishop of Chicago.[93]

Like the changes in the curriculum of the college, the principal change in the curriculum of the seminary during the early years of the twentieth century was driven by outside influences. In this case it was not secular universities but the Church itself that brought about the change. Pope Pius X's condemnation of Modernism in the 1907 encyclical *Pascendi Dominici Gregis* caused bishops throughout the world to make a careful examination of theological programs in their seminaries. In the wake of the encyclical the Holy See issued guidelines, later codified in the Code of Canon Law (1918), which set the curriculum of major seminaries at two years of philosophy and four years of theology, sacred scripture, history, liturgy, and canon law.

Change occurred immediately at Saint Vincent Seminary, which by the end of the 1907–8 school year became the first Catholic theologate in the United States to expand the traditional three-year theology curriculum to four years.[94] The courses remained relatively stable and continued to consist primarily of dogmatic and moral theology, sacred scripture, church history, canon law, liturgy, and homiletics. In the new curriculum, seminarians continued their studies of these subjects for a fourth year and attended classes in patristics and pastoral theology as well. Four, rather than three years of a modern language (German, Slovak, or Italian) were now also required. Following further instructions of the Holy See, an even greater emphasis than before was placed on the scholastic theology of St. Thomas Aquinas in the seminary classrooms at Saint Vincent.

The eagerness with which the entire Saint Vincent community attempted to show its support for the pope's teaching and its loyalty to the Holy See in the aftermath of the controversy caused by *Pascendi Dominici Gregis* is reflected in an editorial that appeared in the *St. Vincent Journal* several months after publication of the encyclical. "Indifference is the great evil of our day," the editorial began.

> It is widespread and all the more harmful because it is subtle and insidious. It is fast becoming a menace. The Pope, always on the alert to point out dangers to his flock, saw this danger and warned the faithful in the recent Encyclical. . . . Pope Pius X acts as the real teacher of God's children, by pointing out the errors of the day and by exposing fallacies. He acts, too, as counsellor by enjoining upon those in ecclesiastical authority the duty of removing abuses and of warning their people of the dangers in their path. Some of the American magazines, heretofore considered leading periodicals, have taken up a fight against the Encyclical, but in this they have only proved that the reputation they formerly possessed as being authorities was a sham. They have belittled themselves. They try to undermine the "Rock of Peter," but it is the "Pillar and Ground of Truth" and cannot be moved.[95]

Though some Catholic schools of theology in the United States fell under suspicion of heterodoxy and lost the support of the hierarchy after the pope's condemnation of Modernism, Saint Vincent Seminary, under the leadership of such outstanding seminary "prefects" (later called "rectors") as Fathers Candidus Eichenlaub, Vincent Huber, Leopold Probst, and Aurelius Stehle, grew in stature and reputation and came to be known among the hierarchy of the United States as a center of conservative theology and unquestioned orthodoxy.[96] Between 1906 and 1917 enrollment expanded from thirty-two to eighty-one students of theology. Not only Pittsburgh and the other Pennsylvania dioceses, but also Seattle, Dallas, Sacramento, St. Cloud, LaCrosse, Toledo, Columbus, Belleville, Covington, Wheeling, and Brooklyn sent seminarians to the theologate at Saint Vincent for study.

The theology faculty of the seminary continued to be staffed by some of the most talented and best-educated members of the monastic community. Among professors of theology during the first decade of the twentieth century were Fathers Julian Kilger (moral theology and canon law), Baldwin Ambros (sacred scripture), Ernest Gensheimer (scholastic philosophy), Leopold Probst (liturgy and sacred scripture), and Vitus Kratzer (dogmatic theology). All but Gensheimer, a native of Erie, Pennsylvania, were Bavarian-born, and all had received their theological training in Rome. In August 1912 the Holy See gave official recognition to the quality of the theology faculty at Saint Vincent by granting pontifical degrees to three of its senior members. The Sacred Congregation of Studies awarded Kilger and Ambros doctorates of sacred theology and Gensheimer a doctorate of philosophy. During the ceremony in the archabbey church at which the degrees were conferred, Bishop Regis Canevin noted that "these titles, coming as they do from the Holy Father, are a public approval of the excellent work done by this institution."[97]

The awarding of pontifical degrees to three members of the Saint Vincent Seminary faculty was only the first of the honors the Holy See bestowed upon the institution in the period before World War I. In April 1912 Archabbot Leander petitioned Rome to grant the seminary itself pontifical status with the right to confer pontifical degrees. Schnerr wrote to Bishop Leo Haid of North Carolina: "I need not tell you how highly we would cherish such a favor and consider it a joyful acknowledgement of our past labors in having educated in [the] college and seminary at least, if not more than, 1150 young men for the priesthood."[98]

The justification for such an honor, the archabbot said, was clear. Boniface Wimmer had come to the United States in 1846 to train young men for the priesthood, and from the beginning the monks of Saint Vincent had shown their loyalty and fidelity to the Holy See by ensuring that only the most orthodox theology was taught to priesthood candidates. Wimmer had safeguarded the integrity of the seminary by sending many young monks, at great expense, to Rome for advanced studies in philosophy and theology, and "his noble example was faithfully followed at all times as a holy tradition." As a result, not only had more than a thousand American priests been educated at Saint Vincent in an ambience of "rigid orthodoxy," but also eleven of them had been "deemed worthy on account of their deep learning and virtuous life to be raised to the dignity of bishops." The strongest point in favor of the petition, Schnerr reminded Bishop Haid, was "the thorough Catholic orthodox education the candidates [for the priesthood] receive here without the least suspicion of Modernism (for *inter nos,* it is known that some of our seminaries [in the United States] are under such a cloud). . . . [T]hank God there is nothing of the kind in our Seminary."[99]

Bishop Haid, together with Bishops Canevin of Pittsburgh and Schrembs of Toledo, supported the petition, and on the feast of Saint Benedict, March 21, 1914, the Holy See issued a decree elevating the seminary at Saint Vincent to pontifical rank with the right of granting pontifical degrees in theology and philosophy. In May Archbishop Giovanni Bonzano, apostolic delegate to the United States, and Archbishop Bonaventuro Cerretti, a member of the Washington nuntiature who had recently been named apostolic delegate to Australia, came to Saint Vincent and promulgated the papal decree. Bishops Schrembs and Canevin participated in the ceremony in the archabbey church, and at the solemn pontifical Mass celebrated by Archbishop Bonzano, Bishop Canevin preached a sermon praising the educational work of the Benedictines at Saint Vincent and at other Benedictine monasteries throughout the United States. "In their schools," he said,

> we find the Scholastic System of philosophy and theology, recommended by Pope Leo XIII and Pope Pius X, as the model, the true Catholic system to be followed in the higher education of this twentieth century. Out of this patristic learning and treasuries of philosophy and theology given to us by the early fathers of the Church, and put into form [by] the medieval Catholic universities, has come the Scholastic System. The great framer of this system is the Angelic Doctor, St. Thomas Aquinas, and St. Thomas Aquinas acquired his stability of character, his reverence and love of truth, his calm and steady progress towards the one great perfection in the knowledge and love and service of God—the great Angelic Doctor acquired the first rudiments of his science in Benedictine Schools![100]

Archabbot Leander named Father Vitus Kratzer, a thirty-nine-year-old Bavarian who had entered the novitiate at Saint Vincent in 1893, as the first rector of the pontifical seminary. Father Vitus had completed his theological studies in Rome, where he had received doctorates in theology and canon law. He had taught dogmatic theology and canon law in the seminary since 1903. When the Holy See instructed American bishops to appoint vigilance commissions to prevent the spread of Modernism, Bishop

Canevin had appointed Kratzer as a member of the commission in the Diocese of Pittsburgh. He was also associate *censor librorum* in the diocese. At the same time, the archabbot confirmed Father Aurelius Stehle as prefect (later called "academic dean") of the seminary, and summoned home Father Ambrose Kohlbeck, who for the previous seven years had been a professor at the Collegio di Sant' Anselmo in Rome, to teach dogmatic theology.[101] In 1914 the Saint Vincent Seminary became the official seminary of the Diocese of Pittsburgh.

THE MONASTERY

Developments in the monastic community kept pace with those of the college and seminary during the period leading up to the First World War. In 1912, two years after the independence of St. Bede's Abbey, there were 201 monks working in the various apostolates of Saint Vincent Archabbey. One hundred and twenty of them were priests, twenty clerics, five novices, and fifty-six lay brothers.[102] There was a notable decline in the number of lay brothers, for German military conscription laws prevented young candidates from emigrating to the United States and few American men were attracted to this very special monastic vocation. Political conditions in the fatherland also resulted in a decline in the number of German-born candidates who now came to Saint Vincent to become Benedictine priests, though there was a steady stream of American-born candidates who entered the novitiate from year to year. Still, the average age of the community was increasing. More than one-third of the archabbey's priests in 1912 were over fifty years old, and illness and age prevented many of these from active involvement in the community's many apostolates.

For the first time in the history of the monastery there was a vocation crisis, and Archabbot Leander, at seventy-five the third oldest member of the community, was hard-pressed to meet the growing demands of Saint Vincent's many apostolates. The independence of St. Bede's had siphoned off nineteen monks, all but two of whom were in their twenties or thirties, and those monks who remained at the archabbey were stretched thin to meet the personnel requirements of the college and seminary in Pennsylvania, the college in Colorado, and the parishes throughout the United States. A conspicuous result of the decline in vocations and the aging of the community during the period leading up to the First World War was that the monastic community was forced to focus its energies on meeting the demands of existing apostolates and found itself unable to accept the numerous offers of parishes and schools that continued to come in from bishops around the country. Dozens of requests for the community to take over parishes were refused, and attractive offers to establish new schools in such dioceses as Boise, Nashville, and Pittsburgh were politely declined.[103] It was not, as in the time of Archabbot Andrew Hintenach, monastic ideology that prevented the community from accepting new parochial and educational commitments, but rather the reality that Saint Vincent no longer possessed sufficient human resources to do so.

Meanwhile, monastic life at the archabbey itself flourished. Under the capable direction of Archabbot Leander, priors Edgar Zuercher and Ildephonse Brandstetter, subpriors Joseph Keller and Anthony Wirtner, and novice masters Athanasius Hintenach and Baldwin Ambros, a renewed zeal for conscientious monastic observance permeated the community. Monks young and old followed the traditional Benedictine horarium of prayer, study, and work with painstaking devotion, and in the process created a communal atmosphere of harmony, stability, and peace at Saint Vincent that was in marked contrast to the troubles and anxieties of the war-threatened world beyond the cloister. Perhaps nowhere was the Saint Vincent monks' commitment to monastic tradition and time-honored Benedictine values better illustrated than in the renewal of the monastic liturgy that took place during this period.

As a consequence of Pope Pius X's 1903 *motu proprio* on church music, the Benedictine community rededicated itself to achieving the highest standards of liturgical observance at the archabbey. The pope's instruction had focused the attention of the Catholic world on the importance of restoring Gregorian chant to its proper place in Catholic worship. This was the chant, said the pope, which the Church "had inherited from the ancient fathers, which she has jealously guarded for centuries in her liturgical books, which she proposes to the faithful as her own, which she prescribes exclusively for some parts of the liturgy."[104] Gregorian chant, also known as Vatican chant, had first been introduced at Saint Vincent in 1878 by Father Ignatius Trueg, but for twenty-five years the community had resisted making it the exclusive form of liturgical music at the archabbey. Staunchly adhering to their Bavarian traditions, they had continued to use Regensburg chant and to embellish the liturgy with sacred polyphonic music by classical composers such as Mozart, Haydn, Handel, and Beethoven. In these practices they followed the tradition established at Saint Vincent by Boniface Wimmer, who had said that he could not conceive of music, even in the liturgy, "without *Pauken, Hörner, and Flöten* . . . kettledrums, horns, and flutes."[105]

It was precisely this form of music that Pope Pius X criticized in his *motu proprio,* and in a spirited defense of the pope's teaching, Father Louis Haas, one of the musicians at the archabbey, wrote that

> The more pretentious church choirs devote themselves to Haydn, Mozart, Cherubini, Beethoven, etc., whose religious compositions are unexcelled, and classical sacred cantatas, rather than music suitable to the service of the Church. Some of the reasons for their unfitness as church music are that these great masters payed only secondary attention to the sacred text, which is often garbled in the most senseless manner; that the sentiment of their music is at variance with that of the sacred text; and that many of their musical settings are so long-drawn as to interfere with the integrity of the liturgical function.[106]

What Father Louis wrote was perhaps true, and it certainly conformed to the Church's new official policy, but it flew in the face of a long tradition at Saint Vincent of making use of the music of eighteenth-and nineteenth-century German masters in the monastic liturgy. Among the older monks it was especially painful to see this tradition die.

But the monks of Saint Vincent were obedient sons of the bishop of Rome, and they immediately began the process of instituting Gregorian chant as the exclusive music of their liturgies. Under the direction of monastery liturgist Father Aurelius Stehle and musicians Fathers Louis Haas, Valerian Winter, and Ignatius Groll (who had been sent to the German abbey of Beuron to perfect his knowledge of plainchant) the monks were trained in the new forms and Gregorian chant was gradually introduced into all the community's divine services. The kettledrums, horns, and flutes were now relegated to nonliturgical concerts and performances. In 1904 the Gregorian Society was established in the college to instruct students and clerics in the plainsong of the Church, and the liturgy at Saint Vincent—both the Divine Office and the Mass—became a model of profound simplicity, great beauty, and inspiring religious devotion.

A cause for general concern in the community during this period was the precarious state of Archabbot Leander's health. For several years he had been suffering from debilitating pains in his neck and arms, but the illness did not prevent him from maintaining his accustomed hectic pace. In October 1903 he set out on his annual visitation of Saint Vincent parishes and missions, going first to Colorado and then to Illinois. He spent two months in Chicago undergoing electric and hot water treatments for his illness, and upon the advice of his physicians he traveled to Manistee, Michigan, in December to take the salt baths. Finding little relief there, he paid a visit to his friend Monsignor Joseph Schrembs, pastor of Saint Mary's Parish,

Grand Rapids, Michigan, and there, in the early days of February, he suffered a stroke that paralyzed him. Father Rudolph Rupprecht, the archabbot's secretary who had accompanied him on the journey, reported to Prior Edgar Zuercher of Saint Vincent that the doctors who had examined the archabbot declared that there was "no chance of his getting well any more," and conveyed Archabbot Leander's request that the community begin a novena to St. Benedict and St. Scholastica for his recovery.[107]

Despite the grim prognosis, Schnerr recovered sufficiently to return to the archabbey by train on February 25, 1904, but he remained bedridden and was unable to say Mass or attend Divine Office for ten months. During this time he considered resigning, but the memory of the turmoil and anxiety caused in the community by the resignation of Archabbot Andrew twelve years earlier prevented him from taking this step. Prior Edgar and the council of seniors took over the spiritual and temporal administration of the archabbey and its widespread educational and parochial apostolates, and Archabbot Leander remained an invalid in his cell.

To the amazement and joy of the entire community, Schnerr began to show signs of recovery toward the end of the year, and though still weak, he was able to say Mass on the feast of the Immaculate Conception, December 8, 1904. By March the *St. Vincent Journal* could announce "the cheerful tidings that [the archabbot] is stronger and healthier and more active than at any period since his illness began." Schnerr never fully recovered his formerly robust good health, however, and although he returned to his office and reassumed direct administration of the monastery and its dependencies, for the remaining fifteen years of his life he suffered chronic illness, the effect of both the stroke and his advancing age, which prevented him from being the dynamic leader the community had elected in 1892.

With their abbot ill and fewer young men coming to the monastery with monastic vocations, the monks of Saint Vincent entered a period of communal introspection and spiritual and temporal consolidation. Rather than issuing forth from the monastery, as in the past, to establish missions, parishes, and schools throughout the United States, they remained at home and built stronger monastic and educational structures at Saint Vincent upon the firm foundations laid by their predecessors. Though living within the walls of the monastery, they certainly were not isolated from the world, for the world often came to Saint Vincent. In 1907 the community celebrated the golden jubilee of Archabbot Leander's monastic profession, and though the archabbot's poor health precluded the kind of grand celebration many of the monks wanted, the ceremony was attended by Bishop Canevin and the abbots of the American Cassinese Congregation. Other important visitors to Saint Vincent during this period included Archabbot Boniface Krug of Montecassino, who had begun his monastic life at Saint Vincent under Boniface Wimmer and had served for a short time as director of Saint Vincent College; Abbot Primate Hildebrand de Hemptinne, who visited the archabbey in 1910; the apostolic delegate, Archbishop Giovanni Bonzano, who came three times between 1912 and 1914; Abbot Aidan Gasquet, president of the English Benedictine Congregation, who visited in 1913; and Father Alphonse J. Donlon, S.J., president of Georgetown University, who gave the annual retreat to the college students in October of 1913.

An important group that frequently came to Saint Vincent were laymen attending retreats sponsored jointly by the archabbey and the Diocese of Pittsburgh. The annual laymen's retreat at Saint Vincent began in August 1913 when sixty-eight men of the Holy Name Society of the Diocese of Pittsburgh came to the archabbey for a week of spiritual conferences, reflection, and prayer. The retreat master at this first retreat was Benedictine Bishop Leo Haid of North Carolina, who was assisted by Prior Ildephonse Brandstetter, Father Walter Stehle, and Father Aurelius Stehle of Saint Vincent. In his conferences to the retreatants Haid emphasized "the need for lay Catholics to remain faithful to the teachings of the Church in the midst of a Protestant culture." In addition to the conferences and "spiritual discussions," the laymen attended Mass in the morning, prayed the Rosary and Stations of the Cross in common during the day, and attended benediction of the Most Blessed Sacrament each evening. Clerics from the archabbey sang at morning Mass and evening Benediction, and it was the first time that many of the men "were able to appreciate the wisdom of the Holy Father's late pronouncement in favor of the singing of the Gregorian chant." The account of the first retreat, published in the *St. Vincent Journal,* noted that the retreatants

> enjoyed the very atmosphere of the place, because they all appreciably felt hovering about the place an air of sanctity. They secured books for spiritual reading, and they were aided in their reading and discussions of the matter they had read, by the atmosphere of religious devotion about them. They were also keenly interested in everything about the place; they inspected the buildings, the art gallery and the museum; they visited the library, the flour mill and the barns; and from this examination they obtained a very high idea of the exceptional advantages, spiritual as well as material, possessed by St. Vincent.[108]

The laymen's retreat was held each summer in subsequent years and became an extremely popular annual event. By 1917 two hundred retreatants were gathering at Saint Vincent each August for a week of withdrawal from their ordinary routines and the opportunity for spiritual renewal.

BUILDING AND FARMING

During Schnerr's abbacy a significant development in the physical facilities at Saint Vincent took place, with farming on the monastery lands continuing to expand to meet the growing needs of the monastic and academic community.

Under Boniface Wimmer construction had been continuous, and from "an obscure hut in the wilderness" Saint Vincent had grown into a large interconnected group of buildings that housed the monastery, seminary and college. By 1888 the institution's core structure had been completed and consisted of a three-and four-story quadrangle of brick buildings intersected in the middle by the old church that divided the space within the quadrangle into two courtyards. The buildings on the west range of the quadrangle (later called Benedict Hall) housed the college and seminary, and those on the east range (later called Anselm and Gregory Halls), the monastery. In the south range (later Placid Hall) were a kitchen, bakery, student dining halls, seminary dormitories, and the college infirmary, while the north range (Maur Hall) contained the monastery kitchen, refectories, and the scholasticate. The west and east ranges were 398 feet in length; the north and south ranges 220 feet.[109] In 1872 a bell tower, 128 feet high and supporting three large bells, was built within the quadrangle on the northeast corner of the church. The bell tower was the most prominent feature of the campus and could easily be seen from the surrounding farmlands and the roads leading to Saint Vincent. It had thus become the symbol of Saint Vincent, and pictures and drawings of it were used on many of the institution's publications. As for the red-brick buildings of Saint Vincent, though hardly distinguished architecturally, they were quite serviceable and reflected the practical-minded policies of Wimmer and the Bavarian monks. These structures were built to endure and to serve the needs of the community, which some of them continued to do well into the 1990s.

Sportsman's Hall, the "obscure hut in the wilderness" built by Theodore Brouwers in 1790, was razed in 1880 when it became too dilapidated to be used, and the school house, built by Father Michael Gallagher in 1845 and used by Wimmer and the pioneer Benedictines as their first residence, was taken down in 1896; but two of the buildings the Benedictines found when they arrived at Saint Vincent in 1846—the church (1835) and parochial residence (1835) built by Father James Stillinger—were in whole (as in the case of the church) or in part (as with the parochial residence, which was remodeled in 1857 to form part of the north range) still standing in the second decade of the twentieth century.

Other structures from Wimmer's time that continued to be used well into the twentieth century included the gristmill (1854), the brewery (1855) and malthouse (1870), the icehouse (1876), the barn (1877), the carriage shed (1879), and the boiler house (1886). The boiler house was replaced in 1917 by a power plant that supplied steam heat and electricity to the community. Like the quadrangle of main buildings, all these structures had been designed and built by the lay brothers of Saint Vincent, using lumber cut and prepared at the sawmill on Chestnut Ridge and bricks fabricated at the Saint Vincent brickyard. Master craftsmen among the brothers who had charge of the design and construction of the early buildings included Theobald Baumann (1814–67), Coloman Reingruber (1826–73), Stephen Weber (1817–70), Andrew Binder (1812–91), Ewald Horn (1827–1900), and Wolfgang Traxler (1854–1931).

Between 1891 and 1905 much of the construction effort of the community was devoted to building the archabbey church, but under Schnerr other buildings rose on the campus as well. In 1892 a library and second-story choir chapel were built as an extension (later called Andrew Hall) east of the old church and connected with the east range of the monastery to meet at the rear of the new church. In 1894 the community erected a freestanding gymnasium building of five stories southwest of the quadrangle to serve the athletic needs of the students and to house the music department of the college. The gymnasium was later named Bede Hall. In addition, new workshops and service buildings were erected in 1900 to replace nineteenth-century structures that had outlived their day. These included one building which housed the blacksmith shop, the machine shop, the butcher shop, and living quarters for lay workmen, and another housing the carpenter shop, the paint shop, the print shop, the book bindery, and additional space for workmen.

An ellipse-shaped water tower of red brick was constructed west of the quadrangle in 1893 to supply water for the monastery, college, and seminary. The water tower contained five tanks capable of holding seventy thousand gallons of water. In 1912 it was raised eighteen feet by the addition of a wooden story that was painted white. The strange-looking structure caught the fancy of the students, who first dubbed it "Mont Blanc" because of its white cap but later settled on the name "The Sauerkraut Tower," speculating that this must be the place where the lay brothers, who had charge of the college kitchens, stored the enormous quantities of a delicacy that appeared on their tables with disconcerting frequency.[110]

In 1904 the lay brothers built a new barn to replace the 1877 structure which had burned to the ground the previous year. The new barn was a 222-by-67-foot, three-story structure that contained stalls for thirty-four horses and sixty-four cows, shelter for farm implements and vehicles, and storage capacity for the farm's produce of hay, wheat, oats, rye, and corn. In 1906 an annex to the barn was constructed to house the laundry for the monastery and schools.

Expanding enrollment in the college resulted in the construction of a new college building in the years after the completion of the archabbey church. Begun in 1905 and completed in 1907, the new building, later named Alfred Hall, was located on the southeast side of the quadrangle, parallel to the gymnasium, and was connected to the south range by a covered brick archway. From its eastern windows it commanded a beautiful view of Chestnut Ridge. The building was 172 feet long, 72 feet wide, and four stories high. Its basement was constructed entirely of Cleveland stone, while the building itself was constructed of pressed brick with stone trimmings. This was the first structure at Saint Vincent since 1846 built with bricks that had not been fabricated by the lay brothers. Also, it was the first building at Saint Vincent to be completely wired for electricity. Parts of both the college and the seminary were located in the new building, which held classrooms, laboratories, a small library, the museum of natural history, and student and faculty dormitories.[111]

Another important building constructed during Schnerr's abbacy was the new monastery. Begun in 1913 and completed a year later, this red-brick structure was designed by E. Brielmeier & Sons of Milwaukee and constructed by the Philadelphia firm of Thomas Reilly, the construction firm that had recently built the Catholic cathedral in Pittsburgh. Located off the northeast corner of the quadrangle, with which it was connected by a covered archway, the four-story building was 170 feet long and 56 feet wide and contained the archabbot's private rooms and chapel, guest rooms, a suite reserved for the bishop, the monastery chapter room, the monastery infirmary, the novitiate, and the archives. Though most of the monks continued to live in the old monastery on the east range of the quadrangle, the porter's room, the pastor's office, several reception rooms, and a few rooms for priests were located in the new building.[112] For years the building was known simply as "the new monastery," but after Schnerr's death it was named Leander Hall.

Farm production in the first years of the twentieth century expanded to meet the food requirements of the growing student body. An important goal of the monastic administrators was to make Saint Vincent as self-sustaining as possible, and virtually all the food consumed by monks and students during this period was produced on archabbey lands. About two hundred acres were under cultivation, producing thousands of bushels of wheat, buckwheat, oats, and potatoes each year. In addition, the truck farm produced beets, beans, carrots, peas, tomatoes, spinach, currants, gooseberries, strawberries, rhubarb, radishes, celery, endive, cauliflower, and lettuce for the monastery, seminary, and college refectories. It also produced mangel-wurzel as food for the cattle. An interesting statistic that helps explain the students' speculation about the real purpose of the water tower is that in 1917 alone the monastery farm produced eight tons of cabbage.

Worked by the lay brothers and increasingly by hired hands, the Saint Vincent farm also had a dairy herd of more than sixty head and raised chickens, beef cattle, pigs, and sheep as well. The hennery produced between thirty and fifty thousand eggs, and the butchery produced more than 150,000 pounds of meat (beef, pork, and lamb) each year. In addition, the farm produced lard, hides, and tallow, which were used at Saint Vincent and sold to local farmers. The gristmill produced flour from the home-grown wheat, and the bakery each year produced an average of 150,000 loaves of the famous Saint Vincent bread. Indeed, the farm was one of the most economically successful operations that the Benedictines of Saint Vincent managed in the early years of the twentieth century.

WORLD WAR I

At the outbreak of the First World War in 1914 Saint Vincent, like America itself, was more focused on internal matters than on events in the great world beyond its borders. The issues occupying the attention of the institution had more to do with local religious, academic, and administrative affairs than with the social, economic, and geopolitical conflicts coming to a head in Europe. Of course, monks and students alike took note of events in the world beyond the cloistered halls of the monastery, seminary, and college. The diverse ethnic identities of those who made up the Saint Vincent community were still very strong, and many monks and students had relatives in the warring countries about whose welfare they were concerned.

Certainly at the beginning of the war, at least, there was no unanimity of opinion among monks and students of German, Irish, Italian, and eastern European heritage as to which side in the conflict represented the forces of truth and justice. In general, sympathies both in the monastery and schools tended to move in the direction of Germany and the Central Powers. More than three-quarters of the monks were German-born or of German heritage, and though the majority of students were of Irish ancestry, they too tended to sympathize with Germany as it confronted the ancient enemy, England. Still, everyone was sensitive to the need for discretion, and if there was an "official" position at Saint Vincent, it was the same as the "official" position of the United States: neutrality. The institution was so "neutral," in fact, that any suggestion the United States government was aiding England brought forth denunciations in the *St. Vincent Journal.* "If we are a neutral nation," a *Journal* editorial declared, "then we should be in reality what we declare to be in words and keep strictly the international laws of neutrality. . . . But we have been furnishing arms, munitions of war, and things out of which munitions of war are made to France, to the United Kingdom, to Russia, and Japan. Hence our neutrality is a fraud, a make-believe, a flagrant lie in the face of the world."[113]

Other published expressions of concern about the war tended to reflect an attempt at evenhandedness within a volatile political climate. In the fall of 1914 Alfred Reynolds, a Saint Vincent student, published an essay entitled "Our Sympathies in the War" in which he said that "the sympathies of our hearts go out in the first place to the soldiers of the Austrian and the Belgian and the English and the French and the German and the Serbian armies. To the poor soldiers, therefore, who are in the front and must bear the brunt of the battle . . . the sympathy of our hearts goes out in unstinted measure."[114]

Initially, the impact on Saint Vincent of the war in Europe was minimal, and life went on as usual. Among other things, the monastery continued to send young monks to Rome for their theological training. In January 1915 Brother Francis Mersinger, a cleric in solemn vows who had been studying at Sant' Anselmo since 1912, returned to the Eternal City after several months' vacation at the archabbey, accompanied by the recently ordained Father Bernardine Pendl and by Brother John Nepomucene Hruza, another cleric preparing for the priesthood. They arrived in Rome at the beginning of February 1915 and took up residence at the college of Sant' Anselmo with fifty-one other Benedictine students from the United States and Europe.[115] Within three months, however, Italy declared war on Austria, and the Holy See closed the schools in Rome. The German and Austrian monks at Sant' Anselmo returned to their homelands, where many of them were drafted into the army, and the three Saint Vincent monks set out on an odyssey that eventually took them to Freiburg, Switzerland.

Mersinger, Pendl, and Hruza traveled to Florence, Bologna, and Milan, passing troop trains filled with Italian soldiers, and from Milan took a train to Lake Como. Crossing the lake by boat, they arrived in Lugano and then journeyed by rail through the Gothard Pass to Fluelen. At Fluelen they crossed Lake Luzern to the city of Luzern, and from that city went to the Abbey of Einsiedeln where they rested. Their initial goal was the Abbey of Engelberg, like Einsiedeln one of the Swiss abbeys that had established a Benedictine community in the United States during the nineteenth century. But before going on to Engelberg, they decided to enter Germany and visit the Abbey of Beuron where they were hospitably received. They learned that seventy young monks of the Beuronese Congregation had been drafted into the German army and that seven had already fallen in battle. At the famous abbey they also encountered ten Russian prisoners of war who had been sent to Beuron as laborers by military officials. Impressed with the condition of the Russians, Mersinger, a native of Baltimore who had family in Mannheim, wrote that he "wished the editors of some English and American papers would come and see for themselves how well the Germans treat their prisoners, and then give reports to the public." The Saint Vincent monks were impressed with the resilience and piety of the Bavarian people and sent a report to the *St. Vincent Journal* saying that "the spirit in all the German villages is marvellous. Everything goes on without a halt, as it does in time of peace. The churches are crowded with the faithful, and we have been told by one of the Fathers [at Beuron] that the number of daily communicants has doubled since the beginning of the war."[116] After several weeks at Beuron, they returned to Switzerland and spent the summer at the Abbey of Engelberg. In the fall they went to Freiburg and entered the Salesianum seminary where they continued their theological studies under the Dominicans for the remainder of the war.[117]

Back in Pennsylvania the monks followed with deep interest the firsthand news of the war in Europe from their displaced confreres. They were shocked and saddened by Mersinger's report that German and Austrian monks at Sant' Anselmo had been obliged to return to their countries in order to enter military service, and that the young Belgian, German, and French monks of the Abbey of Maredsous "were forced to join their respective arm[ies], and are perhaps engaged in actual conflict against one another."[118] The world had gone insane, and it seemed that the Benedictine family, like all of Europe, was being torn asunder.

In December 1915 the prior of Maredsous, Father Aubert Merten, wrote Archabbot Leander and informed him of the desperate straits of that uprooted Benedictine community. After the German invasion of Belgium the monks of Maredsous who had not been conscripted had fled their home and gone with their superior, the saintly abbot Columba Marmion, to Ireland where they were living in impoverished conditions near Enniscorthy in County Wexford. Father Aubert asked the monks in America for aid, and when the Saint Vincent chapter sent several hundred dollars in Mass stipends to the Maredsous community, Abbot Marmion himself wrote to Archabbot Leander that it was "a great consolation at this moment, when the spirit of war is separating nations made to know and love one another, that the spirit of our H. Father S. Benedict & his holy *Pax* unites us in holy Charity. *'Ubi caritas, ibi Deus est.'*"[119]

As war clouds darkened the American horizon the mood at Saint Vincent grew sombre. There was still general opposition on the campus to America's entry into the war. When President Woodrow Wilson called for universal "military preparedness" in 1916, the *St. Vincent Journal* said bluntly: "Military Preparedness is but another name for militarism, and the militarization of Democratic America is a decidedly bad policy."[120] Then, when the United States finally declared war on Germany in 1917, the reaction of the Saint Vincent community was a combination of patriotism and concern. The patriotism manifested itself in editorials, speeches, and campus demonstrations. The *Journal* observed that "the true status of the Church in America was clearly shown by the zeal and enthusiasm with which Catholic citizens throughout the Republic responded" to the call to arms. Under the administration of college director Father Ernest Gensheimer, a 102-foot flag pole was put up and the American flag was ceremoniously raised over the campus each morning. Not everyone, however, was happy with this manifestation of patriotism. Some of the German-born priests objected, but Archabbot Leander quickly admonished them to cease their "criticizing and murmuring" about the flag raising.[121]

The concern of the community was not only for the safety and welfare of students, friends, and family members (both in the United States and Germany) but also for the security and safety of Saint Vincent itself at a time when war-crazed American public opinion was strongly marshaled against individuals and institutions that bore a German identity. Saint Vincent, particularly the monastery, was still demonstrably a German institution. More than a third of the monks were German-born, the German language was the first language of the archabbey, and the German culture and heritage of the institution were still proudly displayed. To offset any negative impact upon the community that its German identity might arouse, Archabbot Leander issued a confidential directive to the monks instructing them to "carefully avoid every word or action that may be interpreted as lack of patriotism and tend to arouse the unfounded suspicion that our Community would fail to stand by our country in the hour of peril."[122]

There is no question that ultimately Saint Vincent did stand by the country in its hour of peril. Prayers were offered daily in the archabbey church for an Allied victory. Students were drafted or voluntarily enlisted in the armed forces, and Saint Vincent priests Fathers Regis Barrett, Timothy Seus, Henry Schwener, and Philip Geeck, and Father George Barry O'Toole, a secular priest on the seminary faculty, entered the army as chaplains. Seus, Schwener, and Geeck spent some time at Camp Colt in Gettysburg, Pennsylvania but were discharged soon after their training began because by then the war had ended; Barrett and O'Toole, however, received commissions and served for the duration as chaplains at training camps in Kentucky and South Carolina.

Despite the war, however, the rhythm of life at Saint Vincent went on as usual during the 1917–18 school year. The laymen's retreat was held in mid-August and the school year opened with a solemn High Mass in the archabbey church on September 5, 1917. The clerics Gervase Schimian, Paul Fife, Frederick Strittmatter, Denis Strittmatter, and Willibald Hoffmann were ordained to minor orders by Archabbot Leander on September 8, and classes began on schedule. In October the community celebrated the silver jubilee of Schnerr's election as archabbot of Saint Vincent, though the celebration was limited to the community. Except for Bishop Canevin of Pittsburgh, guests were not invited, more because of the archabbot's precarious health than because of the war. The debating society began its season with the propositions "that intercollegiate athletics promote the best interests of colleges" and "that limited monarchies better secure the interests of the people than do republics." (The winning teams argued in favor of intercollegiate athletics and republics.) On the feast of All Saints, Father Raymond Balko pronounced his solemn vows in the archabbey church. Throughout the fall intramural football teams vied with one another for mastery on the gridiron. On November 14 the sophomores went on their class day to Seton Hill where "they greatly enjoyed the many beauties revealed during their well-conducted tour of the buildings" of St. Joseph Academy. The Thanksgiving Day play that year was *In the Palace of Caesar,* a melodrama that showed "the obstinate prejudices and hot indignation of pagan Rome against the early Christians, and the joy and religious resignation with which the hardy martyrs of the second century went down to death for

Christ's sweet sake." Christmas was celebrated as usual with solemn High Mass at midnight in the archabbey church. Nearly all the priests in the house went out to assist in parishes on Christmas Day. On New Year's Day the scholastics performed a German comedy, *Nathan der Weise.*

Forty hours devotion was held in the college and seminary in February 1918, and the archabbot's nameday was celebrated on February 28. St. Patrick's Day, St. Benedict's Day, Lent, and Easter were celebrated with the traditional solemn liturgies, and during the Easter vacation those students who remained at Saint Vincent took walking excursions to Latrobe, the Ridge, and Greensburg. On May 25 Bishop Canevin came to Saint Vincent and ordained twenty-one seminarians to the priesthood, including Benedictine clerics Eugene Kornides and Vincent Schlemmer. During the spring the baseball season got underway, and the college team played a full round of games coached by Brother Jerome Rupprecht, a young cleric recently out of the novitiate. The college and seminary students held their annual May Day picnic at Idlewild Park, and the traditional Corpus Christi procession took place on May 30. On June 17 the college held its seventy-second commencement at which three students received master's degrees, and four bachelor's degrees. That year there were 332 students in the college and 138 theologians and philosophers in the seminary.[123]

In September 1918 military training was introduced at the college by the new director, Father Gerard Bridge. Students participated in the training on a voluntary basis, but many joined the newly formed cadet corps, whose purpose was to give the students "manly bearing and strong and healthy bodies." Drill was held for half an hour on Mondays, Tuesdays, Thursdays, and Fridays, and for a full hour on Wednesdays and Saturdays.[124]

More than 250 students and alumni of Saint Vincent entered the armed forces of the United States in 1917 and 1918, and many of them saw action in France. Brothers Hugo Klein, a thirty-one-year-old native of Denver, Colorado, who had entered the lay brotherhood at Saint Vincent in 1904, and Vincent Thiede, a twenty-eight-year-old native of Blue Island, Illinois, who had entered the monastery in 1912, were drafted into the army. Brother Vincent served as a rifleman with the U.S. infantry in France before being transferred to burial duties on the front lines, and Brother Hugo was with the American expedition sent to Russia to oppose the Bolshevik revolution. Brother Vincent, the assistant sacristan at Saint Vincent, sent frequent letters back to the monastery describing his experiences, and some of these were published in the *St. Vincent Journal.* In one he described the final offensive of the war.

About eleven o'clock in the evening, just as we were leaving the woods, the Germans opened up fire upon us with their artillery. A number of our men were killed on the spot, and many of them were wounded. I thought every minute that we would be hit, as the shells were bursting all around us, and we had to duck into holes and trenches to escape the flying fragments. A few times they burst so close to Father Wallace and me that we were splashed with mud and dirt. The following morning about four o'clock, the American and French opened up fire upon the Germans, and, believe me, that was some artillery display. The Germans afterwards said that it was as though all hell had been let loose, and that it was the most terrible they had experienced since the war started. Father Wallace and I were in a dugout behind the French cannon when it began, and we went out to watch it. It certainly was a sight. The sky looked as if it were all on fire. The Americans surely had the Germans on the run. Father Wallace and I stayed a little distance behind to bury the dead, and he and I alone buried twenty or more soldiers soon after it started. It was there that we saw some awful sights. Some of the bodies were terribly mangled. This burying of the dead is gruesome work. At first I thought that I could hardly do it, but I got used to it.[125]

Two Saint Vincent students were killed during the war: Phil Daugherty, a marine who died in France on October 9, 1918, and John J. McKee, who died the following day. McKee had been preparing to become a novice at Saint Vincent when he was drafted into the Army. Both he and Daugherty were 1917 graduates of the college.[126]

The sad news of war-related deaths that came to the Saint Vincent community was not limited to those who had friends and family members fighting in the American armed forces. In the winter of 1919 Father Vincent Schlemmer, a native of Essenbach, Bavaria, who had entered the novitiate at Saint Vincent in 1911 and who was now serving as curate at St. Mary's Parish, Erie, learned that his two brothers had been killed in battle while fighting in the German army. In reporting the deaths of the Schlemmer brothers, the *St. Vincent Journal* noted that the news "brought home to us the truth which many have lost sight of, that the greatest sacrifices of the recent war were frequently made by patriotic Americans of German birth, some of them going forth to do battle against their own kindred and friends to uphold the ideals and rights of the land of their adoption."[127]

On Thanksgiving Day 1918, the Saint Vincent community marked the end of the war with a Mass of thanksgiving in the archabbey church. College students, seminarians, and monks all joined together to celebrate the solemn liturgy, but the joyful news of peace was overshadowed by another catastrophe that had by now struck the nation and the community. The deadly Spanish influenza, so called because of its purported place of origin, arrived at Saint Vincent in the fall of 1918 and lasted for nearly three months. The highly contagious virus had come to America from Europe with the returning troops, and thousands of people in the United States died from it. The college and seminary administrations at Saint Vincent sent the students home in October 1918, at the height of the epidemic, and did not allow them to return to the campus until shortly before Thanksgiving.

The illness wreaked havoc in the monastic community, where more than a third of the monks were confined to their beds. The young clerics and novices were especially hard hit. Monks who did not contract the disease were assigned to care for the sick in the scholasticate, college, and seminary. Brother Alphonse Thumel, the college infirmarian, was sent to Elk County to attend to the sick members of the priory in St. Marys, and Brother Maurus Hoehler took charge of the infirmary at the archabbey. During the outbreak Subprior Remigius Burgemeister was universally praised for his attentiveness to the bedridden, especially among the lay brothers. "With thermometer in hand, [he] watched with an eagle eye over the rising and falling of that treacherous fever, from early morning until late at night, rigidly kept his patients in bed until all danger was past, and administered the potions that drove the enemy of the common health to his lair."[128]

Five monks of the archabbey and one seminarian lost their lives during the epidemic. In St. Marys, Pennsylvania, thirty-seven-year-old Father Alban Seckler died, as did twenty-six-year-old Father Eugene Kornides in Hastings, Pennsylvania. At Saint Vincent itself, Father Raphael Wieland (age fifty-two), Father Alexius Grass (age fifty-eight), Brother Eugene Erb (age sixty), and first-year theologian Carl Druschl succumbed to the disease. Still, the devastating effects of the influenza upon the Saint Vincent community could have been much worse than they were. Father Regis Barrett, who continued to serve as an army chaplain in Kentucky, wrote from Camp Zachary Taylor that the influenza had killed eight hundred soldiers in the camp.[129]

The deadly contagion had run its course by the end of the year, and life went back to normal at Saint Vincent. Father Barry O'Toole, Father Regis Barrett, Brother Hugo Klein, and Brother Vincent Thiede returned from military service and took up their duties once again, and students who had left the college to serve in the armed forces began to drift back to the campus to complete their studies.

In the early days of 1919 word came to the community of the singular achievement of one of the college's alumni. During the war Gregory

Zsatkovich of Homestead, Pennsylvania, a student at Saint Vincent from 1902 to 1905, had become leader of a Pittsburgh-based organization of Ruthenian immigrants who sought independence for the five-thousand-square-mile central European country of Ruthenia, which had long been a part of Hungary. After the war, the Allied Powers declared Ruthenia an independent democratic republic, and Zsatkovich was elected its first president. The *St. Vincent Journal* reported that Zsatkovich proposed "to adapt American methods of business and government to the new state . . . and will also attempt to introduce baseball as its national game." The independence of Ruthenia, however, was short-lived. It became part of Czechoslovakia in 1920, and Zsatkovich became governor with the understanding that the small nation would have semiautonomous status. When the Czechoslovakian government failed to live up to its undertaking of semiautonomy and democracy, Zsatkovich resigned as governor and returned to the United States. He was the first and only alumnus of Saint Vincent to be elected president of a nation.[130]

A COADJUTOR FOR ARCHABBOT LEANDER

By the summer of 1917 the burdens of office had taken their toll on Archabbot Leander, who by then had led Saint Vincent for a quarter-century. He was eighty-one years old and in failing health, and so it was no surprise to the monks of the archabbey when he announced that he was seeking permission from Rome for them to elect another abbot who would serve as his coadjutor, or assistant, and take on the principal administrative duties of the monastery and its apostolates. Schnerr submitted his request to the Holy See in September, and a month later he received word that permission had been granted. On October 16, 1917, Abbot Ernest Helmstetter of Newark, president of the American Cassinese Congregation, arrived at the archabbey and in a meeting with the council of seniors read the Roman decree authorizing the election of an "abbot coadjutor" with the right of succession. He explained that Schnerr would remain the spiritual and administrative head of the community but that the coadjutor would exercise authority in Archabbot Leander's name and with his advice until the latter's death, at which time the coadjutor would assume full jurisdictional powers as Saint Vincent's fourth archabbot.[131]

During the winter of 1917–18, Archabbot Leander was in relatively good health, and the council of seniors saw no need to proceed quickly with the election. They decided, therefore, to wait until the summer when most of the priests of Saint Vincent who lived away from the archabbey could attend. The election began on June 24, 1918, when the priests of the archabbey gathered in the old abbey church for the *scrutinium,* or general discussion, of the candidates. Archabbot Leander absented himself from the meeting, but 118 other capitulars were in attendance. The following morning was "cloudy and stormy" when the community gathered in the old church for a solemn High Mass in honor of the Holy Spirit. After the Mass the doors of the church were shut and locked and the voting began under the direction of Abbot President Ernest Helmstetter.

On the first ballot ten priests of the archabbey received at least one vote, the majority being cast for three candidates: Fathers Aurelius Stehle, Leonard Schlimm, and Linus Brugger. Stehle was a member of the seminary faculty while Schlimm and Brugger were pastors living away from the monastery. On the second ballot, the votes were divided among seven priests, but this time the same three leading candidates garnered more than 90 percent of the total. Stehle remained the favorite with sixty-four votes, almost three times the number for Brugger, his closest challenger. This gave Stehle a simple majority and in an earlier day would have won him the election. But the new statutes of the American Cassinese Congregation required that a monk receive two-thirds plus one of the votes in any of the first three ballots in order to be declared abbot, so a third ballot was necessary. On this ballot Stehle received eighty-two votes, considerably more than the two-thirds plus one required, and Abbot Ernest declared him duly elected. When asked if he would accept, he reluctantly said yes. Archabbot Leander recorded in his diary that the election was "peaceable and friendly."[132]

Aurelius Stehle was born in Pittsburgh in 1877 and as a child had moved with his family to Greensburg, Pennsylvania. There he attended the parochial school attached to the Benedictine church of the Most Blessed Sacrament and at the age of thirteen entered the scholasticate at Saint Vincent. Completing his studies in the college and seminary in 1899, he was ordained to the priesthood by Bishop Richard Phelan of Pittsburgh and for the next nineteen years served at the archabbey in various capacities, first as professor in the classical (college) course, and then, after 1911, as prefect and professor of Latin and Greek in the seminary. He was an accomplished Latinist and for twenty-five years (ever since his novitiate) had also been master of ceremonies in the monastery, in which capacity he had overseen the monastic celebrations of the liturgy. In the course of his career he had gained a reputation both at Saint Vincent and among churchmen throughout the United States as an expert on the liturgy, and after publication of his *Manual for Episcopal Ceremonies* in 1915, he was sought out by diocesan liturgists around the country for advice on liturgical matters.

The election of Archabbot Aurelius marked the beginning of a new era in the history of Saint Vincent. He was the first archabbot of the community not to have been educated by Boniface Wimmer and the first to have been born in the United States. He was also, at forty-one, the youngest. Stehle assumed his position as leader of the community at a time when the First World War was coming to an end and when Saint Vincent, like the rest of America, was ready to embark on a dynamic and outward-looking engagement with the world at large. Just as the United States emerged from the war with a clearer awareness of its global responsibilities and its new international role, so Saint Vincent, under Archabbot Aurelius, entered the 1920s with a deeper understanding of the challenges and obligations of its missionary heritage. Now, however, the community would not limit its apostolic work to the American continent. Its gaze turned eastward, toward China, and the opportunities and challenges for the American Benedictines that lay in that distant land.

SIX

MISSION TO CHINA (1918–1930)

Like the country as a whole, the Catholic Church in the United States during the decade following the First World War experienced a newly discovered self-confidence, an expanding material prosperity, and an almost unbridled optimism about the future. In 1920 the nation's Catholics numbered eighteen million, nearly 17 percent of the total population, and had become an increasingly important presence in American society, both politically and economically. Ten years later their number had grown to over twenty million. Still largely an immigrant community, the American Church during the 1920s benefited from the powerful and firm leadership of the four American cardinals: Patrick Hayes of New York, William O'Connell of Boston, Dennis Dougherty of Philadelphia, and George Mundelein of Chicago (who had received his early theological education at Saint Vincent). One hundred and thirty Catholic colleges and universities and over fifteen hundred Catholic high schools educated the sons and daughters of first- and second-generation immigrants, and more than ten thousand Catholic parishes flourished throughout the nation, half of them with parochial schools that educated more than one and a half million Catholic children. The National Catholic Welfare Council, which had grown out of the wartime National Catholic War Council, was established by the U.S. hierarchy in 1919 to coordinate American Catholic efforts in education, social action, lay organizations, and labor relations; and although Rome attempted to suppress the council in 1922 because of fears it would interfere with the authority of individual bishops, the NCWC was saved by the intervention of the American bishops themselves, whose representative, Bishop Joseph Schrembs of Cleveland, an alumnus of Saint Vincent, successfully defended the organization before the Roman tribunals.[1]

A clear sign that the American Church had come of age was the Holy See's decision in 1908 to remove it from the jurisdiction of the Sacred Congregation for the Propagation of the Faith and to place it under the Sacred Consistorial Congregation. This move signified that the Vatican no longer regarded the United States as a mission country and that the American Church had achieved a degree of maturity and stability that warranted a greater measure of administrative independence. One corollary of this change was a growing awareness among American Catholics, now that America's missionary period had ended, that they had an obligation to help spread the Gospel to other parts of the world. In 1911 the Catholic Foreign Mission Society of America, familiarly known as Maryknoll, was established by Fathers James Anthony Walsh and Thomas Frederick Price as the first American religious congregation created solely for the purpose of supplying missionaries for the foreign missions. The initial group of Maryknoll missionaries went to China in 1918, and there soon followed a steady stream of American Catholic priests and religious from various dioceses and religious orders who dedicated their lives to the missions of the Far East.[2]

At Saint Vincent interest in the Chinese missions had developed even before World War I. The plight of Christian missionaries in China during the Boxer Rebellion (1900) had stimulated considerable concern among Saint Vincent monks and students, and when forty-eight Catholic missionaries were killed during the hostilities, the news became the subject of several articles in the *Saint Vincent College Journal.* The visit to the archabbey of Father John Weig, a Bavarian missionary in China who was a friend of several of the older monks, also stimulated a flurry of interest in the Chinese missions. Father Weig had been driven out of China during the Boxer Uprising, and returning to his mission in Shantung two years later, he spent Holy Week 1902 at Saint Vincent giving firsthand accounts of the Church's work in that distant land.[3]

It was not until 1920, however, that more direct contact between Saint Vincent and the Chinese missions occurred. In that year Father George Barry O'Toole, a priest of the Diocese of Toledo who had joined the Saint Vincent Seminary faculty in 1917 as a professor of philosophy, took a sabbatical to visit China where he hoped to study the Chinese language and familiarize himself with the work of the Catholic missions. O'Toole returned to Saint Vincent in September 1921 and immediately began encouraging the diocesan seminarians he taught to consider volunteering for the Chinese missions.[4]

In the meantime the Saint Vincent community received visits from several Chinese missionaries who fueled the enthusiasm of students and monks alike for the work of evangelizing the Chinese people. Jesuit Father Joseph Chang visited the archabbey in June 1920, and "more than repaid the cordial hospitality extended him by giving . . . a very instructive and enjoyable lecture on the Celestial Kingdom's language and the customs of Chinese life," and a year later Father William Kress of the Maryknoll foreign mission seminary in New York lectured on the Catholic missions in China.[5] Kress, who had studied for the priesthood at Saint Vincent in the 1870s, was one of several alumni who had joined Maryknoll and other missionary societies dedicated to the evangelization of China. These included Maryknoll Father Joseph Donovan and Passionist Father Timothy McDermott, both of whom kept in touch with their friends and former teachers at the archabbey during their years of labor in the Chinese missions. Growing interest in China led to the creation in 1920 of an annual scholarship for a Chinese student at the seminary of the vicariate of Shansi in southern China. For several years the Saint Vincent Seminary provided funds for the education of the Chinese seminarian, naming the scholarship in honor of Archabbot Boniface Wimmer, and in 1921 the Saint Vincent Seminary Mission Society was formed as an affiliate of the American Catholic Students' Mission Crusade.[6]

Thus by 1923 the Chinese missions had become a focus of interest and activity at Saint Vincent, and it was a logical step for the community to decide to move from academic interest and local fund–raising to a more substantial role in the Church's missions in China. But although the decision may have been logical, it was not an easy one for the monks to make.

BEGINNINGS OF THE CHINA MISSION

The origins of Saint Vincent's China mission were in a journey Father George Barry O'Toole made to the Far East in 1920. O'Toole was a thirty-four-year-old native of Toledo, Ohio, who had completed his theological studies in Rome in 1912 and studied biology at Columbia University before becoming chancellor of the Diocese of Toledo under Bishop Joseph Schrembs. At the request of Archabbot Aurelius Stehle, Bishop Schrembs temporarily released O'Toole from the diocese in 1917 to teach philosophy at Saint Vincent Seminary, but his temporary status became permanent and he never returned to work as a diocesan priest in Ohio. At Saint Vincent he affiliated himself with the monastic community as an oblate of St. Benedict and soon became a very popular professor of philosophy and dogmatic theology. His teaching was interrupted in 1918 when he became an army chaplain, but after the war he returned to Saint Vincent where he continued his work in the seminary. At the same time he assisted the Sisters of Charity in developing the department of biology at Seton Hill College in Greensburg.[7]

In October 1920, during his visit to Peking, O'Toole met with Vincent Ying (Ying Lien-chih), a leading Chinese Catholic layman who for eight years had been attempting to establish a Catholic University in China.[8] In 1912 Ying had written the Holy See seeking support for such an institution and the following year had established at Hsiang Shan near Peking the Fu Jen She, or Academy of Chinese Studies, for young Catholic men. In 1917 Ying published an article entitled "An Exhortation to Study" in which he appealed to the Catholic hierarchy and clergy of China to enter the field of Christian higher education which until then had been dominated by Protestant missionaries, but his appeals appeared to fall on deaf ears, and a year later he was forced to suspend the work of the Fu Jen She because of inadequate funds.

Vincent Ying explained to Father O'Toole his hopes for a Chinese Catholic university and asked if the American Benedictines could help. He gave O'Toole copies of the letter he had sent to the Holy See in 1912 as well as the article he had published in 1917, and the American priest promised to do what he could. O'Toole returned to America by way of Europe, and in Rome he met with Benedictine abbot primate Fidelis von Stotzingen who assisted in obtaining for him a private audience with Pope Benedict XV. O'Toole presented a plan to the abbot primate and the pope for the American Benedictines to establish a Catholic university in Peking, and received encouragement from both to pursue the project. Several weeks later, when he reached New York, he met with Abbot Ernest Helmstetter of St. Mary's Abbey, Newark, president of the American Cassinese Congregation, and sought his support, and upon his return to Saint Vincent in September 1921, he presented the plan to Archabbot Aurelius Stehle.[9] Neither Helmstetter nor Stehle was as enthusiastic about the project as Roman officials had been.

Meanwhile in Rome the Sacred Congregation for the Propagation of the Faith was preparing its own strategy for the creation of a Catholic university in China. In December 1921 Archbishop Pietro Fumasoni-Biondi, secretary of the Propaganda Fide, wrote Abbot Primate Fidelis von Stotzingen suggesting that Saint Vincent be charged with responsibility for the undertaking. Stotzingen queried Saint Vincent, and Archabbot Aurelius replied that the resources of a single Benedictine community, even one as large as Saint Vincent, were insufficient for the task. In June 1922 Cardinal William van Rossum, prefect of the Propaganda Fide, wrote Abbot Ernest Helmstetter urging that the entire American Cassinese Congregation take up the work. Van Rossum said that the reason the Holy See had turned to the Benedictines was that the situation confronting the disintegrating Chinese Empire was similar to that which confronted the Roman Empire at the beginning of the European Dark Ages, when Benedictine monks kept the light of Christian faith and classical learning alive and helped rejuvenate European society. Vatican officials believed that the Benedictines were the religious order best suited, by character and tradition, to take charge of the Church's higher educational apostolate in China. Nine months later the cardinal prefect informed Helmstetter that Pope Pius XI himself was eager for the American Benedictines to accept the task and had set aside one hundred thousand Italian lire (about five thousand dollars) for the purpose.[10]

In August 1923 abbots and delegates of the twelve monasteries of the American Cassinese Congregation gathered at St. Procopius Abbey, Lisle, Illinois, for the congregation's twenty-first general chapter, and in the fifth session they took up the question of whether to accept the mission to China. The American Benedictine leaders were reluctant to take on such a monumental challenge, but to decline a mission specifically requested by the Holy See was not considered a viable option for the American abbots. They therefore reluctantly accepted the undertaking, but pointing out that the constitution of the congregation did not allow for enterprises to be conducted by the congregation as such, the abbots entrusted the project to Saint Vincent Archabbey "with the promise of support, both moral and physical, on the part of all the other abbeys of the congregation."[11]

Six weeks later Archabbot Aurelius convened the monastic chapter at Saint Vincent and presented the proposal to the community. He explained that although initially reluctant to take on the China mission, he now felt that the community was obliged to do so not only because the Congrega-

Aurelius Stehle, O.S.B. (1877–1930), fourth archabbot of Saint Vincent.

tion for the Propagation of the Faith had requested it but also because the abbots of the American Cassinese Congregation had put their confidence in Saint Vincent to respond positively to a direct entreaty of the Holy Father. Because most of the Saint Vincent priests were engaged in parochial and educational work away from the archabbey, only 29 of the 120 monks eligible to participate in the chapter were present. These joined in an animated debate over Saint Vincent's capacity to assume so daunting a responsibility, but when the dust settled, they voted by a margin of fourteen to seven, with eight abstentions, to "accede to the request of the Roman authorities to establish a foundation in Pekin, China."[12]

Archabbot Aurelius sought volunteers from among the capitulars to undertake the mission, and in May 1924 he sent Father Ambrose Kohlbeck, rector of the seminary and a former faculty member at the Collegio di Sant' Anselmo, to Rome to discuss with officials of the Propaganda Fide details of the establishment of a Catholic university in Peking. Shortly after his arrival in Rome, Kohlbeck cabled Stehle with an instruction from the Holy See ordering that two monks from Saint Vincent proceed at once to Peking to establish contact with the apostolic delegate to China, Archbishop Celso Costantini, and begin the process of creating a university.[13] A week later Archabbot Aurelius dispatched to China Father Ildephonse Brandstetter, the archabbey's fifty-four-year-old German-born subprior, and thirty-one-year-old Father Placidus Rattenberger, a native of Bavaria and assistant pastor at St. Paul's Church in Chicago.

The departure of Brandstetter and Rattenberger was the occasion of a moving farewell at the archabbey. On the afternoon of June 10, monks and students gathered in the church for pontifical Vespers. In his address to the assembly Archabbot Aurelius said that the departure of the two priests was the cause of both sadness and joy at Saint Vincent: "sadness at the loss of two beloved confreres and joy at the holy undertaking they are about to begin." He drew everyone's attention to the "great harvest . . . awaiting laborers in the China mission field" and commended the generous and self-sacrificing spirit of Fathers Ildephonse and Placidus for enlisting in the cause. He solicited the prayers of students and monks for their success and expressed his personal hope that Saint Vincent's newest foundation would generate many future vocations for the Benedictine Order. At the end of the archabbot's address, the two missionaries chanted the *Itinerarium* with the choir, and the ceremony concluded with the *Te Deum* and the Kiss of Peace. At 6:45 p.m. Brandstetter and Rattenberger bade their last farewells and boarded the westbound train at the Latrobe station. Recalling the missionary trials of Boniface Wimmer and the first Benedictines in Pennsylvania, the *Saint Vincent College Journal* reported:

> And so there have gone from our midst the first two of what we hope will one day be a numerous community of missionaries. To them has been commissioned the difficult and laborious, yet, withal, glorious task of being the pioneers of Benedictine life in China. . . . [I]nnumerable difficulties will confront them. They will, however, ever have before their minds' eye the early history of Saint Vincent's. Many were the days of trial and uncertainty that dawned and darkened to leave

their impress of care and worry on the venerable Boniface Wimmer. More than once was the very existence of his most cherished project seemingly threatened with dissolution. There were times when the future of Benedictinism in America seemed to hang in the balance between immediate succor and the disbanding of the sturdy but well-nigh discouraged group of pioneers. But never once, even in the darkest moments, did the confidence of the Saintly Founder forsake him. Never once did he doubt that God who had inspired him to begin the noble work would provide for its continuance. And his confidence was generously rewarded. . . . So too, they will face days of darkness and uncertainty, but the memory of the doubtful, even threatened, and yet, triumphant, life of their Mother House will urge them on to fuller confidence. Ours is the staunch conviction that God, for the glory of Whose Name they are immolating on the altar of Religion all that this world holds dearest, will abundantly bless their undertaking. Like St. Paul, the great Apostle of the Gentiles, may they have the Faith to say, *Omnium possum in eo qui me confortat,* "I can do all things in Him Who strengtheneth me."[14]

Brandstetter and Rattenberger sailed from Vancouver, British Columbia, aboard the *Empress of Canada* on June 19, 1924, arriving in Shanghai on July 4. From Shanghai they traveled by train to Peking where on July 8 they were welcomed by Archbishop Costantini, Vincent Ying, and Ma Hsiang-po, another distinguished Chinese Catholic layman.[15] They spent the next six months as guests in the residence of the apostolic delegate, where they began at once to investigate the possibilities open to them in China.[16] Archbishop Costantini pledged his support for the enterprise but laid stress on the difficulty of the task. He emphasized the importance of careful planning and diplomacy and advised them to "accept suggestions freely, promise nothing, and only after mature deliberation to draw . . . conclusions."[17]

The Holy See had issued a rescript on June 27, 1924, establishing the Catholic University of Peking as a pontifical university and granting the archabbot of Saint Vincent full powers to appoint professors and regulate the academic programs of the institution.[18] Brandstetter and Rattenberger, however, arrived in China with the thought of establishing first a Catholic college (or secondary school) and then gradually building on that foundation a Catholic university. Within days of their arrival they learned that Bishop Stanislaus F. Jarlin, C.M., vicar apostolic of northern China, did not favor any plan that allowed for only a gradual development of the university. Fathers Ildephonse and Placidus wrote Archabbot Aurelius that Bishop Jarlin insisted upon the immediate establishment of an institution of higher learning and pointed to the monks' mandate from Rome to reinforce his position.

The bishop refers to the word "University," as mentioned in our document, most emphatically. He expresses himself positively against the establishment of a College as such, but is willing to concede a two years preparatory course for the university. This preparatory course he calls a "Gymnasium Major Course." His reasons for opposing the erection of merely a College are as follows: 1. There are already Colleges in Peking and outside of Peking. 2. A mere College will not attract the Chinese students. 3. The document from Rome demands the erection of a University.[19]

The Benedictines both in Peking and Pennsylvania believed that if their enterprise in China were to succeed, they would have to attract to their community young Chinese with vocations to the monastic life. Their experience in both Bavaria and the United States was that young men with such vocations came principally from Benedictine secondary schools, and without such an institution in Peking, they saw their work in China coming to depend in the long run on a continued supply of Benedictines from America. Benedictine tradition called for creating independent communities that drew their membership from the environs of the monastery. Saint Vincent itself had secured its future only when young Americans began to enter its novitiate. Without a secondary school in Peking, the monks doubted that they would be able to establish a permanent Benedictine foundation in China.

For that reason, Brandstetter and Rattenberger returned to the theme in their ongoing negotiations with the apostolic delegate, asking if in lieu of a full-fledged secondary school they might be permitted "to erect an academic course for such boys and young men who might become candidates for the Order." The question

aroused [Costantini's] lively interest immediately, as he had applied to Rome for the erection of such a [minor seminary], before the erection of a university was ever discussed. Since he also advises the erection of a monastery, in his opinion such a school would become a necessity and would meet no opposition. This view also meets the approval of the bishop as expressed in today's interview.

Our work according to the Apostolic Delegate therefore is twofold: the erection of a monastery with a religious training school and the erection of a university. The right to establish a university has been granted by Rome, but for the erection of a monastery and training school for candidates a written petition to the bishop is required.[20]

Brandstetter and Rattenberger urged Archabbot Aurelius to make such a petition.

Meanwhile, Archabbot Aurelius had received a letter from an American priest working in the Chinese missions suggesting an almost providential solution to the problem of a secondary school. Father Francis X. Clougherty, a twenty-nine-year-old native of Braddock, Pennsylvania, who had studied at St. Mary's Seminary, Emmitsburg, Maryland, before being ordained and sent as a missionary to China, wrote Stehle from Kaifeng, a city on the Yellow River four hundred miles southwest of Peking, that he had recently read in the Chinese newspapers of the Benedictines' plans to establish a Catholic university in Peking. Delighted with the news, Clougherty told Stehle that he and four other American priests had been working for several years at an American-style high school in Kaifeng that they had founded. At present, he said, there were more than three hundred young Chinese in the school, and if it were true that the Benedictines were going to establish a Catholic university, then they might consider the Catholic secondary school in Kaifeng as "a feeder to the University." Clougherty urged Stehle to consider the possibility of the Benedictines' assuming charge of the school in Kaifeng. If they would provide additional teachers to augment the five American priests already teaching there, Clougherty said, the school could double in enrollment in a very short time. Moreover, two of the secular priests in Kaifeng—Father Sylvester Healy, a thirty-three-year-old native of Detroit, and Clougherty himself—wanted to join the Benedictine community in Peking as novices.[21]

Father Clougherty's initiative led to a long-term and close relationship between the community of diocesan priests who operated the American school in Kaifeng and the American Benedictines. In 1927 Clougherty and Healy became Benedictine novices at the monastery in Peking, and Father Placidus Rattenberger went to Kaifeng to teach in the Catholic secondary school (the Pei Wen Catholic Academy) there. A year later Clougherty and Healy pronounced vows as Benedictine monks of Saint Vincent Archabbey, though they had never visited the Pennsylvania monastery. In 1928 a third American priest from Kaifeng, thirty-four-year-old Father Carl Rauth, entered the novitiate in Peking.[22]

In October 1924 Archabbot Aurelius issued a "call to arms" to the abbots and monks of the American Cassinese Congregation, urging the monasteries to assist with raising funds and recruiting personnel for the American Benedictine mission in China. In his letter to the American monks he noted that the challenge confronting Saint Vincent was one "that will tax every resource available to us," and he made it clear that the Pennsylvania community could not manage to accomplish the task alone. The Saint Vincent chapter, he said, would therefore depend on the generosity of the other eleven American monasteries that had promised their cooperation at the general chapter of 1923. This cooperation would necessarily involve both financial support and the recruitment of Benedictine volunteers for the mission.

With respect to financial support, Stehle recommended that the monasteries undertake a three-phased approach. First, the abbots should seek the permission of local bishops to take up collections in all the parishes of the dioceses where monasteries were located. The Holy See had authorized the monks of Saint Vincent to make a general appeal to all dioceses and parishes in the United States, so Stehle told the abbots they should expect cooperation from the bishops and pastors they approached. He emphasized, however, that as this was a Benedictine mission, the greatest support should be expected from parishes staffed by Benedictine pastors. Second, he urged that the popular and widespread mission societies that existed in parishes, colleges, and schools under American Benedictine auspices should dedicate the funds they collected each year to the Catholic University of Peking. Third, he encouraged the abbots and monks of the congregation to solicit major contributions from well-known wealthy benefactors.

As for recruitment of personnel for the university faculty, Archabbot Aurelius called on each of the larger American Cassinese monasteries to send at least one volunteer from their communities. The volunteers selected for the work, he said, "should be young and scholarly" because "[y]outh adapts itself readily to new conditions; and, as for scholarship, it is manifest that one unqualified in this respect would be of no value to an undertaking like a university." The archabbot also urged the abbots and priests of the Congregation to recruit monastic candidates specifically for missionary work in China by "broadcast[ing] the fact that now the American Benedictines offer a splendid opportunity for doing far more efficient work toward the conversion of heathendom than the ordinary missionary can ever hope to accomplish." China had many Catholic missionaries, but the archabbot believed it was "especially by the monastic missionary that its ultimate conversion will be achieved," because while the ordinary Catholic missionary was a "soldier," the monk was "a colonist, and herein lies the secret of the [Benedictine's] apostolic efficacy." Just as in the Middle Ages when Benedictines went as missionaries to convert "the uncultivated races of the Western world," American Benedictines were now charged by the Holy See with nothing less than "preserv[ing] and christianiz[ing] Chinese literature, art, and philosophy" and "plac[ing] before the eyes of the Chinese people an ideal exemplar of truly Christian civilization."[23]

The results of Stehle's "call to action" were initially disappointing. By October 1926, two years after the circular, only three American Benedictines—Father Placidus Houtmeyers of St. Martin's Abbey, Lacey, Washington; Father Damian Whelan of Saint Vincent; and Father Callistus

Stehle of Saint Vincent (the archabbot's brother)—had volunteered for the mission. On the other hand, however, fund-raising efforts had met with remarkable success. The monasteries of the congregation had pledged to raise almost $100,000, of which $85,000 (including a $25,000 contribution of the Saint Vincent chapter) had been collected by March 1926. In addition, the Holy See contributed another 100,000 lire ($5,000) to the enterprise.[24]

In January 1925 Archabbot Aurelius appointed Father George Barry O'Toole rector of the Catholic University of Peking, and the following month accompanied him to China. In Peking Stehle authorized the purchase of the palace and grounds of Prince Tsai Tao, uncle of Hsuan Tung, the deposed emperor of China, for the site of the new university. The property consisted of eleven acres located in the so-called "Tartar City" of Peking, in front of the residence of the apostolic delegate. The buildings contained five hundred rooms of various sizes, and there were beautiful paths and gardens throughout the grounds. Stehle reported that the estate was valued at more than half a million U.S. dollars but that with the help of Dr. James H. Ingram, an American Protestant missionary in China who had befriended the Benedictines in Peking, he was able to negotiate the purchase for only $85,000. Prince Tao, he said, had been induced to sell at so low a figure because he feared the possible confiscation of his property by the new Chinese government.[25] As soon as they took over the Manchurian nobleman's palace and lands, the American Benedictines began renovating the buildings, installing steam heat, modern plumbing, and electric wiring, and turning the library on the western side of the estate into a school. They converted the living quarters into a monastery capable of housing thirty monks.

Meanwhile O'Toole set about preparing the groundwork for the university. His plan was to begin by reviving Vincent Ying's Fu Jen She, or Academy of Chinese Studies for young Catholic men, which had closed in 1918 because of financial problems. To help resolve the financial difficulties confronting the project, O'Toole solicited support from a wealthy friend in Detroit, Mr. Theodore MacManus, who pledged to meet the annual expenses of the academy by establishing a trust fund that would yield ten thousand dollars per year. O'Toole then appointed Vincent Ying as dean of the MacManus Academy of Chinese Studies of the Catholic University of Peking and hired four distinguished Chinese scholars to serve as professors: Chen Yuan (a noted historian and former Chinese vice minister of education), Chang Wei Hsi (president of the Chinese Geographical Society), Kuo Chia Sheng, and Li Tai Fen. On October 1, 1925, the school opened with an enrollment of twenty-three students, nearly all of whom were Catholic. By February forty students had enrolled. Archabbot Aurelius reported to the monks of the congregation that the school's faculty consisted of "some of the most eminent scholars and literateurs of Peking" and that the carefully selected student body consisted of young Chinese Catholics chosen on the basis of their ability to write first-rate literary compositions in their native language. "Some of these students," he said, "have already applied to be admitted into the Order of St. Benedict, and we hope that from such as these will arise the future Benedictine Literati whose pens will uphold the intellectual prestige of the Catholic religion in China."[26]

The establishment of the MacManus Academy of Chinese Studies was the first step in the Benedictine plan to create a fully functioning Catholic university in China. The academy (in fact a secondary school) was intended to be the nucleus of a university that the American priests envisioned would eventually consist of five higher education faculties (theology, philosophy, Chinese studies, arts and letters, and science) and two secondary schools (the Chinese Preparatory School and the General Preparatory School). It was an ambitious plan and would require enormous sums of money as well as a large number of professors to accomplish.[27] In order to obtain the necessary financial support and recruit qualified teachers, Barry O'Toole returned to the United States in January 1926 and visited various Benedictine monasteries and parishes. He also took advantage of the trip to help establish the Society of Friends of the Catholic University of Peking, which was based at Saint Vincent but which eventually had branches at Benedictine monasteries in several parts of the United States.[28]

The Saint Vincent Chapter estimated that the annual cost of operating the university would at the beginning approach one hundred thousand dollars a year, and only a small portion of that amount could be expected to come from funds generated by the institution itself. The rest had to be raised by Saint Vincent and the other abbeys of the American Cassinese Congregation. To coordinate fund-raising efforts among the American Benedictine communities as well as to solicit assistance from Catholic contributors throughout the United States, Archabbot Aurelius established a China Mission Office at Saint Vincent and sent a circular letter to the priests of the archabbey reminding them of the support he expected from them. "The Holy See," he said, "has placed on my shoulders the burden of responsibility for the success of the new University, and it is for you, my brethren in Christ, to hold up my hands, that it may never be said of our community that we 'began to build and could not finish.'"[29]

IMMERSION IN CHINESE CULTURE

After an absence of more than a year, Father O'Toole returned to China via Rome and the Middle East in March 1927. He was accompanied by three volunteers for the China mission: Father Callistus Stehle, O.S.B., professor of English at Saint Vincent College; Dr. Victor Maucher, a lay professor of music at Saint Vincent College (who remained only briefly in China); and Father Adelbert Gresnigt, O.S.B., a Belgian monk of Maredsous Abbey who had gained an international reputation as an artist and architect of ecclesiastical buildings and who had accepted an invitation to join the Benedictine mission in order to design the university buildings. Gresnigt had been recommended for the job both by his fellow countryman Cardinal William van Rossum, prefect of the Propaganda Fide, and by the apostolic delegate to China, Archbishop Costantini, who intended to commission the Belgian Benedictine to design several churches and schools in China and at the same time to inaugurate a new "Sino-Christian style of architecture to be used henceforth in the Catholic Missions of that country."[30]

Upon his arrival in Peking in the fall of 1927, O'Toole began at once to prepare for the opening of the university's first faculty, that of arts and letters, but the work was slow and difficult. Political turmoil and civil war hindered progress. The institution had experienced, for example, an invasion of refugees in April 1926 which had severely disrupted its operations. For two months the Benedictines played host to nearly four hundred women and children fleeing the fighting between the troops of the Manchurian warlord Chang Tso-lin and the Kuomintang Nationalist army of Chiang Kai-shek. Father Placidus, the procurator, was hard-pressed to feed so many refugees but managed to do so, and to provide them with shelter, until the fighting ended in June.[31] Then in the spring of 1927 new fighting broke out south of Peking sending a flood of refugees north. Much of the fighting took place in and around Kaifeng, and the result was that in April the American priests and nuns working in Kaifeng—including the teachers at the Pei Wen Catholic Academy and six Sisters of Providence from St. Mary of the Woods, Indiana—sought refuge with the Benedictines.[32] All these difficulties came on top of the loss to the university of Vincent Ying, dean of the school of Chinese studies, who died of cancer on January 10, 1926. His funeral took place in Peking's northern cathedral with Father Ildephonse Brandstetter celebrating the Requiem Mass.[33] To replace Ying, O'Toole named former Chinese vice minister of education and professor of history Chen Yuan, first as dean of the school of Chinese studies and then as vice rector of the university.

Despite these contretemps, however, the effort to create a full-fledged university moved steadily forward. The Benedictines from America were the first group of Catholic missionaries since the Jesuits of the eighteenth century to attempt to work with the educated classes of northern China, and the announcement of their intention to establish a university had stimulated the curiosity and interest of the elite of the region. The primary goal of the American monks was to educate a select core of Chinese Catholic laity and to prepare them for assuming responsible positions in Chinese society. Secondarily they regarded their work as one of evangelizing and Christianizing the Chinese people.[34]

The chief means of achieving their goals was the introduction into China of the American system of liberal higher education as it existed in American Catholic colleges of the day. But the Benedictines from Saint Vincent did not come with the intention of simply imposing American Catholic religious, cultural, and educational values upon the Chinese. They regarded themselves as settlers in a new land whose culture, language, and values they were obliged to learn and, whenever possible, adopt. Father Barry O'Toole wrote that for missionaries to ignore the culture and scholarship of China was "fatuous" and promised that "far from intruding their American nationalism upon the Chinese," the American Benedictines

> would do all in their power to hasten the day when both the University and their own community in China would become indigenous institutions. Though beginning their work as Americans, they would foster the patriotism and befriend the national spirit of the Chinese people. They would spare no pains to make the Church as Chinese in China as it is American in America, or French in France. They would welcome the day when the Catholic religion would cease to be an exotic plant in Chinese soil, and when they themselves might be able to hand over to native successors the task of continuing in China the educational mission recently confided to them by the Holy See.[35]

Soon after he arrived in China, Father Callistus Stehle wrote that the American Benedictines had to become "thoroughly conversant with [the] written and spoken language [of China], a highly difficult task." One of the most perceptive remarks about the importance of understanding and appreciating Chinese culture came from Brother Hugh Wilt, a Saint Vincent cleric who volunteered for the China mission in 1929. "China has a culture of its own," Wilt wrote to his confreres at Saint Vincent:

> [L]ike all else in China it is more or less *sui generis.* Its history and literature antedate our own by centuries. To a mind Westernly trained, however, the cultural element seems to be a minus quality at first for the simple reason that we set up [as] standards of judgement our own ideas and occidental customs, forgetful of the fact

Saint Vincent's first missionaries to China, 1924. Fathers Ildephonse Brandstetter, O.S.B. (1870–1945), and Placidus Rattenberger, O.S.B. (1892–1948), before leaving for the Far East to establish the Catholic University of Peking.

Father Placidus Rattenberger at the Catholic University of Peking in 1926, surrounded by refugee children.

that China has her own *li* (meaning "rite" or "etiquette" in English) and her own standards, some of which existed for centuries before ours began to exist. It is not fair, therefore, to maintain that ours is the only worthwhile culture. The Chinese are a proud people and undoubtedly it is galling for them to sit at the feet of foreigners.[36]

To achieve their goals, the American monks set about learning the Chinese language and immersing themselves in Chinese culture with the help of Chinese colleagues at the university. They also began publishing a series of Chinese Christian classics. The first of these was a Ming dynasty work by Jesuit Father Francis Furtado (1587–1653) and the celebrated Catholic mandarin and scholar Li Chih-tsao (1570–1670) entitled *Ming Li Tan (The Science of Logic),* which the Benedictines published in Peking in 1926. In addition, the Benedictines published an eighteenth-century Chinese work on the Gospel narratives with a Chinese translation of the Acts of the Apostles and the Letter to the Hebrews, as well as a number of devotional and catechetical works in Chinese.[37] The university also became a way station for other Catholic missionaries who desired to learn the Chinese language and study Chinese culture before setting out on their missionary labors.[38]

In order for the new university to function legally, it had to be registered and accredited by the Chinese government, and in June 1927 Father O'Toole submitted a petition for registration to the Ministry of Education. Two government inspectors—Yang Chin-yuan, counselor of the Ministry of Education, and Wu Chia-chen, head of the Department for Supervision of Institutions of Higher Studies—came to the school in July to conduct an evaluation. In their report to the ministry, the inspectors noted that the twofold purpose of the institution was "(1) to introduce the most modern developments of Western scholarship and science; [and] (2) to preserve and vitalize the traditional culture of China." They recommended that the university be registered and accredited by the government, observing that "[w]hen we reflect that these foreigners were able to appreciate the importance of preserving Chinese culture and were willing in the promotion of so great a cause to cross the seas with men and money at the cost of personal sacrifice, and, for the sake of introducing Western science and of reviving Chinese culture, have known how to enlist the service of eminent Chinese scholars and to awaken the enthusiasm of aspiring youth, we cannot withhold the tribute of our admiration."[39]

In August 1927 an exuberant Father Barry O'Toole wrote Archabbot Aurelius that the university's success in obtaining government recognition was an important milestone in its history. "After only two years of existence," he said, "we obtained something that the Jesuits at Shanghai and Tientsin have striven to attain for many years. Even the great Protestant university (the Yan Ching) did not succeed in getting this recognition until last year."[40] And Father Ildephonse Brandstetter wrote that with official government recognition, applications for admission were "pouring in" and that over 250 applications had now been received.[41]

The university opened for its third academic year on September 26, 1927. A hundred and fifty-five applicants had been accepted, of whom sixty were Catholics. The apostolic delegate, Archbishop Celso Costantini, and the Chinese minister of education, Liu Cheh, were present for the opening ceremonies, and both addressed the students and assembled dignitaries. The beginning of the school year was marked by the inauguration of the new Faculty of Arts and Letters, comprised of the departments of history, English, Chinese, and philosophy. The MacManus Academy of Chinese Studies became what it had in reality been from the beginning, a three-year preparatory school. The creation of the Faculty of Arts and Letters marked a major modification in the original plan to establish five faculties and two preparatory schools. The financial realities and personnel problems facing the Benedictines had resulted in their developing a more modest initial plan for the university. In a circular letter to the Catholic clergy of China, Father O'Toole said that

> we are persuaded that a University School devoted to liberal studies is of more immediate importance than schools giving courses in natural sciences and their technical applications. Hence the Catholic University of Peking proposes, for the present, at least, to limit its scope to the teaching of the liberal arts and letters, deferring the establishment of a School of Science until some later date. For we believe that the adoption of this policy will enable us to meet the present needs of our Catholic Missions in the most effective way possible under existing conditions.[42]

In 1930 a faculty of science and a faculty of education were created, but the majority of students continued to study liberal arts in the School of Arts and Letters, which eventually added a department of sociology and economics and a department of psychology.[43]

By the third academic year the faculty had expanded to twenty-three part- and full-time professors. Twelve of these were Chinese laymen[44] and eleven, American and European priests. In addition to Fathers Barry O'Toole, Ildephonse Brandstetter, Callistus Stehle, Damian Whelan, Francis Clougherty, and Sylvester Healy of Saint Vincent, Benedictine faculty members included Father Gregory Schramm of St. Mary's Abbey, Newark, New Jersey; Father Aidan Germain of St. John's Abbey, Collegeville, Minnesota; Father Jehan Joliet of the Abbey of Solesmes, France, and Father Pius de Cocquéau of the Abbey of Sant' André, Belgium. The latter two, who had come to China with the intention of establishing a Benedictine monastery in the province of Szechuan, temporarily served as professors of French.[45] In addition, Father Carl Rauth, a diocesan priest from Hagerstown, Maryland, who had been on the faculty of the Pei Wen Catholic Academy of Kaifeng and who would later become a Benedictine, taught English and geography in the preparatory school.[46]

Thus by October 1927 Saint Vincent's mission in China seemed destined for success, though the problem of how to finance the enterprise remained. Costs were rising and income both from the university itself and from fund-raising efforts in the United States was not keeping up with expenses. In addition, it was becoming clear that the university needed more space for an expanding student population. In view of the increased number of applicants, and to make room for more students, the Benedictines proposed to their confreres in Pennsylvania that they purchase a sixteen-acre tract adjacent to the property they had obtained earlier. This tract was the estate of Prince Kung Wang Fu; and Father Placidus Rattenberger, who had returned to the United States to raise money for the China mission, explained to the Saint Vincent chapter that it could be purchased for about one hundred thousand dollars. Archabbot Aurelius told the chapter "that he could get a loan of $200,000 with 5% interest for the University [of Peking]," and in the discussion that followed "the fact was emphasized that the risk of St. Vincent is very little." The chapter voted by a fourteen to eight margin (with seven abstentions) to purchase the property with money borrowed for that purpose by the archabbot.[47]

Following the chapter in Pennsylvania, Archabbot Aurelius went to Wisconsin to seek financial assistance from Milwaukee's German archbishop, Sebastian Messmer, who had expressed great interest in Saint Vincent's work in China. Messmer recommended him to the Missionary Association of Catholic Women of Milwaukee, which provided a $60,000 loan to Saint Vincent for the China mission. In addition, the Holy See donated $15,000. With this money in hand, the chapter authorized a loan of $110,000 from the Dollar Savings Bank of Pittsburgh to permit the purchase of the Kung Wang Fu estate, which by now had risen in price to $160,000.[48]

In September 1928 the new academic year opened at the university in Peking with an enrollment of 195 students and with three new American priests among the professors: Boniface Martin of St. Bede Abbey, Peru, Illinois; Oswald Baker of Saint Vincent; and Passionist Father Celestine Roddan. Prospects were bright for the future, and with the acquisition of the Kung Wang Fu estate, the Benedictines in Peking now began making plans for the construction of more suitable buildings for the university than the refurbished palace of Prince Tsai Tao had proven to be. Prior Ildephonse Brandstetter commissioned Father Adelbert Gresnigt, who had been busy designing churches and schools in southern China since his arrival the previous year, to design a "Chinese style" university complex that would include a library, an auditorium, classrooms, offices, and dormitories capable of housing four hundred students.[49] Taking note of the progress of the American Benedictines in China, the Catholic lay periodical *Commonweal* announced that "the University is prospering. Almost miraculously it gained official approval in its infancy. It bids fair to become a mighty fortress, a bulwark of Catholicity in China, a pivot on which may swing destinies."[50] Back at Saint Vincent, however, an increasingly worried Archabbot Aurelius began to explore new ways of paying for the expansion in Peking.

SAINT VINCENT COLLEGE IN THE "ROARING TWENTIES"

While the mission to China preoccupied the monastic chapter and absorbed many of the resources of the archabbey during the 1920s, the community continued to engage in other apostolates that also occupied its attention and absorbed its resources. Among these none was more important than Saint Vincent College. In the decade after the First World War American higher education developed dramatically, expanding in terms of both numbers of students and programs and improving in terms of academic rigor and quality. Increased numbers of young men and women sought the intellectual, social, and economic advantages that a college education offered, and colleges and universities themselves began to conform to academic and organizational standards set by regional accrediting associations. Though initially hesitant to allow "outside" agencies to set curricula and influence academic requirements, by the 1920s administrators of Catholic colleges had generally come to realize that if they were to compete with secular institutions, they would have to meet common standards that in great measure were determined by those agencies.

One mark of this recognition among American Benedictine educators was the formation in 1919 of the National Benedictine Educational Association (whose purpose, according to one member, was "to select by stringent criticism the wheat from the chaff of the modern educational systems"). As we have seen, Saint Vincent College was a founding member of the BNEA, and monks from the archabbey continued to play an important role in its annual meetings. In addition, representatives from Saint Vincent—among them Fathers John Ujlaki, Alcuin Tasch, and Louis Haas—took an active part in the National Catholic Educational Association,[51] and in 1921, under the leadership of its vice president and director, Father Gerard Bridge, Saint Vincent College became a member of the Association of Colleges and Secondary Schools of the Middle States and Maryland. At this stage, membership in the regional educational association did not imply formal accreditation and required only minimal compliance with the broadest academic standards, but the Saint Vincent administration's willingness to join what came to be called the Middle States Association was a clear sign that the college aspired to broader recognition in the world of American higher education.[52]

The 1920s were a time of transition for the college. In 1921 the institution began a process of thoroughly revamping its curriculum and academic organization to reflect more clearly the distinction between the classical secondary school (which now came to be known as the preparatory school) and the undergraduate college. By 1923 the restructuring was essentially complete. The new organization marked the administration's effort to create an institutional structure modeled on that of the better undergraduate colleges of the nation. It consisted of a "College of Liberal Arts and Sciences" that offered three courses: a "classical course" leading to a bachelor of arts degree, a "science course" leading to a bachelor of science degree, and a "pre-medical course" that prepared students for entrance into the nation's medical schools.

According to the college catalogue, the principal goal of the program in arts and sciences was "the education of broadly cultured men, men of well-trained will and intellect, and of high religious and social ideals and the knowledge to apply these as guiding principles of life." The administration pointed out that the Church had long recognized the importance of this kind of liberal education "by demanding that its future ministers complete the full college course before entering upon the professional study of Theology."[53] Indeed, the preparation of young men by means of a liberal education for the subsequent professional study of theology, law, or medicine was a primary objective of the College of Liberal Arts and Sciences. To that end the college conducted a careful study of the requirements for admission to regional law and medical schools and fashioned pre-law and pre-med programs at Saint Vincent to meet those requirements.

The study revealed that "only the broadest cultural education" was "the proper preparation for the study of law." The successful lawyer had to be able "to work out the problems that confront him from every point of view; he must know where to seek for special information on a large variety of subjects." To that end the college offered in its bachelor of arts curriculum a "sound program" in logic, psychology, ethics, history, economics, sociology, and literature (both ancient and modern), which gave "the prospective lawyer the broadest possible foundation in general knowledge" and fulfilled the admission requirements "now in force in the leading law schools of the United States."

As for premedical training, the college administration noted that for admission to medical schools, the State of Pennsylvania required two years of college work (after completion of the standard high-school course) with special courses in chemistry, physics, and biology, while leading schools of medicine, such as the School of Medicine of the University of Pennsylvania, had additional requirements. The new curriculum sought to provide two- and three-year programs that would adequately prepare students for entrance into those medical schools that did not require a bachelor of science degree. The premedical student at Saint Vincent was advised to "acquaint himself with the conditions of admission of the school he proposes to enter" and pursue the appropriate curriculum.

The bachelor of science program included "cultural and scientific subjects" and was appropriate for "those intending to enter the ranks of industrial chemists, bacteriologists, etc." The college literature noted that "[t]here is at present a great demand in almost every industrial enterprise for capable men trained in science" but also pointed out that the college's science program "in conjunction with courses in education" was appropriate for those students looking forward to careers in the teaching profession.

Beginning in 1922 students could major in one of several disciplines by taking at last six courses in that discipline, and they could receive minors in related disciplines by taking four courses in the appropriate department. Bachelor of arts candidates could choose from majors in economics, sociology, education, philosophy, and history; and bachelor of science candidates in zoology, botany, chemistry, physics, and mathematics. All students were required to take core courses in religion and English as well as in one modern language (selected from among German, French, Spanish, and Slovak). Bachelor of arts students were required to take Latin and Greek as well. For the bachelor of arts degree, core courses included psychology and science; for the bachelor of science, psychology and history. One hundred and twenty-eight semester hours were required for graduation. The course of studies for both the bachelor of arts and the bachelor of science degrees was largely prescribed, with few opportunities for students to take elective courses.

Latin continued to be stressed for students in the bachelor of arts program since many of these students intended to enter the seminary, but even those not destined for the priesthood were expected to learn Latin thoroughly. Saint Vincent earned a reputation during these years as a place where graduates were often fluent in Latin. Under such outstanding Latin teachers as Fathers Louis Haas and Gerard Bridge students learned not only to read and write the language but to speak it as well. Archabbot Aurelius, himself a Latin teacher and an accomplished linguist, encouraged the students to practice their Latin frequently, at times dropping in on Latin classes to conduct *colloquia latina* (Latin conversations) for up to an hour and a half. Even nonpriesthood students were expected to be able to carry on a conversation in Latin. By the time a student reached the seminary, he was supposed to be fluent in the language. The seminarians held annual debates *(disputationes)* in Latin on philosophical and theological propositions.[54]

In 1927 the college introduced a bachelor of fine arts degree for students who completed a set curriculum that included four courses in art history and eight studio courses in drawing, painting, and architectural design. The program was directed by Benedictine artist Father Benno Brink with the assistance of Brother Fabian Febrey, who taught drawing and design. This was a short-lived program that ended by 1930, but it was replaced by a bachelor of music degree in the 1930s under the direction of Father Raymond Balko. In 1927 a teacher training course was introduced by Father Alcuin Tasch. This consisted essentially of the bachelor of science curriculum with the addition of six courses in education and supervised practical teaching experience at Latrobe High School in conformity with the requirements of the State of Pennsylvania for teacher certification.

In 1929 a course in "aeronautics" was added to the curriculum, making Saint Vincent one of the first colleges in the country to offer students a program in aviation. The college bought a biplane, which was painted green and gold and christened *The Spirit of St. Vincent,* and housed at J. D. Hill Airport near Latrobe (later the Westmoreland County Airport). Benedictine faculty members taught the student pilots physics (Fathers Bernard Brinker and Aquinas Brinker), mathematics (Father Cyprian Yahner), and astronomy (Father Mark Kistner), while experienced pilots and mechanics at the airport provided practical flying and aircraft maintenance instruction. The goal of the course was "to equip air pilots more fully with the requisite knowledge for their work, and to render flying more scientific and safe." Even this program had its liberal arts component. The *Saint Vincent College Journal* said that a "liberal education renders judgment quicker, estimates more accurate, and thought more searching: all necessary qualities of the successful aviator, and the aim of the theoretical part of the [aviation course] is to promote and develop these. Added to this is the distinctive feature that the study may be successfully pursued under Benedictine auspices, an entirely rare and new advantage for the prospective aviator."[55] The program was discontinued during the Depression on account of its high cost but was revived in September 1939 on the eve of the outbreak of World War II.

As for faculty, the decade began with fifteen Benedictines engaged full-time in undergraduate-level instruction and ended in 1930 with thirty-three Benedictine professors, one secular priest (Father James Aloysius Reeves, president of Seton Hill College, who taught psychology), and three laymen who served as athletic coaches and physical education instructors. (It was not until the 1930s that lay professors were hired to teach major courses.) The period saw the college under the direction first of Father Gerard Bridge, who was director and vice president (later dean) until 1927; then of Father Matthew Muething, who served in the new position of dean for one year; and finally, of Father Alcuin Tasch, who became dean in 1928.

The principal challenge to the college administration during this period was providing qualified professors for the expanding curriculum. Archabbot Aurelius and the monastic chapter supported the college by continuing the practice introduced by Archabbot Leander of sending young priests and clerics to U.S. universities to pursue advanced degrees, though Stehle agreed with his predecessor that it was preferable to send young monks to Catholic rather than secular universities. The University of Chicago, he wrote, was "a hot-bed of atheists and even while the price of instruction may be very low, we may pay for going there."[56] Thus most of the priests and clerics who studied away from Saint Vincent during the 1920s did so at Catholic colleges and universities. Fathers Benno Brink and Malachy Brawley, for example, studied art at Saint Anselm College in New Hampshire in 1921, while the clerics Adalbert Kalsch and Kevin Lynskey studied chemistry (Kalsch) and mathematics (Lynskey) at the University of Notre Dame and St. Procopius College respectively. In 1922 Archabbot Aurelius relented somewhat in his insistence upon Catholic universities and sent Fathers Alcuin Tasch and Edward Wenstrup to study education (Tasch) and biology (Wenstrup) at Columbia University in New York, but they like other Saint Vincent monks who studied at Columbia—Leander Pail (English), Bernard Brinker (physics), and Maurice Costello (psychology)—were required to live at St. Anselm's Church in New York, a parish staffed by monks from St. John's Abbey, Minnesota. Tasch eventually received his doctorate from the University of Chicago, and Wenstrup his from the University of Pittsburgh. Still, Catholic universities were preferred, and Notre Dame was the principal school for graduate studies for the young monks of Saint Vincent. During the 1920s Father Camillus Long studied journalism and poetry there; Father Theodore Weber, history; Father Alexius Udavcak, botany; Father Urban Lux, pharmacy; Father Cyprian Yahner, mathematics and physics; Father Aquinas Brinker, mathematics; Father Edmund Cuneo, biology; and Father Rupert Stadtmiller, chemistry.[57]

During the "Roaring Twenties" the total enrollment at Saint Vincent (including the seminary, prep school, and college) remained remarkably steady, reaching an all-time high of 616 in 1923–24. Nonetheless, the distri-

TABLE 1 Enrollment at Saint Vincent College, 1920–1930

	Seminary	*College*	*Prep School*	*Total*
1920–21	120	96	355	571
1921–22	123	98	357	578
1922–23	115	94	361	570
1923–24	115	163	338	616
1924–25	100	176	306	582
1925–26	108	202	296	606
1926–27	124	216	244	584
1927–28	139	203	243	585
1928–29	120	230	195	545
1929–30	124	252	193	569

SOURCE: Saint Vincent College *Catalogue* for the years indicated.

bution of students among the three schools fluctuated significantly. The high school began the decade with an enrollment of 355 students and ended it (as the prep school) with 193 (Table 1). Even as enrollment in the prep school declined, that of the undergraduate college increased. At the beginning of the decade there were only 96 undergraduate students in the college (including the 58 priesthood candidates studying philosophy). By 1929 there were 252 undergraduates studying at Saint Vincent. The number of students in the theology course of the seminary remained fairly constant throughout the period.

Extracurricular activities continued to be a major part of student life at Saint Vincent during the post–World War I period, though the college catalogue reminded the student that his " primary reason for going to school and his first duty in consequence" was "to study and to give his time and attention to study." Other activities, no matter how worthy, would not be allowed to interfere with "the main purpose of college life." Successful academic work, therefore, was "a prerequisite to participation in extracurricular activities." Student organizations continued to be divided into "religious" (e.g., the League of the Sacred Heart, later known as the Apostleship of Prayer), "literary" (e.g., the Debating Society and the College Journal), and "musical" (e.g., the Plain Chant Choir and the Saint Benedict Orchestra). In 1921 the Slovak Literary Society was formed at the college. At its biweekly meetings students engaged in debates, gave short speeches, and read original papers in Slovak. Also during the 1920s a local chapter of the Catholic Slovak Student Fraternity was established at Saint Vincent, and representatives from this chapter regularly attended national conventions of the fraternity.[58]

Members of the sophomore class of 1926 and their professors. Front row: Cosmas Minster, O.S.B.; Flavian Yelinko, O.S.B.; Matthew Muething, O.S.B.; Father Felix Fellner, O.S.B.; Father Walter Stehle, O.S.B.; Father Mark Kistner, O.S.B.; Father Gerard Bridge, O.S.B.; Patrick McKivigan, O.S.B.; Paulinus Hammer, O.S.B. Center row: Philip Metzgar; Joseph Gunderman; Frank Kaminsky, Raymond Dugan, Joseph Meisinger; Philip Kattan; John Kameen; Louis Smith; Joseph Gotwalt; Joseph Metzgar. Top row: Joseph Faix; James McKay; Arthur O'Shea; Daniel McCullough; Leo Fallon; Claude Daly; Raymond Studeny; Martin Birmelin; Rembert Sorg; O.S.B.; Harold Phillips, O.S.B.

In 1929 a career-oriented lecture series was inaugurated by the dean of the college, Father Alcuin Tasch. Its purpose was to provide students with information about various career options open to them. In the first year of the series, lectures were given on the medical profession by Dr. Stephen Nealon of Latrobe, on engineering by Mr. J. J. Laboon of the Chester Engineering Company of Pittsburgh, on public service by Pittsburgh Council member J. J. McArdle, on the artistic profession by Father Benno Brink, and on the music profession by Father Raymond Balko.[59]

Under the direction of Father Bonaventure Reithmeier, drama continued to be a popular pastime at the college, and performances of plays in both English and German attracted visitors to the campus from Pittsburgh and other parts of western Pennsylvania. The scholastics regularly performed their annual German play on New Year's Day—in 1924 it was the two-act comedy *Der Knorappel.* Thanksgiving was another important occasion for dramatic performances. On that day in 1928, for example, the student dramatic association performed an adaptation of Robert Louis Stevenson's *Treasure Island.* In March 1924 the Oberammergau Passion Players from Bavaria performed their famous passion play in Pittsburgh, and several professors and students from Saint Vincent attended. After the performance Archabbot Aurelius invited the players to visit Saint Vincent, which they did on March 16. The players from Oberammergau, a village situated in the shadow of the Bavarian Benedictine Abbey of Ettal, were honored at a banquet, given a tour of Saint Vincent, and introduced to the lay brothers, many of whom were Bavarian-born. In the evening the St. Benedict Orchestra and archabbey choir gave a concert, and Anton Lang, the Christus of the Oberammergau production, spoke to the monks and students, telling them the history of the Passion Play which had been produced every ten years since 1634. The experience of the visit of the Oberammergau players inspired the student dramatic association the following year to revive the tradition at Saint Vincent of producing during Lent the seven-act passion play *Calvary,* by Redemptorist Father F. L. Kenzel.[60]

Team sports also remained extremely popular at Saint Vincent during the 1920s. Varsity baseball was by far the most popular sport. Under the leadership of two Benedictine coaches, Fathers Leander Pail and Jerome Rupprecht, the Saint Vincent baseball squad played local college teams such as Carnegie Tech, Slippery Rock State Normal School, Bethany College, St. Francis College, and Marietta College, as well as local athletic association teams, including the Wilmerding Independents, the Bellevue Athletic Association, and the Carnegie Athletic Association. Saint Vincent also regularly played the Homestead Grays, and on two occasions (in 1924 and 1926) hosted the Pittsburgh Pirates on campus before crowds numbering more than four thousand fans. Saint Vincent lost both games to the Pirates (thirteen to nothing and nine to one), but the college team was praised for its tenaciousness as well as its "fast, heavy hitting" performance.[61] Saint Vincent also fielded varsity football, basketball, track, and tennis teams during the Roaring Twenties.

THE PREPARATORY SCHOOL

The grammar department at Saint Vincent, which had been part of the college since the 1840s, ended operations during World War I. The last mention of it in the college catalogue was for the 1917–18 academic year, when forty-two seventh- and eighth-grade students studied at Saint Vincent in preparation for entering the secondary-level classical and commercial courses.[62] In 1918 the college's secondary curriculum was divided into three separate programs: the first four years of the eight-year "classical course," the "Scientific High School," and the "Commercial High School."[63] Then in 1921 this organizational structure was scrapped and the "College Preparatory School" was formed, consisting of a classical course and a scientific course. The commercial course, which had been part of the secondary curriculum at Saint Vincent since the time of Boniface Wimmer, was eliminated.[64]

The creation of the preparatory school was part of the general reorganization of the college that took place at this time. The college catalogue informed readers that the new school offered programs found "in the best academies and high schools" of the country and was intended to prepare students to enter college. Its classical course furnished "the best foundation for advanced scholarship" and was "taken up by those preparing for the priesthood" and by others who sought a "complete liberal education." The scientific course was intended for "those who are looking forward to professional careers in law, medicine, dentistry, pharmacy, agriculture, and engineering." A few commercial classes were offered in the scientific course for students "to whom some knowledge of business methods will be of advantage," but a full-scale commercial course was no longer part of the secondary curriculum.[65]

In 1923 the formal separation of the preparatory school from the college occurred with the creation of separate administrations for both institutions. Father Gerard Bridge remained director (dean) of the college, and Father Bertrand McFadyen was named by Archabbot Aurelius as director of the preparatory school. McFadyen was succeeded in 1925 by Father Walter Stehle, who held the position of director of the prep school for the next eight years.

The decline in the prep school's enrollment in the late 1920s (see table 1 above) was a side effect of the monastic chapter's efforts to build a strong undergraduate college, which required a significant shifting of financial and human resources away from the prep. The enrollment decline, however, was accompanied by a concurrent improvement in the academic quality of the prep school. Nearly thirty Benedictines taught in the prep, a large percentage of whom were also professors in the college. Many of the younger monks who had benefited from the monastic chapter's policy of sending clerics and young priests to U.S. universities to receive advanced degrees were on the faculty. Both the classical and scientific programs in the prep school included challenging courses in religion, English, Latin, modern languages, history, and mathematics; and all students took courses in biology, chemistry, and physics as well. The classical program included two years of Greek, and the scientific program, courses in commercial law and economics. Students could take elective courses in art (freehand drawing, painting, and illustration) and music (piano, organ, violin, and voice). Those who spent four years in the Saint Vincent Preparatory School received a first-rate secondary education and were fully prepared for college work.

The prep school continued as an integral and important part of academic and communal life at Saint Vincent until 1971.

THE SEMINARY

In many ways the 1920s were a golden age for Saint Vincent Seminary. For one thing, enrollment was higher than it had ever been. Between 1920 and 1930 the number of seminarians studying theology never fell below 100, peaking at 139 in 1927. On the average one out of five theologians in the seminary during this period was a Benedictine cleric. Of the diocesan seminarians, more than half came from the Diocese of Pittsburgh, while most of the others came from the seven Pennsylvania and Ohio dioceses of Erie, Altoona, Harrisburg, Scranton, Columbus, Toledo, and Cleveland. A few seminarians also continued to come to Saint Vincent from the dioceses of Brooklyn, New York, and Trenton, New Jersey.

High enrollment in the seminary stretched housing capacity to the limit, so in 1921 the monastic chapter entered into an agreement with the Diocese of Pittsburgh to construct a new seminary building at Saint Vincent. Completed in 1923, the new building (later called Aurelius Hall) cost $125,000, with the Diocese of Pittsburgh providing $100,000 toward construction. In return the Saint Vincent chapter agreed not to charge tuition for Pittsburgh seminarians, but to collect only actual expenses ($365 dollars per year) for their room and board. This decision went far beyond the papal decree of 1855, by which Saint Vincent was instructed to accept "a few" Pittsburgh students each year at a lower rate than other seminarians were charged, and it reflected the close relationship that existed between Saint Vincent and the Diocese of Pittsburgh throughout the 1920s.[66]

Situated southeast of the monastic quadrangle on a parallel line with the archabbey church, the new seminary, like the other buildings on campus, was constructed of red brick and cut stone. Measuring 38 feet by 168 feet, it was seven stories high and had two hundred single rooms. The *Saint Vincent College Journal* observed that the location of the new seminary, away from the other buildings, isolated the seminarians "in a proper manner" from the rest of the student body.[67]

Father Ambrose Kohlbeck (1869–1931) served as seminary rector throughout the 1920s. In his youth he had studied in Rome where he received a doctorate in dogmatic theology. For seven years at the beginning of the century he had taught theology at the Collegio di Sant' Anselmo in Rome before returning to Saint Vincent to become first a professor of theology and then rector of the seminary. Kohlbeck was assisted in his administrative duties by Father John Nepomucene Hruza, vice rector and prefect, and Father Alfred Koch, spiritual director and professor of scripture. The seminary faculty consisted of about twenty Benedictines, many of whom had received degrees in theology and philosophy in Rome and Germany. In 1923, two young Saint Vincent priests, Fathers Jerome Rupprecht and Andrew Biberger, returned from Sant' Anselmo, where Rupprecht had earned a doctorate in philosophy and Biberger had pursued studies in theology, and took up teaching duties in the seminary. Two years later Father John Evangelist Ujlaki, another Roman-educated Benedictine, transferred his vows from the Archabbey of St. Martin in Pannonhalma, Hungary, to Saint Vincent and joined the seminary faculty as professor of scripture and oriental languages. Father Raymond Balko, director of music at Saint Vincent, returned to the seminary faculty in 1927 after a yearlong study of Gregorian chant in Rome, Solesmes, and Beuron.

The theology program at Saint Vincent continued to enjoy papal accreditation, and pontifical degrees (baccalaureates, licentiates, and doctorates) in both theology and philosophy continued to be granted to those students who fulfilled the standard requirements. The four-year theology course remained essentially the same as it had been when the seminary was granted pontifical rank in 1914; but now, in accordance with diocesan regulations throughout the United States, graduates of the seminary were given additional examinations in theology every year for five years after their ordination. Only if they passed these examinations would their temporary faculties to function as priests within a particular diocese be made permanent. The examinations, given in Latin, were intended to promote continued theological study by young priests and (like the "Oath against Modernism," which every priest was required to take) to ensure orthodoxy. In the Diocese of Pittsburgh the examinations were administered principally by the faculty of the Saint Vincent Seminary.[68]

The extracurricular activities of the seminarians included participation in such organizations as the seminary choir (which "furnished both Plain Chant and polyphonic music at divine services"), the Saint Vincent Seminary Mission Society (which had "for its object the promotion of missionary study and activity"), and the St. Thomas Homiletic and Literary Society (whose goal was "to develop and perfect the literary and oratorical powers of its members"). Beginning in 1923 the St. Thomas H & L Society had English, German, Slovak and Polish divisions. In 1919 the society began publication of an annual volume of essays, poems, and biographical sketches of the seminarians and their professors, *The Seminarists' Symposium.* A combination yearbook and literary journal, the *Symposium* continued in existence for thirteen years, publishing essays on such subjects as the relationship of the priest and the Eucharist, the Thomism of Dante, the Oxford Movement, the Liturgical Movement, Catholicism in Colonial America, and the life of John Henry Newman.[69] The seminarians also participated enthusiastically in campus sports activities, both intramural and varsity. Several of them, including Thomas Cawley, played on the Saint Vincent College baseball team. Cawley, who was ordained for the Diocese of Altoona in 1923, was one of the most renowned pitchers on the team during the period. The college journal honored Cawley by dedicating its April 1923 issue to him, noting that "[c]lub after club with records that would stagger an old timer would leave the College campus with hopes and records shattered" when they came face to face with Thomas Cawley on the pitcher's mound.[70]

Other publications emanating from the seminary during this period reflected the professional interests of the faculty as well as the academic needs of the students. Archabbot Aurelius Stehle's *Manual of Episcopal Ceremonies,* first published by the Archabbey Press in 1915, continued in print through five revised editions and was widely used throughout the country by diocesan and religious order liturgists. Father Daniel Kaib's *Bookkeeping for Parish Priests,* first published by the Archabbey Press in 1910, went through two new editions before 1932 and was used in the seminary's clerical accounting course. Other textbooks and scholarly works published by the Archabbey Press included *Englmann's Latin Grammar,* edited by Saint Vincent professor Father Michael Hlavcak; *Systematic Exercises in Latin Syntax,* by Archabbot Aurelius and Father Louis Haas; *The Rule of Saint Benedict: A Commentary* by the French Benedictine abbot of Solesmes, Paul Delatte, translated by the English Benedictine Justin McCann (1921); *The Science of Education in its Sociological and Historical Aspects* by Otto Willmann, translated from the German by Father Felix M. Kirsch (1922); *Liberalism, the Satanic Social Solvent: A Criticism of Liberalism,* by French Cardinal Louis Billot, translated by Father George Barry O'Toole (1922); Father Gerard Bridge's *Illustrated History of St. Vincent Archabbey* (1922); and the *Gemma Caelestis: Breviary Hymns and Other Hymns in Honor of St. Benedict,* selected and translated from the Latin by Father Matthew Britt of St. Martin's Abbey, Lacey, Washington (1926). In addition, seminary professor and later rector of the Catholic University of Peking, Father George Barry O'Toole, published *The Case Against Evolution* in 1925 (New York: Macmillan) and Father Hubert Macko, language professor in the college and seminary, published his widely used *Grammar of the Slovak Language* in 1926 (Scranton, Pa.: Orbana Publishers).

The 1920s also witnessed the promotion of several graduates of the Saint Vincent Seminary in the ranks of the American hierarchy. In 1921 Father Hugh Boyle, who studied at Saint Vincent between 1888 and 1898, was named sixth bishop of Pittsburgh, succeeding another Saint Vincent alumnus, Bishop Regis Canevin. Archabbot Leander and Archabbot Aurelius attended Bishop Boyle's episcopal ordination at St. Paul's Cathedral, Pittsburgh, where Saint Vincent alumnus George W. Mundelein, archbishop of Chicago, preached the sermon. Also in 1921 Bishop Joseph Schrembs of Toledo, a student at Saint Vincent from 1877 to 1882, was named bishop of Cleveland, later receiving the personal rank of archbishop, and in 1924 Pope Pius XI elevated Archbishop Mundelein to the rank of cardinal, the first Saint Vincent alumnus to be honored with the red hat.[71]

DEVELOPMENTS IN THE ARCHABBEY

The chief focus of the monastic community during the 1920s was the Catholic University of Peking, and the overriding concern was where to find the necessary resources, both financial and human, to support it. In the second half of the decade particularly, the China mission posed such challenges to the community that those who fully understood their implications wondered if these challenges might eventually cause the archabbey's financial ruin.

Archabbot Aurelius bore the greatest burdens on his own shoulders. He kept his own counsel and discussed his apprehensions with few of his confreres. Those to whom he expressed his concerns about the China mission and its cost to the archabbey included the monastery's procurator, Father Victor Lillig, and several members of the council of seniors, including Prior Daniel Kaib and Subprior Felix Fellner; but even they did not fully realize the extent of his alarm, for he tended to keep much of his anxiety over the dire financial plight of the university to himself. Only a few of the monks were aware of the stress that drained the archabbot of his accustomed energy and jeopardized his health.

On the surface, at least, everything at Saint Vincent seemed to be going very well. The college, preparatory school, and seminary were flourishing. The parishes reported that their operations were sound both spiritually and temporally, and young men with monastic vocations continued to seek entrance into the monastery as novices. Between 1920 and 1930 more than a hundred candidates were accepted into the archabbey's novitiate, and the monastic community expanded from 190 members at the beginning of the decade to 224 at the end, an increase of almost 20 percent (Table 2). Unlike in previous decades, virtually all the young men who sought admission to the monastery during the 1920s were American-born. Nonetheless in 1925 more than half the professed monks of Saint Vincent were still foreign-born (principally from Germany, but also from Hungary and Slovakia), and as late as 1932 33 percent of them were immigrants from Europe.

On September 3, 1920, the retired archabbot, Leander Schnerr, died at the age of eighty-four. He had been a monk of Saint Vincent for sixty-seven years and for twenty-six years had served, before his retirement in 1918, as abbot of the community. Hundreds of clerical and lay friends came to Saint Vincent for the funeral. Bishop Regis Canevin of Pittsburgh officiated at the pontifical Requiem Mass, and Bishop Joseph Schrembs of Toledo preached the eulogy. Afterwards the much-loved archabbot was buried in the rain under the twenty-five-foot sandstone cross that marked the grave of Boniface Wimmer.[72]

Another death the following year affected the local community as well. Sebastian Wimmer, the founder's nephew, had come to live at the archabbey in 1918 after a long and successful career as a civil engineer. Sebastian Wimmer had come to the United States in 1851 and spent a few years at Saint Vincent College before completing his studies in Pittsburgh. During his professional years, he had helped build railroads in New York, Pennsylvania, Ohio, and Mexico, and in 1889 he volunteered his services to Saint Vincent to design the foundations and grounds for the new abbey church. He lost his money in the economic depression of the 1890s, however, and moved to Minnesota to live with one of his children. In 1918 his granddaughter wrote Archabbot Leander that at the age of eighty-seven her grandfather was ill and destitute and had asked to end his days at Saint Vincent. The monastic chapter agreed to care for him, and he came to the

TABLE 2 Monastic Population of Saint Vincent Archabbey, 1920–1930

	Priests	*Clerics*	*Novices*	*Brothers*	*Oblates*	*Total*
1920	119	29	1	41	0	190
1921	121	33	5	39	2	200
1922	124	28	5	37	0	194
1923	118	25	9	36	4	192
1924	119	26	10	36	2	193
1925	122	28	15	34	5	204
1926	121	37	12	36	5	211
1927	126	41	8	36	5	216
1928	129	41	13	35	5	223
1929	128	44	14	37	5	228
1930	132	41	11	35	5	224

SOURCE: The American Cassinese Congregation *Ordo* for the years indicated

archabbey where he remained, a venerable and honored figure, until his death in December 1921 at the age of ninety-one. The monks celebrated a pontifical Requiem Mass for the repose of his soul and then sent his body to St. Marys, Pennsylvania, where he was buried in the churchyard next to his wife.[73]

On September 7, 1927, the monks of the archabbey marked the end of another era when their second archabbot, Andrew Hintenach, died. After his resignation in 1892, Hintenach had served as chaplain of the Benedictine sisters in Canon City, Colorado, and then in Erie, Pennsylvania. In 1921 he returned to the archabbey where he spent the final years of his life in seclusion and prayer, leading a virtual eremitical life, until his death at the age of eighty-three. Bishop Hugh Boyle of Pittsburgh, who had come to Saint Vincent as a student in the year of Archabbot Andrew's election, celebrated the solemn pontifical Requiem Mass. Hintenach was buried under the sandstone cross next to his predecessor, Archabbot Boniface, and his successor, Archabbot Leander.[74]

Distinguished visitors to Saint Vincent during the 1920s included Michael von Faulhaber, cardinal archbishop of Munich, who came to the archabbey in May 1923. In explaining the reason for Cardinal von Faulhaber's visit, the *Saint Vincent College Journal* said that the First World War "not only devastated Germany and destroyed its prosperity, but also cut off all financial support necessary for the sustenance of the orphans, nuns, and ecclesiastical students of the Cardinal Archbishop's jurisdiction." It was therefore to raise money for archdiocesan charitable institutions and to "solicit even greater aid to cope with the ever increasing amount of misery and suffering" that he had come to the United States. No records exist that reveal the amount of the donation made to the Archdiocese of Munich by the monastic chapter at Saint Vincent during the course of the cardinal's visit, but it is certain to have been generous.[75]

The same purpose brought two European Benedictine leaders to Saint Vincent in 1927—Abbot Primate Fidelis von Stotzingen and Archabbot Raphael Waltzer of the Abbey of Beuron. Von Stotzingen visited the archabbey on the feast of St. Scholastica, February 10, as part of his nationwide tour of American Benedictine abbeys to solicit financial support for German Benedictine communities, and Waltzer came to the monastery in April on behalf of his own community. For almost eighty years the Beuronese monks had regarded the American Cassinese houses as less than exemplary in their monastic and liturgical observance, but during his visit to Saint Vincent Waltzer graciously admitted that "his preconceived views of St. Vincent, first as a monastery, and then as a school, received a surprising jolt . . . [of] a pleasant nature" during his sojourn in Pennsylvania. The manner in which the liturgy was conducted by the American monks ("especially the Gregorian Chant of the Archabbey Choir"), he said, was "a source of great edification" for him. Archabbot Raphael, like Abbot Primate Fidelis, departed Saint Vincent with his purse considerably heavier than when he arrived.[76]

Throughout the decade following World War I, at the same time that the China mission was draining so many resources from Saint Vincent, the monastic chapter received many requests for financial assistance from Benedictine communities in Bavaria and Austria, where postwar reparation payments were impoverishing the German people. These requests never met with refusal. Again and again the Saint Vincent chapter sent thousands of dollars to Bavarian and Austrian abbeys, including two contributions of $5,000 each to St. Peter's Abbey, Salzburg.[77] But European monasteries were not the only Benedictine communities that benefited from the generosity of the Saint Vincent chapter during the 1920s. In 1924 when St. Mary's Abbey, Richardton, North Dakota, declared bankruptcy, Saint Vincent joined other U.S. monasteries in coming to the assistance of the beleaguered abbey. The chapter in Pennsylvania made two interest-free loans (of $15,000 and $25,000) to the community in North Dakota and later canceled the debt.[78] After the stock-market crash of 1929, when Holy Cross Abbey in Canon City, Colorado, faced imminent financial ruin, Saint Vincent joined St. John's Abbey in Minnesota in coming to the Colorado monastery's rescue. Because of its own financial crisis at that time, the Saint

Vincent chapter was not able to provide significant amounts of money, but at the request of the abbot president of the American Cassinese Congregation, the archabbot of Saint Vincent did send Father Leonard Schlimm, a fifty-seven-year-old monk with considerable experience as a financial administrator, to Colorado in order to administer the abbey in Canon City for two years.[79]

The community also welcomed several Benedictine refugees from Europe during the period immediately following the First World War. Fathers Rhabanus Goetz and Heribert Thiel from the suppressed Dutch Abbey of Merklebeck were received as members of the community in 1923 and spent the rest of their lives as monks of Saint Vincent. Similarly, Father John Ujlaki arrived at Saint Vincent in 1925 from the Hungarian Archabbey of Pannonhalma and became a well-known professor of Hebrew and sacred scripture in the seminary and of modern languages in the college until his retirement in 1959.[80] During the 1920s Saint Vincent also provided a home to an Ecuadorian secular priest, Father Humberto Chiriboga. Father Chiriboga affiliated with the Benedictine community as an oblate and spent several years teaching in the college and preparatory school. In 1929, during a visit to his family in Quito, he was killed in an automobile accident.

Other European Benedictines came to Saint Vincent during this period to study. In 1922 two clerics, Genadius Diez and Bernardo Lopez, came from the Spanish Abbey of Our Lady of Montserrat to Pennsylvania to complete their theology courses and to study English before moving on to Montserrat's dependent priory and college in Manila.[81] And Father Corbinian Hofmeister of Metten spent 1925 in Pennsylvania perfecting his English. He returned to Bavaria and was later elected abbot of Metten. Young monks from other American Benedictine communities also studied at Saint Vincent at the time. The abbeys that sent novices or clerics to Saint Vincent during the 1920s included St. John's (Minnesota), St. Benedict's (Kansas), St. Mary's (New Jersey), St. Bede's (Illinois), St. Leo's (Florida), and St. Anselm's (New Hampshire).[82]

Liturgical developments at Saint Vincent during the 1920s were influenced by two major factors. The first was that the new archabbot, Aurelius Stehle, was a highly regarded liturgist whose publications on liturgical practice were recognized nationally as authoritative. Archabbot Aurelius was frequently called upon by the bishops of Pittsburgh and other prelates and priests throughout the country for advice on liturgical matters,[83] and with Stehle at the helm, the monastic community in Pennsylvania gained an international reputation for the perfection of its liturgical ceremonies.

The second factor that influenced liturgical life at Saint Vincent in the

1920s was the postwar liturgical revival, a movement that began in Europe and spread to the United States during the period. Following World War I a movement to deepen the understanding of the liturgy developed among European Catholics. Promoted by such Benedictines as Father Lambert Beauduin (1873–1960) of the Belgian Abbey of Mont-César and the monks of Solesmes in France, Maria Laach and Beuron in Germany, Maredsous in Belgium, and Montserrat in Spain, the liturgical revival spread to the United States chiefly through the work of Father Virgil Michel of St. John's Abbey, Minnesota. The primary goal of the movement was to help Catholics better understand the meaning and function of the Mass in the Catholic community. Under the intellectual leadership of Michel, who began the journal *Orate Fratres* in 1926, the movement in America attempted to integrate Pope Leo XIII's social vision and Pope Pius X's call for a spiritual reform with contemporary ecclesiological theories on the Church as the mystical body of Christ.[84]

The impetus and leadership of the liturgical movement in the United States emanated from St. John's Abbey and to a lesser degree from such American Benedictine monasteries as St. Meinrad Abbey in Indiana and St. Anselm's Priory in Washington, D.C. But while Saint Vincent did not assume a role of leadership in the movement, liturgical life at the archabbey in Pennsylvania was certainly influenced by it. It was in response to the interest generated by the liturgical revival that Archabbot Aurelius sent Father Raymond Balko to Europe in 1926 to study music at key continental liturgical centers in Rome, Solesmes, and Beuron, and the movement itself became the theme of animated discussion and debates at Saint Vincent. In 1927 a lengthy article appeared in the *Saint Vincent College Journal* entitled "A Return to the Liturgy" which attempted to explain the significance of the liturgical movement to the uninitiated and called for greater efforts on the part of pastors to implement its programs of liturgical study and the active participation of the laity in the Mass.[85] At student and parish Masses at Saint Vincent the *missa recitata* or "dialogue Mass" was introduced, at which those in attendance, together with the acolytes, responded to the prayers of the priest. As a result of the liturgical movement, a deeper awareness developed generally among the Saint Vincent community of the communal nature of the Mass.

Priests from Saint Vincent also participated in the International Eucharistic Congress held in Chicago, June 18–25, 1926, hosted by Saint Vincent alumnus Cardinal George Mundelein. This celebration of the mystery of the Real Presence attracted one million people, a Catholic gathering which was not to be surpassed until Pope John Paul II visited the United States in 1979. It offered an opportunity for the American Church to demonstrate its strength in the United States at a time when a notable resurgence of anti-Catholic nativism was occurring.[86] Father Alfred Koch of Saint Vincent Seminary attended the Eucharistic Congress and delivered an address in Latin on the place of the Eucharist in Catholic theology, and on the eve of his departure for China, Father Callistus Stehle also went to Chicago and gave a lecture entitled "Life Nourished by the Blessed Eucharist," in which he discussed the origins and nature of the feast of Corpus Christi and the liturgical rites surrounding it. The Corpus Christi procession at Saint Vincent each June continued to be a major public celebration, drawing hundreds of people to the archabbey. Father Callistus said that "it has been called the most exquisite painting brought from the old world to the new reproduced with original freshness of color each year when spring and summer merge. From my early days it has remained a rite 'white with the stainless radiance of eternity.'"[87]

THE PARISH APOSTOLATE

During the 1920s more than half the priests of the archabbey were engaged in the parish apostolate. The number of parishes under the care of the Saint Vincent Benedictines did not increase significantly during the period, but some changes did occur in the organization of those in the immediate vicinity of the archabbey. In 1921 Bishop Regis Canevin confirmed the de facto status of parishes under the care of the pastor of the Saint Vincent Parish. Seven churches were declared "filial or succursal" chapels of Saint Vincent Parish: Sacred Heart, Youngstown; St. Cecilia, Whitney; St. Bartholomew, Crabtree; St. Mary's, Forbes Road; St. James, New Alexandria; St. Boniface, Chestnut Ridge; and St. Benedict's, Marguerite. Saint Vincent Parish was declared the official parish of the district encompassing these chapels, and the Benedictine priests in charge of the chapels were declared assistants to the pastor of the archabbey parish. At the same time, Bishop Canevin raised the Benedictine churches in Ligonier, New Florence, and Saltsburg to the rank of canonical parishes. St. Mary's Parish, New Florence, itself had succursal chapels in Bolivar (St. Mary's) and Seward (Holy Family).[88] Among the new churches placed under Benedictine direction during the 1920s were St. Benedict's in Canton, Ohio (1923), and All Saints in East Vandergrift, Pennsylvania (1924), the former established at the special request of Bishop Joseph Schrembs of Cleveland.[89]

By 1929 priests from Saint Vincent served thirty parishes in the Diocese of Pittsburgh (including St. Mary's and St. Boniface on the North Side of the see city and Blessed Sacrament in Greensburg), as well as others in the dioceses of Erie, Altoona, Covington, and Cleveland and in the archdioceses of Baltimore and Chicago. Altogether they had charge of fifty-four parishes in these seven dioceses. (In 1922 they had turned over their parishes in the Diocese of Denver to the newly independent priory of St. Leander's in Pueblo, Colorado.)[90]

Many of the churches staffed by Saint Vincent Benedictines were "national" parishes. These included St. Boniface in Pittsburgh (German), Fourteen Holy Martyrs in Baltimore (German), St. Ambrose in Avonmore (Slovak), St. Matthew's in Saltsburg (Slovak), St. George in Patton (Slovak), St. Sylvester in Slickville (Slovak and Polish), Forty Martyrs in Trauger (Hungarian), All Saints (Polish), Holy Trinity (Slovak), and St. Casimir (Lithuanian) in East Vandergrift, and Ascension in Jeannette (Italian). By now the archabbey had enough priests fluent in Slovak, Hungarian, Polish, Lithuanian, and Italian to make the staffing of these and other national parishes a less vexing task for Archabbot Aurelius than it had sometimes proven to be for his predecessor, Archabbot Leander.

Priests from Saint Vincent also served as chaplains for the Little Sisters of the Poor and the Benedictine Sisters of Pittsburgh, the Benedictine Sisters of Erie and St. Marys, the Sisters of Charity of Greensburg, and the Sisters of Mercy at St. Xavier Convent, Latrobe.

PROGRESS AND SETBACKS IN CHINA

In February 1926 Father Victor Lillig, the archabbey's procurator (treasurer), reported to the monastic chapter that during the previous year the community's "income was one of the best ever received." With overall enrollment in the seminary, college, and prep school in Pennsylvania approaching six hundred students, tuition alone brought in more than two hundred thousand dollars to the community. In addition, profits from the farm and from the sale of coal mined on the community's property in Westmoreland, Cambria, and Elk counties, annual income from parishes staffed by Saint Vincent priests, and dividends and interest from the community's stock portfolio and bank accounts seemed to many in the chapter to ensure that the archabbey would enjoy financial security for the foreseeable future.[91] As early as 1927, however, it was clear to Archabbot Aurelius, Father Victor, and a few others in the chapter that unless new sources of income were found, the commitment to China could jeopardize the community's financial stability.[92]

In the summer of 1929 Archabbot Aurelius went to Rome at the request of Cardinal van Rossum to discuss the expansion of the Catholic University of Peking. The Propaganda Fide was eager for the university to initiate programs that would directly support the Church's missionary work in the Orient, and Stehle went prepared to offer the Holy See all that it wanted. At meetings with Cardinal van Rossum and in two private audiences with Pope Pius XI, he committed Saint Vincent to establishing a faculty of sacred theology and philosophy at the university. The plan he outlined called for the creation within one year of an "Ecclesiastical Course in Philosophy," together with "the usual collateral branches of study," and then, over the next five years, the development of a complete seminary program in philosophy and theology. This program—consisting of two years of philosophy and four of theology—would constitute a separate faculty whose purpose would be to prepare Chinese students for the priesthood. The new faculty would be organized under the same guidelines for ecclesiastical studies, set by the Holy See's Sacred Congregation of Studies, as those followed by Saint Vincent Seminary. To illustrate the kind of program he had in mind for China, the archabbot submitted with his plan a copy of the Pennsylvania seminary's catalogue.[93]

Meanwhile in Peking events were unfolding that would delay indefinitely the project to establish the faculty of sacred theology and philosophy. In April 1929 twenty disgruntled students attempted to disrupt classes at the university. Their effort was "energetically opposed by the vast majority of the students, both Catholic and non-Catholic," and the short-lived protest came to an end. But when the twenty were then expelled, they brought charges of "cultural aggression" against the administration, and the Ministry of Education sent inspectors to investigate. The inspectors—Chu Ching-nung and Hsieh Shu-ying—cleared the institution of charges of "imperialistic oppression of the students," but in the course of their investigation they discovered that the school's academic program did not provide all the courses required by the Chinese government for a fully accredited university. As a result, they recommended that the university be downgraded to the status of "college." Accepting the inspectors' recommendation, the Ministry of Education issued a decree on June 25, 1929, "demoting" the institution.[94]

The loss of accreditation by the Chinese government had a potentially disastrous effect on the ability of the institution to attract students. If a university was not officially recognized by the Ministry of Education, the diplomas and degrees it granted did not have the stature of accredited institutions, and its graduates were severely limited in job opportunities.[95] The news of the decree, therefore, shocked and demoralized the entire community. Father Barry O'Toole wrote Archabbot Aurelius that as a result of the ministry's action

> we have lost considerable face and we all feel that no pains must be spared to regain our former status before the opening of classes next September. Nanking's chief criticism against our University was based on the fact that we had no scientific equipment and no scientific courses. In order to be recognized by the Nationalist Government, it is necessary for us to inaugurate the School of Science, because according to the present laws no institution may lay claim to the title of university unless it has a School of Arts and a School of Sciences."[96]

Archabbot Aurelius, who received O'Toole's letter in Rome, immediately brought the matter to the attention of officials of the Propaganda Fide and added to his proposal for the expansion of the Catholic University of Peking a caveat that in light of the Chinese government's "pressing demands," unless the Holy See provided immediate financial assistance, it would be virtually impossible to open the proposed faculty of sacred theology and philosophy. Stehle noted that the new buildings required for an expanded university would alone cost $250,000. In response, the Congregation for the Propagation of the Faith offered to pay the interest on a $100,000 loan.[97]

Archabbot Aurelius remained in Rome for two more weeks in order to participate in the celebration of the fourteen hundredth anniversary of the founding of the Archabbey of Montecassino. Leaving Italy at the end of August, he went first to Bavaria, where he visited Saint Vincent's motherhouse at Metten as well as the Benedictine Abbey of Eichstätt, and then to Belgium where he visited the Abbey of Maredsous. At both Metten and Maredsous he unsuccessfully solicited volunteers for the China mission. He returned to the United States aboard the S. S. *Resolute* in the third week of August.

On August 20, 1929, Pope Pius XI issued a papal brief addressed to the archabbot of Saint Vincent expressing his great joy at "not only how much the monks of your Archabbey and the Abbots of the American Cassinese Congregation have achieved in so short a time under your leadership but also how much in the near and distant future you are prepared to accomplish for the glory of God and the welfare of the Chinese people." The Holy Father thanked Archabbot Aurelius for all that he had done to further the China mission, and said he was confident that soon Saint Vincent would establish at the university an "illustrious home" for the study of philosophy and theology in China and that "in the lofty traditions of your holy Father St. Benedict," the monastery in Pennsylvania would "supply the most efficient men to govern, to teach, to lead souls to Religion, and to furnish both equipment and endowment of the University."[98]

The pope's letter was both a commendation for past accomplishments and a mandate for further expansion at the university. The expectation that Archabbot Aurelius and the Saint Vincent community would "furnish both equipment and endowment" for the institution, develop a science program that would satisfy the demands of the Ministry of Education, and establish a faculty of theology and philosophy imposed a heavy burden on the community, and in his attempt to carry that burden, Archabbot Aurelius made a crucial decision that in the long run proved illadvised.

At the beginning of October 1929, not long after his return from Rome and less than a month before the stock-market crash of October 29, the archabbot traveled to New York for the purpose of borrowing money for the China mission. He contacted a friend, Nicholas F. Brady, a wealthy Catholic layman who in the past had provided considerable financial support for Catholic educational projects, including that of the Catholic University of America, and asked his assistance.[99] Brady, a member of the board of directors of the National City Bank of New York, expressed his interest in and willingness to help the Catholic University of Peking, and introduced Archabbot Aurelius to M. D. Currie, an assistant vice president at National City Bank. After a short period of negotiation, the archabbot entered into an oral agreement with Currie, subsequently confirmed by letter, to borrow $250,000, at an interest rate of 7 percent, for the purpose of constructing new buildings and repairing old ones at the university.[100] According to the oral agreement, the loan was to be repaid within eighteen months. Stehle explained to Currie that he wanted to make the loan personally, as chancellor of the Catholic University of Peking, rather than on behalf of Saint Vincent Archabbey, and said that he preferred this course of action for "a variety of reasons." Brady supported the arrangement, to which Currie agreed. The principal reason for preferring to take the loan out in his own name (which Stehle did not feel obligated to explain to the bank officers) was that he had not approached the monastic chapter for authorization to borrow the money in the name of the archabbey, as required by the statutes of the American Cassinese Congregation. Nonetheless, as chancellor of the Catholic University of Peking, he felt that he had the necessary authority to make the loan on behalf not of the archabbey but of the university. He also felt confident that fund-raising efforts currently underway in the United States would generate sufficient income to permit a rapid repayment of the loan.[101]

The National City Bank issued the first twenty-five-thousand-dollar installment of the loan to Archabbot Aurelius on November 15, 1929. The rest of the loan was given directly to the university through National City Bank's office in Peking in periodic installments over the next twelve months.[102] Assistant Vice President Currie informed C. R. Bennett, manager of the National City Bank branch office in Peking, that because the university enjoyed the support of the Holy See and expected to repay the loan within eighteen months, the bank would not require the Benedictines to mortgage their property in Peking, though Currie did give Bennett the option of asking the Benedictine procurator in Peking, Father Boniface Martin, to deposit the title deeds of the university in the bank's Peking office. Bennett decided not to do so "due to [the] understanding regarding the duration of the loan."[103]

Meanwhile, plans were going ahead in Peking for construction of the new building. The design for the expanded university, drawn up by Father Adelbert Gresnigt, had been completed in March 1929, and called for a large facility capable of accommodating four hundred students and including dormitories, classrooms, scientific laboratories, a library, offices, and an auditorium. According to Father Sylvester Healy, Father Adelbert's design embodied "the characteristic spirit of Benedictinism" in that it "reconcil[ed] the old with the new, adapting the traditional forms to the needs of modern school architecture."[104] The structure was laid out in the form of a quadrangle, measuring 450 feet by 200 feet, with towers at each corner. The design was modeled on a traditional Chinese city wall, complete with towers and gates, and included "the distinctly local features of the Grand Old Capital of China." A major contribution to the "Sino-Christian" architectural style that Gresnigt hoped to introduce, the new university building was intended to offer visible proof that the university's mission was "to idealize and purify what is already dear to [Chinese students], and not to deaden their taste for the culture of their native land by overemphasizing that of other countries."[105] Construction began in September, and two months later Archbishop Costantini laid the cornerstone in a ceremony attended by Chinese education officials and members of the Catholic hierarchy.[106]

In the meantime Father Barry O'Toole drew up plans for an administrative reorganization of the university that would meet the requirements of the Ministry of Education. The reorganization plan established three facul-

Catholic University of Peking, 1931.

Chapel at the Catholic University of Peking, 1930.

ties (arts, sciences, and education) and twelve academic departments. The departments of Chinese, English, history, philosophy, and social sciences would comprise the faculty of arts; new departments of mathematics, physics, chemistry, biology, and pharmacy would be created to form the faculty of sciences; and the departments of pedagogy and psychology would make up the faculty of education. Dr. Liu Fu, the university's Sorbonne-educated director of studies, was assigned the task of delivering and explaining the reorganization plan to the Ministry of Education in Nanking, and in August the ministry restored to the institution its status as a university. Two years later the Nanking government went one step further and granted the university permanent accreditation.[107]

The effort to win reaccreditation from the ministry, however, had imposed new and unexpected financial burdens on the university. Now, in addition to constructing a major new building at a cost of $250,000, the administration had to find the resources to purchase the necessary equipment and to hire qualified professors for the faculty of sciences. Archabbot Aurelius sought more volunteers from the monasteries and schools of the American Cassinese Congregation, and in the fall of 1929 Father Damian Smith of St. Mary's Abbey, Newark, who held a master of science degree from the University of Chicago, went to Peking to teach biology and chemistry. Other American monks who went to work at what was now called Fu Jen University included Father Aidan Germain of St. John's Abbey, Minnesota, who held a doctorate in history from the Catholic University of America, and Saint Vincent clerics Columban Gross and Hugh Wilt. In addition, Father Gregory Schramm of St. Mary's Abbey, Newark, returned to China after a year in the United States, having received a Ph.D. in psychology from Johns Hopkins University.[108] On their way to Peking, Gross, Wilt, and Schramm stopped in Kyoto, Japan, to purchase "scientific instruments" for the physics department at Fu Jen, and a few months after his arrival Father Damian Smith went to Shanghai and Fukien to purchase supplies and equipment for the biology laboratory.[109]

The newly reaccredited university opened for the 1929–30 academic year in September with 345 students. Two hundred and forty-eight of these were secondary students in the university's "middle school," formerly the MacManus Academy of Chinese Studies; only 97 were enrolled in the university course itself. There were forty professors, of whom twelve were American or European Benedictines and twenty-eight Chinese laymen. Father Charles Rauth, formerly of the Pei Wen Catholic Academy of Kaifeng and since August a Benedictine in triennial vows, and Professor Tu Lui-sheng were joint directors of the middle school. Father Barry O'Toole continued to serve as rector, but he was assisted by Professor Chen Yuan, who now held the title "president" of the university.

The prominence of Chinese Catholic laymen in the administration of the institution was the result not only of the Benedictines' desire to make Fu Jen a truly Chinese university as soon as possible, but also of government accreditation requirements. Ministry of Education regulations mandated that accredited universities have a majority representation of Chinese citizens both on their boards of directors and in their academic administrations.[110] Chinese members of Fu Jen's largely honorary board of trustees included Ma Hsiang-po, former governor of the province of Kiangsu and president of the National University of Peking; Shen Yin-mo, current president of the National University of Peking; Fu Tseng-hsiang, former Chinese minister of education; Lo Pa-hung, director of the Nanking Central Hospital; Peking banker and prominent Catholic layman H. H. Mu; Lo Ting, the Mongol prince of Karachin; Chang Chi, a member of the executive committee of the Chinese Nationalist Party; Peter Celestine Lu Cheng-hsiang, former prime minister of China and later a Benedictine monk in Belgium; Bishop Peter Cheng of the vicariate of Hsuan-hua-fu; Bishop Simon Tsu, S.J., of Haimen; Bishop Melchior Sun, of Li Hsien; Bishop Joseph Hu of Taichow; and Bishop Evarist Chang of East Mongolia.

Research among faculty members of the university during this period tended to focus on historical studies of Chinese Christianity and Chinese relations with the West. Volumes of the university *Bulletin* between 1927 and 1930 included such articles as Father Barry O'Toole's "Random Notes on Early Christianity in China" and "John of Montecorvino" (a biographical sketch of the fourteenth-century Franciscan missionary to China); Chen Yuan's "Manichaeism in China"; Father Francis Clougherty's "The Franciscan Contemporaries of Marco Polo"; Father Charles Rauth's "China's Relations with the West from the Accession of Yao (2357 B.C.) to the End of the San Tai Period (249 B.C.)"; and Ignatius Ying Quianli's "A New English Translation of the [ninth-century A.D.] Nestorian Tablet" and "The Secularization Decree of Wu Tsung" (on the persecution of Nestorian Christians in China in the ninth century).

The students were primarily non-Catholics, and though no formal proselytizing occurred because of Chinese government restrictions on the religious indoctrination of Chinese students at accredited universities, the Benedictines were always alert to potential converts and conducted private classes in religious instruction for "neophytes." Each year a few of these students were baptized and confirmed in the chapel of the Benedictine priory.[111]

Student life in general at the university in Peking centered around studies and athletics. Intramural athletic events—soccer, tennis, basketball, and track—were part of the school's extracurricular activities from the beginning, and there were two hours of compulsory calisthenics each week. The first extramural contest took place in the fall of 1927 when the university soccer team played two games against the American Marine detachment stationed in Peking. In the spring of 1928 the team played two games against a contingent of Italian sailors, losing both of them. It subsequently defeated the alumni team of the Sacred Heart School, considered the best independent Catholic team in the city.[112]

When Father Boniface Martin, director of athletics at St. Bede's College, Peru, Illinois, joined the staff of Fu Jen in March 1928, he immediately took charge of the athletic program. By July 1929 the university still had not organized varsity teams in any sport but soccer. Nonetheless, there were active intramural programs in basketball and tennis in the first semester of 1928–29, though because part of the athletic field was chosen as the site for the new university building, intramural basketball and tennis were all but discontinued during the second semester. In 1930 a plot of ground next to the university property was purchased for a new athletic field, which was later also used as a parade ground when compulsory military training for students was imposed by the government in Nanking.[113]

In May 1930 Brother Hugh Wilt, who had joined the Benedictine mission in Peking nine months earlier and who was studying Chinese while completing his theological studies for the priesthood, wrote his confreres in Pennsylvania about the students he had encountered at Fu Jen. "The Chinese student," he said, "is no different than any other student when it comes down to work. We have the same two classes here that we have at home, those who really study and are out for knowledge and those who are regular bums. However, the proportion of zealous students seems to be greater here than at home. But the Chinese student is not so easily handled, especially today when they are more or less imbued with the spirit of Communism." The political influence of the Communists was of particular concern to the American Benedictines in Peking. Wilt went on to say that

> [i]t is now an open secret that Russia is handing out large sums of money to the Chinese who help to spread her bolshevistic principles. The young men of China, but especially the student element, are not averse to accepting such money. Russia has gained great headway and I really fear that unless something is done very soon,

it won't be long until Communism is the ruling power here. The civil war is raging at present but that is only a secondary matter when compared with the danger of anarchy which is now rising in the South. One encouraging factor for us at present is the assurance given us by the police that our school is free from any devotee of Moscow. Some of the Universities have them in abundance.

Reflecting the views of all the American Benedictines at Fu Jen, the young cleric observed that in face of the "paganism" that prevailed in China and the growing threat of Communism, "[e]ducation is the Church's only chance in China. . . . It is the greatness of the cause that leads us on. . . . We are confident that the American Benedictines will do their part and bring this all important enterprise to a successful reality."[114]

THE DEATH OF ARCHABBOT AURELIUS

On February 12, 1930, four months after he had negotiated the $250,000 loan for the Catholic University of Peking from the National City Bank of New York, Archabbot Aurelius suddenly and unexpectedly died. It was clear to the monks at Saint Vincent that the stress of responsibility for the China mission was a major cause of his death.

Father Felix Fellner, prior of the community, sent a letter to the monks of the archabbey describing the series of events that led up to the archabbot's fatal stroke. On New Year's Eve, as was customary, all the monks had gathered at the archabbot's office to wish him "health and happiness in the Lord throughout the New Year." That evening he seemed in good health, and in his genial way he spoke with the monks about the work that lay ahead of them in the coming year, particularly the work in China. A few days later he traveled to Detroit where he met with leaders of the national retreat movement and took advantage of the meeting to solicit funds for Fu Jen University. There was no doubt, the prior said, "that his work at that meeting was more than his physical strength permitted."

When the archabbot returned to the archabbey on January 10, everyone who saw him realized that something was seriously wrong. He had lost part of his memory and could not recognize many of the monks who greeted him. Several of the senior priests urged him to take a long rest. Dr. Stephen Nealon of Latrobe, the archabbey's "house physician," who was a special friend of the archabbot, was called in. After a brief examination, Dr. Nealon tried to convince him that absolute rest was essential for his recovery. But Stehle refused to withdraw from his work even for a short time. He was anxious about the heavy financial burdens that the China mission had placed upon both the archabbey and himself, and as the effects of the October stock-market crash became more apparent and the signs of a major economic depression began to appear, he could not see his way clear to taking time off to rest. He faced the daunting task of raising $250,000 to repay the National City Bank loan by April 1931, and when an invitation came to attend a meeting in Cleveland of the Society for the Propagation of the Faith, a diocesan group that raised money for the foreign missions, he announced that he had accepted.

He left Saint Vincent on Sunday afternoon, January 19, and stopped in McKeesport, Pennsylvania, to address a group interested in supporting the China mission. From there he went to Pittsburgh to speak with other potential contributors. On January 21 he rushed back to Saint Vincent because of the sudden death of twenty-nine-year-old Father Alexius Udavcak. The following day he set off again for Cleveland where he was to be the guest of his friend, Bishop Joseph Schrembs. He arrived in Cleveland on January 22, and two days later the prior of Saint Vincent received a curt telegram from the rector of the Cleveland cathedral: "The archabbot does not seem right. Send some good man to the Cathedral for him."

When Father Victor Lillig arrived in Cleveland, he found Archabbot Aurelius disoriented and unable to speak. Bishop Schrembs had brought in doctors who recommended that the archabbot be taken to Pittsburgh for medical treatment. On January 26 Father Victor accompanied him to Pittsburgh where he entered St. Francis Hospital. Father Felix told the community that "everything is being done by the doctors, who love and venerate him, to bring him back to health with God's help."[115]

On February 1 Dr. T. M. Barrett, the physician in charge of the case, wrote Dr. Nealon in Latrobe that the archabbot's condition had improved slightly. His aphasia was not so marked, and he was able to write and speak a little. X-rays revealed evidence of an old skull fracture, apparently sustained the previous year when the archabbot had been in an automobile accident. He had been knocked unconscious but had recovered and no serious problems had appeared at the time. Now his blood pressure was dangerously high and there was evidence of cardiorenal disease. Barrett's diagnosis of the immediate cause of the archabbot's condition was "a Subcortical Hemorrhage (or, less likely, thrombosis) of one of the branches of the middle cerebral artery"—in laymen's language, a stroke—which "would account for practically all the symptoms." The doctor said, however, that he thought the outlook was "fairly good at least for partial recovery."[116]

But the archabbot's condition worsened during the next few days. His blood pressure soared, his vital signs deteriorated, and the physicians informed Prior Felix Fellner that he was dying. On Tuesday, February 4, Fellner administered the last rites. Archabbot Aurelius recognized the prior "but on account of his aphasia he could not express his thoughts plainly." During the visit, the archabbot "twice folded his hands in prayer," Father Felix told the community. "Undoubtedly, he wished thereby to indicate to pray for him. I assured him that we will intercede with God for him."[117]

The archabbot lingered for another week, but after drifting into a coma, he died in his sleep on Wednesday, February 12, at the age of fifty-two. The official death notice, sent to all the monks of the American Cassinese Congregation asking prayers and Masses for their departed confrere, said that the

> countless worries connected with the establishment of [the Catholic University of Peking] slowly exhausted the Archabbot's strength and fast wore out his keen mind. The same man who so sweetly consoled others and encouraged them, when in difficulty, to hope for a better lot, in his own supreme affliction sighed, "He has led me and brought me in darkness and not into light" *(Lam. III, 2)*. Towards the last he was unable to clothe his thoughts with words, but even then he showed a complete and humble submission to the will of God. In His mercy God made the affliction of his servant short; on the 12th of February he sent forth His angel to lift the soul of our Archabbot from her dark prison into the light that knows no darkness.[118]

The funeral took place in the archabbey church on February 18. Five bishops, eleven abbots, three hundred priests, and over eight hundred relatives and friends were in attendance. Bishop Joseph Schrembs of Cleveland delivered the funeral sermon and Bishop Hugh Boyle of Pittsburgh celebrated the pontifical Requiem Mass and officiated at the grave. When they gathered around the sandstone cross in the archabbey cemetery to bid farewell to their spiritual father and with heavy hearts to chant the *In Paradisum,* the monks of Saint Vincent wondered what the days ahead held for them. As economic depression settled on the land, some of them understood that at least with regard to temporal matters their community faced a very bleak future.

SEVEN

DEPRESSION AND JUDGMENT
(1930–1940)

On April 22, 1930, two months and ten days after the death of Archabbot Aurelius, the monastic chapter met at the archabbey under the chairmanship of Abbot Ernest Helmstetter of St. Mary's Abbey, Newark, abbot president of the American Cassinese Congregation, and on the following day elected fifty-year-old Father Alfred Koch as fifth archabbot of Saint Vincent. Koch was born in Arzheim, Bavaria, where he completed his early education before entering the Society of the Divine Word, a religious congregation devoted to missionary work. He continued his schooling in Vienna and later studied at the College of the Propaganda Fide in Rome where he received a doctorate in sacred theology. Ordained in 1905, he was appointed rector of the papal seminary at Sutri and Nepi, near Rome, a position he held for six years. Then in 1912 he was sent by his superiors to the United States to teach at the Society's Sacred Heart Mission House in Girard, Pennsylvania. In 1916, at the age of thirty-seven, he entered the novitiate at Saint Vincent and a year later professed vows as a Benedictine monk. Appointed to the seminary faculty, Koch taught sacred scripture, exegesis, homiletics, and Italian for thirteen years and held, at various times, the positions of spiritual director and prefect in the seminary before being elected fifth archabbot of Saint Vincent.[1]

In the seminary Father Alfred proved himself an affable yet demanding professor and administrator. His approachable personality, together with his clear vision, self-confidence, and decisiveness, made him a popular teacher and spiritual advisor. Unlike the previous three archabbots, he had not come to Saint Vincent as a boy nor had he been nurtured in the archabbey's schools. His experience in the community's apostolates was limited to the seminary, and his relatively recent profession made him junior to all the monks his age and to many of those younger than he. He was considered a newcomer by some and an outsider by a few. But his easy manner and natural brilliance eventually won the confidence of the entire community, who came to consider him the ideal superior to lead the monastery through the difficult days ahead.

It also did no harm that with respect to the China mission Koch had always been a skeptic. Although (or perhaps precisely because) as a member of the Society of the Divine Word he had been trained as a missionary, he had never been a strong supporter of Saint Vincent's work in China. He questioned whether the archabbey had the personnel and material resources to accomplish this mission, and like many of his confreres he did not see the other abbeys of the American Cassinese Congregation eagerly coming to the fore with men and means to sustain the university in Peking.

During the last years of the former archabbot's life, the majority of priests in the community had grown skeptical of the value to Saint Vincent of the China mission as well as of the archabbey's ability to support it. Even early in the mission, none of the important chapter votes on China had won with more than a slim majority, and some had won with a mere plurality, with "no" and "indifferent" outnumbering the "yes" votes.[2] While only a few of the skeptics expressed their views strongly and openly, Archabbot Aurelius was sensitive enough to the sentiments of the majority that he more and more dealt with the business of China without consulting the chapter. His extraordinary decision to borrow $250,000 from the National City Bank of New York in his own name, without seeking the approval of the community, was clearly a consequence of his understanding that the community no longer fully supported the enterprise. He feared that if he sought the approval, it would be denied, so he acted on his own.

The new archabbot had been a voice of reason during the earlier debates

Alfred Koch, O.S.B. (1879–1951), fifth archabbot of Saint Vincent.

over China, and while he advised caution and expressed concern about the wisdom of committing so many resources to a work with so doubtful a future, he never openly opposed Archabbot Aurelius. He nevertheless took a hard line with respect to at least one aspect of the China mission. The Catholic University of Peking, he believed, had to be weaned from financial dependence on the motherhouse in Pennsylvania as soon as possible. In his opinion the mission was not viable as long as it continued to require large infusions of cash and men from Saint Vincent.

In the weeks following the death of Archabbot Aurelius, the monks of Saint Vincent learned of the loan he had made in New York the previous

November. Father Felix Fellner, prior and administrator pro tempore of the archabbey, wrote M. D. Currie of National City Bank on March 8 to inquire about the conditions and liability of the loan and to advise the bank that after a new archabbot was elected, the Holy See would name a new chancellor with full authority to negotiate repayment.[3] When officials at the National City Bank expressed their view that the archabbey itself was responsible for the loan, Fellner responded that "Archabbot Aurelius Stehle had no authority from the [monastic chapter] to borrow money" in the name of Saint Vincent.[4]

Immediately after his election in April, Archabbot Alfred sent Father Victor Lillig to New York "to find out how matters were, to find out just to whom the loan was granted," and to discover whether or not Archabbot Aurelius had mortgaged any of the archabbey's property in order to secure the loan. In his meeting with M. D. Currie, Father Victor learned to his relief that there was no mortgage involved in the transaction. He also learned, to his surprise, that "there was no note . . . or other legal document evidencing the loan" itself. In testimony given at the civil trial seven years later, Lillig recalled the exchange between himself and Currie:

> "Mr. Currie, how is it possible that a bank, an organization of your reputation, international, could grant a single individual who is the president of the Benedictine Society, and Chancellor [appointed by] Rome of the Peking University, such a loan without any evidence of security?" To which question, Mr. Currie replied: "Why, Father Lillig, isn't the whole Catholic Church in back of this project?" and to which Father Lillig rejoined: "Mr. Currie, I cannot answer for the whole Catholic Church, since I am only a single member, but I can and do answer as treasurer of St. Vincent's that St. Vincent Archabbey at no time authorized or gave Archabbot Aurelius permission to take up this loan for the Peking University."[5]

The news that the National City Bank considered Saint Vincent liable for the debt distressed and disconcerted both Archabbot Alfred and the monastic chapter, but the Saint Vincent monks continued to believe they were on solid legal grounds in refusing responsibility for the debt since the chapter had not authorized the loan and in fact had not even known about it until after Archabbot Aurelius's death.[6] At the time of Father Victor's meeting with Mr. Currie in New York, during which the Saint Vincent procurator strongly asserted that the archabbey would not assume responsibility for any loan not authorized by the monastic chapter, a total of $102,100 had been advanced by the bank to the Catholic University of Peking. Subsequently, Fathers Barry O'Toole and Boniface Martin continued to draw money from the credit account set up at National City Bank's

Peking branch. Between May 31 and November 10, 1930, they withdrew an additional $147,900.

It is clear that Archabbot Alfred and the monastic chapter at Saint Vincent considered the Catholic University of Peking as the responsible party because Archabbot Aurelius had borrowed the money in his capacity as papally appointed chancellor of the university and not as archabbot of Saint Vincent. It is equally clear that the National City Bank of New York considered the archabbey ultimately responsible since the Catholic University of Peking was "owned or operated or conducted by [Saint Vincent Archabbey] as a part of its activities."[7] To complicate matters, both Nicholas F. Brady and M. D. Currie died within nine months of Archabbot Aurelius. Thus by the end of 1930 none of the parties directly involved in the loan was still alive, and no formal documents existed to clarify the nature of the transaction. It would take nine years and two law suits to determine the outcome of the dispute.

FU JEN UNIVERSITY: 1930–1933

Meanwhile Archabbot Alfred began to assess the difficulties facing Saint Vincent, not only on account of outstanding loans made on behalf of the China mission (which exclusive of the loan from the National City Bank amounted to nearly two hundred thousand dollars) but also in the light of continuing financial demands on the archabbey in the wake of the stock-market crash and the looming economic depression. On June 25, 1930, two weeks after being blessed as Saint Vincent's fifth archabbot, Koch departed for Rome "to discuss the future of the Catholic University of Peking with Vatican officials."[8] In Rome he met with Cardinals Van Rossum and Francesco Marchetti-Salvaggiani of the Sacred Congregation for the Propagation of the Faith; Cardinal Eugenio Pacelli (later Pope Pius XII), papal secretary of state; and Cardinal Bisleti. He also had a private audience with Pope Pius XI.

Explaining to Roman officials the dire financial straits of the Catholic University of Peking, which required $75,000 a year to operate, he asked for a substantial increase in the Holy See's financial assistance. Cardinal Marchetti-Salvaggiani agreed to increase the Propaganda Fide's yearly subsidy from $15,000 to $25,000, but the archabbot explained that, while generous, this subsidy would cover only a third of the annual cost of the university and that Saint Vincent and the American Cassinese Congregation would find it all but impossible to provide the remaining $50,000 each year. He noted that the economic crisis in America meant that neither

Saint Vincent nor the American Cassinese Congregation as a whole would be able to raise significant sums of money in the foreseeable future.

Cardinal Van Rossum admonished the archabbot that the American monks could not renege on their commitment to China. "[O]therwise it would be a [blemish] for the entire Order," he said. When Cardinal Marchetti-Salvaggiani acknowledged that the University of Peking was "a thorn" for Saint Vincent, Koch replied, "No, it is a crown of thorns"; and when the archabbot explained to Cardinal Bisleti the extent of the financial burden that the Chinese mission imposed upon Saint Vincent, Bisleti responded with a bromide: "Trust in God. A noble work will have difficulties." Even the pope, who was sympathetic, did not offer much help. He listened attentively to Archabbot Alfred's explanation of the financial difficulties confronting the American Benedictines and then advised him to call on the poor and common people for assistance. "The poor are many and generally willing to give," he said. "[This is what] I did when I was archbishop of Milan. We know that the rich are few and often not disposed to give. Therefore organize the people of the parishes and especially the children. The work in China is of the greatest importance and a most noble work indeed."[9]

In the midst of his meetings in Rome, Koch received an urgent telegram from Father Barry O'Toole in Peking that the university needed the one hundred thousand that Archabbot Aurelius, several months before his death, had said the Holy See had promised for the proposed faculty of sacred theology and philosophy in Peking. The archabbot asked officials at the Propaganda Fide about the grant, but no one had ever heard of such a promise. They suggested that he make inquiries at another office, but again he discovered that "no knowledge of any such promise was registered in the records." Someone suggested that perhaps the Holy Father had made the promise personally to Archabbot Aurelius, so Archabbot Alfred sent a letter to Cardinal Pacelli asking whether the office of the Vatican secretary of state had information about such a commitment by His Holiness. Pacelli invited Koch to his office, where he regretfully explained that after searching the archives nothing could be found to confirm the alleged promise. "This left me with the impression that a negative answer would be forthcoming," Koch wrote. The archabbot's impression was later confirmed at his audience with the pope, who blessed the American Benedictines and their work in China but "[made] no definite promise" to provide additional financial support for the university.[10]

Archabbot Alfred returned to the United States in August, shortly after learning that the Holy See had named Father Francis Clougherty, O.S.B., as the new chancellor of the Catholic University of Peking. Clougherty's promotion to the position was in complete accord with the archabbot's own desires. Koch had made it clear during his meetings with officials of the Propaganda Fide that "the chancellorship [was] incompatible with the office of Archabbot of Saint Vincent" because of the heavy responsibilities the archabbot already bore for the monks, students, and other apostolates of Saint Vincent.[11] He was pleased, therefore, that Clougherty, who had served in China for more than ten years (though he had been a Benedictine for only two), was named to the position.

At the university in Peking, meanwhile, the signs of positive progress were everywhere in the fall of 1930. The new university building was nearly finished and would be fully occupied in January. In anticipation of the completion of the building, the academic year began in September with a significant increase in enrollment. A total of 705 students registered for classes, nearly double the number of the previous year. There were 270 undergraduate students, a dramatic rise over the 97 who had registered the previous fall. Two hundred and sixty-nine students were registered in the preparatory or senior middle school, and 166 in the junior middle school. One hundred and fifty-five of the students were Catholics.[12] New faculty members included Father Adrian Stallbaumer of St. Benedict's Abbey, Atchison, Kansas, who taught chemistry; Father Brendan O'Connor, a Benedictine from the Abbey of Fort Augustus in Scotland, who taught physics; Father Genadius Diez of St. Bede's Priory, Manila, who taught European history; Father Franz Feinler, a German secular priest who taught mathematics; Father Carl Hensler, a Pittsburgh diocesan priest who taught sociology and ethics; and Father William O'Donnell, a priest of the Diocese of Cleveland, who taught English. In the course of the year two additional Benedictines arrived from St. Anselm's Abbey, Manchester, New Hampshire, to join the faculty. Father Cuthbert Redmond took charge of the English department, while Father Hubert Sheehan taught biology. In addition, four more clerics—Brothers Nicholas Scoville of Saint Vincent, Edward Chrisman of New Subiaco Abbey (Arkansas), Terence Carroll of St. John's Abbey (Minnesota), and Raphael McGuire of St. Anselm's Priory (Washington, D.C.)—arrived in Peking to complete their theological studies before joining the faculty of Fu Jen University.[13]

In September 1930 six Benedictine sisters from St. Benedict's Convent, St. Joseph, Minnesota, arrived in Peking to establish a women's college at the university. They were Sisters Francetta Vetter, Regia Zens, Ronayne

Gergen, Rachel Loulan, Donalda Terhaar, and Wibora Muehlenbein. The sisters spent their first year in China studying Chinese and giving private lessons as they prepared to establish the women's college. The college (or secondary school) opened in the fall of 1932 with twenty students.[14]

On June 27, 1931, Fu Jen marked a milestone when it held its first commencement exercises. The ceremony was presided over by Chang Chi, president of the university's board of trustees, and the commencement address was delivered by Chou Hsueh-chang, director of education for the municipal government of Peking. Eleven students from the faculty of arts and letters who had successfully completed the four-year undergraduate program received the bachelor of arts degree from Chen Yuan, president of Fu Jen. Three of the graduates had majored in Chinese studies, four in history, and four in English.[15]

The 1931–32 academic year opened with another dramatic increase in enrollment. Slightly more than a thousand students registered for classes in August, a 45 percent rise over the previous year. The Chinese government had granted permanent accreditation to Fu Jen in August, and as a result there had been a large influx of applications for admission. Five hundred and nineteen students were accepted for the undergraduate program; 296 were enrolled in the preparatory or senior middle school, and 202 in the junior middle school. Twenty percent of the students were Catholics.

The organizational structure of the institution had not changed significantly since the reorganization of 1929. Three faculties—arts and letters, sciences, and education—consisting of twelve academic departments continued to make up the university. In the faculty of science, however, the pharmacy department had been eliminated and a new department of fine arts had been added to the faculty of education. Sixty percent of the undergraduates were enrolled in the faculty of arts and letters, 30 percent in the faculty of sciences, and the remaining 10 percent in the faculty of education. In the organizational schema published for 1931–32, the university listed the women's college and the library as constituent divisions of the institution. There were eighty-three members of the faculty, of whom fifteen were American Benedictines (including the six Benedictine sisters) and fifty-two were Chinese laymen. The others were European and American secular priests and laymen, including Dr. Ernest Schierlitz, former librarian of the Bavarian National Library, who was codirector of the Fu Jen University library.[16]

The extent and quality of faculty research also made impressive advances during the period after 1930. At the request of Catholic missionaries in

Mongolia, the university's biology department worked for two years to develop an inexpensive vaccine for typhus. Thousands of people (including about ten missionaries) died of the disease annually. The only available inoculation against it was the costly Weigl vaccine, which was produced only by a long and tedious process. Under the direction of Dr. Stephen Gadjos, a Hungarian biologist, and Dr. Joseph Chang, a Chinese physician, the university's microbiology laboratory prepared a new and inexpensive vaccine to combat the deadly typhus bacterium.[17]

Father Gregory Schramm, head of the psychology department, conducted research in the university's psychology laboratory on the learning patterns of Chinese children, and university registrar and professor of logic Ying Quianli (also known as Ignatius Ying, the son of Vincent Ying Lien-chih) collaborated with Father Barry O'Toole in the writing and publication of a dual-language textbook on Aristotelian logic. Under the editorship of university president Chen Yuan the university press published the *Fu Jen Hsueh-Chih (Fu Jen Sinological Journal),* an English-language journal aimed at introducing the Chinese language, literature, history, philosophy, and arts to the Western world.[18] By 1932 Fu Jen was regarded as one of the top five universities in the city of Peking, and Father James A. Walsh, superior of the Maryknoll mission in China, observed that the university was "a vital step in the progress of the Church in China."[19]

The faculty of sacred theology and philosophy that Archabbot Aurelius proposed to the Propaganda Fide in 1929 was never established at Fu Jen, but a small seminary did come into existence in 1930 when the Benedictine clerics Hugh Wilt and Columban Gross arrived in Peking and needed to complete their theological studies before ordination. Brothers Hugh and Columban were directed in their studies by Prior Ildephonse Brandstetter, Father Francis Clougherty, Father Carl Hensler, and Father Barry O'Toole, who also later taught the clerics Nicholas Scoville, Edward Chrisman, Terence Carroll, and Raphael McGuire. In 1932 Father Basil Stegmann of St. John's Abbey, Minnesota, and Father Donald Murphy of St. Mary's Abbey, Newark, took charge of the seminary, where they taught moral theology, dogmatic theology, and patrology to the Benedictine clerics and a few Chinese seminarians. They were assisted in their work by professor of sacred scripture Father Luigi Polucci, O.F.M.Conv., from the American Franciscan Province of the Immaculate Conception.[20]

The American Benedictines were especially eager to foster vocations to the monastic life among the Chinese, and they were thus delighted when one of the Chinese seminarians who had completed his final year of theology in the small seminary at Fu Jen, Thaddeus Wang, became a postulant for the Order shortly before his ordination in February 1932. Seven months later Aloysius Ching and Joseph Wang, who had recently completed their secondary studies at Fu Jen and entered their first year of university work, were invested with the Benedictine habit as postulants for the Order.[21] Unfortunately the American Benedictines were withdrawn from China before any of these postulants had the opportunity to enter the novitiate.

The progress made by the Benedictines at Fu Jen University between 1927 and 1933 occurred in spite of the political turmoil that vexed the country during the same period. In 1931, in the midst of the Chinese Civil War, the Japanese invaded northern China and in September captured Shenyang, one of the largest cities in the northeast region. Protests sprang up throughout China over the Nationalist government's policy of nonresistance to the Japanese. Thousands of students (including many from Fu Jen) went on the streets of Peking protesting the invasion and the Chinese government's inaction. In December a special delegation of Fu Jen students went to Nanking with other students from Peking to present a petition to Chang Kai-shek and his government to adopt a harder line against the Japanese invasion.[22] The Japanese threat increased in the months ahead, and by April 1933 the inhabitants of Peking expected that their own city would soon be occupied. Father Valentine Koehler, a Saint Vincent monk recently arrived in China, wrote at the beginning of 1933 that "the hard times find us struggling daily to keep going. . . . Regarding the threat of Japanese occupation of the city, the only thing that the people fear is the danger of looting by disorderly forces that would take advantage of the confusion."[23] Though the Japanese occupation of Peking did not occur until after the Benedictines had withdrawn from China, the imminent threat of disorder and war had an unsettling effect upon the university during this most difficult period.

END OF THE CHINA MISSION

In December 1931 Archabbot Alfred wrote to Abbot Ernest Helmstetter of St. Mary's Abbey, Newark, president of the American Cassinese Congregation, that "China is still *mein Sorgenkind* [my problem child]." He informed the abbot president that Prior Ildephonse Brandstetter, without his superior's knowledge or approval, had petitioned Rome to make the American Benedictine monastery in Peking an independent priory. Rome, surprised by the petition because the foundation clearly did not have sufficient funds to maintain itself, had sent an inquiry to Saint Vincent. Now Archabbot Alfred had learned that there was discord between the rector of the university, Father Barry O'Toole, and the prior of the Benedictine community, Father Ildephonse. The apostolic delegate, as the pope's representative, had written that "Prior Ildephonse has made himself impossible" and that he must be removed. Cardinal Van Rossum of the Propaganda Fide concurred and called for a canonical visitation of the Benedictine community in Peking.[24]

The conflict between Prior Ildephonse and Father O'Toole had its roots in misunderstandings about the extent of the jurisdiction of each. As superior of the Benedictine monastery in Peking, Brandstetter held that O'Toole, a Benedictine oblate, was under his authority and that no decisions concerning either the assignment of Benedictine professors or the expenditure of funds for the university should be made without his approval. O'Toole (who would later call Brandstetter "incompetent and treacherous")[25] regarded himself as responsible to the chancellor, Father Francis Clougherty, who supported him in all his actions, and not to Prior Ildephonse. To Brandstetter's distress, the rector continued to make decisions regarding the Benedictine staff and the budget of Fu Jen without consulting him. Moreover O'Toole's affiliation as an oblate with the Benedictine community had become increasingly tenuous.

In May Archabbot Alfred journeyed to Peking for the canonical visitation. He spent two weeks in China investigating conditions at the priory and university, and returned to the United States in August by way of Rome. In Rome he reported to officials at the Sacred Congregation for the Propagation of the Faith that the single most serious obstacle to regular monastic observance at the community in Peking was the lack of a monastery for the monks. The monastic community, which at the time numbered fifteen priests, one subdeacon, three clerics, and two oblates, lived in quarters spread out among the various buildings of Prince Tsai Tao's old palace and in rooms in various parts of the new university. They had plans to construct a suitable monastery when funds became available, but until they did, they found it difficult to live a common monastic life. The archabbot praised Father Ildephonse Brandstetter as *optimus monachus et vir solidae doctrinae ac virtutis* (an excellent monk and a man of solid doctrine and virtue), but said that the prior was unable to govern the monks under the existing very difficult circumstances *(in difficillimis circumstantiis).* Koch told the Holy See that he intended to replace Father Ildephonse as prior as soon as possible. With respect to the university, the archabbot said that the most difficult challenges facing the institution were financial. "On the one hand, the debt is extensive; on the other, the institution lacks adequate means to meet the ordinary operating expenses." He asked for renewed support from the Holy See and help in obtaining greater assistance from the bishops of the United States.[26]

At the twenty-fourth general chapter of the American Cassinese Congregation, held at the end of August 1932 at St. Procopius Abbey, Lisle, Illinois, the archabbot spoke bluntly to the abbots and delegates about the Holy See's disappointment with progress at Fu Jen and about what in his view was the failure of the American Benedictine communities to come to the aid of the university. His view, he said, was one shared by the Roman authorities. He quoted the cardinals of the Propaganda Fide as saying that "it seems as if the zeal of the Benedictines in America has become lukewarm. . . . The whole world is looking at you. A failure would mean a catastrophe to the cause of the Church in China." The cardinals had urged him to "speak again to the Right Reverend Abbots" and promised to "write another letter, pointing out the importance of the China foundation and of its tremendous influence on young China." Such, said the archabbot, "was the expression of the view of the authorities of the Propaganda." If all the abbots shared in the burden, "at least we will have the satisfaction of having tried hard to make the work a success for the honor of God and His Church." But it was clear from his remarks that Archabbot Alfred was far from confident that his efforts and those of the other abbots, no matter how hard they worked, would meet with ultimate success.[27]

In the fall of 1932, upon the recommendation of Abbot Alcuin Deutsch, newly elected president of the American Cassinese Congregation, Koch appointed Father Basil Stegmann, the thirty-nine-year-old prior of St. John's Abbey, to replace Father Ildephonse Brandstetter as prior in Peking. Father Basil, who also taught sacred scripture in the seminary at St. John's, left for the Orient in December, and Archabbot Alfred sent Father Blase Strittmatter from Saint Vincent to St. John's to fill the vacancy on the seminary faculty left by Father Basil's departure. In Peking Stegmann began the difficult task of reforming monastic observance in the priory and reclaiming Benedictine authority over the administration of the university. Unfortunately, he was not in China long enough for his efforts to succeed.

In October 1932 Archabbot Alfred sent a circular letter to the monks of Saint Vincent exhorting them to work harder than ever towards raising funds for Fu Jen University. He noted that Rome had instructed each monastery in the American Cassinese Congregation to raise at least four thousand dollars a year for the China mission, and he directed the Benedictine pastors in the parishes affiliated with Saint Vincent to show a "lively interest in the work" by organizing the sisters, lay teachers, and children in the parochial schools as fund-raisers. He acknowledged that there would be problems. "It is true," he said, "that the depression will, perhaps, prevent us from reaching the desired sum." But he told his monks that it was time "to put aside any prejudice that we may bear against our China foundation. St. Vincent's accepted it and the Holy See confidently hopes that we will do all we can to promote its welfare both temporal and spiritual."[28]

But by December 1932 the financial plight of the university had become desperate. The international value of the American dollar had fallen precipitously and expenses were mounting in Peking. Father Barry O'Toole had returned to the United States in an attempt to raise money from the American bishops, and Father Francis Clougherty, the chancellor, wrote urgently to Abbot Alcuin Deutsch for help. Abbot Alcuin could do nothing. He told Archabbot Alfred that he had not answered Clougherty's cablegram. He was afraid that "there will be a black eye for us with the Holy See, if we fail," but he did not know what to say to Clougherty "except that I have no money."[29]

Koch responded to the abbot president that he had tried and failed to obtain another bank loan. He also faced the problem of growing opposition to the China mission among members of the chapter at Saint Vincent. Even if he were able to find a bank that would agree to lend him money for China, he did not think that the chapter would approve the loan. "This is my personal opinion of our China situation briefly put: Impossible to continue. St. Vincent alone can not do it. Upon the receipt of the first S.O.S. from China for $10,000, I succeeded in getting $1,000 from Abbot Valentine [Kohlbeck of St. Procopius Abbey]—the others could not see their way clear to give because of their own needs. I see myself forced to inform Rome again that I cannot continue. If they want my scalp, let them take it. I am getting tired of prolonging an agony that is very trying to my nerves."[30] What the archabbot did not tell Abbot Alcuin was that two months earlier he had sent a cablegram to Rome acknowledging the inability of Saint Vincent and the American Cassinese Congregation to meet the expenses of the Catholic University of Peking and asking the Holy See to assume financial responsibility for the institution.[31]

Meanwhile Father O'Toole was having a measure of success raising funds from American bishops. In January he wrote from New York that he had raised almost twenty-five thousand dollars from individual bishops who had contributed anywhere from fifty dollars to a thousand dollars. He was now on his way to Rome where he said that if he could "secure Rome's sanction," he had "a good prospect of getting . . . the twenty thousand needed . . . to complete the school year."[32] When he reached Rome, however, he learned that the process was already underway to transfer Fu Jen University from the American Benedictines to another religious order. O'Toole reported that Archabbot Alfred's October cablegram to Rome "virtually throwing back upon the S.C. of the Propaganda responsibility for the University's upkeep" had so "angered the Holy Father and the S.C." that they decided to approve Archbishop Costantini's proposal to replace the Benedictines with priests from the Society of the Divine Word. On March 8, 1933, the father general and the American provincial of the Society of the Divine Word called on O'Toole at the North American College, where he was staying, and asked for information about the Catholic University of Peking. "They got none from me," O'Toole said, "but I received from them the news that the transfer was already a *res acta,* i.e., an accomplished fact."[33]

Father O'Toole immediately wired Abbot Alcuin Deutsch, who was on visitation at St. Bernard's Abbey, Alabama, and urgently called him to Rome. Abbot Alcuin was unable to depart immediately, but on March 22, 1933, he sailed for Italy aboard the S. S. *Europa.* Before his departure he met with Archabbot Alfred at St. Mary's Abbey, Newark, to discuss "the Pros and Cons concerning a change in the administration of the Catholic U. at Peking China." Archabbot Alfred told him that in his opinion the situation was hopeless and expressed his sense of relief that the bitter cup was about to pass from his lips. Koch wrote in his diary that "I did not hesitate to give my view concerning the cooperation of the Abbots in that great work." Abbot Alcuin "admitted that there was no cooperation on the part of the Abbots. And such a lack of conforming our united forces to the project entrusted to us by the Holy See, will accuse us and give us a black eye. Rome seems to be decided to see action. If it fails to save the University we are guilty." The archabbot agreed with Abbot Alcuin that the latter's mission to Rome would be a difficult one.[34]

Six days after the abbot president sailed for Rome, Archabbot Alfred wrote that he had recently learned from Father Basil Stegmann in Peking that Archbishop Costantini himself had left for Rome and that before his departure he had "threatened if the Abbots provide no financial support by the time he gets to Rome, he will take the University out of their hands." For the archabbot it was "the old story: 'If money is not forthcoming, you may go.' It is evident that [Rome's] underlying principle in this procedure is: 'We can help, but we won't.' Certainly an easy statement to make—but what about the present conditions? Are they really unknown to the men in authority?" Koch was exasperated not only by the attitude of the apostolic delegate and the cardinals in Rome but also by the independent actions of O'Toole and Clougherty. The rector and chancellor were embarked upon their own crusade to save the university, and they continued to refuse to acknowledge the authority of the Benedictine prior in Peking to make final decisions concerning the expenditure of funds. The archabbot wrote:

> If we cannot come to an understanding, that the Religious superior has rights, and that the independence in spending money must cease, we never can achieve anything. There ever will be friction, that must naturally affect the development of the Institution. It seems that this [question] never enters the minds of some people—*Who pays the bills[?]*
>
> I have been informed that the Chancellor bought property for the Sisters without asking permission. I am afraid that Father Clougherty heaps debts upon debts—*who will be responsible for them?* I certainly decline to accept them. Can I take from him the Power of Attorney, or are there objections on the part of the Roman appointment? I feel that we must act; otherwise the burden of debts will ruin the University.[35]

But by now the die had been cast, and there remained no hope of saving the university for the American Benedictines. On April 12 Abbot Alcuin wrote Archabbot Alfred that "the University of Peking is no more for St. Vincent's and the American Benedictines. While the last formal step withdrawing it from us has not been taken, it may be regarded as settled that we lose it and the S.V.D.'s get it." Abbot Alcuin explained that when he arrived in Rome, the cardinals had asked him, as president of the American Cassinese Congregation, to guarantee that the American Benedictines would provide the necessary funds to sustain the university. This was something, he said, that he had no authority to do. As a result the Propaganda Fide decided to turn the institution over to the Society of the Divine Word. "I have not yet had an audience with the Holy Father, but expect it by the middle of next week. I shall then leave for home."[36]

Abbot Alcuin never revealed the details of his audience with Pope Pius XI, though in later years he said that it was the most difficult thing he had ever had to do. The pope was severe and said in the course of the interview that the Benedictines were indeed an "Order without order."[37] On his way back to Minnesota the abbot president stopped in Greensburg, Pennsylvania, to meet briefly with Archabbot Alfred before catching the evening train for Chicago. Koch noted in his diary that Abbot Alcuin reported that "the Holy Father was not too friendly" and that Deutsch's attempts to explain the reasons for the Benedictine failure in China were met with the pope's rebuffs. Archbishop Salotti, secretary of the Propaganda Fide "was not smiling either" and told Abbot Alcuin that "the loan of $250,000 [from the National City Bank of New York] should be a debt of St. Vincent." Archabbot Alfred's response upon hearing Salotti's opinion was: "How generous! We give the property over to SVD and then pay the debts besides; they get a property valued [at] half a million and we have the pleasure of paying besides a quarter million of dollars. As long as I have charge of the affairs, no dealing of that kind will take place. I have the law on my side."[38] Unfortunately, within six years both Rome and the American courts would decide otherwise.

On May 10, 1933, Abbot Alcuin wrote the abbots of the American Cassinese Congregation informing them of the Roman decision. "Whether my setting forth of the financial condition of our abbeys and of our country convinced the Holy See that we did all in our power to finance the University, I do not know," he said. But he had his misgivings.

> The Holy See did not doubt the financial condition of our abbeys nor that of our country. But it did doubt that we made a serious effort at cooperative organization. How difficult it was for me to prove the contrary, you can readily imagine. I am afraid that I did not succeed fully with Msgr. Costantini, the Apostolic Delegate to China, nor with Msgr. Salotti, the Secretary of the Propaganda. Cardinal Fumasoni was more sympathetic. The Holy Father, in the audience which he granted me, lamented our failure. It was painfully evident that he was not so friendly as in the audience granted me four years ago. He did not permit me to make any explanations, but interrupted every attempt. Yet he said no unfriendly word, but gave our whole Congregation his blessing. After the audience I wrote him a letter and sent with it a Promemoria setting forth briefly the history of the University and showing that the reasons for our failure to do more lay rather in the manner of its development and in unfavorable conditions than in our lack of good-will.[39]

Meanwhile Archabbot Alfred began the unhappy work of closing down the Benedictine mission in China. Rome had given instructions that the American monks were to remain at the university until the end of the academic term. Until the Society of the Divine Word formally took control of the institution, the Propaganda Fide agreed to cover the expenses of the university, but the cardinals would give nothing for the upkeep of the Benedictine community in Peking, though Archbishop Costantini indicated his desire that the Benedictines maintain a monastic community in China. Archabbot Alfred was "more than hesitant" to acquiesce to the archbishop's desire. "At present," he wrote, "I have enough of China."[40] In June he cabled his monks to return home and told the other abbots who had men in China that they should do the same.[41]

Only Father Ildephonse Brandstetter, the first Saint Vincent monk to go to China in 1924, and Father Francis Clougherty, who had worked in China since the early 1920s and who had pronounced vows as a Benedictine in 1928, expressed a desire to remain on the mission. They had been asked by Bishop Joseph Tacconi of Kaifeng to work in his vicariate, and Archabbot Alfred readily granted them permission to do so.[42] Eventually joined by Father Oswald Baker, another of the Saint Vincent monks who had served in Peking, Fathers Ildephonse and Francis established a Benedictine priory in Kaifeng in December 1934. Archabbot Alfred did not believe the three monks were "fully competent" to found an independent priory in China, and the Saint Vincent chapter refused to support their efforts.[43] In 1936, however, St. Procopius Abbey of Lisle, Illinois, agreed to adopt the monastery as a dependent priory. The three Saint Vincent monks transferred their vows to St. Procopius and were joined by three monks from that abbey.[44] Later Father Sylvester Healy, another of the diocesan priests who had become a Benedictine in Peking, returned to China and was named prior of the community in Kaifeng.

Together with the Benedictine sisters from St. Benedict's Convent, St. Joseph, Minnesota, who had gone to Peking in 1930 and who likewise opted to remain in China, the American monks served the Catholics of Kaifeng until 1941. The sisters operated a medical dispensary and gave catechetical instructions while the priests taught at the Kwang Fu Middle School. In the course of their labors they endured a student riot, an earthquake, the Japanese occupation of Kaifeng, and the serious illness of several of the monks. After the Japanese attack on Pearl Harbor, the American Benedictine sisters and priests were interned by the Japanese army in Kaifeng and remained in custody until 1943. The Communist takeover of China in 1949 frustrated further efforts to establish a permanent American Benedictine foundation on the mainland. The former Saint Vincent monks—Oswald Baker, Francis Clougherty, and Sylvester Healy—returned to the United States about 1948. Father Ildephonse Brandstetter, however, did not join them. The pioneer American Benedictine in China had died on December 30, 1945, shortly after his liberation from a Japanese concentration camp. He was seventy-five years old and had devoted more than twenty years of his life to the Benedictine mission in China. His confreres buried him in Peking, among the people and culture he had come to serve and whom he had grown to honor and to love.[45]

Reflecting upon the causes of the failure of the Benedictine mission to China of the 1920s and 1930s, Father Francis Clougherty wrote Father Felix Fellner, prior at Saint Vincent, that the mission was "too much for us."

> [I]t was from the very beginning built on air and borrowed money, and it was maintained on the same diet for the most part. Since the depreciation of the American Dollar, the cost of operation today is well-nigh $200,000 U.S. dollars. The S.V.D. Fathers, due to the fall in the American dollar will have to raise more than thrice the $50,000 which they presumed would be the very maximum yearly expenditure. This is why I say we should be thankful to be relieved of the heavy responsibility, especially at this time. Had the Abbeys promised and produced the fifty thousand per annum as suggested, it would not be sufficient for more than one-third of the year—and where would the remainder come from? It is ridiculous to hear some of our younger men saying how easy it would have been to maintain the University. Even with the best of will it would have been impossible to get through this year had we continued up till now. If the U.S. dollar reaches par with the Chinese dollar then Techny [Illinois, the American headquarters of the Society of the Divine Word] must produce very nearly half a million American dollars annually! And this sum excludes expansion and new dormitory space which must be provided before one year is passed.[46]

Clougherty's assessment of the financial burden of the Catholic University of Peking upon Saint Vincent was accurate. A financial report that Father Oswald Baker, treasurer of the university, sent to the archabbey in June 1933 revealed the full extent of Saint Vincent's investment, and subsequent loss, in China. According to Baker's report, the cost of operating the university between February 1, 1925, and June 1, 1933, was $1.5 million.[47] Almost $600,000 of this amount came from American donors, income from the university, and the annual subsidy from the Holy See. (The Holy See provided a little less than $200,000 between 1925 and 1933.) The rest of the money came from Saint Vincent and the other monasteries of the American Cassinese Congregation.

THE THORNTON CASE

The money from the American Benedictines was raised principally through loans made by Archabbot Aurelius, but also included direct grants from Saint Vincent and the other American abbeys and salary reimbursements of Benedictine faculty members at Fu Jen. Saint Vincent's contribution was over $800,000, and by the end of 1933 the archabbey's China debt was still in excess of $400,000. Archabbot Alfred and the monastic chapter refused to acknowledge the portion of this debt that had been contracted by Archabbot Aurelius with the National City Bank of New York ($250,000). On the remainder of the debt (approximately $175,000), however, the community was being assessed interest at rates between 7 and 11 percent, which at the height of the Depression the archabbey was hard-pressed to pay. Archabbot Alfred found himself overwhelmed by the financial burden. "I am more than disgusted with this money question," he wrote, "and yet I dare not say anything in public because of the good name of [Archabbot Aurelius]."[48]

One debt that was particularly galling to Koch was owed to Miss Helen J. Thornton, a Pittsburgh resident who in 1925 had given twenty-five thousand dollars to Archabbot Aurelius for scholarships to educate Benedictine students for the priesthood and for Masses to be said for her deceased relatives. Miss Thornton's bequest was made in the form of an annuity investment. Archabbot Aurelius agreed to pay her 5 percent interest annually on the twenty-five thousand dollars until her death, at which time the principal would revert to the archabbey for the educational and spiritual purposes set forth in her bequest.[49]

The Thornton bequest came to Saint Vincent at the time when the community was attempting to raise money for the China mission, and Archabbot Aurelius applied the $25,000 to that purpose, orally instructing the archabbey procurator, Father Victor Lillig, to pay Miss Thornton $1,250 a year in semiannual installments until her death. These payments were regularly made for six years, but in January 1932, after his predecessor's death, Archabbot Alfred ceased to authorize payments based upon his view that because the monastery chapter had never authorized the agreement between Archabbot Aurelius and Helen Thornton, it was invalid. In May 1932 Miss Thornton wrote Archabbot Alfred revoking her bequest and demanding the return of the $25,000 she had given Archabbot Aurelius. When the archabbot refused to reimburse her, she brought suit against him and the Saint Vincent chapter in the Court of Common Pleas of Westmoreland County, Pennsylvania.[50]

The case dragged on for almost two years. In May 1934 the court ordered Saint Vincent to repay the principal to Miss Thornton, together with two years' interest plus court costs, a total of more than $30,000.[51] The Saint Vincent chapter appealed the decision and eventually came to an agreement with Miss Thornton that rather than repay her the $25,000, the archabbey would continue to pay her $1,250 a year until her death. The original $25,000 had already been invested (and lost) in China; therefore, in order to meet the annual payments to Miss Thornton, the community established a $25,000 trust fund by mortgaging part of its farm lands.[52] Payments continued until Miss Thornton's death in 1973 at the age of 89. In the end it was estimated that Saint Vincent paid more than $50,000 for this unusual and controversial bequest.[53]

ST. EMMA INDUSTRIAL AND AGRICULTURAL INSTITUTE

Though the China mission occupied most of the attention and resources of the archabbey between 1927 and 1933, it was not the only new apostolate accepted by the Saint Vincent chapter during the period. Another was St. Emma Industrial and Agricultural Institute in Rock Castle, Virginia, a boarding school for African American boys founded by the Drexel family of Philadelphia. This new work began when Archabbot Aurelius received a letter from John J. Sullivan, a member of the board of directors of St. Emma's, inviting the Benedictines to send two priests to serve as chaplains for the boy's institute as well as for the nearby St. Francis de Sales Academy for African American girls.[54] Recognizing the offer as an excellent opportunity for Saint Vincent to contribute once again to the American Church's educational work among African Americans (as the community had done in the 1870s and 1880s at St. Benedict's Industrial School, Skidaway Island, Georgia), the monastic chapter accepted the invitation in April 1929 by an overwhelmingly affirmative vote of twenty-eight to two. A year later the chapter agreed to take over the administration of the boys' school as well.[55]

The St. Emma Industrial and Agricultural Institute was founded in 1895 by Philadelphia philanthropist Louise Drexel Morrell, stepsister of Mother Katharine Drexel, founder of the American religious congregation, the Sisters of the Blessed Sacrament for Indians and Colored People. After the death of their wealthy father, Francis A. Drexel, both Drexel sisters devoted their lives and fortunes to supporting Catholic educational and missionary work among African Americans and Native Americans. In 1894 Louise Drexel Morrell and her husband, Colonel Edward Morrell, purchased Belmead, a sixteen-hundred-acre estate on the James River, forty miles northwest of Richmond, and turned the buildings into a trade and agricultural school which she named in memory of her mother, Emma Bouvier Drexel. Five years later, Mother Katharine Drexel established St. Francis de Sales Academy for girls on a nearby estate, placing it under the direction of the Sisters of the Blessed Sacrament. From 1895 to 1924 St. Emma's was under the direction of the Christian Brothers, who were followed by a group of Catholic laymen before the Benedictines arrived in 1929.[56]

The first Benedictines to go to Belmead were Father Placidus Rattenberger, who since his return from China had been stationed in Chicago, and Father Benno Brink, professor of art and student chaplain at Saint

Vincent College. Rattenberger became dean of the school and pastor of the local Catholic congregation, while Brink became chaplain at both St. Emma's and St. Francis de Sales Academy and also athletic director at St. Emma's. That summer Father Frederick Strittmatter joined them and became director of the industrial and agricultural departments at St. Emma's. In the fall Father Frederick's brother, Father Denis Strittmatter, joined the staff as well and took over responsibility for teaching "trade mathematics."[57]

In addition to the four Benedictines, twenty-five lay instructors of English, mathematics, social sciences, music, trades, and agriculture taught a hundred young men, most of them boarders. The trades offered at the institute included auto mechanics, baking, cooking, blacksmithing, ironworking, carpentry, electricity, masonry, plastering, painting, plumbing, steam fitting, shoemaking, tailoring, upholstering, and woodworking; while agricultural subjects included animal husbandry, dairying, stock breeding, and horticulture. In addition, all the students were enrolled in the cadet corps which was under the supervision of a U.S. Army officer. The purpose of the institution was "to give to young colored men a thorough religious and secular education, enabling them also to acquire a technical training in modern scientific methods of agriculture, or in such mechanical trades as they may elect."[58]

Later, the Benedictine staff expanded to nine priests. Among the other monks from Saint Vincent who served at Belmead were Fathers Casimir Thomas, Harold Phillips, Constantine Zech, Donald Haggerty, Innocent Farrell, Werner Conwell, and Ermin Smith.

A unique feature of the relationship between Belmead and Saint Vincent was that St. Emma's Institute (later St. Emma's Military Academy) was staffed by the Benedictines but not owned by them. An independent board of directors—including Louise Drexel Morrell and Mother Katharine Drexel—held title to the institution's property and set policy for it. This was the first time since Boniface Wimmer sent monks to Canada in 1862 to take over the administration of Assumption College for the Bishop of Sandwich, Ontario, that the Saint Vincent chapter had accepted charge of a school for which it did not hold the property title and did not control the policy. The monks of Saint Vincent had always regarded their schools as potential nuclei for independent priories or abbeys, and in order for an independent monastery to be established, the property on which it and its educational apostolate were founded had to be legally held in the name of the monastic community. In the case of the St. Emma Industrial and Agricultural Institute, the Benedictines agreed to operate the institution as contract employees of the board of directors. It was not intended that the small monastic community at Belmead, which over the next eighteen years never numbered more than six monks, would ever become an independent priory. It is a measure of Saint Vincent's commitment to the work of educating African American boys that the monastic chapter agreed to these unusual conditions.

The monks of Saint Vincent continued to administer and teach at Belmead until 1947, when the Holy Spirit Fathers of Pittsburgh took over operation of the school. During the Benedictine period the school's enrollment grew to over three hundred students, and under the direction of Fathers Frederick and Denis Strittmatter the educational program increasingly emphasized academic subjects. During the Second World War more than two hundred Belmead graduates served in the armed forces, drawing on the military training they had received at St. Emma's to become leaders in their respective units.[59] One graduate, William Lane, entered Saint Vincent Seminary where he completed his theological studies before being ordained at St. Joseph's Cathedral, Wheeling, West Virginia, in 1933. He later went to work in the Diocese of Port-of-Spain, Trinidad. Lane was the ninth African American priest ordained in the United States and the first to receive his education at Saint Vincent.[60]

Saint Vincent monks continued to staff Belmead through the Depression and the Second World War. By 1945 the school had changed its name to the St. Emma Military Academy and was described in its promotional literature as "an academic, agricultural, military, and trade school for colored youth in charge of the Benedictine Fathers." The school now offered young black men "the opportunity of acquiring Military training, a Senior High School education and at the same time of receiving practical instruction in a mechanical trade, or of making a study of modern scientific methods of agriculture." The annual cost of tuition, board, and fees in 1945–47 was four hundred dollars, and scholarships were provided for those who could not afford to pay the entire cost.[61]

In 1945 the board of trustees proposed a new long-term agreement (of fifty to a hundred years) with the chapter at Saint Vincent under which the Benedictines would assume full financial responsibility for the operation of St. Emma's. The income from the institution's endowment of $890,000 would be turned over to the archabbey, though the endowment itself and the institution's real estate would remain in the hands of the board of trustees.[62] After consulting with his council of seniors, Archabbot Alfred responded to the trustees that Saint Vincent was not prepared to accept the offer. Until now any shortfall between the income generated by the endowment and the annual expenses of the institution had been made up by a yearly contribution from Louise Drexel Morrell. As Mrs. Morrell's health became increasingly impaired (she died on November 5, 1945), the board proposed that under the new agreement Saint Vincent would provide funds to cover the annual deficit of St. Emma's, estimated at about $50,000. The monastic chapter was not prepared to accept this responsibility even if the endowment and property at Belmead were vested in the Benedictine Society of Westmoreland County.[63] Bitter memories of the China mission and what happened there when the community accepted financial responsibilities that it was unable to meet convinced the capitulars that they should not take on any new commitment whose future cost was unknown. Archabbot Alfred wrote bluntly to Father Denis Strittmatter, now director of St. Emma's, that the "Chapter certainly will not accept the Belmead proposition unless we see our way clear in financial matters."[64]

Negotiations dragged on for more than a year, but in the end the monastic chapter decided that it could not "assume any additional charities" and was therefore unable to underwrite the cost of operating the school in Virginia.[65] Early in 1947 Archabbot Alfred informed the board that Saint Vincent would not renew its contract, and in June he recalled the Benedictines at St. Emma's to the archabbey. St. Emma's was turned over to the priests of the Congregation of the Holy Spirit who staffed the institution until it was closed for good in 1972.[66]

THE COLLEGE DURING THE DEPRESSION

Surprisingly, there was an increase in enrollment at Saint Vincent College during the Depression, and the basic annual costs for attending the college remained stable (at $225 for tuition and $300 for room and board) throughout the 1930s. The decade began with an enrollment of 222 students in 1930 and ended in 1939 with a record enrollment of 281 undergraduates. With the exception of slight declines in 1931 and 1933, the increase in enrollment was steady throughout the period. Obviously the cost of education at Saint Vincent was within the range of a middle-class family's financial resources, despite the economic crisis that gripped the nation. Almost thirty scholarships, endowed by alumni and the Benedictine community, were available for "poor and deserving boys."[67]

One result of growing enrollment was an increased need for student housing. The college administration drew up plans for construction of a new dormitory, a dining hall, and a gymnasium, and in June 1930 the Saint

Vincent Alumni Association contributed $52,000 to the building fund. This money was in addition to $26,000 the association had raised as an endowment for scholarships and $66,000 it had contributed to the fund for construction of Lake Saint Vincent on farmland north of the campus. (The fourteen-acre lake had been completed in 1924 and in addition to supplying water to the campus, served as a recreation area for students and faculty members who used it for swimming and ice-skating. The scholarship endowment supplied money for two full scholarships to needy students each year.)[68] The death of Archabbot Aurelius, the Depression, the enormous debt Saint Vincent faced on account of the Catholic University of Peking, and finally the Second World War prevented the college from proceeding with its building plans until the 1950s. The money from the Alumni Association was used to build a convent for the Benedictine Sisters who arrived from Bavaria in 1931 to work in the kitchens of the monastery and college, and a football stadium constructed in 1936. In the meantime, students were squeezed into existing facilities. The college library was turned into a dormitory and the books consolidated with those of the prep school library and moved to another location.[69]

In 1930 Father Bonaventure Reithmeier replaced Father Alcuin Tasch as dean of the college, serving in the position through most of the Depression period. Father Alcuin became registrar and remained intimately involved in promoting the academic development of the college, overseeing the growth of the extension campuses and the night school (see below), introducing a thesis requirement for the bachelor's degree, and creating a faculty advising system for students. As dean, Father Bonaventure oversaw the development of a master of arts program in classics, philosophy, sacred scripture, and theology; fostered the development of the college library, including the creation of an interlibrary loan program with Carnegie Library in Pittsburgh, the state library in Harrisburg, and the libraries of the University of Pittsburgh and the Catholic University of America; and introduced the bachelor of fine arts in music as well as bachelor of science majors in accounting, economics, finance, and business administration.[70]

At the end of 1932 the college learned that its bid to obtain accreditation from the New York Board of Regents had been successful. Father Alcuin Tasch had been the driving force behind the application for recognition by "one of the highest accrediting associations in the country." The most important result of this accreditation was that holders of bachelor's degrees from Saint Vincent were now recognized as eligible for admission to any graduate or professional school in the state of New York.[71] In addition to the New York Board of Regents and the Middle States Association of Colleges and Secondary Institutions, the college was now also accredited by the National Catholic Educational Association, the College and University Council of Pennsylvania, the American Council on Education, and the Association of American Colleges.[72]

The effort to receive wider recognition by accrediting agencies as well as to enlarge the educational opportunities for students by introducing new academic programs led the college administration in the 1930s to begin hiring more lay professors than ever before. Since the 1920s laymen had directed the athletic program at Saint Vincent. Clement Crowe and Eugene Edwards, graduates of Notre Dame and former football players under Knute Rochne at the premier Catholic university in the country, were brought in to develop varsity football and basketball programs. By the mid-1930s laymen were teaching courses in chemistry, psychology, education, business administration, and music at the college. Among them were Harvard graduate James Underwood and University of Pittsburgh graduate Raymond Kent, both of whom taught business administration; Latrobe attorneys Regis Mahady and Paul Mahady, who taught business law, history, economics, and political science; and Daniel Patrick Nolan, a Ph.D. from Notre Dame, who taught chemistry. Still, the majority of the college faculty were Benedictines. In 1932 the faculty numbered forty professors, of whom twenty-eight were monks. As the Depression deepened and the college looked for ways to cut costs, the faculty became smaller and the ratio of Benedictine to lay members widened. By 1935 there were thirty-five professors, of whom only five were laymen.[73] A precedent had been established, however, and when economic times became better, there was a dramatic increase in the number of lay faculty members in the college.

Despite the energetic efforts of the college administration to raise academic standards during the period, moral development continued to be the chief goal of the educational program. The college catalogue stated unequivocally that at Saint Vincent "the formation of character is of more importance than the acquisition of knowledge, because for the well-being of the individual and of society, conduct is more important than learning." Under the heading "Character Training" the catalogue went on to say that "[c]haracter, the foundation of conduct, does not grow noble and strong spontaneously. It must be trained. St. Vincent helps the young man to establish the strong convictions and sound habits upon which character and correct moral habits are built. This is done through Religion, which is not merely a course in the curriculum but is made a guiding influence in every-day college life. Every encouragement is given the students to attend Mass daily and approach the Sacraments frequently."[74]

Courses in religion continued to be a required part of the curriculum for Catholic students, who formed the overwhelming majority of the student body at Saint Vincent during the 1930s. Students took a religion course in each of the eight semesters of their undergraduate program. The courses included "The Catholic Moral Ideal," which stressed that "Religion is the basis of all morality"; "The Motives and Means of the Catholic Life," a study of the fundamental dogmas of the Catholic Religion focusing on the relationship of Catholic dogma to moral principles; "Christ and His Church," which examined the "governing function of the Catholic Church" and provided a brief survey of the Church's "positive legislation" and her relationship to the modern state; and "Life-Problems of the Catholic Layman," which dealt with "some of the practical problems that every college graduate will meet and must solve," including "faith and broad-mindedness," "Catholic marriage and its defense," and "character building [and] progress in virtue."[75]

Contemporary social problems became an important area of discussion and academic study at Saint Vincent during the Depression, and the sociology department offered several courses that focused on some of the burning issues of the day. A three-credit course in "social problems," for example, examined the "causes of industrial unrest as related to distribution of wealth," as well as the ethical approach to the distribution of wealth and the "moral defects of the present system." A course in "labor problems" was a survey of the conditions that led to the rise and development of trade unions in the United States and England. In this course students studied the cause and the factors involved in modern labor problems, collective bargaining, and the rights of workers.[76] The sociology courses were taught by Fathers Augustine Minkel, Gervase Chutis, and Ernest Gensheimer.

The Catholic Worker movement, founded in 1932 by Dorothy Day and Peter Maurin, attracted much interest among the students at Saint Vincent during the 1930s.[77] In the spring of 1937 the *St. Vincent Journal* sent editor Nicholas J. Campbell, a senior at the college (who later, in his professional life, would become president of Standard Oil Company), to New York to report on the phenomenon, and in May he published a lengthy article in the *Journal* explaining the work of the movement to the Saint Vincent community. Though Dorothy Day was unavailable to meet with Campbell because she was in the South working among sharecroppers at the time, he conducted a lengthy interview with Maurin, whom he described as "a short, thick-set man, rather roughly dressed, and resembling a typical ex-prizefighter. . . . The reactionary person would call him a radical, but would soon find that he was anything but a Communist as we understand the term." Maurin explained that the Catholic Worker movement opposed the economic philosophy that prevailed in America. "Listen to our every-day conversation," he said. "[We use the terms] 'law of supply and demand, the almighty dollar, margin of profit' [and we ask ourselves] 'How much can I make today?'" The Catholic Worker believed, however, that the solution to economic problems was "a return to the Sermon on the Mount," though Maurin admitted that "present indications are that the way back will be a long, tedious one." On being asked about the movement's pacifist principles, Maurin said, "We object to all wars." And when Campbell interrupted ("But a just war . . . ?"), Maurin said, "In modern international relations, a just war can hardly be possible. In theory, of course, there is such a thing as a just war. Modern statesmanship is built on lies, and in view of this, it is hard to conceive a situation in which the one side or the other is not to blame."

Campbell explained to readers of the *Journal* that while the Catholic Workers called themselves "Catholic Communists," their communism was a socialism founded upon Catholic principles. "Their community life is basically the same as that of the Benedictines here at St. Vincent," he said. "They are opposed to the rugged individualism of capitalism and the collectivism of Communism. The Works of Mercy are put into practice by this group in every activity they undertake, whether it be in the establishment of a cooperative, the feeding of the hungry, or the clothing of the naked." Pointing out that much criticism had been leveled against the Catholic Workers by clergy and laity alike, Campbell said that they had the strong support of such Catholic leaders as Cardinal Patrick J. Hayes of New York, social activist Monsignor John Ryan, Cardinal George Mundelein of Chicago, and Bishop Hugh Boyle of Pittsburgh, the latter two of whom were Saint Vincent alumni. He concluded his highly positive report by saying that the people who made up the Catholic Worker movement "are often called extremists. If by extremists we mean they are people who *practice* the Works of Mercy as well as preaching and believing in them, it is true. Again, the *Catholic Worker* does not attempt to create a political system based upon their principles. They are merely trying to decrease the gap between avowed ideals and actual practice. They are filling a need—and doing a very fine job."[78]

Racial justice, which was the subject of articles in the college journal as early as 1893,[79] was also a topic that generated discussion during the period. In 1936 several students from the St. Emma Industrial and Agricultural Institute sought admission to the college. The matter came before the monastic chapter, where Father Benno Brink presented the case for admission of students regardless of race and won the chapter's unanimous approval of the motion that Saint Vincent College "shall . . . continue its past policy of not restricting the admission of Negroes for the institution."[80] In the fall of 1936 seven African American students from Saint Emma's entered the freshman class.

When Father Bonaventure Reithmeier stepped down in 1938, Father Maurice Costello became dean. A thirty-eight-year-old native of Lancaster, Pennsylvania, Father Maurice had entered the monastery in 1921, and after ordination in 1928 had studied psychology at Columbia University. He had served as prefect and student chaplain and had taught psychology in the college for more than a decade before being named dean. Father Harold Phillips, who held a Ph.D. in psychology from Johns Hopkins University, was named to the new position of dean of men that same year, while Father Alcuin Tasch continued to hold the positions of registrar, director of vocational guidance, and director of the extension program. This was a time when many of the younger priests of the archabbey who had gone out to graduate school returned to join the college faculty. China veteran Father Hugh Wilt, who had completed graduate studies at Columbia University, returned in 1938 as professor of history. Other Benedictines recently returned from graduate school included Father Colman Lillig, professor of accounting and statistics; Father Bertin Emling, professor of chemistry; Father Maximilian Duman, professor of botany and biology; and Father Eric McCormack, professor of psychology and music. Father Camillus Long was named college chaplain to replace Father Maurice Costello, and Father Valentine Koehler, another China veteran, began his second year as college librarian. Father Vitus Kriegel had completed his Ll.B. at Catholic University the previous year and now taught courses in constitutional law, social legislation, and business law in the social science department. In addition, Father Blase Strittmatter, who held a doctorate in philosophy from the Collegio di Sant' Anselmo in Rome, was assigned to teach in the seminary.[81]

EXTENSION COURSES AND NIGHT CLASSES

In a successful effort to boost enrollment and generate additional income, the college offered extension courses in Erie, Pittsburgh, and St.

Marys, Pennsylvania, during the Depression and in 1932 began evening classes at the main campus in Latrobe. (Students who participated in these courses were not counted among the regular enrollees of the college but were rather considered special students.)

The extension program in Erie was established in 1925 as Cathedral College, a project of Father Joseph J. Wehrle, superintendent of schools in the Diocese of Erie and a 1912 graduate of Saint Vincent College. Cathedral College functioned under the authority of the state charter granted to Saint Vincent in 1870, and academic credit was granted by the Benedictine college, though the faculty consisted of priests and laymen of the Diocese of Erie under the leadership of Father Wehrle, who acted as dean. Cathedral College, Erie, was a fully functioning junior (two-year) college offering programs in the arts and sciences, business administration and commerce, teacher training, and preprofessional subjects to "young men, high school graduates, anxious for higher education under Catholic auspices but unable to realize their aim in schools away from home because of insufficient means."[82] At its height, the Erie extension course had about sixty-five students. In 1941 the college's program in Erie became independent of Saint Vincent when the Diocese of Erie established Gannon College.[83]

A much larger extension program existed in the 1930s in St. Marys, Pennsylvania. The Saint Vincent branch campus in St. Marys offered a two-year college program to about 120 students a year, including some of the Benedictine sisters from St. Joseph's Convent in St. Marys. The program was under the direction of Benedictine Father Timothy Seus and included both Benedictine and lay faculty members. It was conducted four evenings a week at Central Catholic High School. Courses in education, psychology, English, German, Latin, accounting, business law, mathematics, chemistry, and mechanical and engineering drawing were offered. The Speer Carbon Company and the Stackpole Carbon Company provided assistance by making laboratories, scientific instruments, and materials available for the course in chemistry.[84] The St. Marys extension program was in existence only a short time and ended in 1936.[85]

Unlike the extension courses in Erie and St. Marys, which had strong commercial training components, the Pittsburgh extension course was a program designed specifically for diocesan priesthood candidates. Later called the Catholic Institute, it offered the first two years of the classical or liberal arts curriculum of Saint Vincent College, and upon successful completion of the courses students were eligible for admission to the philosophy program of Saint Vincent Seminary. Funded by the Diocese of Pittsburgh, the Catholic Institute, located on Fifth Avenue and Clyde Street, Pittsburgh, was under the general academic supervision of the director of extension programs at Saint Vincent College. The faculty was made up of Christian Brothers of the Diocese of Pittsburgh. The average number of students was around forty.[86] The college's Pittsburgh extension program ended in 1939.

The evening school at Saint Vincent opened in 1932, its purpose "to satisfy the educational needs of many who are handicapped from continuing their studies in the regular day classes at the College." As the Depression worsened, many local students had been forced to withdraw from the college to find work in order to help support their families, and it was primarily for these students that the evening college was begun. Classes were held on Monday and Wednesday evenings and included courses in English, accounting, business administration, mathematics, and "social problems."[87] In addition, the Westmoreland County Chapter of the American Institute of Banking offered a short-lived course in the fundamentals of banking at Saint Vincent beginning in 1932. Local bankers taught these courses, which were supplemented by classes in business law and economics taught by regular members of the college faculty. The courses were "arranged to provide a progressive system of banking education," and were divided into three groups: prestandard, standard, and special graduate. Certificates were awarded to those who completed the courses in each group.[88] The number of students who attended the night school was never greater than forty, but the program did offer an important opportunity to young men who otherwise would have had to withdraw from college altogether.

THE COLLEGE MUSEUM

In 1939 Father Jerome Rupprecht was appointed curator of the college museum. He was assisted by the cleric Alfred Grotzinger and a small staff of students. Established in the time of Boniface Wimmer, the museum was a unique and curious institution. A hodgepodge collection of minerals, plants, insects, stuffed animals, shells, fossils, coins, stamps, antiques, religious objects, art work, historical mementos, and nondescript objects and curios, the museum represented on the one hand the hobbies and scientific interests of many generations of Saint Vincent monks and on the other hand the donations of hundreds of friends and benefactors whose gifts were often put on public display.

The museum, a favorite haunt of students, was open to the public three afternoons a week and at other times by special arrangement. Begun in the

1860s by college president Father Alphonse Heimler (1832–1909), it moved from place to place on campus until in 1917 it was dispersed, its space turned into classrooms for a growing student population. For ten years the contents migrated all over the campus, "trinkets here, trophies there, and museum everywhere."[89] Then in 1927 it found a home on the fifth floor of the "college building" (later called Alfred Hall) where it occupied a space 152 by 58 feet.

The contents of the museum were many and various. The "mineral collection," consisting of rocks, stones, and minerals, was begun by Father Alphonse Heimler as a teaching aid in his science course. Heimler's collection was enhanced in 1863 by a donation from Rudolph Müller of Munich and by another in 1871 from Father George Sterr of Donaustauf, Bavaria, who left his entire collection of more than a thousand specimens of European minerals to the college. The collection also grew through donations from Saint Vincent priests studying abroad and stationed in the American missions. By 1939 the mineral collection had more than three thousand specimens.

The plant (or botanical) collection consisted of twenty thousand specimens of plant life, most of it gathered by Fathers Edwin Pierron (1846–1930) and Dominic Block (1849–91). The botanical collection had been featured in the Centennial Exhibition in Philadelphia in 1876, where it received a blue ribbon.

Hailed as "one of the most complete and most valuable of its kind" in the United States, the insect collection consisted of about fifty thousand specimens mounted according to classification and habitat. The collection was principally the work of Father Jerome Schmitt (1857–1904), professor of science at Saint Vincent College and an internationally renowned entomologist. Father Jerome was the inventor of the famous "Schmitt Box," a sturdy, dermestid-resistant wooden box still used by entomologists to ship specimens.[90] The museum's insect collection also included contributions by Fathers Meinrad Jeggle (1834–1926), Modestus Wirtner (1861–1948), and Edward Wenstrup (1894–1977). The butterfly and moth collection had more than two thousand well-preserved specimens collected by Fathers Jerome Schmitt, Marcellus Rettger (1868–1933), Edward Wenstrup, and Jerome Rupprecht (1896–1982).

The animal and bird collection commenced in the 1870s when Father Cornelius Eckl (1852–94) began to mount animals for display at the college. Before his death Eckl also collected two hundred local specimens of birds. The animal collection featured a bear and two cubs, four foxes, a wolf, squirrels, raccoons, alligators, weasels, and bobcats. The birds included a peacock, six snow owls from Saskatchewan, herons from Florida, two swans, and thirty-five ducks and loons. There was also a collection of reptiles, including a live rattlesnake named Oscar, the pet of Father Jerome Rupprecht. Fathers Edward Andelfinger (1861–1913) and Wenceslaus Sholar (1876–1942) had contributed substantially to the collection of animals and birds.

The museum also housed fossil and shell collections, donated in the nineteenth century by Rudolph Müller and Father George Sterr of Bavaria. The shell collection had been subsequently enhanced by Saint Vincent Father Germain Ball (1860–1918).

A valuable collection of coins and stamps was kept in the museum as well, though because of its value it was not on open display. In the 1880s Archabbot Boniface Krug of Montecassino (1838–1910) donated a large number of ancient Roman coins to Saint Vincent, a nucleus enhanced by additional Roman coins collected by Saint Vincent Father Adalbert Müller (1842–1906) when he was a student and professor in Rome. Other gold, silver, and copper coins, collected over the years by monks of the archabbey, were later added to the numismatic collection. The stamp collection was begun in the 1870s by Father Philip Kretz (1857–1905) and increased by Father Daniel Kaib (1869–1947) and other philatelists among the monks to include more than thirty-five thousand stamps.

The collection of early American antiques included an historically valuable set of furniture from the Johnson family home in Kingston, Pennsylvania. The Indian relics collection included bows and arrows, a wampum belt, clay pipes and utensils, stone hammers, and five hundred projectile points (arrowheads), many of which had been collected on Saint Vincent property. Among the religious objects were the crozier of Boniface Wimmer, three chasubles donated to Saint Vincent by Empress Elizabeth of Austria, the wife of Emperor Franz Josef I, and a set of red vestments for solemn High Mass said to have been made from the coronation gown of King Ludwig I of Bavaria. Hundreds of paintings donated to Saint Vincent in the nineteenth century by King Ludwig I and other Bavarian benefactors were stored in the museum; some were on display. The war trophies exhibit included guns and relics from the Civil War, the Indian Wars, the Spanish-American War, the Boxer Rebellion in China, and World War I. Various other curios capped off the collection, including a model replica of Sportsman's Hall, a banjo made by Ellis Hatfield (of the Hatfield-McCoy feud in West Virginia and Kentucky) while he was serving time in the West

Virginia penitentiary, a mummified hand and foot from the Valley of the Nile, a stone from the reputed tomb of St. Patrick, the first typewriter and microscope used at Saint Vincent College, and relics from the Johnstown Flood of 1889.[91]

VARSITY SPORTS

The 1930s witnessed a dramatic growth in intercollegiate football, basketball, and baseball at Saint Vincent. Among the schools competing with the college's teams were St. Bonaventure College (Olean, New York), Canisius College (Buffalo, New York), St. Francis College (Loretto, Pennsylvania), Indiana State Teachers' College (Indiana, Pennsylvania), St. Thomas College (Scranton, Pennsylvania), Geneva College (Beaver Falls, Pennsylvania), Thiel College (Greenville, Pennsylvania), Slippery Rock State Teachers' College (Slippery Rock, Pennsylvania), and Edinboro State Teachers' College (Edinboro, Pennsylvania). The decade opened in 1930 with winning seasons in basketball (eleven and nine) and baseball (ten and zero) and a losing season in football (four and six).

Baseball was the oldest varsity sport at the college. Popular as an intramural sport as early as the 1860s, it traced its intercollegiate origins back to 1888 when the first Saint Vincent team competed with teams from other schools. Intercollegiate football competition began in 1923, and varsity basketball was introduced in 1928. In November 1930 the Saint Vincent Athletic Association (founded in 1928) awarded 148 baseball varsity letters to former college baseball stars who had played for Saint Vincent between 1888 and 1925. Recipients included Bishop Hugh C. Boyle of Pittsburgh, who was a star pitcher on the 1894 team; Father James Graven of Cresson, Pennsylvania, who played on the 1888 team; Mr. John J. Maloney, who starred in the 1906 season; and Father James Delaney, who played on the undefeated team of 1908. A debate arose at the 1930 athletic association meeting over who was the greatest baseball player in the history of the institution, and the general consensus was that Benedictine Father Cuthbert Gallick (1882–1948), who played and managed the team in the first decade of the century, held that distinction. Gallick, it was said, was "literally rushed by big league offers," including a contract offer from the Chicago White Sox, but he chose to enter the Benedictine novitiate instead.[92] Other baseball stalwarts fondly remembered by alumni included Benedictine Father Jerome ("Smokey Joe") Rupprecht, who pitched for the Saint Vincent team between 1913 and 1915 and later coached the team, off and on, for twenty-five years, and Father Thomas Cawley of the Diocese of Altoona-

Johnstown, who starred on the baseball team at Saint Vincent throughout his days in the prep school, college, and seminary (1914–23).

Toward the end of the 1920s the varsity teams at Saint Vincent adopted the nickname "Bearcats." A note in the college *Journal* in January 1930 said that a new name was needed in order "to get away from the name that papers naturally give to Catholic colleges, namely 'The Saints.'" The *Journal* said that even though there was no such animal as a bearcat, the name was "a combination of the Bear and the Cat, with the fighting qualities of both combined. The Bear with his tenacity and strength, and the Cat for his ripping, tearing, speed, and cunning." An athletic team with those qualifications, it was felt, "was a real team, and every year the St. Vincent teams are coming closer to filling that name in the proper manner."[93] Several years later a letter to the *Journal* pointed out that in fact such a creature as the bearcat did exist in the animal kingdom. A native of Sumatra and Java, the bearcat was a carnivore with a tail like a monkey's. It was said to be "one of the rarest animals ever imported into this country," and three or four specimens existed in zoos in the United States, though the writer did not say where they were located.[94]

In 1932, owing to the high cost of running an intercollegiate sports program and the economic pressures of the Depression, the college's board of trustees voted to suspend varsity football and basketball at Saint Vincent indefinitely. The decision came as a surprise and shock to many. Coach Clement Crowe left the college and accepted a position at Xavier University in Cincinnati. The official reason given for the decision was that there had developed at the college an overemphasis on athletics and the college administration wanted to focus the institution's energies on maintaining the "high academic standards achieved in years past." Students were promised that intramural sports would "receive a new impetus during the coming year" to make up for the loss of intercollegiate athletics.[95]

The announcement spawned immediate public reaction, however, and protests from local fans and alumni forced the board of trustees to reconsider its decision. Perhaps the mildest comment came from the *Greensburg Morning Review,* which said: "Saint Vincent furnished Westmoreland County the only college sports within its borders. It was just beginning to be generally recognized in the district and was building up quite a following. Many will regret the change in policy, although probably realizing that intercollegiate athletics are an expensive proposition and in these times of economic distress few will criticize St. Vincent authorities for trimming their budget."[96] Several weeks after the original announcement was made, the trustees met with a committee of the Latrobe Chamber of Commerce which urged that the college not follow through with its plan to discontinue intercollegiate sports. Pointing out that the sports program at Saint Vincent helped foster economic growth in the area, chamber president Roy C. McKenna promised that local businesses would help provide sufficient financial support to ensure that the program be continued. In the light of the outpouring of public protest and the offer of material help from the chamber of commerce, the board of trustees reversed itself on April 5, and Archabbot Alfred issued a press statement announcing that "business interests in Westmoreland County, the valuable suggestions and proffered material aid of the Latrobe Chamber of Commerce, together with communications of friends and alumni of the institution have brought about the indefinite suspension of the former decision of the Board of Trustees of St. Vincent College." Still, the board insisted that the policy of the college would "continue to be 'Education First,' and above all considerations." Athletic activities, it said, would "continue to be subservient to educational interests."[97]

Not long after the announcement, the Saint Vincent College Athletic Association was reformed, now composed almost entirely of members of the Alumni Association and the Latrobe Chamber of Commerce, and the board of trustees granted it jurisdiction over all athletic activities at the college, "thus removing in great measure athletic matters beyond the pale of the institution." Officers of the newly reorganized association were John J. Maloney of Pittsburgh, president; Victor Stader of Latrobe, vice president; John G. Hulton of Latrobe, secretary; and Father Victor Lillig, O.S.B., treasurer. The athletic association's board of directors was chaired by Roy C. McKenna, head of the chamber of commerce and president of Vanadium-Alloy Steel Company of Latrobe.[98]

The popularity of varsity sports during this period—especially football and baseball—led to a decision to construct a new stadium in 1936. (A sensitive point for years afterwards was that the stadium's construction was never authorized by the monastic chapter but only by college treasurer Father Victor Lillig and college dean Father Alcuin Tasch.) Funded by contributions from the alumni and designed by the Celli architectural firm of Monessen, Pennsylvania, Bearcat Stadium was built on ground west of the quadrangle by the Rust Engineering Company of Pittsburgh. The stadium, with a seating capacity of seventy-five hundred, was used for the first time on September 25, 1936, for the football season opener against Morris-Harvey College of Pittsburgh.[99] Along with the convent for the Benedictine

Sisters, the stadium was the only structure put up at Saint Vincent between 1922 and 1952.

THE SEMINARY

The seminary continued to enjoy high enrollment during the Depression, averaging more than 130 theologians annually throughout the period. About 20 percent each year were Benedictine clerics from Saint Vincent and other American monasteries, and of the diocesan seminarians the vast majority were from the Diocese of Pittsburgh. At the end of 1930 a study conducted by Father Gerard Bridge, secretary of the Saint Vincent Alumni Association, showed that 734 living alumni of the institution had become diocesan or religious order priests serving in sixty-three dioceses of the United States. This number did not include the nearly 200 Benedictine priests of the American Cassinese Congregation who had made all or part of their theological studies at Saint Vincent.[100]

Father Ambrose Kohlbeck, for a decade and a half rector of the seminary, died in August 1931 and was replaced by Father John Nepomucene Hruza. Benedictines who taught on the faculty of the seminary during the 1930s included Fathers John Ujlaki (sacred scripture), Justin Krellner (sacred scripture), Anthony Stromovich (sacred scripture), Rembert Sorg (sacred scripture), Baldwin Ambros (dogmatic theology), Julian Kilger (moral theology and canon law), Wolfgang Frey (moral theology and canon law), Andrew Biberger (patristics), Gilbert Straub (catechetics), Felix Fellner (church history), Otto Wendell (liturgy), Leander Pail (homiletics), Columban Gross (Gregorian chant), Constantine Zech (Gregorian chant), and Dominic Breuss (clerical accounting).[101]

Young monks who had been sent to Rome for philosophical and theological studies, and who had returned to teach in the seminary during the period, included Fathers Blase Strittmatter, Justin Krellner, Oliver Grosselin, Rembert Sorg, Anthony Stromovich, and Paulinus Selle. Father Paulinus, the last Saint Vincent monk to study at the Collegio di Sant' Anselmo before the outbreak of the Second World War, returned to Saint Vincent in 1940 on account of the war and took up duties teaching moral theology in the seminary. That same year Father Matthew Benko went to Catholic University in Washington to begin his studies in canon law.[102] He would later return to teach the subject in the seminary for nearly three decades. In the meantime, Father Wolfgang Frey had completed his doctorate in canon law at Catholic University and had returned to Saint Vincent to assume the dual position of vice rector and prefect of the seminary.

In 1939 seminary scripture professors John Ujlaki and Justin Krellner (who had recently completed his doctoral studies in Rome) joined a team of translators of the American Catholic Biblical Association who were translating the Latin Vulgate into English. The two Saint Vincent monks were assigned the task of translating three books of the Old Testament: I and II Kings and I Paralipomenon (I Chronicles). The aim of the new translation was "to eliminate the archaic expressions of the Douay-Rheims translation of the Latin Vulgate, and to replace the almost meaningless literally translated passages with idiomatic English." In March 1942 the *St. Vincent Journal* reported that Fathers John and Justin had completed their translation and were working on the explanatory notes. The work was painstaking. The two scholars studied the Hebrew, Greek, and Latin texts in making their translation, then compared the draft English version with various modern-language translations, including Italian, German, French, and Hungarian. Once their draft was complete, they submitted it to an editorial board to be further "conned and culled."[103] The American Catholic Biblical Association's translation of the entire Bible was finally published in 1971 and included the work of Ujlaki and Krellner.[104]

Distinguished speakers who came to the seminary during the Depression to address the students included American Catholic Church historian Monsignor Peter J. Guilday of the Catholic University of America; Father Daniel A. Lord, S.J., internationally renowned Catholic author and director of the Sodalities of Our Lady in the United States and Canada, who lectured on Catholic Action and the importance of working among youth in parishes; and well-known Catholic author F. J. Sheed, who spoke on the "Catholic Literary Revival."[105]

Some of the seminary alumni who distinguished themselves during this period included Edward G. Hettinger, a 1928 graduate of the seminary, who was named auxiliary bishop of Columbus, Ohio, in 1941, a position he held until his retirement in 1977. Three years later Monsignor Michael J. Ready, valedictorian of the 1913 college graduating class, was named bishop of Columbus and served as ordinary of the Ohio see until his death in 1957.[106] Another alumnus of the seminary distinguished himself as a labor leader during the Depression. In January 1932, when the number of America's jobless and their dependents had risen to twenty million people, Pittsburgh priest James R. Cox, a 1911 graduate of Saint Vincent, led eighteen thousand unemployed workers to Washington, D.C., to seek government redress. Cox met with President Hoover and a number of congressmen, to whom he presented the workers' petitions.[107] His activism inspired other

Pittsburgh seminarians studying at Saint Vincent at the time, including Charles Owen Rice, who after his ordination in 1934 went on to become a national leader in the cause for workers' rights and social justice.[108]

THE PREP SCHOOL AND SCHOLASTICATE

In 1932 Father Walter Stehle stepped down as director (now called headmaster) of the prep school and was replaced by Father Edmund Cuneo, a twenty-eight-year-old native of St. Marys, Pennsylvania, who had been ordained just two years before. Archabbot Alfred's decision to appoint such a young and talented man as Cuneo to the position of headmaster was driven by a view held by many in the community that the prep school needed to be modernized and updated.

In many ways the prep school had continued to be organized and run along the lines of the old German gymnasium, which Boniface Wimmer had taken as the model for Saint Vincent in the 1840s. Archabbot Alfred and his advisors believed that after almost ninety years, the time had come to make the prep school a modern American institution, and Father Edmund was chosen to undertake the task. Cuneo was assisted in his work by four prefects: Fathers Patrick McKivigan and Norbert Rupprecht, and the clerics Egbert Donovan and Stephen Wendell.

Under its new leadership, the prep school's academic program in the 1930s began to emphasize mathematics and the natural sciences more than it had in the past, and to open itself in general to the outside world. Father Edmund established a forensics program in the prep school which brought Saint Vincent students into contact with students from other institutions through the interscholastic competition of the National Forensics League. He also worked with the administrations of Seton Hill and St. Xavier Academy to organize joint student dances, and he encouraged the prep school's music department to stage joint musical productions with the music departments at Seton Hill and St. Xavier. His efforts to modernize the institution were opposed by what some in the community called "the old German guard," but he enjoyed the strong support of Archabbot Alfred, the council of seniors, and the vast majority of the community.[109]

Under Father Edmund, the prep school faculty was still made up principally of Benedictines—including Fathers Jerome Rupprecht (mathematics and religion), Aquinas Brinker (mathematics and physics), Otto Wendell (Latin and Greek), Genadius Diez (history, Spanish, and Italian), Celestine Huber (German), John Ujlaki (French), Cyril Vlossak (Slovak), Malachy Brawley (Latin and religion), Patrick McKivigan (English and social sciences), and Regis McCoy (English)—but it now also included several laymen: William Rafferty (mathematics and chemistry), Paul Kunkle (German, history, and typewriting), and Louis Smith (Latin and English).[110] Rafferty was also head coach of the prep school's varsity football and basketball teams, the Bearkittens.

Enrollment in the prep school remained fairly stable during the period, averaging 150 students per year and reaching a high of 188 students in 1938. The vast majority of the students were boarders, though between fifteen and twenty day students, primarily from Latrobe, Marguerite, Greensburg, and Jeannette, enrolled each year. About 20 percent of the students came from Pittsburgh. In 1936, a typical year, "prepsters" came to Saint Vincent from New York, New Jersey, Maryland, West Virginia, Kentucky, Indiana, Illinois, and Nebraska, though the majority were Pennsylvanians. On the average 40 percent of the students were scholastics, preparing to enter the Benedictine Order. The scholastics, as in the days of Boniface Wimmer, were housed in separate quarters from the other students, and under the direction of Father Malachy Brawley, and later Father Vitus Kriegel, they followed a regimen of spiritual exercises designed to prepare them for monastic life. The separation between scholastics and regular students, however, did not extend to the classroom. Scholastics attended the same academic classes as their colleagues who were not preparing for the Benedictine priesthood.

All the students, both scholastics and prepsters, followed a highly disciplined schedule that later generations, and perhaps even contemporaries, would consider monastic. The order of the day was as follows.

6:10 a.m.	Rising
6:30	Mass
7:00	Breakfast
7:35	Study
8:00	Classes
11:00	Reading
11:15	Dinner, followed by a visit to the Blessed Sacrament
12:00 p.m.	Recreation
1:45	Studies
3:00	Classes
4:00	Reading and special classes
4:45	Studies
5:30	Supper
6:00	Recreation

7:00 Studies
8:45 Night prayers and retiring[111]

In addition to an active intramural and varsity sports program in the prep, a popular extracurricular activity during the period was drama. Plays were regularly produced on such occasions as Halloween, Thanksgiving, Christmas, and the arrival of spring. Under the direction of Benedictine Fathers Bonaventure Reithmeier and Columban Gross, Sister Antoninus, R.S.M., Sister Rose de Lima, S.C., and Sister Ann Regina, S.C.,[112] joint productions with the girls of St. Xavier Academy in Latrobe and St. Joseph Academy at Seton Hill in Greensburg were also staged.

Interscholastic debating and journalism also became important parts of student life in the prep during the Depression. Under the direction of Father Edmund Cuneo prep debaters competed in forensic competitions throughout western Pennsylvania and at national competitions. In 1935 prepster Hugh Kennedy set a national record when he won first place in both the oratorical and dramatic declamation finals on the same day at the National Forensic Tournament at Kent, Ohio,[113] and in 1942, led by Robert Haight and William Ucker of Mt. Lebanon, Pennsylvania, George Jaeger of Brooklyn, New York, and Joseph Hurley of Latrobe, the debate team won the state debating championship.[114] In 1932 prep students began to produce a weekly mimeographed "gazette" called the *Beacon,* which chronicled events in the prep, especially the results of football and basketball games. In 1936 the *Beacon* was replaced by the *St. Vincent Journalette* ("News and Notes from the College Preparatory School"), which became a regular part of the college-produced *St. Vincent Journal.* Also, in 1935 the first edition of the prep school yearbook, *The Chimes,* appeared.

THE ARCHABBEY

Vocations to the monastic life increased at Saint Vincent during the 1930s and 1940s. Between 1931 and 1940 eighty-five young men entered the clerical novitiate at the rate of about eight a year, while fifteen entered the lay brother novitiate. During the 1940s the number of new vocations continued to be high despite the war, with seventy-eight young men entering the clerical novitiate between 1941 and 1950 and twenty-seven entering the lay brotherhood. On the average 40 percent of those who entered the novitiate persevered to final vows. During the nearly two decades of Archabbot Alfred's abbacy the total monastic population of Saint Vincent rose from 221 in 1930 to 244 in 1949; the number of priests from 135 to 181.[115]

The monastery in Pennsylvania was clearly flourishing, and there developed a critical need for space that would not be fully addressed until the 1960s. Meanwhile, novices and clerics were crowded into dormitories and small cells in Leander, Anselm, and Gregory halls, spaces that in the view of some of them were firetraps. The population of novices and clerics at the archabbey was significantly increased by the presence of young monks from other abbeys of the American Cassinese Congregation (and sometimes the Swiss American Congregation) sent to Latrobe by their communities to undergo their novitiate and pursue philosophical and theological studies. Among the monasteries sending novices and clerics to Saint Vincent during the period were St. Anselm Abbey, Manchester, New Hampshire; St. Bede Abbey, Peru, Illinois; St. Mary's Abbey, Newark, New Jersey; Belmont Abbey, Belmont, North Carolina; St. Andrew Priory, Cleveland, Ohio; St. Benedict's Abbey, Atchison, Kansas; and Conception Abbey, Conception, Missouri. In 1933 there were thirty-seven American Cassinese novices in the novitiate at Saint Vincent, and throughout the period of Archabbot Alfred's reign an average of fifty clerics from Saint Vincent and other Benedictine communities annually studied in the seminary.[116] Saint Vincent's novice masters during this time were Fathers Baldwin Ambros, Celestine Huber, and Malachy Brawley.

One of the most memorable events of the early 1930s at Saint Vincent was the ceremony surrounding the unveiling of the statue of Boniface Wimmer. On his visit to Rome in 1929 Archabbot Aurelius had commissioned Viennese artist Ferdinand Seeboeck to create a bronze statue that would stand as a monument to the founder of Saint Vincent.[117] Seeboeck, who had carved the marble statues on the side altars of the archabbey church, designed and prepared a mold for the Wimmer statue in less than two years. After a delay caused by the inability of the Roman foundry in charge of the work to cast such a large figure in one piece, the statue arrived at Saint Vincent in June 1931, was placed in front of the archabbey church, and was unveiled in a festive ceremony on September 1, 1931. It stood eleven and a half feet high on a base of Vermont granite of equal height, and weighed three thousand eight hundred pounds. To mark the occasion, Bishop Hugh C. Boyle of Pittsburgh celebrated a solemn Pontifical Mass. Abbot Ernest Helmstetter, abbot president of the American Cassinese Congregation, conducted the unveiling ceremony outside the church, and Bishop Joseph Schrembs of Cleveland delivered the dedicatory address. Monks, sisters, students, parishioners, and friends of Saint Vincent gathered for the ceremony. The Latrobe American Legion Drum and Bugle Corps and band were present and led the procession, attended the Mass, and performed both before and after the unveiling.[118] Wimmer was still remembered by some of the older monks in the community, and his achievement against almost insuperable odds of founding Saint Vincent and planting the Benedictine Order in the fertile soil of America had become a virtual legend among the younger monks of the congregation. His imposing bronze image in front of the archabbey church, a copy of the Holy Rule of St. Benedict in one hand, fingers of the other pointing to the Pennsylvania mountains in the east, would now remind future generations of the great work that he had accomplished.

On February 25, 1931, ten Benedictine sisters from St. Walburga Abbey, Eichstätt, Bavaria, led by Mother Leonarda Fritz, O.S.B., arrived at Saint Vincent to establish a new foundation in the United States. Archabbot Alfred had invited them to Pennsylvania and offered them work at Saint Vincent College as a way of assisting the Bavarian abbey through the financial difficulties it faced as a result of the worldwide Depression, whose effects in Germany had been particularly wrenching. Almost eighty years before, sisters from St. Walburga's had come to the United States at the invitation of Boniface Wimmer and had in the course of time established thriving convents and schools in many parts of the United States. The new group of Bavarian Benedictine women came not to establish schools, as their predecessors had done, but to take charge of the kitchen at Saint Vincent. They were accompanied on their voyage from Cherbourg, France, by Father Anthony Stromovich, who had recently completed his theological studies in Rome, and were met in New York by Prior Felix Fellner, who accompanied them to the archabbey.[119]

Within a year six more sisters arrived at the archabbey from St. Walburga's. At least one of the sisters who came to Saint Vincent from Germany in the 1930s, Sister Emmanuel Drey, O.S.B., was of Jewish heritage and had been sent by her superiors to America to escape Nazi persecution. In 1965 Sister Emmanuel became successor to Mother Leonarda as superior of the community in Pennsylvania. In 1932 the monks built a five-story convent for the nuns. Located behind the student gymnasium, the convent had twenty-four individual rooms, a chapel, and a community room. The sisters and their rich Bavarian food quickly became very popular among the college, prep school, and seminary students, and soon the nuns took over responsibilities in the monastery kitchen as well.[120] In 1934 eleven more Benedictine sisters from Eichstätt arrived in the United States. Father Felix Fellner brought ten of them to Saint Vincent immediately, while one remained for a short time in Philadelphia "to make further researches in American cuisine artistry." Two weeks later four of the new arrivals and two sisters who had been at Saint Vincent since 1931 were accompanied by Father Victor Lillig to Holy Cross Abbey, Canon City, Colorado, to take charge of the kitchens at that Benedictine monastery and school.[121]

Settling in Pennsylvania at the height of the Depression, the sisters soon found themselves engaged in an unexpected work of charity. In addition to their regular tasks, they also prepared meals for as many as forty itinerant homeless men each day who came to the monastery seeking food. Impoverished families in the area also came to their kitchens for "care packages." Many of the homeless men camped in abandoned coke ovens by Twelve Mile Run, southeast of the college, and sought work on campus. Even when no work was available, no one was turned away hungry by the sisters.[122] The nuns who took the lead in feeding the poor were Sister Hedwig Scholz, O.S.B., and Sister Reinildis Fieger, O.S.B. By 1934 the sisters were not just providing leftovers to the homeless and needy but preparing special meals for them, which were distributed with the assistance of several lay brothers, including Brothers Jacob Lang (1864–1938), Maurus Hoehler (1871–1943), and Paul Hauser (1879–1969). In addition to food, Brother Maurus distributed rosaries and gave religious instruction to the itinerants, and Brother Jacob preached to them.[123] When one of the homeless inhabitants of the migrants' camp on Twelve Mile Run, Andy Hudic, died in the winter of 1932, a Requiem Mass was celebrated for him in the archabbey church, and he was buried in the Saint Vincent cemetery.[124] The sisters were long remembered for the kindnesses they showed to these "knights of the road," at least one of whom wrote back after the Depression to thank them and to send a small donation of money. "I will never forget the meals I received," he said.[125]

In April 1934 Abbess Benedicta Spiegel von und zu Peckelsheim, O.S.B., of Eichstätt came to the United States for a two-month visit with the Benedictine sisters at Saint Vincent and Holy Cross. She was warmly received at the archabbey, where she gave several addresses to the monks and students and also spoke to a gathering of 150 lay oblates about the social and economic problems facing Germany at the time. At an informal reception in the college auditorium, the prep school students welcomed the abbess in seven of the eight languages in which she was fluent: German, English, French, Italian, Slovak, Latin, and Greek.[127]

The Benedictine sisters who went to Pennsylvania and Colorado in the 1930s eventually withdrew from kitchen work at Saint Vincent and Holy

The Benedictine Sisters at Saint Vincent in April 1934. Front: Sister Veronika; Sister Brigitta; Sister Barbara; Mother Leonarda; Abbess Benedicta von Spiegel of Eichstätt; Sister Laurentia; Sister Aloisia; Sister Leodegaria; Sister Gaudentia. Center: Sister Theresia; Sister Justina; Sister Liberata; Sister Pia; Sister Hedwig; Sister Blandina; Sister Hermelinde; Sister Margareta; Sister Stilla. Back: Sister Benigna; Sister Josefine; Sister Vincentia; Sister Armelia; Sister Felicitas; Sister Johanna; Sister Monica; Sister Richmundis.

Cross and established independent contemplative communities separate from the college campuses where they originally settled. In 1948 the sisters in Pennsylvania established St. Emma's Priory in Greensburg, and those in Colorado, St. Walburga's Priory in Boulder, which in 1991 was elevated to the rank of abbey.

The institution of the lay brotherhood at Saint Vincent went through significant changes during the abbacy of Archabbot Alfred. For one thing, despite a steady stream of candidates who felt themselves called to this very special vocation, the number of lay brothers at the archabbey declined during the 1930s. By 1940 there were only twenty-three of them at Saint Vincent, a dramatic decrease from the more than one hundred lay brothers who served the community in the nineteenth century. One reason for this decrease was that young American men who desired to become brothers often found the environment they entered at the archabbey foreign. The lay brotherhood was the last institution at Saint Vincent that maintained a strong German identity, and new candidates had to deal not only with the unfamiliar climate of nineteenth-century Bavarian piety but also with a language they did not understand. Because of the difficulties of cultural and linguistic adjustment, many of the young brothers did not persevere to final vows, and even as they departed the community, the old German brothers grew old and died.

In an effort to attract new American vocations, the monastic chapter began gradually to eliminate the language barrier. In 1927 English replaced German at the table reading in the monastic refectory. In 1935 the traditional German prayers at meals were replaced by Latin ones. While these changes in the refectory affected the entire community, clerical and lay, an important change took place in 1937 which affected only the lay brothers. Since the time of Boniface Wimmer the brothers had recited their daily rosary in common and conducted all their communal spiritual exercises in the German language. In March of 1937, however, that tradition changed forever when English became the language for the brothers' communal prayers. (The clerical monks, of course, continued to pray communally in Latin.) The announcement of this change stated that "the increasing number of English-speaking brothers necessitated the abandoning of German for spiritual exercises."[128] In 1937 the Archabbey Press published the *Lay-Brothers' Manual of Prayer* in English, a volume that became the standard prayer book for the lay brothers at Saint Vincent as well as in several other abbeys of the American Cassinese Congregation. The change from German to English gradually led to the Americanization of the institution of the lay brotherhood, but it did not result in significant increases in vocations. By 1950 there were still only twenty-six lay brothers at Saint Vincent, and in 1967 the institution disappeared altogether when the lay brothers (or non-clerical monks) and the clerical members of the archabbey were integrated into a single praying community.

In addition to Abbess Benedicta of Eichstätt, other notable Benedictine visitors to the archabbey in the 1930s included Abbot Gislar Stieber. O.S.B., of the Bavarian abbey of Niederaltaich, and Abbot Augustino Antoniolli, O.S.B., of the Abbey of St. Peter, Modena, Italy, who visited U.S. abbeys in 1934 seeking aid for their monasteries suffering from the devastating effects of the Depression.[129] Another important visitor during the peri-

Brother Clement Hausmann, O.S.B. (1853–1948), ringing the bell in the clock tower.

od was Prior Albert Hammenstede of the Beuronese Abbey of Maria Laach, who spent time at Saint Vincent in the summer of 1936. Hammenstede was one of the leaders of the liturgical movement in Europe, and Maria Laach, one of the movement's major centers. He had come to the United States in order to look into prospects for establishing a daughterhouse of Maria Laach here, and he took advantage of the opportunity to visit several U.S. monasteries to discuss the liturgical movement. At Saint Vincent he gave a series of lectures on the "Liturgy and Early Benedictine Ideals," which were well received,[130] and introduced the ideas of the renowned Benedictine liturgists (and members of the Maria Laach community) Abbot Ildefons Herwegen and Father Odo Casel. He later wrote that he "learned a great deal about the true monastic spirit since I came to America. . . . There is so much good will just among the young American monks that our Holy Order will soon become most flourishing in this country."[131]

Later European visitors to Saint Vincent came as refugees from Nazi oppression. In 1938 Father Jerome Gassner, a thirty-seven-year-old Benedictine from the Austrian abbey of Seitenstetten, arrived at the archabbey with Father Felix Fellner, who had been visiting Germany and Austria at the time. A leader of the Austrian Catholic Youth Movement, Gassner had run afoul of the Nazis after the annexation of Austria and was forced into exile. Father Felix brought him to Saint Vincent, where he remained for two months before going to St. John's Abbey, Minnesota.[132] Father Stephen Van der Lee, a diocesan priest in Amsterdam, arrived at the archabbey in December 1939. Active in the family life movement in Holland, Father Van der Lee said that "Nazi inroads into the German family life have almost destroyed even the intimacy which normally exists between parents and their children. The concept of family life is being torn from the hearts of the German people, with the result that the German youth in their most formative stage of development are under the influence and instruction of the Nazi leaders."[133] The Dutch priest came to America with his brother Cornelius, a seminarian. Cornelius Van der Lee completed his theological studies in the seminary at Saint Vincent and was ordained in June 1940. The two brothers then left the archabbey to become missionaries in South Africa.

The purpose of Father Felix Fellner's visit to Europe in the summer of 1938 was to do research in the archives of Bavaria and Rome on the history of the Benedictines in America and the life of Boniface Wimmer. Fellner visited the Abbey of Saint Paul's Outside the Walls in Rome, the Sacred Congregation for the Propagation of the Faith, the Ludwig Missionsverein in Munich, and the abbeys of Metten, Scheyern, and Eichstätt in Bavaria and of Salzburg, Schottenstift (Vienna), and Seitenstetten in Austria, where he photocopied hundreds of Wimmer's letters for his projected biography of Saint Vincent's first archabbot. He also visited the village of Thalmassing, Wimmer's birthplace. Father Felix was accompanied on his travels through Bavaria by Brother Paulinus Selle, who was ordained deacon during that summer by the bishop of Regensburg. When Fellner returned to the United States with Father Jerome Gassner, he told his confreres that Germany was in a "war-fever," and that the abbot of Metten, who had come into conflict with the Nazis, had been arrested, detained for nine days, and "examined about the affairs of his abbey."[134]

Music, both liturgical and nonliturgical, continued to be a major focus of interest and activity among the monks during the 1930s. A key figure in the musical life of Saint Vincent during this period was Father Raymond Balko, who entered the novitiate in 1913 at the age of nineteen and was ordained to the priesthood in 1920. Father Raymond had begun his musical education at Saint Vincent and continued it at the Chicago School of Music, where he received a master's degree. He did further studies in Gregorian chant at Benedictine schools in England, France, Germany, Austria, Hungary, and Rome, and by the opening years of the 1930s he was widely regarded as one of the foremost authorities on Gregorian chant in the United States.[135]

In the 1920s Balko became head of the music department at Saint Vincent College, where he introduced the bachelor of music degree. In 1929 he was invited by Bishop John J. Cantwell of Los Angeles to give a course in Gregorian chant to musicians of the California diocese, and in 1930 he instituted a summer school of music at Saint Vincent that attracted students from throughout western Pennsylvania. Courses included not only Gregorian chant and "Gregorian chant accompaniments," but also piano, counterpoint composition, canon and fugue composition, and modern dance orchestration. In the summer of 1932 he directed the Benedictine School of Gregorian Chant at St. Scholastica Academy in Chicago, and in 1936 he was invited by Father Charles Coughlin, the famous "radio priest" who visited Saint Vincent in October 1936, to take charge of musical and liturgical activities at the Shrine of the Little Flower in Royal Oak, Michigan. In May 1936 Father Raymond went to Michigan, where he directed the men's choir, the boys' choir, and a mixed choir at the shrine for a year before returning to Saint Vincent because of ill health.[136]

Musical concerts remained an important part of the cultural life at Saint

Vincent during the Depression. The college band and glee club, the seminary choir, and the community orchestra (composed of monks, seminarians, college students, and prep school students) performed regularly before audiences that included many music-loving visitors to the campus. The orchestra programs included pieces by Mozart, Beethoven, Brahms, Grieg, Bach, Haydn, and Mendelssohn, and were frequently accompanied by explanatory lectures. Often the glee club, orchestra, and band performed at sites off campus such as Seton Hill College, where at a concert in May 1932 Seton Hill student Catherine Rubino gave a solo soprano performance of Bizet's "Carmen Waltz Song" with the Saint Vincent Orchestra.[137]

Shortly after his return from China Father Columban Gross, himself a talented musician, took charge of the orchestra and conducted concerts that included piano solos by such Benedictine clerics as Brother Eric McCormack of Saint Vincent and Brother Martin Burne of St. Mary's Abbey, Newark, New Jersey. Monks who were members of the orchestra during this period included Fathers Bernard Brinker, Gerald Nessler, and Justin Krellner (all of whom played the violin), Edwin Bender (flute), Camillus Long (oboe), and Florian Bergman (bassoon), and the clerics Aidan Pfiester (violin), Roland Heid (cello), Giles Killoran (bass viol), Terrence O'Connor (cornet), Anselm Ober (cornet), Matthew Benko (French horn), Eugene Polhemus (French horn), Reginald Buerkle (trombone), and Ralph Bailey (drum). Also under Father Columban's direction the *schola cantorum* of the Saint Vincent Seminary Choir broadcast concerts of Gregorian chant over Pittsburgh radio station WCAE.[138] In 1937 Father Constantine Zech, who had been on the staff of the St. Emma Industrial and Agricultural Institute, returned to Saint Vincent to take charge of the music department of the college and direct musical activities at the archabbey.

Saint Vincent priests continued to conduct summer retreats for laymen through the Depression. Fathers Edmund Cuneo and Patrick McKivigan served as directors of these retreats, which during the 1930s became an increasingly important part of the apostolic work of the monastery. Each summer the community sponsored several four-day retreats that attracted as many as one thousand Catholic men to the campus. Since the 1920s the American Catholic retreat movement had garnered significant support from U.S. bishops as a means of promoting spiritual renewal and Catholic Action among the laity, and Saint Vincent, with one of the earliest retreat programs in the country, attracted national attention for its work in the field. In January 1931 the archabbey hosted the fourth national retreat conference, a gathering attended by four bishops (Hugh C. Boyle of Pitts-

Corpus Christi procession at Saint Vincent in the 1930s.

burgh, John Mark Gannon of Erie, Auxiliary Bishop Joseph H. Albers of Cincinnati, and Auxiliary Bishop Gerald P. O'Hara of Philadelphia) and 230 priests and laymen from seventeen states and the District of Columbia. Archabbot Alfred addressed the convention on the topic "Why the Retreat Movement Must Go On," and the meeting concluded with a festive banquet at the William Penn Hotel in Pittsburgh attended by six hundred people.[139]

Another important community apostolate that focused on the spiritual development of lay Catholics was the Benedictine oblate movement. Part of the spiritual work of the monks of the archabbey since the 1890s, the oblate movement promoted Benedictine spirituality among the laity through the activities of oblate chapters in Benedictine parishes and elsewhere. At Saint Vincent the Oblates of St. Benedict met monthly in the crypt of the archabbey church to pray and to hear spiritual talks by Benedictines and other speakers. Fathers Maurice Costello and Cosmas Minster served as spiritual directors of the oblates during the 1930s, and among the speakers at oblate meetings were Father Gilbert Straub, pastor of St. Bruno's Church, South Greensburg; Abbess Benedicta Spiegel von und zu Peckelsheim, O.S.B., of Eichstätt; Father Edmund Cuneo, headmaster of Saint Vincent Preparatory School; and Father Alcuin Tasch, head of the education department at Saint Vincent College.[140] Beginning in 1934 the clerics of the archabbey began publication of *The Saint Vincent Oblate,* a quarterly newsletter whose purpose was to secure "closer union between St. Vincent Archabbey and its secular oblates."[141] By 1937 there were about a thousand laypersons enrolled as oblates of St. Benedict at Saint Vincent.

The most tragic event that occurred at Saint Vincent during the 1930s was the death of Father Columban Gross. On June 23, 1937, the thirty-three-year-old priest drowned while swimming in the Saint Vincent Lake (though there was some speculation afterwards that he had suffered a fatal heart attack before disappearing beneath the water). Father Rembert Sorg, who was swimming with him at the time, made an unsuccessful attempt to rescue him, but Sorg himself nearly drowned as he struggled to save his confrere. Father Columban's body was finally located in eleven feet of water and brought to the surface by Brother Dominic Chonko, a cleric from St. Andrew Abbey, Cleveland. Efforts to revive him failed.

Born in Chicago in 1904, Columban Gross had come to Saint Vincent as a scholastic in 1919, entered the novitiate in 1925, and pronounced solemn vows four years later. In 1929 Archabbot Aurelius sent him to China to join the Benedictine priory in Peking, and there, in June 1932, after completing his theological studies, he was ordained with his classmate Father Hugh Wilt. Father Columban taught English and music at the University of Peking until the Saint Vincent monks were recalled from China, and then he served as assistant pastor of St. Boniface Church on Pittsburgh's North Side before taking charge of the music department at Saint Vincent College in 1935 when Father Raymond Balko went to the Shrine of the Little Flower in Royal Oak, Michigan. Father Columban was highly regarded by his confreres as a generous, devout, and talented monk whose intellectual powers and musical talents were outstanding. The monastic chapter had elected him a member of the monastery's council of seniors at the extraordinarily young age of thirty-two, and many considered him a probable successor to Archabbot Alfred. His sudden and unexpected death caused grief and consternation among both his confreres and the students whom he had taught in the college and seminary. The *St. Vincent Journal,* said that his death came "as a staggering shock to the entire St. Vincent community and to a wide-flung circle of relatives and friends."[142]

ECONOMIC EFFECTS OF THE DEPRESSION

The impressive growth of the seminary, college, preparatory school, scholasticate, and monastery during the 1930s occurred despite the severe financial strains on Saint Vincent caused by the Depression. The negative economic effects of the Depression, moreover, were exacerbated by the burden of debt on the community brought on by the failed mission to China. Archabbot Alfred and the council of seniors, who together controlled and managed the finances of both the archabbey and its schools, were deeply concerned about the financial problems Saint Vincent faced throughout the decade and took steps to trim costs wherever possible. These steps included cutbacks in the athletic program and the decision to limit the number of lay professors in the college and prep school. On the other hand, despite the fact that a large percentage of students in the seminary, college, prep school, and scholasticate were unable to pay their tuition during the worst days of the Depression, the archabbey's council of seniors decided that these students would be allowed to continue their studies in the expectation that their families would settle accounts when times got better.[143]

As a cost-saving measure, the output of the archabbey farms, under the direction of monastery procurators Father Victor Lillig and later Father Dominic Breuss, was increased to reduce the necessity of purchasing meat, eggs, and vegetables from local suppliers. In the 1920s Saint Vincent had moved from an almost totally self-sufficient institution to one that depended in large measure on staples produced by local markets. In the mid-1930s, however, Father Victor Lillig invested some of the community's limited resources into agricultural expansion that resulted, if not in a return to total self-sufficiency, at least in diminished dependence upon outside markets for food. Farm labor was done by lay brothers, novices, clerics, and a small force of hired workmen. By the end of the decade Saint Vincent cattle, pigs, poultry, and bees were "setting [the] tables with milk and meat, eggs and honey; the truck gardens [were] producing vegetables for the year; the potato fields [were] yielding sufficient for needs; the fruit trees [were] bearing" fruit; and the grainfields, gristmill, and bakery were (as in the past) producing all the wheat, flour, and bread that the monks and students required. In addition, a vineyard, begun in the 1920s by the subprior Father Remigius Burgemeister and overseen by Brother Thomas Pertocy, provided sacramental wine for the altars of Saint Vincent.[144] Beer, however, was no longer produced at the archabbey after the Eighteenth Amendment to the U.S. Constitution forced the closing of the Saint Vincent brewery in 1919. Nonetheless, some of the German lay brothers (such as Brother Joseph

Weigl of Windischeschenbach, Bavaria) produced home brew during the 1920s and early 1930s for those members of the monastic community who were used to their beer and who found legal prohibition both inexplicable and intolerable.[145]

During the Depression the energy needs of Saint Vincent were met to a large extent by coal mined on archabbey lands. The monks had been mining coal since the time of Boniface Wimmer for use in the stoves that kept the buildings warm during the long Pennsylvania winters. Beginning in the 1890s and lasting for more than fifty years, commercial coal mining operations were conducted on the monastery properties both at Saint Vincent and in Elk and Cambria counties. After 1915 the archabbey's "coal lands" became heavily exploited by mining companies, and the leases on these lands, and the royalties paid to the monastery for each ton of coal extracted, generated significant income for the community, income used to support Saint Vincent College as well as the archabbey's other apostolates. To a lesser extent, Saint Vincent also leased land for gas and oil exploration, particularly in Elk County.[146]

In an attempt to raise funds for the Catholic University of Peking, Archabbot Aurelius Stehle convinced the monastic chapter to sell outright the coal under the monastery lands, rather than to continue leasing mineral rights to the coal companies for the stable but relatively small income that the leases generated. This decision seemed judicious in 1928, but two years later, when the Depression struck, the monks deeply regretted that in opting for a quick profit, they had sold the mineral rights to most of their coal lands and were now deprived of the steady coal lease income on which they had depended in the past for extraordinary expenses.[147]

Thus an important potential source of financial relief during the worst days of the Depression was denied the community. Nonetheless, the archabbey itself maintained a small mining operation during the Depression. Under the general direction of Father Victor Lillig, and worked by the lay brothers and a few local hired workmen, the Saint Vincent mine produced coal for the powerhouse that provided heat and energy to all the campus buildings.

Commercial coal-mining operations on Saint Vincent property ceased shortly before the Second World War began. The main reason that the coal companies stopped operations was that the price of coal plummeted during the Depression. Also, by 1940 most of the accessible coal under Saint Vincent property had already been mined. Perhaps a less pressing determining factor, from the coal companies' perspective, but nonetheless an important reason for ending the operations from the monastery's point of view, was the question of safety. On Memorial Day 1937, in one of the mines under the monastery property operated by the Frick Coal Company, a wall broke and water from an adjacent mine rushed in, flooding the mine and killing two miners, Bernard Ransel and John Lane.[148] Because it was Memorial Day only a small workforce was below ground. Had the flood occurred on an ordinary work day, many more miners would have died. The mine disaster caused the monastic chapter to worry about the safety of the mining operations beneath Saint Vincent property, and the council of seniors urged the coal companies to close down the mines, which they did before 1940. Mining under lands adjacent to Saint Vincent, however, continued into the 1940s.[149]

The deleterious ecological effects of coal mining at Saint Vincent and in its immediate vicinity soon became apparent. A coal mine dug under the spring that was the main source of water supply for the campus diverted the water and diminished the supply to such an extent that it was necessary for Saint Vincent to contract with the Latrobe Water Company in 1941 to provide water to the campus.[150] Because of undermining, land sank in various places on campus, including at the Saint Vincent cemetery. Plans for new buildings on the property had to be carefully made to avoid collapses caused by earlier mining. When the new auditorium and gymnasium were built in the 1950s, expensive foundations and deep steel piles were required because part of the dual structure was erected over an abandoned mine. Mine seepage contaminated streams and ponds on and around archabbey lands. In the 1990s efforts were begun by the college, in collaboration with the Pennsylvania Department of Environmental Resources and the Loyalhanna Creek Mine Drainage Coalition, to reclaim some of the damaged land and alter the harmful effects on the environment that resulted from the early twentieth-century mining operations.

JAMES BARRY-ROBINSON HOME FOR BOYS

In the summer of 1933 John Baecher, an alumnus of Saint Vincent College, approached Archabbot Alfred Koch with a proposal that the Benedictines take over administration of a newly founded home for boys near Norfolk, Virginia. The home had been established by the will of Virginia real estate developer Frederick J. Robinson. The Robinson will, probated in 1923, called for the creation of a boys' orphanage to be named for Robinson's grandfather, James Barry, a distinguished citizen of Norfolk who had died during the Civil War. Baecher had been named a trustee of the Barry-

Robinson home, which was expected to open in the fall, and had convinced the board of trustees to ask the Benedictines of Saint Vincent to operate it.

Archabbot Alfred brought the proposal to the monastic chapter, which took the matter under consideration on September 1, 1933. The transfer of the Catholic University of Peking to the Society of the Divine Word had recently taken place. The monks in China were on their way home, and vocations to the monastic life had steadily increased over the past decade, so that for the first time since Boniface Wimmer's day it appeared that the monastic population would be more than sufficient in the foreseeable future for the staffing of the archabbey's existing apostolates. The proposal to accept the new work in Virginia thus came at a moment when the community had a surplus of monks and was amenable to committing itself to a new undertaking. As the Depression deepened and the extent of the losses in China were becoming apparent, the new apostolate was also a means of generating much-needed cash for the increasingly costly operations at Saint Vincent.

The arrangement with the board of trustees at the Barry-Robinson Home was similar to that which the monks had made with the board of trustees at the St. Emma Industrial and Agricultural Institute at Belmead. No property transfer was involved. The institution was to be governed by a board of trustees with the Benedictines serving as contracted employees of the board.

The chapter debate preceding the vote indicated the concerns the capitulars had. Was this really an apostolate appropriate for the Saint Vincent community? Were the Benedictines adequately prepared to take charge of young orphan boys? Would the monks sent to Barry-Robinson be able to lead a proper monastic life? Some capitulars pointed out that the work of their confreres at Belmead proved that the community could satisfactorily undertake the work in Norfolk. Others urged that care be taken that those sent to Barry-Robinson be able to observe properly the monastic rule. In the end, the new apostolate was accepted by a decisive majority of thirty-three to four.[151]

Archabbot Alfred assigned Father Sylvester Healy, newly returned from China, as director of the Barry-Robinson Home. The institution opened in January 1934 with about twenty boys between the ages of twelve and eighteen. The property on which the home was situated included eighty acres of cultivated land, worked by the boys and several hired workmen, and twenty acres of woodland. The monks received a monthly allotment of two thousand dollars to operate the institution and were paid an annual salary of one thousand five hundred dollars plus board and lodging. The Benedictine staff eventually consisted of five monks. The salaries they received from the Barry-Robinson trustees went back to Saint Vincent to help meet some of the expenses of the archabbey during the Depression.[152]

In the beginning the institution was simply a residence home for boys who attended St. Mary's School in downtown Norfolk, but in 1937, when the contract with the board of trustees was renewed for another three years, additional monks were assigned from Saint Vincent and a junior high school was begun on the premises. Father Adalbert Kalsch replaced Father Sylvester Healy as director, and Fathers Conrad Patrick and Lucian Malich were assigned to teach in the school.[153] Subsequently Father Cletus Crawford became director, followed by Fathers Urban Lux, Marcian Kornides, and Brinstan Takach. Among the Saint Vincent monks who served at Barry-Robinson were Fathers Terrence Rogan, DeSales Zang, Damian Abbaticchio, Columban Bomkamp, Paschal Kneip, Dunstan Debes, Edmund Kollar, Gordian Burkardt, Blane Resko, Bertrand Dunegan, and Bede Hasso.

Enrollment in what came to be known as "James Barry-Robinson High School" eventually expanded to over a hundred students. Most of them were boarders whose parents could not provide adequate supervision for them. Others remained at the school during the week but returned to their families on weekends. About 80 percent of the boys were Catholics.[154]

Saint Vincent continued to operate Barry-Robinson for thirty-four years. In 1961 the school became a fully accredited four-year high school and began to focus on preparing students for entrance into college. In 1967, when Saint Vincent took over administration of the Benedictine priory and high school in Savannah, Georgia, the monastic chapter in Pennsylvania voted to relinquish the administration and staffing of Barry-Robinson.

CHINA DENOUEMENT

In the years following the Benedictine withdrawal from China, the $250,000 debt contracted in 1929 by Archabbot Aurelius with the National City Bank of New York lay like a sleeping giant. From the moment he learned of it, Archabbot Alfred had insisted that the debt was not Saint Vincent's. It was Koch's contention that his predecessor had made the loan on his authority as papally appointed chancellor of the Catholic University of Peking, not as archabbot of Saint Vincent, and that because the monastic chapter at Saint Vincent had not been consulted and had not approved the loan, it was not the archabbey's responsibility to repay it. The responsibility belonged, in Archabbot Alfred's opinion, to the Catholic University of Peking and its new proprietors, the priests of the Society of the Divine Word. Ultimate responsibility, he believed, lay with the Holy See.

The Society of the Divine Word (S.V.D.) continued to administer Fu Jen University, but escalating costs and political turmoil resulting from civil war and the Japanese invasion of China made their work extraordinarily difficult. The S.V.D. priests were incapable of paying current debts, much less repaying the $250,000 debt to the National City Bank. The Sacred Congregation for the Propagation of the Faith, for its part, continued to insist that the debt was not the Holy See's but Saint Vincent's.[155] As long as the bank did not insist upon repayment, however, no one was concerned greatly about the problem. Between 1929 and the end of 1936 no interest was paid to National City Bank on the loan and no effort was made to resolve the issue; but in November of 1936, with time running out on the statute of limitations for outstanding debts, the National City Bank brought suit against the Benedictine Society of Westmoreland County for $250,000 plus seven years of interest.[156]

Upon learning of the suit, Archabbot Alfred wrote Abbot Alcuin Deutsch of St. John's Abbey, president of the American Cassinese Congregation, that because no interest on the debt had been paid since 1929, and no effort had been made to reduce the principal, "the Bank had to bring suit against somebody to protect itself against a heavy fine—to be imposed by Federal authorities." The bank was therefore suing Saint Vincent for principal and interest, amounting to an "awe-inspiring bill of $362,000." Koch said, however, that he believed the bank would be happy to be paid only the principal and would be willing to "write a greater part of the interest in the chimney." The archabbot told the abbot president that he had informed the cardinals of the Propaganda Fide that the Holy See "would have saved thousands of dollars had they settled the debt question back in 1933 as they promised to do."[157]

At the recommendation of Rome, Archabbot Alfred sought the advice and assistance of Cardinal Patrick Hayes of New York, and Hayes advised him that the Holy See was of the opinion that all the abbeys of the American Cassinese Congregation should share with Saint Vincent the burden of repaying the loan. When the archabbot informed Abbot Alcuin of this advice, Deutsch himself visited Hayes in an attempt to convince the cardinal that such a solution was "quite out of the question." In a letter to Archabbot Alfred following his meeting with Hayes, the abbot president insisted

> that the abbeys never intended to assume any obligation toward the University; that the University was purely a St. Vincent's undertaking, though the Holy See appeared, in some of its utterances to assume that it was an undertaking by the American Benedictines; that the other abbeys had merely promised to give St. Vincent's such support as they could; that with the passing of the University out of the hands of St. Vincent's they considered themselves freed from all obligation to help that may have arisen from their promise, as their promise was never meant to extend to anything but to instructors and such financial assistance as might be obtained from their friends and from the parishes which they administer.[158]

Deutsch went on to say that neither he nor the other abbots considered it just that Saint Vincent should be called upon to shoulder the debt now that the university had been handed over to the Society of the Divine Word. He agreed with Koch that either the university (and the Society of the Divine Word) or the Holy See itself should assume responsibility for the debt. Nonetheless, he recommended that the Saint Vincent chapter "admit the legal responsibility of St. Vincent's to the National City Bank, and consequently [the responsibility] to repay to it the loan made to the University." He recognized that the chapter "might balk at this on the score that it did not give [Archabbot Aurelius] the consent required by our Statutes to contract this loan," but he insisted that this was "the proper legal procedure to get this matter settled." He said, moreover, that if Saint Vincent took this course, Cardinal Hayes, the apostolic delegate in Washington, and the cardinals of the Propaganda Fide would be pleased and could be expected to come to the aid of the archabbey with financial assistance to repay the loan.

Archabbot Alfred responded immediately that the abbot president's suggestions "concerning our Chinese puzzle" were "a cold douche." "We are asked to acknowledge the loan of $250,000 as a loan of St. Vincent's, although all the conditions required both by canon and civil law for a lawful loan are absent. I wonder how in conscience I could do such a thing." He said that the Holy See had "promised at various times to settle the debt question" but that nothing had ever been done owing to the fact that "the Propaganda has no money and . . . the Holy Father himself is in great financial distress." He therefore declined to follow Abbot Alcuin's advice.[159]

These letters initiated a correspondence between Archabbot Alfred and Abbot Alcuin that at times grew heated. On May 9, 1937, Deutsch wrote that the suggestion in his earlier letter was that Saint Vincent recognize the "*legal* claim of the bank" but not the "*moral* responsibility for the debt." "If you will carefully read my letter," the abbot president said, "you must admit that I explicitly stated I hold that, in justice, the present incumbents at the University, the S.V.D., are morally bound, or, if the Holy See gave the

Society the assurance that it would not be responsible for the loan, then the Holy See itself is bound to repay the money." Deutsch went on to repeat that the best way to resolve the problem was for Saint Vincent to acknowledge its *legal* responsibility for the debt. He had been assured by officials in Rome, he said, that "the Holy See recognizes this debt as its *moral* responsibility," and he chided Archabbot Alfred that "the whole affair between you and Propaganda may have been due to a misunderstanding, which may be your fault. At least, the Propaganda seems to feel that it can get nowhere with you. To be frank, if you evaded the issue, as you did in part in your answer to my letter, I am not surprised."[160]

Archabbot Alfred, however, had no intention of admitting responsibility for the debt. His concern was that he had no formal, legally binding agreement with Rome that the Holy See would pay the debt if Saint Vincent accepted "legal responsibility." So he continued to resist acknowledging an obligation that he honestly believed Saint Vincent did not have. He was, moreover, offended by the tone of Abbot Alcuin's letter. In a draft response, which apparently he never sent, he wrote: "I am not surprised that you and the Propaganda prefer to lay the blame for the long drawn out affair of the loan question at my door. I am guilty! Well, let us look a little closer into this affair." In five tightly packed handwritten pages he laid out his case for refusing to acknowledge responsibility for the loan, which, basically, was that the chapter at Saint Vincent had never approved it. He remarked that he was "in the dark why I should take upon myself the settlement of this question. If Rome really intends to pay that loan, why does she not give me an authoritative declaration to that effect[?] Then I [will] have something to propose to my chapter. I do not evade the question at issue, as you stated. I am only too anxious to have that question settled. But let it be settled in justice. It is easy to condemn a man if one is in a safe shelter."[161]

At the end of June 1937 Cardinal Pietro Fumasoni-Biondi, prefect of the Sacred Congregation for the Propagation of the Faith, sent a letter to Abbot Alcuin stating that "the responsibility for this [loan] rests with the archabbey of Saint Vincent and the other Benedictine abbeys of the [American] Cassinese Congregation," and "inviting" Saint Vincent and the other abbeys to contribute $15,000 a year toward interest payment and reduction of principal on the debt. The Propaganda Fide and the American bishops, he said, would contribute $10,000 a year. The invitation to the American abbeys was justified, the cardinal said, because they had all agreed at the general chapter of 1923 to assist Saint Vincent in the task of establishing a Catholic university in China.[162] Abbot Alcuin strongly disagreed with Fumasoni-Biondi's position. He wrote Archabbot Alfred that "I shall not accept this decision without appeal, and I am writing His Eminence the Cardinal a protest against this decision, or 'invitation,' as he calls it euphemistically." Koch himself had grave reservations about the Propaganda Fide's solution. "Who is going to impose that burden upon the various Abbeys 'authoritatively'?" he asked. "I am afraid that there will be fireworks."[163]

In October 1937 the American abbots went to Rome for the international congress of Benedictine abbots, and while there met among themselves to discuss the China debt question. During their meeting they "unanimously decided" to appeal the decision of the Propaganda Fide that all the abbeys be held responsible for the debt to the National City Bank of New York, and Abbot Alcuin composed a carefully reasoned, six-page letter to Cardinal Fumasoni-Biondi explaining the abbots' viewpoint. The abbots and delegates who attended the 1923 general chapter of the American Cassinese Congregation, he said, never intended to accept responsibility for the Catholic University of Peking "because they were convinced that the monasteries of the Congregation could, at that time, provide neither a sufficient number of properly trained professors nor the necessary financial means for such a large undertaking." For that reason, and because "the late Archabbot of St. Vincent's Archabbey greatly favored the proposition," the abbots and delegates had voted to "leave the matter to the decision of the Chapter of the said Archabbey." The responsibility for the establishment of the university "rested therefore on St. Vincent's Archabbey, and on it alone."

Abbot Alcuin went on to say that the abbeys of the American Cassinese Congregation should not be held liable for any debts contracted by the university, and in the case of the loan from the National City Bank of New York, Saint Vincent should not be held responsible either. Archabbot Aurelius "considered the University as a separate moral entity for which he, as Chancellor, could and did enter contractual obligations, which he, as Chancellor, also sought to fulfill." The loan from the National City Bank was just such a contractual obligation entered into by Stehle *as chancellor.* Both Archabbot Aurelius and the bank "considered the University as a moral entity, a corporation distinct from the Archabbey corporation, and therefore responsible for the loan, which was wholly expended for the benefit and advantage of the University." Thus the debt, Deutsch said, belonged to "the University of Peking and not [to] the Archabbey of St. Vincent," and "it does not seem consonant with the demands of natural equity to impose on the Archabbey the obligation of repaying said loan now that it has lost control of the University." In the name of the abbots of the congregation, Abbot Alcuin asked the prefect of the Propaganda Fide, therefore, to hold neither the American abbeys in general nor Saint Vincent Archabbey in particular responsible for the debt.[164]

Deutsch remained in Rome after the abbots' congress to discuss the National City Bank loan with Cardinal Fumasoni-Biondi and Archbishop Celso Costantini, apostolic delegate to China, and after a meeting on October 20, he sent a memorandum to the cardinal summarizing the substance of the discussion and listing the conclusions that he believed he and the Roman officials had come to. The key conclusion was "that the S. Congreg. of the Propaganda does not hold that the Abbeys of the [American Cassinese] Congregation have the obligation in justice to repay the said loan or any part of it."

After his meeting with Fumasoni-Biondi and Costantini, Abbot Alcuin felt that he had settled the matter definitively. He was therefore shocked to receive a letter shortly after Christmas from Archbishop Amleto G. Cicognani, apostolic delegate to the United States, that stated categorically that Deutsch's memorandum to Cardinal Fumasoni-Biondi did not "represent accurately the mind of the Sacred Congregation de Propaganda Fide" nor did it "represent aright either the viewpoint of His Eminence, the Cardinal Prefect, or of His Excellency, Archbishop Costantini." Cicognani informed Abbot Alcuin that the original position of Cardinal Fumasoni-Biondi, that all the abbeys of the congregation should share the burden of paying the debt, "did not change at all in the conversation held with you in Rome" and he trusted that "in the spirit of cooperation with a great Catholic enterprise, which the Catholic University of Peking unquestionably is, the American Cassinese Congregation will undertake to liquidate this debt."[165]

Deutsch waited two weeks to collect his thoughts before responding to the apostolic delegate. On January 15, 1938, he wrote that Archbishop Cicognani's letter had come as "quite a shock," and that his reply had been delayed "simply because I have been at a loss as to the form that I should have given it." He explained again the reasons that the American abbeys should not be held liable for the loan and said that he could not support the Holy See's solution "without doing violence to my conscience and without the fear that, by doing so, I would cause a great disturbance in our communities, who would be shaken in their confidence that the Holy See can be relied on to do justice." He asked that Cicognani convey his concerns to the cardinals of the Propaganda Fide and requested that the Holy See reconsider the matter.[166]

Cicognani responded a few days later that he would bring Abbot Alcuin's appeal to the attention of the Holy See, but he made it clear that Rome's position was still "that the Benedictine Abbeys have an obligation in this matter. Moreover, I am quite certain that the Sacred Congregation will be at a loss to understand your contention to the contrary, which goes so far as practically to deny every common ground of discussion." The apostolic delegate promised to ask the cardinals of the Propaganda Fide to study the question once again, but he noted that reconsideration in such matters usually occurred only when an appellant presented new evidence, which Abbot Alcuin had not done.[167]

Deutsch answered that he could do no more than "stand by my contention, and continue to insist that the Abbeys had no intention of assuming any financial obligation" and that "the responsibility for the loan obtained for the University rests solely upon St. Vincent's, if it does indeed rest even on St. Vincent's, which I feel I must continue to deny." He went on to explain once more that

> since the University has passed out of the hands of St. Vincent's, neither St. Vincent's nor the other Abbeys have any obligation with respect to the repayment of this loan. Neither Your Excellency nor His Eminence, Cardinal Fumasoni, has ever paid any attention to this my contention, the force of which is that, even if the Abbeys had committed themselves, as your Excellency and the Sacred Congregation assert, the transfer of the University out of their hands would automatically carry with it also the transfer of the encumbrances on the University to those into whose control it passed. The principle of justice, on which I base this contention, seems to me clearly implied in Canon 1500. I herewith appeal to this Canon, to confirm my contention already well-based on what is the correct interpretation of the commitment made by the Abbeys at the General Chapter of 1923, that the Abbeys of the American Cassinese Congregation have no obligation with respect to the repayment of the loan made to the Catholic University of Peking by the National City Bank of New York.[168]

For the next several months, as the Sacred Congregation for the Propagation of the Faith reviewed Abbot Alcuin's appeal, the matter lay dormant. In the interim, no further communications passed between the Holy See or the apostolic delegate and the abbot president of the American Cassinese Congregation. Meanwhile, National City Bank's suit against Saint Vincent was proceeding through the legal system. As attorneys took depositions and presented evidence in preparation for the court hearing, Archabbot Alfred wrote Abbot Alcuin that Saint Vincent's lawyers had advised him that "an adverse sentence . . . is beyond doubt. Then what?" If Saint Vincent lost the case, the community would likely have to declare bankruptcy, unless the Holy See came to its assistance. "I informed Rome of the Court trial," Koch wrote. "Next week I shall also pay a visit to the Apostolic Delegate. . . . What the outcome will be is hard to tell."[169] Abbot Alcuin answered that "Rome is likely to sit quietly on the side line and let the case go on, salving itself with the reflection that the American Cassinese Congregation should have supported the University while it was in the hands of St. Vincent's."[170]

The civil trial of *The National City Bank of New York v. The Benedictine Society of Westmoreland County* opened in Pittsburgh on February 14, 1939, before Judge F. P. Schoonmaker of the U.S. District Court for the Western District of Pennsylvania. Greensburg attorneys Edward P. Doran and Vincent E. Williams represented Saint Vincent. The legal team representing the National City Bank was composed of two law firms: Reed, Smith, Shaw and McClay of Pittsburgh and Sherman and Sterling of New York.

In his opening argument, National City Bank attorney Elder F. Marshall said that the bank's suit was being brought not against the Catholic University of Peking but against the Benedictine Society of Westmoreland County because the university was not incorporated but was "solely the creature of the Benedictine Society." The Benedictine Society "was the proprietor of it, the Benedictine Society oversaw its business affairs," and the Benedictine Society benefited directly from the $250,000 loan from the National City Bank of New York. This was the crux of the argument, for if it could be proven that the Benedictine Society was the beneficiary of the loan, then Saint Vincent would be obligated to repay the loan with interest. As the plaintiff's lawyer stated: "[W]e expect to show that this venture, this foundation, was simply an arm or an adjunct or an agency of the Benedictine Society, and that when the loan was made to the Catholic University, it was for the purpose of improving real estate of the Benedictine Society, and that the Benedictine Society is liable, because it is in actuality a loan to it."[171]

Attorneys for the defendant, on the other hand, argued that because the monastic chapter at Saint Vincent had not approved the loan in accordance with the by-laws of the Benedictine Society of Westmoreland County, the Benedictine Society was not responsible for the debt. They also repeated the argument made by both Archabbot Alfred and Abbot Alcuin that Archabbot Aurelius Stehle had taken out the loan not in his capacity as archabbot of Saint Vincent and president of the Benedictine Society of Westmoreland County, but as chancellor of the University of Peking. The University of Peking, therefore, was the beneficiary of the loan and the party responsible for repayment.

A key piece of evidence presented by the plaintiffs was the check for twenty-five thousand dollars issued to Archabbot Aurelius by the National City Bank as initial disbursement of the loan. Archabbot Aurelius deposited this check in the account of the Benedictine Society of Westmoreland County with the First National Bank of Latrobe, and then withdrew the money to pay off part of a previous loan that the Saint Vincent chapter had approved for the Catholic University of Peking. The National City Bank attorneys argued that this action proved in law that the loan had been made to the Benedictine Society.

The hearing lasted only three days, during which evidence was presented based upon bank records, minutes of the monastic chapter and the council of seniors, correspondence between the bank and Archabbot Aurelius, decrees and other documents issued by the Sacred Congregation for the Propagation of the Faith, and depositions taken from bank officials and American diplomats in China. Among the Saint Vincent priests called to testify in the case were Fathers Victor Lillig, Hugh Wilt, Wolfgang Frey, Felix Fellner, and Archabbot Alfred Koch. It was a stressful and sometimes humiliating experience for the monks.

In the end the court found in favor of the National City Bank of New York. On April 27, 1939, Judge Schoonmaker issued a judgment that the Catholic University of Peking "was not autonomous and independent" of the Benedictine Society, "but was simply a branch or an enterprise and activity of the defendant, founded and conducted in accomplishment of one of the purposes for which the defendant was incorporated; and the defendant was the sole proprietor thereof." He concluded that Archabbot Aurelius "had authority to act for defendant in its dealings with plaintiff for a loan to improve its property in Peking, China; and even if there was no express authority, the defendant accepted the benefits of the transaction and is now estopped from repudiating the Archabbot's authority to act for it." On May 1, 1939, the judge ordered the Benedictine Society of Westmoreland County to pay the National City Bank of New York the sum of $382,756.78, which represented the loan principal of $250,000 plus interest from November 15, 1929, to May 1, 1939.[172]

The judgment was a devastating blow to the monks of Saint Vincent, whose lawyers immediately filed an appeal. A stunned Archabbot Alfred wrote Abbot Alcuin of the outcome and said that he was about to inform the Holy See of the results of the suit and to ask for financial assistance in paying the debt. Abbot Alcuin responded that in his opinion "[m]erely advising Rome by cable that the decision has been against you may not even bring you an expression of sympathy. Deal with the bank and afterwards take up the case with the Holy See."[173]

THE AFTERMATH OF JUDGMENT

The days and weeks following the court's judgment were hectic for Archabbot Alfred. He initiated negotiations with the bank to postpone repayment of the loan until he could consult with Church officials in the United States and Rome on how to raise the money, and he prepared to travel to Rome to discuss with the Holy See the problem now facing the archabbey. Meanwhile Saint Vincent's lawyers pressed for a reversal of judgment through the United States Circuit Court of Appeals. When a bitter Father George Barry O'Toole learned of the judgment and of the plan to seek assistance from Rome, he wrote Father Hugh Wilt that

> what [the archabbot] wants is simply to escape the penalty of his own perfidy by demanding that the Holy See refund to him the sum assessed against St. Vincent Archabbey by the courts. In such an undertaking, it would be against my conscience to lend a helping hand to the man, who turned a deaf ear to the pleading of our late Holy Father Pius XI, who deliberately sabotaged the noble work of his predecessor Archabbot Aurelius, who defamed the good name of Archabbot Aurelius in order to save his own skin, who dishonored himself by breaking his own word and promises and by treating as scraps of paper the most solemn and binding contracts.[174]

In the second week of June Archabbot Alfred went to Rome to seek help from the Holy See. He spent a month consulting with the abbot primate and officials of the Propaganda Fide. It was a very difficult time for him, for the abbot primate and the cardinals strongly criticized him for not preempting the court decision by accepting responsibility for the debt two years earlier. They offered the remote hope that the pope would instruct the archbishops of New York and Milwaukee to use funds gathered for the missions to pay part of the judgment, but they said that nothing would be done until the American abbeys, and especially Saint Vincent, came forward with one hundred thousand dollars to partially cover the debt. Koch departed Italy on July 13, 1939, and Father Hugh Wilt, who had accompanied him to Rome as advisor and secretary and who remained at the Collegio di Sant' Anselmo to follow up on negotiations with the Holy See, wrote Abbot Alcuin that the archabbot had "left for home without anything having been accomplished." Father Hugh urged the abbot president to appoint someone other than Koch to carry on the proposed discussions with the archbishops of New York and Milwaukee. "Knowing the Archabbot," he said, "I greatly fear his delays and his ways of avoiding the questions that should be settled."[175] In confirmation of Wilt's fears, an exasperated Cardinal Fumasoni-Biondi wrote the abbot primate that if the American Benedictines "persevere in their passive and contrary attitude, this Sacred Congregation, which has done all that is possible to solve the problem, which would not have arisen if the Benedictines had done their duty in time, will no longer interest itself in the case, and will allow the National City Bank to act as it sees fit."[176]

Archabbot Alfred continued to resist the efforts of the Holy See to "tax" the American abbeys for repayment of the loan, but he clearly viewed the solution to the problem as a responsibility of the entire congregation and not just of Saint Vincent.[177] Abbot Alcuin also hoped to avoid taxing the abbeys, and urged Koch to negotiate with the bank for a reduction of the judgment and at the same time to make contact with Archbishop Samuel Stritch of Milwaukee to discuss the possibility of using the mission funds controlled by Stritch to pay off the debt. "If you have interviewed these parties and gotten definite figures from them, it will be possible to approach the Abbots with some confidence that definite action can be gotten," i.e., that the abbots would consider voluntarily contributing to the payment of the debt.[178]

Archabbot Alfred replied that he wanted to meet with all the abbots before approaching Archbishop Stritch. He said that "[c]onditions force me to find a settlement that will keep the sheriff's sale beyond possibility," and he urged Abbot Alcuin to call a special meeting of the general chapter.[179] In response Deutsch said that he was "quite willing to do anything I reasonably can to help you in the China case. But I greatly doubt whether the calling of a meeting of the Abbots before you have done what I suggested in my last letter will lead to anything." Abbot Alcuin said that he was "certain that our abbeys will be inclined to do something in this matter only when they are satisfied that St. Vincent's has done all that is possible to reduce the burden that is to fall on it and them." Again he urged the archabbot to discuss the matter with Stritch, and he returned to the perennial theme of Saint Vincent's having to bear "sole responsibility."

I am inclined to think that such assumption of sole responsibility on the part of St. Vincent's will not only help wonderfully to rehabilitate St. Vincent's in the eyes of Propaganda, and to justify the contention of no responsibility made by me on behalf of the Congregation; but will, in the end, also help St. Vincent's financially. Propaganda, New York, Milwaukee, and the S.V.D. will surely be moved to greater sympathy and more substantial help, if they know that St. Vincent's alone is bearing the burden. If, then, it is still too heavy for St. Vincent's alone, I am certain the other abbeys will be inclined much more to lend a helping hand, if you appeal to them, than they are now to make a contribution on the score of responsibility towards the University of Peking.

The abbot president, who was clearly vexed by what he regarded as Archabbot Alfred's failure to cooperate with his strategy, concluded his letter on an ominous, almost threatening note. "I shall wait upon your action," he said. "But please do not delay too long and keep me informed of what you are doing. Otherwise I shall feel it incumbent on me to write Propaganda that, in the name of the Congregation, I decline responsibility for the other abbeys and will leave it to your abbey to take the consequences."[180]

Abbot Alcuin's continued insistence upon Saint Vincent's assuming total responsibility for repayment of the National City Bank loan rankled with Archabbot Alfred to the extent that he refused to answer Deutsch's letter. When the abbot president had not heard from him for more than a month, he wrote again on September 30 to remind him "that the Cardinal says that, if the Benedictine Fathers do not accept his proposal, he will let the National City Bank take whatsoever action it pleases. That means that the help which he promises will be withdrawn and that St. Vincent's will have to bear the whole burden alone. . . . The result will be a calamity for you and your abbey and probably a big scandal." To avoid calamity and scandal, Deutsch urged that the archabbot not delay taking action. "Unless you give me a full report on what you have done or contemplate doing, I shall regretfully deem it my duty to consult with the Right Rev. Visitators whether it is advisable for us to go to St. Vincent's to take this matter up with your Chapter."[181]

Even now, Archabbot Alfred delayed responding for more than a week. Finally, he wrote that "I do not exactly know what prompted you to advance such a suggestion [that Saint Vincent assume responsibility for the loan of $250,000] unless it is the fact that by such a procedure you would render your account to the Propaganda very easy and would thereby free the Congregation of the obligation which the Propaganda tries to impose on it." He went on to say that if Saint Vincent accepted the responsibility, "I admit that the Propaganda most probably would greet such a decision with extreme joy," but he wondered if the cardinals might not then "turn against St. Vincent" and refuse to come to the archabbey's assistance in view of the American abbeys' failure to fulfill their earlier promises of supporting the Catholic University of Peking. "I admit that the position of St. Vincent in this case is not to be envied." He concluded by saying that "a meeting will soon be called" in which Archbishop Samuel Stritch of Milwaukee and Archbishop Francis Spellman of New York (who had recently succeeded Cardinal Patrick Hayes) would discuss how much the two archdioceses could contribute towards settlement of the China debt. "Then," he said, "the shares of the S.V.D. and St. Vincent will be discussed. What will happen if the Abbots refuse [to help]? God only knows. I am afraid that it will be *vae victis* ['woe to the vanquished']."[182]

Koch's remark about Abbot Alcuin's motive for insisting that Saint Vincent assume responsibility for the debt infuriated the abbot president. Deutsch replied that it was "not an easy matter to answer your letter. I might ignore it, were it not for the fact that you explicitly ask some questions which, if you had kept in mind what I have more than once written or said to you, you would not have asked." He said that he was indeed trying "to free the Congregation of the obligation which Propaganda has been trying to impose on it." As for the suggestion that he was attempting to "render my account with Propaganda very easy," he said, frankly, that he "wanted to avoid altogether making a reply to Cardinal Fumasoni's letter." He believed that it was Archabbot Alfred's duty to respond to Rome, a duty which he had failed to fulfill. "You know perfectly well and have admitted it to me," he said,

> that your predecessor wanted the University to be regarded as an undertaking of St. Vincent's and acted accordingly. You also know that Rome knows you did not want the University, and charges that you acted accordingly. The University did not get more support from the Congregation precisely because Archabbot Aurelius proudly regarded it as a St. Vincent's undertaking, and you did not want it at all. Both you and your predecessor went to Rome repeatedly and to China in the interests of the University, and you did not go in the name of the Congregation, but in virtue of your jurisdiction over the University. Nothing that my predecessor as President of the Congregation or I have done in connection with the University can destroy or weaken the significance of these facts.

Finally he accused Archabbot Alfred of acting without due consultation with the abbot president. "You write that a meeting will soon be called in which Archbishops Spellman and Stritch will be asked to give an estimate of the amount they will contribute. You do not say when it is likely to be called nor where nor by whom nor who is to be present. You want me to assume responsibility for the Congregation in the matter of this debt, yet you hardly keep me properly informed as to what is going on."[183]

Abbot Alcuin felt as if Archabbot Alfred had closed off all possibility of discussion of the issue and in frustration wrote for help to Father Hugh Wilt, the Saint Vincent monk who had been serving as secretary and advisor to the archabbot. Abbot Alcuin wrote to Father Hugh: "I have been negotiating with the Archabbot in an endeavor to get him to act." Thus far, however, the abbot president had "not made a home-hit [hit a home run?] with him." Koch continued to insist that the American Cassinese abbots meet to discuss how much money they would be willing to contribute to the debt resolution. Deutsch did not want the abbots to meet until Koch had gotten a clear statement from Archbishops Stritch and Spellman concerning how much the Archdioceses of Milwaukee and New York were prepared to contribute. Koch, on the other hand, felt that he could not approach the archbishops or the Propaganda Fide without having a specific offer in hand from the American Benedictine abbots. The archabbot and abbot president had reached an impasse. "I have little hope of coming to an understanding with the Archabbot by letter," Deutsch wrote Father Hugh. "Yet something must be done. Either he must answer Cardinal Fumasoni's proposition, or I must do so as President of the Congregation. He does not seem disposed to take my point of view."[184]

Father Hugh Wilt was equally frustrated by the archabbot's apparent indecisiveness. "I was greatly upset," Wilt wrote the abbot president, "when upon my return [from Rome] I discovered that the Archabbot had taken no definite action." Father Hugh had urged him to meet immediately with the archbishops of New York and Milwaukee, as instructed by the Holy See, and had even offered to meet with the prelates himself, but Koch "didn't even hear the request." Wilt had also urged the archabbot to give the Saint Vincent chapter an opportunity to "accept the Cardinal's solution in the name of St. Vincent's if the Abbots do not see their way clear to accept it in the name of the Congregation." But Koch remained adamant.

> He simply refuses. The basis of his refusal is simply his fear of his own Chapter. As I wrote you from Rome, there can be no solution as long as it is in his hands. In other hands it could have been settled to everybody's satisfaction years ago. There must be a solution soon for the interest is piling rapidly at over two thousand a month. With some kind of solution, that alone could be cut in half—it is now nine months since the trial—or $18,000. To be very frank with you, Father Abbot, I personally have grown very discouraged over it all. After nearly six years of constant suggestions and requests I have yet to see my first suggestion acted upon.[185]

On November 16, 1939, after having received no response to his letter of October 20, Abbot Alcuin sent Archabbot Alfred a strongly worded message designed to elicit action. "Frankly, I do not understand your attitude," he said. "This whole affair will have disastrous consequences for you and your Abbey unless it is settled soon." Though he continued to hold that the debt question "concerns primarily St. Vincent's," he said that he was willing to help "to the utmost of my ability." He was therefore prepared to make an offer to the archabbot, but he threatened that "[i]f you do not accept this offer, we shall have to consider other ways and means to safeguard your community and the Congregation." The "other ways and means" the abbot president had in mind were clearly the institution of canonical proceedings against the archabbot to force him from office. Abbot Alcuin's offer of help was to have Abbot Vincent Taylor of Belmont Abbey accompany Archabbot Alfred to New York for a meeting with National City Bank officials in an effort to reduce the bank's claims on Saint Vincent.[186]

This letter brought an immediate response from Archabbot Alfred. By return mail he sent a formal, businesslike answer in which he thanked Abbot Alcuin for his "kind offer to help us" but said that approaching the National City Bank for the purpose of reducing its claims on Saint Vincent was "at present premature." His lawyers had advised him to wait until after the results of the appeal were known before speaking with bank officials. Koch then pointed out to the abbot president that the questions the capitulars of Saint Vincent were most interested in knowing the answers to were: "Did the Right Reverend Abbots of the Congregation decide anything as to their attitude in the Chinese case? Have any steps been taken in regard to the request of the Propaganda? How much will the Congregation contribute toward the payment of the debt?" Archabbot Alfred said that a clear answer to these questions "is greatly desired because Rome seems to make [the abbots' cooperation] a *conditio sine qua non* for the help she has promised. May I therefore ask: 'Has anything been done in that regard? Is any definite answer available?'" Koch concluded by referring to "the hidden threat contained in your letter." He noted that with regard to Deutsch's implication that the abbot president might institute proceedings to remove him from office, "I leave it in your own judgment and conscience. However I wish to state one thing: Nothing in this world will induce me to willingly assume the responsibility for the loan in question."[187]

By now the disagreement between the archabbot and Abbot Alcuin had developed into an open rift. The abbot president was convinced that Archabbot Alfred's apparent indecisiveness was in fact a delaying tactic designed to force the congregation to take responsibility for the loan. The archabbot, on the other hand, had concluded that Deutsch and the other abbots of the congregation had decided to abandon Saint Vincent to its creditors and had no intention of coming to its assistance. The apparent lack of cooperation from the congregation was a bitter disappointment for the archabbot and the capitulars of Saint Vincent, and in the light of his disillusionment Koch determined that the only way for him to save the archabbey from imminent bankruptcy was to carry on negotiations with the Holy See independently of Abbot Alcuin and the other abbots of the American Cassinese Congregation.

Toward the end of November he learned that Saint Vincent's appeal for a reversal of the U.S. District Court's judgment had been rejected by the appellate court and that Saint Vincent was compelled to pay almost $390,000 to the National City Bank of New York.[188] On December 5, 1939, the archabbot went to Washington to meet with the apostolic delegate, Archbishop Cicognani, to discuss how to resolve the issue, which had by now reached the critical stage. The National City Bank had sent investigators to Latrobe to assess the value of the buildings and property of Saint Vincent with the intention of instituting civil proceedings to seize the property in lieu of satisfactory settlement of the debt. The investigator reported:

> It is estimated that replacement costs for the improved property owned by the Society in Latrobe would exceed $500,000. The land is not very valuable; a considerable part is wild, the coal mines formerly operated are now flooded, but some part of the acreage is cultivated for the benefit of the school. The buildings consist chiefly of dormitories and class rooms for the 500 students, administration building, church, and the usual collateral facilities. Except for the special purpose the property has little utility. . . . We have a debtor whose assets if offered at auction might produce some unknown realization.[189]

At their meeting in Washington, the apostolic delegate told Archabbot Alfred that the Sacred Congregation for the Propagation of the Faith continued to insist that the American Benedictines provide $100,000 toward payment of the settlement. In private conversation with Koch Cicognani assured the archabbot that if the American Benedictines raised the stipulated amount, Rome itself would see to raising the balance required to pay off the debt. In response, Archabbot Alfred committed Saint Vincent to raising $25,000 and asked the apostolic delegate to seek the remaining $75,000 from the abbots of the American Cassinese Congregation. After the meeting on December 5, 1939, Cicognani sent Koch a letter restating with more details Rome's plan for resolving the case. The Holy Father, he said, had given "unlimited faculties" to the archbishops of Milwaukee and New York to do "everything possible toward a diminution of the debt," and the "fine cooperation and financial assistance of Their Excellencies" had resulted in notable success. The apostolic delegate was therefore "able to assure you that by the payment of one hundred thousand dollars in cash in the very near future the Benedictine Fathers will be able to bring this affair to a final settlement." He noted that Saint Vincent had agreed to pay one-fourth of this amount, and he asked the archabbot to write the other abbots asking for their help in providing the rest.[190]

Archabbot Alfred sent the apostolic delegate's letter to Abbot Alcuin and asked his assistance in communicating the necessary information to the abbots of the congregation. Deutsch replied with barely concealed anger that by his recent letter, Koch had now "confirm[ed] my conviction, arrived at from other indications, that you have favored, if you did not actually suggest, that the other abbeys of the Congregation be called upon by Propaganda to help pay this loan. That appears to me to be the reason why I have had no success in my fight against this plan." But now that the decision about "taxing" the abbeys had been finally made by the Holy See, the abbot president saw no alternative and advised the archabbot "to get busy and send a circular letter to all the Abbots at an early date."[191]

Three days after Christmas Archabbot Alfred sent a copy of Cicognani's letter of December 5 to the abbots. Koch explained that he had opposed the Holy See's "taxation plan" but said that since the Propaganda Fide now saw fit to implement it, he would appreciate the abbots' informing him by the middle of January how much each monastery would be able to contribute towards the payment of the debt. Abbot Alcuin followed this letter with one of his own urging the abbots to be cooperative but suggesting that Saint Vincent's share of the burden be more than the $25,000 the community was prepared to offer.[192]

By the end of January 1940 the abbots of the congregation—despite almost universal hardship, some serious misgivings, and a few harsh words expressed in letters to the archabbot of Saint Vincent—had sent checks amounting to more than $55,000 to the abbot president for liquidation of the debt. Only a few of the smaller and poorer abbeys had been unable to contribute. With its check for $15,000 St. John's Abbey, Minnesota, contributed the largest amount. Ten other abbeys contributed between $500 and $9,500 each, and the chapter at Saint Vincent agreed to provide the remaining $45,000.[193] Archabbot Alfred sent individual letters of thanks to each of the abbots whose communities had provided funds. To Abbot Mark Braun of St. Gregory's Abbey, Shawnee, Oklahoma, he wrote expressing his appreciation not just for the check but also for his "kind criticism." Braun was one of several abbots who had recommended that Saint Vincent assume a greater portion of the burden, and the archabbot told him that the archabbey chapter had indeed accepted responsibility for $45,000 of the National City Bank settlement.

> Add to this [another] $75,000, the remainder of the loan of $100,000 which St. Vincent guaranteed, and you have an idea of the burden that has been imposed on us within the space of *one* year. Besides that there is also an annuity of $1250 to be paid on a loan of $25,000 which my lamented predecessor received from a lady in Pittsburgh. Summing it up, the large as well as the small, and you will certainly agree with me that our Chinese venture cost us the staggering sum of over $200,000. And what can we show for it? Only an empty purse.[194]

In fact Saint Vincent's losses were much more than $200,000. For nine years the archabbey had poured all its available resources, human and material, into the China mission. In financial terms alone, more than $1.5 million had been invested in Fu Jen University, and while much of the money had come from the Holy See, from other abbeys of the American Cassinese Congregation, and from individual lay and clerical contributors to the Chinese mission fund, Saint Vincent had invested over $800,000 between 1925 and 1933.[195] The investment had been a total loss. When the American Benedictines withdrew from China, they had left behind property and buildings worth more than $750,000.

The abbots of the congregation sent their communities' contributions for liquidation of the National City Bank debt to Abbot Alcuin, and from Minnesota Abbot Alcuin forwarded the total amount to Archabbot Alfred. Koch, following instructions of the apostolic delegate, then sent a check for $100,000 to the new archbishop of New York, Francis J. Spellman, who had agreed to coordinate negotiations with the bank to settle the debt.[196] At the request of the Holy See, Archbishop Samuel Stritch of Milwaukee also sent $150,000 of a nonobligated mission fund to Archbishop Spellman to help pay the debt, and the archbishop of New York, after negotiating a modest adjustment in the settlement, provided the balance of $100,000.[197]

The China mission had proved disastrous for Saint Vincent, which during the 1940s suffered great economic hardship as a result of the losses it had sustained. More than a decade would pass before the archabbey achieved a measure of financial security. During that period, development of the community's educational and pastoral apostolates was severely constrained, and construction of new buildings necessary to accommodate the post–World War II influx of students had to be postponed. Perhaps the greatest burden Saint Vincent had to bear as consequence of the failure of the China mission and the loss of the National City Bank suit, however, was the strain that resulted in the community's relations with the monasteries of the American Cassinese Congregation on the one hand and with the Holy See on the other. The Sacred Congregation for the Propagation of the Faith blamed primarily the archabbey in Pennsylvania for the failure in China and secondarily other abbeys of the congregation for their supposed lack of support, while in America recriminations were exchanged between the archabbey and its fraternal partners in the congregation. Many of the monks of the American Cassinese abbeys held Archabbot Alfred and the monastic chapter at Saint Vincent responsible for the humiliation the entire congregation had suffered, while the monks of Saint Vincent regarded the other abbeys as unreliable confreres who had come to the aid of the motherhouse a day late and a dollar short. The earlier relationship of friendship and trust between Archabbot Alfred Koch and Abbot Alcuin Deutsch was seriously damaged, and a period of frosty relations ensued between the Benedictine communities in Pennsylvania and Minnesota.

But the American Benedictine mission in China clearly had its positive results as well. More than thirty American Benedictine monks and nuns (including eleven from Saint Vincent) had served on the China mission, and they all brought back to their communities a love for China and a commitment to spreading the Gospel in the Orient that survived the loss of the Catholic University of Peking. The American Benedictine involvement in China, which began with the arrival of Saint Vincent Fathers Ildephonse Brandstetter and Placidus Rattenberger in Peking in July 1924, continued after 1933 with the work of American Benedictine monks and nuns in Kaifeng until their internment by the Japanese in 1941. After the war, monks from St. Procopius Abbey, Lisle, Illinois, and nuns from St. Benedict's Convent, St. Joseph, Minnesota, continued to work in Kaifeng until they were forced to leave with the arrival of the Communists in 1948. The Benedictine women went to Taiwan, where they established a priory in Tanshui, and nearly twenty years later the monks of St. Procopius established a priory in Chiayi, Taiwan.[198]

As for the Catholic University of Peking, the Society of the Divine Word continued against great odds and with heavy losses to build on the foundation laid by the American Benedictines. The university came under the aegis of the German province of the Society of the Divine Word and survived the Second World War as the only university recognized by the government of Japanese-occupied Peking. The S.V.D. missionaries gave up the institution only in 1952 when the Communist government assumed control of Fu Jen and merged it with the Beijing [Peking] Normal University. In its more than a quarter-century of existence on the mainland, nearly five thousand young Chinese students graduated from Fu Jen, which according to one Chinese commentator "became a significant force in the country's social development."[199]

In 1960, at the initiative of the Sacred Congregation for the Propagation of the Faith, Fu Jen University was reestablished on Taiwan under the supervision of three religious groups: the Society of the Divine Word, the Jesuits, and the Chinese diocesan clergy; and four years later, after an absence of three decades, monks from Saint Vincent returned to China to establish Wimmer Priory in Taipei, Taiwan, and to serve on the faculty of the newly constituted Fu Jen University.[200]

EIGHT

BUILDING FOR THE FUTURE (1940–1963)

THE FINANCIAL CRISIS That resulted from the loss of the National City Bank suit was only one of the problems Archabbot Alfred and the monastic community faced as Saint Vincent entered the 1940s. The war in Europe occupied the attention of monks and students alike, and with the rest of America the Saint Vincent community wondered what impact it would have on their country and themselves. In the fall of 1940 the U.S. Congress passed the Burke-Wadsworth Military Conscription Bill, and young men of draft age registered in compliance with the law. At Saint Vincent Fathers Bernard Brinker, Cyprian Yahner, Justin Krellner, Cosmas Minster, Harold Phillips, and Colman Lillig served on the local registration board, and three clerics—Brothers DeSales Zang, Werner Conwell, and Godfrey Burkhardt—were the first from the archabbey to register.[1] Subsequent conscription legislation exempted clerical students from military service, but in the closing days of 1940 no one was certain what was going to happen, so all the clerics of the monastery joined their student colleagues in the seminary, college, and prep school (several of whose seniors were eighteen years old) in registering for the draft.

The general attitude among both students and monks was that America should avoid the conflict. The *St. Vincent Journal* editorialized that "[i]f the American people would only open their eyes, they could easily see how we are being railroaded into war by a publicity stunt that would put even Barnum to shame." The "publicity stunt," in the editor's opinion, was the pro-British propaganda of the American press. Reflecting the views of a majority of professors and students at Saint Vincent, the *Journal* consistently opposed "the many hysterical fools of the nation whose minds [have] been warped by the British propaganda which is being spread throughout the country," and in a moment of unbridled isolationism the student newspaper said that

> [o]nce again the brave American politicians are slowly but surely leading the United States into war, and once again it will be the youth of this Rooseveltized country who will pay the supreme price for the material gain of a few select war profiteers. . . . We—and the vast majority of college students are of the same opinion—will fight tooth and nail if the United States is invaded, but we want no part of a program to defend Great Britain. We, with Charles A. Lindbergh, firmly believe that before the United States rushes to the aid of a tottering British Empire, we should start in our own backyard to reinforce the foundation of our own democracy.[2]

Such were the views of many Americans in the months leading up to Pearl Harbor, but when the Japanese attacked on December 7, 1941, and America went to war, the students and monks of Saint Vincent were, like the rest of the country, stirred to patriotic fervor. "America is at war," Archabbot Alfred wrote in his 1941 Christmas message. "I know that students will be loyal to their country; that they will perform all their duties with a ready willingness and joy; that they will accept the sacrifices which the war will bring with good cheer. Let our actions be guided by that strong and true Christian patriotism which has always been a source of inspiration, sacrifice, and service. Let our slogan be: 'For God and country, through victory to peace.' May God bless America!"[3]

SAINT VINCENT IN WORLD WAR II

The first students drafted from the college were senior class president Louis Slomoff of Arnold, Pennsylvania, and James Wiesen of Sharon, Pennsylvania, editor of the *St. Vincent Journal*.[4] In the course of the next year many more draft notices arrived, and as other students went off to war, enrollment in the college fell, causing concern about the financial viability of the institution. In March 1942 eight students signed up for the reserve officer and pilot training program with the Marine Corps and Navy. Entrance into the program required six college credits in mathematics, and the student newspaper reported that the college was "cooperating with these boys and all others who are thinking of enlisting in the armed forces by offering a course in basic mathematics this summer. The course will comprise algebra, trigonometry, and geometry."[5] A month later the Navy approved the college's proposed curriculum for the Naval Reserve's V-1 officer training program for college sophomores, freshmen, and prospective freshmen. Students who successfully completed the program were eligible to enter the Navy's V-7 officer training program for college graduates. More importantly, they were allowed to remain in college until they completed their degree. Dr. Daniel P. Nolan of the chemistry department was in charge of the program.[6]

In March 1942 Archabbot Alfred named Fathers Camillus Long, Colman Lillig, and Norbert Rupprecht as air raid wardens for Saint Vincent. The appointments were "in keeping with the established policy of lending all possible aid to the surrounding district during the present emergency," and a few days later the Saint Vincent community went through its first scheduled blackout. For a period of fifteen minutes on the evening of March 16 all the lights of Westmoreland County were turned out, and the *Journal* reported that "being in an advantageous position, overlooking the surrounding countryside—Latrobe, Youngstown, and the neighboring hamlets—we could observe the spectacle. It was a great success. . . . The only flaw of a perfect night panorama was the glare on the horizon from lights and fires in the nearby mills."[7] If the blackout proved interesting and exciting to students and monks, a deeper understanding of the tragic realities of war struck home four months later when news reached campus of the first wartime casualty among the alumni of the college. The first Saint Vincent student to be killed in the war was twenty-two-year-old Stephen Bladykas, a 1941 graduate who joined the Army Air Corps shortly after graduation and who died in a training accident at Bolling Field, Washington, D.C., on July 30, 1942.[8]

In January 1942 the administration introduced a "wartime schedule" at the college. Saturday classes were added, hours for classes during the day were extended, and the traditional fifteen-week semester was cut to thirteen weeks. The new schedule consisted of three terms (fall, winter, and summer) of thirteen weeks each. The accelerated program allowed students to complete their degrees in three rather than four years. The committee of studies that developed the program consisted of Fathers Augustine Minkel,

Edward Wenstrup, Alcuin Tasch, and Maurice Costello, and Dr. Daniel P. Nolan.[9]

The 1942–43 academic year opened with a notable decline in the number of undergraduates. The draft, as well as increased opportunities for lucrative employment in the steel mills of western Pennsylvania, resulted in significantly fewer students coming to the college, though enrollment in the seminary remained stable and that of the prep school even rose. Thus by September 1942 there were 292 college students at Saint Vincent, 108 theologians in the seminary, and 209 students in the prep school. The college enrollment was down 15 percent from that of 1940, while the prep school enrollment was up almost 20 percent. The following year, after the Army enlisted reserves were called to active duty, undergraduate enrollment dramatically dropped to 124, while prep enrollment increased slightly to 220 and seminary enrollment remained unchanged.[10] To help offset the decline, the college began to admit freshmen in the winter semester. But by September 1944 the draft had all but dried up the available pool of incoming freshmen, while most of the able-bodied sophomores, juniors, and seniors had been conscripted. The number of nonclerical students in the college for the 1944–45 school year was 102, though enrollment in the prep school had risen to 325 in partial compensation for the loss. Even the prep school, however, was affected by the draft. At the commencement exercises of May 1943, 44 prep seniors received diplomas, but 8 of them were not present because they had been inducted into the armed forces.[11]

Regular student activities, of course, were disrupted by the war, though the faculty and students attempted to maintain as normal an atmosphere as possible, sometimes with impressive results. Interscholastic debating and varsity sports were suspended in 1943, but the annual freshman recognition dance was held, as were other dances throughout the year. The college orchestra and glee club under the direction of Father Ralph Bailey presented regular concerts (including one in December 1943 at which Brother Ildephonse Wortman, a cleric studying theology, performed Mozart's Piano Concerto no. 22); student representatives attended regional meetings of the National Federation of Catholic College Students; the *St. Vincent Journal* continued publication without interruption throughout the war; college clubs and organizations continued to meet and engage in their traditional activities; intramural football, basketball, and baseball remained an important feature of student life; the student production of the passion play *Calvary* was regularly presented each Lent; prep school students put on operettas in conjunction with the students of St. Joseph Academy at Seton

Hill, Greensburg, and of St. Xavier's Academy, Latrobe; and regular liturgical celebrations continued uninterrupted throughout the year, with special ceremonies marking the feasts of Christmas, St. Thomas Aquinas, St. Patrick, St. Benedict, Holy Week, Easter, and Corpus Christi.

Other activities during the war included regular spiritual talks by Saint Vincent monks on Greensburg radio station WHJB. Fathers Norbert Ruprecht, Christopher Fullman, and Egbert Donovan were among the priests who broadcast weekly spiritual advice on the station's Eternal Light radio program. The annual summer laymen's retreats also continued during the war and attracted large numbers of Catholic laymen to the campus. In August 1944, 933 retreatants participated in the five retreats preached by Father Francis Murray, C.Ss.R., of Pittsburgh.[12]

In the spring of 1943 the diocesan students of theology and philosophy vacated their quarters in Aurelius Hall and moved to the college dormitories when more than 350 cadets in the Army Air Corps aviation training program arrived on campus and took up residence in the seminary. The following summer the seminary joined the college in establishing an accelerated academic program that kept the seminarians in classes year-round. The reason for the accelerated seminary program was that local draft boards were beginning to reconsider the exemption status of those clerical students not in academic programs during the summer. The number of incoming diocesan students declined as fewer college undergraduates were able to complete studies in philosophy, but for a while seminary enrollment held steady because of the number of Benedictine clerics studying theology. In 1943 there were still 109 theologians in the seminary, though the number fell to 90 in 1944 and to 80 in 1945. Most of the diocesan students were from the Diocese of Pittsburgh, but there were a few students from other dioceses as well. In the fall of 1943 the Diocese of Trenton sent two seminarians to Saint Vincent—Thomas Jones and Joseph Butler—who became the second and third African American students to enroll in the seminary. Later in the war even ordinations were accelerated, so that after 1944 students who had completed their theology program were immediately ordained to the priesthood. In March 1945, for example, eighteen seminarians (including Benedictines Leopold Krul, Ildephonse Wortman, and Marcellus Kovach) were ordained by Bishop Hugh Boyle just after finishing their last course in theology three months ahead of schedule.[13]

In his Christmas message of 1943 Archabbot Alfred emphasized the religious and moral challenges facing the students during these difficult times. "The upheaval in the moral order which is so generally admitted to be the cause of our world troubles," he said, "is a challenge to the students of our day." He went on to say:

> What is needed nowadays is a firm stand on the eternal grounds of right and wrong. Do not lose sight of the fact that our new America, which is to emerge out of the present chaos, must be based on the foundation stone of the real distinction between right and wrong in accordance with the teachings of natural and divine law. If that loyalty to God's law is discarded in the life of nations and individuals, the downfall of nations is sealed. What we need to make a better America is the reform which Christ inaugurated and exemplified in His life. We need a religious spirit, a spiritual motive power, that animates the lives and work of men. We need men and women who live their faith in daily life. If those fundamental truths of Christianity have lost their place in the affairs of men, if education, social life, and economics are divorced from the guiding principles of religion, things cannot be well with mankind, as our present conditions in this war-torn world fully prove. In view of this fact we cannot but say that our students have a sublime mission assigned to them.[14]

Hundreds of Saint Vincent students and alumni served in all branches of the armed forces during the conflict. Ensign Arthur Hartung (a student in the college from 1934 to 1938) was on board the U.S.S. *Nauset* when it was torpedoed off the coast of Salerno in September 1943. He survived the ordeal in which eighteen men were killed and forty-four wounded. In February 1944 the *St. Vincent Journal* reported that Lieutenant Donald C. McCall, a 1941 graduate of the college and now a B-17 pilot, had heroically saved his crew by bringing his crippled bomber to a successful crash landing in an English wheatfield after a bombing run up the "suicidal Ruhr Valley." McCall, who received the Silver Star for gallantry in action and the Air Medal with two Oak Leaf Clusters, was later shot down over Germany and remained a prisoner of war until 1945. Another graduate who became a prisoner of war was Lieutenant Walter Strosser, a star football player at Saint Vincent in the late 1930s who had been named to the All-American small college football team in 1940. Strosser piloted a B-17 that was shot down over Germany in 1944.

Father Thomas E. Madden of Altoona, a graduate of Saint Vincent Seminary who had enlisted as a chaplain with the U.S. Army, was wounded in the Italian campaign of 1944. Dave Davies, a 1943 college graduate, was also among the American troops who landed in Italy and wrote that he had had the happy opportunity of serving a Mass offered by a Catholic chaplain on the Montecassino front. "The altar was improvised from the hood of a parked jeep," he said; "the blue cloud-studded sky served as a roof; the surrounding high mountain peaks were as lofty spires. For a choir we had the rumbling of our big guns and the death-song of outgoing shells. The Holy Sacrifice that day, in my mind, was more impressive in its simplicity than any colorful ceremony to be witnessed in the most beautiful cathedrals."[15] Major Lawrence C. Buchman, a prep school graduate of 1926, was also at the Battle of Montecassino and wrote afterward to his former professors at Saint Vincent that much of the ancient archabbey of St. Benedict was in ruins. Another prep alumnus at Montecassino was Robert LaBolitta (class of 1937), whose fighter plane crashed near the archabbey; he escaped uninjured.[16]

Captain John Vesely (college class of 1940) was with the Army Medical Corps in France, and First Lieutenant George Lawlor of Latrobe (class of 1936) served in a tank battalion in France, where he was wounded. Lieutenant Albert G. Smith (class of 1938), who flew over Germany, received the Air Medal with three Oak Leaf Clusters and the Distinguished Flying Cross, and Ensign Michael Bernard Rich (class of 1943) won the Purple Heart for wounds received when his ship was sunk during the Normandy invasion. Technical Sergeant Lawrence E. O'Neill of Jeannette, Pennsylvania, who had graduated from the prep school in 1940 and attended the college for one year before enlisting in the Army, was awarded the Distinguished Flying Cross "for extraordinary achievement" while flying bombing raids over Germany; and Staff Sergeant Howell T. McFarland (college class of 1942) of Mount Pleasant, Pennsylvania, was awarded the Air Medal for "meritorious achievement" while flying as aerial gunner aboard a B-17 out of Italy. Another Saint Vincent student who flew as an aerial gunner with the Army Air Corps was Paul Regis Maher of Latrobe, a 1943 graduate of the prep school who had won the gold medal for highest scholastic average in the graduating class. After the war Maher returned to Saint Vincent to join the monastery, and in 1983 he became the tenth archabbot of the community.

Those who served in the Pacific theater included Raymond Testa, first member of the class of 1943 to enlist in the Marine Corps. Testa fought the Japanese on the Solomon Islands where he was wounded in hand-to-hand fighting and evacuated to a naval hospital in California; in January 1944 he returned to Saint Vincent to continue his studies in political science. Marine Lieutenant Steve J. Vucic of Rankin, Pennsylvania, a 1942 college graduate, was also wounded in action in the Pacific, and Marine Captain Lou Ditta (college class of 1940), fought at Guadalcanal and received both a Purple Heart and a presidential citation for bravery. Army Staff Sergeant Norbert Paine (class of 1939) fought in the jungles of New Guinea. Navy

Lieutenant Robert W. Hurley (class of 1942) of Latrobe, who flew a torpedo plane off a U.S. aircraft carrier, was awarded the Navy Cross for his part in sinking the Japanese battleship *Yamato,* and Navy medic Francis R. Statzula (class of 1940) was awarded the Bronze Star for heroism in action on Saipan when he rushed to the rescue of several wounded men.[17]

Among Saint Vincent students and alumni killed during the war were Robert Nordlohne (college class of 1933) of Covington, Kentucky, who was killed in England in March 1944 when his bomber crashed; Joseph Kornish (class of 1928) of Pittsburgh, killed in action in Italy in February 1944; Anthony Rosswog (class of 1923) who died of heart failure in England in March 1944; Lieutenant Leonard Boehm (class of 1941) of McKees Rocks, Pennsylvania, killed over China in December 1944 while piloting a C-87 transport over "the Hump" in the China-India-Burma theater; and Lieutenant William H. Kenah (class of 1939), a dive-bomber pilot killed in action over the South Pacific in November 1944; he had won the Navy Air Medal for successful attacks on Japanese shipping. Captain of the college's tennis team and a leading debater on the debate team during his years at Saint Vincent, Kenah left behind a wife and a son who was born a month before he died and whom he never saw. Also, Father Herbert F. Butterbach, a major in the Chaplain's Corps and a 1934 graduate of the seminary for the Diocese of Pittsburgh, served two years with the Army in England and upon his return to the United States died of a heart attack in 1945.[18]

Along with students and alumni of the college, seminary, and prep school who served in the armed forces, several priests of the archabbey were chaplains. Father Aquinas Brinker, an Army Reserve chaplain since 1936, was promoted to captain and assigned to the 902nd Engineers in Pittsburgh in 1941. He was later posted at Kelly Field in Texas and in 1943 was with American forces in the invasion of North Africa. Father Rupert Stadtmiller entered the Army Chaplain's Corps in April 1942 and went to North Africa in 1943 where he was assigned to the 109th Medical Battalion. Father Rupert participated in the landing at Anzio at the beginning of the Italian campaign. Father Gerald Nessler, former music teacher at the college, became an Army chaplain in May 1943, and Father Patrick McKivigan, debate coach and professor of geography in the college, joined the Chaplain's Corps in the summer of 1944.[19]

After a hiatus of several years because of the Depression, the aviation program was revived at Saint Vincent in September 1939 when the Civil Aeronautics Authority, under the Civilian Pilot Training Act of 1939, selected the college to conduct a pilot training program. Father Aquinas Brinker of the physics department was in charge of the program and was assisted by Father Othmar Waltz. Flying instruction was given by Civil Aeronautics Authority instructors Ray Leeward, Charles B. Carroll, Cecil Smith, George Allen, and Davis S. Petterson at the Latrobe Airport. A certificate of competency as a private pilot was awarded to students who successfully completed the course, for which they earned four college credits. During the first semester of each year ground school instruction in the theory of flight, aeronautical meteorology, aeronavigation, and the construction, control, and operation of "heavier-than-air craft" was given at the college by members of the physics department and specially hired teachers. Flight instruction took place in the second semester.[20]

The college's first eight student pilots took to the air for the first time in January 1940, flying the school's new fifty-five-horsepower Taylor Cub monoplane. The following September twenty-five undergraduates enrolled in the aviation course. In 1941 when Father Aquinas Brinker was called to active duty, Father Ulric Thaner became coordinator of the aviation program, and in January 1942 the college opened the program to high school graduates between the ages of eighteen and twenty-six. Draftees in line for induction who hoped to fly for the Army Air Corps were given a three-month deferment to complete the civilian pilot training course.[21] The program, later called the War Training Service Program, was radically expanded in 1943 when the Army Air Corps established on campus an aviation training school for Army recruits.

On March 1, 1943, 200 Army Air Corps cadets arrived at Saint Vincent, and a month later these were joined by 150 more prospective pilots. The cadets were housed in the seminary building (Aurelius Hall) and attended college classes in mathematics, physics, geography, history, and English given by regular Saint Vincent faculty members. Among the professors who instructed them were Fathers Ulric Thaner, Ferdinand Lillig, Bernard Brinker, Roland Heid, Bertin Emling, Mark Kistner, Felix Fellner, Jerome Rupprecht, Emmeran Rettger, Fintan Shoniker, Leander Pail, Quentin Schaut, Cyprian Yahner, Camillus Long, Xavier Mihm, and Warren Raab—virtually the entire college faculty. In addition to ordinary undergraduate courses, the Saint Vincent professors also had the task of teaching such technical courses to the cadets as aircraft identification, Morse code, meteorology, "avigation" (astronomy for navigators), and "aerology" ("systems of navigation, course plotting, and radio aids"). The *St. Vincent Journal* observed that the college's academic program would have to be modified "to provide some of the highly technical courses required in the training of a pilot. New courses will have to be taught, and some of the courses now being offered will have to be dropped from the curriculum." Flight training was given by military and civilian instructors at the Latrobe Airport, and the Army sent thirteen training planes ("and eighteen parachutes") to the airport for that purpose.[22]

Under commandant of cadets Lieutenant David J. Shapiro, the Army Air Corps training program (designated the 33rd Aircrew Detachment) continued at Saint Vincent for fourteen months. Archabbot Alfred appointed Father Oliver Grosselin chaplain for the trainees, and Grosselin made arrangements with local Protestant and Jewish clergymen to hold services in the college auditorium for those cadets who were not Catholic. College football coach Eugene Edwards was placed in charge of the cadets' physical training and oversaw construction of an obstacle "commando course" for their use.[23] The changes at Saint Vincent resulting from the presence of the cadets were radical. The campus took on the characteristics of a military camp, with cadets marching, singing, and drilling every day within the shadow of the monastery. In August 1943 Father Felix Fellner wrote Abbot Bertrand Dolan of St. Anselm's Abbey, Manchester, New Hampshire, that "St. Vincent is now on the War-Path with 350 air trainees and about a dozen officers within its walls. They occupy the Seminary (which was transferred to the College), but they can be heard everywhere. Drums and fifes and singing and shouting do not well harmonize with the Pax Benedictina, especially when we are at meals and several young men shout (to strengthen their lungs, they told me) right below our windows."[24]

During their time at Saint Vincent the cadets dominated life on the campus. The daily schedule of meals and study halls in the prep school had to be adjusted to accommodate the Army Air Corps program, and the seminarians were hard put to pursue their studies of philosophy and theology undistracted by the noisy activity of 350 young soldiers. The military's presence also served to illustrate sharply the college's need for new facilities. The Army inspection team had approved the facilities in general: the location, housing, kitchen and dining rooms, laboratories, faculty, and the accessibility to the Latrobe Airport. But the team pointed out that there was no adequate gymnasium for drilling and physical exercise during the winter months, and proposed constructing a temporary structure for that purpose. Father Maurice Costello, the college dean, countered with a proposal that the government provide funds for the construction of a permanent gymnasium and also a new dormitory, but when the Army balked, not even a temporary gym was built.[25]

In the end the Army made do with what was at hand, and the program continued successfully despite the lack of suitable indoor training facilities during the winter. If the impact of the cadets on Saint Vincent was great, the reverse was also true. Many of the cadets were highly impressed by the peaceful setting of the campus and the warmth with which they were received by faculty, students, monks, and the German-speaking nuns who served them meals. Private Frank C. Gilkes wrote of the physical beauty of the college, but noted that he had encountered something even more beautiful at Saint Vincent. "This beauty is much more subtle and produces a more powerful effect," he said.

> It is a spiritual beauty. To define it, to put your finger on the exact thing that is this spiritual beauty is difficult. Yet it is there. It is there in the cheery smiles of everyone. It is there in the warm greeting, the firm handclasp, and the encouraging word of all. It is there in the helping hand and acts of kindness. It is important, this spiritual thing. For without it the physical beauty would, in time, appear drab and lifeless. . . . The acts of kindness, of brotherhood and cheerfulness so evident here will serve to aid us when strength is most needed in time and events to follow.[26]

An airplane crash at the Latrobe Airport on the morning of June 1, 1943, was the only event that marred the experience of the young soldiers who trained at Saint Vincent during the war. The civilian flight instructor, Mr. Mowell of Adamsburg, Pennsylvania, was killed, and the cadet pilot, Stillman Copp, was seriously injured.[27] But otherwise no untoward incidents occurred, and the community's experience with the Army on campus was, on the whole, very positive. Indeed, the military training program at Saint Vincent was in certain ways a godsend. With the decline in college enrollment, the already precarious financial condition of the archabbey and its apostolates had become critical, and the income generated by the Army Air Corps program helped the monastic community to remain solvent.

The cadets ended their training in May 1944 and went off to war. A few officers stayed on campus to wrap up administrative details, but by midsummer they too had gone. When regular classes resumed in the fall, the seminarians moved back into Aurelius Hall and a few discharged servicemen returned to the college. Enrollment was still low in both the college and seminary. In October 1944 the former counted 102 undergraduates; the latter, 90 theologians. But the prep school was flourishing with 325 students, and the overall enrollment picture of the three schools was therefore not bad. There were high hopes, moreover, that college and seminary enrollment would improve as soon as the war ended.

In the meantime, the college administration reintroduced the civilian aviation program, opening it to high-school teachers who wished to teach aeronautics in local high schools, and to other civilians as well. The pilot training program consisted of a two-month course, and under the direction of diocesan priest Father Michael Carmody ("Pennsylvania's famous flying priest") it was offered regularly throughout the year. Ground instruction was given three nights a week at the college, and as before, flight instruction took place at the Latrobe Airport. The *St. Vincent Journal* boasted that "St. Vincent . . . is maintaining her progressive outlook on flying as a preparation for post-war developments in air-transportation."[28] The program was terminated, however, in 1945 at the conclusion of the war.

PASSING A CENTURY

When the Japanese surrendered on August 14, 1945, monks, retreatants, lay faculty, students, alumni, and friends of Saint Vincent gathered in the archabbey church for a solemn *Te Deum* and liturgy of thanksgiving to mark the end of the war. It was a joyous celebration, for not only had peace settled on the land but also prospects for the future of Saint Vincent seemed bright again. As hundreds of thousands of young men were discharged from the armed forces, the college—with its faculty intact and its dormitories and classrooms ready—was well positioned to receive the influx of undergraduates that demobilization and the GI Bill portended. Disappointingly, enrollment in the fall of 1945 did not fully meet expectations. Only 162 college students registered that semester. The following summer, however, the number of those who applied for admission to classes for the fall term astonished even the most sanguine prognosticators. More than 700 undergraduates entered the college in September 1946. The following year college enrollment rose to 845, and in 1948 it peaked at over 900 students. Collegians, seminarians, and prepsters that fall totaled an astonishing 1,260 students.[29] After many lean years, the college was bulging at the seams.

The community paused briefly in September 1946 to celebrate the hundredth anniversary of Boniface Wimmer's arrival at Saint Vincent. Plans for the centennial celebration had begun before the end of the war. In the summer of 1945 Archabbot Alfred appointed Father Edmund Cuneo to the newly created position of director of public relations in the college, naming Father Egbert Donovan to replace him as headmaster of the preparatory school. Father Edmund's chief duty was "to acquaint the communities of Westmoreland County with the services which St. Vincent has been rendering for the past century to the intellectual and cultural life of the region and with the extensive plans which are being developed for the future."[30] Those plans included a major building program at the college to accommodate the anticipated postwar influx of students, and Archabbot Alfred named Father Edmund and Father Maurice Costello, dean of the college, as co-chairmen of the executive committee of a "Centennial Building Fund," the purpose of which was to raise money for the expansion of the college.

The Centennial Building Fund Drive opened in October 1945. Roy C. McKenna, president of Vanadium-Alloys Steel Company of Latrobe, accepted Archabbot Alfred's invitation to serve as general chairman of the drive. The goal was to raise five hundred thousand dollars by September 1946. This was the first public fund-raising drive in Saint Vincent history. Previous drives had focused exclusively on the alumni and had been modest in their objectives. This time, however, the board of trustees recognized the need for a broader base of support for the college and therefore extended its fund-raising efforts to the local business community.[31] The hope was to raise enough money to build a much-needed gymnasium and college dormitory, but a design was drawn up for two additional dormitories and an "activities" building as well. Unfortunately, the Centennial Building Fund Drive was only partially successful. A year after the drive began, the fund had reached only two hundred thousand dollars, forty percent of what was hoped for and needed. The college therefore had to postpone plans for the new buildings. The two principal reasons for the lack of complete success in the institution's first major fund-raising drive were clearly that the monks had little experience raising money from business and industry, and that local businessmen and industrialists were to a great extent unfamiliar with the work of the Benedictines at Saint Vincent. Experience would come with time, however, and meanwhile Father Edmund Cuneo led administrators of the college in developing new ties with local business and industry and building closer relations with potential benefactors in Pittsburgh and Westmoreland County.

To mark the hundredth anniversary of the establishment of the monastery and schools at Saint Vincent, the monks undertook other projects as well. One of these was the complete renovation of the crypt of the archabbey church. The crypt was redesigned to commemorate and celebrate the contributions that the Benedictine Order had made over the previous fourteen hundred years to the religious, artistic, and intellectual development of Western civilization. Father Quentin Schaut, the novice master, was put in charge of the project, and liturgical artists Emil Frei of

St. Louis and Jan Henryk de Rosen of Warsaw, Poland, who had resided in the United States since 1937, were commissioned to do the art work.

Frei, whose artistry in glass already graced the Shrine of the Immaculate Conception in Washington and St. Meinrad Archabbey in Indiana, designed the crypt's sixteen stained glass windows, which symbolically depicted important figures in Benedictine history. The windows honored St. Benedict and his Holy Rule; Pope Gregory the Great (sixth century) for his contributions to the church's plain chant; the seventh-century Anglo-Saxon Abbot Benedict Biscop for his contributions to church architecture; Alcuin of York (eighth century) for his work in promoting Christian education; Rhabanus Maurus (ninth century) for his scriptural studies; Roswitha of Saxony (tenth century) for her contributions to European drama; St. Anselm of Canterbury (eleventh century) for his contributions to dogmatic theology; Peter the Venerable of Cluny (twelfth century) for his writings on monastic discipline; Pope St. Peter Celestine V (thirteenth century) for his spirit of worldly renunciation; St. Gertrude (fourteenth century) for her mysticism; the English monk John Lydgate (fifteenth century) for his contributions to poetry; John Trithemius (sixteenth century) for his contributions to humanistic studies; Benedict van Haeften of Germany (seventeenth century) for his ascetical writings; Jean Mabillon of France (seventeenth century) for his scholarship; and Boniface Wimmer (nineteenth century) for his leadership in introducing the Benedictine Order to America. The final window depicted St. B enedict welcoming his faithful followers into heaven.

Jan Henryk de Rosen—whose work embellished the papal chapel at Castelgandolfo, Italy, the National (Episcopal) Cathedral in Washington, D.C., and the Catholic cathedral of Toledo, Ohio—designed and painted the Montecassino triptych above the crypt's main altar. This was the "Montecassino Altar," dedicated to St. Martin of Tours (in whose honor St. Benedict dedicated the first chapel at Montecassino) and commemorating the famed archabbey of St. Benedict which had been destroyed by American forces during the Second World War. The theme of the triptych was the ancient motto of Montecassino, *succisa virescit* ("cut down, it grows again"). The destruction of 1943 was only one in a series of catastrophes that had visited the venerable monastery in the course of its history. Destroyed several times over the centuries, on each occasion it had revived and grown strong again. The triptych featured St. Benedict and some of the famous abbots who had led efforts to restore the abbey and to renew its Benedictine observance: Petronax (d. 750), a native of Brescia who found

Montecassino lying in ruins after its destruction by the Lombards; Abbot Aligernus (d. 986), who had brought Benedictine life back to Montecassino after its destruction by the Saracens; Leo of Ostia, an eleventh-century chronicler of the abbey; Pope Stephen X, who was abbot of Montecassino when Leo of Ostia became a monk there; Desiderius (d. 1087), builder of the great basilica and most celebrated of the abbots after St. Benedict himself (he became Pope Victor III); and Boniface Krug, the Saint Vincent monk who became archabbot of Montecassino at the end of the nineteenth century. In the background of the work, the artist depicted the building of the great basilica by Desiderius, the visit of Charlemagne, the meeting of Eastern and Western monasticism represented by the visit of St. Nilus the Younger, and, finally, the destroyed Montecassino, as it was in 1946, the year the triptych was painted. Over the ruins of the bombed monastery was a new Montecassino rising out of the ashes.

Flanking the Montecassino altar were two altars dedicated to St. Michael the Archangel (patron of Metten Abbey, motherhouse of Saint Vincent) and St. Boniface of Germany. Over the Metten altar hung a wood carving of St. Michael by Polish artist Gleb Derujinsky, and over the St. Boniface altar hung Jean de Marco's carving of St. Boniface of Germany and Boniface Wimmer of Metten.

The crypt's ten side altars, fashioned from Indiana limestone, were dedicated to the ten abbeys that owed their beginnings to the missionary labors of Boniface Wimmer and the monks of Saint Vincent: St. John's in Minnesota, St. Benedict's in Kansas, St. Mary's in New Jersey, Belmont in North Carolina, St. Bernard in Alabama, St. Procopius in Illinois, St. Leo in Florida, St. Bede in Illinois, St. Peter's in Saskatchewan (Canada), and Holy Cross in Colorado. A statue of St. Benedict, carved by Janet De Coux of Gibsonia, Pennsylvania, was placed at the entrance of the crypt, and later André Girard's triptych in oil illustrating the life of St. Bernard was hung above the St. Bernard Altar.[32]

Another project to celebrate the centenary of Saint Vincent was the establishment of an annual lecture to honor the founder of the first Benedictine monastery and school in the United States. The Wimmer Memorial Lecture Series was inaugurated in December 1947 when Professor Kenneth J. Conant of Harvard University spoke at Saint Vincent on Benedictine contributions to architecture in the eleventh century. The following year Professor Erwin Panofsky, art historian at the School of Humanistic Studies of the Institute of Advanced Studies in Princeton, New Jersey, gave the second Wimmer Lecture on the topic "Gothic Architecture and Scholasticism." In succeeding years a host of internationally distinguished scholars gave Wimmer Lectures, which were published by the Archabbey Press. The scholars and their lectures included Father Gerald B. Phelan, director of the Medieval Institute at the University of Notre Dame, who spoke on "The Wisdom of Saint Anselm" (1949); the eminent medievalist and former French ambassador to the Vatican, Jacques Maritain, whose lecture topic was "Man's Approach to God" (1951); Professor William Foxwell Albright of Johns Hopkins University, "Toward a Theistic Humanism" (1952); literary critic Helen C. White, "Prayer and Poetry" (1954); English historian Christopher Dawson, "The Movement towards Christian Unity in the Nineteenth Century" (1959); Renaissance scholar Paul Oskar Kristeller, "Renaissance Philosophy and the Mediaeval Tradition" (1961); American Catholic historian John Tracy Ellis, "A Commitment to Truth" (1965); Henry Margenau, "Scientific Indeterminism and Human Freedom" (1966); Gunnar Myrdal, "The Problem of Objectivity in Social Research" (1967); Howard Mumford Jones, "History and Relevance" (1968); Paul Weiss, "Theology and Verification" (1969); and Paul Goodman, "Silence, Speaking and Language" (1970).

The centennial celebration itself, marking the anniversary of the inauguration of Benedictine life in the United States, took place at Saint Vincent on September 2–4, 1946. The events began on the first morning with a Mass of thanksgiving in the Saint Vincent stadium celebrated by the apostolic delegate, Archbishop Amleto Cicognani. Bishop Hugh Boyle of Pittsburgh and nine other bishops were present, along with eighteen Benedictine abbots, more than five hundred clergy and nuns, and ten thousand laypeople. That afternoon the Benedictine community hosted a banquet for six hundred people in the college gymnasium. Father James Reeves, president of Seton Hill College, Greensburg, and an alumnus of Saint Vincent, was toastmaster at the banquet, and Archbishop Cicognani delivered the principal address.

The next afternoon an academic convocation was held in the stadium attended by representatives of fifty-seven colleges and universities. Archabbot Alfred conferred honorary degrees on fourteen religious, cultural, and civic leaders including Archbishop Cicognani, Bishop Boyle, Pennsylvania Governor Edward Martin, Abbot Alcuin Deutsch of St. John's Abbey, Abbot Corbinian Hofmeister of Metten, Pittsburgh banker Richard King Mellon, United Mine Workers president Thomas Leo Kennedy, and U.S. Senator Francis J. Myers. That evening and continuing into the following day a symposium on the Benedictines in America (entitled "The Challenge

Saint Vincent priests and clerics, with visiting American abbots, gathered to celebrate the one hundredth anniversary of the arrival of the Benedictines in the United States, 1946.

of a New Century") was held. Among the papers delivered by visiting monastic scholars were: "Benedictines and the Liturgy" by Father Rembert Sorg of St. Procopius Abbey, Lisle, Illinois; "The Monastery and Christian Art" by Father Damasus Winzen of St. Paul's Priory, Keyport, New Jersey; "Monastic Life and Scholarship" by Father Anselm Strittmatter of St. Anselm's Priory, Washington, D.C.; and "Through One Hundred Years," a lecture on the history of the Benedictines in America by Abbot Alcuin Deutsch. Plans were made by the Archabbey Press to publish the symposium papers under the title *The Challenge of a New Century,* but the project was never realized.

Other publications that marked the event, however, were a *Centennial Brochure* written by the Saint Vincent clerics and edited by Brothers Maynard Brennan and Demetrius Dumm, a centennial edition of the *St. Vincent Journal,* and a fifty-two-page supplement to *The Pittsburgh Catholic* edited by Father Edmund Cuneo.[33] The supplement to *The Pittsburgh Catholic* was a compendium of Saint Vincent history and detailed the contributions made to the Church and the nation by the archabbey, seminary, and college in the preceding hundred years. Featured in the publication were articles on Benedictine history by Monsignor Paul J. Glenn of Columbus, Ohio; attorney Joseph A. Beck of Pittsburgh; and Fathers Felix Fellner and Christopher Fullman of Saint Vincent; as well as articles on the lay brothers, the Benedictine sisters, the parishes and schools staffed by Saint Vincent priests, the Saint Vincent summer retreats, the Saint Vincent library, and the more than twenty monasteries of the American Cassinese, Swiss-American, English, and other Benedictine congregations established in the United States since 1846. The *Pittsburgh Catholic* supplement also contained an article about the Saint Vincent Women's Auxiliary, an organization of Saint Vincent friends founded in 1939 by Mrs. Harry M. Staley, Mrs. Stephen W. Nealon, Mrs. Nettie Caito, Miss Minna Stratman, and several other women for the purpose of raising funds "to assist Saint Vincent College in the development of its educational program, and, second, to assist deserving young men to obtain the advantages of higher education." Through the 1940s Father Hugh Wilt served as chaplain of the Women's Auxiliary, which by 1946 had raised more than thirty thousand dollars for the college.[34]

An article about the centennial that received less favorable reviews appeared in *Time* magazine two weeks after the gala at Saint Vincent. The centennial celebration had generated considerable local press coverage, but Father Edmund Cuneo wanted national coverage as well, so he had invited some of the leading national magazines and newspapers to send representatives to cover the story. *Time* magazine accepted the invitation and dispatched a reporter who dutifully interviewed Father Edmund and Archabbot Alfred and then spent several hours exploring the campus on his own. One of the places he went was the powerhouse, where he interviewed fifty-six-year-old Brother Victor Orsansky. He also spoke with some of the other lay brothers.

The article that resulted was entitled "The Black Monks" (a name given the Benedictines in the Middle Ages because of the color of their religious habit) and featured a photograph of a bearded, sinister-looking Boniface Wimmer over the caption "Beer, Romanism, and Permanence." Appearing to be a straightforward story about the monastery and college, the article's subtext was that the Benedictines in Pennsylvania had never really fit in well with American ways and modern society. Wimmer had clashed with

German priests in New York, Irish bishops in Pittsburgh, and Protestant neighbors in Westmoreland County. His monks had "scandalized" temperance advocates by brewing beer and had failed to adjust to "the pressure of an increasingly industrialized and secularized society." In a subsection entitled "The Virgin & the Dynamo," the reporter noted that the campus had its own powerhouse, a concession to the Industrial Revolution, but even there the spirit of the Middle Ages prevailed. Brother Victor, the article pointed out, "builds naive, pious grottoes and crèches among his dynamos."[35]

The article deeply upset Father Edmund and the monks of the archabbey. They and other monks of the American Cassinese Congregation sent letters of complaint to the editor of *Time,* who later corrected one misrepresentation in the article. The original piece said that the monastic population at Saint Vincent had dwindled from one hundred monks in the nineteenth century to twenty-five in 1946, implying that the Benedictine presence in America was slowly dying out. A month later, *Time* editors conceded that "[t]hriving St. Vincent's actually has 242 priests, seminarists and lay brothers in its monastic community. It is the number of lay brothers that has dwindled from 100 to 25."[36]

But still the damage had been done. Those monks like Father Edmund, who hoped to promote Saint Vincent as a dynamic and modern institution worthy of support from the secularized society around it, were chagrined by the article. Others in the monastery, however, had a different perspective. To a certain extent, they said, the *Time* reporter had gotten the story exactly right, though unwittingly. Benedictines, like all committed Christians, *were* outsiders in modern society; it *was* their vocation to be in conflict with the world, whose values and materialism they spurned. Brother Victor's "naive and pious grottoes" were much more important in the context of eternity than his dynamo, and monks who sought to make friends with the mammon of iniquity were not being faithful to their call. Thus the *Time* article, among other things, gave occasion for the century-long tension between the "pragmatists" and the "idealists" at Saint Vincent to manifest itself once again.

POSTWAR DEVELOPMENTS

The first former soldiers to enter Saint Vincent College under the GI Bill of Rights arrived in the fall of 1944. There were four of them, two of whom—Raymond Testa, who had been wounded in the Solomon Islands, and Philip Rager—had been students at Saint Vincent before the war. By

January 1946, 188 former GI's had been admitted to the college, 70 of whom had formerly studied there. The *St. Vincent Journal* reported that "with the return of St. Vincent students from the Armed Forces and the entry of new students, the College has assumed its pre-war appearance and spirit. Registration day, for many returning veterans, took on the aspect of a college reunion as they recognized their former classmates and associates and renewed old friendships."[37] Thirty-four of the veterans were studying philosophy with the intention of later entering the major seminary and becoming priests. In September 1945 recently ordained Father Leopold Krul was appointed "coordinator of veterans' adjustment." His duties involved not only assisting former servicemen in solving problems they encountered as they entered academic life but also acting as intermediary between the returned soldiers and the Veterans Administration in Washington.[38] Later Father Patrick McKivigan, a former Army chaplain, was appointed dean of men to replace Father Hugh Wilt. Father Patrick had studied political science at Johns Hopkins University, but his strongest credential for becoming dean of men was his experience with young soldiers in the Army. By September 1947 more than 60 percent of the student body at Saint Vincent were veterans of the war.[39]

These young men arrived on the campus with their own special experiences, talents, and needs. More mature than classmates who had not been tested in the crucible of war, they found much in the incidentals of undergraduate life that they regarded as petty and meaningless. Thus in October 1946 the returning veterans protested the system of Freshman Rules, a traditional feature of college life at Saint Vincent in which freshmen were for a period of six weeks initiated into undergraduate living by means of various activities that were often both puerile and humiliating—wearing silly green caps and bright yellow socks, shining the shoes of upperclassmen, having their faces painted by upperclassmen, being paddled by upperclassmen for supposed offenses, running the gauntlet when the supposed offenses were particularly egregious. The veterans objected to the tradition and the hazing associated with it, and they especially objected to the "bully-victim" aspects of Freshman Rules. The *St. Vincent Journal* observed that "the veteran who has learned military discipline needs no further prodding to develop his respect for superiors, both faculty and upperclassmen. Most veterans are here to obtain a delayed education—nothing should interfere with this aim, including Freshman Rules intended for recent high school grads."[40]

A more significant characteristic that separated veterans from ordinary college students was that some of the veterans were married. As a concession to the new conditions confronting it, the college, for the first time, permitted married students to register. One of these was Joseph Kraus, who had served in both Europe and the South Pacific during the war. A student at Saint Vincent Prep School in the mid-1930s, Kraus returned to the college in 1946 with a wife and child. The responsibilities of marriage and parenthood introduced a new dimension of challenge and maturity to the student body. "The marriage-college combination," the *Journal* said, "rests on a painfully fine knife-edge. Very little extra stress in either direction unbalances the whole system and sends it toppling."[41]

To advance their interests, the former servicemen established the Saint Vincent College Veterans' Association, the purpose of which was "promoting good fellowship among students, aiding veterans in college life, and securing all benefits due honorably discharged members of the armed services." Philip Rager of Ligonier was elected first president of the association, and Father Leopold Krul was named its moderator.[42] By the fall of 1947 veterans held most of the principal positions of student leadership at the college, including all the major positions on the student council and the editorship of the *St. Vincent Journal.*

In December 1946 Father Edmund Cuneo was named dean of the college to replace Father Maurice Costello, who after eight years on the job stepped down because of ill health. Varsity basketball returned to the campus in the fall of 1945, varsity football in the fall of 1946, and varsity baseball in the spring of 1946. By 1948 there were varsity teams in golf and tennis competing in intercollegiate leagues as well. But the college catalogue warned that the administration did "not allow sport to run mad and become its own end to the detriment of that thorough education and that serious moral training which a Catholic college should stand for."[43] Father Oliver Grosselin served as director of athletics and was assisted by Fathers Conall Pfiester and Arnold Weimer. In January 1948 Albert DeLuca of Duquesne University was named head football coach, and William Rafferty, a Saint Vincent alumnus who had been serving as coach of the prep football and basketball teams for more than ten years, was named assistant coach.[44]

After the war, in order to ensure a well-prepared and strong faculty for the burgeoning population of undergraduates, Archabbot Alfred and the college leaders sent many of the young monks away to graduate school for advanced degrees. Among those who went out in the 1940s were Father Roland Heid, who studied physics at Johns Hopkins; Father Xavier Mihm, who studied chemistry at Purdue; Father Owen Roth, who studied biology at Yale; Father Armand-Jean Baldwin, political science at Georgetown; Father Clement Heid, mathematics at the University of Pittsburgh; Father Godfrey Burkhardt, accounting at Northwestern University; Father Leopold Krul, classics at Cornell; Father Jude Coughlin, classics at the University of Michigan; Father Joel Lieb, biology at Fordham; and Father Maynard Brennan, English literature at the University of Wisconsin. Most of these monks received their masters degrees and some their doctorates before returning to Saint Vincent to teach on the college faculty. Among the young monks sent out to study theology during the period were Fathers Germain Lieb and Roderick Baronner, who pursued their work at the Pontifical Institute of Mediaeval Studies in Toronto, and the clerics Demetrius Dumm and Alphonse Meier, who went to Rome for studies at the Collegio di Sant' Anselmo.

Meanwhile, the increased number of students required the appointment of a large number of laymen to faculty positions. In the fall of 1948, for example, Dr. Thomas Jordan was made head of the education department; Charles Houston was appointed to the English department; James Miller and George Zvirblis to the business department; Morgan Litzinger to the music department; and James Beatty to the chemistry department. The college faculty for 1948–49 listed seventy-three professors, of whom twenty-one were lay persons.[45]

The music department, which had suspended classes during the war, was revived in the fall of 1947 and once again, in a tradition that was as old as the college, began to attract talented student musicians. Father Ralph Bailey chaired the department and was assisted by Father Ildephonse Wortman, Dr. J. Vick O'Brien, Dr. Joseph A. Rauterkus, Mr. Gabriel Burda, and Miss Josephine McGrail, the lone woman on the college faculty, who taught voice on a part-time basis. The tradition of regular classical concerts on campus (which had not been interrupted by the war) continued. In April 1948 the college symphony orchestra gave a concert under the direction of Dr. O'Brien featuring Brother Rembert Weakland's performance of Rachmaninov's Piano Concerto no. 2 in D Minor. The following month, under the baton of Dr. Rauterkus, the Saint Vincent–Seton Hill orchestra gave a concert that highlighted Mendelssohn's Violin Concerto performed by Gloria Mawn of Seton Hill. On the same program the combined Saint Vincent–Seton Hill glee clubs, jointly directed by Father Ralph Bailey and Miss Margaret Garrity of Seton Hill, performed the Brahms Motet, op. 29, no. 2.[46]

After the war new life was given to the tradition of dramatic productions at Saint Vincent as well. Fathers Conall Pfiester and Maynard Brennan revived the old college drama society and produced such classic plays as Shakespeare's *Comedy of Errors.* The prep school also continued to produce plays and musicals that attracted large audiences. Under Father Ralph Bailey and Sister Antoninus, R.S.M., the students of Saint Vincent Prep and St. Xavier's Academy performed a full cast production of Gilbert and Sullivan's *H.M.S. Pinafore* in April 1948, and in March 1949 the prepsters put on *The Emperor's New Clothes* under the direction of Father Aelred Beck.[47]

The period of the late 1940s was a time rich in "firsts" at the college. In October 1947 a college radio station was first formed and broadcast its first programs on a frequency of 850 kilocycles under the call letters WSTV, which soon changed to WSVC. The station had its origins when freshman Don Daino set up a homemade amplifier and small oscillator in his room and began playing music for the collegians for an hour before the evening meal. Shortly afterward Daino and student Dean Foote obtained more equipment, got an FCC license, became affiliated with the Intercollegiate Broadcasting System, and convinced the college administration to give them a room on campus for the station.[48]

Comprehensive examinations were first introduced as a graduation requirement in the spring of 1947. The biology department was the first to introduce the requirement, which quickly spread to the political science, chemistry, and business departments, and eventually to all the academic departments of the school.[49]

The first college year book, *The Tower,* was published in May 1948, and the first anti-Communist prayer rally on campus occurred that same month. In an event that would be regularly repeated during the early years of the Cold War, hundreds of students from Saint Vincent College, Seton Hill College, St. Francis College, and the College of Steubenville came together at Saint Vincent to participate in the rally in May 1948. The theme of the rally was "rededication to the Blessed Virgin and prayers for the conversion of those addicted to Communism." The students formed a living Rosary pageant; Father Raymond Finan, C.S.C., assistant director of the National Family Rosary Crusade, spoke; and Bishop John K. Mussio of Steubenville, Ohio, celebrated an "open-air solemn pontifical benediction" in the Saint Vincent stadium. The next year, 1949, Saint Vincent hosted a regional anti-Communist rally of the National Federation of Catholic College Students, an event which drew more than six thousand college students to the campus. Again a living Rosary was staged, and Pittsburgh Bishop John F. Dearden spoke. In addition to Saint Vincent, the colleges represented at the second rally were Seton Hill, St. Francis, Steubenville, Mount Aloysius, and Duquesne.[50]

It was during this period too that, following the lead of distinguished liberal arts institutions throughout the United States, Saint Vincent College first organized its curriculum into departmental majors and a core curriculum, the curriculum model which continued fundamentally unchanged for the next fifty years. In 1948 there were fourteen majors available to students in the divisions of humanities, social sciences, science, and business.

The greatest unfulfilled need at Saint Vincent during the immediate postwar period was for buildings and facilities to accommodate the expanding student population. The 1946 centennial building fund drive had not proven successful, and by the end of the decade the essential new structures that were envisioned and needed had not been constructed. The reason for the delay was that Archabbot Alfred would not authorize building loans. He and the older monks of the community remembered the results of the China loan of 1929, and the seventy-year-old abbot was adamant in his refusal to commence major projects without having all the necessary funds at hand.

The younger monks, however, for whom the China debacle was becoming a distant memory, insisted that new buildings had to be constructed. Existing facilities were entirely inadequate for the new population of students, and if the college were truly to be a modern institution, it needed modern buildings. Still, the archabbot refused to build. Instead, he appointed Father Denis Strittmatter, newly returned to the archabbey after eighteen years of service at St. Emma's Industrial and Agricultural Institute in Rock Castle, Virginia, as director of maintenance, and authorized limited improvements in the existing facilities. Beginning in the fall of 1948 Father Denis initiated an improvement program that included repointing the dormitories, repainting the science hall, extensive renovation of the lavatories and showers, and the installation of new gas stoves and a new ventilation system in the kitchen. Improvements continued, but no new buildings were built.[51]

THE SIXTH ARCHABBOT

Archabbot Alfred Koch had grown old in the service of Saint Vincent. He had been a monk of the archabbey for thirty-two years and superior of the community for almost twenty. He had shepherded Saint Vincent through the troubled waters of economic depression, near bankruptcy, and war; and under his competent leadership the monastery and schools, though battered, had survived intact and were now moving forward. But the archabbot was in poor health, and he realized that it was time to turn the work over to a younger generation. In the summer of 1949 he submitted his request to Rome that he be permitted to retire and that the community be allowed to elect a coadjutor archabbot with full administrative powers and the right of succession.

The Holy See agreed, and on September 7, 1949, at 7:00 in the evening the capitulars of Saint Vincent assembled in the choir chapel for the election. Abbot Mark Braun, abbot of St. Gregory's Abbey, Shawnee, Oklahoma, and president of the American Cassinese Congregation, presided and began the proceedings by informing the electors that the rescript from the Sacred Congregation of Religious granting permission for the election did not specify what powers the coadjutor would have. He said, however, that Archabbot Alfred had agreed in writing to transfer the full jurisdiction to the coadjutor. The capitulars were therefore to elect an archabbot who would not only have the right of succession but who would also possess complete jurisdiction in all matters, spiritual as well as temporal, with Archabbot Alfred retaining his right of precedence.

Father Matthew Benko was appointed secretary of the election, and Prior Celestine Huber announced the names of the proxies who would cast ballots for the capitulars who were unable to be present. The capitulars then elected Fathers John Nepomucene Hruza, Wolfgang Frey, and Leander Pail to act as tellers. A nominating ballot followed in which the names of forty priests who had received at least one vote were put in nomination. When this vote was announced, the meeting adjourned until the following morning.

At 9:00 a.m. on September 8 the capitulars assembled in the archabbey church for the celebration of a solemn votive Mass in honor of the Holy Spirit, and at 10:00 a.m. they convened in the choir chapel for the *scrutinium* (or discussion of the qualifications) of the ten candidates who had received the highest number of votes. These were Fathers Denis Strittmatter, Matthias Auer, Celestine Huber, Hugh Wilt, Quentin Schaut, Frederick Strittmatter, Henry Schwener, Egbert Donovan, Nepomucene Hruza, and Vitus Kriegel. The *scrutinium* continued into the afternoon, and when it ended, capitulars recited the prayers to the Holy Spirit prescribed by the *Rituale Monasticum* and sang the hymn *Veni Creator Spiritus.* Then at the instruction of the abbot president, the secretary called the roll of electors. One hundred and seventy-four electors were present. The twelve who were absent would vote by proxy.

Father Felix Fellner, the subprior, read the sixty-fourth chapter of the

Holy Rule of St. Benedict on the election of an abbot, and gave a general absolution to the capitulars as required by the monastic ritual. Abbot Mark then administered the oath of secrecy to the electors, and the voting began. The winner had to gain a two-thirds majority, or 124 votes.

On the first ballot the leading candidates were Fathers Denis Strittmatter (with 60 votes), Matthias Auer (49 votes), Quentin Schaut (30), and Hugh Wilt (24), with the other votes spread out among nine candidates. On the second ballot Strittmatter received 78, Auer 59, Schaut 28, and Wilt 13. Since none had received a two-thirds majority, the abbot president announced that voting would continue at the fourth session that evening and declared the third session closed. After supper, at 7:30 p.m., the capitulars assembled once again in the choir chapel and immediately proceeded to the third ballot. This time Strittmatter received 95, Auer 63, and Schaut 19. On the fourth ballot, at which only an absolute majority was required, Strittmatter received 120 votes, Auer 49, and Schaut 11.

When the senior teller, Father John Nepomucene Hruza, announced the results, the capitulars "responded with their *placet*" and Abbot Mark declared Father Denis Strittmatter the newly elected coadjutor archabbot of Saint Vincent. He then approached Father Denis, "delivered a brief exhortation," and formally inquired whether he would give his consent and accept the election. Father Denis addressed the capitulars and formally consented to accept the burden of the office. Then amid the joyous ringing of the monastery bells, Archabbot Alfred entered the choir chapel and congratulated his successor. Afterward the community went in procession to the archabbey church where they chanted the *Te Deum* and individually pledged their obedience to the new archabbot with the kiss of peace.[52]

A native of Hastings, Pennsylvania, fifty-three-year-old Denis Omer Strittmatter had come to Saint Vincent as a boy of fourteen and studied in the prep school and college before entering the novitiate in 1916. He completed his philosophical and theological studies in Saint Vincent Seminary and was ordained to the priesthood in 1923. Afterward he served for six years in Saint Vincent's parishes in Youngstown, Ligonier, Wilpen, Pittsburgh, and Jeannette, Pennsylvania, before being appointed assistant director of St. Emma's Industrial and Agricultural Institute in Virginia in 1929, a post he held for fifteen years. In 1944 he became director of St. Emma's, and when the institution was turned over to the Holy Ghost Fathers of Pittsburgh, he returned to Saint Vincent in September 1947 to assume the position of director of maintenance. Strittmatter was blessed as the sixth archabbot of Saint Vincent on November 25, 1949, by Bishop John F. Dearden of Pittsburgh.[53]

Denis Strittmatter, O.S.B. (1896–1971), sixth archabbot.

Under Archabbot Denis Saint Vincent moved forward on several fronts. Increased numbers of young men presented themselves as candidates for the Benedictine life, and a postwar spirit of optimism about the future of the monastic community pervaded the house. Enrollment in the seminary of students for the diocesan clergy more than doubled in the five-year period following the election of Archabbot Denis. The college grew not only in enrollment but in prestige as a better-educated Benedictine and lay faculty assumed teaching duties and a younger and more administratively adept leadership took charge of the college administration. While his predecessors had reserved for themselves the right to make virtually all important decisions concerning the college, the new archabbot, in what at the time was regarded as a real innovation, gave genuine authority to the college board of trustees (still entirely Benedictine) in the areas of financial administration and the setting of academic policy for the college. He also supported the efforts of the college administration to modernize the financial offices of the institution and to update the academic programs, bringing them into conformity with the best contemporary standards of American Catholic higher education. Perhaps the most noteworthy achievements of Strittmatter's fourteen-year abbacy, however, were in the area of building expansion.

In April 1950 the monastic chapter approved an ambitious expansion plan presented by the monastery and college's building committee, a plan necessitated by the increasing number of candidates for the monastic life at Saint Vincent and the dramatically expanding enrollments in the college and seminary. The plan called for (1) enlargement of the monastery to include more rooms for the priests, a suitable dining room, adequate quarters for the brothers, and a "developed" infirmary; (2) a residence hall for the college; (3) an activities building to house a gymnasium, auditorium, and the music department; (4) a library; (5) more and better classrooms for each academic department; (6) better science facilities; (7) a convent for the Benedictine sisters; (8) service department facilities, a warehouse, and water, heat, and light expansion; (9) new campus space for the post office, student recreation facilities, and a snack bar; and (10) the expansion and improvement of kitchen and dining room facilities.[54]

Six months later ground was broken on the three most critically needed structures—the student residence hall, a classroom building, and the activities building. The student dormitory (Wimmer Hall) was essential to accommodate the expanded student population, and along with the classroom building (Aquinas Hall) it was the first of the new structures to be completed. The combined cost of Wimmer and Aquinas Halls was $750,000. The former became the residence of the seminarians, who moved there from Aurelius Hall, and the latter provided classroom space for the seminary. Abbot Primate Bernard Kaelin, O.S.B., blessed both buildings on August 24, 1952.[55] Though groundbreaking for the activities building took place in October 1950, actual construction did not begin until 1952. There were two reasons for the delay. First, the chapter continued to be cautious about financially overcommitting the community and wanted to make sure that it could pay for construction before beginning to build. Second, the architects discovered that the site chosen for the activities building, southwest of the old quadrangle on the site of the varsity baseball field, was badly undermined as a result of earlier coal-mining operations, so the new building required expensive foundations and deep steel supports.

Because the activities building was projected to be built on the site of the old baseball diamond and playing fields, land south and west of the main college buildings was set aside for athletic fields, for which construction began in January 1951. The new outdoor athletic facilities included a baseball diamond, three full-size and five three-quarter-size football fields, and six tennis courts. Meanwhile, the $1.6 million activities building continued under construction, and on February 3, 1954, the gymnasium was inaugurated with a basketball game between the Bearcats and St. Francis College of Loretto, Pennsylvania. To the disappointment of alumni, faculty, and students, the Saint Vincent team was soundly defeated by a score of eighty-five to thirty-nine. The rest of the activities building—including the auditorium/theater, the music department, the art department, and the bowling alleys—was completed in September 1954. The building was solemnly blessed on May 1, 1955, at which time it was christened "Sportsman's Hall" to commemorate the early name for the land that became Saint Vincent.[56]

Another building constructed at Saint Vincent during Archabbot Denis's abbacy was the $750,000 library, completed in 1959 and blessed by the archbishop of New York, Francis Cardinal Spellman. The library was critically needed by the college and seminary if efforts to modernize and improve the academic programs of each were to be successful. The chief motivating force behind the construction of the new library was Saint Vincent librarian Father Fintan Shoniker. At the time that Father Fintan assumed duties as the monastery librarian, there were four libraries on the campus, each located in a different place: the archabbey's, the seminary's, the college's, and the prep school's. In what one observer characterized as "a great act of diplomacy," Father Fintan, with the support of Archabbot Denis, convinced the administrators of each of these libraries to surrender their autonomy and to assist in the establishment of a single Saint Vincent library which would serve the entire community.

Archabbot Denis also initiated construction of a complex of two student dormitories and a student center that honored three early deans of the college: Gerard Hall, named for Father Gerard Bridge; Bonaventure Hall, named for Father Bonaventure Reithmeier; and Alcuin Hall (the student center), named for Father Alcuin Tasch. Work began on the buildings in April 1963. Gerard Hall was completed in the astonishing space of five months and was occupied for the fall semester. Bonaventure and Alcuin Halls were ready for occupancy in 1964. All three buildings were dedicated after Archabbot Denis's resignation.[57]

To move forward in the areas of community relations and fund-raising, the Saint Vincent College Educational Foundation, a lay board of advisors, was established in 1951 by Fathers Egbert Donovan, headmaster of the prep school, and Edmund Cuneo, dean of the college. Twenty-three western Pennsylvania businessmen were invited to be members of the foundation, whose purpose was to assist in the development of the college. Pittsburgh attorney John E. Laughlin, Jr., served as first president of the foundation; and James M. Underwood of Latrobe, president of Vulcan Mold and Iron Company, was the first vice president. Members of the foundation were chosen "on the basis of their varied business activities, with the thought that each member . . . would be qualified to advise the College authorities on a particular phase of the expansion program."[58]

THE SCHOOLS IN THE 1950S

Father Edmund Cuneo continued to serve as chief administrator of the college, first with the title of dean, then as vice president, until the fall of 1954, when Father Quentin Schaut became vice president. As was customary in colleges of the American Cassinese Congregation, the archabbot held the title of president, but the day-to-day operations of the institution were in the hands of the vice president. In the summer of 1955 the abbots and delegates of the congregation's general chapter decided that in order to devote more time to their monastic and spiritual responsibilities, abbots should no longer be college presidents but instead "chancellors," and that the colleges' chief administrative officers should be given the title "president." In the fall of 1955, therefore, Archabbot Denis named Father Quentin the first nonabbatial president of Saint Vincent College since Father Alphonse Heimler held the title in the 1860s. Archabbot Denis then assumed the new position of chancellor.[59]

As chancellor, the archabbot chaired the college's board of trustees, which made all major decisions concerning finances, academics, college administration, and student life. Among the priests who served on the board during the 1950s were Fathers Dominic Breuss, Vitus Kriegel, John Nepomucene Hruza, Edward Wenstrup, Oliver Grosselin, David Yochim, Donald Haggerty, Matthias Auer, Alfred Grotzinger, Edmund Cuneo, Godfrey Burkhardt, Bertin Emling, and Egbert Donovan.

Other new college administrators were appointed in the early years of Archabbot Denis's abbacy. Father Aelred Beck was named academic dean, and Father Clair Gannon replaced Father Patrick McKivigan as dean of men, a position assumed by Father Owen Roth in 1954. Father Owen held the position until 1957 when Father Egbert Donovan became dean of men. In 1950 Father Jude Coughlin replaced Father Aidan Pfiester as registrar, and Father Fintan Shoniker was appointed alumni secretary, replacing Father Gerard Bridge who had held the job for forty-seven years. Father Fintan also served throughout the 1950s and into the 1970s as director of libraries at Saint Vincent.

The Korean War briefly interrupted the steady growth of the college when military conscription was instituted in the nation once again. In November 1950 sixty Saint Vincent students received draft notices ordering them to appear for physical examinations in anticipation of being inducted into the armed forces. By the following January, ten of these students had been inducted. The *St. Vincent Journal* editorialized in favor of the draft and universal military training for American youth, saying that "America and the free world are faced with the alternatives of rearming and holding the aggressor at bay or submitting to world domination and slavery by the forces of materialism and atheism."[60] Several hundred Saint Vincent students and alumni served in the armed forces during the conflict, and one of them was killed in combat. William P. Wehrle of Punxatawney, Pennsylvania, a 1950 graduate of the college and a veteran of World War II, was recalled to active duty in October 1950 and went to Korea where he served with the First Cavalry Division. He was killed during the Inchon landing in March 1951.[61] Following in the footsteps of confreres who had served in the armed forces during World War I and World War II, two priests from the archabbey—Fathers More Herald and Christian LeFrois—became military chaplains during the Korean War. The college was the scene of frequent prayer-for-peace services during the conflict. In August 1951, for example, more than fifteen thousand women from seventy-eight Catholic parishes of western Pennsylvania gathered at the Saint Vincent stadium to pray for peace.[62]

Among the milestones the college passed during the early fifties was the establishment in 1952 of a joint engineering program with Notre Dame University. According to the press release that announced the new initiative, the program was designed to "serve the student who seeks both the broad cultural background of general education and the specific vocational training that a course in engineering can provide." Under the new program, students would attend Saint Vincent for three years, where they would receive instruction in mathematics and core subjects in the liberal arts curriculum, and then go to Notre Dame for two years of engineering courses. In the end, they would earn a B.A. from Saint Vincent and a B.S.

in engineering from Notre Dame. Twenty-nine students enrolled in the program during its first year of existence. Also in the fall of 1952, "in response to a growing need among local industrial and business establishments," the evening college was reinstituted at Saint Vincent with Father Armand-Jean Baldwin as director and Father Aurelius Labuda as assistant director. Courses were offered in the evening college by most of the academic departments of the institution.[63]

An important academic initiative during the period was the college's establishment in 1954 of a reading program as part of the general requirements for graduation. Students were required to read eight books a year during their first three years and six books in their senior year. The books were selected by the faculty "on the basis of value, interest, and diversity of subject matter," and examinations were given twice a year to ensure that the reading requirement had been fulfilled. Books on the required reading list included works by Homer, Aristotle, Virgil, St. Augustine, Dante, Erasmus, Shakespeare, Locke, Molière, Dostoevsky, James Joyce, Ernest Hemingway, and Thomas Merton.[64] Another milestone was passed in September 1954 when Sister Estelle Hensler, S.C., of Seton Hill became the first woman to join the faculty at Saint Vincent. Sister Estelle, who held a master's degree from New York University, was appointed lecturer in fine arts and taught part-time at Saint Vincent while continuing to serve on the faculty at Seton Hill College.[65]

In 1955 the college conducted an in-depth self-evaluation, now required by the Middle States Association of Colleges and Secondary Schools for full accreditation. In the document submitted to the Middle States Association, Saint Vincent identified itself as "a Catholic and Benedictine college of liberal arts and sciences, aiming to serve the local communities and the nation by offering a diversified program of college-level education leading to academic degrees, and by participating in and furnishing leadership for other programs of interest to the neighboring communities." The emphasis on Catholic heritage, Benedictine tradition, and community service had increasingly become central to the college's promotional literature and clearly reflected the institution's self-understanding and identity. The college was Catholic because it provided "spiritual and moral training through the creation of a climate favorable to spiritual and moral development." It was Benedictine because it followed a "tradition of fourteen centuries of education of youth" and affirmed a "life of 'Prayer and Work' [which were] substantial factors in favor of giving the students a correct perspective of the real values of life and the motivation to attain them." And among the ways the college served the community were the participation of faculty and students in local community organizations and the institution's "program of adult education and other programs as determined by the needs of the various groups of the neighboring communities."[66] In 1956 the Middle States Association granted accreditation to the college for a period of ten years.

A more detailed explication of the institution's self-identity, goals, and objectives appeared in the annual college bulletins. Saint Vincent, the bulletins said, was "a Catholic liberal arts college for men, conducted by the members of the Order of St. Benedict." As a Catholic college, Saint Vincent strove "to achieve the aims authoritatively set down by Pope Pius XI in his encyclical on the Christian education of youth." These aims received "practical implementation in the religious and moral area through courses in theology and philosophy, and through generous provision for participation in divine services, with the special emphasis on liturgy characteristic of Benedictines." The college offered "an atmosphere favorable to spiritual growth," and in this atmosphere, with its "elaborate liturgical services difficult to parallel," students were able to "develop a consciousness of the all-permeating nature of religion."

As a liberal arts institution Saint Vincent recognized its obligation "to provide means for that broad and deep cultivation of mind that will enable a man to realize fully his intellectual powers," as well as the obligation "to assist in equipping him for the practical task of making a living." The college met these obligations by providing "a core curriculum of languages, literature, history, science, and philosophy" together with programs of studies "that in some cases prepare a student to enter immediately upon a career in the business, industrial, or professional world; in other cases to enter upon a program of professional or graduate study. Always the accent is on thoroughness."

The Benedictine character of the college was expressed in the fact that the institution was "a firmly-knit community, that it has a corporate character in a deeper sense than would obtain from the mere fact of having men gather together in an educational unit." The communal character of the school stemmed "from the basic doctrine and the profound truth embodied in the idea of the Mystical Body of Christ. A Benedictine community constitutes a supernatural family, with consequent close relations between members, a condition from which students benefit in a manner that goes quite beyond the formal guidance program." The Benedictine character of Saint Vincent was also found in "the imprint of stability." A Benedictine institution "sinks its roots in the soil; it becomes a permanent part of the larger community in which it is situated. In a variety of ways and emphases this element reveals itself. For instance, the aim of the Founder of St. Vincent was above all the preservation of the Faith in this region. This objective is still an important one, and no inconsiderable portion of the resources of the institution are devoted to it." In addition, "the teacher training and the adult education programs are efforts to contribute to the well-being of the larger community of which the College is a part."[67]

College enrollment declined slightly in the early 1950s as the number of veterans applying under the GI Bill decreased. An average of 750 undergraduates attended the institution each year, though the number fell to a little more than 600 during the Korean War. By 1959, however, enrollment had more than recovered, and there were 860 students in the college. Figures published in the *St. Vincent Journal* indicated that the most popular areas of study were philosophy (for those preparing to enter the seminary), business, pre-law, pre-medical, engineering, and teacher training, which together accounted for 70 percent of the undergraduate majors. Other students majored in chemistry, biology, sociology, psychology, predental, mathematics, music, history, political science, and humanities.[68]

The undergraduate college continued to be organized into four divisions. The humanities division, led through most of the period by Father Melvin Rupprecht, consisted of the departments of classics, English, modern languages, music, philosophy, and religion. The division of social sciences, headed by Father Harold Phillips, consisted of the departments of economics, education, history, political science, psychology, and sociology. The science division, headed by Father Roland Heid, consisted of the departments of biology, chemistry, mathematics, and physics. And the division of business administration, headed by Father Godfrey Burkhardt, consisted of the department of accounting and finance and the department of management. Students could major in any of eighteen subjects, but all had to complete a core curriculum consisting of courses in religion (eight courses), philosophy (four courses), English (four courses), history (two courses), psychology (one course), natural science (two courses), and physical education (four courses).[69]

Faculty growth during this period kept pace with student enrollment. In 1955 the faculty numbered sixty-four professors, of whom twenty were laymen. The decline in the faculty's size from the late 1940s reflected both the temporary drop in student enrollment resulting from the Korean War and the decrease in applications from veterans under the GI Bill. Four years later, however, the number of faculty members had grown to eighty-six professors, of whom thirty-one were laymen.[70] Several lay and clerical faculty members were refugees from Communist Europe. Dr. Peter Stercho, a native of the Ukraine, had received his doctorate from the Ukrainian Institute of Economics and joined the economics faculty at Saint Vincent in 1955. Dr. Balis Marsilionis, a native of Lithuania who had studied in German universities before the Second World War and had earned his doctorate at the University of Graz, Austria, was appointed professor of economics in 1957. Father Ludwig Cepon, a diocesan priest from Slovenia with a doctorate from the University of Ljubljana, joined the faculty in 1957 to teach theology. From 1948 until his arrival at Saint Vincent he had taught at the Swiss-American Benedictine Abbey of St. Benedict at Benet Lake, Wisconsin. In December 1958 another diocesan priest from Slovenia, Father Alphonse Cuk, became assistant professor of psychology at the college, replacing Father Harold Phillips who had suffered a heart attack. Father Cuk had come to the United States in 1948 and taught at Fordham University before joining the Saint Vincent faculty. Paul Voyda-Szabo, a Hungarian who held a master's degree from the University of Debrecen, Hungary, joined the mathematics department in 1958, and in 1960 Jaroslav Slezak and his wife Vera Slezak, refugees from Czechoslovakia who had earned advanced degrees at Charles University, Prague, began teaching at Saint Vincent. Jaroslav Slezak was appointed an instructor in the physics department, and Vera Slezak (the first woman to hold a full-time faculty position in the college) became an instructor in the modern languages department where she taught German and Russian.[71]

During the 1950s young Benedictine faculty members continued to pursue advanced degrees at graduate schools around the country and in Europe. Father Roland Heid finished his doctorate in physics at Johns Hopkins University and returned to Saint Vincent to chair the college's physics department and head the science division. Father Joel Lieb returned from St. Louis University with a doctorate in biology. Father Colin Paul Maher earned a doctorate in philosophy at the Collegio di Sant' Anselmo and came back to teach in the college and the seminary. Father Christopher Fullman completed his doctorate in English literature at the University of Wisconsin and later did research at Oxford University before returning to teach in the college. Father Maynard Brennan completed his doctorate at the University of Michigan and came back to chair the English department. At the University of Toronto, Father Eric McCormack studied philosophy and completed his doctorate, and in New York Father Rembert Weakland studied musicology at Juillard and Columbia University. Father

Omer Kline finished a master's degree in history at the Catholic University of America before going on to earn a doctorate in speech at Columbia University. Father John Murtha studied history at Columbia and Catholic University; Father Emeric Pfiester, fine arts at Carnegie Institute of Pittsburgh and Catholic University; Father Callistus Milan, economics at the University of Chicago; and Father Austin Staley, sociology at the University of Wisconsin and the University of Pittsburgh. In addition, Fathers Alphonse Meier, Demetrius Dumm, and Maurus Wallace completed advanced theology degrees in Rome during this period.

Saint Vincent faculty members were also engaged, to varying degrees, in scholarly research and writing during this period. Father Roland Heid carried out research in radio astronomy, a relatively new field that sought to discover the composition and properties of heavenly bodies by analyzing the waves they emitted. Father Edward Wenstrup of the biology department conducted research in genetics. Father Austin Staley, chairman of the sociology department, went to São Paulo, Brazil, in the second semester of the 1956–57 academic year to do research on race relations. In 1957 Father Armand-Jean Baldwin, chairman of the political science department, completed a textbook entitled *Christian Principles of Political Science.* Published by the Archabbey Press, the book was intended "to combat the secularistic philosophy characteristic of present-day political thinking in the world." Father Rembert Weakland of the music department helped produce a scholarly edition of the thirteenth-century musical drama *The Play of Daniel,* and advised the New York Pro Musica Society on its performance of the play at the Cloisters in New York in January 1957. Weakland, who had studied at the Conservatory of Santa Cecilia in Milan and at the Abbey of Solesmes, France, had by now gained an international reputation as an expert in early liturgical music.[72]

Also in 1957 Father Maximilian Duman, associate professor of biology at Saint Vincent and an internationally renowned expert on Arctic plants, was named associate professor of biology in the graduate school of the Catholic University of America. Father Maximilian had earned his doctorate in botany from Catholic University in 1941 and since then had taught botany and biology at Saint Vincent. He had spent eight summers in northern Canada photographing, studying, and collecting specimens of plant life in the Arctic regions, and several of his research trips had been funded by the U.S. Department of Defense. Father Maximilian remained on the faculty of Catholic University until he was recalled to Saint Vincent and appointed president of the college in 1962.[73]

Varsity sports, always a popular part of undergraduate life, underwent several significant changes during the 1950s. The decade began with the college football team gaining national renown for an undefeated season against such regional small college teams as Indiana State Teachers College, Steubenville College, Alliance College, Geneva College, St. Francis College, and Westminster College. The result of the winning season was an invitation to the Tangerine Bowl in Orlando, Florida. The Bearcats, under head coach Al DeLuca and athletic director Father Oliver Grosselin, played Emory and Henry College of Emory, Virginia, in the fourth annual Tangerine Bowl on January 2, 1950, before a capacity crowd of ten thousand. This was the team's first and only bowl game, and in an exciting contest attended by a large contingent of fans from Pennsylvania, the Saint Vincent eleven defeated Emory and Henry by a score of seven to six.[74] Subsequent seasons were not so successful, however, and the team lost all eight of its games in 1954. In 1963 varsity football was dropped at Saint Vincent, and Bearcat Stadium was demolished, making way for the science center which was built on the site.

Varsity basketball was temporarily suspended in 1950 owing to the lack of a gymnasium where the team could practice and host home games, but the sport was reinstated in 1953 as the Sportsman's Hall gymnasium neared completion. That year Orlando (Dodo) Canterna of the University of Pittsburgh was named head basketball coach.[75] Varsity baseball was also dropped in 1951 because of inadequate facilities, but was reinstated in April 1954 after completion of the new baseball diamond. The college administration continued to downplay the role of varsity sports at Saint Vincent, however, for fear that high-profile and successful varsity teams would dominate the interest and attention of students and alumni to the detriment of the school's commitment to high academic quality. The college bulletin, reflecting the views of the administration and board of trustees on this matter, made it clear that athletics existed on campus solely for educational purposes. The bulletin stated that "[t]he athletics program contributes importantly to the achievement of the objectives of the College by stimulating interest on the part of prospective male teachers in athletics and in every major area of secondary education, consistent with the aims of the College, by improving morale and by effectively promoting the physical education program."[76]

Student life in the 1950s continued to be enriched, as it had been for over a hundred years, by frequent musical and dramatic entertainments on campus. The annual "Show-Off" variety show, sponsored by the college glee club, was a popular event during the cold month of February. The glee club, under the direction of Father Ralph Bailey, also performed annual Christmas concerts that featured such sacred works as the Alleluia from Bach's Cantata no. 142, as well as such modern works as pieces from the opera buffa of Giancarlo Menotti. Under the direction of Professor Richard Karp, general director of the Pittsburgh Opera and a member of the music faculty at Saint Vincent, the combined orchestras of Saint Vincent and Seton Hill College continued to present programs of classical and popular music, and when Father Rembert Weakland returned from studies in New York and Italy, he gave regular organ recitals in the archabbey church. On at least one occasion, the Pittsburgh Symphony, under the direction of William Steinberg, performed a concert in Sportsman's Hall.[77]

Drama, too, flourished at Saint Vincent during the fifties. Under the direction of Fathers Ralph Bailey and Maynard Brennan students at the college produced such operas and musicals as *Amahl and the Night Visitors,* Sigmund Romberg's *The Student Prince* ("an operetta of beer, moonlight, and Heidelberg"), an adaptation of Charles Dickens' *Christmas Carol* entitled *The Stingiest Man in Town,* a lavish production of the Broadway hit *Finian's Rainbow* with a cast of seventy-five students and local amateur actors, and a presentation of the medieval liturgical drama *The Play of Daniel.*[78] Nonmusical student dramatic productions during the period included *Murder in the Cathedral, Epicoene, As You Like It,* and *Twelve Angry Men,* all directed by English department chairman Father Maynard Brennan.[79] In October 1957 the Dublin Players, the touring group of the famed Abbey Players of Dublin, visited the campus and performed George Bernard Shaw's *Arms and the Man* and Paul Vincent Carroll's *Shadow and Substance* in the newly completed auditorium of Sportsman's Hall.[80]

Student achievements during the period included senior Fred McAlpine's capturing the national championship in original oratory at Mary Washington College, Fredericksburg, Virginia, in April 1950, and the election of Saint Vincent junior Louis Manderino as president of the National Federation of Catholic College Students. Manderino succeeded another Saint Vincent student, Thomas A. Brickley, in the position of president of the NFCCS, and three years later Saint Vincent senior Bernard Scherer was elected vice president of the organization. In 1955 junior Thomas J. Reinstadtler was elected president of the NFCCS, the third Saint Vincent student to hold the position in a period of five years.[81]

Campus life also continued to be enriched by visiting lecturers. Among them was Matt Cvetic, an FBI undercover agent and a student at Saint

Vincent from 1922 to 1924, who spoke to the students in 1951 about how he had posed as a Communist during the 1940s in order to discover the workings of the Communist party in the Pittsburgh area. He alarmed his audience by telling them that the United States was host to some five hundred thousand thoroughly organized Communists, and he "stressed the importance of education in combating the forces of materialism."[82] Frank Sheed, noted British Catholic lecturer, author, and cofounder of the Sheed and Ward publishing house, spoke at the college in 1956 and urged the students as Catholic laymen "to vigorously participate in the intellectual and religious war which is currently being fought the world over" against atheism, Communism, and rampant materialism.[83] And two years later British lecturer, author, and former Communist Douglas Hyde spoke to the students on the topic "The Psychology of Communism." At one time a leading English Communist and editor of London's Communist newspaper the *Daily Worker,* Hyde had abandoned the party after twenty years' membership and converted to Catholicism. He now maintained that Communism and Christianity could not coexist and was traveling the world lecturing on the evils of Communism and seeking its downfall.[84]

Despite the strong anti-Communist climate at Saint Vincent during this period of cold war and international tension, the *Saint Vincent Journal* (which became the *St. Vincent Review* in 1956) expressed strong opposition to the methods and tactics of United States Senator Joseph McCarthy. "Though Senator McCarthy may have the nation's best interests in mind," the *Journal* editorialized in 1954, "he apparently has forgotten, possibly wilfully, two very important principles: the end never justifies the means, and secondly, man is the possessor of an inherent dignity not subject to attack. If the Senator would recall these two primary maxims, his road would become certainly more ethical and just, and his results perhaps more noteworthy." When the Senate censured McCarthy, the student journal applauded. "Let us hope this censure improves the senator's way of thinking," the editors wrote. In the same edition of the journal, the editors came out strongly in favor of the Supreme Court's May 1954 ruling against segregation in public schools, expressing their hope that "desegregation of public schools in the United States is but another step toward the realization of that ideal expressed by Thomas Jefferson: 'the most sacred of the duties of a government is to do equal and impartial justice to all its citizens.'"[85]

The students' awareness of and involvement in world events were enhanced by the presence on campus of a number of international students during the 1950s. The archabbey chapter had voted in 1950 to fund two four-year scholarships for German students who wished to attend the college. Also in the fall of 1950, the institution received its first Fulbright student when Alphonse Selzle of Donauwörth, Bavaria, arrived on campus. Selzle, one of two hundred and fifty German Fulbright students in the United States in 1950, was a priesthood candidate who spent a year studying philosophy at Saint Vincent.[86] In 1956, after the failed Hungarian uprising against the Russian occupation, two young Hungarian freedom fighters from Budapest, Frank Molnar and Andrew Pechany, came to Saint Vincent as refugees and were given full scholarships to study science in the college.[87] Other foreign students who received scholarships at the college in the 1950s included Henry Musamali from Uganda and Peter Kanari from Kenya, whose studies were funded by the Benedictine community.[88]

A highlight of this period, long remembered by students and faculty, was the address given by John F. Kennedy at the annual honors convocation in February 1958. Kennedy, at the time junior senator from Massachusetts, received an honorary doctor of letters degree from the college and afterward gave the principal speech at the honors convocation held in the auditorium of Sportsman's Hall. He spoke on the topic "The Challenge Ahead," and told his audience that "the devotion of the followers of St. Benedict has been one of the most inspiring chapters in the story of the Church. Their successors in communities, priories, and colleges all over the world have unfailingly demonstrated the qualities of great courage and wholehearted dedication. These are the qualities without which all that we hold dear would surely wither and perish, and qualities which I know those of you who have been fortunate enough to study at this college with its motto of Pax and its atmosphere of peace will be reluctant to leave behind."

Senator Kennedy urged the students of the college to consider politics as a career and said that their liberal arts education at Saint Vincent well prepared them for public service. He warned them that it was "not enough to lend your talents to merely discussing the issues and deploring their solutions." They needed to become actively involved in solving the problems of the nation and the world, to become leaders "capable of making hard, unpopular decisions." He concluded his speech with an exhortation: "Students and faculty of Saint Vincent College, we who are here today are concerned with the dark and difficult task ahead. We ask that you bring candles to illuminate our way."[89] Kennedy was the strong favorite at Saint Vincent during the presidential campaign that began a year later, and when he was assassinated in 1963, the Sportsman's Hall activities building where he had spoken was renamed Kennedy Hall.

The seminary experienced remarkable growth during the 1950s. Beginning in 1950 with an enrollment of 57 theology students, the school had expanded to include 135 theologians by 1955. The combined total of theology students and philosophy students for the rest of the decade averaged a little more than 200 a year. About a quarter of these were Benedictine clerics from Saint Vincent and St. Mary's Abbey, New Jersey. The rest were diocesan students chiefly from Pittsburgh, Greensburg (after its establishment as a diocesan see in 1951), Washington, and Brooklyn. Other dioceses that sent students to Saint Vincent during the period included Harrisburg, Altoona, Erie, Scranton, Covington, Columbus, Steubenville, Trenton, and Camden. Father John Nepomucene Hruza stepped down as rector in 1952, and Father Oliver Grosselin took his place. Father Oliver, who held a doctorate in philosophy from the Collegio di Sant' Anselmo and had pursued postdoctoral studies at the University of Louvain, served as rector of the seminary for the rest of the decade.[90]

The prep school, too, continued to enjoy healthy enrollment. Throughout the fifties the number of students remained well above 200 per year. The decade began with 276 boys registered in the preparatory program and ended with 244. When Father Egbert Donovan stepped down as headmaster in 1954 to become director of public relations, Father Warren Raab took his place. Father Warren died suddenly in March 1956, however, and was replaced by Father Louis Sedlacko, a veteran instructor and administrator in the prep school. Father Louis remained headmaster for eight years. The majority of students in the prep school continued to come from Pennsylvania, though some also came from neighboring states, especially Ohio and West Virginia, and from Washington, D.C. More than 70 percent of them were boarders, and of these about half were scholastics preparing to enter the Benedictine Order. The scholastics continued to follow a stricter religious regimen than that of the other prep students and lived in separate quarters from their classmates, but the academic programs of the two groups of students in the prep school were fully integrated. Father Aidan Pfiester served as director of the scholasticate from 1950 to 1960 and was succeeded by Father Germain Lieb.[91]

MONASTIC DEVELOPMENTS

In 1951 the Holy See divided the Diocese of Pittsburgh and created the Diocese of Greensburg, naming Philadelphia auxiliary bishop Hugh L. Lamb as first ordinary of the new see. Saint Vincent fell within the new diocese, which comprised the western Pennsylvania counties of Westmoreland, Indiana, Armstrong, and Fayette. The Benedictine church of the Most Blessed Sacrament in Greensburg, established by Boniface Wimmer in 1847, became the Greensburg cathedral, and Benedictine Father Gregory McAtee, pastor of Blessed Sacrament Parish, was named cathedral rector.[92] After 105 years of close relations with and service to the Diocese of Pittsburgh, the monastery of Saint Vincent now entered into a new and fruitful era of service to the Diocese of Greensburg.

Priests from the archabbey, however, continued to staff and operate parishes in the Diocese of Pittsburgh, as well as in the dioceses of Greensburg, Erie, Altoona, Youngstown, and Covington and the archdioceses of Chicago and Baltimore. Among the most important parishes staffed by the Benedictines of Latrobe during the 1950s were Blessed Sacrament Cathedral, Greensburg; St. Mary's Church and St. Boniface Church, both on Pittsburgh's North Side; St. Mary's Church, Erie; St. Joseph's Church, Johnstown; St. Benedict's Church, Canton; St. Paul's Church, Chicago; St. Joseph's Church, Covington; Fourteen Holy Martyrs Church and St. Benedict's Church, Baltimore; St. Benedict's Church, Carrolltown; St. Mary's Church, St. Marys; and Saint Vincent Church, Latrobe. Altogether, Saint Vincent priests continued to have charge of nearly forty parishes in American dioceses during the decade of the 1950s.

The archabbey also established a mission band in the 1940s, and throughout the 1950s and early 1960s priests from Saint Vincent—including Fathers Norbert Rupprecht and Charles Weber—visited dioceses in the eastern United States and Canada giving parish retreats and missions.[93] The annual summer retreats at Saint Vincent continued to draw large numbers of Catholic laymen from throughout western Pennsylvania. In 1951, for example, the monastery hosted nearly two thousand retreatants in seven retreats preached by Monsignor Andrew J. Pauley of St. Paul's Cathedral, Pittsburgh.[94] Other types of public religious celebrations sponsored by the archabbey during this period included the annual Corpus Christi processions held each June; the previously mentioned prayer-for-peace rally during the Korean War, which brought fifteen thousand Catholic women to the campus; and a Marian rally in May 1954 held to commemorate the Marian Year proclaimed by Pope Pius XII. Seven thousand people attended the 1954 rally in the Saint Vincent stadium, which included a "living Rosary pageant" and a sermon by Monsignor Joseph E. Schieder, director of the youth department of the National Catholic Welfare Conference.[95]

Archabbot Alfred Koch, who had been living in retirement at the archabbey for a little more than two years, died on November 7, 1951, after an extended illness. His abbacy had been marked by severe financial difficulties stemming from the Depression and the failure of Saint Vincent's China mission, but in his final years he was gratified to witness the community's financial recovery and a steady movement forward under his successor, Archabbot Denis Strittmatter. New buildings were rising on campus, and the community was solvent at last. What Archabbot Denis had managed to accomplish was a tribute not only to his own administrative and organizational abilities but also to Archabbot Alfred's careful stewardship of the monastery's temporal affairs through one of the most difficult periods of its history. Archabbot Alfred's funeral took place in the archabbey church on November 13. Bishop John Dearden of Pittsburgh celebrated the solemn pontifical Requiem Mass, and Abbot Lawrence Vohs of St. Bede Abbey, Peru, Illinois, delivered the eulogy.[96]

Koch's funeral was the second burial of an archabbot from the archabbey church within a year. In November 1950 Saint Vincent had been the scene of obsequies for Archabbot Chrysostom John Keleman of St. Martin's Archabbey, Pannonhalma, Hungary. Archabbot Chrysostom had come to the United States as a refugee after the Communist takeover of Hungary. He had visited Saint Vincent but then took up residence at St. Joseph's Convent in Elizabeth, Pennsylvania, where he served as chaplain. After the funeral services he was buried on the convent grounds in Elizabeth.[97]

Another refugee who came to Saint Vincent in the 1950s was Brother Lambert Berens. Originally a monk of the Benedictine monastery of Ilbenstadt, Germany, he had been drafted into the German army during World War II and served first on the Russian and then the French front. He was at Normandy when the Allies landed and there was wounded and taken prisoner by the American Army. He came to the United States as a prisoner of war and spent a year in a prison camp in Delaware where he made contact with Benedictine priests of St. Mary's Abbey, Newark, New Jersey, who were attending to the spiritual needs of the German Catholic prisoners. After the war he returned to Germany but later sought admission to Saint Vincent. He arrived at the Pennsylvania monastery in December 1952.[98]

Other arrivals at the monastery during this period included Father Oliver Kapsner of St. John's Abbey, who joined the Saint Vincent library staff in February 1951 to organize and direct procedures for the classification and cataloguing of the monastery library and the reclassification of the college library according to the Library of Congress system, following the consolidation of the libraries under the leadership of Father Fintan Shoniker. The consolidated library contained nearly one hundred thousand volumes, with particularly fine collections of works in the fields of medieval history and philosophy, ecclesiastical and monastic history, and patrology. Father Oliver's work in the early fifties was essential for the reorganization of the Saint Vincent library. In 1958 the reorganized library moved into the new library building which had been constructed on the knoll south of the Sauerkraut Tower.[99]

Vocations to the monastic life continued to flourish at Saint Vincent during the 1950s. An average of eight to ten novices entered the monastery each year, and the number of Benedictines increased from 244 in 1950 to 265 1960. During this period the community's monastic leaders included Priors Celestine Huber and Hugh Wilt, Subpriors Felix Fellner and Roland Heid, and Novice Masters Quentin Schaut, Otto Wendell, and Germain Lieb.[100] This was a time when American Benedictine monasteries were attracting large numbers of monastic vocations, and those in charge of monastic training programs for novices and clerics, as well as the novices and clerics themselves, benefited from a wide range of new monastic and spiritual works that helped make monastic life more accessible and comprehensible to contemporary Americans. No longer did monastic formation programs depend upon such timeworn books of spirituality as those of the Sulpician writer Adolphe Tanquerey or the *Tyrocinium Religiosum,* which had been used by novices in Benedictine communities of the United States since the first monks had arrived from Bavaria. Now a book that extolled monastic spirituality—Thomas Merton's *Seven Storey Mountain*—was on the *New York Times* bestseller list, and other modern works of monastic history and spirituality were readily available to the young men who came to Saint Vincent to enter the monastery in the 1950s. Among the authors whose works helped shape the archabbey's monastic observance and spiritual life after World War II were Abbot Columba Marmion and Dom Germain Morin of Maredsous, Abbot Ildephonse Herwegen and Dom Odo Casel of Maria Laach, Abbots Cuthbert Butler and John Chapman of Downside, Abbot Justin McCann of Ampleforth, Louis Bouyer, and Romano Guardini.[101]

In the wake of the 1946 centennial celebration of the establishment of the Benedictine Order in the United States, a renewed interest in the history of Saint Vincent and of the American Benedictine experience also developed during the decade of the fifties. As part of their studies in monastic history, novices thoroughly examined American Benedictine history in the light of new research and books by American Benedictine historians Father Colman Barry of St. John's Abbey, Father Peter Beckman of St. Benedict's

Abbey, and Father Felix Fellner of Saint Vincent. Father Felix, who had devoted a lifetime to researching the history of the Benedictine Order in the United States and the life of the first archabbot of Saint Vincent, completed his five-volume biography of Wimmer, entitled *Abbot Boniface and His Monks,* and saw it through a limited edition that was published by the Archabbey Press in 1956.[102]

Improving the quality of the community's monastic observance continued to be a priority at Saint Vincent during the 1950s. The integrated Benedictine life of prayer and work, as formulated by St. Benedict in his sixth-century Rule, was the root and foundation of all the activities the monks engaged in. The celebration of the liturgy and daily attendance at Mass and Divine Office were public manifestations of the community's interior spiritual life. Together with meditation, private prayer, spiritual reading, and faithful adherence to the Gospel counsels of poverty, chastity, and obedience, they constituted essential elements of the proper observance of the Benedictine Rule. Archabbot Denis Strittmatter, like all his predecessors, sought to strengthen and revitalize monastic observance among the monks, and whenever he saw signs that their work in the schools and the other apostolates might be drawing their attention away from the careful observance of the monastic regimen, he was quick to admonish them to remember what their vocation was and to call them to greater zeal in developing the community's spiritual life.[103]

At the thirty-second general chapter of the American Cassinese Congregation, held in 1953 at St. Andrew Abbey, Cleveland, Archabbot Denis was elected president of the congregation, the first archabbot of Saint Vincent since Boniface Wimmer to hold that position. In September 1953 he accompanied the other American abbots to Rome to attend the international congress of Benedictine abbots and at that time was elected one of the four members of the abbot primate's council.[104] And at the thirty-third general chapter of the congregation, held at Saint Vincent from June 22 to 25, 1959, Archabbot Denis was reelected the congregation's abbot president for another six-year term. In 1962, as president of the congregation, he returned to Rome as a participant in the Second Vatican Council, the sessions of which he attended between 1962 and 1964. It was the second time in the history of the community that an abbot of Saint Vincent had been called to Rome to represent the American Benedictines at an ecumenical council. Boniface Wimmer, as president of the American Cassinese Congregation, had been a father of the First Vatican Council in 1869–70.

In August 1955 the monks celebrated the one hundredth anniversary of

Pontifical High Mass in the archabbey basilica celebrating the one hundredth anniversary of the elevation of Saint Vincent to the rank of abbey, 1955. Celebrant is Archbishop John O'Hara, C.S.C., of Philadelphia.

the elevation of Saint Vincent to the rank of an abbey. The three-day event was attended by several hundred guests, including thirteen bishops and thirty Benedictine abbots. Among the bishops were five who had pursued their theological studies at Saint Vincent Seminary: Michael Ready, bishop of Columbus, Ohio; George Ahr, bishop of Trenton, New Jersey; Jerome Hannon, bishop of Scranton, Pennsylvania; Edward Hettinger, auxiliary bishop of Columbus; and Coleman F. Carroll, auxiliary bishop of Pittsburgh who in 1958 would become the first bishop of Miami. During the celebration the Saint Vincent clerics performed Father Christopher Fullman's original play, *The Shadow of Glory,* which depicted the life and work of Boniface Wimmer, and in honor of the anniversary of the abbey (and of the concurrent fiftieth anniversary of the consecration of the archabbey church), the Holy See raised the church to the rank of a minor basilica.

In conjunction with the celebrations of 1955, the community also undertook extensive renovation of the archabbey basilica. The lighting and sound systems were completely reconstructed; the church was cleaned and repainted; and a new main altar, designed by Saint Vincent cleric Brother Rene Gracida, a graduate architect, was placed in the church. The new altar consisted of two base blocks of Botticino marble, each weighing five thousand pounds, and a cross-slab, or *mensa,* of Verde Scuro Fraye marble weighing ten tons and measuring five by ten feet. Dr. Leo Ravazzi of Pietrosanto, Italy, designed and carved the four panels on the base blocks, representing key sacrifices of the Old Testament: that of Cain and Abel; Abraham's preparations for the sacrifice of Isaac; Moses' sacrifice of the Paschal Lamb; and Melchizedek's sacrifice of bread and wine. A canopy of bronze and wood was hung above the altar, symbolizing the kingship of Christ. Brother Rene had designed the table-like altar to reflect contemporary theological emphasis on the Eucharist as both a sacrifice and a meal, and later, when liturgical changes resulted in priests celebrating Mass facing the people, the altar in the archabbey basilica, unlike altars in most Catholic churches of the world, needed no further modifications. In addition, the organs were rebuilt during the basilica's renovation.[105]

The restoration of the archabbey church was part of the overall building program in the 1950s that included construction of the activities building (Sportsman's Hall), the library, the Aquinas Hall seminary classroom building, a seminary residence building (Wimmer Hall), and the new athletic fields. Even as new buildings were planned and constructed, however, Archabbot Denis and the monastic chapter continued to focus on problems related to the older buildings on campus. The heart of the campus was still the double quadrangle, consisting of the old church (used as a students' chapel), the monastery, the prep school, the scholasticate, and various offices, laboratories, workshops, classrooms, dormitories, refectories, and kitchens. This was the oldest part of Saint Vincent, with buildings dating back to 1835, and maintaining them was a major problem. Archabbot Denis, even before his election, had been involved in renovating and modernizing these buildings. Under his direction new electric wiring, plumbing, and heating had been installed, but the buildings were old and to a great extent unsafe, and there was general concern about their structural soundness, as well as about the ever-present danger of fire.

Blacksmiths at Saint Vincent, 1897. Left to right: Brother Aloysius Wernet, O.S.B.; Brother Maximilian Schneider, O.S.B.; and Pius Robel.

Brothers James Brown, O.S.B., and Gerard Klaric, O.S.B., on the Saint Vincent farm, about 1955.

Benedictine Sisters Leodegaria and Liberata, 1961.

Everyone recognized that ordinary maintenance work was not sufficient to ensure the safety of the buildings, and the cost of complete restoration and renovation was prohibitive. In 1959, when a large piece of molding over the high altar in the students' chapel fell, an inspection revealed that the structure, now nearly 125 years old, was unsafe for further use. It was closed, and the students' chapel was moved to the ground floor of the new library.[106] But the greatest hazard at Saint Vincent in the 1950s was the possibility of a catastrophic fire. Many considered the buildings of the double quadrangle "a conflagration waiting to happen." Though built of brick, their frames, flooring, and internal partitions were made of wood that had been drying, in some cases, for more than a century. Moreover, these buildings were all interconnected, and such fire safety features as they contained (several thick fire walls, for example) had been installed in the nineteenth century and did not meet modern safety standards.

To help protect the campus against fire, a Saint Vincent fire department was formed and regular fire drills were held. Archabbot Denis appointed Father Ferdinand Lillig as campus fire chief, and a number of young monks underwent fire training at the Westmoreland County Fire School. Among them were the clerics Fidelis Lazar, Luke Callahan, Earl Henry, and Lawrence Hill, and lay brother Patrick Lacey. During the late 1950s Latrobe Fire Chief Earl Dalton came to Saint Vincent several times with members of the local fire company to tour the buildings, offer fire safety instructions, and study the layout of the campus in the event that they were ever called there to fight a fire. In the summer of 1959 the Pennsylvania state fire inspector inspected Saint Vincent and ordered that portions of the buildings be remodeled to conform with state requirements for fire prevention and safety. In August of that year the monastic chapter authorized the expenditure of one hundred thousand dollars for improvements that would allow the buildings to meet the standards of the state fire code.[107]

On December 8, 1959, Bishop Hugh L. Lamb of Greensburg died unexpectedly of a heart attack. Three days later the monks of Saint Vincent gathered in the archabbey basilica for a solemn pontifical Requiem Mass for the dead bishop, and on December 15 many of them, including Archabbot Denis, attended the funeral Mass in the Greensburg cathedral. Lamb had served as bishop of Greensburg for nearly eight years. His successor was named in February 1960, and the entire archabbey community was pleased to learn that the new bishop was Monsignor William G. Connare of Pittsburgh, an alumnus of Saint Vincent Seminary. Bishop Connare, who had been a student at Saint Vincent from 1932 to 1936, was consecrated on May 4, 1960, by Archbishop Egidio Vagnozzi, apostolic delegate to the United States, at a solemn ceremony in Blessed Sacrament Cathedral, Greensburg, attended by Archabbot Denis and a large contingent of monks from the monastery in Latrobe. Under Bishop Connare ties between Saint Vincent and the Diocese of Greensburg were solidified with the bishop's decision to send the seminarians of the newly established diocesan minor seminary of St. Joseph's Hall to the Saint Vincent Prep School for their academic program. Most of the diocese's major seminarians continued to study theology in the seminary at Saint Vincent.

A year after his installation as ordinary of Greensburg, Bishop Connare came to an agreement with Archabbot Denis that the diocese would take charge of the Benedictine parishes of St. Sylvester in Slickville and St. James in New Alexandria. These parishes had been founded by monks of the archabbey in Archabbot Leander's time, but there were now sufficient diocesan priests in the Diocese of Greensburg to assume responsibility for churches that formerly had been staffed by religious order priests. Under Bishop Lamb the diocese had earlier assumed charge of Blessed Sacrament Cathedral from the Benedictines. Thus, after more than a hundred years of serving the parochial needs of the Church in western Pennsylvania, the Benedictines of Saint Vincent began to relinquish control of some of the parishes they had founded and nurtured for decades, not only in the Greensburg diocese but in other dioceses as well. While surrendering these parishes was sometimes a difficult and painful experience for both the monks and the parishioners whom they served, it was clear to all that the changing of the guard was indeed a sign that the Benedictine mission had been a success. Since 1846 priests of Saint Vincent had provided pastoral care for thousands of people and had built parish communities in times when the number of diocesan priests was insufficient. Now, when the moment came to turn over their parishes to the diocesan clergy, the Benedictines were proud that over the years they had been successful in helping build strong communities of faith whose charge they could now confidently relinquish to others. In some cases the diocesan priests who assumed charge of the former Benedictine parishes had themselves been educated for the priesthood at Saint Vincent.

Even as the number of Benedictine parishes declined, the final years of Archabbot Denis's abbacy were marked by important new initiatives that extended the apostolic work of the archabbey. Twenty-seven years had elapsed since the end of Saint Vincent's China mission, and during that time no new missions had been founded by the community. An opportunity now arose for the Pennsylvania monks to become involved once again in Catholic higher education in the Orient. In 1959 the Holy See asked Archbishop Paul Yu Pin, exiled archbishop of Nanking, to determine the feasibility of reopening Fu Jen Catholic University on the island of Taiwan. The archbishop sought the aid of various religious societies, including the Jesuits and the Society of the Divine Word; Pope John XXIII donated one hundred thousand dollars to the project; and Cardinal Richard Cushing of Boston pledged a million dollars. In September 1960 Archabbot Denis accepted an invitation from Archbishop Yu Pin to meet with him in New York to discuss how Saint Vincent could participate in the restoration of Fu

Jen University. Accompanying the archabbot to New York was Father Hugh Wilt, a veteran of Saint Vincent's first mission to China and, until recently, prior at the archabbey. During his meeting with Archbishop Yu Pin, Archabbot Denis committed the archabbey to providing monks to help reestablish Fu Jen, and a few days later he assigned Father Hugh the task of going to Taiwan to assist in the project. Father Hugh left for the Orient in October 1960 and for the next three years worked with the archbishop and the university's board of trustees in a successful effort that resulted in the reopening of Fu Jen University near Taipei, Taiwan, in October 1963. In July 1963 the monastic chapter in Pennsylvania authorized the establishment of a dependent priory on Taiwan where monks from Saint Vincent would observe monastic life while teaching in the university. To honor the founder of Saint Vincent, the monastery was called Wimmer Priory.[108]

A second initiative of Archabbot Denis that resulted in a new field of apostolic work for the monks of Saint Vincent was the decision to send priests from the archabbey to the Pennsylvania State University in State College, Pennsylvania, in order to establish a Catholic center for the four thousand Catholic students at the university. The opportunity came when Bishop J. Carroll McCormick of Altoona-Johnstown asked the monks of Saint Vincent to assume the Catholic chaplaincy of the university. The chapter agreed to accept the mission on a trial basis, and Archabbot Denis demonstrated its importance to Saint Vincent by sending the president and dean of men of Saint Vincent College to initiate the new apostolate. Father Quentin Schaut, who was replaced as college president by Father Maximilian Duman, and Father Egbert Donovan, replaced as dean of men by Father Omer Kline, left Saint Vincent for Penn State on February 5, 1962. Four months later they reported back to the chapter and recommended that the mission to the students of the Pennsylvania State University be taken on permanently by the archabbey. On June 15, 1962, the chapter voted to accept the mission and authorized a loan of five hundred thousand dollars to build the Catholic Center at Penn State. The loan would be repaid from the income of the Catholic Center. Meanwhile, at the recommendation of Fathers Quentin and Egbert, the chapter also authorized the purchase of a fifty-thousand-dollar building to be used as a temporary residence for the chaplains, as well as pastoral offices and meeting spaces for the students, until the permanent center could be completed.[109]

The third new mission from Saint Vincent, the seeds of which were planted in the final years of Archabbot Denis's reign, was to Brazil. In the closing months of 1962 the archabbot, in his capacity as president of the

American Cassinese Congregation, received inquiries from Abbot Placidus Staeb, president of the Brazilian Benedictine Congregation, about the possibility of an abbey of the American Cassinese Congregation taking charge of the Priory of São Bento, a small independent monastery in the Brazilian Congregation the future of which was in doubt because of a lack of vocations. Archabbot Denis decided to propose to the monastic chapter that Saint Vincent assume responsibility for the monastery as a dependent priory and brought the matter up for discussion before the chapter.

Father Martin Roth, prior of São Bento, came to Saint Vincent in January 1963 to discuss the matter with the archabbot and community. During this visit he attended a meeting of the chapter at which he formally proposed that the archabbey take over the priory. The Priory of São Bento had been founded in 1650 in the seaport of Santos, thirty miles southeast of São Paulo, and in 1947 it had moved to Vinhedo, Brazil, an 800-acre plantation near Campinas, some seventy miles northwest of São Paulo. The priory operated a vineyard at Vinhedo (which in Portuguese meant "large vineyard") and also owned and cultivated 160 acres near the village of Indaiatuba. Father Martin explained to the Saint Vincent capitulars that the lack of vocations was a critical problem for the community, which consisted of four priests (all of German heritage) and a Brazilian lay brother, and he proposed that Saint Vincent assume charge of the priory and its property and allow the monks there to transfer their vows of stability to the monastery in Pennsylvania. The capitulars welcomed the project, and Archabbot Denis informed them that he would send a delegation from Saint Vincent to Vinhedo in the summer of 1963 to examine the matter in greater detail.[110]

Another mission, though a temporary one, undertaken by Saint Vincent during this period was to Ethiopia. In the spring of 1962 Archabbot Denis received a request from the Vatican's Sacred Congregation for Religious, delivered through the apostolic delegate in Washington, to assist the Vatican in making contact with monks of the Coptic Church in Ethiopia. Strittmatter assigned Father Ermin Smith, novice master at the archabbey, and Father Demetrius Dumm, vice rector of Saint Vincent Seminary, to the mission, which they undertook in the summer of 1962. The two Saint Vincent priests spent six weeks in Ethiopia visiting the Coptic monasteries there. They returned to the United States by way of Rome, where they made their report to the Holy See, and in September 1962 they reported to the monastic chapter at Saint Vincent some of their experiences in Ethiopia.[111]

In addition to turning their attention to new missions and foundations in the United States and abroad, the monks of Saint Vincent also came to the financial assistance of several foreign and American Benedictine houses in the early 1960s. Though the community was by no means wealthy, it had managed by careful stewardship of its temporal resources to achieve solvency in the years following World War II, and by the beginning of the 1960s it had even built up a modest financial reserve. The archabbey was therefore able to join with other abbeys of the American Cassinese Congregation in providing financial support to the Collegio di Sant' Anselmo for construction of new classroom space at the international Benedictine house of studies in Rome, and to assist the Benedictine Priory of São Geraldo in São Paulo, Brazil, when that community sought funds to construct a school. Later, when St. Bernard Abbey in Cullman, Alabama, found itself in financial difficulties, the monastic chapter in Pennsylvania voted to come to the aid of this daughterhouse of Saint Vincent with an interest-free loan.[112]

DISCORD AND DISSENT

Increased financial security, building expansion, growth in the college, and a rise in monastic vocations all characterized Saint Vincent during the decade of the 1950s. With respect to what the monks traditionally called their "temporal" affairs, all seemed well with the community as the college flourished, new buildings rose, and the halls of the monastery buzzed with the activity of those monks engaged in the community's educational and pastoral apostolates. But even as Saint Vincent became stronger with respect to its temporal affairs, many of the monks expressed concern that all was not well with the spiritual life of the archabbey. It was an old story, but one no less serious and divisive on account of its familiarity.

Tangible evidence of this latest concern for the spiritual welfare of the community first surfaced during the regular triennial visitation of the archabbey in February 1954. The congregational visitators, Abbot Lawrence Vohs of St. Bede Abbey, Peru, Illinois, and Abbot Cuthbert McDonald of St. Benedict's Abbey, Atchison, Kansas, reported to Archabbot Denis that during their interviews with individual members of the community, many expressed dissatisfaction with what they regarded as the poor quality of monastic observance at Saint Vincent as well as with the monastery's purported lack of spiritual development. Much of the dissatisfaction focused on the lack of regular conferences by the archabbot on the religious life, the alleged neglect of spiritual reading and meditation by individual monks, and the failure of some of the confreres to meet their obligations of daily participation in communal prayer, meals, and recreation. Many were of the opinion that the demands of the community's academic commitments and educational apostolates were "crowding out and destroying the monastic spirit." Others noted that the professors were so overworked that they often had no time to attend Divine Office or even the daily conventual Mass. The visitators remarked that the stress of academic and administrative responsibilities was so great that not a few of the monks were "becoming disinterested both in monastic life and teaching activities," and they pointed out that the rapid expansion of the college, and the desire on the part of certain monastic and academic leaders to expand still further, were causing serious division within the community.

The archabbot himself came under strong criticism during the visitation for his purported undemocratic style of leadership. Some of the monks complained that he was excessively involved in minor details of administration that should be left to others, and that he often made unilateral decisions affecting important aspects of the community's life and work without consulting the chapter. Abbots Lawrence and Cuthbert reported to Archabbot Denis some of the details of the monks' complaints, and urged him to "try to be more congenial and pleasant with your confreres and more accessible to them." The visiting abbots said that because of what many perceived as rebuffs from the archabbot during meetings of the chapter, some of the monks hesitated to speak openly of the concerns they had. The monks feared rather than loved and respected their spiritual father, the visiting abbots said, and they urged the archabbot to demonstrate "a greater generosity in words of commendation and encouragement," which would "result in a more congenial and family relationship between the Father of the Community and [his] confreres."[113]

Archabbot Denis took these criticisms seriously, bore them patiently, and attempted to resolve the tensions in the community as best he could. He urged the monks to more faithful observance of the monastic regimen and sincerely sought to create a more cordial and familial ambience in the community. His aloof manner, innate reticence, deeply ingrained traditionalist outlook, and rigorous sense of duty, however, caused many of his confreres to regard him as a rigid and inflexible autocrat and made it difficult for him to foster the kind of personalist leadership that so many in the community desired. Archabbot Denis seemed at a loss as to how to restore unity to the divided community. His relative failure to achieve success in this effort was reflected in the visitation reports of 1957 and 1960, which essentially raised the same issues that the visitation report of 1954 had raised.[114]

Nonetheless, the visitators were not entirely negative in their assessment of the archabbot's leadership. They commended him for improving the monastic formation program in the novitiate and the clericate and spoke favorably about the positive changes that had occurred in the care of sick and infirm monks. In the visitation of 1960 they also noted that the community generally believed "in the sincerity of their Abbot. . . , appreciate[d] his great charity toward them, . . . [and] esteem[ed] him for his edifying example."[115]

Despite the fact that Archabbot Denis continued to be the focus of much criticism for both his expansionist projects and his purported failure to foster an appropriate environment for the monastic community's spiritual growth, he continued to retain the support of a significant number of the monks. Those who approved of the way he was conducting the work and prayer of the community included the two priests who held the office of prior during this period, Fathers Hugh Wilt and Leopold Krul, as well as Father Edmund Cuneo, director of college development, and Father Frederick Strittmatter, the archabbot's brother. Indeed, the archabbot enjoyed the support of many of the older members of the community, who shared his traditionalist views and regarded his ambitious building plans as critical for the future security of both the monastery and the schools. He also enjoyed the support of the majority of monks assigned to the parish apostolate. There were many who genuintely liked the archabbot personally, recognized his many virtues, and could not understand the animosity that he seemed to evoke in some of the brethren. One of those who knew him well, and who had a deep awareness of the benevolent character that lay concealed beneath the austere facade, noted years later that Archabbot Denis "was a kind and generous person, a much misunderstood man."[116] And young monks who entered the monastery after Strittmatter's retirement were struck and even inspired by his piety, humility, and kindness.

Lack of space continued to be a serious problem at Saint Vincent throughout this period. Monks and students found themselves uncomfortably crowded in their living quarters, work areas, and classrooms despite the steady construction taking place under Archabbot Denis's leadership. The monastic chapter therefore met on August 18, 1959, to consider the needs of the community for new buildings. By a majority vote of ninety-nine to nineteen the capitulars authorized the expenditure of fifty thousand dollars for preliminary studies for a master construction plan as well as for preliminary drawings for a monastic infirmary, a new chapter room, offices, new parish facilities, new college residence halls, and a new science hall, and Archabbot Denis appointed a development committee, chaired by Father Alfred Grotzinger, to conduct a search for an architect.[117]

The development committee discussed the community's needs with a number of architectural firms and then recommended to Archabbot Denis and the council of seniors the firm of Victor Christ-Janer and Associates of New Canaan, Connecticut. The council accepted the recommendation, and the Connecticut firm was invited to submit ideas for consideration. In April 1960 Mr. Christ-Janer came to Saint Vincent and presented a preliminary report to the chapter, which then proceeded by a vote of forty-nine to eight to approve the initial plan and to authorize the architect to complete a master plan.[118]

Eight months later, in December 1960, Christ-Janer returned to Latrobe and presented the detailed master plan to the capitulars. The monks took advantage of the occasion to pose many questions about the plan and to make suggestions for improvement. When the architect left the meeting, a lively discussion ensued. There was considerable disagreement among the monks about the nature and feasibility of the plan, which some estimated would cost more than $3 million. Even members of the development committee, now called the building committee, were in disagreement. Some thought the master plan a visionary and aesthetically pleasing response to the community's practical needs for new physical space, while others regarded it as extravagant and excessively expensive. Remembering the crisis that resulted from the community's financial overcommitment in China thirty years before, opponents of the plan accused its supporters of "wanting artistic buildings regardless of cost" and called for a more conservative, less costly building program. Those who supported the plan pointed out that it was farsighted and ultimately achievable because the community was solvent and fully capable of taking on the burden of debt that the plan would require. In the end, because the monks could not reach a consensus, the chapter decided to postpone the vote for approval.[119]

In March 1961 Mr. Christ-Janer met with the chapter once again to discuss revisions in the plan designed to keep costs down. At that time he also presented his proposal for initiating the building program with construction of two student dormitories, a high priority on account of the rapidly expanding number of students applying to the college. After the architect had made his presentation, he left the meeting, and Archabbot Denis asked the capitulars if they were prepared to vote on the question of whether to build the dormitories. During the ensuing discussion, the question of the master plan was brought to the floor, and someone pointed out that the chapter had never officially approved it. Christ-Janer was invited back to the meeting where he once again explained the fundamental ideas of the master plan as well as its "philosophical" basis. Following this presentation, the monks discussed the proposal at length and in the end voted by a margin of thirty-nine to two "to adopt the Christ-Janer plan as a philosophical and practical framework for long-range planning." Three weeks later the chapter reassembled and, with the addition of capitulars living in parishes and missions outside the monastery who had returned for the occasion, voted by a margin of 102 to 8 to allocate $1,620,000 for construction of the student dormitories. The capitulars also agreed to borrow $1,233,000 from the Federal Housing Administration to meet the cost.[120]

More than two years would pass, however, before ground was broken on the project. The delay was caused by intense disagreement within the Benedictine community over the design and cost of the new buildings. The key issue for many of the monks was the question of design. Archabbot Denis insisted that the Christ-Janer plan was too elaborate, and as a consequence too costly. He wanted a simple, functional, unembellished design such as those that characterized the other buildings constructed on campus during his abbacy—Wimmer Hall, Aquinas Hall, Sportsman's Hall, and the library. He and his supporters pointed out proudly that these buildings had been constructed without the community's having incurred any debts at all. The plans of independent professional architects, the archabbot insisted, resulted in nothing but "expensive gingerbread."

An increasing number of the members of the community, however, strongly disagreed with the archabbot's point of view. They regarded the earlier buildings constructed during his abbacy as perhaps functional but indisputably ugly, and they called for more careful attention to the character and beauty of any new buildings that would be built. The community was building for the future, they insisted, and the monks had an obligation to insure that the structures they put up were aesthetically pleasing as well as functionally efficient. In Christ-Janer they were convinced they had found an independent professional architect who would provide the character and beauty that they believed the campus urgently needed.[121]

Several members of the building committee were among those who believed that the character and beauty of the new buildings were as important as their functional efficiency, and consequently they insisted that the design of the proposed dormitories should be in conformity with Christ-Janer's overall master plan, a plan that was "based upon needs and spirit, rather than expediency and budget." Following this principle, the architect prepared a detailed design for the dormitories that would have resulted in structures whose cost would have exceeded by $1 million the amount authorized by the chapter. While the additional cost did not seem excessive to those who supported the Christ-Janer plan, other members of the community feared that committing more than $2.5 million dollars to the construction of new student housing would involve an unwise financial risk that neither the monastery nor the college should assume. Some opposed the Christ-Janer plan because they believed it did not meet the practical needs of the students.[122]

Among those who vigorously opposed taking on the additional burden of debt was Archabbot Denis, and when it appeared to him that the architect was moving ahead with his design without taking into consideration the cost limits established by the monastic chapter in April 1961, Strittmatter decided to cancel the contract with the firm of Christ-Janer and Associates and to seek another architect. At a meeting held in Pittsburgh on August 17, 1962, and attended by Father Alfred Grotzinger, chairman of the building committee, and two members of the St. Vincent College Board of Lay Advisors, Mr. John Laughlin and Mr. John Davis, Archabbot Denis informed Christ-Janer that his services would no longer be required.[123]

On September 25, 1962, Strittmatter formally announced to the chapter the termination of the architect's contract. He also announced that the college's lay advisory board would help select a new architect who would develop new plans for the student dormitories. Although the announcement resulted in a firestorm of protest from those members of the monastic chapter who supported the master plan, the chapter secretary noted simply that there were "many questions, such as why a new committee, why a new architect, and other pertinent questions. The discussion that followed brought out nothing definite," and the archabbot ended the questioning by introducing a totally different subject for the chapter's consideration.[124]

The months that followed were among the most difficult and contentious in Saint Vincent's history. To many of the monks the manner in which the decision concerning construction of the dormitories had been handled was another, perhaps the worst, example of the archabbot's autocratic and high-handed style of leadership. They protested that the precipitous decision to dismiss the architect was not the archabbot's to make. It was the chapter that had selected the architect; it was therefore the chapter's right to determine when and if that decision was to be reversed. But Strittmatter, confident of his authority, refused to acknowledge the chapter's right to decide and proceeded with his own agenda. He appointed a new building committee, worked with the lay advisors to identify a new architect, and did not reassemble the chapter for almost three and a half months. When he finally did call another meeting, on January 9, 1963, it was simply to announce that a new architectural firm had been chosen. Triggs, Myers, McQuade & Associates of Pittsburgh, he said, had been contracted to develop new plans for the student dormitories. These plans would be brought to the chapter as soon as they were ready. Again, the dissidents objected strongly to both the archabbot's decisions and his procedure. Some pointed out that the firm of Triggs, Myers, McQuade & Associates was not an independent, professional architect at all but rather a construction contractor. Impassioned voices accused the community's superior of violating congregational regulations as well as simple justice in his dismissal of the previous architect and his abandonment of the master building plan. Neither he nor the lay board of advisors had the right to select a new architect or commission a new design without the chapter's prior approval. The majority of the monks still supported the original Christ-Janer plan. The debate was divisive, and the lengthy arguments which the archabbot's critics made were again summarized by the chapter secretary in abbreviated and laconic form: "In general," the minutes reported, "the Capitulars were reluctant to abandon these previously adopted plans."[125] But Strittmatter would allow no vote to be taken.

TRIAL BY FIRE

The chapter of January 9, 1963, resulted in increased bitterness and frustration on the part of those in the community who considered Archabbot Denis's behavior despotic and even erratic. Already there were those who were prepared to seek redress for his purported abuse of power by calling for a special visitation by the American Cassinese Congregation's visitators. Some even suggested that his allegedly unjust treatment of architect Victor Christ-Janer should be reported to the apostolic delegate in Washington. The possibility of bringing the matter before the apostolic delegate, however, was never seriously pursued, and the difficulty of bringing the case before the congregational visitators was complicated by the fact that Archabbot Denis, in addition to being superior of Saint Vincent, was also abbot president of the American Cassinese Congregation. His position as abbot president would not have prevented those who thought an injustice had been done from pursuing such a course of action, but it would have put the two abbots who served as visitators in a very awkward position.

As it happened, however, catastrophe struck Saint Vincent before the dissident monks had an opportunity to organize effective opposition to the archabbot's decisions regarding the student dormitories. On Monday, January 28, 1963, the fire, which for decades many had feared, succeeded in bringing the monks together, uniting them in a common effort for survival, and making the chapter squabbles and the disagreements within the community seem insignificant by comparison.

The fire began in the biology laboratory, in one of the oldest parts of the double quadrangle, where Old Main (or Benedict Hall) met Father James Ambrose Stillinger's church of 1835. The church had for many years served as the students' chapel, but in 1959 it had been closed for safety reasons and was now used merely as a storage area. No satisfactory explanation was ever offered as to exactly how the fire started, but speculation later focused on faulty electrical wiring.

Monday morning dawned cold and grey in western Pennsylvania, with ice and snow on the ground and a slight wind blowing out of the west. A blizzard had passed over the countryside the previous day, and thermometers at Saint Vincent registered ten degrees below zero. The college students were home on semester break, but the seminarians and prep school students were on campus and preparing to begin the week's classes. Brother Colman McFadden, a cleric who served as prefect in the scholasticate, had accompanied the scholastics to Mass and breakfast earlier in the morning and had already made his usual inspection of the dormitories to see that all the beds had been properly made. He was now on duty in the study hall, where the students were preparing for the first class of the day. About 8:20 a.m., as McFadden sat reading in the study hall, Ronald Palenski of Alexandria, Virginia, a sophomore in the scholasticate, came up to his desk and asked if there was a chimney in the biology laboratory, which adjoined Benedict Hall. "My heart almost stopped," Brother Colman wrote, "[because] I knew there wasn't." Palenski said that he saw smoke coming from the roof of the lab. Brother Colman went to look, and just as he too caught a glimpse of the smoke, Father Louis Sedlacko, headmaster of the prep school, announced over the loudspeaker that all students were to take their heaviest jackets and proceed immediately outside and across the road to the Sportsman's Hall activities building on the southwest side of Benedict Hall. By now smoke was pouring from the eaves of the biology lab and the adjacent chapel, and after assisting the students to make their escape, Brother Colman returned to the prep study halls and dormitories in Benedict Hall to make sure that no one had been left behind. While checking the freshman dormitory next to the biology laboratory, he was startled by a loud explosion as an air vent on the nearby laboratory roof blew off. The explosion frightened him, but he finished checking for any remaining students before making his own escape.[126]

Father Leo Rothrauff, assistant business manager in the college, had risen early and gone to the monastery choir chapel at 4:15 a.m. to say his private prayers before the community gathered for Lauds at 5:00 a.m. At 7:00 a.m., after Divine Office and conventual Mass, he had breakfast and then went to his office in Benedict Hall to deal with papers on his desk. At 8:15 a.m. he heard the prep school fire alarm atop Maur Hall sound, and thought it entirely too early in the day for a fire drill. He looked out of the window and saw smoke coming from the area of the prep school. He immediately grabbed his topcoat and without bothering to lock the door of his office, began running to his monastery room in order to save his uncompleted doctoral thesis. As he ran through the monastery he looked out of the hall window and saw smoke coming from the roof of the biology laboratory. Taking two steps at a time, he rushed up to the clericate and yelled down the hall that the biology lab was on fire. Clerics were coming out of their rooms all along the hall and looking out of the windows. Father Leo then rushed up another flight of stairs to his room on the top floor of the monastery, a warren of monastic cells and storage closets dubbed "Chinatown" because of its overcrowded condition. There he scooped up his thesis and a box of research material and with the aid of a cleric who was standing in the hallway, carried them back to the hallway outside the college bookstore. He met Father Conall Pfiester at the foot of the stairs that went up to the biology lab. Father Conall told him to help collect fire extinguishers, and Father Leo returned to the bookstore to get the heavy soda and water extinguisher that was hanging on the wall there. When he returned to the stairwell, he found Father Owen Roth, and together they climbed the stairs and approached the door of the upstairs lab. Father Owen unlocked the door and pushed it open. Heat and smoke rushed out of the room, and the two priests jumped back. "We can't go in there," Father Leo said, and Father Owen closed the door on twenty-five years of work.[127]

At 8:20 a.m. Brother Philip Hurley, sacristan of the Saint Vincent Basilica, was setting out vestments for the next day's Masses. Most of the priests of the archabbey had already said their private Masses, though a few were still at the basilica's side altars. Brother Philip heard the fire alarm and smelled smoke just as Father Ferdinand Lillig, the Saint Vincent fire chief, entered the sacristy after his morning Mass. When the sacristan asked Father Ferdinand what was burning, the fire warden "took a deep breath, exclaimed, 'O my God!' and dashed out of the door." Just then another priest came into the sacristy and said that the old students' chapel was on fire, but Brother Philip wasn't concerned, "presuming everything would be under control."[128]

Latrobe fire chief Earl Dalton got the call—"Fire at Saint Vincent"—on his two-way radio at 8:20 a.m., just as Brother Philip was setting out Mass vestments and prep sophomore Ron Palenski was asking Brother Colman about the existence of a chimney on the roof of the biology lab. Dalton immediately jumped in his car and headed out of Latrobe toward Saint Vincent, his siren wailing. As he passed the lumberyard in west Latrobe, he received a second call informing him that the old students' chapel was burning. He immediately radioed orders for backup assistance from the Greensburg fire department, nine miles away, and issued a request to local factories to release all volunteer firemen so that they could join the fire trucks from Latrobe that were already making their way to the archabbey. At Robles' Corner he noticed for the first time smoke hanging above the monastery and college, and he pressed his foot on the accelerator as he saw ahead of him the first fire truck making its way up the hill. He passed the truck as it entered the road to the campus and pulled his car around to the front of Benedict Hall. As he got out of the car he saw people standing on the road pointing to the smoke coming from the chapel and now from the roof of Benedict Hall as well. He quickly put on his service coat and helmet and ran over to speak with Father Ferdinand Lillig who was on the scene. Father Ferdinand told him that the main part of the fire was in the chapel, so Dalton ordered the first truck that arrived to run water lines to the chapel in the hope that the fire could be contained there. In quick succession four more trucks from Latrobe arrived and began to connect hoses to the cistern near the Sauerkraut Tower, the cistern on the main road leading to campus, and the fire hydrant in front of the library. The aerial ladder truck from Latrobe was positioned in front of Benedict Hall and within minutes water was being poured onto the fire from the ladder hose. Dalton later said that reports suggesting that it took forty-five minutes to get water on the fire were incorrect.[129]

Nonetheless, frustration followed frustration for the next half-hour as the brass nozzles of the fire hoses froze and initial streams of water slowed to a trickle. Water from the cisterns also froze, and men were sent to the reservoir below the basilica to break through the foot of ice on the surface and run lines to the water. All this caused delay, and it wasn't until at least half an hour after the first fire trucks arrived that steady streams of water could be played on the fire. By then, however, the old students' chapel was an inferno. The glass windows were exploding outward because of the intense heat, and the slate roof was starting to collapse. The firemen focused their efforts on preventing the blaze from spreading to adjacent buildings.

As usual, at 6:15 a.m. Brother Placid Cremonese, the monastery baker, had begun to prepare the day's loaves of the famous Saint Vincent bread for baking. He had mixed the yeast with flour and water in the large vats used for that purpose and then switched on the mechanical kneader. This morning's batch of the rich brown bread that the monks of Saint Vincent had been baking daily for over a century would be smaller than usual—only sixty six-pound loaves—because the college students were away, so Brother Placid took his time, feeling under no compulsion to "break any records in the history of our bakery." By 8:00 a.m. the loaves were shaped and covered with long towels, and after another half hour of proofing they would be ready for the oven. About 8:15 a.m. Brother Placid heard a steady buzzing sound which he realized only afterward was the house fire alarm. Several minutes later he began to smell something burning. He looked out of the window towards the old students' chapel, several yards from the bakery, and immediately saw black smoke pouring from the north windows of the biology lab. A minute later flames burst from windows of the lab, and he realized the danger he was in. He quickly put the finished loaves in the oven and "ran for dear life . . . to a place of safety." Brother Placid watched the fire trucks arrive on campus and the firemen begin to unwind the hoses for the battle ahead. At about 9:30 a.m. he remembered the loaves and realized that they were ready to be taken from the oven. By now, however, flames had spread to the top story of Benedict Hall, and firemen were pouring water into the rooms two floors above the bakery. He knew it would not be safe to attempt pulling the loaves from the oven, but since the flames and smoke had not yet reached the bakery, he decided to make an effort to save the bread anyway. He dashed into the bakery, where he remained only long enough to open the oven's draft control, which allowed the heat to escape up the chimney and thus prevented the bread from burning.[130]

By 9:00 a.m. a general alarm had been issued throughout Westmoreland County, and volunteer fire companies from Greensburg, Ligonier, Derry, Hempfield Township, Jeannette, Irwin, Mt. Pleasant, Scottdale, Youngwood, and ten other communities were converging on Saint Vincent. Latrobe chief Earl Dalton ordered his men to train their hoses on the critical points of the fire, but it was clear that the firefighters were losing the battle to prevent the flames from spreading. Wind whipping in from the west was causing the fire to lick at nearby buildings, and despite initial success in getting water on the old students' chapel, pumps and water lines continued to freeze in the bitter cold. Dalton's men found that they were unable to get sufficient water on the hottest spots to prevent the fire from advancing to the monastery and prep school in the east and west ranges of the double quadrangle. The old students' chapel was already a total loss and flames were entering the monastery choir chapel, which was connected with the basilica. The fire had even reached the landmark monastery bell tower, next to the old students' chapel.

At about 9:15 a.m. Brother Philip Hurley left the basilica sacristy to see what was happening. He later wrote: "I had prayed to God that I would not panic, and when I did look outside, the horror that met my eyes was unbelievable. The front of the choir chapel and the base of the [bell] tower were completely enveloped in black smoke. I lost no time in getting back into the sacristy and telling the seminarian[s] to start taking all the vestments outside. . . . The whole responsibility of [saving] the sacred vestments and chalices and other furnishings of the basilica fell upon me. God did not let me panic."

Elsewhere crews of monks, seminarians, and prep students, after helping evacuate the older monks from their rooms in the threatened monastery to the safety of Leander Hall, were hastily removing the contents of rooms on the two floors of the monastery known as Fifth Avenue and Shotgun Row. Father Emeric Pfiester and another crew had already taken the portable items—vestments, chalices, missals—from the St. Boniface Chapel, which was located behind the old students' chapel. By 9:30 a.m. the fire had destroyed the St. Boniface Chapel and had spread to the top floor of the monastery—Chinatown—where it was quickly consuming the rooms of the clerics and lay brothers. As additional fire companies arrived on the campus, monks and seminarians stepped forward to help firemen unwind hoses and run them to the places where they were most needed. Brother Earl Henry, a member of the Saint Vincent fire department, was among the first of the monks to don helmet, fire coat, and hip boots and help train water on the old students' chapel. Other monks who were in the thick of the battle included Brothers Luke Callahan, Lawrence Hill, Patrick Lacey, and other members of the community fire company. When firemen noticed any of the monks and seminarians standing around watching the blaze, they would abruptly draft them, at times with harsh orders to "get the lead out" or to "pick up that damned hose; it's your building!" Chief Dalton later remarked that he himself had been "mighty short, direct, and probably down right nasty when I ran into some of those people who we have been telling for five years the fire potential that was St. Vincent's."

By 10:00 a.m. there were about four hundred volunteer firemen and eighty monks and seminarians fighting the blaze. By now flames were shooting from the top floor of the monastery, and those manning the hoses below could see through the windows that it was already about two-thirds of the way along the hallway of Chinatown. Another hook and ladder truck, one from Greensburg, sped up the road by the seminary and paused as firemen and bystanders knocked down the ornamental brick wall that led into the seminary's St. Thomas Courtyard. Within minutes the wall was down and the truck moved quickly under the seminary arch and into the courtyard. Father Leo Rothrauff shouted at the fireman steering the rear section of the truck to duck his head a moment before the fireman's helmet skimmed under the arch with only two or three inches to spare. In another five minutes one of the firemen was fastened to the top of the ladder, manning a hose that sent a large stream of water cascading into the falling timbers of Chinatown. The ladder moved back and forth through the dense smoke that poured from the building, and several times bystanders lost sight of the firefighter atop the ladder. Father Leo feared for the man's life amidst the suffocating smoke, but each time the firefighter disappeared, he reemerged, though sometimes after what seemed like an eternity. Those below cheered when they saw that he was continuing to pour water on the flames.

About 10:30 a.m. the three bells fell from the blazing bell tower with a crash. The two smaller ones rolled into the pit at the base of the tower; the larger one struck those already below and bounced and rolled into the ground floor of the monastery where it came to rest outside the room of Father Edmund Cuneo. One of the monks who saw where the bell now lay commented, "That's very appropriate. Father Edmund is so often late for his appointments."[131]

As the fire entered the choir chapel and threatened the basilica, several dozen seminarians went to help Brother Philip move valuables from the church to the seminary. The rapid progress of the flames through Chinatown, which Brother Philip and the seminarians could plainly see as they bore sacred vestments and vessels to the seminary, stunned them and spurred them on to work even faster in stripping the basilica. When the lights went out all over the campus, Brother Philip put candles in the

The Saint Vincent fire, January 28, 1963.

church's basement storage room while seminarians rescued the pontifical vestments and other valuables stored there. Even if the fire didn't reach that far, it was clear that the water would.

By now firemen were entering the basilica with ladders and hoses to attempt to reach the fire in the choir chapel, behind and above the basilica sacristy. Father Marcian Kornides, pastor of Saint Vincent Parish, directed their work. He showed them how to enter the rear of the choir chapel through a door high in the back wall of the sacristy, and fifteen firefighters, with oxygen masks on their faces and hoses slung over their shoulders, climbed a ladder to gain this access. For an hour they fought the fire from the floors of the choir chapel, facing heat that was almost unbearable. Flames licked the windows at the opposite end of the chapel, and the firemen were ordered not to advance any closer than halfway along the chapel floor since it was feared that at any moment the bell tower, which was then belching flames, would crumble and shower its burning debris on the heat-weakened roof of the choir chapel. Afterward everyone said that it was the heroic defense put up by these men in the monks' choir chapel that marked the turning point of the struggle. While the chapel was scorched, the flames did not reach the basilica. When it had appeared that the fire had been halted outside the choir chapel, one of the firemen who had been in the vanguard of the fight there paid spontaneous tribute to Father Marcian. "That priest down there is the guy who saved the church for you fellows," he told seminarian Shane MacCarthy. "If we had to wait another fifteen minutes, then we wouldn't have been able to get up there. But he showed us where to go and what to do. He's done the work of five of us, and believe me, Sonny, we've all worked like hell today."[132]

At 10:30 a.m., before it was clear that the church would be saved, Archabbot Denis Strittmatter, who appeared to be in a state of semishock, agreed with a suggestion that the Blessed Sacrament should be removed from the basilica, and Prior Leopold Krul went to the sacristy with Father Leo Rothrauff and several other priests and clerics to do so. Threading their way through the firefighters, each of the priests took two ciboria from the tabernacle. Then they formed a procession, led by clerics with candles and a bell, and proceeded to the new students' chapel in the library. As the procession passed through the smoky halls and then outside the buildings into the cold, seminarians, monks, sisters, and students paused, bowed their heads or knelt in the ice and snow. One of the local newspapers reported the next day that the prior had gone through the buildings blessing the walls to prevent the fire from spreading, but this was an inaccurate and garbled account of the procession that transferred the Blessed Sacrament to the library chapel.

Though the basilica now seemed to be safe, time appeared to stand still as the fire continued to move in four directions, forming an almost perfect H in the double quadrangle. The crossbar of the H was the biology lab and the old students' chapel, which by now were smoldering ruins. The two lines connected by the crossbar were the east range of the quadrangle (Anselm and Gregory Halls), where the monastery was located, and the west range (Benedict Hall) where the prep school and the scholasticate were located. On the west range the top floor of the central part of Benedict Hall was ablaze, and flames approached the fire walls on either end. Everyone knew that if these fire walls were breached, there would be little hope of saving the north and south ranges (Maur and Placid Halls) of the quadrangle. The firefighters aimed their hoses in the direction of the fire walls on either side of the west range, and on the east range they poured water on the north and south ends of Anselm and Gregory Halls. In Gregory Hall firemen from Latrobe fought the fire inch by inch in the hallways and monastic cells. They made a courageous stand at the monastery tailor shop, where they broke through the ceiling and walls to get at the fire which was burning in the hallway above them. There they broke its progress and began to force it back toward the old students' chapel. In the other wing of the monastery, Anselm Hall, firefighters from Greensburg made an equally courageous stand. Only one room in Chinatown still had a roof on it when the fire was finally stopped on this side of the monastery, but thanks to the valor of the Greensburg volunteers, the floors below were saved.

The Red Cross first aid station sent out from Greensburg and set up in Sportsman's Hall was fully occupied caring for firemen who suffered from frostbitten hands, ears, faces, and feet, and from smoke inhalation. The Salvation Army from Latrobe established a soup kitchen on campus and with the help of the Benedictine sisters provided hot coffee and food to exhausted and hungry firemen throughout the day. Latrobe fireman Bob Blazek was hit on the shoulder by falling debris, and it was feared that he might have a fracture. But Blazek did not want to withdraw from fighting the fire and had to be argued into going to the first aid station and then to the hospital where X-rays revealed a bad bruise but not a fracture. Jim Martin, another Latrobe fireman, was rushed to the hospital with what at first appeared to be a heart attack but which turned out to be exhaustion.

Meanwhile, Brother Placid Cremonese, who had been helplessly watching the fire burn, ran into Frank Zarzeczny, a layman who had worked as the Saint Vincent baker for forty-seven years and had recently retired. Brother Placid, who later said he regarded the meeting as providential, commented that the sixty loaves of bread still in the oven would almost certainly be destroyed. He half-jokingly said to George Hoehler, another lay worker at Saint Vincent, that if he and Zarzeczny were up to it, he would join them in trying to save the bread. "Let's go," said Hoehler, and without debating the wisdom of the move, the three men immediately hurried to the bakery. Zarzeczny was the first to reach the oven, where he immediately began to pull "the last batch of bread from the oven that he had cherished for forty-seven years." After finding the way to the college kitchen blocked by fire hoses and fallen debris, Brother Placid and his companions took the sixty loaves to the shoe shop, some thirty feet from the bakery, where they stored them until the following day when the bread was served to monks, students, workers, and firemen at Saint Vincent.

The battle continued into its fourth hour. Older monks stood by the library and wept as they witnessed what seemed to them the apocalyptic destruction of their monastery and schools. Some had to be led away to the shelter of the new students' chapel to avoid frostbite. Prior Leopold ordered a head count of monks and students and discovered that one priest could not be found. Word spread among the community that Father Fintan Shoniker, the director of libraries, was missing. Many feared that he had not escaped the monastery in time. A call went out to search for him.

As midday approached, the prior passed word to all the monks that the community would pray the Minor Hours, as usual, at noon. Those not engaged in fighting the fire gathered in the students' chapel on the ground floor of the library and began to chant the psalms they had prayed every day at this time since Boniface Wimmer had introduced Benedictine life at Saint Vincent more than 116 years earlier. Brother Philip Hurley wrote afterward: "I have never seen a more beautiful sight than those burnt-out monks saying Office while the firemen were still fighting the fire across the street from the chapel." When the noon office was over, the monks went to the "Shack" in Sportsman's Hall for a lunch of hot dogs, chili, and coffee.

By 12:30 p.m. the fire seemed to be under control. The fire walls in Benedict Hall had held, and the defense at the north and south ends of the monastery had been successful. Still, the fire continued to burn vertically, though not horizontally, for four more hours, gradually diminishing in intensity; and it was necessary to keep pouring water on those parts of the buildings that had been wholly or partially destroyed. The firemen chopped holes in floors of some of the rooms in Benedict, Anselm, and Gregory Halls to allow the accumulated water to drain out, and "bucket brigades" of monks and seminarians moved into the basilica to clear out the water that had flooded the church.

At 4:00 p.m. the monks gathered in the chapter room in Leander Hall for their afternoon recreation period and beer haustus. Some of them objected to this apparent frivolity in the wake of the tragedy the community had just experienced—"It was like fiddling while Rome burned," one monk complained—but the majority agreed that having the afternoon recreation period with the traditional mug of beer was a psychologically important confirmation that the community had not been defeated by the disaster and that, as far as possible, things would go on as normal. Bishop Connare joined the monks for haustus and assured them of his and the diocese's help in the rebuilding of Saint Vincent. At 5:00 p.m. the monastic community gathered again in the library chapel for Vespers and afterward ate supper in the Sportsman's Hall gymnasium. The supper was prepared by the Benedictine sisters and served by women of the parish and lay employees of the college. During the meal everyone was delighted to see Father Fintan Shoniker, who had been thought lost. Father Fintan explained that early in the morning, before the fire began, he had left campus to help raise money for one of the college alumni, Lawrence Gerthoffer, who with his family had been burnt out of his home two weeks before.

About 5:00 p.m., with the fire dying down, Chief Earl Dalton began to release trucks from the Greensburg units and the companies that had come in support of them. The Latrobe Fire Department remained on station, however, manning the pumps and hoses required to spray down the hot spots burning under the rubble that had developed as debris fell from the buildings. Dalton recognized the need to relieve the men who had been fighting the fire all day in the bitter cold. He said he felt "rather cruel" telling the Latrobe volunteers, and some from nearby communities, to stay at their posts in order to prevent a fresh outbreak of the fire. He did ask for dry clothes to be brought to them, and he set up a schedule that allowed small groups to change clothes and rest a little before being sent back to battle the more stubborn pockets of fire. As night fell, the weather grew colder, and the men had to rest oftener and longer. But the Latrobe firefighters maintained their stations until midnight, when a reserve company from Ligonier and another from Blairsville came up to relieve the local volunteers, some of whom had been battling the fire for fifteen hours, and all of whom, in the words of their chief, "were dead on the job."

The prep students and seminarians had been sent home in the afternoon, after the fire had been brought under control and transportation could be arranged for them. Administrators of the college, prep school, and seminary announced that classes would be suspended until further notice. The unanticipated vacation lasted only a week, however, and the following Monday the students were back on campus attending classes in virtually every available free space and doubling up in the dormitories that survived the blaze. Some classes, including the biology labs, were held at Seton Hill College. The Sisters of Charity at the Greensburg institution generously offered Saint Vincent's professors and students whatever facilities they required for the remainder of the semester. As for the monastic community, almost a hundred monks had been burned out of their rooms, but before they went to bed on Monday night, accommodations had been found for everyone in Leander, Aurelius, and Wimmer Halls as well as in other buildings that had escaped destruction. The following day a heavy freezing rain fell, coating the burnt-out buildings with several inches of ice.

Initial estimates were that the fire had caused almost $2 million in damage, and insurance adjusters later confirmed that figure. The old students' chapel, biology laboratory, and bell tower had been completely destroyed. The top floor of Benedict Hall had been burned out and much of the second floor had been damaged. In the monastery the top floor was destroyed and the floors below rendered uninhabitable, while the basilica, as well as the choir chapel and monastic refectory in Andrew Hall, had sustained extensive damage from smoke and water. In addition, the life's work of the college's biology professors had gone up in the flames. The loss included twenty-five thousand biology slides collected over the years by Father Edward Wenstrup, the entire Arctic plant collection gathered by Father Maximilian Duman during the ten trips to the Arctic that had earned him international fame and the nickname "the Arctic Priest," and the famed herbarium collection of Father Edwin Pierron (1846–1930), which was regarded as one of the finest in the country. Also, the clothes, books, and personal effects of more than eighty priests, brothers, and clerics were lost. Some of the monks escaped the destruction with only the clothes on their backs. Everyone, however, thanked God that despite the extensive material loss and damage, no one had died in the disaster.

A COADJUTOR ARCHABBOT

The monastic chapter met three days after the fire to determine how best to proceed in the wake of the catastrophe. Physically ill and emotionally distraught, Archabbot Denis sat silently, huddled in his overcoat, as the community discussed the need to begin planning at once for construction of new buildings at Saint Vincent. The majority of capitulars agreed that as a result of the fire, it was now more necessary than ever to move forward with a building project such as the one embodied in the Christ-Janer master plan. Critical need existed not only for student dormitories, but also for a new science building and a new monastery.

Two unanswered questions, however, occupied most of the chapter's attention. The first was how the new buildings were to be paid for, and the second, whether construction should proceed in conformity with the Christ-Janer plan. Those who attended to the community's financial affairs addressed the first question. The principal means of paying for the necessary buildings, they said, would be loans, fire insurance reimbursements, and a professionally organized fund-raising drive. Father Aelred Beck, academic dean of the college, proposed that the Community Counseling Service of Pittsburgh, a financial planning organization with considerable experience collecting funds for Catholic institutions, be contracted to launch a campaign to raise at least a million dollars for rebuilding Saint Vincent. The chapter members passed the motion by an almost unanimous vote. The second question, however, was more difficult to answer. Many favored proceeding with the Christ-Janer plan, pointing out that it had already been approved by the chapter at an earlier meeting. Others, however, noted that Christ-Janer had been dismissed by the archabbot and another architect had been hired. The discussion was extensive, but it was not until the meeting held almost three weeks later that the issue was resolved, at least temporarily. Archabbot Denis, whose health had improved sufficiently for him to participate fully in the chapter of February 19, explained once again that the former plans had been abandoned and that new plans would be developed. There was an animated debate over the suitability of this decision, and many capitulars felt that the community should restudy the former plans, while others felt that the community should go ahead with new plans. In the end, when a vote was taken, sixty-eight capitulars voted in support of the archabbot's position, while sixty-three opposed it.[133]

The narrow vote illustrated once again how divided the community continued to be over the question of the building program. The vote also reflected the extent of dissatisfaction with Archabbot Denis's leadership that continued to exist among a significant number of the monks. Now, however, the ranks of those who thought that it was time for Stittmatter to step down were increased by those who had grown increasingly concerned about the archabbot's health. For more than a year Archabbot Denis had shown signs of physical disability. An inner ear problem had affected both his hearing and his equilibrium, and in general his health had deteriorated noticeably. The illness that struck him following the disastrous fire was a culmination of many infirmities that had become increasingly manifest in the previous twelve months, and which were exacerbated by the emotional impact of the fire.

The chapter in which the monks voted by a slim margin to abandon the original master plan and to support Archabbot Denis's decision to develop new plans occurred during the first days of the regular triennial visitation of the archabbey. On February 16, 1963, the visitators, Abbot Bede Luibel of St. Bernard Abbey, Cullman, Alabama, and Abbot Raphael Heider of St. Martin's Abbey, Olympia, Washington, arrived at Saint Vincent. Concerns were deep and tensions high at the archabbey as a result of the recent fire and the continued divisions in the community. As a consequence not only of the fire but also of the malaise that had troubled the monastery for almost a decade, the community was suffering both materially and spiritually in February 1963. Almost everyone agreed that Saint Vincent needed the help of some external, disinterested agency in order to resolve its many problems. One means that church legislation provided for such help to Benedictine communities was regular canonical visitation. Thus, although expectations varied, hopes were high among virtually all members of the Saint Vincent community that some resolution to their problems would be found and proposed by the visitators.

Abbots Bede and Raphael arrived at the archabbey bearing a heavy and unenviable burden of responsibility and expectation. For a week they met with the monks of the archabbey, listening to all points of view and weighing the views of those who took various positions in the controversies dividing the community. In the end, after much thought and prayer, the visitators decided to urge Archabbot Denis to relinquish the administration of the archabbey and to seek the Holy See's permission for the community to elect a coadjutor archabbot who would have full jurisdictional authority and the right of succession. As reasons for their recommendation, the abbot visitators cited Archabbot Denis's continuing ill health as well as the overwhelming burden of responsibility he bore not only as superior of the Saint Vincent community but also as president of the American Cassinese Congregation and participant in Vatican Council II. They pointed out that in the aftermath of the disastrous fire, which had occurred just three weeks earlier, Saint Vincent was in need of energetic leadership, and they noted that all of the archabbot's confreres were concerned about his physical well-being. Many of the monks were convinced that it would be "cruel" to insist that he continue bearing the multitude of responsibilities which he had always borne "with generous and sacrificing zeal." The visitators therefore said that he must submit a petition for a coadjutor within a week of the visitation.[134]

Archabbot Denis acceded to the wishes of the community and the directives of the visitators and immediately sent his request for a coadjutor to Rome. In the interim between his submission of the letter to Rome and the Holy See's response, he continued to move forward on the building program. He directed the building committee to work with the firm of Triggs, Myers, McQuade & Associates to develop an acceptable design, and he met with the college's lay board of advisors to solicit their support. Two months after the fire he launched a $1 million development campaign, directed by the Community Counseling Service, and on April 9, 1963, he presided at the ground breaking ceremony for the new student residences. On the day of the groundbreaking, he was able to announce that the development campaign, less than two weeks after it had been launched, had already received seventy-five thousand dollars in donations, including a ten-thousand-dollar contribution from Bishop William Connare of Greensburg.[135]

But Archabbot Denis's fourteen-year tenure as superior at Saint Vincent was coming to an end. During his time as archabbot, he had contributed significantly to the postwar development of the community, overseeing dramatic increases in monastic vocations as well as notable growth in the college and seminary. He had led Saint Vincent into the second half of the twentieth century with a singleminded commitment to continuing the traditions of his predecessors. He had made key improvements in the old buildings and had built an impressive array of new ones, including a new seminary, a new library, and a spacious activities building for sports and cultural events. Under his leadership the monastery, college, and seminary had all made astonishing progress in the postwar period. But now it was time for him to step down and turn the administration of the institution over to a new leader, and he did so with humility and a quiet grace that impressed even his critics.

On April 29, 1963, the Holy See issued a rescript granting the monks of Saint Vincent the privilege of electing a coadjutor archabbot with right of succession and full jurisdiction, and on June 24, 184 priests of the community gathered at the archabbey for the election. Thirteen others, who were unable to attend, were represented by proxies. Abbot Bede Luibel of St. Bernard Abbey, Cullman, Alabama, presided. On the evening of June 24 Abbot Bede met with the electors in the monastic refectory, appointed Father Matthew Benko secretary of the election, and oversaw the choosing of tellers. The following morning, after a solemn votive Mass in honor of the Holy Spirit celebrated by Prior Leopold Krul, the election itself commenced. The nominating ballot was cast, followed by the *scrutinium,* or discussion of the merits of the various candidates. Voting for the coadjutor archabbot began that evening and carried over to the next morning, when on the fourth ballot thirty-six-year-old Father Rembert Weakland was elected seventh archabbot of Saint Vincent.[136]

Like his predecessor, Archabbot Rembert was a native of Cambria County, Pennsylvania, who had come to Saint Vincent as a boy of fourteen to study for the priesthood. He had completed his secondary and undergraduate education in the schools of Saint Vincent and in 1951 had finished his theological studies at the Collegio di Sant' Anselmo in Rome. He later pursued graduate studies in music in New York, Italy, and France. Fluent in Italian, French, and German, he was an internationally renowned scholar of medieval liturgical music, and at the time of his election he was serving as chairman of the music department of Saint Vincent College and as a member of the archabbey's council of seniors.

Even after the election of Rembert Weakland as coadjutor archabbot, Archabbot Denis retained his office as president of the American Cassinese Congregation in accordance with the directives of the Holy See, and as abbot president he continued to represent the congregation at the Vatican Council. He held the presidency of the congregation until 1965, but though he continued to live at the archabbey, where he retained the right of precedence in the community, he surrendered all administrative responsibilities for the Pennsylvania monastery to his coadjutor.

Upon assuming leadership of Saint Vincent, Archabbot Rembert faced several formidable challenges. In the previous ten years the monastic community had experienced internal divisions and a spiritual malaise that had seriously fractured its unity and brought disharmony among the confreres in ways that were difficult to resolve. A complicating factor in the tensions that the community experienced at this time was that the winds of change blowing through the Church in the opening years of the 1960s had raised the hope of renewal for many and caused grave anxiety for others. It was still too early to draw final conclusions about the full implications of the decrees emanating from the Vatican Council, but those who were eager for renewal and reform in the Church were in the ascendancy while traditionalists who feared the consequences of altering familiar structures and methods of worship and governance were on the defensive. To a great extent tensions within the Saint Vincent monastic community reflected the debate between reformers and traditionalists in the universal Church. Archabbot Denis had consistently adhered to the point of view of the traditionalists, but the new archabbot was clearly aligned with the reformers, and his greatest achievements during his brief, four-year abbacy were to restore a spirit of unity among his confreres and to establish and maintain a balanced perspective within the community as it embarked on the often turbulent waters of spiritual and monastic renewal.

But leading the community in its effort to recover from the devastating fire of January 1963 was the new archabbot's most immediate challenge. After consulting with the chapter, he appointed a development committee that initiated plans for the demolition of the burnt-out buildings and the construction of a new monastery, science building, and student dining facility designed by architect, Tasso Katselas of Pittsburgh. His tenure witnessed the completion of the monastery, the beginning of modernization and academic development of the college, the formal establishment of dependent priories in Brazil and Taiwan, and the Saint Vincent community's acceptance of responsibility for a dependent priory and high school in Savannah, Georgia.

During his administration Archabbot Rembert also laid the groundwork for the post–Vatican Council renewal that marked a new era in the history of the archabbey. Working in concert with other American abbots, he introduced the vernacular in the Divine Office at Saint Vincent, eliminated the moribund institution of the lay brotherhood, and obtained for the brothers the right to make solemn vows (thus integrating them more fully into the life of the community). In addition, he instituted the practice of permitting young candidates to enter the monastery and pursue their monastic and theological studies with the intention of becoming nonordained choir monks, and he led the members of the Saint Vincent community in a reexamination of and a recommitment to their role as Benedictines in the modern world. In September 1967, after serving little more than four years as seventh archabbot of Saint Vincent, Weakland was elected abbot primate of the Benedictine Order by the world's Benedictine abbots meeting in Rome. He served two terms as abbot primate, and in 1977 Pope Paul VI named him archbishop of Milwaukee.[137]

THE MISSION CONTINUES

The Benedictines of Saint Vincent had passed through a difficult decade, and the years ahead would pose new problems and challenges that

Rembert Weakland, seventh archabbot of Saint Vincent, greeting Pope Paul VI.

were even more daunting than those of the 1950s. But the community proved resilient, and under the fortunate leadership of Archabbot Egbert Donovan (1967–79), Archabbot Leopold Krul (1979–83), and Archabbot Paul Maher (1983–90), Saint Vincent managed to meet the problems and challenges with wisdom, discretion, and, ultimately, with success.

In the 1960s and 1970s the social upheavals of the nation, the profound changes taking place in the Catholic Church, and the often painful process of aggiornamento, or updating, within religious communities that followed in the wake of the Second Vatican Council all touched Saint Vincent and profoundly affected the lives of both monks and students. Following a trend seen throughout the Catholic world, there occurred a notable decline in the number of monastic vocations at the archabbey, and the number of students in the seminary fell precipitously. The Benedictines of Saint Vincent, however, continued their tradition of parochial, educational, and missionary work, concentrating their efforts in Pennsylvania, Georgia, Brazil, and Taiwan, and by the early 1980s it was clear that the community had emerged not merely intact but reinvigorated from an epochal experience of challenge and change in the nation, the Church, and the monastic order.

The story of these challenging decades remains to be told. The telling, however, must await a future moment when time and distance provide the perspective necessary for accurate and objective analysis.

It is nonetheless clear that at Saint Vincent the seeds planted by earlier generations have taken root and thrived, their harvest surviving storms that wreaked havoc in many American religious communities during the decades that followed the Second Vatican Council. The 1990s witnessed a stabilization of monastic vocations at the archabbey as well as the community's recommitment to parochial, educational, and missionary work. Under Archabbot Douglas Nowicki (elected in 1990), monastic life was reinvigorated; the seminary experienced unexpected growth and expansion, and the college underwent administrative and academic developments that improved the quality of its programs and brought it acclaim as one of the finest liberal arts undergraduate institutions in the nation.

In 1996, as the community celebrated the 150th anniversary of Boniface Wimmer's arrival in the United States, it was clear that the monks of Saint Vincent, the first Benedictine monastery in the United States, had indeed remained faithful to their call to live and teach the Gospel, to work and pray according to the Rule of St. Benedict, and to create in their own corner of the world a school for the Lord's service.

APPENDICES

APPENDIX I

THEODORE BROUWERS' WILL

OCTOBER 24, 1790

IN THE NAME OF GOD, AMEN.

I, the Reverend Theodore Browers, being weak in Body but of sound mind and memory and understanding and calling to mind the Mortality of my Body Do make ordain and Constitute this to be my last will and Testament viz. First I recommend my soul to God who gave it, my Body to the Earth to be buried in a decent Christian like manner on the Place I now live Called Sportsmanns Hall, And a small neat stonewall to be built around my grave, All my just debts and funeral Expenses is next to be paid, Item I Give and Bequeath to my beloved Sister Gartudas Browers, Fifty Dollars all the aforesaid expenses and Legacees is to be paid by my Executors herein after named out of the mony I have in the Bank at Philadelphia. Item, all my Horses, Cows and all other farming Utensils, to be left on the place I now live on for the use thereof untill Christian Andrises year shall expire, then to be sold, and the mony arising there from to be appropriated to the payment of said Christian and Wife. And if the aforesaid Articles should amount to more than will pay the aforesaid sums, the remainder to be appropriated by my Executors to the improvement of the Place. Item I Give and Bequeath all my Books clothing and Furniture and all the residue of my personal estate that shall not be otherwise disposed of, to Jams Pennane, in Trust and for the use of the Poor Roman Catholic Priest [Irish?], that does or shall live at the Chappel, on Connewagga. Item I give and bequeath all my Real Estate viz. my place on which I now live called Sportsmans Hall, and one other Tract of Land on Loyalhanna Creek called ONeals Victory, with their appurtenances to a Roman Catholic Priest that shall succeed me in this said place, to be Entailed to him and to his Successors in trust and so left by him who shall succeed me to his successors and so in trust and for the use herein mentioned in succession forever, and that the said Priest for the time being shall strictly and faithfully say Four Masses Each and every year for ever viz. One for the soul of the Reverend Theodorus Browers, one the day of his death in each and every year for ever and three others the following days in each year as aforesaid at the request of the Reverend Theodorus Browers And further it is my Will that the Priest for the time being shall Transmitt the Land so left him in Trust as aforesaid to his successor clear of all incumbrance as aforesaid And I do Nominate Constitute and appoint Christian Ruffner and Henry Coons Executors to this my last Will and Testament. Signed, sealed, Published, Pronounced and declared by the said Theodorus Browers, to be his last Will and Testament this twenty fourth day of October in the year of our Lord One thousand seven Hundred and Ninety in the presence of us

Christian Andrews (L.S.)	R. Mr. Theodore Browers.
William Maghee.	R. Mr. John Bapt. Cause.

Register of Wills, Westmoreland County Court House, Greensburg, Pa. Printed in Oswald Moosmüller, *St. Vincenz in Pennsylvanien* (New York: F. Pustet, 1873), 363–65; and Vincent Huber, "Sportsman's Hall," *Records of the American Catholic Historical Society of Philadelphia* 3 (1888–91): 148–49.

APPENDIX 2

BONIFACE WIMMER'S PROPOSAL FOR ESTABLISHING THE BENEDICTINE ORDER IN THE UNITED STATES, *AUGSBURGER POSTZEITUNG*

NOVEMBER 8, 1845

CONCERNING THE MISSIONS

Every Catholic who cherishes his faith must take a deep interest in missionary labors. But religion as well as patriotism demands that every German Catholic should take a special interest in the missions of America. To us it cannot be a matter of indifference how our countrymen are situated in America. I, for my part, have not been able to read the various and generally sad reports on the desolate condition of Germans beyond the ocean without deep compassion and a desire to do something to alleviate their pitiable condition. Thus I have given much thought to the question of how they might be practically assisted. It is not difficult to understand what should be done—more German-speaking priests should be found laboring for the spiritual welfare of our countrymen in America. The only question is how to get priests and what kind of priests will do the work most successfully. The answer to the second question will also give the solution for the first. I do not wish to offend anyone, but my opinion is that secular priests are not the best adapted for missionary labors. History shows that the Church has not availed herself of their services to any great extent in missionary undertakings. I do not mean to say that a secular priest cannot labor effectually within a limited territory in America, for there are many who labor successfully even at the present day. But they cannot satisfy themselves. They are in great danger of becoming careless and worldly-minded. I cannot agree with Dr. Salzbacher[1] when he says that the spiritual needs of our countrymen can be provided by perambulating missionaries, who go about like the Wandering Jew from forest to forest, from hut to hut; for unless such a missionary be a *Saint* not much of the spiritual man would remain in him, and even then by such transient visits not much lasting good could be accomplished. The missionary, more than any other priest, stands in need of spiritual renewal from time to time, consolation and advice in trials and difficulties. He must, therefore, have some place where he can find such assistance: this may be given by his bishop but he will find it more securely in a religious community—in the midst of his confreres.

He should also have a home to receive him in his old age or when he is otherwise incapacitated for missionary labors; he should have no worldly cares, otherwise he might neglect or even forget his own and others' spiritual welfare. All this can be had only in a religious community. For this reason, therefore, religious are better adapted to missionary work than secular priests. In a community the experiences of the individual become common property; all have a common interest, stand together and have the same object in view. A vacancy caused by death or otherwise can be filled more readily and having fewer temporal cares, they can devote themselves more exclusively to the spiritual interests of themselves and others. Thus, all other things being equal, a religious priest in a community should be able to work more effectively in the missions than the secular priest who stands alone.

The next question is: What religious Order is most adapted for the American missions, not to convert the native Indians but to provide for the spiritual necessities of German immigrants?

As far as I know the only Religious in the strict sense of the word now found in America are the Jesuits and Redemptorists. The missionaries of the Middle Ages, the Benedictines, Dominicans, and Franciscans, are not yet represented in the New World, except by a few individuals who do not live in monasteries.[2] The Jesuits devote their energies principally to teaching in colleges; their students are mostly from the higher classes of society and many of them belong to Protestant families. Many Jesuits are also doing excellent work among the Indians, and others have charge of congregations in cities near their colleges. But while they accomplish so much in their sphere of labors, they can do little for Germans, because few of them speak their language. The Redemptorists are doing noble work for our countrymen in the States: in cities and thickly settled country districts they have large congrega-

1. Canon Joseph Salzbacher of Vienna had been sent to the United States in 1842 by the *Leopoldinen Stiftung,* the Austrian mission society, to investigate conditions among German Catholics there. The report of his journey *(Meine Reise nach Nord-Amerika in Jahre 1842)* appeared in 1845, shortly before Wimmer wrote this anonymous article for the *Augsburger Postzeitung.*

2. Wimmer was unaware that Edward D. Fenwick, O.P. (1768–1832), first Bishop of Cincinnati, had opened St. Rose Priory near Springfield, Kentucky, the first Dominican convent in the United States, as early as December 1806.

tions, and also do what they can for others as traveling missionaries. Some secular priests likewise go about among the scattered Catholics doing good, but they naturally and necessarily concentrate in cities where there is a large Catholic population.

We see, therefore, that much is being done in America; very much, indeed, when we consider the small band of priests and the difficulties under which they labor. But as yet nothing has been done for the stability of the work, no provision has been made for an increase of German-speaking priests, to meet the growing demand for missionary laborers. It is not difficult to see that secular priests, whose labors extend over a district larger than a diocese, can do nothing to secure reinforcements to their own number. But why have the Redemptorists and Jesuits not accomplished more in this line? By his vows neither the Jesuit nor the Redemptorist is bound to any particular place, but he must always be prepared to leave his present position at the command of his superiors, and may also request, if not demand, his removal for weighty reasons. This has many advantages, but for America it seems to me also to have disadvantages. For the successor of the one who has been removed will require a long time to be acquainted with all the circumstances with which his predecessor was familiar, and even the uncertainty as to how long he will remain at any particular place will be an obstacle in his way. Moreover, the fact that Jesuits generally receive only the children of richer families, many of whom are Protestants, into their institutions, because they depend upon them for their sustenance, and that the Redemptorists are by their statutes required to devote themselves to missionary work, and can, therefore, not be expected to take charge of seminaries, gives us no reason to hope that the spiritual wants of Americans, particularly of German-Americans, will be provided for by native German-speaking priests. And if the mission societies of Europe should unexpectedly be rendered incapable of supplying money or reinforcements in priests, the situation would become even more serious. But even supposing that everything remains as it is, we cannot hope to have an efficient supply of priests as long as we have no means of securing a native clergy for the United States of America. For the number of those who are educated at Altötting[3] or elsewhere in Germany is not in proportion to the continually increasing emigration to America, not to speak of the natural increase of Germans in America itself. Jesuits and Redemptorists are, therefore, doing noble work in America and their number should be increased as much as possible; but they will scarcely be able to remove the chief cause of the deficiency of German-speaking priests. We need not speak of the Dominicans and Franciscans; there are very few German Dominicans, and the present social condition of America seems not to call for Mendicant Friars.

We now come to the Benedictines, who are not as yet represented in the United States. In my opinion they are the most competent to relieve the great want of priests in America. In support of my opinion I will adduce some facts: but I must again state that I have not the remotest intention of belittling the efforts and successes of other religious orders; on the contrary, I am desirous of seeing them labor in the same field, side by side with the Benedictines.

History abundantly proves:

3. Site of a seminary for missionary priests located in the diocese of Passau, Bavaria. Wimmer had once served as a secular priest at the famous Marian shrine of Altötting.

(1) That we owe the conversion of England, Germany, Denmark, Sweden, Norway, Hungary, and Poland almost exclusively to the Benedictines, and that in the remaining parts of Europe Christendom is deeply indebted to them.

(2) That the conversion of these countries was not transient but lasting and permanent.

(3) That this feature must be ascribed to the fact that the Benedictines are men of stability; they are not wandering monks; they acquire lands and bring them under cultivation and become thoroughly affiliated to the country and people to which they belong, and receive their recruits from the district in which they have established themselves.

(4) That the Benedictine Order by its Rule is so constituted that it can readily adapt itself to all times and circumstances. The contemplative and practical are harmoniously blended; agriculture, manual labor, literature, missionary work, education were drawn into the circle of activity which St. Benedict placed before his disciples. Hence they soon felt at home in all parts of Europe and the same could be done in America.

When we consider North America as it is today, we can see at a glance that there is no other country in the world which offers greater opportunities for the establishment and spread of the Benedictine Order, no country that is so much like our old Europe was. There are found immense forests, large uncultivated tracts of land in the interior, most fertile lands which command but a nominal price; often for miles and miles no village is to be seen, not to speak of cities. In country districts no schools, no churches are to be found. The German colonists are scattered, uncultured, ignorant, hundreds of miles away from the nearest German-speaking priest, for, practically, they can make their homes where they please. There are no good books, no Catholic papers, no holy pictures. The destitute and unfortunate have no one to offer them a hospitable roof, the orphans naturally become the victims of vice and irreligion—in a word, the conditions in America today are like those of Europe 1000 years ago, when the Benedictine Order attained its fullest development and effectiveness by its wonderful adaptability and stability. Of course the Benedictine Order would be required to adapt itself again to circumstances and begin anew. To acquire a considerable tract of land in the interior of the country, upon which to found a monastery, would not be very difficult; to bring under cultivation at least a portion of the land and to erect the most necessary buildings would give employment for a few years to the first Benedictine colony, which should consist of at least three priests and ten to fifteen brothers skilled in the most necessary trades.

Once the colony is self-supporting, which could be expected in about two years, it should begin to expand so that the increased number of laboring hands might also increase the products and revenues to be derived from the estate. A printing and lithographing establishment would also be very desirable.

Since the Holy Rule prescribes for all, not only manual labor and the chanting of the Divine Office, but also that the monks should devote several hours a day to study, this time could be used by the Fathers to instruct the Brothers thoroughly in arithmetic, German grammar, etc., thereby fitting them to teach school, to give catechetical instruction and in general to assist in teaching children as well as grown persons.

Such a monastery would from the very start be of great advantage to German settlers, at least to those who would live near it. They would have a place where they could depend upon hearing Mass on Sundays and hear a sermon in their own language; they would also have a place where they could always be sure to find a priest at home to hear their confessions, to bless their marriages, to baptize their children, and to administer the last sacraments to the sick if called in time.

Occasionally the Superior might send out even the Brothers two by two to hunt up fallen-away Catholics, to instruct children for their first Communion, etc. All subsequent monasteries that might be established from the motherhouse would naturally exercise the same influence.

So far the services rendered by the Benedictines would not be extraordinary; any other priests or religious could do the same, except that they would not likely be able to support themselves without assistance from Europe; whereas a community of Benedictines, when once firmly established, would soon become self-sustaining.

But such a monastery if judiciously located would not long remain isolated; all reports from America inform us that the German immigrants are concentrating themselves in places where churches have been erected or where a German-speaking priest has taken up his residence. This would also be found, and to a greater extent, if there were a monastery somewhere with a good school. In a short time a large German population would be found near the monastery, much as in the Middle Ages, villages, towns, and cities sprang up near Benedictine abbeys. Then the monks could expect a large number of children for their school, and in the course of time, as the number of priests increases, a college with a good Latin course could be opened. They would not be dependent upon the tuition fee of the students for their support, which they could draw from the farm and the missions (though these would not be a source of much income in the beginning). Thus they could devote their energies to the education of the poorer classes of boys who could pay little or nothing, and since these boys would daily come in contact with priests and other monks, it could scarcely be otherwise but that many of them would develop a desire of becoming priests or even religious. I am well aware that to many readers these hopes and expectations will appear too sanguine, since all efforts at securing a native American clergy have hitherto failed so signally. But we must remember that the annals of the missions as well as the oral reports of priests who have labored in America, inform us that these efforts were more theoretical than practical, that there was a desire of making such efforts, but that they were not really made, and that those which were really made were more or less restricted to the English-speaking clergy, and that in general there were neither sufficient means nor sufficient teachers to train a native German-speaking clergy. It is said that the young American is not inclined to devote himself to the sacred ministry because it is so easy for him to secure a wife and home; that the American has nothing in view but to heap up the riches of this world; that fathers need their sons on the farms or in the workshops and, therefore, do not care to see them study. But, let me ask, is it not the same here in Europe? Are the rich always pleased when their sons study for the priesthood? Are all Germans in America well-to-do or rich? Are they not as a rule the very poorest and to a certain extent the menials of the rest? Moreover, is the first thought of a boy directed to matrimony? Is it any wonder that he should show no inclination for the priesthood when he sees a priest scarcely once a year; when divine services are held in churches which resemble hovels rather than churches, without pomp and ceremony, when the priest has to divest himself of his priestly dignity, often travels on horse-back, in disguise, looking more like a drummer than a priest, when the boy sees nothing in the life of a priest but sacrifice, labor, and fatigue?

But all this would be quite different if boys could come in daily contact with priests, if they received instructions from them, if the priest could appear to advantage, better dressed and better housed than the ordinary settler, if young men could learn from observation to realize and appreciate the advantages of a community life, if they could learn to understand that while the life of a priest requires self-denial and sacrifice, his hopes of a great reward are also well grounded. Yes, I do not doubt but that hundreds, especially of the lower classes, would prefer to spend their lives in well regulated monasteries in suitable and reasonable occupations, than to gain a meager livelihood by incessant hard labor in forest regions. Let us remember that here in Bavaria from the year 740 to the year 788 not less than 40 Benedictine monasteries were founded and the communities were composed almost entirely of natives from the free classes, who had enjoyed the advantages of freedom in the world and could have chosen the married state without any difficulty or hindrance. Why should we not reasonably expect the same results in the United States where the conditions are so similar?

But such a monastery in North America would not draw its recruits exclusively from the surrounding country, but also from the great number of boys, who either during the voyage or soon after their arrival in America lose their parents and thereby become helpless and forsaken. An institution, in which such unfortunate children could find a home, would undoubtedly be a great blessing for that country. And where could this be done more easily than in Benedictine monasteries as described above, in which young boys could not only attend school, but also do light work on the farm or in the workshops and according to their talents and vocation become priests or at least educated Christians and good citizens? Surely, many of these would gladly join the community as brothers or priests, and thus repay the monastery for the trouble of educating them.

In this way a numerous religious clergy could soon be secured, and then some of the Fathers might be sent out to visit those Catholics who scarcely ever see a priest; occasionally at least they might preach the word of God and bring the consolations of religion even to those who live at a great distance from the monastery; small congregations could be established, and the seminary could soon furnish a goodly number of the secular clergy.

But where could the Benedictines be found to establish such a monastery in North America, and where are the necessary means for such an undertaking? The writer is informed that there are several Fathers in the Benedictine Order in Bavaria who would gladly go upon such a mission, and with regard to Brothers there would be no difficulty whatever; within a few years not less than 200 good men have applied for admission into one of our monasteries. It is a well known fact that of those who are studying for the priesthood many are joining the Redemptorist Order simply because it offers them the hope of becoming missionaries in America.

The necessary funds could easily be supplied by the Ludwig Missionsverein. Bavaria annually pays 100,000 florins into the treasury of this Society. Would it be unfair to devote one tenth of this sum to the establishment of monasteries in America, especially since just now hundreds of our own nationality are seeking homes in the United States, and consequently the money contributed would be used to further the interests of Germans in general and our countrymen in particular? Could a better use of such contributions be made or could anything appeal more loudly to our national patriotism? Is it right that we should continually look after the interests of strangers and forget our own countrymen? Moreover, whatever would be done for the Germans would advance the well-being of the entire Church in America. We must not stifle our feelings of patriotism. The Germans, we hear it often enough, lose their national character in the second or third generation; they also lose their language because like a little rivulet they disappear in the mighty stream of the Anglo-American population in the States. Is this not humiliating for us Germans? Would this sad condition of affairs continue if here and there a German center were established, to which the stream of emigration from our country could be systematically directed, if German instruction and sermons were given by priests going forth from these centers, if German books, papers and periodicals were distributed among the people, if German boys could receive a German education and training, which would make themselves felt in wider circles?

Let us, therefore, no longer build air castles for our countrymen in America. Let us provide for their religious interests, then their domestic affairs will take care of themselves. Benedictine monasteries of the old style are the best means of checking the downward tendencies of our countrymen in social, political, and religious matters. Let Jesuits and Redemptorists labor side by side with the Benedictines; there is room enough for all and plenty of work. If every Religious Order develops a healthy activity within its sphere, the result will be doubly sure and great. North America will no longer depend upon Europe for its spiritual welfare, and the day may come when America will repay us just as England, converted by the Benedictines, repaid the continent of Europe.[4]

[Printed in Colman J. Barry, *Worship and Work: Saint John's Abbey and University 1856–1992,* 3d ed. (Collegeville, Minn.: Liturgical Press, 1993), 479–85; and John Tracy Ellis, ed., *Documents of American Catholic History,* 3 vols. (Wilmington, Del.: Michael Glazier, 1987), 1:279–88.]

4. Wimmer refers here to the historical fact that England, converted to Christianity by Benedictine monks from Italy at the end of the sixth century, sent English monks to the German lands in the eighth century to convert the people there. The leader of the English monks in the conversion of Germany was St. Boniface.

APPENDIX 3

BONIFACE WIMMER'S LETTER TO STUDENTS ASPIRING TO JOIN THE MISSION TO AMERICA

FEBRUARY 19, 1846

Munich, February 19, 1846

My Dear Candidates: In reply to your communication regarding our proposed mission to America I wish to submit the following. If I rightly understand the tenor of your letter, you wish to inform me that, as matters now stand, you are not satisfied with the mere prospect of becoming Benedictines and missionaries in America, but that you are anxious to know whether I intend to take you with me at once, or leave you in the Institute until you complete your regular course of studies, or send you to one of our monasteries to become acquainted with the Holy Rule. You also intimate that unless you first live here under the same Rule, you might later regret the step which you are planning to take. I can even see the beginning of wavering in your resolution to follow me. I do not find fault with you for submitting these questions, and in response I wish to send you the following reflections for your serious consideration:

(1) You must above all be determined to become priests and good priests.

(2) You must be determined to become religious not only to be united to Christ more closely and follow Him more faithfully, but, if necessary, do more for Him, to

suffer for Him, and not by any means to go with the intention of becoming priests more easily or, still less, to escape temporal cares.

(3) The vocation to the priesthood in itself is a great grace, and that to the religious state a greater one, because it is a state of perfection, and that to the missionary life still greater, because it is an apostolic vocation.

(4) We should consider it a great privilege that God deigns to use us as instruments in founding an institution which, if the foundation is well laid, will confer untold benefits on the people of the United States. If you consider this well, you will not put yourself forward without vocations. But if you feel the call within you, you will not allow yourselves to be deterred by obstacles from following this impulse, because the greater the sacrifice, the greater the reward. We will be able to say to Our Lord with Peter, "Behold we have left everything and have followed Thee; what therefore will we have?" Undoubtedly he will give us the same answer that he gave to Peter, recorded in the Gospel of St. Matthew, chapter 19, verse 28.[5]

If these are your sentiments, you will never have cause to regret having followed me when you are in America. The main reason is not that you are in quest of beautiful surroundings, a comfortable home, or a life of ease, but that you are seeking the opportunity to carry the cross of self denial after the crucified Jesus, to save or regain souls that otherwise would be lost and for which His blood would have been shed in vain.

What I know of America I have learned only from hearsay and from what I have read about it. I must be prepared to meet all possible emergencies. I am giving up a comfortable and honorable position and cannot reasonably expect another. I am leaving behind relatives who are poor and therefore stand in need of me. I am parting from kind superiors and confreres who honor me and only reluctantly consent that I go. I am renouncing a position in which everything is well ordered to enter upon an entirely new state of life in which everything has to be started anew and be put in order.

I do this because I am interiorly urged, although I take upon myself difficulties, cares, and hardships. My heaviest burden, however, will be that I must carry out my plans with men whose willingness, confidence, and vocation have first to be tested.

You see, therefore, that I have no advantage over you. I am willing to take you along because I am confident that you will gladly share my joys and sorrows in the service of God and of our neighbor. If you join me, you must be animated by the same confidence in me. If you cannot have this confidence in my integrity, my honesty, my zeal, my experience, and my determination, do not go with me. Under such conditions you would not obey, and I could not keep you. We must all be animated by a mutual love and confidence in one another. Perhaps next to confidence in God, these qualities will often be the only means to console and support us in our difficulties and hardships. Through harmony small things grow; through dissension great things are destroyed.

5. "I tell you this: in the world that is to be, when the Son of Man is seated on his throne in heavenly splendor, you my followers, will have thrones of your own, where you will sit as judges of the twelve tribes of Israel."

To that end you should consider it a privilege to be allowed to take part in a work like this. I will be glad to have good and zealous helpers. But you must not imagine that you are doing me a favor by going with me. The reception into a religious Order is something that must always be sought and asked for, no matter how welcome an applicant may be to a community. For this reason, do not go with me to please me, but on the contrary, consider yourselves fortunate and honored if you are found worthy to take part in such an undertaking. God is able to raise up children of Abraham from stones. He made Paul out of Saul. If my undertaking is from Him, He will send me co-laborers, wherever they may come from. I am sure of this. Therefore I will not persuade or entice you to go and thus render you unhappy if you have no vocation. You will never have cause to cast this up to me. I do not know the future. I only show you the cross. If you take it upon your shoulders, very well. But do not complain afterwards when from time to time you feel its weight. Jesus said to his apostles, "Behold, I have told you beforehand," and "Behold, I send you as lambs among the wolves." He said it to us also, and I say it to you: If you are frightened when you hear their howling and see their gnashing teeth, then stay at home. If with the grace of God you have not the courage to do and suffer these things for Him, to go wherever obedience requires, to allow yourselves to be used as willing tools, then do not enter the monastery and by no means go with me to America. It is true that in America men are free to profess whatever religion they please. Non-Catholics are more numerous, powerful, and wealthy than are the Catholics. We cannot tell how long they will respect the laws. It is possible that they may persecute us and put us to death. I can vouch for nothing. I am prepared for everything. Whoever wishes to follow me must also be prepared.

As you desire to go with me, it will not be necessary to complete your course of studies. In America no one will ask you whether you have completed your entire course of studies. However, if you wish to finish it, it must be done before July, and I hope to obtain this favor for you. The preparations for it will have to be made here.

I would not advise you to enter a monastery here to make your novitiate before you leave. You would soon become accustomed to many things that you will not find in America, and this would result in unpleasant comparisons. I know of a religious community that receives no one who belonged for even an hour to another community.

Whether it would be better for you to accompany me or to remain and continue your studies is a difficult question to answer. Although I have given the matter much thought, I am unable to say which is preferable. If you wish to accompany me at once, I will take you along without much ado. But your decision must be made soon because I will have to make arrangements accordingly, as two may have some difficulty in getting released from army service. You will have time to become acquainted with the Holy Rule before you leave. As soon as the copies I ordered arrive, we can begin instructions without delay. It will not take long to read it and you need not fear it, for it is very moderate. You must also get the consent of your parents and guardians. Only after a written statement of this is on hand will I be able to arrange matters with the government, and I shall do so before Easter.

Each one will take along what he possesses. Whatever may be left after the fare to America has been paid will be his until he makes his religious profession. After that it will belong to the community. However, if one has poor relatives, he may leave it to them, according to the Holy Rule. He who has little will take little. Let each one endeavor to get as much as may be required to secure an outfit, namely, the necessary books, a habit, clothing, etc. The money that I have will be sufficient for a time if we work a little. Work in the fields and other hard work will naturally devolve upon the lay brothers, but at times we may be obliged to lend a helping hand. The housework, apportioned according to each one's physical condition and with regard to the fact that they are preparing for the sacred ministry, will fall to the lot of the clerics. When I begin to explain the Rule, I will inform you of the order of the day, insofar as it may be determined at present. The details can be arranged only after our arrival. We will have everything that can reasonably be expected: a house, clothing, food and drink (at least good, fresh water). We will have time for prayer, meditation, and study, for practice in teaching and preaching, and for other useful occupations so necessary to ward off the evils that result from idleness.

If to all this everyone adds good will and cherishes a kind regard for his brother, then our little monastery will be a veritable paradise. Even if suffering, sickness, poverty, or persecution should occasionally be our lot, as they are not wanting in any place, still they will be like pepper and salt to season the monotony of our daily routine. They will remind us that there is nothing perfect here below and that we must carry the cross of affliction because the road to heaven is narrow and thorny. Let there be no Judas among us. Let no temporal considerations motivate us. Let not ambition be our goal. Do not render my life nor yours miserable through such aims. If you feel that you are weak, it is no disgrace to stay at home, but to come along without being animated by pure and holy intentions would be acting the part of Judas.

From this you know my opinion in the matter. Consider well whether you are satisfied with what I have said. May God guide you in your decision. I will not entice you, nor will I tempt you to go; but I will take you along if you desire to follow me. P. Boniface

Printed in Felix Fellner, *Abbot Boniface and His Monks,* 5 vols. (Latrobe, Pa.: Privately published by Saint Vincent Archabbey, 1956), 1:41–44; Gerard Bridge, *An Illustrated History of St. Vincent Archabbey* (Beatty, Pa.: Saint Vincent Archabbey Press, 1922), 60–64; and Vincent Huber, "Sportsman's Hall and St. Vincent Abbey," *St. Vincent Journal* 2 (1893–94): 267–71.

APPENDIX 4

SAINT VINCENT PARISHIONERS' LETTER OF INVITATION TO BONIFACE WIMMER

OCTOBER 11, 1846

Rev. Sir: Having learned that it is your intention to establish a monastery of the Benedictine Order in this country, the members of which devote themselves to the care of souls and to the education of youth, and feeling convinced that you cannot find in Pennsylvania a place better suited for these purposes than the farm attached to St. Vincent's church, we the undersigned do earnestly request you to come here and establish here the monastery above alluded to.

In our own name and in the name of the other members of this congregation, every man of whom, if he had time, we feel assured, would join with us in the sentiments we now express, we beg leave to assure you that we shall be always ready to do everything in our power to aid you in your benevolent undertakings, and console you in the discharge of your arduous mission. This farm has been given for the support of the pastor of the church for the time being. Trustees were appointed to preserve the property for the purpose for which it was granted, but being in your hands it could be used for this purpose in the most effectual manner. When worthy clergymen are living here attending this congregation and this farm, not destroyed nor injured, the people neither have nor claim any right to interfere with it. No one at the present moment would be inclined to give the least trouble or annoyance but on the contrary all would be delighted at your coming amongst us. Lest, however, anything of the kind should be anticipated in the future, we pledge ourselves to do everything in our power to make your position independent, so that when the above objects are secured you may feel certain that no one shall even have it in his power to give you the least annoyance.

Henry Coon, Jacob Kintz, Jacob Coon, Conrad Henrich, Trustees

John Showalter	Patrick McGirr, M.D.	Daniel Rinsel
Joseph Kintz	Henry Rinsel	I. J. Cantwell
John Toner	George Miller	Andrew Kuhn
A. J. Kuhn	Daniel Flanigan	Francis Steder
John Sneder	James Gloss	James Toner, Sr.
Thomas Kirk	Johannes Roesch	George Menne
Daniel B. Kuhn	Daniel Kuhn	Chas. Conroy
Adam Stoup	Peter Miller	James Watterson
James Hitsman	James McBride	Adam Kuhn
Joseph Georg	Hermann Hufeler	Edward Kelly
Joachim Noel	Arthur Toner	Blasius Noel
John Kuhn	John K. Henry	John Rowen
Joseph Gosch	Conrad Henry	George Bridge
Frederick Kintz	Patrick Ward	Michael Palmer
Lewis Keiflin	Elihu J. Schowalter	G. W. Jelly
John C. Stoup	Gregory Harkinson	George A. Neumann
John S. Henry, Jr.	George Stein	Francis Denning
Alois Zoller	Johann Miller	Conrad Rinsel

ASVA: Saint Vincent Parishioners to Wimmer, Youngstown, October 11, 1846. Printed in Bridge, An Illustrated History of St. Vincent Archabbey, 68–69; Fellner, *Abbot Boniface and His Monks,* 1:63–64.

APPENDIX 5

BONIFACE WIMMER'S LETTER TO KING LUDWIG I OF BAVARIA

JANUARY 25, 1851

Munich, January 25, 1851

Most August, Most Mighty King! Most Gracious King and Lord! I fully realize and appreciate the fact that Your Royal Majesty has deigned to become the founder and the real donor of the first Benedictine monastery in America by granting most kindly an endowment in the amount of 10,000 florins, just as Your Highness became the restorer and donor of other Benedictine monasteries in Bavaria. Therefore I feel obligated to submit most humbly to Your Royal Majesty a comprehensive description of the locality of this first Benedictine monastery as well as the story of its first beginnings, and along with this an indication of how meaningful this foundation is for the Catholic Church and for our German countrymen in particular. On my return to America I shall try to complete this description as best I can by sending you a roughly drawn sketch of both the buildings and the surrounding countryside.

Our state of Pennsylvania, the largest industrial state in the Union, is approximately one-third the size of the kingdom of Bavaria but has only about 1,800,000 inhabitants, half of whom are Germans. The largest city, with close to 250,000 inhabitants, is Philadelphia, not far from the mouth of the Delaware River as it flows into the sea. This river is navigable, even for the largest merchant ships and battleships, as far as Philadelphia, which is its port. Harrisburg is the seat of government and the governor. It is a city of about 8,000 inhabitants, situated on the Susquehanna River, which is of enormous width, yet navigable by rafts only in the spring, and never by ships because of the many ledges in its bed.

The Alleghenies, a rough mountain range, run from southwest to northeast right through the middle of the state; generally, however, they do not quite reach the height of 3,000 feet. East of this mountain range the land takes on a distinctly European character, with its pleasant rolling hill country strewn with many nice-looking homes of settlers or small farms, surrounded by rich grain fields, meadows, and even some vineyards, and large orchards everywhere. There are also many rather thickly populated cities in this region, containing the liveliest manufacturing districts, which are linked with one another and with Philadelphia by railroads and canals.

In the mountains themselves, which are divided into several sections, the soil is not very productive but the hills contain an inexhaustible supply of iron and coal; stock farming, on the other hand, is practically out of the question.

West of the Alleghenies one must distinguish between the north and the south. Both are dotted with hills, which rise up at random, as it were, and close together, without any order or continuous chain, so that any talk of level ground is completely out of the question. Even the Allegheny, Monongahela, and other rivers, which in size closely resemble the Danube in Bavaria, become very narrow as they make their course through the valleys, generally hemmed in on both sides by steep rocky banks. The southern portion of this stretch of Pennsylvania land, however, is very fertile and well cultivated, whereas the northern section, for the most part, is covered over with horrible-looking woodland and, besides, is less populated, and its soil is not as good and is often very poor. The German colony of St. Marys is located in this northern part; that certainly was an unwise venture, although it is unbelievable how much the untiring diligence and hard work of the Germans there, mostly Bavarians, have accomplished. The location, however, is so unfavorable that you cannot expect any good to come of it.

What Philadelphia is for eastern Pennsylvania, Pittsburgh, a city of sixty thousand inhabitants, is for western Pennsylvania: that is, the business and commercial center. And just as eastern Pennsylvania ships its products across the Atlantic Ocean by means of the Delaware River, so western Pennsylvania carries on shipping to the far west and to some extent as far as the Gulf of Mexico by way of the Monongahela, Allegheny, and Ohio rivers, the latter being formed by the confluence of the Monongahela and the Allegheny at Pittsburgh.

Until now, besides the many large, excellent, and picturesque roads, domestic commerce has been handled principally by the large canal that runs from Philadelphia to the small town of Hollidaysburg at the foot of the Allegheny Mountains. There it is replaced by a railroad which starting from Hollidaysburg goes over the mountain until it reaches the village of Johnstown on the other side. The boats that go through the canal are transported over the mountain on this railroad since they are so constructed and fitted together that they can be separated into three parts. In Johnstown the canal takes over again, after the boat is reassembled, and transports it to Pittsburgh where freight and passengers often go down the Ohio on the same steamer. But if their destination is to the northwest, they proceed again by canal to the city of Erie on the lake of the same name. This lake separates the United States from Canada, but at the same time it serves as a wonderful waterway binding together the eastern and western states of the Union. Recently, however, they have begun to set up a more rapid communication between Philadelphia and Pittsburgh by means of a railroad which already runs as far as Hollidaysburg, for the most part alongside the canal. From there an ambitious effort to extend the railroad to Pittsburgh has been made and should be completed by 1852.

This railroad is expected to be continued from Pittsburgh as far as St. Louis, and if the gigantic plan can be realized, it should, in not too long a time, be extended throughout all America, as far as the Pacific Ocean.

Here, where this railroad passes over the last stretch of the Allegheny Mountains on the other side of Chestnut Ridge, an hour's walk distant from these mountains, on a pleasant hill with a fine view overlooking the mountain range and the beautiful surroundings, in Westmoreland County, 280 miles west of Philadelphia and 40 miles east of Pittsburgh, at forty-nine degrees north latitude—here it is, I believe, that God has created a cradle for the Order of St. Benedict in America. In any event, we can see here an unmistakable manifestation of Divine Providence.

Already in the eighties of the last century there came to this hill a German missionary from the Lower Rhineland province of the Franciscan Order. His name was Theodore Brower, or Brauer, a devout, zealous, godly man who no doubt will survive for a long time in the grateful memory of the Catholics of western Pennsylvania. He bought a piece of land, 315 acres in size (an acre is about forty-two thousand square feet), and built on the hill a small poverty-stricken log hut which served at the same time as his dwelling and church. It is still standing today. At that time there were only a few Catholics, and even fewer Germans, mostly descendants of people who once lived in the vicinity of the Mosel and the lower Rhine. Because they were so few and scattered far and wide, this German missionary sought to gather them as near to his dwelling as possible, to save them from going astray among the Protestants. Where this was not feasible, he would at least visit them from time to time and in this way recovered the buds of the first promising German congregations from the other side of the mountains. Even Pittsburgh, which was then a poor and unattractive place with a fort, did not yet have a Catholic church or priest, and pastoral duties there were carried on from the "hill."

In order that the little flock after his death, being without a shepherd, might not be scattered again, and in order to make it easier for them to obtain and support a shepherd, this valiant man of God ordained in his will that the 315 acres of land on the "hill," together with another 174 acres about six English miles away, also bought by him, should be passed on to all his successors in the pastorate of this congregation, and it was further stipulated that no pastor could sell it, though each one could make use of it for his own support. The local authorities confirmed the will and later incorporated all the property to the state, that is, put it under the special guarantee of the state.

At the beginning the congregation had priests, but sad to say, there were soon no more German priests, partly because of the general shortage [of German priests], and partly because many English and Irish Catholic settlers banded together and were in need of an English priest.

Soon the small room in the log hut was no longer adequate for the needs of the faithful. Therefore a chapel made of stone was constructed, and then in 1834 a church, which together with the priest's residence cost eight thousand dollars, but which is already in danger of collapsing and serves as nothing more than a hall of prayer. Although it is of considerable size, it has no church atmosphere whatsoever. It was dedicated to St. Vincent de Paul in 1835 by Bishop Kenrick of Philadelphia.[6] Such was the state of things for 23 years [sic] until I arrived with my confreres.

My destination at first was the congregation of St. Joseph in the Allegheny Mountains where, next to a very large Irish congregation that Prince Gallitzin[7] had gathered together in and around the village of Loretto (perhaps the only village in America that is entirely Catholic), a large German congregation had also developed. I had made arrangements earlier with the priest there, a German missionary named Lemke, for the purchase of his property. But when he saw that I had little money and had with me just a troop of twenty young men, of whom some were farmers and some craftsmen, and four students, he, like all the German priests whom I met on my first arrival in America, lost all confidence in the success of my undertaking. And so after a stay of sixteen days in that colony, I had to leave again without being able to close a decent bill of sale with him.

Nevertheless as soon as I arrived in New York I informed the bishop of Pittsburgh about this matter. (I did the same from Bavaria, but without receiving an answer from him.) He then invited me to come to Pittsburgh, and as we traveled together to St. Vincent, he persuaded me to establish a monastery there. I did not want to accept this offer so long as there was still hope of coming to an agreement with Father Lemke. Since, however, the latter place [St. Joseph's] turned out to be a failure, and not only the Germans but also the English-speaking Catholics, in a special letter, urgently invited me to take charge of St. Vincent—and though for my own part I was not sure where to turn—I finally consented and gave orders for departure.

That, however, was easier said than done. We could, to be sure, travel a distance of fifty-five miles, but no German could be induced to take along our thirty-nine trunk loads of belongings. They all wanted us to remain, and as remonstrances and pleadings were of no avail in trying to explain that under the circumstances it was not possible, I was, as a consequence, compelled to listen to some rather harsh language, with the net result that I was ready to give up again.

Since, however, there was nothing else to be done, and the Germans among us did not want to do any more hauling, I accordingly had recourse to some Irishmen who thereupon offered their services in return for good pay. Thus on October 20, 1846, we arrived at the church of St. Vincent where we were given a very friendly reception, not only by the congregation but also by the most reverend bishop, Michael O'Connor, who right then and there installed me as pastor after my Irish predecessor had resigned the parish in my favor. Then on October 24 I gave all my associates, upon their urgent request, the habit of St. Benedict and thus started a new monastery.

But what a monastery! At that time there were several Sisters of Mercy living in

6. Francis Patrick Kenrick (1796–1863), bishop of Philadelphia (1830–51).

7. Father Demetrius Gallitzin (1770–1840), the son of a Russian prince who became a Catholic priest and served as a missionary in western Pennsylvania from 1799 until his death.

the rectory itself. They had built a convent about half an hour from the church, which however could not be occupied until the spring. In the old mission house a German-American, who had leased the parish property, was living with his family. For us there was left only the school house, which had two rooms and an attic. One of these rooms had to serve as a kitchen and refectory and also as a museum [study hall] for the lay brothers where they made their meditation and spiritual reading and were given the necessary instructions in Benedictine asceticism. The other room was a museum for me and my students and served at the same time as an office for the local pastor. The attic was our dormitory, where we slept on our straw mattresses, for we didn't have any bedsteads. We were only too glad to get up in the morning, since it was so cold that we were freezing even under the woolen blankets.

The little money I still had with me was quickly used up in the acquisition of implements needed to run the farm, in the purchase of horses and cattle, etc. Our food and board during the first year was paid entirely out of our own purse; hence I was soon up to my ears in debt and my credit was very low because people still had doubts about the feasibility of my plan, since all similar projects attempted by others in various places had turned out to be failures.

My plan, then, was as follows: first of all, in the Benedictine fashion, to acquire some land and then to cultivate the soil, a task to be left in the hands of the hardworking lay brothers. We hope in this way to gain a livelihood not just for the monastery alone; over and above the needs of the monks there will be many more mouths to feed. We have in mind a considerable number of German boys who are poor but very talented and who want to become priests and feel they have a vocation. We hope then to be able to educate them and give them priestly training so that on the one hand they may help to preserve and spread the Catholic religion among our fellow countrymen and on the other hand may win respect and recognition for the German elements in the population through the sound and thorough education of youth; and in particular to preserve the German culture and language among the Germans themselves.

My own most reverend bishop was himself one of the skeptics. Accordingly, when in order to make sure of my position I strongly urged him to assign the parish not just to me but to the Benedictine Order in perpetuity in such a way that every lawful successor of mine in the monastery to be erected would also be ipso facto the pastor and as such should be authorized to hold the two church properties, he for a long time would not go along with the idea and in any case wanted to obligate me to maintain parity in the seminary, that is, to admit as many English-speaking as German-speaking boys, enjoying the same favors and privileges. I, however, firmly rejected these demands and insisted just as firmly that my request be granted. Negotiations in the matter lasted from May 1847 until the following October and brought no results. I thereupon declared my firm intention to leave the place again and made the necessary arrangements to that end. Only when it was seen that I was really in earnest in my intention, and because in the meantime Father Peter Lechner arrived from Scheyern with a new band of twenty lay brothers, thereby manifesting his interest in our undertaking and bringing from Bavaria a new guarantee for its success, did the bishop grant my request and refrain from his previous demands. This was on December 6, 1847.

Thus ended a year full of troubles and frustration, of uncertainty and insecurity. I really lost that year because it was precisely on account of the state of uncertainty that plagued me that I could neither think about building projects nor did I want to. Meanwhile I instructed the men under me, as best I could, in the practice of the Holy Rule. I also sought out the Germans in their homes round about [St. Vincent] and occasionally made visits even to far-off places where I knew or suspected there were German Catholics without a priest. On these tours I baptized many children and adults and formed two small congregations in Indiana County.

Through the lively personal interest on the part of the most reverend archbishop [of Munich], and the unwearying solicitude of the Reverend [Joseph Ferdinand] Müller, the court chaplain, I received help again and again, especially when my needs were the greatest. For this reason I was able to put my finances in order and, for the present at least, put up the most necessary buildings. First of all we added on to the rectory a building 60 feet long and 40 feet wide and three stories high; then we built a barn 126 feet long and 40 feet wide. Both were built of solid brick. The latter was so constructed that it could later be easily changed into a building with living quarters as circumstances required. This year we added another 36 feet to our monastery floor, thus closing the side in the back of the house. Next summer I will probably put up a mill, and after that we shall again have to take up the problem of enlarging the monastery building so that it will be completed in two or three years.

The lay brothers mold the bricks themselves and carry out all the construction without the help of craftsmen from the outside. The only things I had to buy were boards, shingles, and nails—for the simple reason that we have no sawmill and also because in America shingles are made only of pine, and pine trees are to be found nowhere in our county. Moreover, tile is absolutely unheard of here. This is true of the cities as well as out in the country.

As I have already mentioned above, our foundation now consists of two pieces of property, one of 315 acres and the other of 175 acres. In addition to that, in 1848 I purchased from Father Lemke, the priest with whom I was previously unable to join, the property owned by him[8] and consisting of 300 acres. I paid $3,000 for it, laying down $1,000 in cash. Afterwards I paid $600 in two yearly installments, thus leaving $1,400 still to be paid. On this piece of property there are now two of my priests together with six lay brothers who take care of tilling the soil. The priests are engaged in the care of souls for the congregation of St. Joseph and especially for the Germans of Cambria and Clearfield counties.

Furthermore, I bought in the little town of Indiana a house with three fine building sites for the price of $3,700, on which I also made a first payment of $1,000 in cash, the remainder to be paid in yearly installments. At first I established a congregation there, but it is my desire and plan to convert the house we acquired into a little monastery as soon as possible so that Indiana County may also be brought forever within the sphere of our activities, and in order to maintain a link between St. Joseph and St. Vincent, since it is situated midway between these two places.

Then I bought and paid for 425 acres up in the mountains, and even though

8. In Carrolltown, Cambria County, Pennsylvania.

only a very tiny section of it is cultivable, it is still very good for grazing. Also, the numerous oak trees there supply the tannin needed for our tannery. In addition, we still have sixteen good horses, which I had to purchase, eight colts which I had to break myself, and seventy-odd head of horned cattle, along with six hundred sheep and about six hundred pigs, etc.

All necessary equipment has been procured for the operation of the farm. It must be noted that we need many other things—such as the threshing machines now in use in America, which cost as much as one hundred dollars or more each.

It is understandable that all this requires large expenditures, which to some extent have not yet been met. I was able, however, in this way to feed and clothe ninety-three men, that is to say eight in St. Joseph and eighty-five at St. Vincent, among whom there are twenty-seven boys whom I had to supply with books. There are also six students of philosophy and theology, eight priests, and forty-six lay brothers. Each year our monastic community grew at a rate of about twenty persons a year, but through hard work and good economy our production also increased at the same rate. Besides, with the money I received from the Ludwig Missionsverein I was able again and again to purchase or procure those things that would be of use in the future, whereas the buildings alone that we put up with our own hands, if we had to have recourse to craftsmen in order to build them, would have cost us so much that we would never have been able to erect them with the money we got from Bavaria.

Thus I believe that the correctness and feasibility of the plan I have undertaken have been established. At least those who have had doubts or misgivings must stand confounded by the successes up until now. They will also have to admit that in the Benedictine Order, if it is allowed to develop freely and unhampered in its own primitive way and has the will to do so, there are to be found sources of energy far greater than in any other Order for advancing the common good of the Church and state.

In America, at least, the Benedictine Order appears to be called to fulfill an urgent need, which is to come to the aid of this country; up to now this has indeed been the common feeling everywhere, except that no one as yet has been able to figure out the ways and means of providing this aid.

Indeed, there are to be found here among Catholics (not for the Germans, of course, but at least for the English) quite a lot of fine institutions where the children of wealthy Americans, both boys and girls, can obtain an adequate education. To be sure, this is only a rather superficial kind of education because the period of instruction is for only three years. For the ordinary people, however, this is sufficient and qualifies a young man, according to the American requirements, which are not too demanding and give no thought to classical education, to take up immediately special studies in law, medicine, or technical subjects.

There is, however, a dearth of educational institutions for Germans generally, and especially institutions where German Catholics can get a classical and truly religious education. On the part of the state nothing at all is done in this matter, since it wants the German element to disappear entirely and is seeking to replace German institutions with English ones. The Germans, however, being tossed indiscriminately among the poor and the English, and furthermore being divided into conflicting interest groups because of the diverse religious denominations among them, have had neither the sufficient courage and confidence that characterize German dignity, nor the necessary spirit of cooperation, to be able to accomplish anything. Since German history has not been taught at all, already the first generation no longer knows from what German district their parents come, much less the many reasons they ought to have for being proud of their German origin.

Here only a religious institution can help, one which enjoys earthly security in the possession of large landed property and in the productivity of the soil, and which thus remains independent and consequently has no need, for its own self-preservation, to beg the patronage of wealthy factory barons and, in return for fat pensions, to put itself in their employ in the tutorship of their children.

There is, however, something still more distressing, namely, the shortage of seminaries where German priests can be educated in order to meet the needs of the German people. Here in this country, with respect to German schools, you cannot expect anything from the government; in the same way you cannot expect anything on the part of the bishops. Almost all of them are English, or in some instances French, and like the government they are not interested in what is German, much less in promoting German interests, and in many ways show themselves fearful of anything that is German. (There is no doubt that in many cases the Germans have given reason for this attitude toward them.) Moreover, the means are lacking to put up buildings, to support pupils, to find professors, and to pay them their salaries.

Thus, it is again only the Benedictines who can be helpful in the manner mentioned above. This appears to be the most natural way, and at the same time the simplest and the surest. If there were just one monastery like ours in every diocese, a great deal could have been accomplished by this time. Then not only would provision be made for the Germans everywhere with regard to the care of souls, not only would the German character be represented, preserved, and respected everywhere in the school, in the pulpit, in the confessional, and in books, but, as the individual monasteries grow stronger and more prosperous, one would always find that the number of young men undergoing training in the seminaries would enjoy numerical superiority over the English and also would be far ahead of them in learning and culture.

Even if, however, for the present that is not to be quickly realized, it is extremely important that the Germans should at least be concentrated in a place that is a railway center, which at the same time could serve as a central place from which, time and circumstances permitting, they could fan out in all directions, and then settle wherever and as soon as existing conditions are found to be most favorable. Really it is not too difficult, once you know America, to form and establish a new foundation in virtually any place. I have already had practical experience of this inasmuch as I was able to erect a Benedictine priory in St. Joseph, whereas upon my arrival I met with insurmountable difficulties trying to establish myself there.

In the beginning what was lacking most of all was not chiefly money but good personnel and a knowledge of conditions in America. In many cases, of course, there was a lack of money, and it is still lacking. One must have some at his disposal if he is to undertake any project. Money, however, is not everything. If you know the country and the character of the people, and at the same time have a good staff under your command, you can also make money or replace the deficit with credit. In the beginning I was alone. My companions were students, rather shy and timid, or simple and plain laymen who had hardly ever seen a monastery. These students are now fine priests, whereas the laymen are good Benedictines; I can rely upon them and know what each one is capable of doing and also to what kind of employment I can assign him. The blessed outcome of our efforts up till now has given high hopes to all of them. The difficult and trying circumstances in which we often found ourselves turned out to be a good school for them. They know now that such trials occur everywhere and that we can surmount them by perseverance and courage. They would therefore be willing to make a beginning anywhere and at any time, since they are given such good assurances of success.

When starting out, it would not be good to have too many irons in the fire. Much is accomplished once a place is put on a firm footing and so made ready, as it were, for doing something worthwhile. I will therefore make such use of the most gracious endowment of Your Royal Majesty that the means of subsistence of our first foundation be constantly on the increase so as to make it possible for us to take in a considerable number of poor German boys. In this way Your Royal Majesty will be acclaimed as the founder of the first German seminary in the United States and also as the benefactor, not only of all our pupils, but of all in general who, in the days to come, shall have a share in the beneficent effects of your endowment. I have full confidence that your beneficence will be richly rewarded by a return in kind made to Your Royal Majesty Yourself, as well as to Your Highness's most illustrious family.

My most heartfelt thanks as well as that of my monastery cannot be better expressed than by the assurance that I shall arrange for Holy Mass to be said every Monday, in perpetuity, for King Ludwig, our founder, in order to insure a lasting remembrance of the generous endowment of Your Royal Majesty as well as of our obligation to remain forever grateful for the same.

May it please Your Royal Majesty to accept most graciously this small tribute of a gratitude that is most becoming and appropriate and to permit me to bid you farewell with the most profound sense of reverence and devotion. Your Royal Majesty's most humble, most loyal, and most faithful, P. Boniface Wimmer, Superior of the Benedictine Monastery of St. Vincent in Pennsylvania

Translated by Bede Babo, O.S.B. The letter is printed in German in Willibald Mathäser, *Bonifaz Wimmer O.S.B. und König Ludwig I von Bayern* (Munich: J. Pfeiffer, 1938), 14–24.

APPENDIX 6

APOSTOLIC BRIEF ERECTING SAINT VINCENT AS AN ABBEY

AUGUST 24, 1855

THE DECREE NAMING WIMMER ABBOT

SEPTEMBER 17, 1855

PIUS IX,

FOR PERPETUAL REMEMBRANCE.

Among the spiritual duties which, in the exercise of Our pastoral office are incumbent upon Us, the greatest and most important is this, that the eternal salvation of the faithful, wherever they are located, be provided for, and that We zealously promote whatever is conducive to this end. Among other things which in recent years have been accomplished for the benefit of religion in the United States of America, We must undoubtedly include the Benedictine monastery, which, through the efforts of Our beloved son, Boniface Wimmer, favored by the cooperation of Our venerable brother, Michael O'Connor, Bishop of Pittsburgh, has been erected on the Hill of St. Vincent, in the diocese of Pittsburgh, and sanctioned by the authority of the Holy See. Since the mode of life of the young religious residing there has been arranged according to the norm of religious profession, and since lay-brothers, called also *conversi,* endowed with suitable qualities, according to a praiseworthy plan and taking into account the prevailing conditions of that region, have been admitted into the Order, with the result that the precepts of the Benedictine Rule can be observed there and that furthermore the monks, as priests, can be active in the care of souls not only at St. Vincent's but also in other places in the adjoining region, in the name of the aforementioned Boniface Wimmer and of the monks of the aforesaid monastery, We have therefore been petitioned that We, through the proper constitution of government, as has been granted for the welfare of the Order of St. Benedict in other localities, and through our Apostolic Authority, make further provisions for the firm foundation and the prosperity of this undertaking. After deep reflection upon these matters and following the advice of their Eminences, the Cardinals of the Roman Church, who are placed at the head of the Congregation for the Propagation of the Faith, We, therefore, through our Apostolic Authority, by this present document, erect the monastery on the Hill of St. Vincent, in the diocese of Pittsburgh, into an abbey, exempt in the smallest degree, that is, without territory in any diocese. We ordain further that monks who are now members of the community or who in the future will become members of the community be held together as a special Congregation of the Order of St. Benedict, which Congregation, in addition to the common Rule of St. Benedict, shall be bound by those particular statutes which by the Apostolic letters of Our Predecessor, Innocent XI, of happy memory, *Circumspecta,* and *Militanti Ecclesiae,* have been approved for the Bavarian Benedictine Congregation, and that they be considered connected with or as we say affiliated with the Cassinese Congregation. We decree further by our Apostolic Authority that the election of the abbot rest with the monastery chapter and that the proceedings of the same shall be submitted to the Holy See for approval. We desire also that the abbot enjoy all rights and privileges which in the Benedictine Order are regarded as belonging to an abbot exempt in the smallest degree, in accordance with the statutes mentioned before regarding the time of his incumbency in office, and in compliance with the decree regarding the insignia and honors, which was issued by Our Predecessor, Alexander VII, of happy memory. Finally, taking into account the peculiar condition of the region, and particularly the lack of priests, We ordain that as regards the care of souls, in addition to the precepts of the law of the Church, also those laws be observed which apply generally for the missions. We desire further that in the same monastery of St. Vincent a monastic seminary be maintained into which secular clerics be admitted, provided that they meet the expenses of their education, and that the Bishop, as Apostolic Delegate, have the right to watch over the education and morals of these clerics.

We confirm and ordain, etc.

Given in Rome at St. Peter's, under the seal of the Fisherman, on the 24th day of August, in the tenth year of Our Pontificate (A.D. MDCCCLV).

[L.S.] V. Card. Macchi

DECREE OF THE SACRED CONGREGATION OF THE PROPAGANDA.

Our Holy Father, through divine Providence Pope Pius, the ninth of this name, on the 29th of July 1855, according to a vote of the Sacred Congregation for the

Propagation of the Faith, has sanctioned and given the force of law to several matters concerning the spiritual government of the monastery of the Order of St. Benedict on the Hill of St. Vincent, in the diocese of Pittsburgh, and on the 24th of August of the present year His Holiness has therefore deigned to issue an Apostolic Breve confirming these matters. In consideration of the eminent services of the Very Reverend Boniface Wimmer in behalf of the monastery, in accordance with a former decree of the Sacred Congregation, His Holiness has deigned to order that for the first time there be no binding force to what has been decreed regarding the election of an abbot, and has raised the said Boniface Wimmer to the abbatial dignity and has appointed him abbot of the aforementioned monastery for the space of three years, in the same manner as if he had been elected according to the customary legal form. After the lapse of three years, however, the election of an abbot should take place according to the regular method.

Given at Rome in the palace of the Sacred Congregation on the 17th of September 1855.

[L.S.] J. Th. Card. Fransoni, Praef.
Al. Barnabo, a Secretis.

ASVA: Apostolic Breve, August 24, 1855, and Decree of the Propaganda Fide, September 17, 1855; printed in Bridge, *An Illustrated History of St. Vincent,* 99–101.

APPENDIX 7

WIMMER'S TEN-YEAR REPORT TO THE LUDWIG MISSIONSVEREIN

FEBRUARY 1856

St. Vincent, February 1856

Esteemed Directors of the Ludwig Missionsverein: During my last visit to Munich, after my return from Rome following the happy and favorable completion of my business there, the wish was often strongly expressed that I should write a short chronicle of my monastery and send it to the Central Committee.[9] I hereby acquit myself of this commission as well as I can, although I do not conceal that it is a rather difficult task. I feel like the man who is supposed to write his autobiography. I hope, however, that I succeed in giving a true picture of the foundation and gradual development of my monastery in terse brevity, without speaking about myself more than is necessary and yet so that my patrons and friends can receive the correct impression.

The founding of the monastery was occasioned first by the question: how can the shortage of priests in the United States be remedied, a shortage felt most acutely by our German countrymen, and whose consequence is the loss of so many

9. Wimmer had gone to Europe in February 1855 and spent ten months in Bavaria and Rome garnering support for the Benedictine mission in the United States and working for the elevation of Saint Vincent to the rank of abbey. The Holy See issued the decree establishing the abbey in August 1855 and Wimmer returned to Pennsylvania in December.

Catholics. The answer was simple and easy, namely, through the education of German missionaries. But further questions arose: where is the seminary for this purpose? Where are the professors? Where are the students? Where is the endowment? Who should assume its direction?

I myself had thought many times about the matter since the idea of becoming a missionary occupied me for years and only obedience hindered me from carrying it out. I was amazed that while these questions were being asked no one thought of the Benedictines, as though it were obvious that they were neither missionaries themselves nor could they prepare missionaries. I considered it my duty therefore to defend my Order, and did so in an article in the *Augsburger Postzeitung* in which I attempted to show that the Benedictine Order would be more suitable than any other to found and direct mission seminaries and to alleviate the lack of priests, if the Order would be introduced into the United States and if it once again would take on the character of those times in which it flourished. My suggestion was therefore that the mission seminary should not be in Germany, nor in Europe at all, but in America. But because in any case it would require a great deal of money to build and maintain a suitable building, a sufficient endowment for the salaries of the professors and for the sustenance of the students, because it is difficult to find the right people who would be suitable for and capable of administration and teaching, and finally because the suitability of such an institution is always endangered and unsure, I desired rather to see the money used for the establishment of Benedictine monasteries that would make it their primary task to work actively on the project of missions and educate talented boys and young men as missionaries for the American people. And in order to do that the monasteries had to acquire a significant amount of land, farm it with lay brothers, and from this create the necessary means to support the personnel of the monastery and the seminary.

This idea found approval. The papal nuncio to Munich, Monsignor Morichini, the then coadjutor and later archbishop, Count von Reisach, and the members of the Central Directory of the Ludwig Missionsverein all approved it and had the business manager at that time, Court Chaplain Müller, offer 6,000 florins for me to attempt to execute the plan. The abbot of Metten also agreed to release me for this purpose.

I was at that time prefect in the Royal Academy in Munich. My intention was soon known among my charges and students and naturally then became known among the people. Gradually 15 young men applied—partly farmers, partly tradesmen—who wanted to go with me as lay brothers. Four students, who felt they had a vocation to the religious life in the missions, did the same. Most of the brothers had the necessary travel money; some had a little more, some not quite enough. Personally known to me were only one of the students and two of the brothers; but all had the best recommendations.

I had not neglected to write Bishop O'Connor in Pittsburgh to make known my plan and to request admission into his diocese. He had sent me this, as I later heard, but it had not reached me. Bishop Quarter of Chicago had also granted me admission, but this had not come into my hands either.

Meanwhile I prepared myself as well as possible for departure, had habits made in Munich for my candidates, procured some beautiful robes, the necessary vestments, chalices, ciboria, missals, etc. In all of this I was supported considerably by many benefactors. Former Bishop Ziegler of Linz, who also approved the undertaking, supported me with a sum of 500 florins and promised further contributions for the future. The abbots of Metten and Scheyern, the prior of Weltenburg, and several good friends among the clergy supported me likewise. Several ladies of highest station and from the middle class sent linens and appointments for the altar. The library was not insignificant. Sailing contracts were made at the proper time.

July 25, 1846, was set as the day of departure. The coadjutor archbishop celebrated the mission Mass at 5:00 a.m. in St. Michael's Church and distributed communion to my companions. There was present a considerable number of the faithful, friends, and acquaintances of the small group which had three days before armed themselves through spiritual exercises against the dangers of the journey. After a hurried breakfast we left for the train.

We traveled by way of Augsburg, Ulm, and Stuttgart to Mannheim. From Mainz we went down the Rhine to Rotterdam. From there we went to Havre de Grace where we had to wait several days. On August 10 we went to sea in the three-masted *Iowa* and reached the harbor of New York on September 16 after a safe voyage. I was in a terrible dilemma when I found no word in New York from either Bishop O'Connor or Bishop Quarter as to whether they wanted to admit me and my company into their dioceses or not. The dilemma became greater when all the German priests, to whom I was directed, received me with a sympathetic shrug of the shoulders and downright refused to wish me luck. They wanted me to dismiss the brothers on the spot because, as these priests believed, they would soon leave me anyway. In regard to the students, they advised me to get in someplace where I could find a little parish for myself in order that I might then perhaps get them into some diocesan seminary. The whole thing, they felt, was an adventurous plan which could not be carried out, and they had to marvel how people in the old country knew so little about American circumstances that they hoped to found a monastery and mission seminary with a crowd of farmer boys and clumsy students. Certainly one could have used the money for something better, etc.

This talk almost robbed me of the confidence with which I had made my plans. However, I did not want to leave the project untested. I stayed in the city only as long as necessary to bring my baggage which consisted of 42 cases and trunks through customs and to make arrangements for the trip deeper into the country. Saint Joseph, now called Carrolltown, in western Pennsylvania, located in the Pittsburgh diocese, 300 miles west of Philadelphia in the Allegheny Mountains, was now our destination. I had to try to settle someplace soon, for otherwise the money with which I was to lay the foundation of a monastery would melt away. Traveling in America is expensive, especially for those who are not familiar with the English language. One is cheated or ceremoniously deceived everywhere. It did not go any better for us.

On September 19 we left New York to go to Philadelphia by train. Just as we arrived at the station with our baggage, the missionary Peter Lemke, coming from Saint Joseph, met us. He was a welcome guide and he actually turned right around, since he had come because of us. We remained only one day in Philadelphia. Then we had a short stretch on the train and the rest of the way by canal. It took eight days to travel in this fashion to Hollidaysburg, a small city at the foot of the Allegheny Mountains, whereas now one can make it in eight hours, now that the rail line is finished.

There two of the brothers were attacked with dysentery. Father Lemke was well known here, so our baggage and the two sick brothers—one of whom quickly recovered, the other of whom lay in pain for half a year—we had transported over the mountains to the little city of Ebensburg, while the healthy followed in good spirits on foot. From Ebensburg we had another four hours to Carrolltown or Saint Joseph where we arrived on September 30. We were full of anticipation to see how the place would look. The area was largely uncultivated, the roads were stony and rough, we were constantly going up and down hills. The farther we went, the less friendly it became. At last we had the view of a narrow valley, closed in by hills; at the northern end there was a barn, a farm house, and another not yet completed house nearby at the foot of a steep hill. This was Saint Joseph! Here lived the missionary Father Lemke. The church was an hour away. So here was where we were to stay and found the first Benedictine monastery!

We moved in and set ourselves up as best we could. The space was far too limited for so many guests. However, we were satisfied—our travels were at least at an end and we were again among Germans. Our German countrymen were happy to see us, helped us kindly, and considered themselves fortunate to have a German priest among them permanently.

One of my first points of business was to write to Bishop O'Connor in Pittsburgh to announce my arrival and, in reference to my earlier letters from Germany, to offer him my services. He answered by return mail, welcomed me, and warmly invited me to visit him in Pittsburgh at my earliest convenience. I accepted the invitation, traveled to Pittsburgh, and paid the bishop my respects. Naturally the subject of our conversation was immediately the purpose of my immigration. And when I told him, as I had earlier written, that it was my aim to found a monastery which at the same time was to be a mission seminary, he said to me that St. Joseph was not suited for this purpose. He said he had a far better place, which he could and wanted to give me, which was much better situated for such a purpose and where also many Germans lived. He asked me to take a trip there with him—it was only a bit out of the way—when I was returning to St. Joseph. I could not reject the invitation and traveled with the bishop the next day to this place. It was Saint Vincent. Saint Vincent, like St. Joseph, was neither a village, market town, nor city; it was nothing more than a church with a rectory, but it lay in a well-cultivated, very beautiful countryside on a gentle hill between two streams which, with their pleasant valleys, joined at the foot of this hill. It was an hour west of the mountains and with a beautiful view of them. The ground was far more fertile than in Carrolltown. Many Catholic and Protestant Germans lived in the neighborhood, but most of them were already first generation Americans and not immigrants, and they embodied more of the American than of the German. The next morning the bishop called together the most influential and notable members of the parish, held a conference in which he detailed my plan to them, and expressed his wish that I should settle at Saint Vincent. The Germans were very glad about this. Although they had had a German priest by the name of Häres for the previous six months, before him they had not had a German priest for 17 years, and they saw that the present one would not remain long with them. The English were glad to hear that a monastery would be founded at Saint Vincent, and they promised their support and active participation.

Nonetheless, I was more in favor of St. Joseph and took leave of Saint Vincent without giving a definite promise that I would take over the place. When I returned to St. Joseph, the brothers were busy with the fall planting, but they were downcast. The poor soil, the many stumps and roots of cut-down trees, which made plowing uncommonly difficult, made them despondent. They thought we could not make ends meet there. As once the Romans were aghast at the Herculean stature of the old Germans, so the immigrant Germans were aghast here at the immense trees of the American virgin forests, before they mastered the techniques which experience and practice taught them how they might destroy these magnificent woods. When I told them about Saint Vincent, they immediately asked me if there were as many stumps and roots in the fields there as at St. Joseph, and as I could report that not a single stump was left in a large field there and that the ground was as fertile and stone-free as in the best regions of Bavaria, they immediately exclaimed that we should move to Saint Vincent.

Stones and stumps were for me no reason to leave this place and trade it for another, for there were still woods at Saint Vincent which had to be cleared and so one naturally had to face huge trees there too. I saw that one must not avoid obstacles but overcome them. At Saint Vincent there was also a difficulty of a different kind. This place was namely not free property but was in trust. This trust consisted of two pieces of land. The one was 175 acres, the other 325 acres. (One acre is 42,000 square feet.) The two properties had been purchased more than 70 years earlier by a German missionary, Theodor Brauer [sic] from the Lower Rhineland, and was left by will as a parish benefice for the use and support of his successors at this place. As a consequence of a court case which took place later, it was enacted by the government that three men from the Catholic parish should be named as trustees, who under their own responsibility had to take care that both places were maintained in good condition and used in the best interests of whoever was pastor at the time. This decision protected the two properties from the danger of being sold or lost, but it also bound the hands of the bishop and the parish as well, so that they could not administer it in any other way, and it became a rich source of discord among the priests, trustees, and parish. There was also a debt of more than $3,000 (7000 florins) on the church. The church itself was not strongly built (1835), and it threatened to collapse suddenly. All of this left me little inclined to take over Saint Vincent, and I certainly would not have done it if I had not been almost forced to do so. In St. Joseph the conditions made to me for the purchase of 300 acres of land which I considered necessary for the foundation of a monastery were such as I could not keep and therefore could not enter into. I saw well that there was here also the conviction, which especially the clergy had, that my undertaking could not succeed. It was this which drove me out. They had expected that I would have considerable sums of money with me, but when they saw that of my 6,000 florins hardly more than 4,000 were left (the long overland journey had caused considerable expense), they tried to get rid of me or place me in such a condition that I ran the danger of losing everything while the other party would be totally protected.[10]

Meanwhile, a written invitation also had come to me from the Saint Vincent

10. The "other party" was apparently Father Peter Henry Lemke who had offered to sell three hundred acres in Carrolltown to Wimmer.

parishioners, signed by most of the members of the parish, [expressing the wish] that I might yet settle there with my people. I therefore decided to follow the call. On October 15 [1846] this decision was formally made. Our effects were packed again, and we prepared for departure. The German inhabitants did not want to let us go. None of them could be moved to transport our baggage away, not even when we offered to pay. Pleas, tears, threats, and insults were used in order to induce me to stay there. The way things stood, it was not possible to remain. I stuck to my decision and finally found Irishmen who were ready to transport us. On October 16 we left for Saint Vincent. The distance was only 22 hours. We reached it with the vanguard after two days. The main army, transporting in his bed on a wagon the sick brother whose dysentery had developed into a very painful arthritis [gout?], through bad treatment, arrived only on the third day. The trip cost $200 or 500 florins.

At Saint Vincent we found a rather long, but very narrow, one-story wooden house, originally the dwelling of whoever was pastor or missionary, but occupied at the time by a German-American farmer and his family of three daughters and six sons. Somewhat lower towards the east stood a building which was supposed to be a barn, but it had almost no roof anymore; the threshing floor was useless for threshing, the beams were half rotted so that they no longer really stretched, but hung. Underneath there was also a stall for horses, carelessly covered with a few boards and bundles of straw of Turkish wheat (corn), so that the poor animals had protection from neither rain nor snow. The cattle had to stay outside. The grain was arranged in front of the barn in stacks which ran up in a point and were protected as much as possible against the penetration of water.

South of the old parish house was a new building of brick originally intended for a schoolhouse, but at that time inhabited by the parish priest. It was only half completed, without floor, without ceiling. However, it was covered with a good shingle roof. It contained two rooms of the same size, which were separated from one another by a narrow hall. One could get to the attic only by ladder. There were no stairs. West of this building, about 150 paces away, stood the church. It was a friendly, roomy building, square like a prayer hall and without tower or bell, but with an organ and three altars. The whole [church] was made of bricks. However, as already mentioned, it was not solidly built. East of it stood the parish house, a two-story building, 40 by 40 feet. But it was occupied by English Sisters of Mercy who were building a convent half an hour away. In the meantime, until they moved in [to the convent], they had found refuge here and had immediately opened a school in which at that time there were 10–12 girls from good families as pupils.

The American farmer had the parish benefice on lease; we could serve him notice on the lease but he had the right to remain until April 1. We therefore moved into the school house. The then pastor or missionary, a rather aged Irish priest,[11] had readily resigned in favor of me, and the bishop named and installed me as pastor in his stead. The above-mentioned German priest received another station and immediately left. But the earlier pastor remained for a time as assisting priest for the English[-speaking] faithful of our parish until I would myself have made such progress in the English language that I could forego his help. Moving in proceeded

11. Father Michael Gallagher.

quickly without any special ceremonies. The mattresses which we had brought along were filled with straw and dragged up the ladder to the loft under the roof where they were laid in two rows on the floor. Each received, in addition, his straw pillow, a sheet, and two woolen blankets (all Bavarian products), and his bed was finished. Bedsteads were not there, nor were they necessary. That was the dormitory for the brothers and students. One of the two rooms was used for a kitchen, for a general refectory, for a place for the brothers at times when they were not at work but at meditation or spiritual reading. At the same time the sick brother lay there. The other room had a board partition behind which I and my assistant slept. The remaining part we used as a lecture hall and study room for the four students. Thus were we lodged and heartily satisfied. This happened on October 18 and 19, 1846.

Now I began to organize my people. On October 24 I gave them the habit in the church. Then we observed regularly the following order of the day: at 3:45 a.m. we rose each day; at 4:00 we went to the church which, as mentioned above, was 150 paces from our dwelling. I went with the students into the choir[loft], the brothers went into the pews. These latter prayed there a rosary with litany and several other prayers; they were finished before 4:45, returned to the house, made a fire, swept up, and made the beds. I prayed Matins and Lauds with my students; the time up until five o'clock was fully taken up with this, and then we also returned to our room. From 5:00 until 6:00 there was meditation; at 6:00 I held Prime while the brothers ate their soup. After Prime was the conventual Mass. After this the brothers worked until 10:45. I and the students took no breakfast; I instructed them until nine o'clock in the Divine Office and when they knew this, in dogmatic and moral theology. At nine o'clock was Terce and Sext, afterwards study time until 10:45. Then we all went to the church again and held there our particular examination of conscience. At 11:00 we all went to table and took a very frugal meal while during it one read aloud. After this we went, praying the *Miserere,* to the church again, held a short adoration there, and then Nones which ended before twelve o'clock. After this there was free time until one o'clock.

At one o'clock the brothers went to the church again and prayed their second rosary and then worked until five o'clock. I studied with my students until three o'clock; then we held Vespers in the church. There was a quarter of an hour free time after this, and then there was class and study until five o'clock. At five o'clock I explained the Holy Rule for half an hour; then there was spiritual reading until six when we had supper with reading from an edifying book. From 6:30 to 7:30 there was free time. At 7:30 we had Compline and the brothers their third rosary until 8:15, when we returned to our house, read and prayed until nine o'clock, and then went to bed. Silence was most strictly observed at night, and also during the day it was not broken without necessity outside of free time. This order was observed also in the summer with the exception that Holy Mass took place at 5:30, the noon rosary was at 12:30, and in the evening the spiritual reading began only at 5:30 so that more time remained for work. Then the students too had to work after noon until Vespers, and for the sake of good example I could not exclude myself from the work.

So the first winter we lived a rather quiet, retired life and zealously schooled ourselves in the observance of the Holy Rule. There was a lively zeal and a very edifying behavior observable in almost all of my comrades. But because of pastoral duties I was sometimes hindered from holding lectures and often even had to stay out overnight on distant visitations of the sick. I had the oldest student, who had already finished theology in Munich, ordained as a priest on the feast of St. Joseph, in order to take my place in emergencies.[12]

In the meantime, the convent for the Irish Sisters of Mercy had been completed and the German-American tenant farmer had also left. We bought from him five horses, five cows, pigs, sheep, wagons, harrows, and everything necessary for conducting a farm. One-half of the grain in the fields belonged to the assisting priest, the other half to the farmer, and this I also purchased from him. With this my treasury was completely drained. When we moved into the parish house on May 14, we were so poor that there was not a penny in the house. As we had to buy all our provisions and had no money, we were obliged to get everything on credit. A German butcher supplied the meat, an American Catholic grocer supplied the other articles we needed. No answer had come to several letters which I had sent to Bavaria, so I did not know whether the letters had become lost or if I had been entirely forgotten. At last in August 1847 I received notice that all my letters had arrived and that under the leadership of one of my confreres a new group of lay brothers who wanted to enter the Order at Saint Vincent would arrive.

On August 17, 1847, Father Peter Lechner from Scheyern arrived with twenty companions and brought (what was the principal item) a significant sum of money, namely 5,000 florins which the Central Directory of the Ludwig Missionsverein had contributed. Now I paid my debts, reestablished my credit, and improved my standing with the public when it was seen that our plan was supported and fostered by benefactors in Europe. In Father Peter I gained an energetic co-worker, a good novice master and professor, and in the 19 [*sic*] brothers, among whom were various craftsmen, I obtained many strong and skilled hands for work. The number of consumers had indeed increased, but the summer's crop already belonged to us. We had a very good crop of corn, though the wheat crop was less. I had acquired sufficient knowledge of English to hear confessions, to teach the children catechism, and even to preach if it was necessary. In our Westmoreland County I had already searched out and found all the scattered Catholics and established several missions where I occasionally during the week said Mass and administered the sacraments. I had also taken charge of Indiana County and made arrangements whereby I had to be away from home five days each month while Father Peter and the novice-priest, Father Charles Geyerstanger, attended to the pastoral and monastic affairs at home.

But we were still on weak foundations, for it was yet very uncertain whether we could remain at Saint Vincent or not. As I remarked earlier, neither the bishop nor the parish could sell or give us the two tracts of land which belonged to Saint Vincent since they had been bequeathed for the use only of whoever might be pastor at the time. Since the bishop had appointed me pastor, the two tracts belonged in the first place to me, but also to my brothers insofar as I was their superior. Therefore everything depended on me. In case of my death, the bishop would have a free hand to give the parish to another, and my brothers would have to move on. But my own appointment was not irrevocable, and I would not be able to object if the

12. Charles Martin Geyerstanger (1820–81), one of the four pioneer students at Saint Vincent, was ordained on March 18, 1847, by Bishop Michael O'Connor of Pittsburgh.

bishop would decide to remove me for any reason. (I had not overlooked this possibility when I left St. Joseph; but I had to patiently accommodate myself to it once I was at Saint Vincent, for winter was at the door and I had to have a place where I could stay if I did not wish to fulfill those prophecies made by the clergy in New York that all the brothers would leave me.) Nor could I blame the bishop that he wanted to be sure with regard to me. Although I was able at my arrival to present him with the best testimonials from the abbot of Metten as well as from the two bishops of Munich-Freising and Regensburg, this was still no proof that I was also capable of leading my project to a happy and successful end. The good priest who resigned the parish had at the bishop's wish tried himself to found a similar institution with six young men, some of whom were Americans and some German, and had completely failed. The bishop thought the same could happen to me and therefore did not want to tie his hands, as he certainly would have done had he appointed me as pastor for life.

But things could not remain as they were. (Through the momentary necessity and the urgency of the situation, but partly also through my unfamiliarity with American circumstances, I had come into a singular position. Now that I had more experience, had won and secured the trust of my people, and had formed them from generous but clumsy farmer boys and craftsmen into good monks, I had to boldly work my way out [of this position] if I did not want to get caught or at least hobbled in all future undertakings. And if that did not work, then there was nothing else to do but to pull out and to settle down at a more suitable place.)

Therefore as early as May 1847 I asked the bishop to transfer the parish and the church *in perpetuum* to the Benedictine Order, with the condition that the superior of the future monastery would be *ipso facto* pastor and therefore owner of the two tracts which belonged to the church. He was not opposed to fulfilling my desire, but he felt he could make conditions with regard to the future seminary which I could not accept. The negotiations over this protracted themselves to some length and were still in process when Father Peter arrived. I doubted the feasibility of a favorable outcome and thought seriously again about leaving Saint Vincent, when on December 6, 1847, an agreement was reached which satisfied both parties. During this period of painful uncertainty, much valuable time was lost. I could build nothing because I did not know whether I could stay or not. Except for the manufacture of tables, benches, bedsteads and the management of the summer and winter crop, nothing significant was done by the brothers. Because a single building could not hold us, we occupied the priest's house, the school house, and the farmer's house.

The next spring we set vigorously to work on the preparations for construction. Bricks were struck and baked, trees felled, timber brought to the sawmill to make boards and lath, limestone cut and burned. The masons could begin their work only on September 29, 1848, and it was Christmas before we had the first construction under roof. It was 60 feet long, 3 stories high, and 40 feet wide. Only in the summer of 1849 was the construction completely done and habitable. The following year we built a barn and stalls in the American fashion, 3 stories high, so that the stalls are on the ground floor and the threshing floor above. We finished it in 1851. The building is 126 feet long and 40 feet wide, built entirely of brick. In 1852 and 1853 we lengthened the monastery building by 50 feet and also a wing of 50 feet. The following year [1854] we started on the steam gristmill to which we added the sawmill in 1855. In the mountains[13] we had already built a small sawmill and several adjoining buildings. Last fall we began a new building which touches the monastery on the front side. It has large cellars and a ground floor. It is four stories high and is 65 feet long. It will not be ready for occupancy before the middle of April [1856]. Between this and the earlier new construction lies the old priest's house which we will tear down right after Easter and then we will fill the resulting area with a new building. The whole will then have a frontage of 200 feet, with two other fronts at right angles to it, the western one 93 feet and the eastern one 65 feet, which will connect in about two years with the church which lies to the south and thus will form a complete square with it. A few auxiliary buildings must also be finished in the meantime so that the monastery will have three courtyards. The mill lies apart at the foot of the hill.

Besides these buildings, we have in the mountains a dwelling and a large barn; in Indiana a barn; in St. Marys a gristmill. This mill was first of wood, but when it burned it was rebuilt with stone. The sawmill [in St. Marys] which was built before we came and which was already dilapidated, has been repaired. In short, for the past eight years we have been building continually, both winter and summer, or have been preparing to build. Only in St. Marys did other skilled laborers join the brothers. At home only during last fall were a few masons called on for help. Otherwise everything was completed by the brothers with the single exception of the millwork which the millwright really had to do, though our carpenters and cabinet makers helped out.

Meanwhile, the number of brothers and priests grew, as did also our field of labor. Already in 1848 I purchased [property at] Carrolltown for $3,000 (7,500 florins), and Father Peter was sent with some brothers to take charge of the place and conduct a parish. In 1849 three priests were ordained in the monastery, of whom one soon took Father Peter's place in Carrolltown and another took over at St. Marys and helped out at other places at times. In August [1849] we took over at St. Marys for good, occupied it with two or three priests and twelve to fifteen lay brothers. Two or three priests were at the same time stationed in Carrolltown in order to expand their effectiveness. In 1852 Indiana was taken over permanently, in 1854 Butler and Cooper's Settlement. Now all of western Pennsylvania, with the exception of only those counties immediately lying along the Ohio border, is under our care as far as Germans are concerned. This is an area of over 500 German square miles in the three dioceses of Pittsburgh, Erie, and part of Philadelphia. Where there is no English-speaking priest we have the care also of the English-speaking Catholics. Several of these missions are very arduous, especially those at St. Marys and Cooper's Settlement, where the locality is still very rough and wooded, sparsely populated, and endangered by wild animals—bears, wolves, panthers, and poisonous snakes. The priests have to travel 40 to 80 miles to their stations, at times on roads where they seldom see a house. The Catholics of these regions, living in small clusters or often quite scattered, often saw no priest for years; some had never seen one. Civil marriages were common; children of ten to fifteen years of age were often not yet baptized, let alone instructed; the parents were indifferent to the faith or attended the Protestant churches. Mixed marriages with their sad con-

13. At the Benedictines' property on Chestnut Ridge, nine miles from the monastery.

sequences occurred everywhere. There were no churches except in the cities. Now churches have been built almost everywhere and schools erected. The priests come regularly on certain Sundays, conduct the service, preach, baptize, bless marriages, visit the sick, instruct the children, attempt to help the scattered Catholics get to know one another and organize themselves into congregations, distribute good books, introduce Catholic newspapers, attempt to ban corrupting books and newspapers, and in every way awaken and strengthen religious life through brotherhoods and societies. In truth, their efforts have been accompanied with blessed success which has not been curbed by the latest persecution of Know-Nothings but rather has been furthered by it.

Besides this pastoral care we have directed our main concern to the training of young men for the priesthood. In the beginning all the candidates for the Order came from Europe and primarily from Bavaria. In 1848 we opened a seminary into which we admitted American boys. We had little success with them at first. Our food was too poor for them and most of them left us. But by and by we received others who persevered. We are now twenty priests, of whom sixteen were ordained in America. Three others have already been taken by premature death after they had worked zealously in the care of souls. More than twelve have entered the diocesan clergy and work in other dioceses. Currently thirty-seven young men are studying theology and philosophy [for the Order] and six others are preparing for the diocesan clergy. Some 50 are in the gymnasium, of whom 17 are candidates for the Order. We now have a complete course of studies, so that we can lead young men from the elementary school through the gymnasium, then through philosophy and theology into the sanctuary of the priesthood. Father Peter Lechner was at the beginning the animating spirit of this institution. We have much to thank him for and regret that we no longer have him. Currently Father Ulrich Spöttl is director of the gymnasium. The higher studies are under the direction of Prior Demetrius Marogna.

We have good professors in Latin, Greek, English, German, French, and Italian. Our drawing school is not surpassed by any in the United States, and its collection of paintings is equal to any in Bavaria. Music is most zealously practiced, not only vocal but string and wind instruments and organ playing. Father Luke Wimmer has charge of the art school, and Father Leonard Mayer is director of music.

Besides the seminary for the training of clergy, we also have an institute for orphans or abandoned children who otherwise would be in danger of moral or spiritual ruin. They leave us after they have received their schooling; or, if they show signs of ability and calling, they are prepared for the clerical state. The expense of the seminary is very high because not only the food but also the clothing, books, etc. must be provided by the monastery and only a few pay. We have this year a total of one hundred students from whom we receive only $800, or an average of $8 each, whereas it costs us at least $50 a student to keep them. Therefore the monastery assumes the burden of at least $4,000, or 10,000 florins. Since last year, 1854, our crops were a complete failure, we consumed this sum. In the spring we had to buy $125 (315 florins) worth of bread or flour each week. But we preferred assuming these debts to sending the students away, for it was to be feared that some of them would lose their vocations.

The monastery owns about 4,000 acres of land of varying quality in different places. Most of it is still woodland and since wood has no value here, it is useless until it is brought under cultivation. Had we not been completely occupied with continuous construction, more land would be cultivated; however we have tilled many acres each year, and the more progress we make with the monastery buildings, the more we will be able to devote ourselves to agriculture. Up until now we have not been able to produce as much as was required for the needs of the community and the students, since our best hands were busy with construction. But since we have the steam gristmill, its income covers the deficit in grain; so that this year we did not need to buy any, although we use ten Bavarian bushels of flour a day. There is no doubt that in a short time production will be so high that it will be able to provide for twice the present number of students. But even if things should remain as they now are, much has been accomplished: priests are being provided for two dioceses and each year some are being prepared for ordination for other dioceses. The beginnings of new seminaries in other dioceses are being planted in the priories which we have founded or will be able to found. The money which has been or will be spent for this work has been fruitfully used and not simply squandered. If such a seminary had been founded in Germany, the buildings could not have been constructed for less than 100,000 florins. That doesn't even take into account the need for an endowment; to support 100 students in Bavaria would require, as a minimal estimate, an endowment of more than 300,000 florins. Moreover, the students would still be in Germany and perhaps would remain there. There would be no bond here in America to keep them together. And the seminary could not be sure of its existence for as much as a year, since this is always dependent upon the government of the nation where it would have been established.

It is entirely different here. The monastery was already approved in its initial growth by Pope Pius IX in 1848 and recognized as a monastery in 1850. Bishop Michael O'Connor of Pittsburgh did everything he could to establish the legal foundation and to assure its continuance. On April 19, 1853 the Benedictine Order in Pennsylvania was recognized by the highest authorities in the land, namely the two houses and the governor, under the name of the "Benedictine Society at Saint Vincent in Westmoreland County," as a corporation with all corporative rights: the right of a seal, its own laws, capacity to receive gifts, testaments, etc. and to procure land property up to $3,000 clear yearly income. Finally on August 24, 1855, His Holiness deigned to elevate the monastery to an abbey, to grant it exemption, and to enact that it should form with its existing dependencies of St. Marys and Carrolltown as well as priories or abbeys which would later arise from them a congregation following the statutes of the former Bavarian Benedictine Congregation in order to promote and maintain unity and mutual cooperation so that the two great aims striven after by the Order in the Middle Ages as well as at its beginnings could be more strongly pursued and therefore more strongly achieved: promotion of Christian art and scholarship through good discipline at home in a quiet monastery and the promotion of the salvation of others through pastoral work outside. Far from being opposed to the formation of a congregation and the related status of exemption, the bishops have expressed their friendly agreement and full satisfaction. And several have since then sent emphatic invitations that we introduce the Order into their dioceses.

The Order, and with it the monastery and seminary, is therefore as far as it is humanly possible, built upon a firm foundation, and the civil and ecclesiastical authorities have done all that could be done to foster its growth. To the same degree that the Order grows in effectiveness and number of its members and spreads out, the monasteries and seminaries will multiply and the scarcity of priests will disappear. The classical and theological sciences and religious art will find teachers and students, souls who are weary in the turmoil of the world or threatened by its dangers will find havens of refuge. This is the case with all religious orders and therefore there can never be enough of them in a country.

Since we probably will be able to have eight or ten priests ordained for several years in a row, we not only can but must think about founding new monasteries. We will have to choose the Far West as our field of labor since priests are scarcest there, Germans are most numerous there, and land the cheapest. Since we have the advantage of almost ten years of experience and know the language, laws, and customs of the inhabitants, it will not take nine years before a second abbey is established, especially if we will continue to enjoy the support of the Ludwig Missionsverein.

At present (February 1856) the personnel of Saint Vincent is made up of 20 priests, 5 clerics, 32 theologians and philosophers of whom 15 are in solemn vows, 22 novices, 17 scholastics in the gymnasium; there are 82 brothers at the abbey, 12 in St. Marys, 10 in Carrolltown, 4 in Indiana, 2 in St. Severin, 2 in Butler. Of the priests 2 are in Butler, 3 in St. Marys, 2 in St. Severin, 3 in Carrolltown, 1 in Indiana; the rest are at home. The priests who are for Indiana reside in the monastery but spend three days a week in Indiana. Relatively speaking, this is a small number, but in America there is hardly another place where there are so many priests in one place. The number of candidates is encouraging and consists mainly of native Americans. If more means had been at our disposal, or even if this were now the case, we could have done more. But it would be ungrateful not to appreciate the assistance given us or not to recognize God's blessing which visibly rested on our benefactors. His Majesty King Ludwig of Bavaria, to whom all the monasteries in Bavaria and several in America are indebted for their existence, stands in the first place as founder of our monastery. His Royal Highness encouraged the project from the beginning, supported it through a contribution of 10,000 florins in 1851 at a time when help was badly needed, and was personally instrumental in 1855 towards having Saint Vincent elevated to an abbey and placed under the immediate jurisdiction of the Holy See. For these benefactions of our Order's noble patron, a weekly Mass is offered in our monastery. The former bishop, now Cardinal Count von Reisach is the next on the list of patrons to our monastery, and with him all the members of the Central Directory of the Ludwig Missionsverein which, despite many doubts concerning the successful growth of the undertaking, did not neglect to promote the foundation and growth of the monastery through the yearly contribution of 5,000 florins—and in the last two years 7,000 florins.

The blessed Bishop Ziegler of Linz has also established a monument of perpetual thanksgiving in Saint Vincent in that he repeatedly during his life time, and now through his last will, remembered the monastery with the considerable sum of over $5,000. Therefore an annual memorial has been established for him. Abbots Gregory of Metten and Rupert of Scheyern have also cooperated according to their abilities towards the spreading and establishing of our Order in America.

The abbot of Metten sent me, at it was expressed in the testimonials which he issued to me, to America in order to found at least one monastery or if possible several monasteries, so that through them the spiritual needs of the Catholic inhabitants of America could be best served. At that time, when Metten itself had but few priests, was in need of many, and therefore could not spare any, the abbot made a great sacrifice for this good cause. That is not all. He supported me with money and sent me help in the person of Father Thaddeus Brunner. Abbot Rupert of Scheyern did the same thing by sending Father Peter Lechner who for three years rendered the most useful service to the young monastery; he also sent money.

There is still a long list of benefactors to mention, among whom are names from the highest ranks of society and from the clergy, but I prefer not to offend their modesty by giving their names. There is however one name which I cannot leave unmentioned, although he is already included in the above-mentioned benefactors of the monastery. Reverend Court Chaplain Joseph Ferdinand Müller, former business manager of the Ludwig Missionsverein has a special right to the thanks of the Pennsylvania Benedictines. He went to astounding efforts to direct many good men as brothers and students to our monastery and always proceeded with so much prudence and circumspection that almost without exception the men whom he recommended to us became exemplary members of the community. He also supplied the generous service of procuring for us all those things required for the furnishing of the monastery and seminary. He procured all the musical instruments, the patterns for drawing, books in the library, a large amount of church vessels, vestments, chalices, etc. and many other things which cannot be gotten here or only at a very high price, and he strove to be useful in every way. There is hardly a brother, student, or priest who came here from Europe who is not indebted to him. Seminary Inspector and Professor G. Sterr of Regensburg also sent the monastery several good people and helped in other ways, for which we also owe him thanks.

It gives me great pleasure to often look over the list of our benefactors. I see then that my share in all the good which has been accomplished is very small, especially when I remember that the prayers of all the members of the Missionsverein must be considered when one speaks about the success of a good work. Because perhaps a pious old lady or some innocent soul with a rosary in hand has done more for this success than I with all my labors and cares.

But it was always my earnest endeavor to labor for the spreading of our holy Catholic religion, for I am convinced, and always was, that this can best occur through the spread of the Benedictine Order. That I found such a general and active cooperation and support from among nobility and common people, from clergy and laity has afforded me much pleasure and has spurred all of us on to greater effort, dedication, and perseverance in the continuation of our work.

Permit me at the end to make a remark. The mention of so many benefactors, besides the regular subsidies of the Ludwig Missionsverein, must give the impression that much, very much, money was given for Saint Vincent, so that one should easily have been able to do much more with it and that at least there should be no debts. However, there is a debt of $6,000. Whoever has undertaken construction knows well how much money it takes. But when one builds in one place for nine years and constructs many shops for which much expensive work and material must be used, as is the case with the three mills, very considerable outlays [of money] must necessarily be made. But I have never received the subsidies in cash. Some years almost half of it remained in Munich for the purchase of church accessories (for some 20 churches and missionaries): musical instruments, books, cloth, etc. Many such things I received as gifts it is true, but the freight costs and the import duty caused high costs which in no year amounted to under $200 (500 florins), more often over $500 (1,300 florins). If I were to show exactly the income and expenditures, certainly anyone would have to come to the opposite conclusion, namely that with so little money so much could be accomplished and through a special blessing of God the money, so to speak, grew. Last year the expenditures exceeded 40,000 florins!

The question whether we should think now or later about the foundation of new monasteries in the West occupies us intensely. There are reasons for it and against it. I would not be in America if I had not believed resolutely that now is the time and need for the Benedictine Order to spread out. I am of this opinion even yet because I believe it is easier to lock the gates of the fortress to the enemy when you occupy it before him than to throw him out of the fortress if he gets there first. Also, if the general is not too neglectful, discipline is more strictly observed in the field than in the barracks. Therefore I will miss no opportunity to establish a new colony of our Order in the West where the stream of emigration now presses, and I hope for this to have the support of the Central Directory.

With deepest respect and humility, Boniface Wimmer, O.S.B., Abbot

Archives of the Ludwig Missionsverein, Munich. Copy and translation in the Archives of Saint Vincent Archabbey, Latrobe, Pennsylvania.

APPENDIX 8

CHARTER OF SAINT VINCENT COLLEGE

APRIL 18, 1870

AN ACT TO INCORPORATE THE ST VINCENT COLLEGE IN THE TOWNSHIP OF UNITY IN THE COUNTY OF WESTMORELAND

Section 1 Be it enacted by the Senate and House of Representatives of the Commonwealth of Pennsylvania in General Assembly met and it is hereby enacted by the authority of the same That there be and is hereby established in the township of Unity in the county of Westmoreland in the Commonwealth of Pennsylvania a college for the education of youth in the various branches of science literature and the arts by the name and style of the St Vincent college in the State of Pennsylvania

Section 2 That the said college shall be under the management direction and government of a number of trustees not exceeding seven a majority of whom shall be a quorum and competent to fill vacancies in their own body who shall appoint a president and faculty and to prescribe the duties to be performed by said president and faculty

Section 3 That the first trustees of said college shall consist of Luke Weimer Rev Boniface Wimmer Giles Christoph Alphonse Heinler Otto Huber John Lommer and Ignatius Trucy[14] which said trustees and their successors to be appointed as

14. *Recte,* Luke Wimmer (1825–1901), Boniface Wimmer (1809–87), Giles Christoph (1830–87), Alphonse Heimler (1832–1909), Utto Huber (1819–96), John Sommer (1815–86), and Ignatius Trueg (1854–1910).

often as occasion may require by said trustees shall be forever hereafter and they are hereby erected into and declared to be a body politic and corporate with perpetual succession with all the incidents corporation in deed and in law to all intents and purposes whatsoever under the name and style of the St Vincent college in the State of Pennsylvania by which name and title the said Rev Boniface Wimmer Giles Christoph Luke Wimmer Alphonse Heimler Otto Huber John Lommer and Ignatius Trucy and their successors shall be able and capable in law and in equity to take to themselves and their successors for the use of the said college any estate in any messuages lands tenements hereditaments goods chattels moneys or other effects by gifts grant bargain sale conveyance assurance will devise or bequest of any person or persons or corporation whatsoever *Provided* The annual income of the same exclusive of the income from students does not exceed the yearly value of five thousand dollars and the same messuages lands tenements hereditaments and estates real and personal to grant bargain sell convey assign demise and to farm let and place out at interest or otherwise dispose of or invest the proceeds of same for the use of said college in such manner as to them shall seem most beneficial for the said college and to receive the rents issues profits and income of the same and to apply the same to the proper use of said college and by the same name to sue commence actions prosecute and defend implead and be impleaded in any courts of law and equity in all manner of suits and actions whatsoever and generally by and in the corporate name style and title aforesaid to do and transact all and every business the education of youth and others or touching the property belonging to the said college or which shall be in any manner incident thereto as fully and effectually as any natural person or body politic or corporate have power to manage their own concerns and to hold enjoy and exercise all such powers and authorities as are held enjoyed or exercised by any other college or university within this Commonwealth

Section 4 That said corporation may cause to be made for their use a common seal with such devices and inscriptions thereon as they may deem proper and by and with which all deeds diplomas certificates appointments and acts of the said corporation shall pass and be authenticated and the same seal at their pleasure to alter and renew

Section 5 The corporators named in this act or a majority of them shall at all times constitute a quorum for the transaction of business They shall have power to transact all business of the said college and to exercise all the powers conferred by this act on the corporation and of electing and removing officers and professors and appointing and authorizing a person or persons to carry into execution any resolution or business of the board or to exercise any of the corporate powers to attend to the duties of the college and manage the affairs of the corporation

Section 6 The president and professors for the time being of the said college shall have power to grant and confer such degrees in the arts and sciences to such students of the college and others when by their proficiency in learning professional eminence or other meritorious distinction they shall be entitled thereto as they may see proper or as are granted in other colleges and universities in the United States and to grant to graduates or persons on whom such degrees may be conferred diplomas or certificates as is usual in colleges and universities

Section 7 The corporators or a majority of them and the president and professors by authority of the trustees shall have power to make rules laws and ordinances and the same to alter and repeal and to do every thing needful for the support and government of the college *Provided* The said rules laws and ordinances be not in violation of the Constitution and laws of the United States or of the State of Pennsylvania

Section 8 No misnomer of the said corporation shall defeat or annul any gift grant conveyance assurance demise or bequest to the said corporation

[Signed] B. B. Strang, Speaker of the House of Reps
Charles H. Stinson, Speaker of the Senate

Approved, the Eighteenth day of April Anno Domini one thousand eight hundred and Seventy

[Signed] Jno. W. Geary

Legislature of Pennsylvania, File of the Senate, no. 1057; copy in ASVA.

APPENDIX 9

ARCHABBOT AURELIUS STEHLE TO THE MONKS OF THE AMERICAN CASSINESE CONGREGATION ON THE FOUNDING OF THE CATHOLIC UNIVERSITY OF PEKING

OCTOBER 5, 1924

Saint Vincent Archabbey, Beatty, Pennsylvania

Dearly-beloved Brethren: The steady advance of the work inaugurated by St. Benedict has brought his sons to the uttermost confines of the Western World. And now the hour has struck, when they must cross the Pacific, to plant the standard of Christ upon still another continent—"*Vexilla regis prodeunt!*" The Holy See hails with joy the advent in China of the Benedictine Fathers, and sees in their presence there a new and striking evidence of the miraculous universality of the Catholic Church.

The Benedictine is no mere preacher. He brings with him, in his monasticism, a complete miniature of the ideal Christian society. This is what makes him an apostle par excellence. "By the mere fact of settling among a people," says Cardinal Gasquet, speaking of the monks who converted Europe, "and exhibiting to them the excellence and beauty of the Christian life, they won them insensibly to adopt the Christian creed, as by exhibiting the arts of peace in operation before the eyes of the uncultivated races of the Western world the monks taught them the value of a civilised life." And again His Eminence observes: "It is not too much to say that few nations of the modern world have been converted to Christianity, or tutored in the arts of peace except through the medium of monasticism." It is for this reason that the Holy See augurs great things for the Church from the extension of Benedictine influence to China. The religious is a soldier; the monk is a colonist, and herein lies the secret of the latter's apostolic efficacy. China has had many religious missionaries, but it is especially by the monastic missionary that its ultimate conversion will be achieved.

We draw inspiration and confidence from the glorious past of Benedictinism, but we may not rest upon the laurels earned by the sweat of those, who have preceded us. Rome admonishes us that a "mighty task" *(magnum opus),* one that is "assuredly difficult" *(sane difficile)* lies before us, and has, in consideration of this fact, authorized us to appeal for aid not alone to our Benedictine confreres, but likewise to all the Bishops and all the faithful of America. The task, which confronts us, is one that will tax every resource available to us, and we cannot, therefore, afford to neglect any legitimate source of revenue. Our non-Catholic competitors in China have richly-endowed universities, with learned faculties and splendid equipment. To vie with them, we must muster all the resources at our command. There are sites to be purchased, faculties to be trained and organized, laboratories to be equipped, libraries to be collected, etc., etc. Rome insists that the university shall be a genuine one, in every respect, and His Eminence, Cardinal Van Rossum,[15] warns us that the Holy See expects great things of us.

Under such circumstances, the monks of St. Vincent Archabbey might well be appalled at the magnitude of the task assigned to them, were it not for the consciousness that they bear a commission from the General Chapter backed by a promise of co-operation on the part of all the abbeys of the American-Cassinese Congregation. The present circular has been drawn up, in consultation with the Rt. Rev. President of our Congregation,[16] in order to suggest the form which this co-operation may most advantageously take. It goes without saying that the new university will require assistance mainly in two respects, namely, first, in the raising of necessary funds, and second, in the recruiting of personnel. Consequently, it is under these two headings that ways and means of co-operation must be discussed.

I. *Raising of Funds:* In this matter, the monasteries of our Congregation can be of assistance in the following ways:

(1) As regards collections: They can use their influence with the local Ordinaries and the local clergies to secure a welcome in the various parishes for such of our representatives as will be sent to preach collections in said parishes, and this will be especially feasible in the case of Benedictine parishes. In fact, one document from the Holy See makes particular mention of the advisability of an appeal to parishes presided over by Benedictine pastors. Nevertheless a general appeal to all dioceses and parishes is authorized, as the enclosed document indicates. Copies of this letter of Cardinal Van Rossum will be gladly furnished, on application, by St. Vincent

15. William Cardinal van Rossum, Prefect of the Sacred Congregation for the Propagation of the Faith.

16. Abbot Ernest Helmstetter, O.S.B., of St. Mary's Abbey, Newark, New Jersey

Archabbey. The collections, if managed with tact and prudence, can be taken up *pro opportunitate,* without entailing much inconvenience to anyone concerned.

(2) As regards mission-societies: In parishes, colleges, schools, etc. under Benedictine auspices and otherwise, there are generally mission-societies, whose contributions could not be better utilized than in supporting a project so dear to the heart of the Holy Father as that of the Catholic University of Peking.

(3) As regards private donations: One often meets with individuals both of the laity and of religious communities, who have the desire as well as the means, to do something for the Foreign Missions. A timely suggestion given to such persons would induce them to espouse the important cause of furthering the success of the aforesaid University.

N.B. Literature dealing with the subject in hand will be cheerfully furnished for distribution by the Archabbey Press.

II. *Recruiting a Personnel:* In the matter of providing a teaching staff for the new University, the Archabbey of St. Vincent is prepared to make every sacrifice. We do not expect the smaller and weaker abbeys of the Congregation to furnish recruits. For the larger abbeys, however, the concession of at least one volunteer to the cause does not seem to be an excessive expectation. In any case, the volunteers selected for the work should be young and scholarly. Youth adapts itself readily to new conditions; and, as for scholarship, it is manifest that one unqualified in this respect would be of no value to an undertaking like a university.

Finally, there is one important way, in which all our abbeys, both great and small, can co-operate most effectively toward ensuring a desirable personnel for the various Faculties of the Benedictine University of Peking. One and all, they can present and urge our project to young men contemplating the missionary vocation. They can broadcast the fact that now the American Benedictines offer a splendid opportunity for doing far more efficient work toward the conversion of heathendom than the ordinary missionary can ever hope to accomplish. Candidates, who respond to this appeal, can either be trained in local novitiates, or be sent to St. Vincent Archabbey.

Solemn and momentous is the charge, which the Holy See has confided to our Congregation and to St. Vincent Archabbey. Rome bids us to do for China what the first members of our Order did for Europe during the Middle Ages. This means that we must preserve and christianize Chinese literature, art, and philosophy. This means that we must place before the eyes of the Chinese people an ideal exemplar of truly Christian civilization. The monks of St. Vincent will do their best to prove worthy of this trust, and in their effort to do so, they are consoled and heartened by the encouraging pledge of the General Chapter: *"ceteris monasteriis nostrae Congregationis pro viribus co-operantibus."*[17]

Saint Benedict of Nursia, pray for us!

Aurelius, O.S.B., *Archabbot of St. Vincent*
Feast of St. Placidus, October 5, 1924

Located in ASVA.

17. "that other monasteries of our Congregation will provide such assistance as is in their power."

ENDNOTES

NOTES TO CHAPTER I. A PARISH ON THE FRONTIER

1. *The Rule of St. Benedict* (Collegeville, Minn.: The Liturgical Press, 1980), Prologue, 45.

2. RAB: Wimmer to Ludwig I, St. Vincent, July 23, 1849.

3. James B. Griffin, "Late Prehistory of the Ohio Valley," in *Handbook of North American Indians: Northeast,* Vol. 15, ed. Bruce G. Trigger (Washington, D.C.: Smithsonian Institution, 1978), 557–59.

4. William A. Hunter, "History of the Ohio Valley," in *Handbook of North American Indians: Northeast,* 15: 588–93; and John N. Boucher, *Old and New Westmoreland,* Vol. 1 (New York: The American Historical Society, 1918), 162–63.

5. W. F. Dunaway, *A History of Pennsylvania* (New York: Prentice-Hall, 1935), 119–33; Boucher, *Old and New Westmoreland,* 1:11–69.

6. Boucher, *Old and New Westmoreland,* 1:142–44.

7. Dunaway, *A History of Pennsylvania,* 134–35; Boucher, *Old and New Westmoreland,* 1:121–36.

8. Boucher, *Old and New Westmoreland,* 1:146–53; Dunaway, *A History of Pennsylvania,* 234–35.

9. Boucher, *Old and New Westmoreland,* 1:249–57; Felix Fellner, "Colonel George Washington and a Forgotten Camp in Unity Township," *St. Vincent's Journal* 49 (1939–40): 13, 15.

10. Dunaway, *A History of Pennsylvania,* 188–191; Boucher, *Old and New Westmoreland,* 1:261–362.

11. Boucher, *Old and New Westmoreland,* 1:85–86.

12. James Hennesey, *American Catholics: A History of the Roman Catholic Community in the United States* (New York: Oxford University Press, 1981), 49–52; Jay P. Dolan, *The American Catholic Experience: A History from Colonial Times to the Present* (New York: Doubleday, 1985), 87; William H. Maloney, *Our Catholic Roots: Old Churches East of the Mississippi* (Huntington, Ind.: Our Sunday Visitor Publishing Co., 1992), 195–96, 227–29, 253–54, 259–60; Lambert Schrott, *Pioneer German Catholics in the American Colonies* (1734–1784) (New York: United States Catholic Historical Society, 1933); and Dunaway, *A History of Pennsylvania,* 352–53.

13. Gerard Bridge, *An Illustrated History of St. Vincent Archabbey* (Beatty, Pa.: St. Vincent Archabbey Press, 1922), 1. See also Felix Fellner, "Early Catholicity in Western Pennsylvania," in *Catholic Pittsburgh's One Hundred Years,* ed. William J. Purcell (Chicago: Loyola University Press, 1943), 9–16.

14. Edmund Adams and Barbara Brady O'Keefe, *Catholic Trails West: The Founding Catholic Families of Pennsylvania,* vol. 2 (Baltimore: Gateway Press, 1989), 446–55; Maloney, *Our Catholic Roots,* 227–28; A. A. Lambing, *A History of the Catholic Church in the Dioceses of Pittsburg and Allegheny from Its Establishment to the Present Time* (New York: Benziger Bros., 1880), 20–21.

15. Thomas O'Brien Hanley, ed., *The John Carroll Papers,* 3 vols. (Notre Dame, Ind.: University of Notre Dame Press, 1976), 2: 256–57.

16. The most thorough and detailed account of the first Catholic congregation in Westmoreland County is Father Omer U. Kline's *The Sportsman's Hall Parish, Later Named Saint Vincent, 1790–1846* (Latrobe, Pa.: Archabbey Press, 1990), from which I have drawn extensively for the discussion that follows. The story of the Sportsman's Hall parish has been told many times over the years; among the more important discussions are those by Adams and O'Keefe, *Catholic Trails West,* 567–79; Bridge, *Illustrated History of St. Vincent Archabbey,* 1–43; Felix Fellner, *Abbot Boniface and His Monks,* vol. 1 (Latrobe, Pa.: Privately published, 1956), 68–75; Louis Haas, *St. Vincent's: Souvenir of the Consecration of the New Abbey Church, August 26, 1905* (Latrobe, Pa.: St. Vincent Press, 1905), 3–10; Vincent Huber, "Sportsman's Hall and St. Vincent Abbey," *St. Vincent's Journal* 1 (1892): passim, and "Sportsman's Hall," *Records of the American Catholic Historical Society of Philadelphia* 3 (1888–91): 142–73; Lambing, *A History of the Catholic Church in the Dioceses of Pittsburg and Allegheny,* 359–72; and Oswald Moosmüller, *St. Vincenz in Pennsylvanien* (New York, Cincinnati: F. Pustet, 1873), 43–87.

17. Adams and O'Keefe, *Catholic Trails West,* 2: 453, 567.

18. The deed of transfer is printed in Moosmüller, *St. Vincenz in Pennsylvanien,* 357–60.

19. See the deed ibid., 361–63. For a discussion of ownership of the land prior to Brouwers' purchase of it, see Omer U. Kline, "The Origins of Saint Vincent and the 'Sportsman's Hall Tract,'" *Saint Vincent* 18 (Summer 1984): 4–6.

20. AAB: Carroll to Cause, Baltimore, August 16, 1785 (*John Carroll Papers,* 1:193–94).

21. Peter Guilday, *The Life and Times of John Carroll, Archbishop of Baltimore, 1735–1815,* vol. 2 (New York: Encyclopedia Press, 1922), 646–47.

22. The will, dated October 24, 1790, is filed in the registry of wills at the county court house, Greensburg, Pa., under the date of registry, November 5, 1790. It is printed with typographical errors in Moosmüller, *St. Vincenz in Pennsylvanien,* 363–65, and Huber, "Sportsman's Hall," 148–49. See Bridge, *Illustrated History of St. Vincent Archabbey,* 6–8; Huber, "Sportsman's Hall," 146; and Adams and O'Keefe, *Catholic Trails West,* 568–69.

23. Fellner, *Abbot Boniface and His Monks,* 1:86.

24. Bridge, *Illustrated History of St. Vincent Archabbey,* 9–10; Huber, "Sportsman's Hall," 147–48; Guilday, *John Carroll,* 2:647.

25. ACPF: Carroll to Antonelli, Baltimore, April 23, 1792 (*John Carroll Papers,* 2:32). See also Carroll to Plowden, Baltimore, March 1, 1792 (*John Carroll Papers,* 2:21–22); Carroll's sermon to the Holy Trinity Congregation (*John Carroll Papers,* 2:56–57); and Raymond Schroth, ed., "The Excommunication of Reverend John Baptist Causse: An Unpublished Sermon by Bishop John Carroll of Baltimore," *Records of the American Catholic Historical Society of Philadelphia* 81 (1970): 42–56.

26. AAB: Carroll to Cause, Baltimore, June 4, 1793 (*John Carroll Papers,* 2:92).

27. ACPF: Carroll to Antonelli, Baltimore, August 6, 1789 (*John Carroll Papers,* 2:377–78).

28. AAB: Carroll to Fromm, Baltimore, February 16, 1791 (*John Carroll Papers,* 2:493).

29. AAB: Carroll to Fromm, [Baltimore], April 5, 1791 (*John Carroll Papers,* 1:502–3).

30. The document is printed by Huber in "Sportsman's Hall," 150.

31. AAB: Carroll to [a Pennsylvania lawyer], Georgetown, August 24, 1798 (*John Carroll Papers,* 2:241–45). "I observed before, that the Archbishop of Mainz did not write the letter, produced by Fromm under his name."

32. AAB: Carroll to Fromm, Baltimore, August 23, 1791 (*John Carroll Papers,* 1:511–12).

33. ASVA: Fromm to executors, Philadelphia, August 11, 1791; printed in Vincent Huber, "Sportsman's Hall and St. Vincent Abbey," *St. Vincent's Journal* 1 (1891): 111–12. See also Huber, "Sportsman's Hall," 151.

34. AAB: Carroll to Brancadoro, Baltimore, February 9, 1799 (*John Carroll Papers,* 2:264–65).

35. AAB: Carroll to Fromm, Baltimore, May 13, 1793 (*John Carroll Papers,* 2:91).

36. AAB: Carroll to Pembridge, Baltimore, September 19, 1794 (*John Carroll Papers,* 2:128–29); Carroll to Plowden, Baltimore, November 15, 1794 (ibid., 2:131–32). See Rene Kollar, "Plans for an 18th-Century Benedictine Settlement in Western Pennsylvania: Bishop John Carroll and the English Benedictine Congregation," *Word and Spirit: A Monastic Review* 14 (1992): 3–11; and Hennesey, *American Catholics,* 81.

37. AAB: Carroll to Fromm, [Baltimore], April 18–30, 1794 (*John Carroll Papers,* 2:115–16).

38. Kline, *Sportsman's Hall Parish,* 14–16. See AAB: Carroll to the congregation of Westmoreland County, [Baltimore], August 5, 1775 (*John Carroll Papers,* 2:148).

39. AAB: Phelan to Carroll, Greensburg, October 17, 1795; quoted in Kline, *Sportsman's Hall Parish,* 17–18.

40. AAB: Westmoreland trustees to Carroll, Greensburg, January 23, 1796; quoted in Bridge, *Illustrated History of St. Vincent Archabbey,* 13.

41. AAB: Carroll to Fromm, [Baltimore], October 18, 1795 (*John Carroll Papers,* 2:152).

42. Kline, *Sportsman's Hall Parish,* 18–20.

43. AAB: Carroll to [a Pennsylvania lawyer], Georgetown, August 24, 1798 (*John Carroll Papers,* 2:241–45).

44. The transcript of the civil trial is filed in the Westmoreland County Court House, Greensburg, Pa., December Term, 1768, and printed in Moosmüller, *St. Vincenz in Pennsylvanien,* 365–76, and Huber, "Sportsman's Hall," 152–59.

45. Quoted in Huber, "Sportsman's Hall," 160.

46. ASVA: Helbron to Friend, Greensburg, August 20, 1800; quoted in Bridge, *Illustrated History of St. Vincent Archabbey,* 19.

47. Huber, "Sportsman's Hall," 163. See *Catholic Baptisms in Western Pennsylvania, 1799–1828: Father Peter Helbron's Greensburg Register* (Baltimore: Genealogical Publishing Co., 1985); reprinted from *Records of the American Catholic Historical Society of Philadelphia,* September 1915–December 1917.

48. Bridge, *Illustrated History of St. Vincent Archabbey,* 18.

49. ASVA: Helbron to friend, Greensburg, January 30, 1801; quoted in Bridge, *Illustrated History of St. Vincent Archabbey,* 20.

50. Kline, *Sportsman's Hall Parish,* 28.

51. Ibid., 30–32; and Adams and O'Keefe, *Catholic Trails West,* 572–74.

52. See *Father Peter Helbron's Greensburg Register;* ASVA: Subscription list for the church at Sportsman's Hall, 1810; Bridge, *Illustrated History of St. Vincent Archabbey,* 27; Huber, "Sportsman's Hall," 162–63; and Adams and O'Keefe, *Catholic Trails West,* 572–74.

53. Kline, *Sportsman's Hall Parish,* 28–29; and Adams and O'Keefe, *Catholic Trails West,* 574–79.

54. ASVA: Subscription list for altar at Sportsman's Hall, May 1816. The list is printed in Bridge, *Illustrated History of St. Vincent Archabbey,* 29.

55. Act of the Pennsylvania Assembly, March 7, 1821; printed in Bridge, *Illustrated History of St. Vincent Archabbey,* 32.

56. Patrick Carey, "The Laity's Understanding of the Trustee System, 1785–1855," *Catholic Historical Review* 64 (1978): 358.

57. Dolan, *The American Catholic Experience,* 110.

58. Quoted in Carey, "The Laity's Understanding of the Trustee System," 358.

59. See Dolan, *The American Catholic Experience,* 111, 165–68.

60. Huber, "Sportsman's Hall and St. Vincent Abbey," 370; quoted in Kline, *Sportsman's Hall Parish,* 42.

61. ASVA: Minutes of the meetings of the trustees of Sportsman's Hall Parish, August 29, 1825; printed in Huber, "Sportsman's Hall," 170.

62. ASVA: Gallitzin to Maguire, Loretto, November 23, 1828; printed in Huber, "Sportsman's Hall," 167–68.

63. ASVA: Minutes of the meetings of the trustees of Sportsman's Hall Parish, October 12, 1829, and September 4, 1830; printed in Huber, "Sportsman's Hall," 170.

64. *Diary and Visitation Record of the Rt. Rev. Francis Patrick Kenrick, Administrator and Bishop of Philadelphia, 1830–1851,* ed. Francis E. Tourscher (Lancaster, Pa.: Wickersham Print Co., 1916), 39.

65. Archives of Mount St. Mary's College: Kenrick to Purcell, Philadelphia, November 8, 1830 (copy in ASVA); printed in Bridge, *Illustrated History of St. Vincent Archabbey,* 36–37, and Kline, *Sportsman's Hall Parish,* 57.

66. ASVA: Kenrick to the congregation at Sportsman's Hall, August 24, 1831; printed in Bridge, *Illustrated History of St. Vincent Archabbey,* 37–38, and Kline, *Sportsman's Hall Parish,* 60–61.

67. ASVA: Minutes of the meetings of the trustees of Sportsman's Hall Parish, May 28, 1832; printed in Huber, "Sportsman's Hall," 172.

68. ASVA: Kenrick to Stillinger, Philadelphia, July 4, 1833.

69. ASVA: List of contributors to the construction of the church at Sportsman's Hall, July 24, 1833; printed in Bridge, *Illustrated History of St. Vincent Archabbey,* 39–40.

70. *Diary and Visitation Record of the Rt. Rev. Francis Patrick Kenrick,* 108–10; Kline, *Sportsman's Hall Parish,* 63–66.

71. Thomas J. Quigley, "The School System in the Diocese," in *Catholic Pittsburgh's One Hundred Years,* 128–29.

72. *Diary and Visitation Record of the Rt. Rev. Francis Patrick Kenrick,* 165, 175, 210; Kline, *Sportsman's Hall Parish,* 68.

73. Henry Szarnicki, *Michael O'Connor, First Catholic Bishop of Pittsburgh, 1843–1860* (Pittsburgh: Wolfson Publishing Co., 1975), 17–35.

74. Ibid., 43.

75. ASVA: Bruté to Stillinger, Mount St. Mary's, July 6, 1831.

76. *Diary and Visitation Record of the Rt. Rev. Francis Patrick Kenrick,* 210.

77. Archives of the Archdiocese of Omaha: Michael O'Connor to James O'Connor, Cambria County, September 16, 1844; quoted in Szarnicki, *Michael O'Connor,* 56.

78. Szarnicki, *Michael O'Connor,* 63, 193, and Kline, *Sportsman's Hall Parish,* 82–83. See University of Notre Dame Manuscript Collections: O'Connor to Purcell, Pittsburgh, April 30, 1845; June 17, 1845; and December 16, 1845; and ASVA: Wimmer to the Ludwig Missionsverein, St. Vincent, February 1856.

79. Szarnicki, *Michael O'Connor,* 54, and Kline, *Sportsman's Hall Parish,* 81–82.

80. Szarnicki, *Michael O'Connor,* 54; Kline, *Sportsman's Hall Parish,* 82; "Looking Backward: St. Xavier's Farm Before the Sisters Came and After," *St. Xavier's Journal* 36 (April–June 1926): 6–11; Kathleen Healy, *Frances Warde: American Founder of the Sisters of Mercy* (New York: Seabury Press, 1973); and ASVA: Wimmer to Ziegler, St. Vincent, November 6, 1846.

81. On Lemke's formidable life, see Peter Beckman, *Kansas Monks: A History of St. Benedict's Abbey* (Atchison, Kans.: Abbey Student Press, 1957), 9–13; Lawrence M. Flick, "Biographical Sketch of Reverend Peter H. Lemke, O.S.B., 1796–1882," *Records of the American Catholic Historical Society* 9 (1898): 184ff.; Terence Kardong, "Peter Henry Lemke: 'Brave Soldier of the Lord' or Gyrovague?" *Tjurunga: An Australian Benedictine Review* 24 (1983): 44–65; Peter Henry Lemke, "Autobiography," *The Northern Cambria News* (Carrolltown, Pa.), June 7–November 22, 1879; Willibald Mathäser, ed. *Haudegen Gottes: Das Leben des Peter H. Lemke* (Würzburg: Kommissionsverlag Echte Gesamtherstellung, 1971); and Modestus Wirtner, *The Benedictine Fathers in Cambria County, Pennsylvania* (Carrolltown, Pa.: Privately published, 1926), 27–66.

82. Lemke, "Autobiography," *The Northern Cambria News,* November 8, 1879. Lemke indeed proposed a Benedictine establishment in western Pennsylvania long before Wimmer did. In a letter published in the *Mainzer Monatschrift* on January 29, 1835, he had written: "What do you think, my dearest friend? Would it not be a great thing if a number of con-

genial religious and lay brothers would settle among these plain, honest people, and would, according to the old Benedictine custom, clear up forests and engage in teaching the arts and sciences, pray and educate the people? The necessary freedom for such work exists here and land can be bought, many thousands of acres, at from one to two dollars an acre, but where is the money to come from for such a purpose? If the ground were purchased, the rest would follow. The messengers of the gospel did not thrive in our German forests in carriages; nor did they in the beginning live in palatial monasteries. This is really the only way in which Catholicity will ever get a proper foothold here in this country. Everything else is lamentable patchwork, and, depend upon it, I have already learned the full meaning of this proposition." Quoted in Wirtner, *The Benedictine Fathers in Cambria County,* 52.

83. AMA: Wimmer to Scherr, Munich, May 28, 1845.

NOTES TO CHAPTER 2.
THE *PROJEKTENMACHER* OF METTEN

1. Karl Bihlmeyer, *Church History: Modern and Recent Times,* revised by Herman Tüchle, translated by V. E. Mills and F. J. Muller (Westminster, Md.: Newman Press, 1968), 306.

2. Chester Penn Higby, *The Religious Policy of the Bavarian Government during the Napoleonic Period* (New York: AMS Press, 1967–1919]) and Georg Schwaiger and Paul Mai, *Johann Michael Sailer und seine Zeit* (Regensburg: Verlag des Vereins für Regensburger Bistumsgeschichte, 1982).

3. Egon Caesar Corti, *Ludwig I von Bayern* (Munich: Bruckmann, 1979); Michael Dirrigl, *Ludwig I: König von Bayern, 1825–1848* (Munich: Hugendubel, 1980); Heinz Gollwitzer, *Ludwig I von Bayern, Königtum im Vormärz: Eine politische Biographie* (Munich: Süddeutscher Verlag, 1986).

4. Wilhelm Fink, *Beiträge zur Geschichte der bayerischen Benediktiner-Kongregation: Eine Jubiläumsschrift 1684–1934* (Munich: Kommissionsverlag R. Oldenbourg, 1934).

5. For a detailed account of Wimmer's life, see Jerome Oetgen, *An American Abbot: Boniface Wimmer, O.S.B., 1809–1887,* 2d ed. (Washington, D.C.: Catholic University of America Press, 1997). Other accounts include Colman J. Barry, "Boniface Wimmer, Pioneer of the American Benedictines," *Catholic Historical Review* 41 (1955): 272–96; Felix Fellner, *Abbot Boniface and His Monks,* 5 vols. (Latrobe, Pa.: Privately published by St. Vincent Archabbey, 1956); Felix Fellner, "Archabbot Boniface Wimmer as an Educator," *The National Benedictine Educational Association Bulletin* 25 (1942): 90–106; J. S. "Rt. Rev. Boniface Wimmer, O.S.B., Founder of St. Vincent's," *St. Vincent Journal* 18 (1909): 151–66; Bernhard Lester, "Erzabt Bonifaz Wimmer: Das Bild eines deutschen Mannes in Amerika," *Frankfurter Zeitgemaesse Broschueren* 12 (1891): 397–424; Willibald Mathäser, *Bonifaz Wimmer O.S.B. und König Ludwig I von Bayern* (Munich: J. Pfeiffer, 1938); Oswald Moosmüller, *Bonifaz Wimmer, Erzabt von St. Vincent in Pennsylvania* (New York: Benziger, 1891); and Sebastian Wimmer, "Biographical Sketch of Rt. Rev. Arch-Abbot Wimmer, O.S.B., D.D., Patriarch of the American Cassinese Benedictines," *Records of the American Catholic Historical Society of Philadelphia* 3 (1891): 174–93.

6. AMA: Wimmer to Nebauer, Altötting, May 22, 1832. Translated by Conrad Zimmerman and Meinulph Schmiesing in "Wimmer Letters," *The Scriptorium* (St. John's Abbey) 17 (1958): 55.

7. AMA: Wimmer to Scherr, Munich, n.d., n.m., 1842. See Oetgen, *An American Abbot,* pp. 27–31.

8. See Colman J. Barry, *The Catholic Church and German Americans* (Milwaukee: Bruce Publishing Co., 1953), 6; and Roger Daniels, *Coming to America: A History of Immigration and Ethnicity in American Life* (New York: HarperCollins, 1990), 145–46. For additional details see Philip Taylor, *The Distant Magnet: European Emigration to the United States of America* (New York: Harper and Row, 1971); Howard B. Furer, *The Germans in America 1607–1970*

(Dobbs Ferry, N.Y.: Oceana, 1973); Theodore Roemer, *The Leopoldine Foundation and the Church in the United States* (New York: U.S. Catholic Historical Society, 1933); and Theodore Roemer, *The Ludwig Missionsverein and the Church in the United States* (Washington, D.C.: Catholic University of America Press, 1933).

9. "Severus Brandus," *Die Katholisch-irisch-bischöfliche Administration in Nordamerika* (Philadelphia, 1840) and Josef Salzbacher, *Meine Reise nach Nord-Amerika im Jahre 1842* (Vienna: Wimmer, Schmidt, & Leo, 1845).

10. AMA: Wimmer to Scherr, Munich, July 22, 1843. See Oetgen, *An American Abbot,* 36–38.

11. AMA: Wimmer to Scherr, Munich, May 28, 1845.

12. AMA: Wimmer to Scherr, Munich, June 5, 1845, June 15, 1845, and June 30, 1845.

13. AMA: Fransoni to Morichini, Rome, July 3, 1845 (copy).

14. AMA: Wimmer to Scherr, Munich, August 5, 1845.

15. AMA: Wimmer to Scherr, Munich, October 29, 1845. The letter is printed in *The Scriptorium* (St. John's Abbey): 18 (1959), 69–70.

16. "Über die Missionen," *Augsburger Postzeitung,* November 8, 1845. For a translation of the complete text, see appendix 2.

17. AMA: Scherr to Wimmer *(exeat),* Metten, February 14, 1846. See ALMV: Wimmer to the Ludwig Missionsverein, Munich, February 26, 1846.

18. AMA: Wimmer to Scherr, Munich, March 16, 1846, and May 6, 1846. See *The Scriptorium* 18 (1959): 71–73.

19. ASVA: Wimmer to clerical students, Munich, February 19, 1846. The letter is translated and printed in Fellner, *Abbot Boniface and His Monks,* 1:44–45, and Gerard Bridge, *An Illustrated History of St. Vincent Archabbey* (Beatty, Pa.: St. Vincent Archabbey Press, 1922), 60–64. For the entire text see appendix 3.

20. *Necrologium Congregationis Americano-Cassinensis, O.S.B., 1846–1946* (Collegeville, Minn: St. John's Abbey, 1948).

21. See Colman J. Barry, *Worship and Work: Saint John's Abbey and University 1856–1992,* 3d ed. (Collegeville, Minn.: Liturgical Press, 1993), 9, and Oetgen, *An American Abbot,* 65–66.

22. Peter Henry Lemke, "Autobiography," *The Northern Cambria News,* November 8, 1879.

23. Fellner, *Abbot Boniface and His Monks,* 1: 56–57. See ASVA: Wimmer to Meyringer, St. Vincent, December 30, 1846.

24. Modestus Wirtner, *The Benedictine Fathers in Cambria County, Pennsylvania* (Carrolltown, Pa.: Privately published, 1926), 16–21, 46–55.

25. Fellner, *Abbot Boniface and His Monks,* 1: 60–63, and Oetgen, *An American Abbot,* 68–71. See also ASVA: Wimmer to Meyringer, St. Vincent, December 30, 1846.

26. ASVA: St. Vincent parishioners to Wimmer, St. Vincent, October 11, 1846. The letter is printed in appendix 4.

27. ALMV: Wimmer to the Ludwig Missionsverein, St. Vincent, March 1847.

28. Wirtner, *Benedictine Fathers in Cambria County,* 53–57, and Fellner, *Abbot Boniface and His Monks,* 63–65.

29. ASVA: O'Connor to Wimmer, St. Vincent, November 5, 1846. See ADL: Wimmer to Ziegler, St. Vincent, November 5, 1846, and ALMV: Wimmer to the Ludwig Missionsverein, St. Vincent, March 1847.

30. ALMV: Wimmer to Müller, St. Vincent, October 26, 1846.

31. ADL: Wimmer to Ziegler, St. Vincent, November 5, 1846.

32. ALMV: Wimmer to Müller, St. Vincent, October 26, 1846, and ADL: Wimmer to Ziegler, St. Vincent, November 5, 1846.

33. David Knowles, *Christian Monasticism* (New York: McGraw Hill, 1969), 72–74. See also Louis Lekai, *Cistercians: Ideal and Reality* (Kent, Ohio: Kent State University Press, 1977).

34. ALMV: Wimmer to the Ludwig Missionsverein, St. Vincent, March 1847. See also AMA: Wimmer to Scherr, Munich, May 6, 1846 (*The Scriptorium* 18 (1959): 72–73).

35. Bruce Seymour, *Lola Montez: A Life* (New Haven, Conn.: Yale University Press, 1996), 238.

36. AMA: Wimmer to Scherr, St. Vincent, November 9, 1847.

37. ALMV: Wimmer to the Ludwig Missionsverein, St. Vincent, March 1847.

38. ADL: Wimmer to Linz, St. Vincent, November 9, 1847, and RAB: Wimmer to King Ludwig I, Munich, January 25, 1851. Wimmer's letter to King Ludwig is printed in Mathäser, *Bonifaz Wimmer O.S.B. und König Ludwig I von Bayern,* 14–24. A translation is provided in appendix 5.

39. ALMV: Wimmer to Müller, St. Vincent, October 26, 1846.

40. ALMV: Wimmer to the Ludwig Missionsverein, St. Vincent, March 1847.

41. Fellner, "Archabbot Boniface Wimmer as an Educator," 9.

42. ASVA: Wimmer to Oertel, St. Vincent, December 14, 1846 (a letter to the editor of the *Katholische Kirchenzeitung* of Baltimore, published on December 25, 1846); ADL: Wimmer to Ziegler, St. Vincent, November 5, 1847; ALMV: Wimmer to von Reisach, St. Vincent, March 1, 1847, and Wimmer to the Ludwig Missionsverein, St. Vincent, March 1847.

43. ALMV: Wimmer to von Reisach, St. Vincent, March 1, 1847.

44. ALMV: Wimmer to the Ludwig Missionsverein, St. Vincent, March 1847.

45. See appendix 4.

46. ALMV: Wimmer to von Reisach, St. Vincent, March 1, 1847.

47. Ibid.

48. ALMV: Wimmer to the Ludwig Missionsverein, December 1847, printed in *Annalen der Verbreitung des Glaubens* (Munich, 1848): 296–98.

49. ASVA: Schell to Wimmer, Kittanning, April 1847. Quoted in Fellner, *Abbot Boniface and His Monks,* 1:84.

50. *Pittsburgh Catholic,* December 18, 1847.

51. ADL: Wimmer to Ziegler, St. Vincent, June 11, 1848.

52. ASA: Wimmer to Leiss, St. Vincent, October 12, 1847.

53. ASVA: O'Connor to Wimmer, Pittsburgh, April 14, 1847.

54. Wimmer's side of his correspondence with O'Connor is lost, apparently destroyed by the bishop. The Benedictine position in the controversy must therefore be gleaned from the letters of O'Connor and Wimmer's complaints about the bishop in his correspondence with Bavaria. A detailed description of the gymnasium and major seminary eventually established at Saint Vincent is given later in this chapter.

55. ASVA: O'Connor to Wimmer, Pittsburgh, May 8, 1847. See Fellner, *Abbot Boniface and His Monks,* 1:95–105; Oetgen, *An American Abbot,* 80–83; and Henry Szarnicki, *Michael O'Connor: First Catholic Bishop of Pittsburgh, 1843–1860* (Pittsburgh: Wolfson Publishing Co., 1975), 82–87.

56. See Barry, *The Catholic Church and German Americans, passim; James Hennesey, American Catholics: A History of the Roman Catholic Community in the United States* (New York: Oxford University Press, 1981), 194–96; and Jay P. Dolan, *The American Catholic Experience: A History from Colonial Times to the Present* (New York: Doubleday, 1985), 297–99.

57. ASVA: Wimmer to O'Connor, St. Vincent, May 10, 1847.

58. ASVA: O'Connor to Wimmer, Pittsburgh, May 13, 1847. See Fellner, *Abbot Boniface and His Monks,* 1:94–96.

59. ASA: Wimmer to Leiss, St. Vincent, October 12–31, 1847.

60. ASVA: O'Connor to Wimmer, Pittsburgh, November 2, 1847.

61. ASVA: O'Connor to Wimmer, Pittsburgh, December 6, 1847.

62. ALMV: Wimmer to the Ludwig Missionsverein, St. Vincent, 1855. Printed in *Annalen der Verbreitung des Glaubens* (Munich, 1856): 85.

63. ALMV: Wimmer to von Reisach, St. Vincent, March 27, 1850; AMA: Wimmer to Scherr, St. Vincent, August 14, 1850.

64. ACPF: Wimmer to the Propaganda Fide, Munich, January 20, 1851, and RAB: Wimmer to Ludwig I, Munich, January 25, 1851. See Oetgen, *An American Abbot,* 115–22, and Fellner, *Abbot Boniface and His Monks,* 2:136. Wimmer's letter to King Ludwig I is found in appendix 5.

65. ASVA: O'Connor to Kirby, Pittsburgh, August 13, 1851 (copy). See Szarnicki, *Michael O'Connor,* pp. 89–91.

66. ASVA: Fransoni to Wimmer, Rome, February 14, 1852.

67. ASA: Wimmer to Leiss, St. Vincent, March 12, 1849.

68. ASA: Wimmer to Leiss, St. Vincent, March 12, 1849.

69. ASA: Wimmer to Scherr, St. Vincent, August 14, 1850.

70. AMA: Lechner to Scherr, St. Vincent, April 21, 1849; Brunner to Scherr, St. Vincent, June 18, 1849; Brunner to Scherr, Carrolltown, July 2, 1849.

71. ASA: Wimmer to Leiss, St. Vincent, March 12, 1849.

72. ASA: Wimmer to Leiss, St. Vincent, July 4–8, 1849.

73. ASA: Wimmer to Leiss, St. Vincent, March 27, 1850.

74. ASA: Wimmer to Leiss, Munich, December 28, 1850.

75. On Catholic colleges founded in America between 1796 and 1850, see Edward J. Power, *Catholic Higher Education in America: A History* (New York: Appleton Century Crofts, 1972), 60, 121–22; and Edward J. Power, *A History of Catholic Higher Education in the United States* (Milwaukee: Bruce Publishing Co., 1958), 255–275.

76. James J. Sheehan, *German History: 1770–1866* (Oxford: Clarendon Press, 1989), 514, 519; Friedrich Paulsen, *German Education: Past and Present* (New York: Charles Scribner, 1912), 200–202; and Friedrich Paulsen, *The German Universities and German Study* (New York: Charles Scribner, 1906), 275–80.

77. This discussion of the early years at Saint Vincent College and Seminary is based principally upon the letters of Wimmer and documents located in the archives of Saint Vincent Archabbey. For summary discussions see also Oetgen, *An American Abbot,* 103–10; Fellner, *Abbot Boniface and His Monks,* 2:163–74; and Fellner, "Archabbot Boniface Wimmer as an Educator."

78. ALMV: Wimmer to von Reisach, St. Vincent, March 1, 1847.

79. ALMV: Wimmer to von Reisach, St. Vincent, March 3, 1848.

80. ALMV: Wimmer to Müller, St. Vincent, December 1848.

81. ALMV: Wimmer to the Ludwig Missionsverein, St. Vincent, November 7, 1851. See also ASA: Wimmer to Leiss, St. Vincent, March 27, 1850.

82. ALMV: Wimmer to von Reisach, St. Vincent, August 9, 1852.

83. ASVA: Biographical records of early monks.

84. ALMV: Wimmer to the Ludwig Missionsverein, St. Vincent, February 1856.

85. ASVA: Manuscript catalogue of Saint Vincent College, 1854–55. Printed in Vincent Huber, "Sportsman's Hall and St. Vincent Abbey," *St. Vincent's Journal* 3 (1893–94): 133–43.

86. For more on the Pilz brothers, see Paschal Baumstein, *My Lord of Belmont: A Biography of Leo Haid* (Kings Mountain, N.C.: Herald House, 1985), pp. 41, 46, 126–28.

87. Alfonso Capecelatro, *Commemorazione di Don Bonifacio Maria Krug, Abate di Montecassino* (Rome: Desclée & Cie: 1910) and "Archabbot Boniface Krug," *St. Vincent's Journal* 19 (1909–10): 1–8.

88. "Father Adalbert Muller," *St. Vincent's Journal* 15 (1905–6): 278–32.

89. See Donald S. Raila, "The Enigma of Archabbot Andrew: A Man Who Knew His Limits," *Saint Vincent* 22 (1988): 6–7.

90. Peter Beckman, *Kansas Monks: A History of St. Benedict's Abbey and College* (Atchison, Kans.: Abbey Student Press, 1957), 136–37.

91. Peter J. Meaney, "Valiant Chaplain of the Bloody Tenth," *Tennessee Historical Quarterly* 41 (1983): 37–47; and Aloysius Plaisance, "Emmeran Bliemel, O.S.B., Heroic Confederate Chaplain," *The American Benedictine Review* 17 (1966): 106–16.

92. Beckman, *Kansas Monks,* 30, 44–42.

93. Jerome Oetgen, "Oswald Moosmüller: Monk and Missionary," *The American Benedictine Review* 27 (1976): 1–35.

94. Fellner, "Archabbot Boniface Wimmer as an Educator," 22.

95. "Father Alphonse Heimler," *St. Vincent's Journal* 19 (1909–10): 22–24.

96. ASVA: Biographical records of Benedictine monks at Saint Vincent Archabbey.

97. See Wirtner, *Benedictine Fathers in Cambria County,* 23, 58, and 104–11; Fellner, *Abbot Boniface and His Monks,* 1:109–15; Oetgen, *An American Abbot,* 133; and Huber, "Sportsman's Hall and St. Vincent Abbey," 102–3.

98. Remigius Burgemeister, *History of the Development of Catholicity in St. Marys* (St. Marys, Pa.: Privately published, 1919); Fellner, *Abbot Boniface and His Monks,* 2:149–62; Oetgen, *An American Abbot,* 133–36; Huber, "Sportsman's Hall and St. Vincent Abbey," 104; and Ephrem Hollermann, *The Reshaping of a Tradition: American Benedictine Women 1852–1881* (St. Joseph, Minn.: Sisters of the Order of St. Benedict, 1994), 57–66.

99. Fellner, *Abbot Boniface and His Monks,* 2:175–76; Oetgen, *An American Abbot,* 136–37; and Huber, "Sportsman's Hall and St. Vincent Abbey," 103.

100. Huber, "Sportsman's Hall and St. Vincent Abbey," 103.

101. Fellner, *Abbot Boniface and His Monks,* 2:177.

102. ASVA: Act of Incorporation of the Benedictine Society in Westmoreland County, April 19, 1854. See Fellner, *Abbot Boniface and His Monks,* 2:176–77.

103. Cooperation among the communities that sprang from a common foundation and tradition was maintained by the loose confederation of these communities in a congregation that followed certain practices and interpreted the Benedictine Rule in specific ways agreed upon by all and spelled out in written statutes. The 17th-century Bavarian Congregation, suppressed at the beginning of the 19th century, was restored in the 1850s after four monasteries reestablished from Metten had gained their independence. When Saint Vincent became an abbey in 1855, Rome concurrently established the American Cassinese Congregation to which all subsequent monasteries founded from Saint Vincent belonged.

104. ACPF: Wimmer to Pius IX, St. Vincent, November 10, 1853; Wimmer to Morichini, St. Vincent, November 11, 1853; and Wimmer to Fransoni, St. Vincent, December 11, 1853.

105. ACPF: O'Connor to Fransoni, Pittsburgh, April 12, 1854. See Szarnicki, *Michael O'Connor,* 101–3.

106. ASJA: Wimmer to di Marogna, Rome, June 27, 1855.

107. ACPF: O'Connor to Fransoni, Pittsburgh, December 1854, and February 13, 1855. See Fellner, *Abbot Boniface and His Monks,* 2:200–202, and Szarnicki, *Michael O'Connor,* 101–3.

108. RAB: Wimmer to Ludwig I, Rome, June 4, 1855.

109. ACPF: Pescetelli to Fransoni, Rome, March 12, 1855.

110. ASJA: Wimmer to di Marogna, Rome, May 13, 1855.

111. ASJA: Wimmer to di Marogna, Rome, July 29, 1855.

112. ASVA: Roman Documents, July 30, 1855, and August 24, 1855. The decree establishing Saint Vincent as an exempt abbey is printed in Appendix 6.

113. ASVA: Roman Documents, September 17, 1855. Printed in Appendix 6.

114. ASVA: O'Connor to Wimmer, Pittsburgh, December 14, 1855. For more details on events surrounding the elevation of Saint Vincent to an abbey, see Fellner, *Abbot Boniface and His Monks,* 2:184–242, and Oetgen, *An American Abbot,* 138–52.

NOTES TO CHAPTER 3.

MONKS, MISSIONARIES, AND TEACHERS

1. Colman J. Barry, *Worship and Work: Saint John's Abbey and University 1856–1992,* 3d ed. (Collegeville, Minn.: Liturgical Press, 1993), 26.

2. *Annalen der Verbreitung des Glaubens* (Munich, 1856): 374.

3. AMA: Wimmer to Scherr, St. Vincent, March 10, 1856. The letter is translated in *The Scriptorium* (St. John's Abbey), 19 (1960): 65–68.

4. Felix Fellner, *Abbot Boniface and His Monks,* 5 vols. (Latrobe, Pa.: Privately published at Saint Vincent Archabbey, 1956), 2:233.

5. AACC: Acts of the First General Chapter 1856. The Congregation did not become fully constituted until two more monasteries achieved independence, which did not occur until 1858. Future general chapters considered that of 1856 a local rather than a general chapter. Thus the chapter of 1858, which declared the Minnesota and Kansas foundations independent, was also called the First General Chapter, and all future general chapters were numbered consecutively from 1858 and not 1856. See Jerome Oetgen, *An American Abbot: Boniface Wimmer, O.S.B. (1809–1887),* 2d ed. (Washington, D.C.: Catholic University of America Press, 1997), 222.

6. ASJA: *The Record,* February 1889. Quoted in Barry, *Worship and Work,* 65–68. Barry's is the definitive study of the history of Saint Vincent's foundation in Minnesota. That foundation achieved canonical independence in 1858 and eventually became St. John's Abbey.

7. ASJA: Memoirs of Father Bruno Riess, *The Record,* February 1889.

8. Callistus Edie, "Demetrius di Marogna," *The Scriptorium* 9 (1949): 7–31; "Bruno Riess," ibid., 10 (1950): 5–39; and Thomas Whitaker, "Brothers of St. John's Abbey: 1856–1866," ibid., 13 (1953): 38–53.

9. Barry, *Worship and Work,* 28–37.

10. ASJA: Memoirs of Father Bruno Riess, *The Record,* March 1889. Quoted in Barry, *Worship and Work,* 43.

11. Peter Henry Lemke, trans., *Eine Vertheidigung katholischer Lehren, und eine Appellation an das protestantische Publikum: Zwei Controvers-Schriften von Demetrius A. Gallitzin* (Reading, Pa.: Arnold Puwelle, 1849), and *Leben und Wirken des Prinzen Demetrius Augustin Gallitzin: Ein Beitrag zur Geschichte der katholischen Missionen in Nordamerika* (Münster: Coppenrath, 1861).

12. Modestus Wirtner, *The Benedictine Fathers in Cambria County, Pennsylvania* (Carrolltown, Pa.: Privately published, 1926), 58–63; Peter Beckman, *Kansas Monks: A History of St. Benedict's Abbey* (Atchison, Kans.: Abbey Student Press, 1957), 5–43; Willibald Mathäser, ed., *Haudegen Gottes: Das Leben des Peter H. Lemke* (Würzburg: Kommissionsverlag Echte Gesamtherstellung, 1971); and Terrence Kardong, "Peter Henry Lemke: 'Brave Soldier of the Lord' or Gyrovague?" *Tjurunga: An Australian Benedictine Review* 24 (1983): 44–65.

13. AMA: Wimmer to Scherr, St. Vincent, March 10, 1856. See Fellner, *Abbot Boniface and His Monks,* 2:262, and Oetgen, *An American Abbot,* 161–62.

14. Peter Beckman's *Kansas Monks* (see note 12) is the history of the Kansas Benedictine foundation's first hundred years. See also ASVA: Lemke to Wimmer, Kansas Territory, February 8, 1856, quoted in Wirtner, *Benedictine Fathers in Cambria County,* 60–61.

15. Beckman, *Kansas Monks,* 29–43.

16. ASVA: Biographical records of the monks of Saint Vincent.

17. ASVA: Seitz to Wimmer, Doniphan, June 4, 1857. Quoted in Beckman, *Kansas Monks,* 34.

18. Oswald Moosmüller, *St. Vincenz in Pennsylvanien* (New York: F. Pustet, 1873), 264–74; Willibald Mathäser, "San José in Texas," *Studien und Mitteilungen* 60 (1946): 309–30; Fellner, *Abbot Boniface and His Monks,* 3:356–68; and Oetgen, *An American Abbot,* 193–96.

19. ASPA: Wimmer to Pescetelli, St. Vincent, December 18, 1859.

20. ADN: Wimmer to Bayley, Newark, October 3, 1854. The letter is edited and published in Giles P. Hayes, "Early Bayley-Wimmer Correspondence (1854–1857)," *The American Benedictine Review* 14 (1963): 480–81.

21. ASVA: Felder to Wimmer, Newark, May 19, 1857.

22. ADN: Wimmer to Bayley, St. Vincent, June 1, 1857. See Hayes, "Early Bayley-Wimmer Correspondence," 491–92.

23. See Malachy McPadden, *The Benedictines in Newark 1842–1992* (Newark, N.J.: Published by Newark Abbey, 1993); Giles Hayes, "St. Mary's Abbey, Balleis to Zilliox: 1838–1886," *The Scriptorium* 20 (1961): 123–84; Fellner, *Abbot Boniface and His Monks,* 2:274–88; and Oetgen, *An American Abbot,* 169–73.

24. Wimmer to Leiss, St. Vincent, January 16, 1859. See Oetgen, *An American Abbot,* 187.

25. Ephrem Hollermann, *The Reshaping of a Tradition: American Benedictine Women 1852–1881* (St. Joseph, Minn.: Sisters of the Order of St. Benedict, 1994), 108–10.

26. ASA: Wimmer to Leiss, Carrolltown, February 25, 1859.

27. Oetgen, *An American Abbot,* 190–91.

28. RAB: Wimmer to Ludwig I, Newark, December 2, 1862, and AMA: Wimmer to Scherr, St. Vincent, February 26, 1863. See Oetgen, *An American Abbot,* 250.

29. ASPA: Wimmer to Pescetelli, St. Vincent, February 12, 1861.

30. Aloysius Plaisance, "Emmeran Bliemel, O.S.B., Heroic Confederate Chaplain," *The American Benedictine Review* 17 (1966): 106–16; Fellner, *Abbot Boniface and His Monks,* 3:351–53; Peter J. Meaney, "Valiant Chaplain of the Bloody Tenth," *Tennessee Historical Quarterly* 41 (1983): 37–47.

31. AMA: Wimmer to Scherr, St. Vincent, February 26, 1863. Louis Haas, O.S.B., *Saint Vincent* (Latrobe, Pa.: Abbey Press, 1905), 27. For statistics on students at Saint Vincent during this period, see *St. Vincent College Catalogue, 1863–1864* (Saint Vincent, 1864).

32. ASVA: Civil War Papers (VH-41). The document of release, signed by Brigadier General C. P. Buckingham of the War Department and dated November 28, 1862, reads: "Francis Patrick Kenrick, Archbishop of Baltimore, and Right Reverend B. Wimmer, Abbot of the Benedictine Monastery, Latrobe, Pennsylvania, having represented to this Department that four monks of the Order of Saint Benedict have been drafted into military services of the United States, that by their religious belief and doctrine it is unlawful for them to bear arms and that the monks are bound irrevocably to the order by solemn vows, their mission being a mission of peace, it is hereby ordered that the members of the Benedictine Order are relieved from military duty."

33. ASVA: Wimmer to Lincoln, St. Vincent, June 10, 1863 (copy). This letter, as well as one of June 11, 1863, that Wimmer sent Secretary of War Edwin M. Stanton, is published in *Official Records of the War of the Rebellion,* Series 101, vol. 3 (Washington, D.C.: Government Printing Office, 1880), 33–36 and 341–45.

34. ASVA: Gaul to Wimmer, Virginia, March 12, 1865; Gaul to Hoffmann, Virginia, April 12, 1865. "Obituary: Brother Bonaventure Gaul, O.S.B.," *St. Vincent Journal* 6 (1896): 38–39. See Fellner, *Abbot Boniface and His Monks,* 3:349–50.

35. ASPA: Wimmer to Pescetelli, St. Vincent, December 15, 1859. See Moosmüller, *St. Vincenz in Pennsylvanien,* 178; Fellner, *Abbot Boniface and His Monks,* 3:333–40; *Barry, Worship and Work,* 68, 79–81; and Oetgen, *An American Abbot,* 256–81.

36. *Pittsburgh Dispatch,* February 26, 1860; *Cincinnati Wahrheitsfreund,* March 15, 1860; and *Pittsburgh Catholic,* March 17, 1860.

37. ASJA: Wimmer to di Marogna, St. Vincent, August 10, 1860. See Barry, *Worship and Work,* 66.

38. ASPA: Wimmer to Pescetelli, St. Vincent, May 12, 1861.

39. AMA: Wimmer to Scherr, St. Vincent, February 26, 1863.

40. ACPF: Wimmer to Barnabo, St. Vincent, June 20, 1863.

41. Ibid.

42. AMA: Wimmer to Scherr, St. Vincent, February 26, 1863.

43. ASVA: Pescetelli to Wimmer, Rome, June 24, 1863.

44. ACPF: Wendelin Mayer to Pope Pius IX, St.Vincent, April 29, 1863.

45. ASVA: Roman Document, October 11, 1865. See Fellner, *Abbot Boniface and His Monks,* 3:340.

46. ASVA: Wimmer to Wirtz, Rome, October 17, 1865. See also ASVA: Paul Keck papers (MV-92), November 13, 1865.

47. ASVA: Wirtz to Mayer, St. Joseph, Minnesota, December 26, 1865. See Barry, *Worship and Work,* 81.

48. ASVA: Roman Document, December 26, 1866.

49. *Annalen der Verbreitung des Glaubens* (Munich, 1848): 384. See also, ADL: Wimmer to Ziegler, Munich, June 9, 1846. "The motherhouse [Metten] has a large choir of priests and clerics. We will have only five. The absence of priests will be keenly felt. Therefore we might try to recite the same office and after considering this question for a time, I came to the conclusion that it would be best to instruct the Brothers sufficiently to recite the office with the clerical members." Quoted in Fellner, *Abbot Boniface and His Monks,* 3:340.

50. ACPF: Sailer to Pius IX, St. Vincent, April 30, 1861. See Fellner, *Abbot Boniface and His Monks,* 3:330–31.

51. ACPF: Domenec to Propaganda, Pittsburgh, September 1861.

52. ACPF: Young to Propaganda, Erie, September 1861.

53. ACPF: St. Vincent monks to Propaganda, St. Vincent, October 3, 1861.

54. ACPF: Wimmer to Barnabo, St. Vincent, August 5, 1861.

55. See Fellner, *Abbot Boniface and His Monks,* 3:328–32; and Oetgen, *An American Abbot,* 235–39.

56. ASPA: Wimmer to Pescetelli, St. Vincent, September 18, 1858. See Fellner, *Abbot Boniface and His Monks,* 3:318–19; and Oetgen, *An American Abbot,* 179–84.

57. ASVA: Roman Documents, December 20, 1858; Barnabo to Wimmer, Rome, December 29, 1858.

58. ASVA: Pescetelli to Wimmer, Rome, April 12, 1859.

59. ASVA: Roman Documents, September 15, 1861.

60. ASPA: Wimmer to Pescetelli, St. Vincent, October 1, 1862. See Oetgen, *An American Abbot,* 247–48.

61. The most complete recent study of the controversy between Wimmer and the Benedictine sisters is found in Hollermann, *The Reshaping of a Tradition,* 91–179. For documents related to the controversy see Incarnata Girgen, *Behind the Beginnings: Benedictine Women in America* (St. Paul, Minn.: St. Benedict's Convent, 1981). Judith Sutera's *True Daughters: Monastic Identity and American Benedictine Women's History* (Atchison, Kans.: Mount St. Scholastica, 1987) is a careful and competent examination of the canonical and ecclesiastical context within which the conflict played out. See also, Oetgen, *An American Abbot,* 193–221.

62. RAB: Wimmer to Ludwig I, St. Vincent, April 9, 1859; Girgen, *Behind the Beginnings,* 148.

63. ACPF: Wimmer to Barnabo, St. Vincent, July 11, 1858; Girgen, *Behind the Beginnings,* 122.

64. ASVA: Roman Documents, December 6, 1859; Girgen, *Behind the Beginnings,* 156.

65. ASJA: Wimmer to Seidenbusch, Rome, July 3, 1865.

66. ASVA: Roman Documents, June 23, 1866, and July 27, 1866. See Oetgen, *An American Abbot,* 280–81.

67. *Cincinnati Wahrheitsfreund,* October 24, 1866. See Fellner, *Abbot Boniface and His Monks,* 3:386–87.

68. Barry, *Worship and Work,* 93–95.

69. ACPF: Wimmer to Smith, Newark, October 18, 1866.

70. ALMV: Wimmer to Missionsverein, St. Vincent, February 25, 1868.

71. *Catalogus Monachorum Ord. S. P. Benedicti Congregationis Americano-Bavaricae Cassinensi Affiliatae* (St. Vincent: Abbey Press, 1873).

72. Fellner, *Abbot Boniface and His Monks,* 4:497–99; Moosmüller, *St. Vincenz in Pennsylvanien,* 321–23.

73. Fellner, *Abbot Boniface and His Monks,* 4:499; *Pittsburgh Catholic,* November 4, 1871; *Cincinnati Wahrheitsfreund,* November 8, 1871.

74. *Pittsburgh Catholic,* November 4, 1871.

75. The bell tower, constructed in 1871, was a landmark at St. Vincent until its destruction in the fire of 1963. Moosmüller's history *(St. Vincenz in Pennsylvanien)* survived the ravages of time and remains one of the most important sources of early American Benedictine history.

76. AMA: Wimmer to Lang, St. Vincent, November 2, 1871.

77. ASVA: College Charter, April 18, 1870. See Fellner, *Abbot Boniface and His Monks,* 3:407.

78. *St. Vincent College Catalogue, 1870–1871* (Pittsburgh, Pa.: Urben & Bro., 1871).

79. Fred Moleck, "Nineteenth-Century Musical Activity at St. Vincent Archabbey" (Ph.D. Diss., University of Pittsburgh, 1971).

80. Heimler owed more to Wimmer than his position as president of Saint Vincent College. In 1855, when he was refused ordination in Bavaria because of a deformed right hand, he came to Saint Vincent where Abbot Boniface first arranged for a surgeon to make an incision in the deformed hand so that he could hold the Host and then obtained a dispensation from Rome so that Heimler could be ordained. He completed his novitiate at Saint Vincent in 1856 and was ordained in 1857. See Fellner, *Abbot Boniface and His Monks,* 3:401 and 409.

81. Felix Fellner, "Archabbot Boniface Wimmer as an Educator," *The National Benedictine Educational Association Bulletin* 25 (1942): 90–106; Fellner, *Abbot Boniface and His Monks,* 3:391–401.

82. *St. Vincent College Catalogue, 1868–1869* (Beatty, Pa.: St. Vincent Press, 1869).

83. ALMV: Wimmer to Missionsverein, St. Vincent, February 25, 1868.

84. See Fellner, *Abbot Boniface and His Monks,* 5:620.

85. Francis X. Reuss, "Base-Ball at St. Vincent's in 1867 & 1868," *St. Vincent's Journal* 5 (1895–96): 389–90. For more on student life at Saint Vincent during the late 1860s, see excerpts from the student diary of Francis X. Reuss published intermittently in volumes 18 through 20 of the *St. Vincent College Journal* (1908–11).

86. *Annalen der Verbreitung des Glaubens* (Munich, 1853): 396.

87. Gerard Bridge, *An Illustrated History of St. Vincent Archabbey* (Beatty, Pa.: St. Vincent Archabbey Press, 1922), 179–82. See also Oetgen, *An American Abbot,* 108–9.

88. ALMV: Wimmer to von Reisach, St. Vincent, July 3, 1851.

89. Fellner, *Abbot Boniface and His Monks,* 2:165.

90. Bridge, *Illustrated History of St. Vincent,* 176–79; and Oetgen, *An American Abbot,* 109–10.

91. *St. Vincent College Journal* 20(1910–1911): 34.

92. Fred J. Moleck, "Music at St. Vincent Under Abbot Boniface Wimmer," *The American Benedictine Review* 14 (1963): 259.

93. Fellner, "Archabbot Boniface Wimmer as an Educator," p. 24.

94. ASVA: MS. Collection, "Fugitive Recollections Musical and Unmusical, 1868–1878, by an Old Alumnus [Henry Ganss]," 4–5. Details of student life contained in the paragraphs that follow are taken from Ganss's memoirs. On Ganss, see "Ganss, Henry George," *New Catholic Encyclopedia,* and Georgina Pell Curtis, *The American Catholic Who's Who* (St. Louis: Herder, 1911), 230.

95. ASVA: Gibbons to Wimmer, Richmond, August 1, 1875. For a discussion of Gibbons' invitation, and some of the misleading statements he made to Wimmer in his letter, see Paschal Baumstein, *My Lord of Belmont: A Biography of Leo Haid* (King's Mountain, N.C.: Herald House, 1985), 31–32.

96. ASVA: Wimmer to Hegele, St. Vincent, January 20, 1876.

97. ASVA: Chapter Records, January 19, 1876; and ASJA: Wimmer to Edelbrock, St. Vincent, February 13, 1876.

98. ASVA: Wolfe to Wimmer, Richmond, January 26, 1876.

99. ASVA: Wolfe to Wimmer, Richmond, April 5, 1876.

100 ASVA: Wolfe to Wimmer, Mariastein, July 5, 1876.

101. Fellner, *Abbot Boniface and His Monks,* 4:517. The name of the mission soon changed

to "Mary Help of Christians" abbreviated as "Maryhelp." Still later the monastery became known as Belmont Abbey. In 1965 the stone after which it had first been named was moved to the baptistery of the Belmont Abbey Cathedral and today serves as a baptismal font. A plaque on the font reads: "UPON THIS ROCK, MEN WERE ONCE SOLD INTO SLAVERY. NOW UPON THIS ROCK, THROUGH THE WATERS OF BAPTISM, MEN BECOME FREE CHILDREN OF GOD."

102. ASVA: Cassidy to Wimmer, Mariastein, October 27, 1876. See Fellner, *Abbot Boniface and His Monks,* 4:514–18. The early history of the Benedictines in North Carolina is told by Baumstein in *My Lord of Belmont.*

103. ASVA: Chapter Records, August 30, 1875.

104. ASVA: Quinlan to Wimmer, Mobile, March 20, 1876; Chapter Records, March 26, 1876. For the early history of the Alabama mission see Ambrose Reger, *Die Benediktiner in Alabama* (Baltimore: Benziger, 1898), translated by Gregory Roettger in *An Historical Overview of St. Bernard Abbey 1891–1991* (Cullman, Ala.: St. Bernard Abbey, 1991).

105. *Historical Overview of St. Bernard Abbey,* 8.

106. Joseph Murphy, O.S.B., *Tenacious Monks: The Oklahoma Benedictines (1875–1975)* (Shawnee, Okla.: Benedictine Color Press, 1974). In 1924 Sacred Heart Abbey became part of the American Cassinese Congregation and in 1929 changed its name to St. Gregory's Abbey.

107. Jerome Oetgen, "The Origins of the Benedictine Order in Georgia," *Georgia Historical Quarterly* 53 (1969): 165–83, and Fellner, *Abbot Boniface and His Monks,* 4:556–71.

108. ASVA: Moosmüller to Wimmer, Isle of Hope, March 20, 1877.

109. Oetgen, *An American Abbot,* 347–49.

110. ASVA: "Prospectus of the Manual Labor School for Colored Boys on Skidaway Island." Quoted in Oetgen, "Origins of the Benedictine Order in Georgia," 173–74.

111. ASVA: Moosmüller to Wimmer, Skidaway, December 9, 1878.

112. Cyprian Davis, *The History of Black Catholics in the United States* (New York: Crossroad, 1995), 123–25; and Baumstein, *My Lord of Belmont,* 57–62.

113. Baumstein, *My Lord of Belmont,* 209–10.

114. ASVA: G. Pilz to Wimmer, San Antonio, May 14, 1886.

115. Fellner, *Abbot Boniface and His Monks,* 5:693–700.

116. Oetgen, *An American Abbot,* 349–50.

117. See Fellner, *Abbot Boniface and His Monks,* 5:619, and Oetgen, *An American Abbot,* 359–60.

118. ASBA: Wimmer to Wolf, St. Vincent, July 14, 1879.

119. Oetgen, *An American Abbot,* 370–72.

120. ASVA: Simeoni to Wimmer, Rome, February 25, 1882.

121. ASBA: Wimmer to Wolf, St. Vincent, March 18, 1882.

122. ASVA: Edelbrock to Wimmer, St. John's, April 3, 1882.

123. ACPF: Tuigg to Propaganda, Rome, February 6, 1882.

124. ASBA: Haid to Wolf, St. Vincent, April 5, 1882.

125. ASBA: Wimmer to Wolf, St. Vincent, April 7, 1882; ASJA: Wimmer to Edelbrock, St. Vincent, June 21, 1882.

126. ASVA: Jaeger to Wimmer, Chicago, November 3, 1885.

127. For a history of St. Procopius Abbey see Vitus Buresh, *The Procopian Chronicle: St. Procopius Abbey 1885–1985* (Lisle, Ill.: St. Procopius Abbey, 1985).

128. Quoted in Urban J. Schnitzhofer,"First Monks in the Colorado Rockies," *The American Benedictine Review* 12 (1961): 234.

129. ASVA: Gutmann to Wimmer, Breckenridge, December 19, 1886; January 3, 1887; Schnitzhofer, "First Monks in the Colorado Rockies," 242, 244. See also Fellner, *Abbot Boniface and His Monks,* 5:702–03. For a brief history of the Colorado community that became Holy Cross Abbey see Martin J. Burne, "Holy Cross Abbey—One Hundred Years," *The American Benedictine Review* 37 (1986): 423–32.

130. ASJA: Wimmer to Seidenbusch, St. Vincent, December 27, 1880.

131. Fellner, *Abbot Boniface and His Monks,* 5:646.

132. Ibid., 651.

133. ASVA: Wimmer to L. Wimmer, St. Vincent, August 20, 1887.

134. ASVA: Wimmer to Sister Hildegard, August 5, 1887. See Joel Rippinger, *The Benedictine Order in the United States: An Interpretive History* (Collegeville, Minn.: The Liturgical Press, 1990), 83.

135. ASVA: Müller to Hofmayer, Rome, December 25, 1887.

NOTES TO CHAPTER 4. CONSOLIDATION AND RENEWAL

1. The abbey church at this time was still the parish church built by Father James Ambrose Stillinger in 1835. The choir chapel was a "comparatively small apartment" where the abbey church was joined to the monastery. See Paulinus Selle, " Building Construction at St. Vincent" (B.A. thesis, St. Vincent College, 1936), 51–52.

2. ASVA: Election Records, February 8, 1888; ASBA: Innocent Wolf Diary, February 8, 1888. See Peter Beckman, *Kansas Monks: A History of St. Benedict's Abbey* (Atchison, Kans.: Abbey Student Press, 1957), 211–12; Louis Haas, *St. Vincent's: Souvenir of the Consecration of the New Abbey Church, August 24, 1905, on the Fiftieth Anniversary of the Elevation of St. Vincent's to an Abbey* (Latrobe: St. Vincent Press, 1905), 43–44; Gerard Bridge, *Illustrated History of St. Vincent Archabbey* (Beatty, Pa.: St. Vincent's Press, 1922), 202–3.

3. ASBA: Innocent Wolf Diary, February 8, 1888; quoted in Beckman, *Kansas Monks,* 211.

4. ASVA: Biographical Files, Andrew Hintenach; see Donald S. Raila, "The Enigma of Archabbot Andrew: A Man Who Knew His Limits," *Saint Vincent* 22 (1988): 6–7.

5. ASVA: Hintenach to Abbot Bernard Smith, St. Vincent, April 6, 1888.

6. ASVA: Hintenach to priests, St. Vincent, May 7, 1888.

7. ASVA: Laufenberg to Hintenach, Anna, Ill., May 24, 1888.

8. ASVA: Moosmüller to Müller, St. Vincent, April 5, 1891.

9. ASVA: Moosmüller to Müller, St. Vincent, April 1, 1889.

10. ASVA: Chapter Minutes, September 7, 1888, and December 7, 1888.

11. AACC: Visitation Report, October 1, 1890.

12. ASVA: Moosmüller to Müller, St. Vincent, May 8, 1890. During his time in Georgia Moosmüller had raised money for the agricultural school for African American boys by publishing a German historical monthly, *Der Geschichtsfreund.* He later established the independent Priory of New Cluny in Wetaug, Illinois, and partially supported the community by publishing another monthly journal, *Die Legende.* For New Cluny Priory, see Jerome Oetgen, "Oswald Moosmüller: Monk and Missionary," *The American Benedictine Review* 27 (1976): 1–35, and chapter 5 below.

13. ASVA: Document in Ecuador File, July 11, 1888. The document reads: "To all whom it may concern: Hereby I state and swear, that by leaving St. Vincent Abbey for our Mission in the Diocese of Portoviejo, South-America, in the Republic of Ecuador, I will give up all claims, rights and privileges which I had on said Abbey, be they civil or ecclesiastic, and acquit them forever. At the same time I promise to work faithfully and zealously in said Mission in Ecuador, for the best of our Holy Order and the salvation of Souls. St. Vincent Abbey, July 11th, 1888." The document was signed by Augustine Schneider, Clement Stratman, Conrad Ebert, and Macarius Schmitt.

14. ASVA: Schneider to Pope Leo XIII, Bahía, October 1888.

15. ASVA: Roman Documents, December 4, 1888.

16. ASVA: Schneider to Smith, Bahía, October 10, 1888.

17. ASVA: Schneider to Hintenach, Bahía, February 2, 1889.

18. ASVA: Stratman to Hintenach, Bahía, May 9,1889; Chapter Minutes, May 27, 1889, and Hintenach to Stratman, St. Vincent, July 26, 1889.

19. *Sterbechronik des hochwürdigsten Herrn Abtes Miguel Kruse, O.S.B. [1864–1929]* (São Paulo, Brazil: S. Paulo-Cayeiras-Rio, 1929). See Joel Rippinger, *The Benedictine Order in the United States: An Interpretive History* (Collegeville, Minn.: The Liturgical Press, 1990), 225. Also *St. Vincent's Journal* 6 (1896–97): 384; 17 (1907–8): 407–8; 29 (1919–20): 299; 43 (April 1934): 23; and 43 (March 1, 1935): 16.

20. ASVA: Corrigan to Hintenach, New York, May 23, 1889. The Archdiocese of New York had been charged by the Sacred Congregation for the Propagation of the Faith with the responsibility of ministering to the Catholics of the Bahama Islands. Archbishop Corrigan was eager to enlist the American Benedictines for this mission and had first turned to the monks of Maryhelp Abbey in North Carolina. When they and the Saint Vincent Benedictines turned down the offer, he sought help from St. Mary's Abbey, Newark. Rejected a third time, he persisted and offered the mission to the monks of St. John's Abbey, Minnesota, who assumed the responsibility and sent two priests to Nassau. See Colman J. Barry, *Upon These Rocks: Catholics in the Bahamas* (Collegeville, Minn.: St. John's Abbey Press, 1973).

21. Consuela Marie Duffy, *Katharine Drexel: A Biography* (Cornwell Heights, Pa.: Mother Katharine Drexel Guild, 1966). See Rippinger, *Benedictine Order in the United States,* 134.

22. ASVA: Chapter Minutes, October 7, 1888.

23. ASVA: Drexel to Hintenach, Philadelphia, January 12, 1889.

24. ASVA: Chapter Minutes, January 17, 1889; Drexel to Hintenach, Philadelphia, January 30, 1889.

25. ASVA: Chapter Minutes, April 8, 1889. See also Peter Beckman, *Kansas Monks: A History of St. Benedict's Abbey* (Atchison, Kans.: Abbey Student Press, 1957), 214–16, and Rippinger, *Benedictine Order in the United States,* 140.

26. ASVA: Hintenach to Mora, St. Vincent, [May 1889].

27. ASVA: Block to Hintenach, Banning, August 29, 1889.

28. ASVA: Block to Hintenach, Banning, October 1, 1889.

29. ASVA: Block to Hintenach, Banning, December 12, 1889.

30. ASVA: Stephan to Hintenach, Washington, January 13, 1890, and January 27, 1890.

31. ASVA: Sierra to Hurley, Banning, October 23, 1983. Father John A. Sierra of Precious Blood Parish, Banning, California, provided Brother Philip Hurley, archivist at Saint Vincent, with information about the subsequent history of St. Boniface Indian School. In 1921 Franciscan priests took charge and operated it for the next thirty years. In 1969 the school moved to Beaumont, California, and became Boys Town of the Desert. The Diocese of San Diego relinquished control of the school in 1978, and it became an institution known as Children's Village.

32. ASVA: Priests of St. Joseph's Priory to Saint Vincent Chapter, Chicago, 1889.

33. ASVA: Moosmüller to Müller, St. Vincent, April 20, 1891.

34. *St. Vincent's College Journal* 1 (1891–92): 25–27.

35. Ibid., 81–87, 238.

36. Theodore Fuertges, "The History of Saint Bede's Abbey and College, Peru, Illinois, 1889–1941" (M.A. thesis, Catholic University of America, 1941).

37. ASVA: Moosmüller to Müller, St. Vincent, April 20, 1891.

38. ASVA: Hintenach to capitulars, St. Vincent, May 9, 1890.

39. Ambrose Reger, *Die Benediktiner in Alabama* (Baltimore: Benziger, 1898), translated by Gregory Roettger in *An Historical Overview of St. Bernard Abbey 1891–1991* (Cullman, Ala.: St. Bernard Abbey, 1991), 18–22.

40. ACPF: Hintenach to Bernard Smith, St. Vincent, July 24, 1890; ASVA: Roman document, May 9, 1891.

41. Roettger, *Historical Overview of St. Bernard Abbey,* 19.

42. *St. Vincent's Journal* 2(1892–93): 15.

43. ASVA: Matz to Hintenach, Denver, March 26, 1890.

44. ASVA: Matz to Hintenach, Denver, December 26, 1890.

45. *Catalogus Monachorum Congregationis Americano-Cassinensis sub titulo Sanctorum Angelorum Custodium* (Collegeville, Minn.: St. John's Abbey Press, 1893).

46. ABelA: Hintenach to Haid, St. Vincent, November 19, 1890.

47. Joseph Chinnici, *Devotion to the Holy Spirit in American Catholicism* (New York: Paulist Press, 1985), 61; Rippinger, *Benedictine Order in the United States*, 201–2.

48. Modestus Wirtner, *The Benedictine Fathers in Cambria County, Pennsylvania* (Carrolltown, Pa.: Privately published, 1926), 321–22. One of the students who lost most of his family in the flood was Hugh C. Boyle, who later became bishop of Pittsburgh. See *St. Vincent's Journal* 1 (1891–92): 27. For an account of the flood by another student who lost his family see V. A. Oswald, "A Personal Experience of the Johnstown Flood," *St. Vincent's Journal* 4 (1894–95): 352–58.

49. *Catalogus Monachorum Congregationis Americano-Cassinensis sub titulo Sanctorum Angelorum Custodium* (1893).

50. Haas, *St. Vincent's*, 46.

51. *St. Vincent's Journal*, 1 (1891–92): 103–4, 135, 179–80.

52. Ibid., 236–37.

53. The discussion that follows of the curriculum, student enrollment, and faculty in the college and seminary from 1888 to 1900 is based upon information in the *Catalogue of the Officers and Students of St. Vincent College*, published annually by the St. Vincent Abbey Press.

54. *Acta et Decreta Concilii Plenarii Baltimorensis Tertii* (Baltimore, 1886). See Francis P. Cassidy, "Catholic Education in the Third Plenary Council of Baltimore," *Catholic Historical Review* 34 (1948–49): 257–305, 415–36.

55. *St. Vincent's Journal* 1 (1891–92): 14.

56. "The Rt. Rev. Bishop of Pittsburgh very wisely insists that his English-speaking students shall also learn sufficient German to enable them to attend to the spiritual needs of those Germans that may be found within the limits of congregations to which these students will afterwards be assigned as pastors." *St. Vincent's Journal* 1 (1891–92): 15.

57. A summary discussion of the "Americanist Crisis" cannot do justice to the divisive issues confronting the American Church in the 1880s and 1890s. For more detailed analyses see John Tracy Ellis, *The Life of James Cardinal Gibbons: Archbishop of Baltimore, 1834–1921*, 2 vols. (Milwaukee: Bruce Publishing Co., 1952), vol. 2; James Hennesey, *American Catholics: A History of the Roman Catholic Community in the United States* (New York: Oxford University Press, 1981), chap. 15; Gerald P. Fogarty, *The Vatican and the Americanist Crisis: Denis J. O'Connell, American Agent in Rome, 1885–1903* (Rome, 1974) and *The Vatican and the American Hierarchy from 1870 to 1965* (Collegeville, Minn.: Liturgical Press, 1985), chaps. 3–7; Colman J. Barry, *The Catholic Church and German Americans* (Milwaukee: Bruce Publishing Co., 1953); and Philip Gleason, *Keeping the Faith: American Catholicism Past and Present* (Notre Dame, Ind.: University of Notre Dame Press, 1987), 41–43, 133–34, 160ff.

58. *St. Vincent's Journal* 1 (1891–92): 15.

59. Barry, *Catholic Church and German Americans*, 112; Rippinger, *Benedictine Order in the United States*, 106–7, 121–22.

60. Moosmüller's publications included *St. Vincenz in Pennsylvanien* (New York: F. Pustet, 1873), *Europaër in America vor Columbus* (Regensburg: G. J. Manz. 1879), and *Bonifaz Wimmer, Erzabt von St. Vincent in Pennsylvanien* (New York: Benziger Bros., 1891). He also published several articles in the Bavarian historical journal *Studien und Mitteilungen*, and edited *Der Geschichtsfreund* (1882–83) and *Der Legende* (1892–98).

61. *St. Vincent's Journal* 4 (1894–95): 23.

62. Ibid., 245.

63. Ibid., 70–71.

64. Ibid., 16.

65. Ibid., 395–401.

66. ASVA: Simeoni to Haid, Rome, January 14, 1891.

67. ACPF: Haid to Simeoni, Belmont, January 31, 1891.

68. ASVA: Haid to Smith, Belmont, January 31, 1891.

69. ASVA: Hintenach to Smith, St. Vincent, January 7, 1892.

70. See Raila, "The Enigma of Archabbot Andrew: A Man Who Knew His Limits," 6–7.

71. ASVA: Hintenach to Smith, St. Vincent, January 7, 1892.

72. ASVA: Haid to Smith, Belmont, April 12, 1892.

73. ASVA: Haid to Smith, Belmont, April 22, 1892.

74. ASVA: Roman Documents, May 25, 1892; Hintenach to St. Vincent monks, St. Vincent, June 14, 1892.

75. ASVA: Haid to Huber, Baltimore, June 12, 1892.

76. ASVA: Hintenach to St. Vincent monks, St. Vincent, June 14, 1892.

77. Haas, *St. Vincent's,* 48.

78. *St. Vincent's Journal* 2 (1892–93): 19.

79. ASVA: Huber to Haid, St. Vincent, June 15, 1892.

80. ASVA: Andelfinger to Haid, St. Vincent, June 15, 1892.

81. ASVA: Chapter Minutes, June 16, 1892.

82. ASVA: Huber to St. Vincent priests, St. Vincent, June 18, 1892.

83. ASVA: Huber to St. Vincent priests, St. Vincent, June 25, 1892.

84. ASVA: Huber to Haid, St. Vincent, June 29, 1892.

85. ASVA: Hintenach to Müller, Covington, Ky., July 4, 1892.

NOTES TO CHAPTER 5. ENTERING THE NEW CENTURY

1. *St. Vincent Journal* 2 (1892–93): 20–22.

2. ASVA: Biographical files, Leander Schnerr.

3. Louis Haas, *St. Vincent's: Souvenir of the Consecration of the New Abbey Church, August 24, 1905, on the Fiftieth Anniversary of the Elevation of St. Vincent's to an Abbey* (Latrobe, Pa.: St. Vincent Press, 1905), 49.

4. *St. Vincent Journal* 2 (1892–93): 48–61.

5. *Catalogus Monachorum Congregationis Americano-Cassinensis sub titulo Sanctorum Angelorum Custodium* (Collegeville, Minn.: St. John's Abbey, 1893), 5–24.

6. ASVA: Roman Documents, August 30, 1892.

7. *Die Legende: Eine katholische Monatsschrift zur Belehrung und Erbauung* (Chicago, 1893–1898). Complete volumes of *Die Legende* are located in the libraries of St. Meinrad's Archabbey, St. Meinrad, Ind., and St. John's Abbey, Collegeville, Minn. Partial collections can be found at St. Bede's Abbey, Peru, Ill.; St. Peter's Abbey, Saskatchewan, Canada; Assumption Abbey, Richardton, N.D.; and St. Vincent Archabbey, Latrobe, Pa.

8. *Die Legende* 1 (1893): 385.

9. ASVA: Moosmüller to Haid, New Cluny, July 8, 1892.

10. For more on Moosmüller and New Cluny see Jerome Oetgen, "Oswald Moosmüller: Monk and Missionary," *The American Benedictine Review* 27 (1976): 1–35.

11. John Sperling, *Great Depressions: 1837–1844, 1893–1898, 1929–1939* (Chicago: Scott, Foresman, 1966), 57–104.

12. Colman J. Barry, *The Catholic Church and German Americans* (Washington, D.C.: Catholic University of America Press, 1953), 211–12.

13. ASVA: Diary of Leander Schnerr, April–July 1893. See also Schnerr's letters from Rome and accounts of the Congress of Abbots in *St. Vincent Journal* 2 (1892–93): 234–41, 284–86, 311–12.

14. *Acta et Decreta Capituli Generalis Undecimi Congregationis Benedictinae Americano-Cassinensis* (Latrobe, Pa.: St. Vincent Press, 1893), 15.

15. Peter Beckman, *Kansas Monks: A History of St. Benedict's Abbey* (Atchison, Kans.: Abbey Student Press, 1957), 227.

16. ASVA: Diary of Leander Schnerr, August 1893. On the Saint Vincent display at the "World's Columbian Exposition" in Chicago, see *St. Vincent Journal* 2 (1892–93): 153; and 3 (1893–94): 194–95, 224. See also Brother Maurelian, F.S.C., *The Catholic Educational Exhibit at the World's Columbian Exposition, Chicago, 1893* (Chicago: J.S. Hyland and Co., 1896), 217–18 ("Benedictine Fathers").

17. ASVA: Diary of Leander Schnerr, October 1895 and May–June 1896.

18. *The Rule of St. Benedict* (Collegeville, Minn.: The Liturgical Press, 1980), 48: 1.

19. ASVA: Schnerr to "Dilecte Confrater," St. Vincent, October 25, 1895, and May 10, 1897.

20. *St. Vincent Journal* 3 (1893–94): 247–53.

21. Ibid., 6 (1896–1897): 374, 378.

22. Ibid., 6 (1896–97): 2–13, 16–24; 7 (1897–98): 327–32.

23. Ibid., 1 (1891–92): 126.

24. Joseph Wieczersak, *Bishop Francis Hodur: Biographical Essays,* ed. Theodore L. Zawistowski (Boulder, Colo.: East European Monographs, No. 523. Distributed by Columbia University Press, N.Y., 1998).

25. Ibid., 2 (1892–93): 34–45.

26. Ibid., 6 (1896–97): 97.

27. Ibid., 7 (1897–98): 195–96, 368.

28. Ibid., 7 (1897–98): 380.

29. Ibid., 7 (1897–98): 244, 284; 8 (1898–99): 193; 9 (1899–1900): 108–10, 400–401; 10 (1900–1901): 33. The following editorial statement in the *Journal* is typical: "An officer of our Army insults Sisters in Manila; another refuses a priest entrance to a hospital in Honolulu, where the remembrance of Father Damien must still be vivid; another, in Puerto Rico, cumulates in his person the offices of preacher and warrior; and so on, wherever our eagle flies, the American Army cad is in evidence."

30. Charles O'Fahey, "Gibbons, Ireland, Keane: The Evolution of a Liberal Catholic Rhetoric in America" (Ph.D. diss., University of Minnesota, 1980), 119–20, and Joel Rippinger, *The Benedictine Order in the United States* (Collegeville, Minn.: The Liturgical Press, 1990), 107.

31. ASVA: Kittel to Schnerr, Loretto, July 24, 1895. Quoted in Omer U. Kline, "An Historical Narrative: The Saint Vincent Archabbey Gristmill and Brewery, 1854–1992" (ASVA: Manuscript collection), 31.

32. ASVA: Satolli to Schnerr, Washington, August 1, 1895. See Kline, "The Saint Vincent Archabbey Gristmill and Brewery," 32, and *St. Vincent Journal* 5 (1895–96): 18–21, 49.

33. George Zurcher, *Monks and Their Decline* (Buffalo, N.Y.: Privately published, 1898). See Rippinger, *Benedictine Order in the United States,* 113. American church historian Colman J. Barry called Zurcher a "fervent temperance advocate but a man of proved intemperance both in word and idea." Zurcher opposed not only beer brewing among American Benedictines but also the efforts of German-American Catholics to preserve their language and culture within a pluralistic American Catholic Church. In 1896 he had written another pamphlet, entitled *Foreign Ideas in the Church of the United States* (Buffalo, N.Y.: Privately published, 1896), in which he accused German Catholics of attempting to divide the American Church. See Barry, *Catholic Church and German Americans,* 169–70.

34. *New York Voice,* April 21, 1898.

35. Ibid.

36. *St. Vincent Journal* 7 (1897–98): 383.

37. See the *Catalogue of the Officers, Faculty, and Students of St. Vincent College, Beatty, Westmoreland Co., Pennsylvania* (Beatty, Pa.: St. Vincent Archabbey Press) for the years 1900 to 1910. An analysis of the family names of students in the college and seminary during this ten-year period is the basis for this observation.

38. Anthony X. Sutherland, "The Role of St. Vincent's in Slovak-American History," *Jed-*

nota Annual Furdek 28 (1989): 279. Quoted in Rene Kollar, *Saint Vincent Archabbey and Its Role in the Development of Slovak-American Culture and History* (St. Vincent Archabbey: Privately published, 1995), 4.

39. *St. Vincent Journal* 6 (1896–97): 181–82.

40. Ibid., 15 (1905–6): 47.

41. Ibid., 2 (1892–93): 69.

42. ABelA: Schnerr to Haid, St. Vincent, March 9, 1913.

43. *Catalogus Monachorum Congregationis Americano-Cassinensis sub titulo Sanctorum Angelorum Custodum* (Collegeville, Minn.: St. John's Abbey Press, 1913).

44. *St. Vincent Journal* 22 (1912–13): 89–91; Cyprian Davis, *The History of Black Catholics in the United States* (New York: Crossroad, 1995), 124.

45. Archives of the Archdiocese of Denver: Schnerr to Matz, St. Vincent, May 1895. The letter is recorded in the Abbey Chronicle of Holy Cross Abbey, vol. 1, pp. 68–69 (Archives of Holy Cross Abbey) and quoted in Martin J. Burne, "Holy Cross Abbey—One Hundred Years," *The American Benedictine Review* 37 (1986): 428.

46. ASVA: Schnerr to Pope Leo XIII, St. Vincent, July 1895 (copy).

47. ASVA: Roman Documents, November 26, 1895.

48. Burne, "Holy Cross Abbey," 429.

49. AACC: Schnerr to Haid, St. Vincent, March 23, 1896.

50. Burne, "Holy Cross Abbey," 430.

51. AHCA: Abbey Chronicle of Holy Cross Abbey, vol. 1, p. 112. Quoted in Burne, "Holy Cross Abbey," 430.

52. ASVA: Diary of Archabbot Leander Schnerr, entries for February 10 and May 12, 1903.

53. *St. Vincent Journal* 13 (1903–4): 25, 35; 14 (1904–5): 49.

54. ASVA: Grass to Schnerr, Pueblo, January 5, 1907.

55. *St. Vincent Journal* 18 (1908–9): 191–92.

56. ASVA: Schnerr to Kaib, St. Vincent, June 10, 1910.

57. ASVA: Kaib to Schnerr, Pueblo, [June 1910].

58. ASVA: Stehle to Schnerr, Pueblo, April 29, 1915.

59. ASVA: Stehle to Schnerr, Pueblo, August 12, 1915.

60. ASVA: Stehle to Schnerr, Pueblo, May 22, 1916, and January 17, 1918.

61. ASVA: Minutes of the Large Chapter, March 19, 1918; Diary of Leander Schnerr, March 19 and 20, 1918.

62. *St. Vincent Journal* 32 (1922–23): 11–13.

63. ASVA: Huber to Schnerr, Peru, January 20, 1898, and September 11, 1898.

64. Theodore Fuertges, "The History of Saint Bede College and Abbey, Peru, Illinois, 1889–1941" (M.A. thesis, Catholic University of America, 1941), 51.

65. *St. Vincent Journal* 17 (1907–8): 47–48, and Fuertges, "The History of Saint Bede College and Abbey," 52–53.

66. *St. Vincent Journal* 15 (1905–6): 242.

67. Fuertges, "History of Saint Bede College and Abbey," 57–59.

68. *Acta et Decreta Capituli Generalis Decimi Sexti Congregationis Benedictinae Americano-Cassinensis* (Atchison, Kans.: Abbey Student Press, 1908).

69. ASVA: Schnerr to chapter members, St. Vincent, September 12, 1909.

70. ASVA: Roman Documents, January 20, 1910. In 1908 the Holy See had removed the American Church from the jurisdiction of the Sacred Congregation for the Propagation of the Faith (the Vatican's missionary congregation) and placed it under the Sacred Consistorial Congregation. This action effectively removed the United States from the list of "missionary countries" and, among other things, established a new relationship between the Holy See and the exempt Benedictine monastaries of America.

71. Fuertges, "History of Saint Bede College and Abbey," 61–69.

72. *St. Vincent Journal* 12 (1902–3): 467.

73. Ibid., 12 (1902–3): 467–69; 13 (1903–4): 380–82; 14 (1904–5): 468–75; and Haas, *St.*

Vincent's: Souvenir of the Consecration of the Abbey Church, August 24, 1905, 51–56. See also Melvin C. Rupprecht, "Saint Vincent Archabbey Church" (B.A. thesis, St. Vincent College, 1938), 21–51.

74. *St. Vincent Journal* 14 (1904–5): 245; 17 (1907–8): 298–307.

75. Ibid., 15 (1905–6): 17–27.

76. Both were published at Latrobe by the St. Vincent Press in 1905.

77. *Catalogue of the Officers, Faculty, and Students of St. Vincent College, Beatty, Westmoreland Co., Pennsylvania, 1904–5* (Latrobe: St. Vincent Archabbey, 1905), 31.

78. *Catalogue of the Officers, Faculty, and Students of St. Vincent College, Beatty, Westmoreland Co., Pennsylvania, 1916–17* (Latrobe, Pa.: St. Vincent Archabbey Press, 1917), 6.

79. *Catalogue 1904–5,* 11–12.

80. Ibid., 11.

81. *Catalogue of the Officers, Faculty, and Students of St. Vincent College, Beatty, Westmoreland Co., Pennsylvania, 1905–6* (Latrobe, Pa.: St. Vincent Archabbey Press, 1906), 9–10.

82. *St. Vincent Journal* 14 (1904–5): 228–29.

83. ASVA: Huber to Schnerr, St. Bede's, April 26, 1899; Schnerr to Huber, St. Vincent, May 1 and 15, 1899.

84. *St. Vincent Journal* 10 (1900–1901): 29.

85. Incarnata Girgen, "The Schools of the American-Cassinese Benedictines in the United States: Their Foundation, Development, and Character" (Ph.D. diss., St. Louis University, 1944), 315–16. See Rippinger, *Benedictine Order in the United States,* 123; and Colman J. Barry, *Worship and Work: Saint John's Abbey and University 1856–1992,* 3d ed. (Collegeville, Minn.: Liturgical Press, 1993), 231.

86. Rippinger, *Benedictine Order in the United States,* 125, and Debora Wilson, "Benedictine Higher Education and the Development of American Higher Education" (Ph.D. diss., University of Michigan, 1969).

87. In American Benedictine communities, "cleric" was the term used to designate young Benedictine monks who had completed their one-year novitiate and who were now engaged in six years of philosophical and theological study in preparation for ordination to the priesthood.

88. ASVA: Minutes of the Small Chapter, January 7, 1912; Tasch to Schnerr, Baltimore, July 12, 1915. See *St. Vincent Journal* 26 (1916–17): 27.

89. Ibid., 25 (1915–16): 50–54.

90. Ibid., 15 (1905–6): 47.

91. Ibid., 20 (1910–11): 493. *The Juniors of St. Bede's,* by T. H. Bryson, was published in New York by Benziger Brothers in 1911.

92. Except where otherwise noted, this discussion of the seminary at Saint Vincent is based upon an analysis of information about the institution published annually in the *Catalogue. . .of Saint Vincent College* from 1900 to 1918.

93. *St. Vincent Journal* 21 (1911–12): 242.

94. Ibid., 30 (1920–21): 2.

95. Ibid., 17 (1907–8): 119–20.

96. On the difficulties some American seminaries faced in the aftermath of the condemnation of Modernism, see Jay P. Dolan, *The American Catholic Experience: A History from Colonial Times to the Present* (New York: Doubleday, 1985), 318–19.

97. *St. Vincent Journal* 22 (1912–13): 24–27.

98. ABelA: Schnerr to Haid, St. Vincent, January 30, 1912.

99. ABelA: Schnerr to Haid, St. Vincent, February 15, 1912.

100. *St. Vincent Journal* 23 (1913–14): 609.

101. Ibid., 25 (1915–16): 60; and 26 (1916–17): 185–86.

102. *Catalogus Monachorum Congregationis Americano-Cassinensis sub titulo Sanctorum Angelorum Custodum* (1913), 3–15.

103. ASVA: Schnerr to Bishop of Boise, St. Vincent, March 4, 1894; Schnerr to Cardinal

Gibbons, Baltimore, January 21, 1902; McCook to Schnerr, Pittsburgh, April 12, 1902; Byrnes to Schnerr, Nashville, St. Vincent, September 8, 1905.

104. Pope Pius X, *motu proprio* "Tra le sollecitudini" (November 22, 1903).

105. ASVA: MS. Collection, [Henry Ganss], "Fugitive Recollections Musical and Unmusical, 1868–1878, by an Old Alumnus," 41.

106. *St. Vincent Journal* 13 (1903–4): 266–67.

107. ASVA: Rupprecht to Zuercher, Grand Rapids, February 14, 1904; and Schnerr Diary, October 1903–February 1904. See also *St. Vincent Journal* 13 (1903–4): 269.

108. Ibid., 23 (1913–14): 18.

109. Gerard Bridge, *Illustrated History of St. Vincent Archabbey* (Beatty, Pa.: St. Vincent's Press, 1922), 162–63. See also Paulinus Selle, "Building Construction at St. Vincent" (B.A. thesis, St. Vincent College, 1936). Except when otherwise noted, information in this section is taken from these two sources.

110. *St. Vincent Journal* 23 (1913–14): 216–18.

111. Ibid., 17 (1907–8): 102–4.

112. Ibid., 23 (1913–14): 52–53.

113. Ibid., 24 (1914–15): 309–10.

114. Ibid., 24 (1914–15): 81.

115. ASVA: Prendl to Schnerr, Rome, February 1, 1915, and *St. Vincent Journal* 24 (1914–15): 322–23.

116. ASVA: Mersinger to Schnerr, Engelberg, June 11, 1915, and *St. Vincent Journal* 24 (1914–15): 714.

117. ASVA: Mersinger to Schnerr, Freiburg, October 28, 1915, and March 21, 1916; and Hruza to Schnerr, Freiburg, December 3, 1915.

118. ASVA: Mersinger to Schnerr, Rome, August 23, 1914.

119. ASVA: Marmion to Schnerr, Enniscorthy, January 21, 1916; Merten to Schnerr, Enniscorthy, December 9, 1918.

120. *St. Vincent Journal* 25 (1915–16): 290.

121. ASVA: Diary of Leander Schnerr, June 12, 1918. See *St. Vincent Journal* 26 (1916–17): 583–84; 27 (1917–18): 413–15.

122. ASVA: Schnerr to monastic community, St. Vincent, March 30, 1917.

123. *St. Vincent Journal* 27 (1917–18): 121, 179, 230.

124. Ibid., 28 (1918–19): 38, 128.

125. ASVA: Thiede to Subprior Remigius Burgemeister, France, December 10, 1918; printed in *St. Vincent Journal* 28 (1918–19): 321.

126. *St. Vincent Journal* 28 (1918–19): 644–45, 665. A month before he died, McKee wrote a moving letter to newly elected Archabbot Aurelius Stehle describing his attendance at a "field Mass" with Brother Vincent Thiede and fellow Saint Vincent alumnus William Kelly (Ibid., pp. 185–87). In 1921 McKee's body was brought back from France and buried in his home parish of Blessed Sacrament, Greensburg, with full military honors. Father Edgar Zuercher of Saint Vincent celebrated the solemn Requiem Mass, assisted by Fathers Gilbert Straub and Francis Mersinger. Archabbot Aurelius spoke the eulogy. (Ibid., 31 [1921–22]: 29–30.)

127. Ibid., 28 (1918–19): 341.

128. Ibid., 132, 208–10.

129. Ibid., 132–33.

130. Ibid., 29 (1919–20): 43–44. See Charles J. Hokky, *Ruthenia: Spearhead toward the West* (Gainesville, Fla.: Danubian Research and Information Center, 1966), 18–21.

131. ASVA: Leander Schnerr Diary, October 15 and 16, 1917.

132. ASVA: Election Records, June 25, 1918; Schnerr Diary, June 24–25, 1918.

NOTES TO CHAPTER 6. MISSION TO CHINA

1. James Hennesey, *American Catholics: A History of the Roman Catholic Community in the United States* (New York: Oxford University Press, 1981), 234–53, and Gerald P. Fogarty, *The Vatican and the American Hierarchy from 1870 to 1965* (Collegeville, Minn.: Liturgical Press, 1990), 214–28.

2. Fogarty, *The Vatican and the American Hierarchy*, 205. See also Thomas A. Breslin, *China, American Catholicism, and the Missionary* (University Park, Pa.: Penn State University Press, 1980) and Robert Carbonneau, "The Passionists in China, 1921–29: An Essay in Mission Experience," *Catholic Historical Review* 66 (1980): 392–416.

3. *Saint Vincent College Journal* 10 (1900–1901): 2–16, 87–88; 11 (1901–2): 309–16.

4. Ibid., 29 (1919–20): 671; 30 (1920–21): 175; 31 (1921–22): 9, 127–28.

5. Ibid., 29 (1919–20): 671–72; 30 (1920–21): 335–36.

6. Ibid., 30 (1920–21): 389–91; 31 (1921–22): 141–43; 33 (1923–24): 54–55; 32 (1922–23): 325.

7. ASVA: Schrembs to Stehle, Toledo, September 10, 1917; also, *Fu Jen News Letter (Peiping, China)* (March 1931): 2.

8. See Donald Paragon, "Ying Lien-chih (1866–1926) and the Rise of Fu Jen, The Catholic University of Peking," *Monumenta Serica* 20 (1961): 165–225.

9. [George Barry O'Toole], "Chronicle," *Bulletin: Catholic University of Peking,* (September 1926), 63.

10. ACSA: Fumasoni-Biondi to Stotzingen, Rome, December 17, 1921; AACC: Van Rossum to Helmstetter, Rome, June 22, 1922, and February 24, 1923. See "Chronicle," Bulletin: Catholic University of Peking, (September 1926), 64.

11. *Acta et Decreta Capituli Generalis XXI Congregationis Benedictinae Americano-Cassinensis* (Latrobe, Pa.: Archabbey Press, 1923).

12. ASVA: Chapter Minutes, October 5, 1923.

13. ASVA: Kohlbeck to Stehle, Rome, June 3, 1924.

14. *Saint Vincent College Journal* 33 (1923–24): 313.

15. See Paul Taylor, "The Development and the Role of Proselytizing in Christian Education in China Culminating in the Expression of the Benedictines at Fu Jen University in Peking," paper presented at Boston College, April 3, 1996. On Ma Xiangbo, see Ruth Hayhoe and Lu Yongling, eds., *Ma Xiangbo and the Mind of Modern China* (New York: M. E. Sharpe, 1996), and Ruth Hayhoe, "Jesuits and the Modern Chinese University," *International Higher Education* 4 (Spring 1996): 8–9. On Vincent Ying, see Paragon, "Ying Lien-chih (1866–1926)" and "Obituary of Sir Vincent Ying, K.S.G.," *Bulletin: Catholic University of Peking* 1 (September 1926): 29–34.

16. ASVA: Stehle to capitulars, St. Vincent, July 14, 1924, and Rattenberger to Stehle, Peking, July 21, 1924. Rattenberger's letter is published in the *Saint Vincent College Journal* 34 (1924–25): 14–16.

17. ASVA: Brandstetter and Rattenberger to Stehle, Peking, July 17, 1924.

18. ASVA: Roman Documents, June 27, 1924 (Protocol N. 2244–24). The Catholic University of Peking, along with the French Jesuit universities in Shanghai and Tientsin, was one of three Catholic universities in China, but the only one with pontifical status. The Holy See made a strategic decision in 1921 to support the establishment of an American rather than a French institution in China. Part of the reason for this was the perception in Rome that the United States was in a better position to provide the resources for a pontifical Chinese Catholic university than was France, which still suffered from the devastation of the First World War. See Taylor, "The Development and the Role of Proselytizing in Christian Education in China," 6–8; Anthony C. Li, *The History of Privately Controlled Higher Education in the Republic of China* (Washington, D.C.: Catholic University of America Press, 1954); Ruth Hayhoe, "China's Universities and Western Academic Models" in *From Dependence to Autonomy,* ed. Philip G. Altbach and V. Selvaratnam (Dordrecht: Kluwer Academic Publishers, 1989),

25–61; J. G. Lutz, *China and the Christian Colleges* (Ithaca, N.Y.: Cornell University Press, 1971); and Edward J. Malatesta, "Two Chinese Catholic Universities and a Major Chinese Catholic Thinker: Shendan Daxue, Furen Daxue, and Ma Xiangbo," in *Historiography of the Chinese Catholic Church: Nineteenth and Twentieth Centuries,* ed. Jeroom Heyndrickx, Louvain Chinese Studies 1 (Leuven: F. Verbiest Foundation, 1994), 235–45.

19. ASVA: Brandstetter and Rattenberger to Stehle, Peking, July 17, 1924.

20. Ibid.

21. ASVA: Clougherty to Stehle, Kaifeng, July 14, 1924.

22. "Chronicle," *Bulletin: Catholic University of Peking,* (May 1928), 79.

23. ASVA: Stehle to abbots and priests of the American Cassinese Congregation, St. Vincent, October 5, 1924. The letter is printed in appendix 9.

24. ASVA: Stehle to abbots and priests of the American Cassinese Congregation, St. Vincent, February 22, 1926.

25. Ibid. See also "Chronicle," *Bulletin: Catholic University of Peking,* 1 (September 1926), 66.

26. ASVA: Stehle to abbots and priests of the American Cassinese Congregation, St. Vincent, February 22, 1926.

27. [George Barry O'Toole], "Kung Chiao Ta Hsüeh (The Catholic University of Peking)," *Saint Vincent College Journal* 35 (1925–26): 192–94.

28. "Chronicle," *Bulletin: Catholic University of Peking,* (September 1926), 69–70; (March 1927), 41.

29. ASVA: Stehle to "Dear Confrere," St. Vincent, June 1, 1926.

30. "Chronicle," Bulletin: Catholic University of Peking, (March 1927), 42–43. See Celso Costantini, "The Need for a Sino-Christian Architecture for our Catholic Missions," Ibid., (September 1927), 7–16; and Adelbert Gresnigt, "Chinese Architecture," Ibid., (May 1928), 33–46.

31. "The University Shelters Refugees," Ibid., (March 1927), 36–39.

32. "Chronicle," Ibid., (September 1927), 62–63.

33. Paragon, "Ying Lien-chih (1866–1926)," 212–13; and "Chronicle," *Bulletin: Catholic University of Peking,* (September 1926), 69.

34. Wu Xiaoxin, "A Case Study of the Catholic University of Peking during the Benedictine Period (1927–1933)" (Ed.D. Diss., University of San Francisco, 1993), 132–33.

35. [George Barry O'Toole], "Pei-Ching Kung Chiao Ta Hsüeh (The Chinese Name of the Catholic University of Peking)," *Bulletin: Catholic University of Peking,* (September 1926), 7. See also George B. O'Toole, "The Catholic University of Peking," *America,* April 10, 1926, 610.

36. ASVA: Callistus Stehle, "The Catholic University of Peking," *The Call of the Mission,* October 20, 1929. 1–2; and Wilt to "Dear Confreres," Peking, May 24, 1930.

37. Francis Clougherty, "The Publications of the Catholic University of Peking," *Bulletin: Catholic University of Peking,* (July 1929), 67–91; and "Chronicle," Ibid., (March 1927), 42–43.

38. "Chronicle," Ibid., (September 1926), 69; (September 1927), 64.

39. ASVA: English translation of the inspectors' report on the Catholic University of Peking to the Ministry of Education, June 29, 1927. See Wu Xiaoxin, "A Case Study of the Catholic University of Peking," 69–78.

40. ASVA: O'Toole to Stehle, Peking, August 15, 1927.

41. ASVA: Brandstetter to Stehle, Peking, August 7, 1927.

42. ASVA: O'Toole to Rt. Rev. Prelates and Rev. Fathers, Peking, July 15, 1927. The English translation of this Latin letter is printed in *Bulletin: Catholic University of Peking,* (May 1928), 17–19.

43. Wu Xiaoxin, "A Case Study of the Catholic University of Peking," 89–100.

44. The Chinese professors during the 1927–28 academic year were: Chen Yuan, Shen

Chien-shih, Chu Shih-chen, Yin Yen-wu, Liu Fu, Chang Hsing-lang, Chu Hsi-tsu, Ying Chien-li, Kuo Chia-sheng, Hung Ta, Huang Lung-fang, and Wu Kuo-chang. See *Bulletin: Catholic University of Peking,* (May 1928), 21–24.

45. Christian Papeians de Morchoven, "The China Mission of the Benedictine Abbey of Sint- Andries (Bruger)" in Heyndrickx, *Historiography of the Chinese Catholic Church: Nineteenth and Twentieth Centuries,* 305–10; and Henri-Philippe Delcourt, *Dom Jehan Joliet (1870–1937): Un projet de monachisme bénédictin chinois* (Paris: Editions du Cerf, 1988).

46. *Bulletin: Catholic University of Peking,* (May 1928), 21–24.

47. ASVA: Chapter Minutes, October 28, 1927.

48. ASVA: Chapter Minutes, August 1, 1928; and Stehle to "Dear Confrater," St. Vincent, December 10, 1927. See also *Saint Vincent College Journal* 37 (1927–28): 150 and ASVA: Notes on the financial transactions of Saint Vincent on behalf of the Catholic University of Peking. The loan from the Dollar Savings Bank of Pittsburgh was repaid by the archabbey in 1936–37.

49. "Chronicle," *Bulletin: Catholic University of Peking,* (July 1929), 132.

50. *Commonweal,* December 12, 1928. See also Ibid., April 7, 1926.

51. *Saint Vincent College Journal* 39 (October 1929): 18.

52. ASVA: Jones (chairman of the Commission on Higher Education for the Middle States Association) to Stehle, New York, June 27, 1921; and *Saint Vincent College Journal* 31 (1921–22): 134.

53. *St. Vincent College and Ecclesiastical Seminary, Beatty, Penna., 1922–1923* (Beatty, Pa.: Archabbey Press, [1923]), 32. Except where otherwise noted, the following discussion of the academic and extracurricular programs at Saint Vincent College from 1921 to 1930 is based upon an analysis of the college's annual catalogues issued during the period.

54. In 1923 Archabbot Aurelius wrote Pittsburgh's Bishop Hugh Boyle, a proponent of rigorous Latin studies: "I spent an hour and a half yesterday morning in the Sophomore class conducting a Colloquium Latinum. It was intensely interesting. How I wished that you could be present and convince yourself that we are attempting to carry out your excellent advice in this matter." ASVA: Stehle to Boyle, St. Vincent, January 12, 1923.

55. *Saint Vincent College Journal* 37 (1927–28): 270.

56. ASVA: Stehle to Helmstetter, Saint Vincent, December 18, 1920. Quoted in Joel Rippinger, *The Benedictine Order in the United States: An Interpretive History* (Collegeville, Minn.: The Liturgical Press, 1990), 125.

57. *The Saint Vincent College Journal* between 1920 and 1930 regularly reported on where the young priests and clerics of Saint Vincent were studying.

58. *Saint Vincent College Journal* 31 (1921–22): 205–6; 39 (October 1929): 18.

59. Ibid., 38 (1928–29): 212.

60. Ibid., 33 (1923–24): 122–23, 229–30; 34 (1924–25): 266–68; 38 (1928–29): 82.

61. Ibid., 31 (1921–22): 266–68; 33 (1923–24): 283; 34 (1924–25): 346–47; and 35 (1925–26): 320.

62. *St. Vincent College and Ecclesiastical Seminary, Beatty, Pa., 1917–1918* (Beatty, Pa.: Archabbey Press, 1918), 19–21.

63. *St. Vincent College and Ecclesiastical Seminary, Beatty, Pa., 1918–1919* (Beatty, Pa.: Archabbey Press, 1919), 17.

64. *St. Vincent College and Ecclesiastical Seminary, Beatty, Pa., 1921–1922* (Beatty, Pa.: Archabbey Press, 1922), 17.

65. Ibid., 17–18.

66. ASVA: Stehle to Mons. P. C. Danner, Saint Vincent, September 28, 1922; Stehle to Bishop Boyle, Saint Vincent, November 28, 1923; January 27, 1924; February 27, 1924.

67. *Saint Vincent College Journal* 33 (1923–24): 11.

68. ASVA: Bishop Canevin to Stehle, Pittsburgh, July 26, 1919.

69. ASVA has a complete set of *The Seminarists' Symposium,* 1919 to 1932.

70. *Saint Vincent College Journal* 32 (1922–23): 241.

71. Ibid., 29 (1919–20): 317–18, 364–69; 31 (1921–22): 11–14, 23; 33 (1923–24): 220.

72. Ibid., 30 (1920–21): 1–4.

73. ASVA: Nanita Wimmer to Schnerr, Minnesota, October 29, 1918; Schnerr Diary, November 3, 1918, and December 2, 1918; "Obituary: Mr. Sebastian Wimmer," *Saint Vincent College Journal* 31 (1921–22): 135–36.

74. *Saint Vincent College Journal* 37 (1927–28): 21.

75. Ibid., 32 (1922–23): 318–19.

76. Ibid., 36 (1926–27): 197–98, 236.

77. ASVA: Stehle to Abbot Alcuin Deutsch, St. Vincent, January 3, 1924, and January 31, 1924.

78. ASVA: Minutes of the Small Chapter, November 18, 1924; Minutes of the Large Chapter, February 18, 1926. See Valerian Odermann, "Abbot Placid Hoenerbach and the Bankruptcy of St. Mary's Abbey, Richardton," *The American Benedictine Review* 29 (1978): 100–114.

79. Colman J. Barry, *Worship and Work: Saint John's Abbey and University 1856–1992,* 3d ed. (Collegeville, Minn.: Liturgical Press, 1993), 305.

80. ASVA: Stehle to Bishop Boyle, St. Vincent, March 29, 1923; Minutes of the Large Chapter, August 19, 1925.

81. ASVA: Father Augustino Costa to Stehle, Montserrat, May 26, 1920.

82. See, for example, *Saint Vincent College Journal* 39 (October 1929): 19–20.

83. ASVA: See Stehle's correspondence with Bishops Canevin and Boyle of Pittsburgh for examples of his liturgical concerns.

84. Joseph P. Chinnici, *Living Stones: The History and Structure of Catholic Spiritual Life in the United States,* 2d ed. (Maryknoll, N.Y.: Orbis Books, 1996), 178; and Rippinger, *The Benedictine Order in the United States,* 185–89. On Virgil Michel and the liturgical movement, see R. W. Franklin and Robert L. Spaeth, *Virgil Michel: American Catholic* (Collegeville, Minn.: Liturgical Press, 1988); Jeremy Hall, *The Full Stature of Christ: The Ecclesiology of Dom Virgil Michel* (Collegeville, Minn.: Liturgical Press, 1976), and Paul Marx, *Virgil Michel and the Liturgical Movement* (Collegeville, Minn.: Liturgical Press, 1957).

85. W[olfgang] F[rey], "A Return to the Liturgy," *Saint Vincent College Journal* 36 (1926–27): 251–54.

86. Fogarty, *The Vatican and the American Hierarchy,* 229–30.

87. *Saint Vincent College Journal* 36 (1926–27): 4.

88. ASVA: Canevin to Stehle, Pittsburgh, February 10, 1921.

89. *Saint Vincent College Journal* 33 (1923–24): 20, 317.

90. *The Official Catholic Directory for 1929* (New York: P. J. Kenedy), 1929. See entries for the dioceses of Altoona, Baltimore, Chicago, Covington, Cleveland, Erie, and Pittsburgh.

91. ASVA: Minutes of the Large Chapter, February 18, 1926.

92. See, for example, ASVA: Brandstetter to Stehle, Peking, August 7, 1927, and August 27, 1927.

93. ASVA: Notes entitled "Suggestions for the Propaganda Fide Submitted in Reference to the Establishing at the Catholic University of Peking of the Faculty of Sacred Theology and Philosophy by Rt. Rev. Aurelius Stehle, O.S.B., Chancellor," no date, but by internal evidence written in July 1929.

94. Archives of Beijing Normal University, Beijing, China: Demotion of Fu Jen University to a College, June 25, 1929. Quoted in Wu Xiaoxin, "A Case Study of the Catholic University of Peking," 75. See also "Chronicle," *Bulletin: Catholic University of Peking,* (December 1930), 131–32.

95. See Wu Xiaoxin, "A Case Study of the Catholic University of Peking," 76–77.

96. ASVA: O'Toole to Stehle, Peking, June 21, 1929. Quoted in Wu Xiaoxin, "A Case Study of the Catholic University of Peking," 76.

97. ASVA: "Suggestions for the Propaganda Fide Submitted . . . by Rt. Rev. Aurelius Stehle" [July 1929].

98. ASVA: Roman Documents [Pope Pius XI to Archabbot Aurelius, Rome], August 20, 1929. A translation of the Latin letter is printed in the *Saint Vincent College Journal* 39 (1929–30): 16.

99. During his lifetime Brady was a notable supporter of Catholic causes. Because of his generous contributions to the Catholic University of America, one of the buildings on campus, Brady Hall, was named after him. Pope Pius XI made Brady a knight of the Supreme Order of Christ, an honor usually reserved for Catholic heads of state. See Hennesey, *American Catholics,* 239.

100. See United States Circuit Court of Appeals for the Third Circuit, Greensburg, Pa., *The Benedictine Society, Defendant-Appellant, v. The National City Bank of New York, Plaintiff-Appellee: Brief for Appellant* (No. 7121 October Term, 1939), 8., and original trial transcript, 12–16.

101. M. D. Currie wrote the manager of National City Bank's Peking Office that "this University, while part and parcel of the work of the Society for the Propagation of the Faith, is under the charge and management of St. Vincent Archabbey, and that the Rt. Rev. Archabbot Aurelius, O.S.B., besides being Archabbot of St. Vincent Archabbey, is also Chancellor of the Catholic University of Peking. . . . While we would have preferred to make the loan direct to the St. Vincent Archabbey, the Archabbot explained that for a variety of reasons he did not wish to follow this procedure and we agreed that after all our request was made on more or less technical grounds. He explained of course that the entire Catholic Church is behind this project, and he also showed us a message from Pope Pius XI, evidencing the interest of the Holy See in this particular Mission." Currie to Bennett, New York, November 15, 1929. Quoted in *Brief for Appellant,* pp. 39–41.

102. Ibid., 7.

103. Ibid., 41–42.

104. Sylvester Healy, "The Plans of the New University Building," *Bulletin: Catholic University of Peking,* (July 1929), 3.

105. Ibid., 7–8.

106. Ibid., 7 (December 1930): 4.

107. Ibid., 133–34.

108. *Saint Vincent College Journal* 39 (1929–30): 18.

109. *Bulletin: Catholic University of Peking,* (December 1930), 135, 141.

110. Wu Xiaoxin, "A Case Study of the Catholic University of Peking," 79; *Bulletin: Catholic University of Peking,* (December 1930), 134, 136; and ASVA: Wilt to "Dear Confreres," Peking, May 24, 1930.

111. *Bulletin: Catholic University of Peking,* (December 1930): 145; (December 1931), 158.

112. Ibid., (October 1928), 103–4.

113. "University Athletics," Ibid., (July 1929), 125.

114. ASVA: Wilt to "Dear Confreres," Peking, May 24, 1930.

115. ASVA: Fellner to "Reverend and Dear Confrere," Saint Vincent, January 27, 1930. At the beginning of February the *Saint Vincent College Journal* reported on the archabbot's condition: "With the laying of the cornerstone of the new building at the Catholic University of Peking on November 13, came new labors and worries for the Rt. Rev. Aurelius Stehle, O.S.B., who was reappointed Chancellor of the University during his recent sojourn in the Eternal City. There were also new difficulties that had to be met and overcome. Thus the Rt. Rev. Archabbot was forced to make extraordinary efforts to secure the needed assistance.

"With his customary zeal, the Rt. Rev. Archabbot set forth to do the Holy Father's bidding, although handicapped by a weakened condition brought on by a severe cold which clung to him through the Christmas holidays.

"In order to make the University better known and to increase its possible assistance, the

Rt. Rev. Aurelius Stehle, O.S.B., attended the Propagation of the Faith meeting in Cleveland, Ohio, on January 23. But the work was too much and the overexertion on his part debilitated his condition to such an extent that he suffered a nervous breakdown while in Cleveland. He was brought to Pittsburgh by the Rev. Victor Lillig, O.S.B., and is now taking a complete rest in St. Francis Hospital. His condition, however, is not critical, and the latest report from the doctors shows a slight improvement.

"Several prominent physicians are doing all they can to bring the Rt. Rev. Archabbot back to health. This, we realize, must be done with the aid of the Great Physician, and we ask you to make a special memento in your prayers for his speedy recovery" (39 [1929–30]: 281).

116. ASVA: Barrett to Nealon, Pittsburgh, February 1, 1930.

117. ASVA: Fellner to "Dear Confreres," Saint Vincent, February 5, 1930.

118. *Saint Vincent College Journal* 39 (1929–30): 174.

NOTES TO CHAPTER 7. DEPRESSION AND JUDGMENT

1. ASVA: Election Records, April 22–23, 1930. See also *Saint Vincent College Journal* 39 (1929–30): 234, and *The Seminarists' Symposium* (1931): 72–73.

2. ASVA: Chapter Minutes 1924–1929. Even the crucial vote on whether to accept the China mission in the first place won by only a plurality of those chapter members who happened to be at Saint Vincent at the time. The vote was fourteen "yes," seven "no," and eight "indifferent." More than ninety of the eligible capitulars did not vote. See Chapter Minutes, October 5, 1923.

3. ASVA: Fellner to Currie, St. Vincent, March 14, 1930. See District Court of the United States for the Western District of Pennsylvania, *National City Bank of New York v. Benedictine Society* (No. 8659, May 1939), 191–202.

4. United States Circuit Court of Appeals for the Third Circuit, Greensburg, Pa., *The Benedictine Society, Defendant-Appellant, v. The National City Bank of New York, Plaintiff-Appellee: Brief for Appellant* (No. 7121, October Term, 1939), 52.

5. Ibid., 49.

6. Ibid., 46, 52.

7. Ibid., 3.

8. *Saint Vincent College Journal* 40 (1930–31): 11, 16. Koch was blessed in the archabbey church on June 10, 1930, by Bishop Hugh C. Boyle of Pittsburgh. Abbot Vincent Taylor of Belmont Abbey, North Carolina, preached the sermon.

9. ASVA: Alfred Koch, "A Brief Report of My Visit to Rome," July 14, 1930 (typescript).

10. Ibid. The mystery of the $100,000 promise is probably best ascribed to a misunderstanding on Father Barry O'Toole's part over another verbal promise made by officials of the *Propaganda Fide* to Archabbot Aurelius in 1929. When Archabbot Aurelius returned from Rome he told the council of seniors that *Propaganda* had agreed to pay *interest* on a loan of $100,000 taken by the archabbey. See p. 322.

11. AACC: Koch to Abbot Ernest Helmstetter, St. Vincent, September 9, 1930. See also "A Brief Report of My Visit to Rome."

12. *Bulletin: Catholic University of Peking,* (December 1931), 124.

13. William O'Donnell, "Progress at the Catholic University of Peking," Ibid., (December 1930), 115–19. See also *Saint Vincent College Journal* 41 (1931–32): 38.

14. For the story of the Benedictine sisters in China see Mary Wibora Muehlenbein, *Benedictine Mission to China* (St. Joseph, Minn.: St. Benedict's Convent, 1980) by one of the missionaries, and Grace McDonald, *With Lamps Burning* (St. Paul, Minn.: North Central Publishing Co., 1957), 267–80. See also *Fu Jen Magazine* 1, no. 2 (May–June 1932): 27, and 1, no. 5 (Christmas 1932): 3–6.

15. Archives of St. Benedict's Convent (St. Joseph, Minn.): Program of the First Commencement of the Catholic University of Peking. The program is reproduced in Wu Xiaoxin,

"A Case Study of the Catholic University of Peking during the Benedictine Period (1927–1933)" (Ed.D. diss., University of San Francisco, 1993), 116–17.

16. *Bulletin: Catholic University of Peking,* (December 1931), 125–30.

17. *Fu Jen Magazine* 1, no.5 (Christmas 1932): 20, and 1, no. 6 (January–February 1933): 2. See Wu, "A Case Study of the Catholic University of Peking," 96.

18. *Fu Jen News Letter* (May 1931): 5–6, 9. See Wu, "A Case Study of the Catholic University of Peking," 97–100, 105.

19. See "Father Walsh's Tribute" in *Fu Jen Magazine* 1, no. 4 (September–October 1932): 27, and George Barry O'Toole, "A Gateway to a New China," ibid., 1, no. 5 (Christmas 1932): 20.

20. Ibid., 1, no. 6 (January–February 1933): 26.

21. Ibid., 1, no. 2 (May–June 1932): 28–29; 1, no. 5 (Christmas 1932): 25.

22. Wu, "A Case Study of the Catholic University of Peking," 100–104.

23. *Saint Vincent College Journal* 43 (1932–33): 184–85.

24. ASVA: Koch to Helmstetter, St. Vincent, December 9, 1931; Minutes of the Council of Seniors, January 19, 1932.

25. ASVA: O'Toole to Hugh Wilt, Toledo, August 7, 1934.

26. ASVA: [Alfred Koch], "Promemoria de Prioratu S. Benedicti in Urbe Pekino necnon de Universitate Catholica Benedictinorum Pekinensi," July 5, 1932.

27. ASVA: Archabbot Alfred Koch's address to the abbots and delegates of the 24th general chapter of the American Cassinese Congregation, St. Procopius Abbey, Lisle, Ill., August 30, 1932.

28. ASVA: Koch to "Reverend and dear Confrere," St. Vincent, October 4, 1932.

29. ASVA: Deutsch to Koch, St. John's, December 16, 1932.

30. AACC: Koch to Deutsch, St. Vincent, December 20, 1932,

31. ASVA: Koch to Propaganda Fide, St. Vincent, October 23, 1932.

32. ASVA: O'Toole to Hugh Wilt, New York, January 27, 1933.

33. ASVA: O'Toole to Hugh Wilt, Rome, April 25, 1933.

34. ASVA: Diary of Archabbot Alfred Koch, March 21, 1933.

35. AACC: Koch to Deutsch, St. Vincent, March 28, 1933.

36. ASVA: Deutsch to Koch, Rome, April 12, 1933.

37. Colman J. Barry, *Worship and Work: Saint John's Abbey and University 1856–1992,* 3d ed. (Collegeville, Minn.: Liturgical Press, 1993), 309.

38. ASVA: Diary of Archabbot Alfred Koch, May 3, 1933.

39. ASVA: Deutsch to "Right Rev. and dear Father Abbot," St. John's, May 10, 1933.

40. AACC: Koch to Deutsch, St. Vincent, May 28, 1933.

41. ASVA: Minutes of the Council of Seniors, June 5, 1933.

42. AACC: Koch to Deutsch, St. Vincent, January 19, 1934.

43. AACC: Koch to Deutsch, St. Vincent, March 8, 1935.

44. Vitus Buresh, *The Procopian Chronicle: St. Procopius Abbey, 1885–1985* (Lisle, Ill.: St. Procopius Abbey, 1985), 95–98.

45. Ibid., 99–107; McDonald, *With Lamps Burning,* 275–76; and Joel Rippinger, *The Benedictine Order in the United States: An Interpretive History* (Collegeville, Minn.: Liturgical Press, 1990), 232.

46. ASVA: Clougherty to Fellner, Kaifeng, November 25, 1933.

47. ASVA: Catholic University, Peking, China, Financial Report: Feb. 1, 1925–June 1, 1933. The amounts listed in this report were given in Mexican dollars, a standard international currency used in China at the time. The Mexican dollar was valued at between one-half and three-fourths the U.S. dollar during the period in question. For the sake of uniformity, the U.S. dollar amounts given in the following discussion are estimated to be one-half the value of the recorded amount in Mexican dollars. Exact U.S. dollar figures are given when known.

48. AACC: Koch to Deutsch, St. Vincent, August 22, 1933. See also Koch to Deutsch, St. Vincent, January 19, 1934, and October 25, 1935.

49. ASVA: Bequest of Helen J. Thornton, May 1, 1925. (The bequest was "accepted, vouched for, and guaranteed" by Archabbot Aurelius Stehle on May 1, 1925.)

50. Court of Common Pleas of Westmoreland County, *Helen J. Thornton vs. Rt. Rev. Alfred Koch, O.S.B., Archabbot of St. Vincent's Monastery, Beatty, Pa., and The Benedictine Society* (No. 1538, May 1934).

51. Ibid., 3a.

52. ASVA: Chapter Minutes, April 25, 1935.

53. Miss Thornton's longevity astonished the Saint Vincent monks. She had, after all, made the original agreement with Archabbot Aurelius in 1925 at a time when she asserted that she was "ill in mind and body" (*Thornton vs. Koch and the Benedictine Society,* 6a). She had moved from Pittsburgh to California, and in 1964, as they continued to send the annual check to her lawyers, the Council of Seniors wondered whether she had died, and they hired a private investigator to find out. The report came back from California that Miss Thornton was indeed still alive. She died on June 14, 1973.

54. ASVA: Sullivan to Stehle, Philadelphia, February 14, 1929.

55. ASVA: Chapter Minutes, February 20, 1929, April 29, 1929, and March 16, 1930.

56. Consuela Marie Duffy, *Katharine Drexel: A Biography* (Cornwell Heights, Pa.: Mother Katharine Drexel Guild, 1966), 199–202. See also Marie Barat Smith, "A History of St. Emma's Military Academy and St. Francis de Sales High School" (M.A. thesis, Catholic University of America, 1949).

57. *Saint Vincent College Journal* 38 (1928–29): 244; 39 (1929–30): 18, 50.

58. ASVA: *Catalogue of the St. Emma Industrial and Agricultural Institute* (1930–31): 9.

59. ASVA: *The Belmeadian,* Rock Castle, Va. (October 1944): 1–2.

60. Though several African Americans from Maryland, Georgia, and Louisiana became monks at Saint Vincent during the nineteenth century, only one, Siricius Palmer of Georgia, studied for the priesthood. Palmer, however, did not complete his studies and left the community before ordination. See p. 164.

61. ASVA: *Catalogue of the Saint Emma Military Academy* (1945–1947): 3–4, 21–22.

62. ASVA: Morrell to Koch, Philadelphia, July 27, 1945.

63. ASVA: Koch to Morrell, St. Vincent, September 14, 1945, and October 5, 1945. See also Minutes of the Board of Trustees of the St. Emma Industrial & Agricultural Institute, October 11, 1945.

64. ASVA: Koch to Strittmatter, St. Vincent, May 7, 1946. See also Father Vitus Kriegel's notes on the "Status of Our Relation with Bel Meade," c. June 1946.

65. ASVA: Chapter Minutes, December 16, 1946.

66. *The Catholic Virginian,* May 5, 1972, 3. According to the board of directors, the decision to close was "motivated by a drastic decrease in enrollment, rising costs and changes in societal attitudes toward military and segregated facilities." By 1972 enrollment had dropped to ninety-three students; the endowment now covered only a fifth of the operating costs, and "it was the feeling of the board that a racially 'isolated' institution is out of date." In addition, the military character of the school had "drawn objections from a number of former students, parents and some of the present students themselves." The closing of St. Emma's followed by two years the demise of its sister institution, St. Francis de Sales Academy for girls.

67. This information is taken from the Saint Vincent College catalogues published annually between 1930 and 1940.

68. *Saint Vincent College Journal* 39 (1929–30): 284–85.

69. Ibid., 40 (1930–31): 10.

70. Ibid., 40 (1930–31): 9; 44 (March 15, 1935): 1; 49 (December 15, 1939): 1; and (January 15, 1940): 3. See also the Saint Vincent College catalogues for the years 1931–40.

71. *Saint Vincent College Journal* 42 (1932–33): 84–85.

72. See *Saint Vincent College Catalogue* (1934–35): 13–14.

73. Ibid., (1931–32): 7–9; (1935–36): 7–9.

74. Ibid., (1935–36): 23–24.

75. Ibid., (1934–35): 131–32.

76. Ibid., (1934–35): 135.

77. On Day, Maurin, and the Catholic Worker Movement, see Robert Coles, *Dorothy Day: A Radical Devotion* (Reading, Mass.: Addison Wesley, 1987) and Mel Piehl, *Breaking Bread: The Catholic Worker and the Origin of Catholic Radicalism in America* (Philadelphia: Temple University Press, 1982).

78. Nicholas J. Campbell, "Local Student Visits 'Catholic Worker' in New York City," *St. Vincent Journal* 46 (May 1, 1937): 10–11.

79. Ibid., 2 (1892–93): 138–46.

80. ASVA: Chapter Minutes, May 1, 1936.

81. *Saint Vincent College Journal* 48 (October 1, 1938): 1, 5, 8.

82. See *Saint Vincent College Catalogue* (1934–35): 71.

83. Robert G. Barcio, *"That You Love One Another": The Life and Times of Archbishop John Mark Gannon*, vol. 2 of *A History of the Diocese of Erie* (Erie, Pa.: Diocese of Erie, 1996), 159–62.

84. *Saint Vincent College Journal* 43 (October 1, 1934): 6; (November 1, 1934): 5.

85. The Depression-era extension program was not the first effort of the monks to establish a college in St. Marys, Pennsylvania. In 1871, at the time the Benedictines received the state charter allowing them to grant degrees at Saint Vincent College, they also received a charter from the Commonwealth of Pennsylvania for "St. Gregory's College" in St. Marys, Pennsylvania. St. Gregory's College, however, was never established, probably because Boniface Wimmer feared that a Benedictine college in St. Marys would attract students who would otherwise have gone to Saint Vincent.

86. *Saint Vincent College Catalogue* (1936–37): 68–69.

87. *Saint Vincent College Journal* 42 (1932–33): 23, 54.

88. *Saint Vincent College Catalogue: School of Commerce and Business Administration, Evening Classes* (1932–33): 9.

89. Joseph Crew, "The College Museum," *Saint Vincent College Journal* 37 (1927–28): 241. The discussion which follows is based upon this article, which appeared in two installments in volume 37 of the *Journal* (pp. 241–44 and 276–78). See also *Saint Vincent College Catalogue* (1935–36): 14–15.

90. Walter R. Suter and Jerome Rupprecht, "The Father of the Schmitt Box," *Entomological News* 85 (November/December 1974): 298–300. Dermestid are beetles that are very destructive to organic material of animal origin, such as leather, wool, and insect specimens collected by entomologists.

91. For more on the college museum see Gerard Bridge, *An Illustrated History of St. Vincent Archabbey* (Beatty, Pa.: St. Vincent Archabbey Press, 1922), 188–91. The museum was dismantled in 1983 when the college turned the space it occupied into offices and classrooms. The entomological collection was donated to the Carnegie Museum of Pittsburgh. Other collections were dispersed among various college departments. Some collections and items were sold or returned to donors.

92. *Saint Vincent College Journal* 40 (1930–31): 81–83; 44 (April 1, 1935): 1, 7.

93. Ibid., 39 (1929–30): 125.

94. Hugh A. McNeill, "On Bearcats," Ibid., 41 (1931–32): 76–77.

95. Ibid., 41 (1931–32): 132.

96. *Greensburg Morning Review*, March 12, 1932, 7.

97. ASVA: Small Chapter Minutes, April 5, 1932; see also *Saint Vincent College Journal* 41 (1931–32): 156.

98. Ibid., 158.

99. Ibid., 46 (October 1, 1936): 1, 11.

100. Ibid., 40 (1930–31): 119.

101. See the annual catalogue of Saint Vincent Seminary (*Seminarium Majus Ecclesiasticum penes Archiabbatiam Sancti Vincenti* [Latrobe, Pa.: Archabbey Press]) for the years 1930 to 1940.

102. *St. Vincent Journal* 50 (October 1, 1940): 3, 9.

103. Ibid., 51 (March 15, 1942): 7. See also Ibid., 48 (February 15, 1939): 3, and 50 (March 15, 1941): 4.

104. *The New American Bible* (New York: Thomas Nelson, 1971).

105. *Saint Vincent Journal* 44 (April 1, 1935): 1; 48 (January 15, 1938): 2–3; 51 (November 1, 1941): 1.

106. *St. Vincent Journal* 51 (March 1, 1942): 1; 54 (November 1, 1944): 1.

107. Edward Robb Ellis, *A Nation in Torment: The Great American Depression 1929–1939* (New York: Coward-McCann, 1970), 398. See *St. Vincent Journal* 41 (1931–32): 111.

108. See James Hennesey, *American Catholics: A History of the Roman Catholic Community in the United States* (New York: Oxford University Press, 1981), 264; and Jay P. Dolan, *The American Catholic Experience: A History from Colonial Times to the Present* (New York: Doubleday, 1985), 77–78.

109 Author's interview with Archabbot Egbert Donovan, April 24, 1998.

110. *St. Vincent Journal* 46 (October 1, 1936): 5.

111. *Catalogue: The Preparatory School, Saint Vincent College* (Latrobe, Pa.: Archabbey Press, 1937), 20.

112. *St. Vincent Journal* 46 (April 15, 1937): 8.

113. Ibid.

114. Ibid., 51 (May 1, 1942): 7.

115. These figures are based on data found in the annual *Ordo* of the American Cassinese Congregation between 1930 and 1950.

116. See, for example, *Saint Vincent College Journal* 40 (1930–31): 16–20; 43 (1933–34): 21–22.

117. ASVA: Seeboeck Correspondence File.

118. Felix Fellner, *Abbot Boniface and His Monk*, 5 vols. (Latrobe, Pa.: Privately published by Saint Vincent Archabbey, 1956), 5:724–26. See also *Saint Vincent College Journal* 40 (1930–31): 205; 41 (1931–32): 2–4.

119. *Saint Vincent College Journal* 40 (1930–31): 205.

120. Ibid., 41 (1931–32): 9, 39; 42 (1932–33): 169.

121. Ibid., 43 (March 1934): 22.

122. William A. Beaver, "'And Who is My Neighbor?' St. Vincent Archabbey Responds to Its Neighbors in the Depression," *Word and Spirit: A Monastic Review* 14 (1992): 98. See also the unpublished paper of Carolyn E. Attneave, "Saint Vincent College in Transition: Coeducation 1983–1984" (ASVA).

123. Beaver, "'And Who is My Neighbor?' St. Vincent Archabbey Responds to Its Neighbors in the Depression," 100–101.

124. *Saint Vincent College Journal* 42 (1932–33): 23–24.

125. Beaver, "'And Who is My Neighbor?' St. Vincent Archabbey Responds to Its Neighbors in the Depression," 102.

126. *Saint Vincent College Journal* 43 (May 1934): 18, 21–22.

127. *Saint Vincent College Journal* 43 (May 1934): 18, 21–22.

128. Ibid., 46 (March 1, 1937): 2. See also ASVA: Diary of Brother Mark Bauer, March 7, 1937, and *St. Vincent Journal* 44 (March 15, 1935): 1; 46 (March 15, 1937): 2.

129. *Saint Vincent College Journal* 43 (June 1934): 21.

130. Ibid., 46 (October 1, 1936): 3.

131. ASJA: Hammenstede to Deutsch, Mount Angel, Oregon, October 3, 1943, quoted in

Barry, *Worship and Work: Saint John's Abbey and University 1856–1992,* 567. See also Rippinger, *The Benedictine Order in the United States,* 187–88.

132. *St. Vincent Journal* 48 (November 1, 1938): 1; 48 (December 1, 1938): 4.

133. Ibid., 49 (January 15, 1940): 1.

134. Ibid., 48 (October 15, 1938): 8, 11.

135. Ibid., 40 (1930–31): 17, 45; 41 (1931–32): 108–9.

136. Ibid., 45 (May 1, 1936): 1; 46 (October 15, 1936): 3.

137. Ibid., 41 (1931–32): 133–34, 181.

138. See Ibid., 46 (December 15, 1936): 2; 46 (March 15, 1937): 2; 46 (June 1, 1937): 1.

139. Ibid., 40 (1930–31): 129–79.

140. Ibid., 43 (May 1934): 21; 46 (October 1, 1936): 3.

141. Ibid., 46 (March 15, 1937): 2.

142. Ibid., 46 (June 15, 1937): 1.

143. ASVA: Koch to Alcuin Deutsch, St. Vincent, January 19, 1934.

144. *St. Vincent Journal* 50 (October 15, 1940): 3; 51 (November 15, 1941): 5.

145. The author interviewed Brother Joseph Weigl on this topic in 1967.

146. See, for example, ASVA: Chapter Minutes, November 7 and 9, 1917.

147. ASVA: Koch to Alcuin Deutsch, St. Vincent, August 22, 1933.

148. ASVA: Diary of Brother Mark Bauer, May 30, 1937.

149. For details on coal mining at Saint Vincent, see ASVA: Chapter Minutes for the years 1890 to 1940.

150. *St. Vincent Journal* 56 (June 1947): 12.

151. ASVA: Chapter Minutes, September 1, 1933.

152. ASVA: Chapter Minutes, January 7, 1937.

153. *St. Vincent Journal* 47 (October 1, 1937): 5.

154. "Boys Enjoy Learning Citizenship at Barry-Robinson Home," *Norfolk Virginia-Pilot,* April 13, 1948, 18. See also ASVA: "James Barry Robinson High School" (brochure c. 1962).

155. ASVA: Diary of Archabbot Alfred Koch, May 3, 1933.

156. District Court of the United States for the Western District of Pennsylvania, *National City Bank of New York v. The Benedictine Society* (No. 8659, May 1939).

157. AACC: Koch to Alcuin Deutsch, St. Vincent, January 20, 1937.

158. ASVA: Deutsch to Koch, St. John's, April 24, 1937.

159. AACC: Koch to Deutsch, St. Vincent, April 28, 1937.

160. ASVA: Deutsch to Koch, St. John's, May 9, 1937.

161. ASVA: Koch to Deutsch, St. Vincent, no date, but from internal evidence, probably May 11, 1937 (draft).

162. AACC: Fumasoni-Biondi to Koch, Rome, June 30, 1937.

163. ASVA: Deutsch to Koch, St. John's, August 2, 1937; AACC: Koch to Deutsch, St. Vincent, August 3, 1937.

164. ACPF: Deutsch to Fumasoni-Biondi, Rome, October 7, 1937 (copy in AACC).

165. ACPF: Pro-memoria of Abbot Alcuin Deutsch to Cardinal Prefect, October 24, 1937; AACC: Cicognani to Deutsch, Washington, December 23, 1937.

166. AACC: Deutsch to Cicognani, St. John's, January 15, 1938 (copy).

167. AACC: Cicognani to Deutsch, Washington, January 25, 1938.

168. AACC: Deutsch to Cicognani, St. John's, February 9, 1938 (copy).

169. AACC: Koch to Deutsch, St. Vincent, October 6 and 22, 1938.

170. ASVA: Deutsch to Koch, St. John's, October 27, 1938.

171. District Court of the United States for the Western District of Pennsylvania, *National City Bank of New York v. The Benedictine Society* (No. 8659, May 1939), 27.

172. Ibid., 339, 344–48.

173. ASVA: Deutsch to Koch, St. John's, May 9, 1939.

174. ASVA: O'Toole to Wilt, Washington, May 28, 1939.

175. AACC: Wilt to Deutsch, Rome, July 14, 1939, and July 15, 1939.

176. AACC: Fumasoni-Biondi to Abbot Primate Fidelis von Stotzingen, Rome, July 14, 1939.

177. ASVA: Archabbot Alfred's Report to the chapter of Saint Vincent on his visit to Rome, July 28, 1939.

178. ASVA: Deutsch to Koch, St. John's, August 10, 1939.

179. AACC: Koch to Deutsch, St. Vincent, August 21, 1939.

180. ASVA: Deutsch to Koch, St. John's, August 23, 1939.

181. ASVA: Deutsch to Koch, St. John's, September 30, 1939.

182. AACC: Koch to Deutsch, St. Vincent, October 12, 1939.

183. ASVA: Deutsch to Koch, St. John's, October 20, 1939.

184. ASVA: Deutsch to Wilt, St. John's, October 19, 1939.

185. AACC: Wilt to Deutsch, St. Vincent, October 23, 1939.

186. ASVA: Deutsch to Koch, St. John's, November 16, 1939.

187. AACC: Koch to Deutsch, St. Vincent, November 18, 1939.

188. United States Circuit Court of Appeals for the Third District, Greensburg, Pa., *Benedictine Society v. National City Bank* (No. 7121, October Term 1939).

189. ASVA: D. C. Borden to G. S. Rentschler (President of the National City Bank of New York), New York, February 7, 1940 (copy). A copy of this memorandum and other materials related to the case were provided courtesy of Father Thomas J. Connellan, C.S.P., whose father was an executive with the National City Bank. of New York.

190. ASVA: Cicognani to Koch, Washington, December 5, 1939.

191. AACC: Koch to Deutsch, St. Vincent, December 7, 1939; ASVA: Deutsch to Koch, St. John's, December 14, 1939.

192. ASVA: Koch to "Right Reverend and Dear Confrere," St. Vincent, December 28, 1939; Deutsch to "Right Rev. and dear Father Abbot," St. John's, January 10, 1940.

193. ASVA: Deutsch to Koch, St. John's, January 30, 1940; AACC: Koch to Deutsch, St. Vincent, February 10, 1940.

194. ASVA: Koch to Braun, St. Vincent, February 16, 1940 (copy).

195. ASVA: Catholic University, Peking, China, Financial Report: Feb. 1, 1925–June 1, 1933. See note 47 above.

196. Francis J. Spellman, auxiliary bishop of Boston, had been named successor to Cardinal Patrick Hayes as archbishop of New York on April 15, 1939. The evening before his installation a month later, he met with Archbishop Amleto G. Cicognani, the apostolic delegate, who told him that there were "four grave matters that required his immediate attention" when he assumed the See of New York. One of these was settlement of the Benedictines' debt to the National City Bank of New York. See Robert I. Gannon, *The Cardinal Spellman Story* (Garden City, N.Y.: Doubleday, 1962), 140.

197. AACC: Deutsch to Stritch, St. John's, January 30, 1940; and ASVA: Notes on the settlement of debt to the National City Bank of New York. See also ASVA: Cicognani to Koch, Washington, December 5, 1939.

198. ASVA: Nicholas Koss, "The Benedictines in China: Background Material to be Distributed at the 1996 Congress of Abbots," 2–7. See also Rippinger, *The Benedictine Order in the United States,* 232; McDonald, *With Lamps Burning,* 271–81; and Buresh, *The Procopian Chronicle,* 99–107.

199. Wu Xiaoxin, "A Case Study of the Catholic University of Peking,"115. See also Hugh Wilt, "Saint Vincent Archabbey and China," *Benedictine Confluence* 6 (Winter 1972): 35.

200. Wilt, "Saint Vincent Archabbey and China," 36–39; Koss, "The Benedictines in China," 6–7.

NOTES TO CHAPTER 8. BUILDING FOR THE FUTURE

1. *St. Vincent Journal* 50 (November 1, 1940): 5; (November 15, 1940); 3.

2. Ibid., 50 (May 15, 1941): 4. For editorials expressing similar sentiments, see ibid., (February 1, 1941): 2; (March 1, 1941): 4; 2 (June 1, 1941): 1.

3. "Archabbot Alfred's Christmas Message," ibid., 51 (December 15, 1941): 1.

4. Ibid., 51 (October 1, 1941): 2; (October 15, 1941): 2.

5. Ibid., 51 (April 1, 1942): 8.

6. Ibid., 51 (June 1, 1942): 1.

7. Ibid., 51 (April 1, 1942): 2.

8. Ibid., 51 (September 1, 1942): 1.

9. Ibid., 51 (February 1, 1942): 1; (May 1, 1942): 1; (September 1, 1942): 1.

10. Enrollment figures are taken from the catalogues of the college, seminary, and prep school for the years indicated.

11. *St. Vincent Journal* 52 (June 1, 1943): 9.

12. Ibid., 54 (September 1944): 3–4.

13. Ibid., 53 (September 1943): 2; (April 1944): 1; 54 (February 1945: 1; 54 (March 1945): 3.

14. "Archabbot Alfred's Christmas Message," ibid., 53 (December 1943): 1.

15. Ibid., 53 (March 1944): 6. See also ibid., 53 (September 1943): 5; 53 (January 1944): 1; 53 (February 1944): 1.

16. Ibid., 53 (March 1944): 6, 11.

17. Information about Saint Vincent students and alumni who served in the armed forces during World War II abounds in the pages of the *St. Vincent Journal* for the years from 1943 to 1946 (volumes 53–55). Details in the preceding two paragraphs are drawn from this source.

18. Ibid., 53 (April 1944): 1; 54 (December 1944): 6; 54 (February 1945): 8; 55 (September 1945): 6.

19. Ibid., 50 (February 15, 1941): 5; (May 15, 1941): 1; 52 (April 1, 1943): 3; 52 (April 15, 1943): 3; 53 (May 1944): 8; (November 1943): 3; and 54 (September 1944): 1.

20. Ibid., 49 (October 1, 1939): 3. See *Saint Vincent College Catalogue* (1941–42): 68– 69, 76.

21. *St. Vincent Journal* 49 (February 1, 1940): 1; 49 (June 1, 1940): 1; 51 (March 1, 1942): 3.

22. Ibid., 52 (February 15, 1943): 1–2; 52 (March 1, 1943): 2–3. See also *Saint Vincent College Catalogue* (1943–44): 70–71.

23. *St. Vincent Journal* 52 (March 15, 1943): 3; 52 (April 1, 1943): 8.

24. ASVA: Fellner to Dolan, St. Vincent, August 10, 1943.

25. *St. Vincent Journal* 52 (March 15, 1943): 8; 53 (September 1943): 1.

26. Frank C. Gilkes, "As St. Vincent Appears from One Barracks Window," ibid., 52 (April 1, 1943): 3.

27. Ibid., 52 (June 1, 1943): 7.

28. "St. Vincent Marks 15th Anniversary of Aviation Program," ibid., 54 (December 1944): 4–5.

29. The college, seminary, and preparatory school catalogues for 1948–49 indicate that there were 924 undergraduates in the college, 57 theologians in the seminary, and 281 students in the preparatory school.

30. *St. Vincent Journal* 55 (September 1945): 1.

31. Ibid., 55 (October 1945): 1.

32. [Quentin Schaut], *The Crypt* (Latrobe, Pa.: Archabbey Press, 1949). See also Maurice Lavanoux, "Go West, Young Man . . . Latrobe, Pennsylvania," *Liturgical Arts* 15 (November 1946), 11–12, 21–23; "Saint Vincent Archabbey, Latrobe, Pennsylvania," ibid., 18 (August 1950), 93–94; André Girard, "Illustrating the *Canticle of Canticles,*" ibid., 85–86; and "At St. Vincent's: Something New in Religious Art," *The Pittsburgh Press Magazine,* April 22, 1951, 24–25.

33. Maynard Brennan and Demetrius Dumm, eds., *A Centennial Brochure* (Latrobe, Pa.: Published by the clerics of St. Vincent, 1946); *St. Vincent Journal* 56 (September 1946) (centennial edition); "Saint Vincent Archabbey and College: 1846–1946," special supplement to *The Pittsburgh Catholic,* August 29, 1946. See ASVA: Centennial Celebration.

34. Hugh J. Wilt, "The Women's Auxiliary," *The Pittsburgh Catholic,* August 29, 1946, 49. See also *St. Vincent Journal* 49 (November 1, 1939): 1; and ASVA: Minutes of the Small Chapter, December 14, 1949.

35. "The Black Monks," *Time,* September 16, 1946, 69–70.

36. *Time,* October 14, 1946, 7–8.

37. *St. Vincent Journal* 55 (February 1946): 1; (April 1946): 3.

38. Ibid., 55 (October 1945): 2.

39. Ibid., 57 (September 1947): 1, 11; 57 (October 1947): 1.

40. Ibid., 56 (October 1946): 7.

41. Ibid., 56 (January 1947): 2.

42. Ibid., 55 (December 1945): 4.

43. *Saint Vincent College Catalogue* (1947–48): 24.

44. *St. Vincent Journal* 57 (January 1948): 7.

45. Ibid., 58 (September 1948): 1; and *Saint Vincent College Catalogue* (1948–49): 6–10.

46. Ibid., 57 (March 1948): 7; 57 (May 1948): 5.

47. Ibid., 57 (May 1948): 11; 58 (January 15, 1949): 1; 58 (February 15, 1949): 7.

48. Ibid., 57 (January 1948): 3.

49. Ibid., 57 (January 1948): 1; 58 (April 15, 1949): 1.

50. Ibid., 57 (April 1948): 1; 58 (May 1, 1949): 1.

51. Ibid., 58 (September 1948): 5.

52. ASVA: Minutes of the Election of the Coadjutor Archabbot, September 7–8, 1949.

53. ASVA: Election of Denis O. Strittmatter, September 8, 1949. See also *St. Vincent Journal* 59 (September 1949): 1, 3.

54. ASVA: Chapter Minutes, April 6, 1950.

55. *St. Vincent Journal* 62 (September 25, 1952): 1.

56. Ibid., 63 (February 15, 1954): 1; 64 (September 1954): 5–6; (May 1955): 2.

57. ASVA: Building construction file in the Archabbot Denis Strittmatter Files. See also *Saint Vincent Review* 2 (March 25, 1958): 1.

58. *St. Vincent Journal* 61 (December 15, 1951): 1.

59. Ibid., 65 (September 1955): 1.

60. Ibid., 60 (February 28, 1951): 2. See also ibid., 60 (November 15, 1950): 2, (January 18, 1951): 6.

61. Ibid., 60 (March 21, 1951): 2.

62. Ibid., 61 (September 1951): 2.

63. Ibid., 62 (September 25, 1952): 1–2.

64. *St. Vincent College Bulletin* (1958–59): 34.

65. *St. Vincent Journal* 64 (October 1954): 3.

66. ASVA: "A Report Submitted to the Commission on Institutions of Higher Education of the Middle States Association of Colleges and Secondary Schools by Saint Vincent College, Latrobe, Pennsylvania," January 21, 1956.

67. *St. Vincent College Bulletin* (1958–59): 13–15.

68. *St. Vincent Journal* 62 (October 8, 1952): 1; 63 (September 1953): 1.

69. See *St. Vincent College Bulletin* (1955–56): 32–46.

70. Ibid., (1955–56): 6–9, and (1959–60): 7–11.

71. *St. Vincent Review* 2 (October 8, 1957): 6; 3 (December 17, 1958): 1.

72. Ibid., 2 (February 11, 1958), 4. See Noah Greenberg, ed., *The Play of Daniel: A Thirteenth-Century Musical Drama . . . Based on the Transcription from British Museum Egerton 2615 by Rembert Weakland: Narration by W. H. Auden* (New York: Oxford University Press, 1959).

73. *St. Vincent Review* 1 (February 5, 1957): 1, 4.

74. *St. Vincent Journal* 59 (January 15, 1950): 1.

75. Ibid., 59 (March 1, 1950): 6; 62 (May 18, 1953): 4; 63 (September 1953): 6.

76. *St. Vincent College Bulletin* (1958–59): 33.

77. *The Review* 3 (April 18, 1959): 1.

78. See *St. Vincent Journal* 65 (December 1955), 3; 65 (April 1956): 3; *St. Vincent Review* 2 (April 25, 1958): 1; and *The Review* 8 (October 31, 1962): 1.

79. *St. Vincent Journal* 65 (February 1956): 1; *St. Vincent Review* 1 (February 21, 1957): 2.

80. *St. Vincent Review* 2 (October 21, 1957): 1, 6.

81. *St. Vincent Journal* 59 (April 15, 1950): 1; 63 (September 1955): 1; 64 (October 1954): 3; 65 (September 1955): 1.

82. Ibid., 60 (February 15, 1951): 1. See also ibid., 59 (March 1, 1950): 3.

83. Ibid., 65 (April 1956): 1.

84. *St. Vincent Review* 2 (March 4, 1958): 1.

85. *St. Vincent Journal* 63 (May 29, 1954): 2; 64 (October 1954): 5.

86. ASVA: Chapter Minutes, March 16, 1950; *St. Vincent Journal* 60 (November 1, 1950): 3.

87. *St. Vincent Review* 1 (March 18, 1957): 1.

88. *The Review* 6 (October 6, 1961): 5.

89. *St. Vincent Review* 2 (February 11, 1957): 1, 3.

90. See the *St. Vincent Seminary Catalogue* for the years 1950 through 1960.

91. See the *Preparatory School Catalogue* for the years 1950 through 1960.

92. *St. Vincent Journal* 61 (January 1952): 1.

93. Ibid., 65 (November 1955): 3.

94. Ibid., 61 (September 1951): 1.

95. Ibid., 63 (May 29, 1954): 1.

96. Ibid., 61 (November 30, 1950): 7.

97. Ibid., 60 (November 15, 1950): 2.

98. Ibid., 62 (January 1953): 4.

99. Ibid., 60 (February 15, 1951): 1; ASVA: Saint Vincent Library Dedication Booklet, April 17, 1958.

100. See the *Ordo . . . Congregationis Americano-Cassinensis O.S.B.* for the years 1950 to 1960 for statistics about the monastic population at Saint Vincent during this period.

101. See Joel Rippinger, *The Benedictine Order in the United States: An Interpretive History* (Collegeville, Minn.: Liturgical Press, 1990), 208–9.

102. Felix Fellner, *Abbot Boniface and His Monks,* 5 vols. (Latrobe, Pa.: Privately published by St. Vincent Archabbey, 1956).

103. See, for example, ASVA: Minutes of the Small Chapter, February 9, 1950: "The archabbot spoke about the necessity of improvements in general [in the spiritual condition of the monastery]. He stressed especially the poor attendance at choir, the want of silence, and the disregard of some as regards the vow of poverty."

104. *St. Vincent Journal* 63 (September 1953): 1; (October 20, 1953): 1.

105. Ibid., 65 (November 1955): 4–5.

106. ASVA: Brother Philip Hurley's Chronicle of the History of Saint Vincent (1959).

107. ASVA: Chapter Minutes, August 18, 1959. Also, ASVA: Earl Dalton to Fr. Fidelis Lazar, Latrobe, February 3, 1963.

108. ASVA: Hugh Wilt, "The Fu Jen Catholic University of China" (April 29, 1966) (MS. Collection). See also, Hugh Wilt, "Saint Vincent Archabbey and China," *Benedictine Confluence* 6 (Winter 1972): 35–39.

109. ASVA: Chapter Minutes, December 30, 1960; December 21, 1961; January 25, 1962; June 15, 1962.

110. ASVA: Chapter Minutes, January 2, 1963; January 9, 1963; July 29, 1963.

111. ASVA: Chapter Minutes, September 25, 1962.

112. ASVA: Chapter Minutes, December 20, 1960; November 6, 1964.

113. AACC: St. Vincent Archabbey Visitation Report, February 22–27, 1954.

114. AACC: St. Vincent Archabbey Visitation Reports, February 17–11, 1957; February 15–21, 1960.

115. Ibid.

116. Interview with Archabbot Egbert Donovan, eighth archabbot of Saint Vincent, November 14, 1996.

117. ASVA: Chapter Minutes, August 18, 1959.

118. ASVA: Chapter Minutes, April 11, 1960.

119. ASVA: Chapter Minutes, December 6, 1960.

120. ASVA: Chapter Minutes, March 28, 1961; April 18, 1961.

121. Interview with Father Demetrius Dumm, April 24, 1998.

122. For example, Father Egbert Donovan, who had earlier been dean of students in the college, said that he opposed the Christ-Janer design for the dormitories because "the rooms were too small, the concrete slabs for the beds would have made the dorms look like Sing Sing, and they were located too close to the road." Interview with Archabbot Egbert Donovan, April 24, 1998.

123. ASVA: Minutes of the Lay Board of Advisors, August 17, 1962. See also ASVA: Christ-Janer to Weakland, New Canaan, Connecticut, August 27, 1962.

124. ASVA: Chapter Minutes, September 25, 1962.

125. ASVA: Chapter Minutes, January 9, 1963.

126. ASVA: Colman McFadden to Fidelis Lazar, St. Vincent, March 1, 1963. The following account of the fire is based upon letters and reminiscences written soon after the event by monks, prep school students, seminarians, and firemen; upon contemporary press reports; and upon personal interviews with witnesses of the disaster. The letters, reminiscences, and newspaper reports are located in ASVA: St. Vincent Fire, January 28, 1963.

127. ASVA: Leo Rothrauff to friends, St. Vincent, February 12, 1963.

128. ASVA: Philip Hurley, notes on the fire of January 28, 1963.

129. ASVA: Earl Dalton to Fidelis Lazar, Latrobe, February 3, 1963.

130. ASVA: Placid Cremonese, "Fire Tragedy" [February 1963].

131. ASVA: Jerome Rupprecht, "The Fire" [February 1963].

132. ASVA: Shane MacCarthy, notes on the fire of January 28, 1963.

133. ASVA: Chapter Minutes, January 31, 1963; February 19, 1963.

134. AACC: Visitation Report, February 17–24, 1963.

135. ASVA: Minutes of Board of Advisors, April 9, 1963.

136. ASVA: Minutes of the election of the coadjutor archabbot, June 24–26, 1963.

137. See Paul Wilkes, *The Education of an Archbishop: Travels with Rembert Weakland* (Maryknoll, N.Y.: Orbis Books, 1994).

BIBLIOGRAPHY

1. ARCHIVES

Archives of the American Cassinese Congregation, Latrobe, Pennsylvania
Archives of the Archdiocese of Baltimore, Maryland
Archives of Belmont Abbey, Belmont, North Carolina
Archives of the Congregation for the Propagation of the Faith, Rome
Archives of the Collegio di Sant' Anselmo, Rome
Archives of the Diocese of Linz, Austria
Archives of the Diocese of Newark, New Jersey
Archives of the Diocese of Pittsburgh, Pennsylvania
Archives of Holy Cross Abbey, Canon City, Colorado
Archives of the Ludwig Missionsverein, Munich, Germany
Archives of Metten Abbey, Metten, Germany
Archives of Scheyern Abbey, Scheyern, Germany
Archives of St. Benedict's Abbey, Atchison, Kansas
Archives of St. John's Abbey, Collegeville, Minnesota
Archives of the Abbey of St. Paul's Outside the Walls, Rome
Archives of Saint Vincent Archabbey, Latrobe, Pennsylvania
Royal Archives of Bavaria, Munich, Germany

2. SERIALS AND PERIODICALS

Annalen der Verbreitung des Glaubens (Munich), 1840–60. Annual publication of the Ludwig-Missionsverein.

Augsburger Postzeitung (Augsburg), 1845–50. Daily newspaper.

The American Benedictine Review (Atchison, Kansas), 1950– . Quarterly journal of the American Benedictine Academy.

Benedictine Confluence (Latrobe, Pennsylvania), 1968–73. Biannual journal of Benedictine studies.

Bulletin: Catholic University of Peking (Peking), 1926–31. Biannual journal of the faculty and staff of the Catholic University of Peking.

The Catholic Accent (Greensburg), 1954– . Weekly newspaper of the Diocese of Greensburg, Pennsylvania.

Cincinnati Wahrheitsfreund (Cincinnati), 1847–68. German Catholic Weekly.

Der Geschichtsfreund: Eine katholische Monatschrift für Recht und Wahrheit (Savannah), 1882–83). Monthly German Catholic historical magazine published by the Benedictines in Georgia.

Katholische Kirchenzeitung (Baltimore), 1846–60. Weekly German Catholic newspaper.

Die Legende: Eine katholische Monatsschrift zur Belehrung und Erbauung. (Chicago, Illinois),

1893–98. Monthly Benedictine religious and historical journal published by the monks of New Cluny Priory.

Fu Jen Magazine (Peking), 1932–35. Quarterly magazine of the Catholic University of Peking.

Fu Jen News Letter (Peking), 1931–32. Quarterly newsletter of the Catholic University of Peking.

National Benedictine Educational Association Bulletin (Atchison, Kansas), 1928–43. Quarterly journal of the National Benedictine Educational Association.

Ordo: American Cassinese Congregation (Collegeville, Minnesota), 1865– . Annual liturgical calendar and personnel list of the American Cassinese Congregation of Benedictines.

Pittsburgh Catholic (Pittsburgh), 1850– . Weekly newspaper of the Diocese of Pittsburgh.

The Review (Latrobe), 1957– . Periodic student newspaper of Saint Vincent College.

Saint Vincent (Latrobe), 1954– . Quarterly alumni magazine of Saint Vincent College.

Saint Vincent College Catalogue (Latrobe), 1859– . Annual college bulletin of Saint Vincent College. Early editions included information about secondary school and seminary programs. Beginning in 1932 the preparatory school and seminary issued separate catalogues.

St. Vincent Journal (alternately titled *St. Vincent's Journal* and *Saint Vincent College Journal*) (Latrobe), 1891–1956. Monthly journal of Saint Vincent monastery, seminary, college, and prep school.

Saint Vincent Oblate (Latrobe), 1934– . Quarterly newsletter of Benedictine spirituality.

Scriptorium (Collegeville, Minnesota), 1940–63. Quarterly journal of St. John's Abbey.

The Seminarists' Symposium (Latrobe), 1919–32. Yearbook of Saint Vincent Seminary.

Studien und Mitteilungen zur Geschichte des Benediktiner-Ordens und seiner Zweige (Munich), 1880– . Quarterly journal of Benedictine historical and monastic studies.

Vineyards Abroad (Latrobe), 1963– . Quarterly newsletter of Benedictine missionary activity.

3. UNPUBLISHED SOURCES

Attneave, Carolyn L. "Saint Vincent College in Transition: Coeducation 1983–1984." National Science Foundation Study #PRM–8212011, 1985 (ASVA).

Fuertges, Theodore. "The History of Saint Bede College and Abbey, Peru, Illinois, 1889–1941." M.A. thesis, The Catholic University of America, 1941.

Ganss, Henry. "Fugitive Recollections Musical and Unmusical, 1868–1878, by an Old Alumnus." ASVA, Manuscript Collection (1909).

Girgen, Incarnata. "The Schools of the American Cassinese Benedictines in the United States: Their Foundation, Development, and Character." Ph.D. diss., St. Louis University, 1944.

Hurley, Philip. "Guide to Saint Vincent Archabbey Archives" (1980).

———. "History of Saint Vincent: Chronicle." ASVA, Manuscript Collection (1987).

Kline, Omer U. "An Historical Narrative: The Saint Vincent Archabbey Gristmill and Brewery, 1854–1992." ASVA, Manuscript Collection (1992).

Koss, Nicholas. "The Benedictines in China: Background Material to be Distributed at the 1996 Congress of Abbots." ASVA, Manuscript Collection (1996).

Moleck, Fred J. "Nineteenth-Century Musical Activity at St. Vincent Archabbey." Ph.D. diss., University of Pittsburgh, 1971.

O'Fahey, Charles. "Gibbons, Ireland, Keane: The Evolution of a Liberal Catholic Rhetoric in America." Ph.D. diss., University of Minnesota, 1980.

Rupprecht, Melvin. "Saint Vincent Archabbey Church." B.A. thesis, Saint Vincent College, 1938.

Selle, Paulinus. "Building Construction at St. Vincent." B.A. thesis, Saint Vincent College, 1936.

Smith, Marie Barat. "A History of Saint Emma's Military Academy and Saint Francis de Sales High School." M.A. thesis, Catholic University of America, 1949.

Taylor, Paul. "The Development and Role of Proselytizing in Christian Education in China as It Culminated in the Expression of the Benedictines at Fu Jen University in Peking." Paper presented at Boston College, April 3, 1996. ASVA, Manuscript Collection (1996).

———. "Boniface Wimmer and Saint Vincent College: The Beginning of American Benedictine Education." Ph.D. diss., Boston College, 1998.

Wilson, Debora. "Benedictine Higher Education and the Development of American Higher Education." Ph.D. diss., University of Michigan, 1969.

Wilt, Hugh. "St. Vincent Archabbey's Involvement in China." ASVA, Manuscript Collection (1964).

Wu Xiaoxin. "A Case Study of the Catholic University of Peking During the Benedictine Period (1927–1933). Ed.D. diss., University of San Francisco, 1993.

4. PUBLISHED SOURCES

Acta et Decreta Capituli Generalis Decimi Sexti Congregationis Benedictinae Americano-Cassinensis. Atchison, Kans.: Abbey Student Press, 1908.

Acta et Decreta Capituli Generalis Undecimi Congregationis Benedictinae Americano-Cassinensis. Latrobe, Pa.: St. Vincent Press, 1893.

Acta et Decreta Capituli XXI Congregationis Benedictinae Americano-Cassinensis. Latrobe, Pa.: St. Vincent Press, 1923.

Acta et Decreta Concilii Plenarii Baltimorensis Tertii. Baltimore, 1886.

Adams, Edmund, and Barbara Brady O'Keefe. *Catholic Trails West: The Founding Catholic Families of Pennsylvania.* Vol. 2. Baltimore: Gateway Press, 1989.

Album Benedictinum. Beatty, Pa.: St. Vincent Press, 1869.

Album Benedictinum. Latrobe, Pa.: St. Vincent Press, 1880.

"Archabbot Boniface Krug." *St. Vincent's Journal* 19 (1909–10): 1–8.

Barcio, Robert G. *"That You Love One Another": The Life and Times of Archbishop John Mark Gannon,* vol. 2 of *A History of the Diocese of Erie.* Erie, Pa.: Diocese of Erie, 1996.

Barry, Colman J. "Boniface Wimmer, Pioneer of the American Benedictines." *Catholic Historical Review* 41 (1955): 272–96.

———. *The Catholic Church and German Americans.* Milwaukee: Bruce Publishing Co., 1953.

———. *Upon These Rocks: Catholics in the Bahamas.* Collegeville, Minn.: St. John's Abbey Press,1973.

———. *Worship and Work: Saint John's Abbey and University 1856–1992.* 3d ed. Collegeville,Minn.: Liturgical Press, 1993.

Baumstein, Paschal. *My Lord of Belmont: A Biography of Leo Haid.* Kings Mountain, N.C.: Herald Press, 1985.

Beaver, William. "'And Who is My Neighbor?' St. Vincent Archabbey Responds to Its Neighbors in the Depression." *Word and Spirit: A Monastic Review* 14 (1992): 96–104.

Beckman, Peter. *Kansas Monks: A History of St. Benedict's Abbey.* Atchison, Kans.: Abbey Student Press, 1957.

Bihlmeyer, Karl. *Church History: Modern and Recent Times,* revised by Herman Tüchle, translated by V. E. Mills and F. J. Müller. Westminster, Md.: Newman Press, 1968.

"The Black Monks." *Time,* September 16, 1946, 69–70.

Boucher, John N. *Old and New Westmoreland.* Vol. 1. New York: The American Historical Society, 1918.

"Brandus, Severus". *Die katholisch-irisch-bischöfliche Administration in Nordamerika.* Philadelphia, 1840.

Breslin, Thomas A. *China, American Catholicism, and the Missionary.* University Park, Pa.: Penn State University Press, 1980.

Bridge, Gerard. *An Illustrated History of St. Vincent Archabbey.* Beatty, Pa.: St. Vincent Archabbey Press, 1922.

Bryson, T. H. *The Juniors of St. Bede's.* New York: Benziger, 1911.

Buresh, Vitus. *The Procopian Chronicle: St. Procopius Abbey, 1885–1985.* Lisle, Ill.: St. Procopius Abbey, 1985.

Burgemeister, Remigius. *History of the Development of Catholicity in St. Marys.* St. Marys, Pa.: Privately published, 1919.

Burne, Martin J. "Holy Cross Abbey—One Hundred Years." *The American Benedictine Review* 37 (1986): 423–32.

Campbell, Nicholas J. "Local Student Visits 'Catholic Worker' in New York City." *St. Vincent Journal* 46 (May 1, 1937): 10–14.

Capecelatro, Alfonso. *Commemorazione di Don Bonifacio Maria Krug, Abate di Montecassino.* Rome: Desclée & Cie., 1910.

Carbonneau, Robert. "The Passionists in China, 1921–1929: An Essay in Mission Experience." *Catholic Historical Review* 66 (1980): 392–416.

Carey, Patrick. "The Laity's Understanding of the Trustee System, 1785–1855." *Catholic Historical Review* 64 (1978): 231–64.

Cassidy, Francis P. "Catholic Education in the Third Plenary Council of Baltimore." *Catholic Historical Review* 34 (1948–49): 257–305, 415–36.

Catalogus Monachorum Congregationis Americano-Cassinensis sub titulo Sanctorum Angelorum Custodium. Collegeville, Minn.: St. John's Abbey Press, 1893.

Catalogus Monachorum Congregationis Americano-Cassinensis sub titulo Sanctorum Angelorum Custodium. Collegeville, Minn.: St. John's Abbey Press, 1913.

Catalogus Monachorum Ord. S.P. Benedicti Congregationis Americano-Bavaricae Cassinensi Affiliatae. St. Vincent: Abbey Press, 1873.

Catholic Baptisms in Western Pennsylvania, 1799–1828: Father Peter Helbron's Greensburg Register. Baltimore: Genealogical Publishing Co., 1985. Reprinted from *Records of the American Catholic Historical Society of Philadelphia* between September 1915 and December 1917.

Chinnici, Joseph. *Devotion to the Holy Spirit in American Catholicism.* New York: Paulist Press,1985.

———. *Living Stones: The History and Structure of Catholic Spiritual Life in the United States.* 2d ed. Maryknoll, N.Y.: Orbis Books, 1996.

Coles, Robert. *Dorothy Day: A Radical Devotion.* Reading, Mass.: Addison-Wesley, 1987.

Corti, Egon Caesar. *Ludwig I von Bayern.* Munich: Bruckman, 1979.

Costantini, Celso. "The Need for a Sino-Christian Architecture for Our Catholic Missions." Bulletin: Catholic University of Peking, (September 1927), 7–16.

Court of Common Pleas of Westmoreland County, Pa. *Helen J. Thornton vs. Rt. Rev. Alfred Koch, O.S.B., Archabbot of St. Vincent's Monastery, Beatty, Pa., and The Benedictine Society.* No. 1538, May 1934.

[Cuneo, Edmund.] "Saint Vincent Archabbey and College: 1846–1946." Special supplement to the Pittsburgh Catholic, August 29, 1946.

Daniels, Roger. *Coming to America: A History of Immigration and Ethnicity in American Life.* New York: HarperCollins, 1990.

Davis, Cyprian. *The History of Black Catholics in the United States.* New York: Crossroad, 1995.

Delcourt, Henri-Philippe. *Dom Jehan Joliet (1870–1937): Un projet de monachisme Bénédictin chinois.* Paris: Editions du Cerf, 1988.

Dirrigl, Michael. *Ludwig I: König von Bayern, 1825–1848.* Munich: Hugendubel, 1980.

District Court of the United States for the Western District of Pennsylvania. *National City Bank of New York v. Benedictine Society.* No. 8659, May 1939.

Dolan, Jay P. *The American Catholic Experience: A History from Colonial Times to the Present.* New York: Doubleday, 1985.

Doppelfeld, Basilius. *Mönchtum und kirchlicher Heilsdienst.* Münsterschwarzach, Germany: Vier-Turme-Verlag, 1974.

Dries, Angelyn. *The Missionary Movement in American Catholic History.* Maryknoll, N.Y.: Orbis Books, 1998.

Duffy, Consuela Marie. *Katharine Drexel: A Biography.* Cornwell Heights, Pa.: Mother Katharine Drexel Guild, 1966.

Dunaway, W. F. *A History of Pennsylvania.* New York: Prentice-Hall, 1935.

Edie, Callistus. "Bruno Riess." *The Scriptorium* 10 (1950): 5–39.

———. "Demetrius di Marogna." *The Scriptorium* 9 (1949): 7–31.

Ellis, Edward Robb. *A Nation in Torment: The Great American Depression, 1929–1939.* New York: Coward-McCann, 1970.

Ellis, John Tracy. *The Life of James Cardinal Gibbons: Archbishop of Baltimore, 1834–1921.* 2 vols. Milwaukee: Bruce Publishing Co., 1952.

Ellis, John Tracy, ed. *Documents of American Catholic History.* 3 vol. Wilmington, Del.: Michael Glazier, 1987.

Fellner, Felix. *Abbot Boniface and His Monks.* 5 vols. Latrobe, Pa.: Privately published by Saint Vincent Archabbey, 1956.

———. "Archabbot Boniface Wimmer as an Educator." *The National Benedictine Educational Association Bulletin* 25 (1942): 90–106.

———. "Colonel George Washington and a Forgotten Camp in Unity Township." *St. Vincent's Journal* 49 (1939–40): 12–18.

———. "Early Catholicity in Western Pennsylvania." In *Catholic Pittsburgh's One Hundred Years.* Ed. William J. Purcell. Chicago: Loyola University Press, 1943. Pp. 3–24.

———. *Die St. Vincenz Gemeinde und Erzabtei.* Latrobe, Pa.: Archabbey Press, 1905.

Fendl, Josef, ed. *Thalmassing: Eine Gemeinde des alten Landgerichts Haidau.* Regensburg: Studio Druck, 1981.

Fink, Wilhelm. *Beiträge zur Geschichte der bayerischen Benediktinerkongregation: Eine Jubiläumsschrift 1684–1934.* Munich: Kommissionsverlag R. Oldenbourg, 1934.

Flick, Lawrence M. "Biographical Sketch of Reverend Peter H. Lemke, O.S.B., 1796–1882." Records of the American Catholic Historical Society 9 (1898): 184–91.

Fogarty, Gerald P. *The Vatican and the American Hierarchy from 1870 to 1965.* Collegeville, Minn., Liturgical Press, 1985.

———. *The Vatican and the Americanist Crisis: Denis J. O'Connell, American Agent in Rome, 1885–1903.* Rome: Gregorian University Press, 1974.

Franklin, R.W., and Robert L. Spaeth. *Virgil Michel: American Catholic.* Collegeville, Minn.: Liturgical Press, 1988.

Frey, Wolfgang. *The Act of Religious Profession: A Historical Synopsis and Commentary.* Washington, D.C.: The Catholic University of America Press, 1932.

[Frey, Wolfgang.] "A Return to the Liturgy." *Saint Vincent College Journal* 36 (1926–27): 251–54.

Furer, Howard B. *The Germans in America 1607–1970.* Dobbs Ferry, N.Y.: Oceana, 1973.

Gannon, Robert I. *The Cardinal Spellman Story.* Garden City, N.Y.: Doubleday, 1962.

Girard, André. "Illustrating the *Canticle of Canticles.*" *Liturgical Arts* 18 (August 1950): 85–86.

Girgen, Incarnata. *Behind the Beginnings: Benedictine Women in America.* St. Paul, Minn.: St. Benedict's Convent, 1981.

Gleason, Philip. *Keeping the Faith: American Catholicism Past and Present.* Notre Dame, Ind.: University of Notre Dame Press, 1987.

Gollwitzer, Heinz. *Ludwig I von Bayern, Königtum im Vormärz: Eine politische Biographie.* Munich: Süddeutscher Verlag, 1986.

Greenberg, Noah, ed. *The Play of Daniel: A Thirteenth-Century Musical Drama . . . Based on the Transcription from British Museum Egerton 2615 by Rembert Weakland. Narration by W. H. Auden.* New York: Oxford University Press, 1959.

Gresnigt, Adelbert. "Chinese Architecture." *Bulletin: Catholic University of Peking* (May 1928), 33–46.

Griffin, James B. "Late Prehistory of the Ohio Valley." In *Handbook of North American Indians: Northeast,* vol. 15, edited by Bruce G. Trigger. Washington, D.C.: Smithsonian Institution, 1978. Pp. 557–59.

Guilday, Peter. *The Life and Times of John Carroll, Archbishop of Baltimore, 1735–1815.* 2 vols. New York: Encyclopedia Press, 1922.

Haas, Louis. *St. Vincent's: Souvenir of the Consecration of the New Abbey Church, August 24, 1905, on the Fiftieth Anniversary of the Elevation of St. Vincent's to an Abbey.* Latrobe, Pa.: St. Vincent Archabbey Press, 1905.

Hall, Jeremy. *The Full Stature of Christ: The Ecclesiology of Dom Virgil Michel.* Collegeville, Minn.: Liturgical Press, 1976.

Hanley, Thomas O'Brien, ed. *The John Carroll Papers.* 3 vols. Notre Dame, Ind.: University of Notre Dame Press, 1976.

Hayes, Giles P. "Early Bayley-Wimmer Correspondence (1854–1857)," *The American Benedictine Review* 14 (1963): 485–507.

———. "St. Mary's Abbey, Balleis to Zilliox: 1838–1886." *The Scriptorium* 20 (1961):123–84.

Hayhoe, Ruth. "China's Universities and Western Academic Models." In *From Dependence to Autonomy,* edited by Philip G. Altbach and V. Selvaratnam. Dordrecht: Kluwer Academic Publishers, 1989.

———. "Jesuits and the Modern Chinese University." *International Higher Education* 4 (Spring 1996): 8–9.

Hayhoe, Ruth, and Lu Yongling, eds. *Ma Xiangbo and the Mind of Modern China.* New York: M. E. Sharpe, 1996.

Healy, Kathleen. *Frances Warde: American Founder of the Sisters of Mercy.* New York: Seabury Press, 1973.

Hennesey, James. *American Catholics: A History of the Roman Catholic Community in the United States.* New York: Oxford University Press, 1981.

Higby, Chester Penn. *The Religious Policy of the Bavarian Government during the Napoleonic Period.* New York: AMS Press, 1967 [1919].

Hlavcak, Michael, ed. *Englmann's Latin Grammar.* Latrobe, Pa.: Archabbey Press, 1928.

Hokky, Charles J. *Ruthenia: Spearhead toward the West.* Gainesville, Fla.: Danubian Research and Information Center, 1966.

Hollermann, Ephrem. *The Reshaping of a Tradition: American Benedictine Women, 1852–1881.* St. Joseph, Minn.: Sisters of the Order of St. Benedict, 1994.

Huber, Vincent. "Sportsman's Hall." *Records of the American Catholic Historical Society of Philadelphia* 3 (1888–91): 142–73.

———. "Sportsman's Hall and St. Vincent Abbey." *St. Vincent Journal* 1 (1892): passim.

Hunter, William A. "History of the Ohio Valley." In *Handbook of North American Indians: Northeast,* vol. 15, edited by Bruce G. Trigger. Washington, D.C.: Smithsonian Institution, 1978. Pp. 588–93.

J. S. "Rt. Rev. Boniface Wimmer, O.S.B., Founder of St. Vincent's." *St. Vincent Journal* 18 (1909): 151–66.

Kaib, Daniel. *Bookkeeping for Parish Priests.* Latrobe, Pa.: Archabbey Press, 1910.

Kardong, Terrence. "Peter Henry Lemke: 'Brave Soldier of the Lord' or Gyrovague?" *Tjurunga: An Australian Benedictine Review* 24 (1983): 44–65.

Kline, Omer U. "The Origins of Saint Vincent and the 'Sportsman's Hall Tract.'" *Saint Vincent* 18 (Summer 1984): 4–6.

———. *The Saint Vincent Archabbey Gristmill and Brewery, 1854–1999.* Latrobe, Pa.: Saint Vincent Archabbey Press, 1999.

———. *The Sportsman's Hall Parish, Later Named Saint Vincent, 1790–1846.* Latrobe, Pa.: Saint Vincent Archabbey Press, 1990.

Knowles, David. *Christian Monasticism.* New York: McGraw Hill, 1969.

Kollar, Rene. "Bishop John Carroll and the English Benedictine Congregation: Plans for an 18th-Century Benedictine Settlement in Western Pennsylvania." *Word and Spirit: A Monastic Review* 14 (1992): 3–11. Reprinted in Kollar, *A Universal Appeal: Aspects of the Revival of Monasticism in the West in the 19th and Early 20th Centuries.* Bethesda, Md.: International Scholars Publications, 1996. Pp. 287–96.

———. *Saint Vincent Archabbey and Its Role in the Development of Slovak-American Culture and History.* Saint Vincent Archabbey: Privately published, 1995.

Lambing, A. A. *A History of the Catholic Church in the Dioceses of Pittsburg and Allegheny from Its Establishment to the Present Time.* New York: Benziger Bros., 1880.

Lavanoux, Maurice. "Go West, Young Man . . . Latrobe, Pennsylvania." *Liturgical Arts* 15 (November 1946): 11–12, 21–23.

Lekai, Louis. *Cistercians: Ideal and Reality.* Kent, Ohio: Kent State University Press, 1977.

Lemke, Peter Henry. "Autobiography," *The Northern Cambria News* (Carrolltown, Pa.), June 7–November 22, 1879.

———. *Leben und Wirken des Prinzen Demetrius Augustin Gallitzin: Ein Beitrag zur Geschichte der katholischen Missionen in Nordamerika.* Münster: Coppenrath, 1861.

Lemke, Peter Henry, trans. *Eine Vertheidigung katholischer Lehren, und eine Appellation an das protestantische Publikum: Zwei Controvers-Schriften von Demetrius A. Gallitzen.* Reading, Pa.: Arnold Puwelle, 1849.

Lester, Bernhard. "Erzabt Bonifaz Wimmer, Das Bild eines deutschen Mannes in Amerika." *Frankfurter Zeitgemässe Broschueren* 12 (1891): 397–424.

Li, Anthony C. *The History of Privately Controlled Higher Education in the Republic of China.* Washington, D.C.: The Catholic University of America Press, 1954.

"Looking Backward: St. Xavier's Farm Before the Sisters Came and After." *St. Xavier's Journal* 36 (1926): 6–11.

Lutz, J. G. *China and Christian Colleges.* Ithaca, N.Y.: Cornell University Press, 1971.

McDonald, Grace. *With Lamps Burning.* St. Paul, Minn.: North Central Publishing Co., 1957.

McDowell, John B. *Water, Death, and Grace: The Life and Works of Hugh Charles Boyle, Priest, Pastor, Bishop, October 8, 1873–December 22, 1950.* Pittsburgh, Pa.: Privately published, 1999.

McPadden, Malachy. *The Benedictines in Newark 1841–1992.* Newark, N.J.: Newark Abbey, 1993.

Macko, Hubert. *Grammar of the Slovak Language.* Scranton, Pa.: Orbana Publishers, 1926.

Malatesta, Edward. "Two Chinese Catholic Universities and a Major Chinese Catholic Thinker: Shendan Daxue, Furen Daxue, and Ma Xiangbo." In *Historiography of the Chinese Catholic Church: Nineteenth and Twentieth Centuries,* edited by Jeroom Heyndrickx. Louvain Chinese Studies no. 1. Leuven: F. Verbiest Foundation, 1994. Pp. 235–45.

Maloney, William H. *Our Catholic Roots: Old Churches East of the Mississippi.* Huntington, Ind.: Our Sunday Visitor Publishing Co., 1992.

Marx, Paul. *Virgil Michel and the Liturgical Movement.* Collegeville, Minn.: Liturgical Press, 1957.

Mathäser, Willibald. *Bonifaz Wimmer O.S.B. und König Ludwig I von Bayern.* Munich: J. Pfeiffer, 1938.

———. "Erzabt Bonifaz Wimmer im Spiegel seiner Briefe." *Studien und Mitteilungen* 60 (1946): 234–302.

———. *Der Ludwig Missionsverein in der Zeit König Ludwigs I von Bayern.* Munich: Druck der salesianischen Offizin, 1939.

———. "San José in Texas." *Studien und Mitteilungen* 6 (1946): 309–30.

Mathäser, Willibald, ed. *Haudegen Gottes: Das Leben des Peter H. Lemke.* Würzburg: Kommissionsverlag Echter Gesamtherstellung, 1971.

Maurelian, Brother. *The Catholic Educational Exhibit at the World's Columbian Exposition, Chicago, 1893.* Chicago: J. S. Hyland and Co., 1896.

Meaney, Peter J. "Valiant Chaplain of the Bloody Tenth [Emmeran Bliemel]." *Tennessee Historical Quarterly* 41 (1983): 37–47.

Moleck, Fred J. "Music at St. Vincent under Abbot Boniface Wimmer." *The American Benedictine Review* 14 (1963): 248–62.

Moosmüller, Oswald. *Bonifaz Wimmer, Erzabt von St. Vincent in Pennsylvania.* New York: Benziger, 1891.

———. *Europaër in Amerika vor Columbus.* Regensburg: G. J. Manz, 1879.

———. *St. Vincenz in Pennsylvanien.* New York: F. Pustet, 1873.

Morris, Charles R. *American Catholic: The Saints and Sinners Who Built America's Most Powerful Church.* New York: Random House, 1997.

Muehlenbein, Mary Wibora. *Benedictine Mission to China.* St. Joseph, Minn: St. Benedict's Convent, 1980.

Murphy, Joseph. *Tenacious Monks: The Oklahoma Benedictines (1875–1975).* Shawnee, Okla.: Benedictine Color Press, 1974.

Necrologium Congregationis Americano-Cassinensis, O.S.B., 1846–1946. Collegeville, Minn.: St. John's Abbey Press, 1948.

Oderman, Valerian. "Abbot Placid Hoenerbach and the Bankruptcy of St. Mary's Abbey, Richardton." *The American Benedictine Review* 29 (1978): 100–114.

O'Donnell, William. "Progress at the Catholic University of Peking." *Bulletin: Catholic University of Peking* (December 1930), 115–19.

Oetgen, Jerome. *An American Abbot: Boniface Wimmer, O.S.B., 1809–1887.* 2d ed. Washington, D.C.: The Catholic University of America Press, 1997.

———. "Belmont Abbey—Historical Notes." *The Crescat Chronicle* 1 (1972): 4.

———. "Benedictine Women in Nineteenth-Century America." *The American Benedictine Review* 34 (1983): 396–423.

———. "Boniface Wimmer and the American Benedictines: 1856–1866." *The American Benedictine Review* 23 (1972): 283–313.

———. "Boniface Wimmer and the American Benedictines: 1866–1876." *The American Benedictine Review* 24 (1973): 1–28.

———. "Boniface Wimmer and the American Benedictines: 1877–1887." *The American Benedictine Review* 25 (1974): 1–32.

———. "Boniface Wimmer and the Founding of St. Vincent Archabbey." *The American Benedictine Review* 22 (1971): 147–76.

———. "King Ludwig I and the American Benedictines." *Saint Vincent* 20 (1986): 7–12.

———. "The Origins of the Benedictine Order in Georgia," *Georgia Historical Quarterly* 53 (1969): 165–83.

———. "Oswald Moosmüller: Monk and Missionary." *The American Benedictine Review* 27 (1976): 1–35.

———. *St. Vincent: History and Heritage.* Latrobe, Pa: Archabbey Press, 1986.

Oswald, V. A. "A Personal Experience of the Johnstown Flood." *St. Vincent's Journal* 4 (1894–95): 352–58.

O'Toole, George B. "The Catholic University of Peking." *America,* April 10, 1926, 610.

——— "A Gateway to a New China." *Fu Jen Magazine* 1, no. 5 (Christmas 1932): 31–33.

Papeians de Morchoven, Christian. "The China Mission of the Benedictine Abbey of Sint-Andries (Bruger)." In *Historiography of the Chinese Catholic Church: Nineteenth and Twentieth Centuries,* edited by Jeroom Heyndrickx. Louvain Chinese Studies no. 1. Leuven: F. Verbiest Foundation, 1994. Pp. 305–10.

Paragon, Donald. "Ying Lien-chih (1866–1926) and the Rise of Fu Jen, The Catholic University of Peking." *Monumenta Serica* 20 (1961): 165–225.

Piehl, Mel. *Breaking Bread: The Catholic Worker and the Origin of Catholic Radicalism in America.* Philadelphia: Temple University Press, 1982.

Pius X, Pope. *Motu Proprio "Tra le sollecitudini."* Rome, 1903.
Plaisance, Aloysius. "Emmeran Bliemel, O.S.B., Heroic Confederate Chaplain." *The American Benedictine Review* 17 (1966): 106–16.
Power, Edward J. *Catholic Higher Education in America: A History.* New York: Appleton Century Crofts, 1972.
———. *A History of Catholic Higher Education in the United States.* Milwaukee: Bruce Publishing Co., 1958.
Purcell, William J., ed. *Catholic Pittsburgh's One Hundred Years.* Chicago: Loyola University Press, 1943.
Quigley, Thomas. "The School System in the Diocese." In *Catholic Pittsburgh's One Hundred Years,* edited by. William J. Purcell. Chicago: Loyola University Press, 1943. Pp. 128–43.
Raila, Donald S. "The Enigma of Archabbot Andrew: A Man Who Knew His Limits." *St. Vincent* 22 (1988): 6–7.
Reger, Ambrose. *Die Benediktiner in Alabama.* Baltimore: Benziger, 1898.
Reuss, Francis X. "Base-Ball at St. Vincent's in 1867 & 1868." *St. Vincent's Journal* 5 (1895–96): 389–90.
Rippinger, Joel. *The Benedictine Order in the United States: An Interpretive History.* Collegeville, Minn.: Liturgical Press, 1990.
Roemer, Theodore. *The Leopoldine Foundation and the Church in the United States.* New York: U.S. Catholic Historical Society, 1933.
Roemer, Theodore. *The Ludwig Missionsverein and the Church in the United States.* Washington, D.C.: The Catholic University of America Press, 1933.
Roettger, Gregory. *An Historical Overview of St. Bernard Abbey 1891–1991.* Cullman, Ala.: St. Bernard Abbey Press, 1991.
"Saint Vincent Archabbey, Latrobe, Pennsylvania." *Liturgical Arts* 18 (August 1950): 93–94.
Salzbacher, Josef. *Meine Reise nach Nord-Amerika in Jahre 1842.* Vienna: Wimmer, Schmidt, & Leo, 1845.
[Schaut, Quentin.] *The Crypt [of Saint Vincent Archabbey Basilica].* Latrobe, Pa.: Archabbey Press, 1949.
Schnitzhofer, Urban J. "First Monks in the Colorado Rockies." *The American Benedictine Review* 12 (1961): 232–56, 369–89.
Schroth, Raymond, ed. "The Excommunication of Reverend John Baptist Causse: An Unpublished Sermon by Bishop John Carroll of Baltimore." *Records of the American Catholic Historical Society of Philadelphia* 81 (1970): 42–56.
Schrott, Lambert. *Pioneer German Catholics in the American Colonies (1734–1784).* New York: United States Catholic Historical Society, 1933.
Schwaiger, Georg, and Paul Mai. *Johann Michael Sailer und seine Zeit.* Regensburg: Verlag des Vereins für Regensburger Bistumsgeschichte, 1982.
Seymour, Bruce. *Lola Montez: A Life.* New Haven, Conn.: Yale University Press, 1996.
Sheehan, James J. *German History: 1770–1866.* Oxford: Clarendon Press, 1989.
Sperling, John. *Great Depressions: 1837–1844, 1893–1898, 1929–1939.* Chicago: Scott, Foresman, 1966.
Stehle, Aurelius. *Manual of Episcopal Ceremonies.* Latrobe, Pa.: Archabbey Press, 1915.
Sterbechronik des hochwürdigsten Herrn Abtes Miguel Kruse, O.S.B. [1864–1929]. São Paulo, Brazil: S. Paulo-Cayeiras-Rio, 1929.
Sutera, Judith. *True Daughters: Monastic Identity and American Benedictine Women's History.* Atchison, Kans.: Mount St. Scholastica, 1987.
Sutherland, Anthony X. "The Role of St. Vincent's in Slovak-American History." *Jednota Annual Furdek* 28 (1989): 278–86.
Szarnicki, Henry. *Michael O'Connor, First Catholic Bishop of Pittsburgh, 1843–1860.* Pittsburgh: Wolfson Publishing Co., 1975.
Taylor, Philip. *The Distant Magnet: European Emigration to the United States of America.* New York: Harper and Row, 1971.

Tourscher, Francis E., ed. *Diary and Visitation Record of the Rt. Rev. Francis Patrick Kenrick, Administrator and Bishop of Philadelphia, 1830–1851.* Lancaster, Pa.: Wickersham Print Co., 1916.

United States Circuit Court of Appeals for the Third Circuit, Greensburg, Pa. *The Benedictine Society, Defendant-Appellant, v. The National City Bank of New York, Plaintiff-Appellee: Brief for Appellant.* No. 7121, October Term, 1939.

Whitaker, Thomas. "Brothers of St. John's Abbey: 1856–1866." *The Scriptorium* 13 (1953): 38–53.

Wilkes, Paul. *The Education of an Archbishop: Travels with Rembert Weakland.* Maryknoll, N.Y.: Orbis Books, 1994.

Wilt, Hugh. "Saint Vincent Archabbey and China." *Benedictine Confluence* 6 (Winter 1972): 35–39.

[Wimmer, Boniface.] "Über die Missionen." *Augsburger Postzeitung,* November 8, 1845. Translated as "Boniface Wimmer Outlines the Future of the Benedictine Order in the United States, November 8, 1845" in *Documents of American Catholic History,* ed. John Tracy Ellis, 3 vols. (Wilmington, Del.: Michael Glazier, 1987), 1:279–88.

Wimmer, Sebastian. "Biographical Sketch of Rt. Rev. Arch-Abbot Wimmer, O.S.B., D.D., Patriarch of the American Cassinese Benedictines." *Records of the American Catholic Historical Society of Philadelphia* 3 (1891): 174–93.

Wirtner, Modestus. *The Benedictine Fathers in Cambria County, Pennsylvania.* Carrolltown, Pa.: Privately published, 1926.

Zimmerman, Conrad, and Meinulph Schmiesing. "Wimmer Letters." *The Scriptorium* 17 (1958): 53–64; 18 (1959): 69–82; 19 (1960): 61–83.

Zurcher, George. *Foreign Ideas in the Church of the United States.* Buffalo, N.Y.: Privately published, 1896.

———. *Monks and Their Decline.* Buffalo: Privately published, 1898.

INDEX

Mission To America: A History of Saint Vincent Archabbey, The First Benedictine Monastery in the United States was designed and composed in Adobe Garamond by Kachergis Book Design, Pittsboro, North Carolina; and printed on 60-pound Natural Smooth and bound by Sheridan Books, Ann Arbor, Michigan.